Copyright Law

Copyright Law

Seventh Edition

Stephen M. McJohn
Professor of Law
Suffolk University

ASPEN PUBLISHING

To contact Customer Service, e-mail customer.service@aspenpublishing.com, call 1-800-950-5259, or mail correspondence to:

Aspen Publishing
Attn: Order Department
1 Wall Street
Burlington, MA 01803

1 2 3 4 5 6 7 8 9 0

ISBN 979-8-8920-7377-6

Library of Congress Cataloging-in-Publication Data application is in process.

ABOUT ASPEN PUBLISHING

Aspen Publishing is a leading provider of legal education content and digital learning solutions in the United States and globally. Our innovative products and platforms—designed based on best practices in learning science—engage students and enhance outcomes. From textbooks and audiobooks authored by renowned experts to digital platforms and products like LEAF, Connected eBooks, Connected Quizzing, PracticePerfect, and JD-Next, we empower the next generation of legal professionals with innovative, trusted, and accessible resources.

The Aspen Casebook Series, affectionately known as the "red and black" casebooks among law faculty and students, includes hundreds of highly regarded textbooks across more than 80 disciplines. These range from foundational courses like Torts and Contracts to emerging electives such as Sustainability and the Law of Policing. Our study aids, including the popular *Examples & Explanations* series, help law students master complex topics with clarity and confidence.

Aspen's expertise extends to undergraduate education with our Paralegal, Criminal Justice, and Business Law series, offering the same hallmark quality to a broader audience. JD-Next, our groundbreaking online law school prep course and admissions test, provides a realistic preview of law school, equips students with essential skills for academic success, and evaluates their readiness for legal studies.

Aspen Publishing Is Proud to Be a UWorld Company

Since 2003, UWorld has been a global leader in developing high-quality learning tools for students preparing for high-stakes exams. With a commitment to excellence, UWorld has helped millions of students in undergraduate, graduate, and professional programs in fields such as medicine, nursing, finance, and law achieve their academic and career goals.

Founded by Chandra S. Pemmasani, M.D., during his medical residency, UWorld began focusing on medical education and has since expanded into various academic fields, including law. In 2020, UWorld launched its Legal vertical, starting with its comprehensive Multistate Bar Exam (MBE®) Question Bank, followed by the acquisition of Themis Bar Review, which integrated resources to provide a complete bar exam preparation experience. In 2024, UWorld expanded its offerings by acquiring Aspen Publishing, enhancing its suite of legal education products.

Today, UWorld offers an unparalleled range of study materials that blend active learning methods with expert content, ensuring students and educators can access the most effective resources. From bar preparation to law school success, UWorld is committed to supporting the next generation of legal professionals. Learn more at uworld.com.

For Lorie, Ian, and Heart's Bend

Summary of Contents

PART IV. COPYRIGHT LITIGATION

Contents

Preface

This book provides the necessary tools for learning the basics of copyright law. Written for law students taking a copyright law survey course or anybody seeking an introduction to the fundamentals of copyright law, the book is divided into four primary areas: copyrightable subject matter, ownership and transactions, statutory rights, and copyright litigation. Copyright law is part of intellectual property law, which governs rights concerning information, but the legal subject matter of copyright overlaps only slightly with patents and trademarks.

Copyright law applies to works of authorship but goes beyond authors. Copyright concerns starving artists, grazing capitalists, crafty hackers, hopeful investors, conspicuous consumers, rulemakers, keepers of secrets, software devotees, rummaging downloaders, rappers, writers, gamers—potentially anyone. In the digital world, copyright spreads everywhere. Its practical rules govern a most protean subject matter: creative expression from Montesquieu to Monty Python. Copyright affects freedom of expression, moral rights of artists and other innovators, allocation of economic resources, interests of consumers, and more.

The book follows the method of the Examples and Explanations series. Each section is followed by examples and corresponding explanations that provide substance to the legal rules and guide students in applying them to other situations. The examples are drawn from many sources: judicial opinions, news reports, student questions, and daily life. Learning the law is not merely learning the rules. Learning the law means learning to apply those rules to a variety of cases. By working with concrete examples and explanations, active readers will develop such comprehensive skills.

The examples can also be used to review the concepts. Readers can work through the examples in a section without rereading the text. They also can change the facts in an example and ask whether the result would be different—or ask how the facts would have to change for the result to be different in a specific way.

I greatly appreciate help from students and colleagues, from the readers who generously provided comments on drafts, from my publishers (Joe Terry, Elizabeth Dobkowski, Troy Froebe, Carol McGeehan, Susan McClung, Tony Perriello, Barbara Roth, Peter Skagestad, Kathy Langone, Paul Sobel, Eric Song and Joseph Antoine), and especially from my family. Special thanks go to the students at the Northwestern Journal of Technology and Intellectual Property. Our annual "Top Tens" analyses of intellectual property law were sources of updates for this book.

Thoughts, comments, suggestions, examples, and explanations are always welcome at smcjohn@suffolk.edu.

Copyright Law

CHAPTER 1

An Overview of Copyright

Suppose Ozzie authors a novel (or sculpture or song or dance or computer program or database or photograph or movie or biography or pantomime or painting or letter or . . .). As soon as she writes it, she holds the copyright in the work. She need not apply for a copyright; it arises automatically. The copyright will last her life plus 70 years. (If it were a work made for hire, her employer would own the copyright, which would last 95 years.) To obtain copyright protection, she need not register the copyright with the U.S. Copyright Office or put "© 2023 Ozzie" on published copies of the work. She may register the copyright and use a copyright notice, because they provide practical advantages. Among other things, the remedies for infringement are greater (statutory damages and attorney's fees are available for infringement only of registered copyrights), and proving infringement is easier when the work is registered before infringement. But Ozzie doesn't have to register in order to hold copyright and benefit from the set of exclusive rights it provides. As copyright holder, she possesses the exclusive right to:

1. reproduce the copyrighted work in copies or phonorecords (often called the *reproduction right* or the *right to make copies*)
2. prepare derivative works based on the copyrighted work (*adaptation right*)
3. distribute copies or phonorecords of the copyrighted work to the public by sale or other transfer of ownership, or by rental, lease, or lending (*public distribution right*)
4. perform the copyrighted work publicly (*public performance right*)
5. display the copyrighted work publicly (*public display right*)

People might infringe Ozzie's copyright by doing such things as the following without Ozzie's permission:

- making or selling copies of the novel
- copying creative elements of the novel into another book
- making a movie based on the novel
- publicly performing a scene from the novel
- downloading the text of the novel

But they might also be protected by various limitations on Ozzie's rights. Certain elements of the work would not be protected by copyright, such as ideas (such as the plot of the novel), elements not created by the author (facts about Chicago that Ozzie puts in the book), and functional elements (such as the rules of a game or the functions that software performs, not an issue with most novels). Other authors may freely copy a clever idea for a novel, or facts uncovered through research, or rules of an accounting system. Moreover, even copyrighted elements may be used under such limitations as fair use. Fair use might permit writing and selling an unauthorized parody of Ozzie's novel, or handing out photocopies of a chapter to a class, or including portions in a book review.

Ozzie's exclusive rights give her control over several types of commercial uses of the work: printing and selling the novel, selling chapters online, performing the work, and so on. She also controls (subject to fair use and the nonprotection of ideas) how the work is adapted into other forms, such as sequels, translations, and other offshoots. The basket of exclusive rights allows the author not just to exploit the work commercially but also to control its public life (to a limited extent—the author cannot dictate how critics review it or whether the public pays attention to it). An author can control the artistic uses of the work, such as by licensing the performance of a play, subject to restrictions (e.g., "You cannot change the ending or stage it as a parody"). Copyright also can be used to prevent dissemination of a work. An author may prevent a work (such as an unfinished novel or a diary) from being published, which can protect artistic values and even privacy interests. But the hazard exists that authors will use copyright to censor or to limit the flow of information, such as by claiming copyright in e-mails discussing important issues, or even in a cease-and-desist letter threatening a lawsuit. Copyright law must often balance incentives to authors and protection of author's artistic creations against legitimate expressive interests of others.

Ozzie may sue an infringer in federal court. She may get remedies like damages, an injunction, and impoundment of infringing copies. If she had registered the copyright before the infringement, she may choose statutory damages rather than actual damages, and she may also seek attorney's fees.

All of these issues are introduced in this chapter, which outlines copyright law, the reasons that justify the law, and the extent of the rights to which the copyright holder is entitled (and, conversely, the extent of others' rights to use her work).

JUSTIFICATIONS FOR COPYRIGHT LAW

Copyright law can prohibit such activities as distributing copies of music, writing plays based on novels, performing songs in concert, publishing letters by famous authors, and selling artworks. One might argue that all of these activities are of a kind that the law should encourage, not deter. What is the purpose of a law that specifically prohibits some uses of creative works? The reasons for copyright law are often grouped into two sets: economic justifications and philosophical justifications.

Economic Bases for Copyright

Samuel Johnson said, "No man but a blockhead ever wrote, except for money." Copyright is usually justified as providing an incentive for the creation of works. The incentive-to-create theory draws its legal basis from the Constitution:

> The Congress shall have Power . . . to Promote the Progress of Science and the useful Arts, by securing for limited Times to Authors and Inventors the exclusive Right to their respective Writings and Discoveries.

U.S. Const. art. I, §8, cl. 8. Under this view, copyright exists to overcome the free-rider problem with public goods. Without copyright law, authors have a diminished incentive to produce works. A potential author might not spend all the time and money required to write a book or make a movie if others could freely make and sell copies. Copyright law gives them an exclusive set of rights in their works, and that set of rights is an incentive to create. The language of several Supreme Court cases is consistent with the incentive-to-create approach.

The benefits conferred by copyright do not come without costs. Costs of copyright can include transaction costs (hiring lawyers, negotiating for permission to use works, locating authors, and asking permission), rent-seeking (the use of copyright to get revenue from nonprotected elements, or even making frivolous claims for their settlement value), dead-weight losses (uses of works that do not take place because of copyright, such as where an author does not write a book or song because of an inability to get the necessary permission from certain copyright holders, or where a copyright holder chooses to sell fewer copies at a higher price), and distorted incentives (channeling resources toward copyrightable works). The Supreme Court has recognized that copyright protection can discourage innovations in distributing works: "The more artistic protection is favored, the more technological innovation may be discouraged; the administration of copyright law is an exercise in managing the trade-off." *MGM Studios Inc. v. Grokster, Ltd.*, 125 S. Ct. 2764, 2775 (2005). In deciding how much copyright protection to provide, the incentive-to-create approach might counsel balancing the benefits against the costs. For example, in considering how broad fair use is, one could balance the benefits of the proposed use against the costs in decreased incentives to authors.

Copyright law doctrine has not been strictly limited by the incentive rationale; the scope of copyright law is much broader. Copyright applies to *any* creative work as soon as it is fixed in a tangible form, including works that are created without the incentive of copyright, such as personal letters, school projects, and legal memoranda. Moreover, there are many incentives other than copyright for people to produce creative works. Diarists may write for catharsis, artists create for art's sake, scientists may write to gain peer recognition, professors may write to get tenure, and software developers write free software. The urge to create is instinctual. In William Faulkner's words, "An artist is a creature driven by demons. He doesn't know why they choose him and he's usually too busy to wonder why." Even nonblockheads creating for money can find other sources of revenue from their creations: musicians sell concert tickets, gag writers get salaries, artists sell the original work (a copy of a Picasso does not get the same price as the original[1]). Finally, copyright's duration (life of the author plus 70 years, or 95 years for works made for hire) is longer than necessary to spur creation of works. The present value of royalties 70 or more years in the future is negligible, even for the few works that have such long-lasting commercial value. So the incentive-to-create theory provides a strong argument for copyright generally, but not one that closely matches the particular copyright law that we have, which is much broader than the incentive rationale alone would support. In some areas, lack of intellectual property protection may mean that freedom to copy speeds innovation. *See* Kal Raustiala and Chris Sprigman, *The Piracy Paradox: Innovation and Intellectual Property in Fashion Design*, 92 Va. L. Rev. 1687 (2006).

The other leading set of economic theories of copyright have been called *property theories* or *ex post theories*. *See* Mark A. Lemley, *Ex Ante Versus Ex Post Justifications for Intellectual Property*, 71 U. Chi. L. Rev. 129 (2004) (skeptical). Rather than looking to copyright as simply providing an incentive to create

1. *See* Amy Adler, *Why Art Does Not Need Copyright*, 86 Geo. Wash. L. Rev. 313 (2018).

works, they also look to copyright as providing an incentive to efficiently exploit works. An analogy is made to real property law. If someone owns a home and yard, she has an incentive to expend resources to manage, maintain, and improve the home efficiently, because she gets the benefits. If she paints it, fixes things that break, and tends the garden, she can get the benefits of those costs (whether she lives there, rents it out, sells it, or lets her kids use it). She can decide how much costs to expend in view of the benefits she will get. But without property rights, anyone could use the home and yard. No one would have much incentive to manage, maintain, and improve things, because others would get the benefit. Why fix everything up if that would just attract strangers to come in and live there? This is the well-known "tragedy of the commons." In economic terms, property serves to avoid externalities—situations where a decision-maker does not bear the resulting costs or benefits.

Some apply the real property analogy to copyright to support arguments for very broad copyright protection. *See* Lemley, *supra*. By making works into private property, we give an incentive to manage, maintain, and improve the works. Copyright holders will preserve copies of old works (like delicate films), devise ways to improve works (like making sequels or other spin-offs), and seek new markets for works (bring them to a wider audience). So unlike the incentive-to-create approach, which counsels balancing the costs of protection against the benefits of providing incentives, the property approach leads some to say, "The more protection the better."

The two approaches can lead to different views about copyright law. Take fair use as an example. Fair use allows some uses of copyrighted works without permission for such uses as education, criticism, research, and the creation of other works. An incentive-to-create theory of fair use might measure the costs (decreased incentives to authors) against the benefits (the favored use). A property theory might counsel that the copyright owner should generally decide how the work is used, so fair use would be applicable only where transaction costs or other obstacles to negotiation would prevent getting permission from the copyright owner. The property approach would lead to a narrow view of fair use (and in general, to broader copyright protection).

There are differences between real property and intellectual property that undermine the analogy. The key difference is the danger of overuse. *See* Lemley, *supra*. If land is open to all, it may be overused. If everyone can graze their cattle in the common, it may be overgrazed (and no one has incentives to plant, because other people's cows will eat the crop). Likewise, if everyone can use the house, no one has the incentive to maintain it. But information is not subject to that hazard. If everyone can read an author's book, so much the better. Rather, the key is to get the author to write it to start with—the problem addressed by the incentive-to-create approach. Having said that, the property approach, which supports broader copyright protection, may better reflect the broad copyright protection that we have.

Certainly, intellectual property has broad economic effects in the tangible world. Cities like Seattle have been transformed by Microsoft, Starbucks, and Amazon. Universities like Carnegie-Mellon, MIT, and Northwestern feature innovation as part of education, while licensing intellectual property supports the schools' expansion. The historical port of Charleston, South Carolina, is now called "Silicon Harbor."

"Public choice," another kind of political/economic theory, might explain why copyright protection is so broad. Congress creates copyright law. Legislation is often more affected by particular interests than broad public policy. Copyright law affects everyone, but the people (from authors to various industries) who own copyrights tend to be the most involved in creating copyright legislation. As a result, it may be that copyright leans toward authors (or really, copyright owners), as opposed to the users of works. As always with politics, opinions differ about that.

Economic analysis of law has recently paid increasing attention to norms: informal, nonlegal standards of behavior. Some see copyright as the legal version of the norms that condemn plagiarism or even theft. Others view copyright as going beyond relevant norms. When the social standard of behavior differs from the legal standard, the law may not accomplish its goals, especially where the purpose of a law is to provide incentives for behavior. Some have questioned whether copyright law is rapidly diverging from norms about use of creative works—in short, whether copyright prohibits acts that are considered socially acceptable, even beneficial. This arises especially in such areas as music downloading or artistic uses of commercialized works.

Philosophical Justifications for Copyright

Copyright may also be supported by philosophical theories. These come in many varieties. For simplicity's sake, one could divide them into "personality" theories and "natural rights" theories.

Under the personality approach, an artist's personality is seen as linked to the works she has created. Anyone who makes use of the work indirectly affects the person of the author. Authors should control the uses of their work, and especially be entitled to prevent distortion or destruction of the work, or misattribution of authorship. Under this approach, copyright might be as broad as necessary to protect the author. There might be broader protection for categories of works that are more closely linked to the author: A work of art might get more protection than a commercial advertisement.

Under the natural rights approach, an author has a natural right to what she has created through her labor. It may be limited by the fact that in creation she has reduced the resources available to others and also relied on elements created by others. So her rights should also let others likewise make some use of what she has created. Cf. Wendy J. Gordon, *A Property Right in Self-Expression: Equality and Individualism in the Natural Law of Intellectual Property*, 102 Yale L.J. 1533 (1993); Alfred C. Yen, *Restoring the Natural Law: Copyright as Labor and Possession*, 51 Ohio St. L.J. 517 (1990).

These views get less explicit recognition in U.S. law than economic theories, but they may influence the sense of fairness of judges, lawmakers, and commentators, even when they do not show up in judicial opinions or statutory language. They are also more widely accepted in other countries, and international/comparative law is increasingly influential in copyright. Indeed, the copyright statute even grants some artworks rights against distortion, destruction, and misattribution in a provision, adopted with international treaties in mind.

The particular doctrines or case outcomes supported by philosophical theories can, of course, vary widely along with the many varieties of the theories. But they provide a good framework for analyzing the issues.

Intellectual property law draws on our intuitive understandings—for better or worse. Origin stories in every culture assign meaning to institutions, provide an explanation and justification of social arrangements, and support cultural unity through common belief. Courts often look to the original language, or original purpose of the rule, or how it responded to a problem, or how the rule's author viewed the rule, such as with legislative history or the Federalist Papers. Intellectual property law provides a special twist on origin stories by assigning control of information to the author or inventor who originated information. Jessica M. Silbey, *The Mythical Beginnings of Intellectual Property*, 15 George Mason L. Rev. 319 (2008). Similarly, cognitive science tells us that "the mind understands every entity in terms of four causes: who or what brought it about; what it's made of; what shape it has; and what it's for." Steven Pinker, *The Stuff of Thought* 61 (2007). Intellectual property mirrors this cognitive structure, giving legal rights to the party that brought the information about. *See* Lorie Graham and Stephen McJohn, *Cognition, Law, Stories*, 10 Minn. J. L. Sci. & Tech. (Fall 2008).

THE LEGAL STRUCTURE OF COPYRIGHT

Intellectual Property Law: Where Copyright Fits In

Copyright is part of intellectual property law. Utility patents give inventors rights in their useful inventions (from drugs to machines to methods of manufacturing rubber). Sellers of goods or services can prevent others from using their trademarks (symbols that distinguish them from other sellers) in ways that are likely to confuse consumers. Authors have copyrights in their creative works. The subject matter of patents, trademarks, and copyrights has limited overlap. Patents on inventions apply only to useful products or processes, whereas copyright does not protect useful elements of works (as opposed to creative elements). Trademark protects identifying symbols against deceptive or confusing uses, whereas patent and copyright infringement does not depend on deception. Most trademarks are uncopyrightable phrases. The Supreme Court has ruled against the use of trademark law to effectively extend the term of a patent or a copyright.

The legal subject matter may differ, but the commercial products overlap a lot. Suppose Mangosoft sells a computer program called Liddles. Mangosoft might have a patent covering a useful process that the program performs (such as a method for controlling machines that manufacture nanotechnology products), trademarks in the names Mangosoft used on software products and Liddles used on nanotechnology software, and a copyright in the code of the Liddles program. People who wrote, used, and sold a program that performed the same processes would not infringe the copyright (if they did not copy creative expression, only the functional aspects of the program) but would infringe the patent (by using and by offering for sale the patented invention). If they sold it under the name "Liddles" or a confusingly similar name (perhaps "Lidles"), they would also infringe the trademark.

Other bodies of law also neighbor copyright. A person who bribed a Mangosoft employee to get the secret source code of the program could be liable under trade secret law. Someone who misrepresented the merits of his product or engaged in other anticompetitive conduct might be liable under unfair competition law. Someone who ran an ad using the likeness of the founder of Mangosoft might violate her right to publicity.

A major practice area for copyright lawyers (and most intellectual property lawyers) is good old-fashioned contract law. Copyrights are part of many contractual transactions. Authors sell book rights to publishers and movie rights to producers. Businesses hire contractors and employees to create copyrightable works, from books to software to photographs to music. Contracts can also be an alternative to copyright. For example, ideas are not copyrightable. So if an author tells a publisher the idea from a book, the publisher would not infringe copyright by using the idea in another book. But if the publisher first signs a nondisclosure contract (good luck getting them to agree!), then it would be a breach of contract to use the idea. Employers, inventors, investors, and others often use a contract to control rights in ideas—as between the parties to the contract.

The U.S. Copyright Statute

Copyright is a statutory area of the law, passed by Congress and signed by the President, after much lobbying by interested parties, such as publishers and entertainment companies. The physical layout of Washington, D.C., affects the shape of copyright law, with Congress looming over the Library of Congress, which houses the Copyright Office. The federal Copyright Act of 1976, as amended, provides the rules governing copyright law. To analyze a copyright case, then, the first thing to do is determine whether the applicable rule is set forth in the copyright statute. Generally it is: The copyright statute provides a comprehensive set of rules governing such things as the subject matter and scope of copyright; copyright ownership and transfer; duration of copyright; copyright notice, deposit, and registration; copyright infringement and remedies; and the operations of the copyright office.

The statute sets out the rules, but case law remains very important. Cases set out authoritative interpretation of the statute, giving shape to important but broad terms like "idea," or "fair use." The Copyright Office also has interpreted many provisions, an authority that courts often follow. Courts also interpret how the various statutory provisions work together. They would, for example, resolve apparent conflict between the first sale doctrine and liability for importation. Courts also fill gaps. The statute does not cover everything. Some doctrines, like secondary liability, have been created and shaped by judicial interpretation. *See MGM Studios Inc. v. Grokster, Ltd.*, 125 S. Ct. 2764 (2005). A related point is that copyright is governed by a federal statute and litigated in federal court. State legislatures and courts can do little in the area, and are instead left to use neighboring areas of law where Congress has not enacted preempting legislation.

The Copyright Act of 1976 provides the copyright law in force today, but copyright lawyers still must often refer to the 1909 Act, which was in effect until 1978. Copyrights last a long time. Many works published after 1922 are still under copyright. Deciding whether a pre-1978 work is under copyright, who owns the copyright, and other issues often requires applying the rules of the 1909 Act. If the author published without a copyright notice in 1940, or failed to renew the copyright in 1968, she may have lost her copyright (even though it would otherwise have lasted until 2035). Understanding the 1909 Act is also very helpful in understanding the 1976 Act, because many of its provisions were drafted with the 1909 Act, and the cases interpreting it, in mind.

Constitutional Basis for Copyright

As stated, the U.S. Constitution specifically authorizes Congress to grant copyrights and patents:

> The Congress shall have Power . . . to promote the Progress of Science and useful Arts, by securing for limited Times to Authors and Inventors the exclusive Right to their respective Writings and Discoveries.

U.S. Const. art. I, §8, cl. 8. Congress has exercised that power by enacting the Copyright Act and its many amendments.

The Supreme Court has given some guidance on how broadly Congress's power may be exercised. *Feist Publications v. Rural Telephone Service*, 499 U.S. 340, 369 (1991), held that copyright could not protect facts against copying. Rather, copyright can protect only original expression, elements independently created by the author, with at least some minimal degree of creativity. *Feist* held that originality is required by the Constitution's reference to granting exclusive rights to "Authors" in their "Writings." As of now, courts hold it includes only humans, not artificial intelligence.

Eldred v. Ashcroft, 537 U.S. 186 (2003), gave Congress latitude. The issue in *Eldred* was the constitutionality of the Copyright Term Extension Act of 1998, which added 20 years to the terms of existing copyrights—extending the copyrights in works dating back to the 1920s. *Eldred* rejected two challenges to the constitutionality of the copyright extension. The first challenge contended that Congress had exceeded its power to grant copyrights for "limited Times" in order to "promote the Progress of Science." That clause, the plaintiffs argued, implies that Congress's authority is limited by the incentive-to-create rationale. Nothing Congress did in 1998 could provide an incentive to create works in the 1920s. But the Court held that the Constitution left it to Congress to choose the intellectual property regime that best serves the purposes of the clause.

Eldred also rejected a First Amendment challenge to the constitutionality of the term extension. Copyright, by its nature, is a limit on freedom of speech. The plaintiffs had argued that the term extension was a content-neutral regulation that should be subject to intermediate scrutiny under the First Amendment. The Court, however, reasoned that First Amendment scrutiny was unnecessary where Congress had not "altered the traditional contours of copyright." The Copyright Clause was adopted around the same time as the First Amendment. Moreover, copyright law itself provides traditional First Amendment safeguards, such as fair use and the freedom to copy ideas from protected works. After *Eldred*, it appears the Congress has considerable latitude in fashioning copyright protection. But *Eldred*'s reliance on the fair use doctrine and the idea/expression dichotomy is likely to strengthen those limitations on copyright protection.

International and Comparative Copyright Law

Copyright is domestic law, but it is increasingly influenced by international law. As the COOL casebook puts it, the United States has gone from pirate to holdout to enforcer. In its early years, U.S. publishers freely published works of foreign authors without permission. The early U.S. copyright statute even expressly barred protection for the works of foreigners. This state of affairs allowed U.S. publishers to get material more cheaply, which may have made some books cheaper for consumers. In 1841, Charles Dickens lamented "the exquisite justice of never deriving sixpence from an enormous American sale of all my books." Katharina de la Durantaye, *Finding a Home for Orphans: Google Book Search and Orphan Works Law in the United States and Europe*, 21 Fordham Intell. Prop. Media & Ent. L.J. 229, 274 (2011). But it hurt U.S. authors abroad (because other countries reciprocated by denying protection to U.S. authors) and at home (it is hard to compete with *free*). The United States gradually entered into agreements with other countries and lowered the barriers to protection for foreign authors. The United States is now party to a number of treaties affecting copyright, most notably the Berne Convention for the Protection of Literary and Artistic Works and the Agreement on Trade-Related Aspects of Intellectual Property Rights (TRIPS). Other relevant treaties include the WIPO Copyright Treaty and the WIPO Performances and Phonograms Treaty. Countries rely on their authors not just to produce creative products but to burnish their reputation to attract visitors.[2]

The Berne Convention requires member countries to provide a certain level of copyright protection. As Professor Patry puts it, Berne is a convention for foreigners. It requires the United States to provide a certain level of copyright protection for authors from other Berne countries, but does not actually require the United States to give such protections to its own authors. But of course the United States does so anyway, giving the same treatment to U.S. authors and authors of other Berne countries (with slight differences).

TRIPS brought copyright into the international trade law arena. TRIPS makes most of the Berne requirements part of the U.S. obligations under the World Trade Organization. This means that if the United States does not live up to its obligations, the WTO may impose penalties on the United States. TRIPS gives bite to Berne. International law is followed by international enforcement, often lead by rights holders.[3]

Neither Berne nor TRIPS nor any of the other treaties gives rights directly to individuals. So an author can neither sue someone for infringing her rights under Berne nor sue the United States for failing to give sufficient rights as required by Berne. But knowledge of the treaties is important in studying and applying copyright law for several reasons. The treaties constrain the United States and put limits on proposals to amend copyright

---

2. Andrew McCarthy, *Ireland's Aran Islands, Hiding in Plain Sight*, New York Times (Sept. 10, 2018), https://www.nytimes.com/2018/09/10/travel/aran-islands-ireland-jm-synge.html ("Just as in the days of J.M. Synge, who wrote his celebrated plays there, the Arans can feel like a place lost in time. Part of the considerable allure of Aran lies in what it lacks. There are no movie theaters and few cars; electricity only arrived in the 1970s.").

3. Danny O'Brien, *Cracking the DVD Code*, The Irish Times (May 11, 2007).

law. Someone might think it is a good idea to pass a law that immunizes schools from claims of copyright infringement, but that law might violate TRIPS. Courts also consider international and comparative considerations in interpreting the copyright statute. If the copyright statute was amended to meet a U.S. treaty obligation, then it may be interpreted in light of that obligation. Similarly, in upholding the constitutionality of the Sonny Bono Copyright Term Extension Act of 1998), the *Eldred* court considered that copyright extension could be justified as bringing the United States into harmony with other jurisdictions, thereby securing longer protection for U.S. authors abroad.

Comparing U.S. copyright law to other copyright regimes can be instructive. U.S. copyright law is generally pretty similar to copyright law in most other countries, in part because so many are party to Berne and TRIPS. But U.S. law still differs in a number of respects. Notable examples include fair use (more broadly defined in the United States); formalities (the United States is unique in having a copyright office with extensive functions, such as registering copyrights and recording transactions involving copyrights, and U.S. law strongly encourages copyright registration, deposit of works, and use of copyright notices); moral rights (U.S. copyright law gives authors fewer moral rights, such as rights of attribution and protection of works from distortion); work-made-for-hire doctrine (under U.S. law, an employer has the copyright in a work created by an employee in the scope of employment; other jurisdictions have narrower rules); and statutory damages (in the United States, infringement of a registered work gives $750 to $150,000 in damages, even without showing harm).

A TOUR THROUGH THE COPYRIGHT STATUTE

Suppose Anna wrote a novel titled *White Castle*, a retelling of Shakespeare's *Hamlet* set in Chicago in 2019. Anna used the plotline of *Hamlet* and bits of the dialogue but added many new elements. She transformed the various characters into twenty-first-century analogs, often with a humorous twist. She recast various scenes with contemporary angles.

Copyrightable Subject Matter

Anna will have a copyright in the work if it is an original work of authorship fixed in a tangible medium of expression. She will easily meet those requirements. Her work is not completely original, being based on the preexisting play *Hamlet* and including many other elements that Anna did not originate, such as facts about Chicago. But to meet the originality requirement, a work need only originate with the author and show a minimal spark of creativity. Anna would be well beyond that standard. It would also have to be a work of authorship. The novel would qualify, as a literary work. The work must also be fixed in a tangible form. Anna would meet this by writing the work down on paper, or typing it into a computer, or dictating it into a tape recorder. So Anna would meet the rather minimal substantive requirements for copyright protection.

Ideas, Nonoriginal Elements, and Other Excluded Subject Matter

Although the work would be protected by copyright, not all elements of the work would be protected by copyright. Copyright applies only to original creative expression. It does not apply to nonoriginal elements. Anna would have no protection in the elements that she copied from *Hamlet* or in facts about Chicago or in other elements of the novel that she did not create. Copyright also does not apply to ideas. Anna would not have protection in her idea of setting *Hamlet* in contemporary Chicago, or in the ideas that constituted the structure of the novel's plot, or in other ideas expressed in the work. Copyright also excludes protection in functional elements of a work, such as the function of a copyrighted computer program. This exclusion may not matter much to a work like Anna's. Copyright also excludes protection for certain government works and for works that infringe on other copyrights. These exclusions likewise would not apply to Anna's work. Her work does not infringe on a copyright in *Hamlet*, because *Hamlet* is far too old to be under copyright.

Rights of the Copyright Owner

Anna, as copyright owner, would have a set of exclusive rights:

1. *Reproduction right:* Anna has the exclusive right to make copies, such as printing copies of the novel or copying expressive elements into other novels.
2. *Adaptation right:* Anna has the exclusive right to adapt the work into new works, such as creating an annotated edition of the novel, or translating the novel into Danish, or making a movie from the novel, or writing a sequel to the novel.
3. *Public distribution right:* Anna has the exclusive right to distribute copies of the work to the public, such as selling copies of the novel, or operating a website that allows people to download the novel as an e-book.

4. *Public performance right:* Anna has the exclusive right to perform the work in public, such as reciting the novel or playing a recorded version of the novel to the public.
5. *Public display right:* Anna has the exclusive right to display copies of the work to the public.
6. *Anticircumvention and copyright management information rights:* If Anna uses technological measures to prevent copying, to limit use of the work, or to implement digital rights management systems, it may be illegal for others to tamper with that technology.

Some authors have an additional set of rights of integrity and attribution. For works of visual art, such as paintings or sculpture, the author may prevent others from destroying or distorting the work itself or from failing to properly attribute authorship of the work. Anna's novel is not a work of visual art, so she would not have those specific rights. But other legal rules might give her a measure of similar protection. If someone published a distorted version of her novel, they would likely infringe her right to make copies and her right to adapt the work. If they misattributed authorship, they might be liable for false advertising or unfair competition.

Copyright owners also have legal protections for certain technological protections they might use. A copyright owner (and other distributors) might use anticopying technology (such as computer code that makes it difficult to make a copy of a CD) or antiaccess technology (such as scrambling a movie transmitted over cable or by satellite). It can violate §1201 of the Copyright Act to circumvent antiaccess technology or to traffic in devices or services to circumvent either anticopying or antiaccess technology. Anna might distribute her novel in e-book form, using encryption to attempt to prevent the novel being read by unlicensed users. Someone who circumvented that encryption or sold software that enabled others to circumvent the encryption might be liable to Anna.

Copyright Ownership

Anna, the author, would be the initial owner of the copyright. It would be different if Anna created the work as an employee, in which case the copyright would belong to her employer, because it would be a work made for hire. If Anna had worked with a joint author, the two would each own the copyright in the joint work. If the work were included in a collective work, the author of the collective work would have the copyright in the work as a whole, but Anna would retain her copyright in the novel. The parties often contract around these rules, such as by agreeing that an employee will retain the copyright in her work (rare), or that the hiring party will have the copyright in a work created by an independent contractor, such as a freelancer or consultant (common).

Note that the copyright says nothing about Anna's ownership of physical objects embodying the work. The copyright in a novel is entirely separate from ownership of the manuscript of the novel or copies of the novel. Someone who simply buys a painting gets ownership of the painting. They do not get ownership of the copyright in the painting unless the parties also agree to a transfer of copyright. Rather, the buyer would get the painting, but the artist would retain the copyright (the exclusive rights to make copies, adapt the work, distribute copies to the public, or publicly display copies—other than displaying the particular copy sold). The buyer would own the painting and could display it, but the artist would have the rights to make posters showing the painting, to display it on a website, or to adapt it into new images.

Copyright Notice, Registration, and Deposit

Simply by fixing the work in a tangible form (e.g., writing her novel on paper or on a computer), Anna would own the copyright in the novel. To have the copyright, it is not necessary to comply with such formalities as putting a copyright notice ("© 2019 Anna") on copies of the work, registering the work with the Copyright Office, or depositing copies with the Library of Congress. But Anna is permitted to take those steps, and there are considerable advantages to doing so. A copyright notice lets others know that she claims the copyright in the work and tells them whom to contact if they wish to license the work. Registration greatly increases the potential remedies for infringement, gives her a presumption of the validity of her copyright, and is necessary if she wishes to file an infringement action. Deposit is technically required if she registers and if she publishes the work, subject to a small risk of a fine.

Copyright Transactions

Anna initially owns the copyright. Many authors engage in transactions involving the copyright. As owner of the copyright, Anna has the exclusive rights to do such things as publish the book, sell copies to the public, have the book translated into other languages, and adapt the book into other works, such as a movie or a sequel. Anna can do those things herself or authorize others to do them. She could simply sell her copyright. She could also sell (or, in effect, rent) portions of the copyright. She could grant a publisher the exclusive rights to publish the book, or a movie studio the exclusive rights to make a movie from the book. Anna could even use the copyright as collateral for a loan. She could borrow money from a bank, putting her copyright up as security. Such grants would require a written agreement, signed by Anna. She could also make nonexclusive licenses, such as allowing another author to print excerpts of the novel. Such nonexclusive licenses could be written, oral, or even be implied from the conduct of the parties.

Whoever entered into a transaction with Anna involving the copyright could record it with the Copyright Office. As with registration, recordation is not required but offers considerable advantages. If Anna sells her copyright to Buyer, and Buyer records the transaction, then Buyer will be protected in the event that Anna sells the copyright again. An open question remains with respect to using copyrights as collateral: Should the lender file in the federal Copyright Office or in the relevant state office for filing notices of a lender's interest in collateral? Courts have not resolved this issue, so a careful lender will file in both places.

The contract under which Anna transfers her rights is also subject to contract law. The terms of copyright contracts sometimes require interpretation. Suppose Anna sold Publisher the exclusive right to publish her novel "in book form." The two might later disagree about whether that meant publishing the book in paper form only, or whether Publisher had acquired the right to publish it as an e-book. Courts use the same interpretive tools that they apply in other contract cases.

Termination of Grants and Licenses

Licensing is key to copyright practice. An author will enter into contracts with publishers and perhaps movie studios. Music companies buy rights from songwriters and performers. Any of the grants made by Anna would be subject to her right of termination. This means that, around 35 years after making the grant, Anna could cancel it and have the rights back. She would retain this right of termination even if she had made an unconditional grant or even if she had expressly waived her termination rights, because such waivers are ineffective. The right of termination does not apply to works made for hire, so employees do not get the right to their 35-year-old works.

Duration of Copyright

Anna's copyright would last for her life and an additional 70 years. So Anna's book would be under copyright for a long time. A work made for hire has a term of 95 years, rather than being linked to the life of the author.

For pre-1978 older works, ownership and duration of copyright may require application of the 1909 version of the copyright statute. Copyright law has changed over time. Some of the rules above would apply quite differently if Anna's book had been written and published in earlier decades. If, for example, Anna had written a book before 1978, she would not have copyright in it simply by fixing it in a tangible form. Rather, copyright would not apply unless she published the book and included a copyright notice (© 1996 Anna). If she had published the book without including the copyright notice, the book would have been a "divestive" publication—meaning Anna would have no copyright and the book would go into the public domain. The term of copyright also varies for works published before 1978. In very broad terms, works published before 1923 are no longer under copyright; works published between 1923 and 1978 may have up to a 95-year term, provided that the copyright owner followed necessary formalities such as providing copyright notice when publishing the work and filing a copyright renewal some 28 years after publication; works published after 1976 generally have the present term (life plus 70 for individual works, 95 years for works made for hire). From 1978 until 1989, it was still possible to forfeit copyright by publishing without a copyright notice, but the rule was more forgiving than the pre-1978 standard.

Fair Use and Other Limitations on Copyright

Anna's exclusive rights are subject to some important limitations. Others are permitted to make fair use of Anna's work. Quoting some lines in a book review, or handing out copies of pages to a literature class, or even writing a parody of Anna's novel might all qualify as fair use. In deciding whether fair use applies, courts look to four factors: the nature of the use, the nature of the copyrighted work, the amount taken, and the effect on the market for the copyrighted work. Anna's copyright is also subject to the first sale doctrine, a limit on her exclusive rights of distribution and display. The owner of a lawfully made copy may distribute it or display it without infringing. Someone who buys an authorized copy of Anna's book and resells it is not liable for infringing Anna's right to distribute copies to the public.

Copyright Litigation

Anna may sue in federal court for infringement of any of her exclusive rights. Potential defendants could be a seller of unauthorized copies or another novelist who copied from Anna's work. To prevail, Anna will have to show several things. First, she must show actual copying. There is no liability if the other novelist independently created elements similar to Anna's book without copying from Anna. Second, she must show copying of protected expression. There is no infringement for copying noncopyrighted elements.

If the other novelist copied only Anna's ideas or facts about Chicago, there would be no liability. Finally, the works must be substantially similar, or there is no infringement. The alleged infringer may raise various defenses, the most common of which is fair use.

There is liability for a direct infringer (one who copies, adapts, distributes, publicly performs, or publicly displays the work) and for any secondary infringer. Secondary infringers are those who are liable for contributory infringement (such as by inducing another to infringe, by running a website that facilitates filesharing) or vicarious infringement (controlling and profiting from infringement, such as running a bar where copyrighted songs are performed without a license).

If Anna can prove infringement, the court may award a range of remedies: actual damages, an injunction governing the infringer's future behavior, and impoundment and destruction of unauthorized copies and even equipment used to make them. If Anna registered her copyright before infringement, she has two more options. She may choose to seek statutory damages, rather than actual damages (downloading an unauthorized copy may be a few dollars of actual damages, but statutory damages will be at least $750 and possibly much more). She may also seek attorney's fees, the painful remedy of paying for the other side's lawyer.

Copyright law faced a new set of challenges with the Internet, a worldwide machine for making and distributing copies. Now artificial intelligence likewise raises many questions as a technology that may make copies of millions of copyrighted works, then use that data to train a program to, among other uses, generate new works. As with the Internet, the law and the technology will change interdependently.

PART I

Copyrightable Subject Matter

CHAPTER 2

Works of Authorship

The U.S. Copyright Act of 1790 covered only books, maps, and charts. Since then, Congress has exponentially broadened the scope of copyright. Now copyright covers books, movies, and songs—but also advertisements, blueprints, computer programs, diaries, dances, finger paintings, T-shirt designs, sculpture, speeches. . . . As this chapter discusses, copyright casts a broad net, applying to works of all categories. Copyright applies to any original work of authorship fixed in a tangible medium of expression. The first three chapters address those three requirements: what qualifies as a work of authorship; what it takes to meet the originality requirement; and when a work is fixed, thereby triggering copyright protection. As section 102 says:

> (a) Copyright protection subsists, in accordance with this title, in original works of authorship fixed in any tangible medium of expression, now known or later developed, from which they can be perceived, reproduced, or otherwise communicated, either directly or with the aid of a machine or device. Works of authorship include the following categories:
>
> (1) literary works;
> (2) musical works, including any accompanying words;
> (3) dramatic works, including any accompanying music;
> (4) pantomimes and choreographic works;
> (5) pictorial, graphic, and sculptural works;
> (6) motion pictures and other audiovisual works;
> (7) sound recordings; and
> (8) architectural works.

WHAT CONSTITUTES A "WORK OF AUTHORSHIP"?

Copyright applies only to original "works of authorship." 17 U.S.C. §102(a). The category "works of authorship" is very broadly construed. Copyright protection could have been limited to works of fine art or high literary merit. It could also have been limited to established categories, such as novels, short stories, poems, paintings, and the like. Likewise, copyright could include some genres (such as literary fiction, history, documentary) and deem others unworthy of protection (risqué works, detective novels, comic books). One could reason that because copyright confers a bundle of exclusive rights, only certain works deserving of such rights should be copyrighted. One could measure whether they deserve copyright on grounds of aesthetic merit, or social value, or some other measure. But that is emphatically not the approach that copyright law takes.

To the contrary, copyright applies without regard to artistic merit. A work does not have to meet any standard of artistic merit to qualify as a work of authorship. Nor is copyright limited to particular categories of creative works. Creative expression takes many forms. Judges are ill equipped to act as critics of art or literature. Any work that qualifies as an original work of authorship is copyrightable, irrespective of whether it is high art, popular art, commercial art, idiosyncratic doodling, or any other form of expression. As Justice Holmes put it, in holding that advertisements are copyrightable:

> It would be a dangerous undertaking for persons trained only to the law to constitute themselves final judges of the worth of pictorial illustrations, outside of the narrowest and most obvious limits. At the one extreme some works of genius would be sure to miss appreciation. Their very novelty would make them repulsive until the public had learned the new language in which their author spoke. It may be more than doubted, for instance, whether the etchings of Goya or the paintings of Manet would have been sure of protection when seen for the first time. At the other end, copyright would be denied to pictures which appealed to a public less educated than the judge. Yet if they command the interest of any public, they have a commercial value—it would be bold to say that they have not an aesthetic and educational value—and the taste of any public is not to be treated with contempt.

Bleistein v. Donaldson Lithographing Co., 188 U.S. 239, 252 (1903).

One could also reason that copyright should be shaped to fit its purpose. Under the Constitution, the purpose of copyright is to provide an incentive to create works: Congress has the power to "promote the Progress of Science and useful Arts, by securing for limited Times to Authors and Inventors the exclusive Right to their respective Writings and Discoveries." U.S. Const. art. I, §8. Copyright could be given out only where necessary to provide an incentive for production. Again, the statute does not take this approach. The categories of protected works are not limited by the incentive purpose of copyright. Absent copyright, many works would not be produced. If authors had no exclusive rights, some books, movies, recordings, and artworks would not be created. A movie may cost millions of dollars to produce. If others were free to copy and distribute the movie, it might be difficult for the producers to recoup their costs, let alone make a profit. The producer would have difficulty competing with other sellers of the same movie who did not have to spend anything on production. There are non-copyright means that the producers could use to protect their investment, such as imposing limitations on distribution and use, employing measures to prevent copying (such as prohibiting video cameras in theaters or putting anticopy technology on DVDs), and exploiting consumers' preference for the authorized version of the film. Other areas of law offer some protection against copying, such as contract, trade secret, and unfair competition laws. But certainly some producers, absent copyright, would invest their resources elsewhere. The same is true for other categories of works. Writers of books, software developers, and many other creative workers are provided an incentive by copyright, meaning that copyright results in more works being produced.

On the other hand, absent copyright, many works would still be created. Many other reasons exist for people to create works. Even without copyright to protect their right to exploit the works, artists would still create art, academics would write articles, and people would write letters and fiction. Some categories of works do not rely on the exclusive rights of copyright for remuneration. An advertising agency creates original works but seeks payment from its client rather than from paying customers. Even authors who usually rely on copyright protection do not depend absolutely on copyright law. Some books, movies, and music, for example, would still be produced without copyright. Creative impulses, desire for expression and recognition, and many other forces motivate the production of creative works. But copyright law does not limit protection to works that would not be produced absent copyright protection. Rather, copyright applies to all original works of authorship.

Example

1. *Coveted cover.* TV Land magazine sues a competitor magazine, alleging that the competitor infringed copyright by copying the cover of an edition of TV Land. The competitor did not literally copy the text and layout, but rather the size, shape, and graphic design of the cover. The design is composed of basic elements composed into a pleasing package likely to catch the eye of someone standing in line at a grocery checkout counter. Competitor argues that the design of a magazine cover is product

packaging, not a work of authorship. Is the design of the magazine cover a work of authorship?

Explanation

1. The design of a magazine cover may be a work of authorship. The layout of a magazine cover may not qualify to hang in an art gallery, and its purpose may be to attract readers' attention rather than to express artistic impulses, but the commercial character of a work does not bar it from being a work of authorship. *See Reader's Digest Association v. Conservative Digest*, 821 F.2d 800 (D.C. Cir. 1987).

   To preview material later in this book, a cover design does fit within the definition of a "pictorial, graphic, or sculptural work" (discussed in the next section) as a two-dimensional work of applied art. To receive copyright protection (discussed in the next chapter), it would also have to meet the requirements of originality. Even though the design employed nonoriginal components, the requisite creativity could be shown in the choices of how to put those components together.

THINGS THAT FALL OUTSIDE THE CATEGORY OF "WORKS OF AUTHORSHIP"

The requirement that something be a work of authorship does exclude some fruits of human creativity from copyright protection. Conversation often includes creative expression such as witty remarks, vivid descriptions, silly stories, or perceptive critiques of artistic works. Everyday behavior can likewise be quite creative. Behavior such as children's play, sidewalk encounters (or avoidance thereof), or practical jokes can all be quite creative. But granting copyright to conversation or personal conduct would greatly inhibit human interaction. If such everyday activity were copyrighted, others would be excluded from repeating it. It would also be difficult to know when someone could claim copyright in such activity if they needed to show only that it was original (and had been somehow preserved in a tangible form, which in our digital area is pretty easy). To prevent such uncertainty, under the leading decision, it would

> be required that the speaker indicate that he intended to mark off the utterance in question from the ordinary stream of speech, that he meant to adopt it as a unique statement and that he wished to exercise control over its publication.

Estate of Hemingway v. Random House, 23 N.Y.2d 341 (1968). Such a statement reserving rights is not a general requirement—a short story, letter, or painting is protected by copyright without any explicit claim by the author. But those works fall within the categories where one might expect copyright to apply. They also have natural boundaries that separate them from other communications. Explicit claims would be necessary only for claims to copyright things like conversation or everyday behavior as a "work of authorship," where others would think it unrestricted. Likewise, the requirement that something be a "work of authorship" could be used to deny claims to copyright protection to such creative activities as crime sprees, tantrums, and practical jokes. Such "works" have the necessary originality but would not be taken by others to be the creation of protected works.

Under similar reasoning, a game of soccer or basketball would not be a work of authorship. Such a game is likely to feature lots of creativity. Like conversation and everyday behavior, however, there would be little guide to what constituted the claimed work, not to mention deciding who the author was. By contrast, a scripted soccer game, a choreographed dance, or a football playbook might be works of authorship (although nonoriginal or functional elements, as discussed later in the book, are not protected). A video of a soccer game or a newspaper story about the game could be a work of authorship. The game itself would not be subject to the copyrights, because the videographer and reporter did not author the game.

The limitation of copyright to "works" can also exclude other creative expression. The U.S. Copyright Office (an authoritative source, although not definitive) takes the position that copyright is not available for words and short phrases, such as names, titles, and slogans. 37 C.F.R. §202.1. Several cases are in accord. The rule seems a necessary one—if a word or short phrase could be copyrighted, then any use of the word or phrase would be potential copyright infringement. Words or short phrases should receive, if anything, the narrower protection of trademark law. "Coca-Cola" is a trademark, but one can still utter the word without infringing the trademark—only using the mark in ways that interfere with Coca-Cola's use to accurately identify its product to consumers is barred. If short phrases were copyrighted, then titles of books and names of songs would be copyrighted, which would mean it would be potential infringement to refer to a book or song. Likewise, clever words like "threepeat" could belong to the first person to utter them, taking copyright far beyond its moorings.

The rule is often justified by stating that words or short phrases are not sufficiently original (as discussed later in the book). But certainly even a single word could originate with the author and have much more than the requisite minimal spark of creativity—like such coinages as "copyleft," "copywrong," and "copybroke." A broader rationale might be that a word or phrase does not constitute a work of authorship. As Gertrude Stein said to Ernest Hemingway, "Remarks are not literature." Another rationale for the rule is the merger doctrine (discussed later in the book). Copyright protection for a word or short phrase would effectively give protection to the idea it expresses.

Recall, however, that a copyrighted work may be made up of noncopyrightable elements. So although a short statement may not be copyrightable, a compilation of short statements (such as a book of short jokes or slogans) could be. Likewise, copying a short phrase from a work could potentially be infringement, although it would likely be permitted under fair use or excused as de minimis.

The limitation of copyright to "works of authorship" also implies an author. This appears to mean that a human created the work, using the requisite creativity. In a work made through a completely mechanical process, copyright might be denied on the basis that no one was the "author." If a security camera mounted in a lobby, recording 24 hours a day, captured a dramatic event, the video might be deemed uncopyrighted, for lack of an author.

Computer-generated works also raise the issue of authorship. If works are generated automatically, or are the product of artificial intelligence, there may be no human author. Courts and the Copyright Office have held that only humans can qualify as authors. A human could qualify as an author if they contributed some creativity to the work. The question would likely be whether the work reflected originality on the part of a human, or whether the choices were actually made by computer.

"Works" created by natural processes or by nonhuman animals would also not be "works of authorship." Lava flows from volcanoes may form fantastical shapes, but they are not copyrighted, not being the product of a human author. Elephants and gorillas have both been taught to paint. The paintings are not copyrightable, not being works of authorship. Nor does copyright apply to video made when a seagull stole a camera or to photos made by macaques monkeying around with an unattended camera. The Ninth Circuit looked at the structure of the Copyright Act as a whole in deciding that a monkey, which somehow took a selfie, did not have standing to sue when the photo went viral.

> "For example, the 'children' of an 'author,' 'whether legitimate or not,' can inherit certain rights under the Copyright Act. Also, an author's 'widow or widower owns the author's entire termination interest unless there are any surviving children or grandchildren of the author, in which case the widow or widower owns one-half of the author's interest.' The terms 'children,' 'grandchildren,' 'legitimate,' 'widow,' and 'widower' all imply humanity and

> necessarily exclude animals that do not marry and do not have heirs entitled to property by law."

Naruto v. Slater, 888 F.3d 418 (9th Cir. 2018) (statutory citations omitted). Courts have held that an AI cannot be an author, for the purpose of copyright law.[1]

The Copyright Office has interpreted the statute to require a human author:

> In order to be entitled to copyright registration, a work must be the product of human authorship. Works produced by mechanical processes or random selection without any contribution by a human author are not registrable. A linoleum floor covering featuring a multicolored pebble design which was produced by a mechanical process in unrepeatable, random patterns, is not registrable. Similarly, a work owing its form to the forces of nature and lacking human authorship is not registrable; for example, a piece of driftwood even if polished and mounted is not registrable.

Compendium II: Copyright Office Practices 503.03(a).

Copyright's exclusions for purely mechanical works and for everyday behavior and conversation are starting to overlap. Increasingly, what we say and do is recorded by various devices: security cameras, communications technology, virtual worlds, chat rooms. More than one person wears a camera intended to record his entire life—and wearable technology may soon do that for the average consumer. Are all those captured moments subject to copyright? One could well argue that they do not constitute works of authorship. In the same way that a conversation does not have boundary lines that mark it as a "work," so do 24/7 automatic recordings of data lack the authorial intent and announcement that would stake a copyright claim. The incentive of copyright is not needed to encourage the creation of such collections of information—they are already created for other reasons. Without showing that someone set out to create a work, courts should hesitate before affording copyright protection to such information.

Finally, a person's identity is also not a work of authorship. One might think of the persona of some people as their own creation, whether Muhammad Ali, Truman Capote, or Madonna. Someone's character, persona, or likeness is in part created by the person—but also by other factors (their genetic makeup and experiences, including the influences of others).

1. *Thaler v. Perlmutter*, Civil Action No. 22-1564 (BAH), 2023 U.S. Dist. LEXIS 145823, at *19-20 (D.D.C. Aug. 18, 2023) ("On the record designed by plaintiff from the outset of his application for copyright registration, this case presents only the question of whether a work generated autonomously by a computer system is eligible for copyright. In the absence of any human involvement in the creation of the work, the clear and straightforward answer is the one given by the Register: No.").

More important, such elements are not embodied in a tangible form, which would set the boundaries of the protected work. *See Brown v. Ames*, 201 F.3d 654 (5th Cir. 2000). Someone can create a work imbued with their persona, such as an autobiography, self-portrait, or ballad. But the work, not the persona, would be copyrighted.

To sum up, the scope of "works of authorship" is broad indeed. It does, however, exclude:

- everyday conversation and behavior (unless the author does something to claim ownership and specifically mark it as a work), even if the words and deeds are randomly recorded by a mechanical device
- words and short phrases
- works with no human author (e.g., works created by animals or AI)
- the identity or persona of a person

Examples

1. *Everyday people*. Welles uses her phone to record video over hours, capturing people going through life in a city day. She modestly edits it into an untitled documentary. Copyrightable work of authorship?
2. *Instant messaging*. Author and Writer have an extended interchange over a computer network via instant messaging. They carry on a far-ranging discussion of literature, including many witty remarks and incisive analyses of famous works. Author subsequently claims copyright in her contributions to the conversation. Were her instant messages (either individually or together) works of authorship?
3. *Same product, different package*. Rather than having the instant messaging conversation, Author writes down her views in an essay, likewise composed of witty remarks and incisive analyses of famous works. Is her essay a work of authorship?
4. *Prepared remarks*. Literary Critic writes to Author, requesting a meeting to discuss Author's works. Anxious to come off well, Author sits down over several days and writes out a lengthy analysis of his own work. During the videotaped meeting, Author then delivers the analysis interview paragraph by paragraph in response to questions posed by Literary Critic. Does Author have a copyright in his remarks?
5. *Whale songs*. Cetologist makes a number of recordings of humpback whales singing off the islands of Hawaii. Cetologist has studied the whales for years and draws on her experience in positioning the microphones, setting the recording levels, and deciding when to make the

recordings. The recordings capture a number of noises made by the whales, with many musical qualities. Merchant gets access to the tapes, makes copies, and sells them to whale enthusiasts. When Cetologist claims copyright infringement, Merchant contends that the recordings are not works of authorship. Are the recordings works of authorship?

6. *Funded*. Herzog wishes to film a documentary about modern life in towns on the Mississippi River. Herzog receives a grant from the Philo Foundation, which fully funds the production of the film. Herzog sends copies of the film to a number of universities, hoping to encourage interest in the work. Several months later, Herzog learns that Movie House has been running Herzog's film for several weeks, making a nice profit. When Herzog seeks compensation, Movie House argues that the work is not copyrighted. Copyright exists to provide an incentive to produce works, and that rationale does not support copyright in works that are funded from the outset, argues Movie House. Does copyright apply to works that would be created anyway?

7. *Hand of nature*. The coastline of Oregon regularly receives driftwood. Bonnie, a local, often walks the beaches looking for pieces of driftwood that have been shaped and textured by the elements. She finds one piece that has a particularly enigmatic shape, which she calls the Portland Pretzel. She leaves it on display in her shop window. Angelo, a sculptor, takes a photo of the piece and produces an iron sculpture with exactly the same shape. Is he liable to Bonnie for copyright infringement?

8. *What's a voggle?* Sitting in calculus class one day, Tango raises his hand and asks the instructor, "What's a voggle?" Having looked in the dictionary, Tango knows that there is no such thing. The closest is a Siberian language known as Vogul. So his question causes confusion and a little respite from mathematical rigor. Other students adopt the same trick, asking, "What's a voggle?" to English teachers, gym teachers, and even the security personnel. For no apparent reason, the phrase becomes extremely popular, and soon the catchphrase "What's a voggle?" appears online, on television, and in the papers. Tango wonders if he should be receiving copyright royalties on the word "voggle" and the phrase "What's a voggle?" Should he?

9. *Photoshopper*. Pixel has assembled a considerable collection of public domain photographs from around 1900, all of which are now in digital form. Using Photoshop, a popular piece of software for manipulating images, she creates a series of pictures. Although her pictures appear to be photos taken during 1900, they are actually made by cutting and pasting elements from many pictures. For example, one shows a boy

wearing a policeman's uniform as a Halloween costume, in conversation with a police officer. But Pixel used Photoshop to take the various elements from a number of photos: The image of the boy was taken from a school picture, his bag was taken from a picture of a store, his uniform was taken from a picture of a police officer and then reduced in size, and the police officer was adapted from the image of a mail carrier. Photoshop automatically adjusts many aspects of the pictures to ensure that they do not look like cut-and-paste collages but rather like single images. After Vader Publishing uses some of the images without Pixel's permission, she sues for copyright infringement. Vader defends on the basis that the pictures were all made by Photoshop, not Pixel, and are therefore the product of software, not works of an author. Are the manipulated images works of authorship?

10. *Elephant see, elephant do*. Shawn, an elephant keeper, patiently teaches Romany the elephant how to paint. After considerable training, Romany learns to pick up a brush, dip it in the palette, and daub paint on a blank piece of paper. Encouraged with treats, Romany covers much of the paper. The zoo sells the painting at a charitable auction for a few dollars. The buyer then sells posters featuring Romany's quite abstract and messy painting. The zoo, feeling cheated, considers suing for copyright infringement. Is the painting copyrighted?

11. *Donkey business*. The Doncaster Donkeys are a popular attraction on Broadway. They perform an intricate act, choreographed by their trainer, Trevor. The donkeys balance on balls, dance in a line, weave in and out in intricate patterns. They also perform a few pratfalls. The show is so successful that it inspires imitators. One production starts up in Las Vegas, closely copying the Doncaster Donkeys' routine. In response to a cease-and-desist letter from Trevor, the new show claims that the donkeys' act is not copyrightable, because it is the work of donkeys, who do not qualify as authors. No work of authorship, no copyright. Is the donkey act in the public domain?

12. *All the world's a stage*. Bolly produces a film about Anoushka, a well-known musician. The screenwriter and lead actress capture Anoushka's quirky and captivating personality well. Anoushka sues for copyright infringement. Is Bolly liable? Would it be different if Anoushka had written her autobiography and a publisher copied that?

13. *Performance anxiety*. Cindy Lee Garcia had a minor role in a film with the working title Desert Warrior. After that film was abandoned, the producer used the footage of her scenes in an anti-Islamic film titled Innocence of Muslims, dubbing offensive lines over her performance. Garcia sued for copyright infringement, claiming copyright in her performance as a work of authorship itself. Should she succeed?

Explanations

1. Welles's documentary is a work of authorship. None of the exclusions apply to her work. She is not claiming copyright in everyday behavior but rather in a film of everyday behavior. Copyright applies to many works that record noncopyrightable elements.

2. Little case law addressing this issue exists. The basic question is whether instant messages are like everyday conversation (unprotected without explicit claims of rights) or letters (protectable without requiring an explicit claim of right, as many cases have held). The interchange here more closely resembles a conversation, with a give-and-take in real time. As technology preserves more and more of our casual communications and daily activity, such copyright issues may proliferate.

3. The essay is a work of authorship. The requirement of an explicit claim of right applies only to things such as conversation or everyday behavior, which otherwise would not be separated out as works by others. Note that this rule arises not from the statute or a line of cases, but rather a single, well-known case. If such cases do become more common, courts may not necessarily adopt the explicit claim requirement, instead relying on the other requirements to play the gatekeeper role.

4. Whether the discussion qualifies as a work of authorship is a moot point. Assuming it had the requisite originality, Author's written version of his analysis would qualify as an original work of authorship (specifically, a literary work). Anyone who made copies of the videotape would potentially infringe the copyright (subject to various limitations discussed in the infringement chapter).

5. The whales are also red herrings. Cetologist has created original works of authorship: the sound recordings. She made a number of creative decisions in how and when to make her recordings. She has created original works of authorship, just as if she had photographed the whales.

6. Herzog's film is copyright protected, even if the copyright's incentive was not necessary for its creation. Nothing in the copyright statute limits copyright in general to works that require the incentive of copyright.

7. Angel is not liable, because Bonnie has no copyright in the driftwood. She did not create the piece of driftwood; rather, the forces of nature created it. It is not a work of authorship. The Copyright Office regulations use the example of driftwood.

8. Tango has no copyright in the word "voggle" or the phrase "What's a voggle?" The weight of authority denies copyright to words or short

phrases. One reason for the rule is that they do not show sufficient originality (although it would seem that the requisite minimal creativity could be met by thinking up a new word or phrase). Another way to justify the rule is that they are simply too short to qualify as works of authorship.

9. The manipulated images are works of authorship. The computer program may do much of the work, but Pixel selects the elements and cuts and pastes them. That would be sufficient to make Pixel the author.

10. A painting by an elephant would not be copyrighted, because there is no human author.

11. The choreography of the donkeys' act is protected by copyright. The author of the choreography is Trevor, although it is performed by the donkeys.

12. Bolly is not liable, because he has not copied a work of authorship. A personality is not a work of authorship, for the purpose of copyright law. It is someone's creation, in a broad sense, but is not embodied in a particular work.

    An autobiography is a work of authorship. So copying the autobiography could be copyright infringement, especially if the copying was simply reprinting and selling copies of the book. As coming chapters discuss, however, many elements of the autobiography would not be copyrighted, such as facts and other material not original to the author, and ideas (even original ones).

13. Garcia was not the author of the film. She may have performed creatively, but her performance was not a separable copyrighted work. "Take, for example, films with a large cast—the proverbial "cast of thousands"—such as *Ben-Hur* or *Lord of the Rings*. The silent epic *Ben-Hur* advertised a cast of 125,000 people. In the *Lord of the Rings* trilogy, 20,000 extras tramped around Middle-earth alongside Frodo Baggins (played by Elijah Wood). Treating every acting performance as an independent work would not only be a logistical and financial nightmare, but it would turn cast of thousands into a new mantra: "copyright of thousands." *Garcia v. Google, Inc.*, 786 F.3d 733, 742-743 (9th Cir. 2015) (en banc).

CATEGORIES OF WORKS

The 1790 copyright statute covered only maps, books, and charts. Things have changed. The copyright statute now provides that works of authorship include the following categories:

1. literary works
2. musical works, including any accompanying words
3. dramatic works, including any accompanying music
4. pantomimes and choreographic works
5. pictorial, graphic, and sculptural works
6. motion pictures and other audiovisual works
7. sound recordings
8. architectural works

17 U.S.C. §102(a). The statute also provides that compilations and derivative works are copyrightable subject matter. 17 U.S.C. §103(a).

The categories are not mutually exclusive, so a work can fall into more than one category. A play may be both a literary work and a dramatic work. The list itself is also not exclusive. The statute and the legislative history indicate that the categories are illustrative, not exhaustive. Whether a work appears to fall into one of the categories may influence a court in deciding whether the work is a work of authorship, but it is not determinative. A work that does not fit into any of the listed categories could still qualify for copyright if it is an original work of authorship. A symphony of odors would not appear to fall into any of the categories but would still qualify as an original work of authorship. In any event, the definitions of the categories (discussed below) are so broad that almost any creative work would fall into at least one category. If a work uses letters or numbers, it is a literary work. If it is in two or three dimensions, it is likely a pictorial, graphic, or sculptural work. That covers almost all potential works already. The list may expand. To look at developments abroad, the Court of Justice of the European Union held that copyright law does not protect the taste of cheese.[2] However, "it added that if in the future, technology could identify tastes with enough precision and objectivity, then copyright could protect tastes."

The importance of the categories lies not in setting the boundaries of copyright, but in applying other rules in the statute. As discussed in more detail in later chapters, certain copyright rules apply only to specific categories of works of authorship. The basic rights of the copyright holder vary somewhat for different categories of works. Copyrights in sound recordings, for example, have much more limited rights of reproduction and public performance. Musical works, to give another example, are subject to a compulsory license that does not apply to other categories of works. It is often important to determine which category a work falls into. The following paragraphs list the categories and provide definitions where applicable. They

2. Estelle Derclaye, *Copyright law does not protect the taste of cheese*, The Conversation http://theconversation.com/copyright-law-does-not-protect-the-taste-of-cheese-108356 (Dec. 12, 2018).

also briefly note some rules applicable to particular categories of works, leaving more detailed discussion of the rules to later chapters.

Literary Works

Finnegans Wake is a literary work. So is the software code for *Minecraft*. This category includes "works, other than audiovisual works, expressed in words, numbers, or other verbal or numerical symbols or indicia, regardless of the nature of the material objects, such as books, periodicals, manuscripts, phonorecords, film, tapes, disks, or cards, in which they are embodied." 17 U.S.C. §101.

Such a broad definition goes well beyond what is normally considered "literature" to include anything made with letters, numbers, or other symbols. Some examples of literary works are plays, short stories, novels, movie scripts, letters, e-mail messages, blogs, computer programs, cooking recipes, souvenir T-shirt messages, mathematical proofs, and municipal zoning ordinances. As with all the categories, any of the foregoing would have to qualify as an original work of authorship to have protection. The definition also emphasizes that the form of fixation is irrelevant. Literary works do not have to be fixed in a form that a human can pick up and read, such as a printed book. Rather, a novel can be fixed by saving it on disk, or a story can be fixed by recording an oral performance.

An important type of literary work is a computer program, also known as software. Software is copyrightable, whether in source code, object code, or other form. This certainly takes the definition of "literary work" beyond its meaning in other contexts. Literature departments in universities are usually quite separate from the computer science program. Literary theory pays much more attention to poetry than computer code. At one time, it was widely debated whether computer programs should be subject to copyright at all. Copyright protects creative expression. Computer programs can be seen as functional works, as opposed to expressive works. They are also sets of instructions for machines, as opposed to creative works experienced by people. Software pervades "the progress of science," as the Constitution puts it. Georgia Tech once offered only a degree in mechanical engineering, but now is a computer science pioneer.

As part of the preparation for the 1976 Copyright Act, Congress established the Commission on New Technological Uses of Copyrighted Works (CONTU). CONTU concluded that computer programs fit within copyrightable subject matter, both as a matter of law and policy. It made two recommendations adopted by Congress. Congress amended the Copyright Act in 1980 to define a computer program as "a set of statements or instructions to be used directly or indirectly in a computer in order to bring about a certain result." 17 U.S.C. §101. It also added section 117, which imposed some limitations on the copyright of a computer program. The two amendments imply that computer programs are copyrightable. Since then, the issue has not been whether computer programs are copyrightable, but rather how broad the scope of protection is.

Example

1. *Literary?* A number of provisions of the Copyright Act apply to "literary works." Which of the following are literary works?
   - A novel, published in book form
   - A novel, available only online as an electronic book
   - A set of instructions for assembling a swimming pool
   - A computer program
   - A mathematical proof
   - The book you are reading
   - A warning label on an energy drink
   - A tweet

Explanation

1. They are all literary works. A novel might be the only one that would be studied in a literature class, but the definition of literary work for copyright law is very broad: any work "expressed in words, numbers, or other verbal or numerical symbols or indicia," regardless of the form in which it is fixed. Literary work lawsuits have included warning labels, course syllabi, legal briefs, letters, T-shirt statements, and more.

Musical Works, Including Any Accompanying Words

"Pretty Woman," "Blurred Lines," "Happy Birthday to You," and "We Shall Overcome" are examples of disputed musical works, as is "Pi Symphony." The category of musical works spans all genres, from a cappella to zigeunermusik. The musical work includes both the music and the words that go with it. A musical work could include both, such as when a songwriter writes the music and lyrics to a new song. A musical work could also include preexisting elements. An old poem could be set to music, or an old tune could be used for a set of new words. Either work would qualify for copyright as a musical work, but the copyright would only protect the new expression.

The statute does not define "musical work." The term is not limited to any particular type or definition of music. New forms and genres of music could be covered, even if they break with traditional forms of music. More recent genres, such as electronic music, rap music, and various avant-garde forms qualify. No particular element of music—such as rhythm, melody, or harmony—is required. Rather, any work that is musical in character would qualify. John Cage's 1952 piece "4′33″," consisting of four minutes and thirty-three seconds of silence, would likely be a musical work, even if it would be difficult to identify specific protected elements.

An important distinction exists between a musical work and a sound recording. A musician who composes music or writes a song is the author of a musical work. A producer who records some sounds creates a sound recording, a separate category of work. A producer who makes a recording of a musician performing musical work is the author of a sound recording. If the recording is put on a compact disc, the CD is a phonorecord of both the musical work and the sound recording. Anyone who copies the recording potentially infringes two copyrights: the musician's copyright in the musical work and the producer's copyright in the sound recording.

Copyright in a musical work is subject to an important limitation. Where recordings of a nondramatic musical work, such as a song, have been publicly distributed, the copyright in the musical work is subject to the compulsory licensing scheme of section 115. Anyone else may record and sell their own version of the song, provided they give the required notice, pay the required royalties, and do not alter the form of the song beyond certain limits. Once one musician releases her version of a song, others are free to market their own versions. The same is not true of other works. The public release of a movie or video game does not authorize others to make their own versions.

Another effect of a work qualifying as musical work is certain limitations applicable to libraries and archives. Section 108 permits libraries to make certain reproductions and distributions of copyrighted works, for such purposes as preservation of works or dissemination of rare works. The scope of the exemption is limited for musical works; audiovisual works; and pictorial, graphic, or sculptural works. It is mostly relevant to literary works.

Musical works have figured large in copyright law. Many musical copyrights are very valuable, so the industry has been active in shaping copyright legislation and pursuing copyright litigation. Music copyright holders have led the way in collective enforcement of copyrights, from creating collective rights societies like ASCAP through recent litigation against music downloading (such as the Napster and Grokster cases). Many songs sound alike, which leads to interesting cases on issues like originality and authorship, not to mention a number of notable cases of infringement claims against well-known musicians.

Example

1. *Musing on musical works.* Which of the following would qualify as "musical works," for the purposes of copyright law?
   - "Happy Birthday to You"
   - "Satisfaction" by Jagger and Richards
   - An opera
   - A symphony
   - The background music for the video game *Cut the Rope*
   - The theme music to *Jeopardy*
   - A song written by some kids as their club's song
   - A recording, available on iTunes, of *Hamlet*

Explanation

1. All would qualify as musical works, except the last. This illustrates the broad reach of copyright. The *Hamlet* example simply serves to remind us that musical works may appear mixed with other works.

Dramatic Works, Including Any Accompanying Music

"Dramatic works" is not defined in the statute, but according to a leading treatise the category includes "any work in which performed actions, speech, or incident, or all three, convey theme, thoughts or character to an audience." Paul Goldstein, *Copyright* (2nd ed. 1996) at 2:110. Examples of dramatic works would include "choreography, pantomimes, plays, treatments, and scripts prepared for cinema, radio, and television." Copyright Office Fl 119. The distinguishing characteristic of a dramatic work is that the actions are "intended to be performed," as opposed to being narrated or described. An opera would be a dramatic work, whereas a novel would not (although many dramatic incidents may be described in the novel). The opera is intended to be performed onstage with the singers playing the roles of characters. A novel is intended to be read. Even some works that are performed in public (such as rock songs) are not dramatic when they are not performed in character to act out the drama in the song.

A dramatic work would likely fall into another category, such as literary work or musical work. The principal effect of a work's qualifying as a dramatic work is that it is not subject to some of the limitations on copyright.

For example, the compulsory license for musical works in section 115 applies only to nondramatic musical works. Nondramatic literary and musical works are subject to use, without requiring permission of the copyright holder, in online education, in religious services, or at certain charitable functions, under section 110.

Example

1. *Dramatic?* "The Ballad of Ethelred the Unready" was written, sung, and recorded by Desmond. The song tells the gripping tale of a medieval monarch's life. Desmond sold a few dozen CDs to the public. He later learned that the group Danegeld had recorded and released its own version of the ballad. Rather than get Desmond's permission, the group used the compulsory license procedure under section 115. Desmond objects. Section 115 applies only to "nondramatic musical works." But, Desmond contends, his ballad is extremely dramatic, telling the story of Ethelred's ascent to the throne at age ten, of his struggles to keep the throne and make the kingdom prosper, and of his battles with the Vikings. Is the ballad a dramatic musical work?

Explanation

1. "The Ballad of Ethelred the Unready" is not a dramatic work, even if it tells a dramatic story. A dramatic work is one where actions are "intended to be performed," as opposed to being "narrated or described." The ballad describes a number of actions, but the singer does not perform them. The ballad would still be copyrightable (as a musical work); it simply would not be subject to certain rules that only apply to dramatic works.

Pantomimes and Choreographic Works

This category includes ballet, mime, jazz dance, and postmodern dance. Note an example of the overlapping categories. Many pantomimes and choreographic works also qualify as dramatic works. They could also be literary works if described by letters, numbers, or symbols.

The Copyright Office has defined choreographic works as follows: "Choreography represents a related series of dance movements and patterns organized into a coherent whole." Compendium of Copyright Office Practices, Compendium II 450.03(a). "Choreography is the composition and arrangement of dance movements and patterns, and is usually intended to be accompanied by music. Dance is static and kinetic successions of bodily movement in certain rhythmic and spatial relationships.

Choreographic works need not tell a story in order to be protected by copyright." *Id.* at 450.01.

Example

1. *Like clockwork.* The playbook of a professional football team diagrams the roles of eleven players for each of the dozens of scripted plays. Is it a choreographic work?

Explanation

1. Football plays carefully coordinate movements of multiple players, which is choreography in a broad sense. But the Copyright Office definition (not binding, because it is not in the statute, but persuasive, because the Copyright Office is the agency with expertise in the area) explicitly limits choreography to dance. So a playbook would probably not be a choreographic work (nor would a choreographed professional wrestling match or a floor exercise routine in gymnastics). But the design could fall into the next category: pictorial, graphic, and sculptural works.

Pictorial, Graphic, and Sculptural Works

The category "pictorial, graphic, and sculptural works" is very broad. It includes "two-dimensional and three-dimensional works of fine, graphic, and applied art, photographs, prints and art reproductions, globes, charts, diagrams, models, and technical drawings, including architectural plans." 17 U.S.C. §101. Recall that the 1790 Act covered only maps, books, and charts. Now maps are simply one item in one of the categories.

As interpreted by the courts, the category includes not only such traditional categories as sculpture and paintings but also any two- or three-dimensional work. Courts have held that belt buckle designs, vodka bottles, lamps, and mannequins fall within the category. A family's vacation photos, the design of their tree house, their toddler's finger painting, and a scarecrow in their garden could all qualify (as always, subject to the requirements of originality).

The most important limitation triggered by this category is the separability requirement for useful articles. "Useful articles" is a subcategory of "pictorial, graphic, and sculptural works." A useful article is protected only to the extent that it has aesthetic features that are separable from its utilitarian features.

Example

1. *Overlap*. Could a work fall into both "literary works" and "pictorial, graphic, and sculptural works"?

Explanation

1. There are many examples of such an overlap, when the letters or other symbols are made or arranged artfully. To name just a few: posters, signs, and concrete poetry, such as "Easter Wings" (not under copyright, being from 1663):

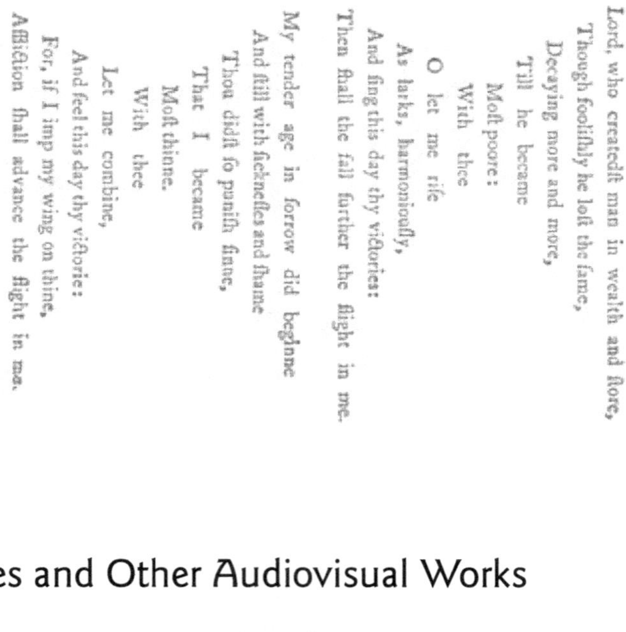
Lord, who createdſt man in wealth and ſtore,
Though fooliſhly he loſt the ſame,
Decaying more and more,
Till he became
Moſt poore:
With thee
O let me riſe
As larks, harmoniouſly,
And ſing this day thy victories:
Then ſhall the fall further the flight in me.
My tender age in ſorrow did beginne
And ſtill with ſickneſſes and ſhame
Thou didſt ſo puniſh ſinne,
That I became
Moſt thinne.
With thee
Let me combine,
And feel this day thy victorie:
For, if I imp my wing on thine,
Affliction ſhall advance the flight in me.

Motion Pictures and Other Audiovisual Works

We know movies are copyrighted, from the FBI warning that starts each film. Movies fall into this category, but its reach is much broader. Audiovisual works are "works that consist of a series of related images which are intrinsically intended to be shown by the use of machines, or devices such as projectors, viewers, or electronic equipment, together with accompanying sounds, if any, regardless of the nature of the material objects, such as films or tapes, in which the works are embodied." 17 U.S.C. §101.

An audiovisual work by definition requires the use of a machine or device like a projector or electronic screen to show it. A play or opera performed on stage would not be an audiovisual work, even if it had some pretty dramatic special effects.

Video games, slide shows (including those using primarily text), and many types of conceptual art fall into the category of audiovisual works. An audiovisual work must have a visual component but need not have any accompanying sounds. The use of some machine or device is required. A play, puppet show, circus act, or other work that has great auditory and visual impact but relies on no device to show it is not an audiovisual work.

The images must be related, but they need not appear on the screen in a particular order. The category is broader than filmed movies, or cartoons, or slide shows, all of which have a sequence of images. Rather, it can also include the screen displays for video games or for other, more boring computer programs, such as tax preparation software. When such programs are used, not all the images may be shown, and they may appear in various sequences. The work would still qualify as an audiovisual work. Courts have also deemed this true even though the content of the image may be dictated partly by the user of the program (such as the player who guides the figures in a video game), rather than completely dictated by the author of the work.

Where the work does have sounds, the sounds are deemed part of the audiovisual work, as opposed to falling into the category of "sound recording." The audio portion of the work is not subject to the various limitations on sound recording copyright (discussed below and later in the book).

The category of "motion pictures and other audiovisual works" receives special attention with respect to works made for hire. If a work is deemed a work made for hire, there are several consequences: The copyright belongs to the hiring party, there are no moral rights in works of visual art, and the duration of the copyright may be different. Of most practical importance, the creator of the work does not have the statutory right to terminate transfers. The definition of "work made for hire" specifically includes such things as screenplays, soundtrack compositions, and other works made as part of motion pictures (provided the parties also agree it is a work made for hire). It includes "a work specially ordered or commissioned for use as a contribution to a collective work, as a part of a motion picture or other audiovisual work." The practical impact of this is that the owner of a copyright in a motion picture need not worry about such things as the possibility that a screenwriter will terminate the transfer of copyright in the screenplay.

Example

1. *PowerPoint point*. Into what category would a slide presentation fall?

Explanation

1. It would certainly be an audiovisual work (as "a series of related images which are intrinsically intended to be shown by the use of machines, or devices such as projectors, viewers, or electronic equipment"). If it used verbal or numerical symbols (alas, slideshows often use them to excess), it would be a literary work. It might also be a choreographic work, if shown to illustrate a dance, or a musical work. Unless intended to be acted out, it would not be a dramatic work. It could possibly be an architectural work (discussed below). It wouldn't be a sound recording, because we will see that that definition excludes the sounds accompanying an audiovisual work. This example emphasizes that works may fall in multiple categories. It often matters only when there is a rule that applies only to specific categories (such as the compulsory license we will see for musical works).

   Long before PowerPoint, film strips were used to present visual information. Often, they had narration with a "beep" signaling time to move to the next slide. They would also qualify as audiovisual works.

Sound Recordings

Sound recordings are "works that result from the fixation of a series of musical, spoken, or other sounds, but not including the sounds accompanying a motion picture or other audiovisual work, regardless of the nature of the material objects, such as disks, tapes, or other phonorecords, in which they are embodied." 17 U.S.C. §101. This category of works was added to the copyright statute in 1972. Pre-1972 sound recordings are excluded from federal copyright protection, but they may be subject to state copyright protection.

The most familiar sound recordings are recordings of music, but a sound recording could be a recording of birdcalls, a student's recording of a lecture, or a recording of the sounds of a hurricane. As noted above, an important distinction must often be made when a sound recording is made of the performance of another work. The author of a sound recording is the one who makes the creative choices about the content of the recording and who controls the making of the recording. The author of the sound recording may be a different person than the author or performer of the underlying work. There may be two separate works, with two different authors. If Producer records Musician singing Musician's new song, the recording captures a sound recording (authored by Producer) and a musical work (authored by Musician). To use the recording in a movie, a movie maker would need licenses from Producer and Musician. Likewise, if Fan (with permission) records Poet reading poetry, Fan is the author of a sound recording, with a separate copyright from Poet's copyright in the poem (a literary work and perhaps also a dramatic work).

Classifying a work as a sound recording is quite important. One basic matter of terminology is that a sound recording is fixed in a phonorecord, not in a copy. More substantively, copyright in sound recordings confers more limited exclusive rights than other categories of works. Record companies persuaded Congress to give protection to sound recordings starting in 1972. But radio companies persuaded Congress to limit the rights, such that radio stations would not need permission from sound recording copyright holders (as they already need permission from the music copyright holder). The exclusive right to reproduce the work and the exclusive right to perform the work are both quite limited. The exclusive right to make copies extends only to reproductions of actual sounds (other works are protected also against nonliteral copying). The exclusive public performance right is limited to performance via a digital audio transmission. Various compulsory licensing provisions also apply to sound recordings.

The practical import of those limitations is as follows. The copyright holder normally has the exclusive right to make copies of the work, both literal copies and nonliteral copies. If Publisher has the copyright in a novel, Copier could infringe by printing literal copies (word-for-word copies) of the novel, or by writing a book that copied expressive elements from Publisher's novel, such as by closely copying the storyline and characters, without any word-for-word copying. With a sound recording, only literal copying is infringement. If Verni makes a sound recording of a performance of the opera he wrote, then Copier will infringe the sound recording copyright only if Copier copies the actual sounds into Copier's own recording. If Copier listens to the recording and makes her own recording, there is no infringement of the sound recording copyright, even if Copier finds elements that closely resemble.

Verni also does not have a general right of public performance in the sound recording, unlike most copyrighted works. If someone performs a play in public (whether by acting it out or simply showing a film of the play), that infringes the public performance right. But playing the sound recording will not infringe the copyright in the sound recording.

The examples above emphasize that nonliteral copying or public performance will not infringe the copyright in the sound recording. Note that a recording is likely to be not only a phonorecord of a sound recording but also a copy of another work of another copyrighted work. If Verni wrote the opera and then recorded a performance, he has a copyright in a musical work and one in a sound recording. Anyone who makes a copy (literal or nonliteral) of the opera or performs it in public will infringe Verni's copyright in the musical work, although not in the sound recording. Sometimes the underlying work in a sound recording will not be under copyright. It could be a recording of an opera published in 1818 (which would be too old to be copyrighted) or a recording of birds singing (no copyright in birdsong as musical works). In that case, the copyright holder would be limited to the sound recording copyright. In other cases, one party may hold the copyright in the musical work on a recording (such as a songwriter), while another party has the copyright in the sound recording (such as the record company).

Example

1. *Sound recording.* Desmond learns that Danegeld is performing in concert a ballad performed by Desmond without Desmond's permission. When his lawyer contacts them, they respond that Desmond's work is a sound recording, which has limited rights with respect to performance. For sound recordings, the public performance right is infringed only if it is performed via a digital audio transmission. Is the ballad merely a sound recording?

Explanation

1. Desmond made a sound recording of the ballad when he recorded himself performing it. But when he wrote the ballad (with its words and music), he created a musical work and a literary work. When Danegeld performs the ballad in concert, it is performing the musical work and potentially infringing. This example gives a preview of rules we will see later in the book, to make an important point early. A recording may embody a musical work as well as a sound recording, and one must keep track of the rights in both. Sometimes they also involve separate copyrights, held by different people.

Architectural Works

An architectural work is "the design of a building as embodied in any tangible medium of expression, including a building, architectural plans, or drawings. The work includes the overall form as well as the arrangement and composition of spaces and elements in the design, but does not include individual standard features." 17 U.S.C. §101.

An architectural work is the design of a building—before the building is built, and even if the building is never built. But the definition limits architectural works to the designs of buildings. Frank Lloyd Wright designed furniture, but furniture designed by an architect is not an architectural work. Not all structures are buildings. The design of a store inside of a shopping mall might not be deemed to be the design of a building (if the mall constitutes the building). The legislative history indicates that "buildings" include places that people enter (such as houses, temples, or schools), but not structures such as bridges and highways. The Copyright Office has further defined the term:

> The term building means structures that are habitable by humans and intended to be both permanent and stationary, such as houses and office buildings, and other permanent and stationary structures designed for human occupancy, including but not limited to churches, museums, gazebos, and garden pavilions.

Copyright Office Circular 41.

By adding the definition of architectural works to the statute in 1990, Congress made clear that architectural works are copyrightable, even though many architectural works are made up of nonprotectable elements. In particular, an architectural work is not subject to the requirement (applicable to useful articles) that there is protection only for aesthetic elements that are separable from the utilitarian elements. All the elements of a building's design, viewed individually, may be unprotected. They may be building features that are unoriginal, because architects tend to use doors, windows, and other features that have already been used. Even newly created features may be unprotectable because they are functional, and copyright does not protect functional elements. But the overall design, and the arrangement and composition of the various elements, may be original to the architect, may be creative, and may have nonfunctional aspects. So the design itself may be copyrightable, even if the individual elements are not.

While clarifying that architectural works were protected, Congress also crafted some provisions recognizing the special character of such works. The exclusive rights in architectural works are subject to some specific limitations. 17 U.S.C. §120. If a building is visible from a public place, the copyright owner has no rights against the making, distribution, or display of images of the building. In addition, the owner of a building may alter or destroy it without obtaining permission from the owner of the copyright in the design of the building. Without this provision, an owner who put an addition on the building could be liable for creating an unauthorized derivative work of the architectural work. The Middle District of Florida is the leader in copyright infringement suits involving architectural works. A visit to Sarasota explains this puzzling fact. The suits largely involve copying of homes in residential developments, not cutting edge architecture. Often, there is no infringement because the copying involved only nonprotected matter, such as functional matter or general floor plans. *See, e.g.*, *Medallion Homes Gulf Coast, Inc. v. Tivoli Homes of Sarasota, Inc.*, 656 F. App'x 450 (11th Cir. 2016).

Example

1. These are the statutory categories in section 102:
   - literary works
   - musical works, including any accompanying words
   - dramatic works, including any accompanying music
   - pantomimes and choreographic works
   - pictorial, graphic, and sculptural works
   - motion pictures and other audiovisual works
   - sound recordings
   - architectural works
   - Into which categories do the following fall?
   - an opera (words and music)
   - a modern dance
   - a recording of birdcalls from the wild
   - the soundtrack to a movie
   - the blueprints laying out the design of a house
   - a tattoo depicting *Hamlet*

Explanation

1. This example serves mainly as a reminder that works may fall into more than one of the statutory categories.

   An opera (words and music): literary work and dramatic work. By tweaking the facts a little, we could also make it fall into the other categories. If there were a choreography of the movements onstage, that would fall under "pantomimes and choreographic works." If there were drawings of the set design, those would be "pictorial, graphic, and sculptural works." If it was filmed, that would fall under "motion pictures and other audiovisual works." If they made a sound recording of a performance, that would be a "sound recording." As to "architectural works," one of the most famous is the Sydney Opera House.

   A modern dance would fall under "pantomimes and choreographic works." It would also likely be a dramatic work. If its choreography were set down in notation, it could be a literary work. If set down in figures, those could be pictorial, graphic, and sculptural works. As above, tweaking the facts would trigger other categories. One could make a sound recording of a performance. Even if there was no music, the sound of feet and breathing could make an interesting recording.

   A recording of birdcalls would be a sound recording. It would not be a musical work, no matter how musical. A bird cannot be an author, only a human can (not to mention that the birdcall may lack originality, if genetically programmed).

The soundtrack to a movie is not a sound recording. The definition of "motion pictures and other audiovisual works" specifically includes "accompanying sounds." The definition of "sound recording" specifically excludes movie soundtracks ("not including the sounds accompanying a motion picture"). The various special rules governing sound recordings do not apply to movie soundtracks.

The blueprints laying out the design of a house would be both an architectural work and a "pictorial, graphic, and sculptural work."

The tattoo would qualify as a "pictorial, graphic, and sculptural work."

Compilations (works created by assembling other works or information) and derivative works (works based on existing works) are also copyrightable.

Compilations

A "compilation" is defined as "a work formed by the collection and assembling of preexisting materials or of data that are selected, coordinated, or arranged in such a way that the resulting work as a whole constitutes an original work of authorship. The term 'compilation' includes collective works." 17 U.S.C. §101. Examples of compilations include a yellow pages telephone directory, a database of astronomical information, a collection of poetry, and a CD containing photographs from *National Geographic*.

Compilations play an important role in copyright. A compilation may be composed of noncopyrightable elements, but the compilation itself may be protected by copyright. If cartographer compiles a list of all the village names in Ireland, cartographer has no copyright protection in those names, which she did not create. But if she selects, arranges, or coordinates the data in an original way, that aspect would be copyright protected. The key issues with compilations are often originality and scope of protection. To be protected by copyright, the compilation must be sufficiently original. It may be completely composed of nonoriginal elements (such as facts or preexisting works), but there may be sufficient originality in the selection, coordination, or arrangement of the elements. Under *Feist* (discussed in Chapter 3), that requires just a minimal level of creativity. The scope of protection becomes an issue when there has been copying from the compilation but the defendant contends that only nonprotected elements were copied. The question could be whether defendant copied the original selection and arrangement of the elements, or copied only unprotected, nonoriginal elements.

Derivative Works

Derivative works raise a number of issues, which will be discussed in later chapters. The two key uses of the term: First, a derivative work is copyrightable. Although *Huckleberry Finn* is long out of copyright, a new work based on it (Huckleberry Finn, the musical—or Huckleberry Swede: The Sequel) would be copyrighted. Second, if a work is under copyright, then the copyright holder has the exclusive right to make derivative works. The holder of the copyright in Evil Genius has the exclusive right to make sequels, adapt it into a musical, have it translated into Finnish, and so on.

A "derivative work" is defined as

> a work based upon one or more preexisting works, such as a translation, musical arrangement, dramatization, fictionalization, motion picture version, sound recording, art reproduction, abridgment, condensation, or any other form in which a work may be recast, transformed, or adapted. A work consisting of editorial revisions, annotations, elaborations, or other modifications which, as a whole, represent an original work of authorship, is a "derivative work."

17 U.S.C. §101.

Examples of derivative works based on *Gone with the Wind* include a film based on a novel, like the film *Gone with the Wind*; *Scarlett*, a sequel to the novel; *Tatt av vinden*, a translation into Norwegian; *The Wind Done Gone*, a parody; an annotated edition of *Gone with the Wind*; and a musical based on *Gone with the Wind*.

A derivative work may have its own copyright, provided it is sufficiently original. The work may be based on another copyrighted work or on a work that is in the public domain. But the copyright in the derivative work applies only to the new creative expression, not to elements copied from the underlying work.

As discussed in more detail later, derivative works raise a number of issues with respect to both copyright ownership and infringement. If a work is under copyright, the copyright owner has the exclusive right to make derivative works based on the copyrighted work. If someone else makes an unauthorized derivative work, it may infringe the copyright. In addition, there is no copyright protection for portions of the new work that use material illegally. But preparation of a derivative work without permission may not infringe; it may be authorized under the fair use doctrine, for example.

As later chapters discuss, the derivative right also plays a role in a number of specific rules. When licenses are terminated, the licensee may retain the right to utilize derivative works. When copyrights are restored in foreign works that fell into the public domain because of failure to comply with the United States' formality requirements, the copyright may not apply to derivative works based on the formerly public domain work. Musical works are subject to a compulsory license that authorizes others to make cover versions, but not to prepare derivative works. The renewal, notice, registration, and remedies rules all have special provisions for derivative works.

Example

1. *Spinoffs?* What derivative works could be made from the novel *The Catcher in the Rye*?

Explanation

1. The reclusive J.D. Salinger did not prepare or authorize many derivative works based on *The Catcher in the Rye* (other than its many translations). He never sold the movie rights (despite interest ranging from Marlon Brando to Jerry Lewis). But derivative works could have included sequels, prequels, translations, a movie (and its sequels), a radio drama, a stage play, a musical, abridgements, annotated editions, and so on.

CHAPTER 3

Originality

A copyright in "We Shall Overcome" (a slightly revised version of the song "We Will Overcome," which is now in the public domain) was registered in 1960 and renewed in 1988. The copyright holders exercised considerable power over the work for decades. But in a declaratory judgment action brought by filmmakers (who wanted to be free to use the work), the court in 2017 held that "We Shall Overcome" lacked sufficient new creative elements to qualify for copyright:

> More specifically, the changes of "will" to "shall" and "down" to "deep" and the melodic differences in the opening measures and the seventh measure, do not create a distinguishable variation. These differences represent "variations of the piece that are standard fare in the music trade by any competent musician."[1]

A work is not protected by copyright unless it is original: created by the author with at least a minimal spark of originality.

Recall that "[c]opyright protection subsists, in accordance with this title, in *original* works of authorship fixed in any tangible medium of expression." 17 U.S.C. §102(a) (italics added). Copyright protects only original creative expression. The originality requirement has two important effects. First, a work that lacks originality is not protected by copyright

1. *We Shall Overcome Found. & Butler Films v. Richmond Org., Inc.* (TRO INC.), No. 16cv2725(DLC), 2017 U.S. Dist. LEXIS 146228, at *36 (S.D.N.Y. Sept. 8, 2017) (citation omitted and "citation omitted" omitted). The parties later settled. *See* Christopher Mele *"We Shall Overcome" Is Put in Public Domain in a Copyright Settlement*, New York Times (Jan. 26, 2018), https://www.nytimes.com/2018/01/26/business/media/we-shall-overcome-copyright.html.

(although it is pretty easy to show the necessary originality). A white pages phone listing, a list of customers, and a mechanically produced copy of an eighteenth-century pirate map all lack originality and so are not copyrighted. But a hack novel, a clumsy drawing, or an awful song are all sufficiently creative to be copyrighted. Adding some original elements to a business certificate, even if not striking, will suffice.[2] Likewise, creative additions to preexisting material qualify for copyright. So a creative arrangement of the list of customers or a creative 2009 adaptation of the eighteenth-century map are copyrighted. Second, nonoriginal elements of a work are not protected. A book may be copyrighted, but nonoriginal elements (such as facts and elements in the book not created by the author) may be freely copied without infringing the copyright. One could freely copy the names of the customers or the data from the underlying map, just not the creative additions of the author.

Originality sets the substantive standard for copyright protection. What works should qualify for copyright protection? Copyright protection could be limited to works of high quality or works showing creative elements that would not be obvious to one working in the field. Copyright could be limited by its incentive-to-create rationale, meaning that copyright would not apply to works with other sufficient incentives (perhaps advertisements, scholarly articles, personal letters). If such standards were too vague, one could use a proxy, such as publication. Copyright could be limited to published works, reasoning that at least someone found the work worth the time and trouble of publishing. Alternatively, copyright could be excluded for works deemed of low social value (depending on one's point of view, this might include video games, comic books, romance novels, abstruse scholarly articles, or advertisements).

In contrast, copyright casts a very wide net. A work in tangible form will qualify for copyright protection, provided it reflects originality—meaning it has elements created by the author with some minimal degree of creativity. For most works, the originality requirement is easily met. But the originality requirement serves important functions. It prevents claims of copyright in elements not created by the plaintiff. It also limits the policy arguments that claimants can make. Even if information has great value, or has been gathered at great time and expense, there is no copyright unless the requisite creativity can be shown.

---

2. *Premier Dealer Servs., Inc. v. Allegiance Adm'rs, LLC*, 93 F.4th 985 (6th Cir. 2024) ("The doctrines of uncopyrightable ideas, merger, and scenes a faire do not excuse Allegiance's imitation. Premier's certificate expresses the idea of a particular type of loyalty program, and comparison of Premier's form to the others in the record shows that companies can choose different ways to express that idea.").

ORIGINALITY: THE *FEIST* STANDARD

A work must be original to the author to qualify for copyright protection. 17 U.S.C. §102(a). Under *Feist Publications v. Rural Telephone Service*, 499 U.S. 340, 369 (1991), originality has two distinct requirements. To be original means that a work is "independently created by the author (as opposed to copied from other works) and that it possesses at least some minimal degree of creativity." *Feist* held that originality is required not only by the copyright statute but also by the Constitution. Congress has the power to grant exclusive rights to "Authors" in their "Writings." Early cases had defined the author as "he to whom anything owes its origin; originator; maker," and described copyright as limited to "original intellectual conceptions of the author," and required showing "the existence of those facts of originality, of intellectual production, of thought, and conception." The words "author" and "writing," then, "presuppose a degree of originality."

Feist nicely illustrates the application of the two-prong originality requirement. Feist concerned the extent of copyright protection in Rural Telephone's telephone directory white pages listings (the names of subscribers, listed alphabetically, together with their respective towns and telephone numbers). Feist Publications, unable to reach an agreement with Rural, simply copied the listings into its own regional directory. The Supreme Court held that Feist did not copy material that is protected by copyright, because there was no creativity in making the listings. The raw data was not original to Rural. Rather, that information existed before Rural ever gathered and published it. Rural could have met the originality requirement if it had selected, arranged, or coordinated the data in an original way. But Rural simply listed the names in alphabetical order, following common practice. Such an arrangement failed to show even the "minimal creativity" required for copyright protection. Rural Telephone did not have copyright in the raw data because of the first requirement (independent creation), and did not have copyright in the selection and arrangement of the data because of the second requirement (a minimal degree of creativity). Therefore, anyone could copy Rural's noncopyrightable listings. So, facts are not copyrightable. But a compilation of facts may be, if the selection, coordination, or arrangement of facts reflects the necessary creativity.

Independent Creation

Under *Feist*, the first requirement of originality is independent creation. An author has copyright protection only in elements of the work that she created. The requirement of independent creation bars copyright protection in facts and other phenomena, even to the person who discovers them first.

Discovery is not creation. If Biologist discovers that elephants can understand sign language, Biologist cannot claim copyright in that information. Even if she was the first to discover or the first to publish the fact, she did not originate the fact. Likewise, if Biologist weighs every elephant in every zoo in the United States, she has no copyright protection in the facts of their respective weights. Originality requires that one be the "maker" or "originator," not merely one that discovers and records a fact. So facts of all stripes—scientific, historical, biographical, news of the day—are unprotected by copyright. Likewise, one that discovers a beautiful gem, flower, or geological formation has no copyright in it.

Facts are not copyrightable, but works containing facts may be copyrightable, because they contain other elements created by the author. As the Copyright Office regulations state, "A fact or event, as distinguished from the manner in which it is described in a particular work, is not copyrightable." Compendium II: Copyright Office Practices 202.02(d). Drawing the line between unprotectable facts and copyrightable expression is not always so clear. For example, if a database consisted of the prices that cars had been sold for, those prices would be facts, information about the actual transactions that had occurred. But some courts have held that "blue book" listings of car values were not mere facts. *See CCC Information Services v. Maclean Hunter Market Reports*, 44 F.3d 61 (2d Cir. 1994). The listings were not reports of actual transactions, but were estimates of value. Although the estimates were based on the prices that cars had sold for, they also required consideration of various other factors. The price listings, therefore, included some elements that originated with the authors, as opposed to mere facts.

The requirement of independent creation by the author also bars copyright in elements created by others. If Anna writes a novel using the plot and characters of *Hamlet*, her copyright would not bar others from copying that plot and characters, only from copying other elements originated by Anna. If Anna writes a historical novel based on the life of Ethelred the Unready, her copyright would not cover historical facts used in her novel (even if she was the one to discover those facts). If Homeowner discovers an unpublished short story in a dusty cabinet, he would not thereby own the copyright in the story. He did not write it. Likewise, if Plagiarist copies the work of another, she would not have any copyright in the copied material. A transcript by a court reporter is not original (however skillfully done), because it is a transcription of others' statements. *A.V. v. iParadigms, LLC*, 562 F.3d 630 (4th Cir. 2009).

Originality does not require novelty. Originality does not require that a work be unique or that it be different from preceding works. Rather, it requires that the author create the work, as opposed to copying it from others. Suppose Painter paints an abstract painting today. By coincidence, the painting closely resembles another painting created decades ago. But Painter had never seen or heard of the first painting. Painter's painting would be original because it originated with him.

Here copyright differs from patent law. If Inventor invents a machine that, unbeknownst to her, is just like a machine that is already in public use, then Inventor is not entitled to a patent. Even though she came up with the invention herself, she would not meet the novelty required by patent law. In copyright, by contrast, it is no bar to protection that someone has already created a similar work.

Courts may nevertheless look at other works in deciding the question of originality. In *Acuff-Rose Music v. Jostens, Inc.*, 155 F.3d 140 (2d Cir. 1998), a songwriter claimed copyright infringement. His song used the phrase "you've got to stand for something or you'll fall for anything," which he alleged had been copied by defendant. The court considered the fact that similar phrases had been used in many different sources: the Bible, Abraham Lincoln, Martin Luther King, Malcolm X, Ginger Rogers, a chaplain of the U.S. Senate, and others that simply refer to it as an "old saying." Moreover, in 1985, popular songwriter and singer John Cougar Mellencamp recorded an album that included a song called "You've Got to Stand for Somethin'," featuring the lyrics "You've got to stand for somethin'/Or you're gonna fall for anything." *Id.* at 144. In light of the widespread use of the phrase, the court held that plaintiff had failed to show that he had originated the phrase, as opposed to copying it from someone else. Note that the court did not deny him protection on the basis that he was not the first one to use such a phrase. Rather, it determined that he failed to show that he came up with the phrase independently. So even though the song as a whole was protected by copyright, that nonoriginal phrase was not.

Examples

1. *Discovered letter.* Historian, sifting through thousands of old documents purchased from a scrap paper dealer, finds a long-lost letter. The letter is covered in grime, making it impossible to read. Nevertheless, Historian imaginatively identifies it as potentially valuable, relying on various subtle clues and her own rich experience. Using great care and skill, Historian spends days cleaning the letter and restoring its colors. The handwriting is atrocious and idiosyncratic. Historian nevertheless manages to decipher it, using creative powers of reasoning, together with lots of research. The letter is anonymous, but evidently was written around 1915. The letter describes 1910s life in Seattle with many evocative details and creative turns of phrase. Historian types up the text of the letter to make it easy for others to read. Historian claims copyright in the letter. If the purpose of copyright is to provide an incentive for the distribution of works, Historian argues, then she is entitled to copyright in

the letter. Otherwise, she may turn her hand to writing trashy historical novels. Does she meet the originality requirement?

2. *Picture this.* Suppose Historian decides to make a photograph of the letter for archival purposes. She carefully positions several lights so that every facet of the letter is shown in the photograph. She also chooses a level of lighting that, together with a colored filter on her camera, lends a somber mood to the picture. Does her photograph meet the requirements of originality?

3. *Peeple's rock.* One day, Peeple discovers a balancing rock worn into mystic shapes by the elements. With great care and much consideration of lighting and angles, he takes a photograph of the rock and publishes it in a newsletter. A week later, Big-City Paper asks him where the rock is so it can send out a photographer. Peeple refuses to tell the secret location. Paper then publishes a copy of his photo. Paper argues that it did not violate copyright because Peeple discovered the rock; he did not independently create it. Has Peeple met the originality requirement?

4. *Souvenir.* Tourist arrives in Chicago and takes a photo of Wrigley Field, the stadium of the Chicago Cubs. Tourist frames the stadium, selects an angle that gives a pleasing shape to the structure, and waits for the moment when the sunlight falls on the stadium as clouds pass overhead. The photo Tourist produces is quite similar to a number of photos that have already been published. Indeed, Tourist can point to nothing that distinguishes her photo from the many thousands of photos that have been taken of Wrigley Field. Is Tourist's photo original?

5. *World heritage.* Anthropologist discovers a number of ancient designs carved into rocks. She painstakingly makes exact copies by skillfully rubbing over specially designed paper placed on the designs. Does she have a copyright in the designs?

Explanations

1. Copyright protection requires that the work be original to the author. The author of the letter does meet the *Feist* standard of originality (independently created by the author and at least a minimal level of creativity). The letter itself is clearly creative and original. But Historian did not write the letter, so it was not original to her. Historian expended great resources, coupled with both historical and material expertise, to locate, restore, and make legible the contents of the letter. Much of her work did require creative thinking, which might meet the second requirement. She also put in a great deal of work and applied considerable skill. But none of those substitutes for meeting both requirements

of originality. Someone else wrote the letter, so Historian did not independently create it.

2. The photograph did originate with Historian, so it meets the first requirement. Unlike Example 1, Historian did not claim copyright in the work of another, but has created a new work (the photograph). The issue is whether it meets the second requirement, a minimal level of creativity. One might argue that she was simply making a "slavish copy"—that all her work and all her decisions were geared not toward creativity but toward making as accurate a copy of the letter as possible. That is the theory used when copyright is denied to works such as digital reproductions of public domain paintings. But Historian went beyond making a copy. She also made creative choices about lighting and color to set a mood for the photograph. So Historian does have a copyright in the photograph. Her copyright protects only the expressive elements that she added to the preexisting work.

3. Peeple did not independently create the rock, but he independently created the photograph. This case illustrates that an author can make an original work that portrays preexisting material. Peeple exercised ample creativity in considering lighting and angles. His photograph meets the originality requirement. In copying the photo, Big-City Paper necessarily copied original elements of Peeple's work.

4. Tourist's photo meets the originality requirement. This case illustrates the fact that originality does not require novelty, uniqueness, or any other high standard. A work need not be unprecedented to qualify for copyright protection. If the work originates with the author and is at least minimally creative, it is original. Tourist did not copy from the other photos, even though her product was similar. The work originated with her. She also made a number of creative choices in making the photo, satisfying the second requirement of originality, so her photo qualifies for copyright protection. An author may create an original work even though she uses preexisting material such as the subject of the work (in this example), facts or a previous work of authorship (as in the examples above), or other preexisting material. The issue is whether the author adds her own creative expression to the preexisting material.

   Does that mean that the next person to take a photo of Wrigley Field infringes Tourist's copyright? No. As the infringement chapter discusses, infringement requires copying. If the next tourist does not copy Tourist's photo, there is no infringement—even if the photo happens to be identical to Tourist's photo.

5. Although Anthropologist used considerable skill, she did not use creativity in making the rubbings. She has no copyright in the rubbings. On

the other hand, she has the rubbings, and as yet controls access to them. Copyright is not the only way in which information can be limited—for better or worse.

Note that the same issue may apply when preexisting designs are used for other purposes. If tattoo artist made an exact copy of a Maori design, there would be no copyright in the tattoo. If the artist used some creativity in adapting the design to a tattoo, then there could be copyright. That issue arose with respect to boxer Mike Tyson's tattoo, which featured in the movie *The Hangover: Part II* and its advertising.

A Minimal Level of Creativity

In addition to independent creation, originality requires creativity on the part of the author. *Feist* emphasized that this is a low standard. The "originality requirement is not particularly stringent," requiring only "some minimal level of creativity." 499 U.S. at 358. Originality will be found in all but a "narrow category of works in which the creative spark is utterly lacking or so trivial as to be virtually nonexistent." 499 U.S. at 359. Originality does not require that the work be innovative or surprising, only that it be more than "so mechanical or routine as to require no creativity whatsoever." 499 U.S. at 379. "The vast majority of works make the grade quite easily, as they possess some creative spark, 'no matter how crude, humble or obvious' it might be." 499 U.S. at 345 (quoting *Nimmer on Copyright*). As the legislative history put it, this "standard does not include requirements of novelty, ingenuity, or esthetic merit." House Report No. 94-1476.

Feist shows just how uncreative the author must be to fail to qualify for protection. The telephone book publisher simply listed the subscribers in alphabetical order. This tried and true arrangement of the information has long been used in telephone books. It was not a creative selection or arrangement of the information.

Subsequent cases have shown that even telephone listings can be sufficiently original to be copyrightable. One compiler selected New York City area businesses of interest to Chinese Americans and arranged them using categories devised to be of interest to that community. *See Key Publications v. Chinatown Today Publications Enterprises*, 945 F.2d 509 (2d Cir. 1991). Alternatively, someone could add creativity to the individual listings. An Icelandic white pages listing is original. Traditional names and the uses of patronyms and matronyms result in many identical names. A substantial portion of the male population is named Magnus Magnusson. So to identify subscribers, Icelandic phone books often include creatively chosen personal information (Magnus Magnusson, the golfing fan, drives an old Volkswagen Beetle).

The author need not show that she engaged in a lengthy creative process, or that she made notably creative decisions. The author need not meet any high standard of artistic creation. Indeed, creativity may be the result of accident. A painter may find that her work did not turn out how she intended or is marked by some accidental brushstrokes. But if she adopts the result as her own, it can be sufficiently creative. Here again copyright law differs from patent law, where an inventor is entitled to a patent only if the invention was not obvious in light of the state of the art in the relevant field. By contrast, in copyright, even the author who turns out obvious but original works is entitled to protection.

The requirement of creativity is so low that most works meet it quite easily. A second grader's T-shirt design (the word "Hi" on the front with a smiley face and the word "bye" on the back with a frowny face) met the requirement.[3] But there have been cases where courts found too little creativity—usually cases where the plaintiff strained to find some original element to prevent others from copying material that was largely nonprotectable. In *Matthew Bender & Co. v. West Publishing Co.*, 158 F.3d 693 (2d Cir. 1998), for example, West published reports of judicial decisions. West had no copyright in the judicial opinions, because they were not created by West, but rather by the judges and their clerks. West did add original, creative elements to its editions, such as summaries of points of law, but the defendant did not copy those elements. The defendants did copy the page numbers in the West volumes, in order to allow users to cite to the page in the West volume. West claimed that the page numbers were its original expression, and therefore protected by copyright. The court rejected that argument on the basis that giving sequential numbers to pages in a book is not even minimally creative (just as in *Feist*, where arranging the listings in a phone book alphabetically is not even minimally creative). The court also noted that West did not have copyright protection in corrections it made to the punctuation and spelling in the opinions, because such changes were too trivial to meet the creativity requirement. In a similar vein, photographs lacked originality, where plaintiffs did not "identify any conscious choices they made regarding lighting or camera angles for the purpose of being 'original.'"[4]

Courts have used the creativity requirement to frustrate other attempts to, in effect, use copyright to protect nonoriginal material. In one such case, the plaintiff hired a builder to build a slightly customized house. The plaintiff took the builder's standard architectural drawings and marked a few places where the plaintiff's house would be different. The house was built, and the plaintiff was quite proud of it. The plaintiff was then dismayed to see that the builder had used the amended drawings to build

3. *I.C. ex rel. Solovsky v. Delta Galil USA*, 2015 U.S. Dist. LEXIS 132052 (S.D.N.Y. Sept. 29, 2015).
4. *Rigsby v. Erie Ins. Co.*, 2015 U.S. Dist. LEXIS 31711 (W.D. Wis. Mar. 16, 2015).

an identical house for another customer. The plaintiff sued for copyright infringement, claiming that the changes to the drawings were sufficiently creative to qualify for copyright. The court rejected that argument, characterizing them as mere editorial changes. *Watkins v. Chesapeake Custom Homes, L.L.C.*, 330 F. Supp. 2d 563, 573 (D. Md. 2004). The plaintiff's real complaint was that the builder had built an identical home for someone else. But where the builder had not copied any creative elements originating with the plaintiff, there was no copyright infringement. The originality requirement prevents copying alone from giving rise to infringement liability.

Courts have likewise rejected attempts to claim copyright in standard product features. Suppose a printer has a popular line of stationery for small business, with envelopes having labels such as "Addressee" and "Sender" and memo pads with "From:" and "To:" lines. A competitor copies the envelopes, memo pads, and other products. The printer claims copyright infringement. A court is likely to hold that there is no copyright in standard labels, because they lack the necessary creativity. Similar issues arise when vendors copy the labels on products. If a ketchup maker uses a picture of a tomato on its goods, a court may hold that it lacks even the minimal creativity required for copyright, meaning there is no infringement if a competitor uses a similar tomato. But where there is any creativity to be found—in how the tomato is drawn, or how several tomatoes are grouped—then that may suffice for copyright protection (which would, however, give protection only against quite literal copying).

Similarly, legal forms that borrow standard language do not qualify for copyright simply because of a few changes in syntax or addition of a few words, done without any independent analysis or legal research:

> Even though word arrangements have been altered, they are at best merely a paraphrasing of earlier forms. There is nothing recognizably different from the language used in form books or earlier business forms. Elementary legal words and phrases are in the public domain and no citizen may gain monopoly thereover to the exclusion of their use by other citizens.

M.M. Business Forms Corp. v. Uarco, 472 F.2d 1137, 1140 (6th Cir. 1973). This is not to say that blank forms never qualify for copyright. If there is creativity in selecting the categories of questions, or in designing the aesthetics of the form, or in drafting the language of the questions, then the originality requirement may be met. Sufficient creativity has been found with such mundane works as a debt collection letter and before and after dental photos. *See Advanced Recovery Sys. v. Am. Agencies*, 923 F.3d 819 (10th Cir. 2019); *Pohl v. MH Sub I LLC*, 770 F. App'x 482 (11th Cir. 2019).

Because the originality standard is somewhat vague, there have been several attempts to make per se rules to guide authors and courts. The

3. Originality

Copyright Office regulations bar registration for certain categories of works that are nonoriginal:

> Works consisting entirely of information that is common property containing no original authorship, such as, for example: Standard calendars, height and weight charts, tape measures and rulers, schedules of sporting events, and lists or tables taken from public documents or other common sources.

37 C.F.R. §202.1(d). The Copyright Office regulations also bar registration for "words and short phrases such as names, titles, and slogans." This rule is frequently justified on the basis that such short phrases lack sufficient originality for copyright protection.

An artificial intelligence, courts and the Copyright Office have held, cannot qualify as an offer. But if a human contributes a little bit of creativity to a work largely put together by AI, the human may qualify as an author with a copyright in the work.

Examples

1. *Minimal spark?* The AudioQuest K2 terminated speaker cable is available on Amazon.com for a mere $8,450 a pair. This offer has spurred a number of reviews, the most popular beginning, "We live underground. We speak with our hands. We wear the earplugs all our lives. . . . We cannot maintain the link for long. . . . DO NOT USE THE CABLES!" Is the Amazon review a copyrighted work?

2. *Prosaic?* Would the following paragraph qualify for copyright?

   > Contains about as much caffeine as a cup of coffee. Limit caffeine products to avoid nervousness, sleeplessness, and occasionally rapid heartbeat. You may experience a niacin flush (hot feeling, skin redness) that lasts a few minutes. This is caused by niacin (vitamin B3) increasing blood flow near the skin.

3. *Creative?* Nova adapts a design for Holiday Inn Express hotel. Nova adds a floor, enlarges the meeting area, changes the closet and door placements in rooms, and changes the size of the pool, exercise, and laundry areas. Nova makes these changes after receiving suggestions, along with graphic designs, from the client. Does Nova's work show sufficient creativity to qualify for copyright?

4. *Formulaic.* Meds sells forms for use during an office visit with a doctor. The forms provide blanks for various categories of specified information: name, date of birth, sex, and ailment. For each ailment, the forms provide information to be obtained: "history of the present illness, a

review of systems, medical and social history, physical exam, medical decision making, clinical impressions, and, finally, consultation, disposition, and instructions." The forms list the common answers for many questions to speed filling out the forms. Meds learns that Formulaic has copied Meds' forms and sold them. Copyright infringement?

5. *Haters gonna infringe.* Would singer Taylor Swift be liable for copying the phrases "playas . . . gonna play" and "haters . . . gonna hate." From one of the many songs playing on those themes?

6. *Borrowing a cookie cutter.* A Florida real estate developer cuts costs by copying the floor plans of a successful nearby development: "In the instant case, as in Home Design Services and Intervest, the Santa Maria and the Duke floor plans are at first glance visually similar. Both plans can be described as four-three split plans, that is, four-bedroom three-bathroom plans with a master bedroom on one end and three other rooms at the other end. In the Santa Maria, the master bedroom is on the right side, and in the Duke plan, the master bedroom is on the left side. Both plans are arranged around a large center open area containing a contiguous great room, dining room, kitchen, and nook. Both plans contain a two-car garage." Copyright infringement?

Explanations

1. The review is a copyrighted work. It is a literary work. It easily meets the requirement of a modicum of creativity. The next question might be who owns the copyright? As discussed later in the book, that might depend on Amazon's terms of service.

2. Courts interpret the creativity requirement quite liberally. "Because the medical caution statements appearing on the energy shots have appreciable differences, and stylistic flourishes may be inserted in the statement, the medical caution label has the minimum level of originality necessary to warrant copyright protection as a matter of law." *Innovation Ventures LLC d/b/a Living Essentials Ltd. v. N2G Distributing Inc.*, No. 2:08-cv-10983-PDB-MJH (E.D. Mich. 2011).

3. Nova did not show creativity. The additions were all made at the prompting of the client, and were relatively routine. So Nova did not contribute creative elements. *See Nova Design Build Inc. v. Grace Hotels LLC*, No. 10-1738 (7th Cir. 2011).

4. The court held that the forms lacked even the minimal creativity to be copyrighted. Rather, they simply called for "the same information that any responsible physician would ask a patient with the given ailment." *See Utopia Provider Sys., Inc. v. Pro-Med Clinical Sys., LLC*, 596 F. 3d 1313 (11th

Cir. 2010)(holding templates were not entitled to copyright protection because they were in the nature of noncopyrightable "blank forms"). Just as every white pages phone book lists all the phone holders in alphabetical order, so too was there no creativity in selecting, arranging, or coordinating the information on the forms.

5. Well, probably not. The trial court dismissed the complaint. "In order for such short phrases to be protected under the Copyright Act, they must be more creative than the lyrics at issue here. [P]layers, haters, and player haters had received substantial pop culture attention prior to 2001. . . . In short, combining two truisms about playas and haters, both well-worn notions as of 2001, is simply not enough." *Hall v. Swift*, 2018 U.S. Dist. LEXIS 43575, at *22-23 (C.D. Cal. Feb. 13, 2018). The appellate court reversed, on the grounds that whether the originality was a question of fact: "Even taking into account the matters of which the district court took judicial notice, Hall's complaint still plausibly alleged originality." *Hall v. Swift*, 786 F. App'x 711, 712 (9th Cir. 2019) (citation omitted). So the case went back down for fact-finding.

6. The developer copied, but did not infringe, because the copied material was not protected by copyright. A basic arrangement of common elements is not sufficient for originality. "[D]espite the fact that the plans share in common the same set of rooms, arranged in the same overall layout, these shared elements are not copyrightable elements. Indeed, the same basic split layout was present in both our Home Design Services and Intervest cases." *Medallion Homes Gulf Coast, Inc. v. Tivoli Homes of Sarasota, Inc.*, 656 F. App'x 450, 454 (11th Cir. 2016).

An Author May Use a Device to Create a Work

An author may use a device in a creative way to produce an original work. *Burrow-Giles Lithographic v. Sarony*, 111 U.S. 53 (1884), rejected the argument that making a photograph was simply a mechanical process lacking in originality. The photograph at issue was a portrait of Oscar Wilde. Defendant argued that the photograph was simply an exact reproduction of the image of Oscar Wilde. But the photographer had made a number of creative choices: posing the subject, selecting and arranging the subject's clothes and other things in the picture, and choosing the lighting. In addition, the author must exercise some creativity to qualify for copyright. A photograph may be copyrightable but only if the author used some creativity in making it. A work made through a purely mechanical or standard process would not be copyrighted (such as a photocopy of an eighteenth-century map).

The author can claim copyright only in elements that originate with her. If an author creates a machine or process, she does not have copyright in the works created by her machine or process. The Copyright Office regulations give a nice example:

> An applicant for registration has developed a novelty item consisting of transparently clear plastic sheets bonded together around their periphery, and having a small amount of colored liquid petroleum in the air space between the laminated sheets. Any slight pressure upon the external surface results in the formation of undulating patterns and shapes, no two of which are ever identical.

Compendium II: Copyright Office Practices 503.02(a). The patterns may have been beautiful, but the toymaker did not create them and therefore was not entitled to claim copyright based on them: "Since the specific outlines and contours of the patterns and shapes formed by the liquid petroleum do not owe their origin to a human agent, it is not possible to claim copyright in such patterns and shapes." *Id.*

Sweat of the Brow Is Not Sufficient to Get Copyright

The amount of creativity to meet the originality requirement is not great. However, under *Feist*, nothing substitutes for creativity. The author cannot win protection by showing that he invested considerable resources (such as the work that went into gathering the information for thousands of telephone listings). If copyright serves as an incentive to produce works, one could argue, there should be copyright protection for databases. Such exclusive rights would give an incentive to people to collect valuable information, just as they give an incentive to authors to create other categories of works. But the *Feist* court held that creativity is required by both the copyright statute and the Constitution as a condition for copyright protection. Whether Congress could grant exclusive rights in databases under another provision of the Constitution, such as the Commerce Clause, is an open question. In the meantime, database owners can still get a measure of legal protection. Copyright protects their original selection and arrangement of data. They can use contracts to impose conditions of use with their customers. Trade secret law and tort law may protect them against wrongful access to the information by others, but the facts themselves are not copyrightable.

New Works (Especially Factual Works, Compilations, and Derivative Works) May Incorporate Nonoriginal Elements

Irish folktales are too old to be protected by copyright, but a compilation of Irish folktales could have copyright protection (in its original selection or arrangement). Shakespeare's *Romeo and Juliet* is too old to be protected by copyright. *West Side Story*, which retells *Romeo and Juliet* in twentieth-century

New York City, is copyrighted. Compilations and derivative works may be copyrighted, by adding original elements to preexisting material.

§103. Subject matter of copyright: Compilations and derivative works

(a) The subject matter of copyright as specified by section 102 includes compilations and derivative works, but protection for a work employing preexisting material in which copyright subsists does not extend to any part of the work in which such material has been used unlawfully.

(b) The copyright in a compilation or derivative work extends only to the material contributed by the author of such work, as distinguished from the preexisting material employed in the work, and does not imply any exclusive right in the preexisting material. The copyright in such work is independent of, and does not affect or enlarge the scope, duration, ownership, or subsistence of, any copyright protection in the preexisting material.

To qualify for copyright, a work must be original, but it need not be completely original or even mainly original. To the contrary, all works incorporate nonoriginal elements. Every novel uses words, phrases, events, personal characteristics, and other elements that the author has learned from others. Even the most abstract painting has elements copied from others—colors, even the very use of paint. A work may still be sufficiently original to qualify for copyright, even though it contains nonoriginal elements (such as facts, or elements for works created by others, or things found in nature or in the trash). The originality analysis considers not how much was copied from others, but whether the author added anything creative of her own.

The issue arises most frequently with factual works, derivative works, and compilations. A factual work (like a book of history or scientific information) may serve to present facts (which are nonoriginal), but it is likely to express those facts in way that meets the requirement of creativity. A derivative work is based on a preexisting work, but it may reflect creativity in elements added by the second author. A compilation is a collection or assembly of preexisting works or data. The compilation's author did not create the preexisting work or data, but she may use creativity in the selection, arrangement, or coordination of those elements.

Facts are not original elements. But a work may be copyrightable even if it incorporates facts. The statute recognizes that a compilation may be a copyrightable work: "a work formed by the collection and assembling of preexisting materials or of data that are selected, coordinated, or arranged in such a way that the resulting work as a whole constitutes an original work of authorship." 17 U.S.C. §101. If an author selects or arranges preexisting facts in an original way, he qualifies for copyright in the compilation. Likewise, facts may be used to create other types of original works.

The author could also take facts and incorporate them into a history text or fictionalized story. A biography is the story of someone's life. It will likely include much nonoriginal material: the humble circumstances of the subject's birth, the various events depicted in the book, the surrounding historical information. But the book will also include much original expression—the author's selection and arrangement of the factual material, and the manner in which the author describes the events. Likewise, a history text will include many facts, but the way those facts are selected and related will likely be original with the author.

Using a camera to record an event captures both uncopyrightable facts and copyrightable creative expression. For example, copyright applied to a bystander's home movie that captured moments of the assassination of President Kennedy. *Time, Inc. v. Bernard Geis Associates*, 293 F. Supp. 130, 133 (D.N.Y. 1968). Defendants argued that "the pictures are simply records of what took place, without any 'elements' personal to Zapruder, and that 'news' cannot be the subject of copyright." The movie showed facts, a historical event that was not created by the moviemaker. But the moviemaker did contribute creative expression. Just as a database compiler may creatively select and arrange the data, the moviemaker selects the moments to film, chooses what will be in the picture, and chooses the vantage point. The court identified several creative choices: "Zapruder selected the kind of camera (movies, not snapshots), the kind of film (color), the kind of lens (telephoto), the area in which the pictures were to be taken, the time they were to be taken, and (after testing several sites) the spot on which the camera would be operated." Anyone who literally copied the film would necessarily copy creative elements, as well as the unprotected facts depicted in the movie.

A work may also be sufficiently creative even if it incorporates expression copied from earlier works. Indeed, an author can make a work that mainly consists of copied material and by adding her own original expression would qualify for copyright. In the landmark case of *Alfred Bell v. Catalda Fine Arts*, 191 F.2d 99 (2d Cir. 1951), the plaintiff, an engraver, made mezzotint engravings that were reproductions of classic paintings. The engraver did not seek simply to duplicate the paintings. Because the engraver had to make creative choices about the depth and shape of the engraving depressions, the work went beyond purely the mechanical to be original. Likewise, changing the size, spacing, and proportions of a graphic design could supply the necessary modicum of creativity.

A work that largely copies from another work may be sufficiently creative to qualify for copyright, like the mezzotint engravings of old master paintings. But there must be some creativity in making the new work. Courts have denied copyright protection where the new work was a "slavish copy" of a previous work or a mere "mechanical reproduction." Even if great skill or technical prowess is used, that does not make up for a lack of creativity.

For example, courts have denied protection in cases in which all the author's efforts are geared toward copying a preexisting work as accurately as possible. It may be technically difficult to make such a "slavish copy," but doing so does not show the necessary creativity. Likewise, a court may deny protection to a "mechanical reproduction." If the new work consists simply of a mere change of medium, such as making a three-dimensional costumes based on characters from a two-dimensional cartoon, the necessary creativity may be lacking. *See Entertainment Research Group v. Genesis Creative Group*, 122 F.3d 1211 (9th Cir. 1997).

Cases involving new versions of old works are not easy to reconcile. One court found sufficient creativity in making a small-scale version of a well-known sculpture. *See Alva Studios v. Winniger*, 177 F. Supp. 265 (S.D.N.Y. 1959). By contrast, making a molded-plastic version of an antique Uncle Sam bank was held to lack the necessary creativity. *See L. Batlin & Son v. Snyder*, 536 F.2d 486 (2d Cir. 1976). The court in *Batlin*, like some other courts, appears to have a different standard for derivative works. Under this approach, there would be one test for most works but a slightly higher test when the new work is based on another work. However, *Feist* (decided after *Batlin*) appeared to set a single standard for all works. The better view is probably to apply the *Feist* standard in all cases. When copyright is claimed in a work based on an earlier work, the key is whether one can identify creative choices made that were not dictated by the desire to put the work into the new medium, but rather were made for aesthetic or artistic reasons.

Many cases involve new works that are composed of nonoriginal elements. The fact that each of the elements is nonoriginal does not mean that the work as a whole lacks originality. Every word in a novel may be found in the dictionary, but the novel can easily meet the requirement of creativity. An original arrangement of even the most mundane elements can qualify for copyright. A video game might use only simple, familiar shapes, such as rectangles and squares, and familiar colors. But sufficient creativity could be shown in selecting the shapes and colors and devising the actions of those elements during play. *See Atari Games v. Oman*, 979 F.2d 242 (D.C. Cir. 1992). Using software, even AI, with a little bit of human creativity, to adapt a work may qualify for a copyright in the adaptation.

The Copyright Office has also addressed the issue of originality in compilations. An author may have copyright in a work consisting entirely of unprotected elements (such as facts, or works created by others) if she shows the requisite creativity in selecting, coordinating, or arranging those unprotected elements. The greater the amount of material from which to select, coordinate, or order, the more likely it is that the compilation will be registrable. Where the compilation lacks a certain minimum amount of original authorship, registration will be refused. Any compilation consisting of fewer than four selections is considered to lack the requisite original authorship, so selecting four elements would be deemed insufficiently creative. But "[t]he selection and ordering of 20 of the best short stories of O. Henry would be registrable as a compilation." *Id.* Compendium II: Copyright Office Practices 307.01. A compilation may also have originality in the coordination or arrangement of the elements. This means more than simply the format in which the items are printed. Rather, it requires an "original ordering or grouping of the items." *Id.* at 307.03.

Examples

1. *Translation.* Historian translates a letter into Spanish. For many of the words and phrases, there are numerous potential Spanish equivalents. Historian seeks to produce a translation that is accurate and pleasing to the ear. She claims a copyright in the translation of the letter. Is her translation original? (We will add the assumption that the letter's author has been located and has given permission for the translation; otherwise, the translation might be denied copyright as an unauthorized derivative work.)

2. *Folk songs.* An old New England fisherman has learned many local folk songs during his years at sea. His younger colleagues prefer other diversions, such as watching videos and listening to recorded contemporary music. Concerned that oral tradition will no longer suffice to pass along the songs, he decides to preserve them. He selects a number of good exemplars and selects the order and grouping for a book of songs. He composes arrangements for the songs and also invents melodies and words for some that he cannot remember. He also visits fishermen in Newfoundland and records them singing their local folk songs. He publishes sheet music of his arrangements of the New England songs and his recordings of the Newfoundland songs. A large music publisher then starts to sell identical copies of the sheet music and the recordings. The publisher argues that it has not copied protected expression because none of the works were original to the fisherman. Rather, they were traditional folk songs, many generations old. Were the new arrangements and recordings original to the fisherman?

3. *Just the facts.* Editor spends years compiling her encyclopedia of sports trivia. She pores through newspapers, books, and other sources to find some of the facts. Other facts she digs up herself from interviews with retired athletes. She uses several innovative techniques to compile the information, devising several new categories and new ways of grouping sports information. She also makes deliberate choices about what information to include, based on numerous factors. Shortly before publishing her book, she learns that facts are not protected by copyright. Does copyright offer her any protection?

4. *Original mint condition?* Medallica makes and sells metallic replicas of U.S. coins and paper currency. Medallica makes three-dimensional silver versions of U.S. folding money. In making each note replica, Medallica makes choices about how to translate color contrasts into a silver medium, how to represent the intricate background detail of U.S. Treasury notes, whether certain features should be dull silver or highly polished silver, and whether certain features should be engraved or set off in bas relief. Medallica also makes three-dimensional replicas of U.S. coins. Its replicas are larger versions of the U.S. coins, made from similar materials. Medallica does not have access to the U.S. Mint materials and therefore faces a number of difficult technical issues in making the coin replicas: deciding what materials to use, choosing the correct manufacturing process, constructing plates that will give the correct images. Medallica's engineers and technicians exhibit enormous skill and expertise in managing to produce astonishingly exact replica coins. Are Medallica's replicas original for the purposes of copyright law?

5. *Mapmaker, Mapmaker.* Mapmaker spends several years gathering information about Boffin Island. Mapmaker researches such sources as geological surveys, satellite photographs, interviews with residents, and Mapmaker's own surveying expeditions. Drawing from this huge amount of information, Mapmaker produces a variety of maps of Boffin Island, both maps of the entire island and of various regions. Some maps emphasize geological information; others show points of historical interest. Rival makes exact copies of Mapmaker's maps and sells them, arguing that the maps are not original. First, they include only facts, which are unprotected by copyright. Second, maps are intended to be exact copies of Boffin Island and therefore lack creativity. Is Rival violating copyright law?

Explanations

1. One might argue that Historian was simply making a slavish copy, but translation from one language to another is not a mechanical task or simply a matter of reproduction. The translator necessarily makes choices that affect the aesthetic quality of the translation. Author did not write the original letter, but many elements of the translation would meet both of the requirements of originality.

2. The folk songs are not original to the fisherman, but the arrangements and some of the melodies and words are. Likewise, his selection and ordering of songs in his book could have the requisite originality. So he could have a copyright in his versions of the New England songs and in the selection and arrangement of the contents of the book. Cf. *Italian Book v. Rossi*, 27 F.2d 1014 (S.D.N.Y. 1928).

3. Originality

The recordings also qualify as sufficiently original. Because he recorded the songs, he did not add any elements such as arrangements, melodies, or new lyrics. However, the recordings are original in the same sense as a photograph. Like a photographer, the recorder makes creative choices, such as what elements to include and where to position microphones.

3. The facts are not copyrightable. Whether Editor drew the facts from other sources or dug them up herself, facts preexist Editor and are not original to her. But her selection and arrangement of the facts is protected by copyright. This compilation is different from the white pages telephone directory in *Feist*. The telephone directory simply listed subscribers alphabetically, following long-standing industry practice. Such arrangement and selection lacked even minimal creativity. But Editor creatively devised new ways of selecting and then arranging information. Therefore, the original elements of her compilation are protected by copyright. Someone who copied only factual material without copying her original selection or arrangement would not infringe her copyright.

4. The designs of the U.S. notes and coins are not original to Medallica, but its designs of the replica notes probably do have sufficient originality. The designs copy many elements from the notes but also include a number of elements beyond "slavish copying." The coin replicas, however, lack originality. Although great technical skill was used, it was used solely toward making as exact copies as possible. *Cf. Medallic Art Co. v. Washington Mint*, 208 F.3d 203 (2d Cir. 2000) (unpublished opinion).

5. Works such as maps can exhibit creativity, even though they serve to represent facts. In deciding which features to include on a map and how to represent them, the mapmaker makes creative choices. *See, e.g., United States v. Hamilton*, 583 F.2d 448 (9th Cir. 1978). Mapmaker could not recover from a rival mapmaker who only copied discrete pieces of information from her maps. But it would likely be infringement to copy the map wholesale, which would copy Mapmaker's selection and arrangement of factual information, together with any creative expression in its representation. This is an example of so-called thin copyright protection, which protects only against very literal, wholesale copying.

   The argument that the map is simply a copy of Boffin Island is fallacious. The lack of originality for "slavish copying" applies to making a copy of a creative work. It does not bar copyright for using photography for capturing realistic images. The use of a map to represent facts is even less like making a duplicate.

COPYING UNPROTECTED MATERIAL IS NOT INFRINGEMENT

The originality standard is quite low, which means that copyright protection is not difficult to obtain. But copyright protection extends only to the original elements of the work. This reflects an important copyright principle. It is not infringement to copy nonprotected elements of a copyrighted work, such as nonoriginal elements, ideas, or functional elements. Infringement requires copying of original, expressive elements of the work. The rule that copyright protects only original elements supplies some balance.

Nonoriginal elements are especially common in two categories of works: derivative works (because they are adaptations of preexisting works) and compilations (which may be collections of facts or preexisting works). The statute expressly states that only the new elements are protected: "The copyright in a compilation or derivative work extends only to the material contributed by the author of such work, as distinguished from the preexisting material employed in the work, and does not imply any exclusive right in the preexisting material." 17 U.S.C. §103.

Suppose a database contains much factual information related to the city of Worcester, such as names of residents and streets, information about utility fixtures, and real estate taxes for properties. The database compiler selects and arranges the information in a creative way, making the database a copyrighted work. Someone who literally copied the entire database without permission would likely infringe the copyright, because she copied both the protected and the nonprotected elements of the work. Suppose someone else copied only some of the factual information from the database and did not copy the selection or arrangement of the information. The second copier would not infringe, because she copied only nonprotected information (the nonoriginal facts). Therefore, copying from a copyrighted work is not necessarily infringement; copying protected elements from a copyrighted work may be infringement.

Derivative works and compilations are especially likely to contain nonoriginal and hence noncopyrighted material, but all works contain nonoriginal elements. As discussed above, Zapruder had the copyright in his home movie, which captured the assassination of President Kennedy. But his copyright would extend only to the creative elements that originated with him. It would not prevent others from copying facts from the film (and even copyrightable elements would be potentially subject to fair use).

The originality analysis, then, arises in two types of cases: cases involving copying of the entire work and cases involving copying part of the work. Where the entire work is copied, the issue may be whether the work as a whole qualified for copyright protection. If the work was unoriginal, then it was not protected by copyright and even copying of the entire work would not be infringement. More commonly, the issue of originality arises where the defendant copied only certain elements from the plaintiff's work. The defendant contends that the elements that were copied were not original, and therefore there was no infringement.

A useful practical distinction is often made between works with thin protection and works with thick protection. A work with thin protection is made mainly of nonprotected elements. Factual works (like telephone directories, books of sports statistics) have thin protection. This means that broad literal copying (such as copying the entire directory) is likely infringement, because it would include copying the creative elements, such as the selection and arrangement of data. Highly creative works (like an imaginative novel) have thick protection, because there would be infringement not just from literal copying but also nonliteral copying (copying not the exact words but the sequence of events and various characters). Because copyright hinges on creativity, creative works receive greater copyright protection.

A practical problem can be identifying which elements of the work are not protected. Nonoriginal elements are not protected, but the author is not required to identify which elements of her work are original. Imagine there were a 1910 book about the Civil War. Publisher has the only extant copy. Publisher scans the book and then has an employee edit and supplement the book, perhaps adding a paragraph here, a chapter there. Publisher publishes the updated book with a foreword explaining that some elements have been added but not specifically identifying the new elements. Publisher would have copyright protection in the new creative elements, but everything from the original book would be unprotected by copyright. However, a reader might be unable to distinguish between the protected and unprotected elements, meaning that copying would risk infringement. The same problem arises in many other types of work. A song may have an original, protected melody or may have copied it from another. A drawing in an advertisement may be new or copied from an old master. So the originality requirement leaves unoriginal material legally unprotected but does not always provide the key to using it.

Example

1. *Recreation.* Photographer Harney took a photo of socialite Clark Rockefeller and his daughter leaving a Boston church. Not too long afterward, Rockefeller went on the run after being exposed as an impostor named Christian Karl Gerhartsreiter. The photo was published widely, including on an FBI "Wanted" poster, as the police hunted Gerhartsreiter. A made-for-TV movie recounted the tale, using its own version of the photo (recreated with actors) without permission from Harney. Is it infringement to make a similar photo using actors?

Explanation

1. The court recognized the creativity in composing the picture but held that Sony copied only unprotected facts: "Harney's creation consists primarily of subject matter—'facts'—that he had no role in creating, including the central element of the Photo: the daughter riding piggyback on her father's shoulders. . . . [W]e do not see how subsequent events can fortuitously transform unoriginal elements of a visual work into protectible subject matter." *Harney v. Sony Pictures TV, Inc.*, 704 F.3d 173 (1st Cir. 2013).

Copyright Estoppel

Even original elements may not be protected if the author presents them as nonoriginal. Under the doctrine of "copyright estoppel," if an author represents information as factual, then she will not have copyright protection in the information—even if she actually originated it. *See Arica Institute, Inc. v. Palmer*, 970 F.2d 1067 (2d Cir. 1992). If an author concocted a story and presented it as fact, the events would be unprotected by copyright (as opposed to events in an avowedly fictional novel). Analogously, original theories could be treated as fact. In *Nash v. CBS, Inc.*, 899 F.2d 1537 (7th Cir. 1990), the author wrote a book about the gangster John Dillinger. The author reported that Dillinger had survived the famous shooting at the Biograph Theater in Chicago and lived out his life under another name in the West. Some television producers copied those elements, along with other specific facts reported by the author, and used them in making a television show. The author then sued for copyright infringement. The courts held that by presenting the information as factual, she had effectively waived any copyright protection. Others should be able to rely on the author's representation that material is not original (and not copyrighted).

Fair Use May Permit Copying Necessary to Access Unprotected Aspects of a Work

Copyright may attach to a work that incorporates nonoriginal material. Data Corp. can creatively arrange information from public tax records through its selection, arrangement, or coordination of the information. Someone who copied the entire database would potentially infringe the copyright. But if they did so not to copy the creative aspects but because it was necessary for accessing the data, they might be protected by fair use (a key subject in copyright, discussed in detail later in the book). Otherwise, the author could effectively have copyright protection in noncopyrighted elements.

3. Originality

The following examples range across the aspects of the originality requirement.

Examples

1. *Originality variations.* Would copyright protect the following?
   a. A researcher discloses many unprecedented facts about Madagascar hissing cockroaches: They sing mating calls, they form social clubs, and they have nicknames for each other, along with many detailed facts from observation.
   b. A book written by the researcher disclosing and analyzing those facts.
   c. The researcher, after others have republished the "facts," reveals she ingeniously made them all up.
   d. The videos made by a worm researcher, cleverly planned, placed, and lighted to capture the day-to-day life of a worm.
   e. The worm researcher's descriptions of dozens of subjects, capturing their individual characteristics but in a whimsical way (e.g., "Looks like Beethoven").
   f. The worm researcher's database, which is cleverly arranged and coordinated to facilitate searching and also by various comical categories.
   g. A kindergartner's drawing of a mousetrap.
   h. The list of names of students in a law school, arranged alphabetically by the registrar.
   i. The same list, arranged to sound as poetic as possible by the registrar.
   j. A video of a sunken ship in Lake Michigan, controlled remotely from the surface.
   k. A selection of violinist jokes, collected, selected, and arranged by a violinist.
   l. Valeria rewrites Shakespeare's *Merchant of Venice* as a political commentary on modern commercial society. She refashions the characters, puts the dialogue into modern idiom, adds topical humor, and tweaks the plot. Her work nevertheless copies thoroughly from the original.

2. *Odd numbers.* Autoparts Manufacture uses a part numbering system. A particular type of carburetor, for example, bears the number 03-11-62. The first pair of digits refers to the category of product, the second pair refers to the particular style of engine, and the third refers to the specific dimensions. Although Autoparts Manufacturer devised the system, it did not choose the specific combination of numbers for each part. Rather, using the system generates the specific numbers. Autoparts Manufacturer discovers that a competitor uses some of the numbers in its service manuals. Are the numbers copyrighted?

3. *"The most beautiful woman in the world."* In a local folktale, a young boy loses his mother. Naturally, he tells searchers that she is the most beautiful woman in the world. Villagers check with all the local beauties, but none is missing her child. Finally, the mother appears—not striking to any but her son. Scriptwriter hears of the story and uses it as the basis for a movie, adding many plot twists, bits of dialogue, and other elements. Novelist sees the movie and writes a novel based on the basic plot. Novelist only copies the elements taken from the folktale. All the other elements of the novel (such as the setting, the dialogue, various incidents that carry the story forward) are different from the film. Is the movie sufficiently original to be copyrighted? If so, did Novelist infringe the copyright?

4. *Butterfly chaos.* Nabokov, a lepidopterist, collects all the information he can about butterflies. Through his own fieldwork and library work, he amasses as many facts relating to butterflies as he can. He then arranges the facts according to his own categories, thereby creating a taxonomy of butterfly information. He publishes a book in which all the information is arranged in various categories Nabokov has devised. Is Nabokov's work copyrightable, or has he failed to exercise sufficient creativity because he has included every fact he could find?

5. *A book about a show about nothing.* A book called *The Seinfeld Aptitude Test* (*SAT*) contains questions about the television show *Seinfeld*. For example:

   1. To impress a woman, George passes himself off as
      a) a gynecologist
      b) a geologist
      c) a marine biologist
      d) a meteorologist
   2. What candy does Kramer snack on while observing a surgical procedure from an operating-room balcony?
   3. Who said, "I don't go for those nonrefundable deals. . . . I can't commit to a woman. . . . I'm not committing to an airline"?

The producers of *Seinfeld* sue for copyright infringement. In defense, the authors of *SAT* argue that they have simply copied unprotected facts, the things that the characters did and said during the show. Have the defendants copied original expression or facts?

6. *Casebook case.* Tibbs assembles materials for an education law casebook. She selects judicial opinions, statutes, regulations, and other published material. From these materials, she chooses which portions to include in the book. Tibbs considers many factors in selecting the material, such as relevance, historical impact, length (some items are heavily redacted), even literary merit. She arranges the materials in a carefully selected sequence. This sequence is intended to help the reader

understand the material, to reflect the history and development of the law, and in some places, to entertain by placing cases in a humorous sequence. Tibbs adds section titles and a few paragraphs of notes but largely lets the material speak for itself, leaving it to the reader to interpret the material. Her book is barely published before Allen comes out with her *Primary Materials on Education Law*. Allen's book has the same material in the same order, omitting only the section titles and paragraphs written by Tibbs. Allen argues that she has not infringed copyright because she has copied only material that was not original to Tibbs. Allen contends that Tibbs did not write the opinions, statutes, and regulations and cannot claim infringement if they are copied. Has Allen copied original material?

7. *GNU twist*. Some software developers decide to write a new version of Unix, a widely used operating system. The first order of business is to think of a name for the software. They hit on the name GNU Project. GNU is pronounced "guh-noo" and stands for "GNU is not Unix." The G in GNU stands for GNU, the name itself. They decide to register copyright in the phrase "GNU Project" (just the phrase itself, not the software). The Copyright Office denies registration on the basis that the word is not sufficiently original. First, there is an animal called the "gnu." Second, words or short phrases are not sufficiently original for copyright protection. Is "GNU Project" original for purposes of copyright law?

8. *Battle of the forms*. Kregos sells a "pitching form" for use by baseball fans. The form lists nine items. Two of the items apply to the entire season: won/lost record and earned run average. Three of the items relate to the opposing team at the site of the game: won/lost record, innings pitched, and earned run average. And four of the items are based on the pitcher's last three games: won/lost record, innings pitched, earned run average, and men on base average. The purpose of the form is to provide information with which a baseball fan could use her own knowledge to predict the likely performance of the pitcher.

   Each item is a type of statistic that was not original to Kregos, but no form had ever listed all these nine items of information together. Some forms had listed some of the items along with other items not on Kregos's form. The information to fill out the forms could be gleaned from publicly available information. The Associated Press began publishing a form copied from Kregos's form, listing the same nine categories of information. The Associated Press claims Kregos has no copyright, because he simply listed preexisting statistical categories. Are the forms sufficiently original for protection?

9. *Tradition.* Lifvon Guo is an elder of the Ami, an indigenous group in Taiwan. He travels to Europe with a group of performers. Unknown to him, someone records him singing the "Ami Song of Joy," a traditional song. The recording is subsequently combined with a twentieth-century dance beat and released by the group Enigma as "Return to Innocence." The song sells millions of copies and is used in advertisements for the Olympic Games in Atlanta. Does Lifvon have a copyright in "Return to Innocence"? Does Enigma?

10. *True fact?* The Bible is copyrighted.

11. *Based on a true story.* Dranker, a forensic psychiatrist in Boulder, writes a book telling the story of her career and many of her cases. She publishes the book, which has quite modest sales. One night, she watches a television show, *FSI: Boulder*, which features a fictional forensic psychiatrist with a background very similar to Dranker. The show revolves around a case much like one described in Dranker's book. As each new episode airs, the show repeatedly shows fictionalized stories based on Dranker's experience. The shows do not use any of the creative expression from Dranker's book but readily plunder her store of facts without giving any credit to Dranker. Does she have an action for copyright infringement? Would it make a difference if Dranker had not published the book but instead had recorded the stories in her diary, which was lost and somehow wound up with the scriptwriters?

12. *Trick or treat.* Suppose that in the last example Dranker confessed that she fabricated her career and the incredible cases she worked on. Rather than a forensic psychiatrist, she was simply a telemarketer with an active imagination. She then decides to pursue her copyright action against the producers of *FSI: Boulder*. They did not copy unprotected facts, she argues, but did copy her creative, and therefore copyrighted, confabulations. Are her fictional facts copyrighted?

13. *"Someone else was using the pencil."* Stuart Silverstein decides to put together a volume of uncollected poems of Dorothy Parker (known also for such remarks as "Everything that isn't writing is fun," and "Unless someone comes near my office, I'm going to write MEN on the door"). Silverstein spends more than a year looking for Parker's poems that have not appeared in previous collections. He goes through hundreds of magazines and newspapers and even locates two of her poems that have never been published. He submits a manuscript to a publisher, Penguin, with 122 poems. He makes "600 copy edits, mainly changes in punctuation, capitalization, indentation, and titling, to standardize the text." He does not tell Penguin of those edits but simply submits

the work as Parker's poems. Penguin declines to publish his proposed volume. Thereafter, Penguin publishes its own *Dorothy Parker: Complete Poems*, which includes a section titled "Poems Uncollected by Parker," containing 121 of the 122 poems compiled in Silverstein's book (but arranged chronologically, rather than following Silverstein's arrangement). Silverstein sues for copyright infringement, claiming originality on two principal bases: the choice to include the uncollected poems and the 600 copy edits made by him. Does the work qualify for copyright protection?

14. *Creative selection?* Lamps Plus sells its "Victorian Tiffany" table lamp. Lamps Plus selected five elements (a base, a finial, a cap, a glass light shade, and a metal filigree) from among the various components offered by its suppliers and put them together in the design of the Victorian Tiffany. Lamps Plus claims copyright in the design of the lamp. Although it did not design any of the components, it claims the requisite originality based on the selection of the components from among the many other possible combinations. Is the design of the lamp copyrightable?

15. *Do re mi*. Biolab sequences the genetic material of various animals and makes the data available online to researchers for a fee. The sequences look like this: CATAGCTAGCC. . . . Biolab is irked to find that DNA gene sequences downloaded by its customers are often passed on to others without Biolab getting a fee. Biolab decides to register the copyrights in gene sequences—as musical works, variations on the four notes C, A, T, and G. Can the sequences be protected from copying as musical works?

16. *Life, uncopyrighted*. Zippy Mart has a contractor install a security camera behind its cashier's station, in industry-standard fashion. One evening, the camera captures inebriated celebrity Rome Sheraton arguing with his dramaturge. After an employee posts the footage on Thoutube, Zippy Mart claims copyright. Is the footage copyrighted?

17. *Digital sculptures or copies?* Meshwerks, under contract with Toyota, made digital models of Toyota vehicles with a two-step process. First, Meshwerks used robotic arms patched into a computer network to precisely measure the form of the vehicle. Second, Meshwerk's digital sculptors tailored the screen images and data points to make the models as accurate as possible. The digital models are very helpful to car designers, who manipulate the models to simulate the effects of design changes, both functional and aesthetic. After Toyota makes use of the models beyond the scope of the original contract, Meshwerks claims copyright infringement. Are the digital models copyrighted?

18. *Coloring book creativity*. Publisher copies a public domain map from a United States census publication and then adds colors, shading, and a new typeface. Is the spruced-up map copyrightable?

19. *Cease and desist posting that cease and desist*. Blogger posts a rant about Big Corp. Soon, Blogger receives a cease-and-desist letter from Big Corp.'s lawyers, alleging defamation and unfair trade practices. Blogger posts a copy of the letter online. Blogger soon receives another cease-and-desist letter, contending that Blogger is infringing the copyright in the cease-and-desist letter. Could a cease-and-desist letter be copyrightable? If so, would it be infringement for the recipient to post it online to tell the world?

Explanations

1. Under *Feist*, originality is a two-part requirement: (i) independently created by the author and (ii) possessing at least some minimal degree of creativity.
   a. The facts are not created by the researcher but instead are discovered. They are not original to her and are therefore noncopyrightable.
   b. Her book would meet both requirements. Many elements of her text would originate with her and show the requisite creativity.
   c. If she represented fiction as fact, she would not have copyright in the material, under the copyright estoppel doctrine. Others are entitled to rely on an author's representation.
   d. The videos capture noncopyrighted facts about worms. But the videos themselves are made by the researcher and reflect a number of creative choices, so they would be copyrighted. Others could copy the facts but not the expression without potentially infringing. Another researcher could use the facts in her book but would potentially infringe if she made copies and sold copies of the video without permission.
   e. The descriptions may capture facts but also have original, creative elements.
   f. The facts in the database are not original, but creative selection, arrangement, and coordination of facts in such a compilation meet the originality requirement. Others could copy the facts but not the original arrangement and coordination.
   g. Copyrighted. The kindergartener originated it with the requisite creativity.
   h. Neither the names (which the registrar did not originate) nor their arrangement (in alphabetical order, completely nonoriginal as in *Feist*'s telephone listings) are original.

i. The registrar's arrangement of the names would be sufficiently creative. Others could copy the names, but not this arrangement of them, without potentially infringing.
j. The facts of the ship are not original, but the making of the video would likely show the necessary creativity. The fact that a device actually fixed the work would not bar copyright when a human made the creative decisions that directed it.
k. The jokes did not originate with the violinist, but she showed originality in her selection and arrangement of the compilation.
l. A work based on a preexisting work can be original if the author adds new creative elements. The adaptation of *Merchant of Venice* would handily clear the low hurdle of a "minimal spark of creativity."

2. The part numbers are not creative expression. They are dictated by the system, rather than by a creative choice of a human. So the numbers are not copyrightable. *Southco v. Kanebridge Corp.*, 390 F.3d 276 (3d Cir. 2004) (en banc) (per Judge Alito). Note that numbers as such are not categorically nonprotectable. A number is not copyrightable, but creative expression that is expressed in numbers may be. For example, the selection and arrangement of used car value listings might be protectable as a compilation.

3. The movie is protected by copyright even though it is not wholly original but based on a preexisting work. By adding original creative expression (the plot twists, dialogue, and other elements), Scriptwriter qualifies for copyright protection. But copyright protects only the original elements of the movie. Novelist did not copy original elements but copied only those elements from the folktale. So Novelist did not infringe the copyright in the movie. *Cf. Reyher v. Children's Television Workshop*, 533 F.2d 87 (2d Cir. 1975).

4. Nabokov has met the creativity requirement. The telephone book publisher in *Feist* published every listing it could identify, in alphabetical order. Nabokov did publish every fact he could find, so he may not have exercised creativity in the selection of information. But he did not simply list the facts in alphabetical order. Rather, he exercised creativity in the coordination and arrangement of the information, because he devised the categories by which the information was organized. As the court that posed this hypothetical put it, "Facts do not supply their own principles of organization. Classification is a creative endeavor." *American Dental Ass'n v. Delta Dental Plans Ass'n*, 126 F.3d 977, 979 (7th Cir. 1997).

5. The defendant did copy original expression. As the court aptly put it:

> The *SAT* does not quiz such true facts as the identity of the actors in *Seinfeld*, the number of days it takes to shoot an episode, the biographies of the actors, the

location of the *Seinfeld* set, etc. Rather, The *SAT* tests whether the reader knows that the character Jerry places a Pez dispenser on Elaine's leg during a piano recital, that Kramer enjoys going to the airport because he's hypnotized by the baggage carousels, and that Jerry, opining on how to identify a virgin, said "It's not like spotting a toupee." Because these characters and events spring from the imagination of *Seinfeld*'s authors, The *SAT* plainly copies copyrightable, creative expression.

Castle Rock Entertainment v. Carol Publishing, 150 F.3d 132, 139 (2d Cir. 1998).

The *Castle Rock* court drew a sound distinction between what it called "true facts" and fictional facts. The reason that facts are not copyrighted is that facts (for purposes of copyright law) do not originate with their discoverer. Rather, facts are information that someone may find, not that someone creates. But the "facts" in *Seinfeld* (such as Jerry placing a Pez dispenser on Elaine's leg during a piano recital) are indeed created by the authors of the show, as opposed to being information that existed beforehand and was later discovered (like facts about the extinction of dinosaurs).

6. Allen has copied original material. Tibbs wrote none of the individual items. But Tibbs's work is a compilation. Tibbs exercised creativity in the selection, coordination, and arrangement of preexisting material. Allen could have copied any particular item without infringing, but Allen copied almost the entire work, omitting only the specific items written by Tibbs. So, Allen copied Tibbs's selection, coordination, and arrangement of the material.

7. This case presents issues as to both requirements of originality: independent creation and a modicum of creativity. Most authorities would agree that a phrase as short as "GNU Project" is not copyrightable. The policy is sound, because otherwise no one could publicly mention the name of the project without risking infringement. Some ground the rule on the originality requirement on the theory that coining a short phrase does not meet even the minimal requirement for originality. But this seems a little dubious, because the phrase is quite creative. A better rationale might be that a short phrase does not constitute a work of authorship, and therefore is not within copyrightable subject matter.

   If short phrases were copyrightable, then the next issue would be whether this one originated with the software developers, given that "gnu" is already a word. But their "work" was the phrase "GNU Project." Like most literary works, it is composed of preexisting words, but nevertheless is itself something that originated with the author.

8. The forms are sufficiently original for protection. *See Kregos v. Associated Press*, 937 F.2d 700 (2d Cir. 1991). Although Kregos did not originate

the various statistical categories, he did originate the listing of those nine categories together. This selection and arrangement would meet the minimal standard of *Feist*.

9. This example, which highlights some troubling outcomes of the originality requirement, is drawn from Angela R. Riley, *Recovering Collectivity: Group Rights to Intellectual Property in Indigenous Communities*, 18 Cardozo Arts & Ent. L.J. 175 (2000) (analyzing the "Ami Song of Joy" case and other cases, and proposing modifications to copyright law to protect indigenous culture). Lifvon Guo does not have a copyright in "Ami Song of Joy," because he is not its author. It is a traditional song, so very likely its author (for copyright purposes) can no longer be identified. Moreover, the song is old enough that it would be out of copyright protection anyway.

   But Enigma does have a copyright in "Return to Innocence." Enigma did not author "Ami Song of Joy," so it does not have a copyright in that musical work. Enigma would have a copyright in the work based on "Ami Song of Joy" (assuming that adding the dance beat met the minimal requirement of creativity) and also the sound recording of the music. So Enigma would appear to have a copyright in music based on the traditional song, as well as the recording of "Return to Innocence." Indeed, even the person who recorded Lifvon Guo's performance probably has a copyright in that sound recording, assuming some creative choices were made in producing it. Such cases raise the question whether there should be adjustments to intellectual property law to address the fact that others may effectively privatize indigenous cultural material, while the indigenous people themselves may not have recognized rights in the material. *See* Lorie Graham and Stephen McJohn, *Indigenous People and Intellectual Property*, 19 Wash. U. J.L. & Pol'y 313 (2005).

10. True. The Bible (reportedly the best-selling book of all time) is under copyright — or, more accurately, various versions of the Bible are copyrighted. *See* Roger Syn, *© Copyright God: Enforcement of Copyright in the Bible and Religious Works*, 14 Regent U. L. Rev. 1, 2-3 (2001-2002) ("All major English Bible translations, except the Authorised Version, are subject to copyright. Copyright also subsists in some standard editions of the ancient biblical manuscripts from which translations are made."). The original texts are in the public domain, but a publisher can use those texts as the basis for another work in several different ways: by translation, by annotation, by editing, by adding pictures, and so on. Provided that the required minimal creativity is met, the work would be subject to copyright (protecting only the new elements, of course). The ethics

of claiming exclusive rights in such texts are another, somewhat controversial, matter.

11. Dranker does not have an action for copyright infringement. Cf. Malcolm Gladwell, *Something Borrowed*, New Yorker, November 22, 2004 (relating the tale of a psychiatrist whose work with serial killers, along with a magazine article about her, was used without attribution in a play). Facts are not protected by copyright, so there is no infringement for copying facts. Assuming that the scriptwriters copied only facts (a big assumption, because there is usually some creative expression mixed in with facts in a literary work), they could not be liable for copyright infringement. Copyright is different from the ethical proscription of plagiarism, which applies to the use of another's work without attribution.

    The result would be the same even if Dranker had written the facts in a private diary. She would have the copyright, but it would not be infringed by copying facts. Of course, the copier would need access to the diary, which might violate some other law (trespassing, trade secret, or possibly rights of privacy).

12. A court would likely hold that Dranker did not have copyright protection in fictional events that she presented as facts. Under the copyright estoppel approach, the public is entitled to rely on the author's representation of what is factual material. Otherwise, any work could present a trap for the unwary. Someone who uses in good faith material that is presented as factual (and therefore unprotected) will not be liable for infringement.

13. Neither argument would succeed. As to selection, "the chief principle of selection is that the poems collected by Silverstein were not collected by Mrs. Parker in her lifetime. The selection was thus made by Mrs. Parker, and it remained for Silverstein only to gather up the poems she selected for exclusion." *Silverstein v. Penguin Putnam, Inc.*, 368 F.3d 77, 84-85 (2d Cir. 2004). Copy edits might be sufficiently original to qualify for protection if they were done in creative fashion and were not simply functional. *Id.* at 83. Perhaps someone could entirely change the meaning of a literary work by revising the punctuation and capitalization. But in *Silverstein*, there was no showing of such creativity in the copyediting. Moreover, even if they were sufficiently creative, copyright would be denied by the doctrine of copyright estoppel. *Id.* Silverstein represented the poems as the work of Dorothy Parker. Once others have relied on that representation, he may be barred from claiming copyright. Finally, although Silverstein expended great resources in compiling the material, that does not give rise to copyright protection.

The result would be different if the facts were slightly different. If rather than including every noncollected poem, Silverstein made creative choices about which to include and which to exclude, that might give his selection the requisite originality. Or if Penguin had copied a creative arrangement of the poems by Silverstein, then it might have infringed. But Penguin's editor rearranged the poems into chronological order.

14. The selection of five preexisting elements would likely be held insufficient to meet the requirements of creativity. *See Lamps Plus, Inc. v. Seattle Lighting Fixture Co.*, 345 F.3d 1140, 1147 (9th Cir. 2003) (relying on Copyright Office regulations discussed in the text). The Copyright Office regulations suggest that a selection of four or fewer elements is insufficient for copyrightability. A court is likely to hold that selecting five elements is likewise insufficient to meet the originality requirement.

15. The DNA sequences are nonoriginal, nonprotectable facts, regardless of how Biolab characterizes them. *See* Stephen R. Wilson, *Copyright Protection for DNA Sequences: Can the Biotech Industry Harmonize Science with Song?* 44 Jurimetrics J. 409-463 (2004). The argument relies on turning the copyright estoppel rule around. If original creations are represented as fact, then they will be treated as nonoriginal, and hence nonprotected, facts. But the converse does not hold. Characterizing facts as creative expression does not turn the facts into creative expression. Biolab could invent lengthy sequences using the four letters C, A, G, and T and would have copyright protection in them (assuming they were done somehow creatively, not just randomly or by computer). But that copyright would be pretty worthless because no one would be interested in copying them. Rather, others are interested in copying actual DNA sequences, exactly because they represent facts.

    One last variation: Suppose, to catch copiers, Biolab invented a DNA sequence and put it in the database. The same sequence shows up in the hands of a noncustomer. Biolab argues that this is copyright infringement. Biolab created the sequence, and the noncustomer must have copied it from Biolab. Copyright infringement? No, because of copyright estoppel, where Biolab represented it as an actual DNA sequence. In short, if Biolab wants legal protection for DNA sequences, it needs to look to patent law, or trade secret law, or contract law.

16. This raises a question that will pop up more and more. As security cameras, personal cameras, communications technology, and virtual and online behavior all proliferate, the question arises whether the recorded information is copyrighted. *Madisonian.net*'s authors often acutely discuss such near future issues. The last chapter discusses the argument that often such information will not be a "work of

authorship." A related argument is that the originality necessary for copyright is lacking. Mounting a security camera behind a cashier is a functional standard industry practice, no more creative than listing all the names in the phone book in alphabetical order. By contrast, if an artist mounted the same camera in the same alley to capture the occurrences over the course of a year, that would be well above the line of a "minimal spark of creativity." So the state of mind may make the difference where creativity is at issue. Even with a security camera, if some creative choices were made in deciding where to mount it or what it should capture, then it might meet the low standard required for creativity.

One can distinguish the mundane security camera example from the Zapruder case, where the home moviemaker happened to capture a historic event. The moviemaker made various creative choices: "Zapruder selected the kind of camera (movies, not snapshots), the kind of film (color), the kind of lens (telephoto), the area in which the pictures were to be taken, the time they were to be taken, and (after testing several sites) the spot on which the camera would be operated." His intent was to film the Kennedy motorcade. Mounting a security camera in standard fashion could be deemed to lack originality.

Copyright is not the end of the story. The owner of a security camera (or cell phone, or permanent personal video recorder, or day care cam) may not have a copyright. But they do have the footage. So unless they permit it to be released, they may still control its dissemination. A person does not have exclusive rights in her life story, but she may control what she discloses, and someone who wants to make a film or book about her may pay for the information.

Bonus (and preview) question: If the security footage were copyrighted, who would own the copyright? The camera was put up not by Zippy Mart or its employees but by an independent contractor. If sufficient creativity went into that process, the author and copyright holder would be the contractor (unless Zippy got an assignment of the copyright in the contract!). Chapter 7 discusses the rules.

17. The Tenth Circuit held that the digital models were not copyrighted because of lack of originality. *Meshwerks, Inc. v. Toyota Motor Sales U.S.A., Inc.* (10th Cir. 2008). The digital models were copies (very good copies) of the cars, representing no independent creation. Despite the skill and even creativity required to create the models, they did not have any creative elements independent from their role as copies (in a different medium). Unlike a photograph, for which the author makes choices about pose, positioning, and lighting, the models served only to accurately reproduce factual data about the configuration of the vehicles.

18. Merely adding commonplace elements such as colors, shading, and a new typeface to an existing map fails to show even the minimal creativity required for copyright. *Darden v. Peters*, 488 F.3d 277 (4th Cir. 2007) (upholding decision of Copyright Office to deny registration).

    Darden makes one wonder about the copyrightability of such items as colorized black-and-white films or remastered sound recordings. Such works certainly require technical skill, but if done in a way that did not include creative choices, would not qualify for a separate copyright (remember that copying such new versions could still infringe the copyright in the original). It would depend on showing that colorizing or remastering does not simply add standard elements but rather requires creative choices. A court might also be sensitive to the hazard of a party capturing public domain material, as by colorizing a public domain film that has not been widely distributed, and effectively precluding others from using it.

19. A cease-and-desist letter could be copyrightable if the author used some menacing creativity rather than just relying on a form letter or standard language. But Blogger's posting the letter online would surely qualify as fair use (to preview a key topic in copyright). Blogger was not seeking to cut into the market for a copyrighted work, but rather to inform the public of the communication from the law firm. Fair use is a key First Amendment safeguard. The case might be different if defendant were copying the letter for a book of legal forms.

    As this example illustrates, fair use may be used to permit parties to use copyrighted works, especially where the purpose of the use is not to exploit the creative expression, but to disseminate unprotected aspects (such as getting facts from a database, or using functional aspects of a work or communicating ideas). A party that has been threatened with legal action must be able to effectively communicate that to the public.

CHAPTER 4

Fixation

When a poet pens a pastoral, she has a copyright:

> Copyright protection subsists, in accordance with this title, in original works of authorship *fixed in any tangible medium of expression*, now known or later developed, from which they can be perceived, reproduced, or otherwise communicated, either directly or with the aid of a machine or device.

17 U.S.C. §102(a) (italics added).

Fixation, the embodiment of the work in tangible form, plays several roles in copyright. First, federal copyright protection begins when a work is "fixed" in tangible form by the author or someone acting with her authority. 17 U.S.C. §102. Fixation draws the line between state copyright law, which may protect unfixed works, and federal copyright, which governs fixed works. See House Report No. 94-1476. Most works are fixed in some tangible form, so copyright law is almost exclusively federal law. Second, copyright infringement may occur when a copyrighted work is fixed in a copy or phonorecord without the authority of the copyright owner. Infringement may also occur by unauthorized adaptation, performance, distribution, or display (as discussed later in the book), but unauthorized copying is perhaps the most commonly raised type of infringement. Third, infringement analysis often requires comparing the allegedly infringing work to the copyrighted work to see if copyrighted expression has been copied. The fact that the work must be fixed in a tangible form makes this comparison easier. Finally, registration of copyright generally requires depositing a copy of the work.

4. Fixation

Copyright protects an original work of authorship as soon as the work has been "fixed in a tangible medium of expression." 17 U.S.C. §102. A novel, for example, may be copyrighted as soon as the author has put it in some tangible form: written it on paper, typed it into a computer, or even dictated it into a tape recorder. To obtain copyright protection, it is not necessary to register the work with the U.S. Copyright Office, or to put the little © on the work, or to publish the work, or to make more than one copy of the work, or even to let anyone know that the work exists.

Without fixation in tangible form, however, there is no federal copyright. Suppose a jazz violinist improvises a complex new tune while playing in concert. The tune may easily qualify as an original work of authorship, far exceeding the minimal creativity required for copyright. But if it has not been fixed in tangible form, the author has no copyright. Even if the concert audience numbered in the thousands, a public performance alone would not cause copyright to apply. If other musicians learned the tune and also performed it, they would not be infringing, because there was no copyright in the tune. Nor would there be copyright if the musician filled out a registration form and mailed it to the Copyright Office. Rather, she would need to fix the work in a tangible medium of expression for copyright to attach. The United States differs here from some jurisdictions, where copyright begins upon creation of the work, whether fixed in tangible form or not.

Fortunately for the musician, fixation is easily done most of the time. Indeed, for writers, sculptors, photographers, and perhaps most authors, fixation occurs naturally as part of the creative process. Even for improvisational artists, such as jazz musicians, comedians, or dancers, who more often do not fix a work in tangible form during the creative process, fixation is easily accomplished. Any tangible form will suffice. Our musician could fix the work by writing the notes down in sheet music, having her playing recorded, having someone videotape the performance, or any other means. A digital recording that transforms it into a long string of zeros and ones would suffice. An architect need not build the house to get copyright protection in the architectural work. Fixing it in the form of drawings will suffice.

Copyright protection is much simpler to obtain than patent protection. If an inventor simply invents a new mousetrap, she has no exclusive rights in the invention. No one would need permission from the inventor to make or use a similar mousetrap, even if they copied directly from hers. Even if she sold millions of the mousetraps, she would not have a patent. To obtain a patent, the inventor must do the following: invent the invention, draft a patent application (a sophisticated piece of work, best done by someone with knowledge of patent law and of the relevant field of endeavor), file the application with the USPTO, convince the patent examiner that the invention is patentable and that the application is valid, and then pay considerable fees for issuance of the patent. That process is likely to take a couple of years.

For copyright protection, by contrast, the author need only create the work and put it in tangible form. The author need not even think of copyright.

The rule that fixation is the moment at which copyright attaches represents a considerable change in copyright law. Before 1978, federal copyright protection attached to a work (generally speaking) when the work was published with a copyright notice on copies of the work (registration conferred copyright for a limited category of unpublished works). To obtain federal copyright protection, the author had to meet two requirements: publication and use of a copyright notice (such as "© 1946 James Baldwin"). Until 1978, unpublished works (with some narrow exceptions) were not subject to federal copyright but could be protected by state copyright law. Therefore, to obtain copyright, an author needed to write and publish the novel. Even until 1989, works that were published without a copyright notice could forfeit their copyright and go into the public domain. Now an author need only write the novel for copyright to attach and remain attached. As later chapters discuss, however, formalities still play an important role in enforcing copyright.

Federal copyright law has expanded considerably: Rather than applying primarily to published works, it now also applies to unpublished works. There are lots of unpublished works—not only novels that did not find publishing contracts but also private letters, art class projects, e-mails, and so on. The number of works subject to copyright has greatly expanded. The role of copyright has likewise expanded. Previously, copyright infringement was usually thought of only where someone had copied a published work. Now, copyright infringement is often claimed in litigation about unpublished works, such as letters, e-mails, drafts of works, computer program source code, and internal memoranda. There is a considerably different paradigm. Before 1978, if a published work did not have a copyright notice, it was probably not copyrighted. Now, works are probably copyrighted whether they have been published or not and whether they have a copyright notice or not.

PURPOSE OF THE FIXATION REQUIREMENT

Several reasons are commonly given for the fixation requirement, the rule that federal copyright will not apply unless a work has been embodied in some tangible form.

One reason is that the U.S. Constitution mandates the fixation requirement. The Constitution grants Congress the power to give copyrights in the "Writings" of authors. The word "writing" implies that the work be recorded in some form. Granting copyrights in unfixed works would exceed the power of Congress. Note that "Writings" has not been limited to its usual literal meaning, which might limit copyright to written works like novels and textbooks. "Writings" is broadly construed to cover any form in which an author's work is embodied, such as books, recordings, notes, photographs, drawings, computer chips, sculpture, or any other tangible, stable form.

Another rationale given for the fixation requirement is that it sets boundaries. By putting the work in tangible form, the author defines what is included in the work. By setting such boundaries, the author informs others of the extent of the author's claimed rights. Just as fences may serve to show the boundaries of real property, the fixation requirement marks the author's intellectual territory. In turn, this facilitates transactions involving copyrights. Markets function better when rights are clearly defined, because that makes it easier to engage in transactions.

The fixation requirement serves a related evidentiary function. In many areas of the law, the rules prompt parties to put things in writing. An oral contract, for example, may not be enforceable. A written contract provides better evidence that the parties had an agreement and what the terms of the agreement were. Likewise, enforcement of copyright in an unfixed work (like an improvised song or dance) would require determining, without the benefit of a recording, just what was performed by the author. It would be very difficult to determine whether expressive elements were copied from a work without a tangible copy of the work showing just what those expressive elements were.

TANGIBLE MEDIUM OF EXPRESSION

The work need only be "fixed" in some tangible form to be copyrightable. The definition of fixed is broad:

> A work is "fixed" in a tangible medium of expression when its embodiment in a copy or phonorecord, by or under the authority of the author, is sufficiently permanent or stable to permit it to be perceived, reproduced, or otherwise communicated for a period of more than transitory duration.

17 U.S.C. §101. The work must be embodied in a copy or phonorecord to be fixed. Most works are fixed in the form of a "copy," which is broadly defined to include almost any medium that can capture a work:

> "Copies" are material objects, other than phonorecords, in which a work is fixed by any method now known or later developed, and from which the work can be perceived, reproduced, or otherwise communicated, either directly or with the aid of a machine or device.

17 U.S.C. §101. A copy of a novel could be a printed book, a file on the hard drive of a computer, a handwritten manuscript, or a film of someone reciting the novel.

"Phonorecord" has a parallel definition as the form in which sounds (other than those in audiovisual works) are fixed. 17 U.S.C. §101. Sound recordings are fixed in phonorecords and other works are fixed in copies. A sound recording could be on tape, in an MP3 file, or any other form.

These definitions are broad enough to clarify that the work need not be fixed in a form that humans can read. Early cases had held that piano rolls (the rolls inserted into player pianos) were not covered by copyright because—unlike things such as music scores, paintings, and books—they were not readable by humans. Under this approach, copyright would not apply to works recorded on tape, disc, or other electronic or magnetic media. Many of the works in today's digital age would not be subject to copyright. However, that narrow approach is clearly rejected by the present form of the statute. The statute now encompasses piano rolls, as well as more modern forms of recordings such as CDs and DVDs. Copyright subsists once works are "fixed in any tangible medium of expression, now known or later developed, from which they can be perceived, reproduced, or otherwise communicated, either directly or with the aid of a machine or device." Note how broadly the statute is drafted to make sure that any physical embodiment will be subject to copyright.

Examples

1. *At what point in time?* In 2006, Concord creates a novella, *Lanes and Games*. She spends several days working out most of the details in her head and then writes it all down over several days. She subsequently types the words into her computer and e-mails them to her publisher. The publisher soon prints 1,000 copies of the book (with a copyright notice, "© 2006 Concord," on each) and delivers them to various bookstores. The books are put on display, and most are sold over the next few months. Meanwhile, just after the book is published, Concord registers the book with the Copyright Office. She downloads the form and mails it in with the fee. Soon, she receives a certificate of registration.

   At what point does Concord have a copyright in the novella? What if all the events had occurred in 1966?

2. *Making a record.* Concord has an idea for another novella. Over several days, she devises an intricate plot and peoples the story with some complex characters. She does not have time to sit down and write out the story. Rather, she simply writes the title of the novella, *Worm Tunnel*, on a postcard and mails the postcard to herself. Does she have a federal copyright

in the story? What if she had carried a tape recorder and dictated the story as she thought it up?

3. *Improvable.* Nick and Tony are improvisational comedians. During their act, they take suggestions from audience members and improvise skits. They learn that local stand-up comedians have copied some of their acts. Can they get copyright protection without resorting to a scripted act?

4. *Lost symphony.* Sergei composes a symphony, working alone in his Alaskan bush cabin. As soon as he finishes, he bundles up the manuscript and jumps in his floatplane, never to be seen again. Several years later, the manuscript floats ashore in Seattle. Local musicians learn of the find and decide to perform the symphony. Just to be sure, they check the Copyright Office records to make sure that Sergei did not register the copyright before his untimely end. Is the symphony uncopyrighted?

5. *Unfixed?* Author writes a story and reads it in public. She then inadvertently destroys the only copy of the story. Moviemaker was at the reading, loved the story, and has a tremendous memory. He would like to copy the story into a script without Author's consent. Does Author lose copyright because her work is no longer fixed?

6. *Lightning in a bottle.* Georgia choreographs a ballet retelling the fable of the tortoise and the hare. Georgia does not care to write the choreography down in annotations or record it in verbal form. Rather, she guides the dancers through the piece bit by bit. At the dress rehearsal, a photographer takes dozens of photos of the performance. Georgia had given permission for the photos to be taken. Does Georgia have a copyright in the dance?

7. *Ever-changing?* Kelly plants and tends a "permanent Wild Flower Floral Display." The bed has aesthetic appeal, partly from how the flowers change with the season. Is the work copyrighted?

8. *Virtual yet tangible.* Firesabre "terraforms" islands in the virtual world Second Life. Is Firesabre's work fixed in a tangible medium even though it's in a virtual world? "Fixed" under the Copyright Act requires only that the work be "sufficiently permanent or stable to permit it to be perceived, reproduced, or otherwise communicated for a period of more than transitory duration." As long as Firesabre's work has a little creativity, it can be a copyrighted work. *FireSabre Consulting LLC v. Sheehy*, 2013 U.S. Dist. LEXIS 139550 (S.D.N.Y. Sept. 26, 2013).

Explanations

1. Concord has a copyright in the novella when she fixes it in a tangible medium of expression. She did this when she wrote the novella. None of the subsequent actions (putting it in a computer, printing and publishing copies with a copyright notice) were necessary to receive protection under the current version of the statute.

   If all this had occurred in 1966, the answer would be different. Until 1978, federal copyright applied primarily to published works. Copyright would not attach until the work was published with a copyright notice (for some works, copyright could be secured by registration). Had it been published without a copyright notice, Concord would have lost her copyright and the work would be in the public domain, free for anyone else to copy.

2. Concord has a copyright in the story when she fixes it in a tangible medium of expression. She has not done this, so she has no copyright. Writing the title alone does not fix the entire work. If, however, she dictated the story into a tape recorder, that would fix it in tangible form and she would have a copyright.

3. Nick and Tony do not need to use a script to have copyright protection. Rather, they could record their act as they improvise it. That would fix it in tangible form, and they would then have copyright in the work. Having said that, comedians reportedly rely less on copyright than on informal norms to reduce free-riding. *See* Dotan Oliar and Chris Sprigman, *The Emergence of Intellectual Property Norms in Stand-Up Comedy*, Va. L. Rev. (2008).

4. Sergei had a copyright in the musical work when he fixed it in tangible form by writing it down in manuscript form. The manuscript may be lost, but that does not affect the intangible right in the copyright. He did not register the copyright, but that is not necessary to have copyright protection. The local musicians could potentially infringe the copyright by a public performance of the symphony. They would be well advised to seek permission from Sergei's heirs.

5. Once fixed, the work is protected by copyright. The statute does not require that the work remain fixed. *See Peter Pan Fabrics v. Rosstex Fabrics*, 733 F. Supp. 174 (S.D.N.Y. 1990) (rejecting even the possibility of such an argument). Author still has her copyright, but proving infringement might be very difficult. To prove infringement, Author must show copying of original, creative expression. It might be difficult without a copy of the story to show which elements were copied. Moreover, as later chapters discuss, Author must register the work to bring an infringement action (assuming Author is a U.S. author). To register the work, Author

must deposit a copy of the work. As discussed later in the book, courts have held that a reconstruction from memory may not be used to satisfy the deposit requirement.

6. The photographs may be sufficient to fix the choreographic work in a tangible form. The question would be whether the choreographic work, the composition and arrangement of dance movements and patterns, could be "perceived, reproduced, or otherwise communicated" through the series of still photographs. As one court aptly described, still images might well suffice to capture choreography:

> A snapshot of a single moment in a dance sequence may communicate a great deal. It may, for example, capture a gesture, the composition of dancers' bodies or the placement of dancers on the stage. Such freezing of a choreographic moment is shown in a number of the photographs in the Switzer book, e.g., at pp. 30, 38, 42, 66-67, 68, 69, 74, 75, 78, 80, and 81. A photograph may also convey to the viewer's imagination the moments before and after the split second recorded. On page 76-77 of the Switzer book, for example, there is a two-page photograph of the "Sugar Canes," one of the troupes that perform in The Nutcracker. In this photograph, the Sugar Canes are a foot or more off the ground, holding large hoops above their heads. One member of the ensemble is jumping through a hoop, which is held extended in front of the dancer. The dancer's legs are thrust forward, parallel to the stage and several feet off the ground. The viewer understands instinctively, based simply on the laws of gravity, that the Sugar Canes jumped up from the floor only a moment earlier, and came down shortly after the photographed moment.

Horgan v. MacMillan, Inc., 789 F.2d 157, 163 (2d Cir. 1986) (discussing a similar issue, whether a series of photos in a book, Ellen Switzer's *The Nutcracker: A Story and a Ballet*, could infringe the copyright in a choreographic work, George Ballanchine's choreography for the ballet *The Nutcracker*).

7. The court, faintly echoing Chauncey Gardiner, held that the work was neither a work of human authorship nor fixed in tangible form: "A garden's constituent elements are alive and inherently changeable, not fixed. Most of what we see and experience in a garden—the colors, shapes, textures, and scents of the plants—originates in nature, not in the mind of the gardener. At any given moment in time, a garden owes most of its form and appearance to natural forces, though the gardener who plants and tends it obviously assists." *Kelley v. Chicago Park District*, 635 F.3d 290 (7th Cir. 2011).

8. "Fixed" under the Copyright Act requires only that the work be "sufficiently permanent or stable to permit it to be perceived, reproduced, or otherwise communicated for a period of more than transitory duration." The work was fixed in computer storage somewhere, even if it portrayed

something in a virtual world. As long as Firesabre's work has a little creativity, it can be a copyrighted work. *FireSabre Consulting LLC v. Sheehy*, 2013 U.S. Dist. LEXIS 139550 (S.D.N.Y. Sept. 26, 2013).

MORE THAN ONE WORK MAY BE FIXED IN THE SAME COPY

A work is fixed in a copy or phonorecord. The same copy may also serve to fix other works as well. This is quite clear with such things as books of poetry, which one would expect to contain many works, but works can also be intermingled in the same copy. An author might write a short story, which a screenwriter adapts into a screenplay or which a director adapts into a film. A copy of the film (on reel, on disc, or whatever form) could be a copy of the story, of the screenplay, songs used on the soundtrack, and of the film, the unified work made up of all those elements, which would have its own copyright. Such multiple fixation is likely to be important less in deciding when copyright attaches (because the copyrights in the story, screenplay, and film attached when each was initially fixed) but more for purposes of infringement analysis. An unauthorized copy or performance of the film could potentially infringe all those copyrights.

Example

1. *Philosophical differences.* Thelma and Louise, two folk singers, write the song "Drumlin Farm" by improvising both tune and words while playing their guitars. When satisfied, they make an audiotape of themselves performing the song. After happily listening to it, they decide to read up on copyright law to figure out their rights. Soon, they are a little confused—do they have a musical work? A sound recording? And is the tape a copy or a phonorecord?

Explanation

1. The authors have two copyrights: a copyright in the musical work "Drumlin Farm" and a copyright in the sound recording of them singing the song. The tape is a copy of the musical work and a phonorecord of the sound recording.

SUFFICIENTLY STABLE FORM: FIXATION AND DIGITAL WORKS

Fixation must be "sufficiently permanent or stable to permit it to be perceived, reproduced, or otherwise communicated for a period of more than transitory duration." 17 U.S.C. §101. The work need not be etched in granite, but it must be in a stable form. A tattoo would be sufficient to fix a "pictorial, graphic, or sculptural" work. An ice sculpture or snowman would be sufficiently stable and so copyrighted if it were sufficiently original. Would the copyright disappear when the copy melted? The work need only be fixed, not eternal, so presumably the copyright would survive. Any alleged infringement, of course, would be difficult to prove without a surviving copy or a witness with a very good memory. To sue for infringement also requires that the work be registered, including deposit of a copy—which now might be impossible.

Just how stable is not clear. Fixation must be "for a period of more than transitory duration." An important issue (which usually arises in the context of infringement, not initial protection) is whether a work is fixed when a computer makes a temporary copy in its memory. A computer very frequently makes temporary copies of works. For example, suppose a user wants to look at some photos that are in digital form on a CD. If the user loads the CD into the CD drive to view the photos, the computer will copy the image file from the CD into the computer's temporary memory to access it. The same is true if the user looks at photos from a website. The images will be stored temporarily in the computer to display them. The same is true for other works. The computer will make temporary copies anytime it runs a program, opens a document, and so on. The temporary copies may be all or part of the work, and will be erased when the computer is turned off. If the user saves one of the pictures, it will be permanently saved on the hard drive of the computer. That looks like the picture has been fixed in a stable form. But does a temporary copy that lasts only as long as the computer is still on (and may be erased to put other things in memory) count as a sufficiently stable copy—and therefore serve to fix a new work or, more important, serve to make an infringing copy of an existing work?

There is a good argument that such temporary copies should not be copies for the purposes of copyright law. Such temporary copies must be refreshed many times per second by the computer and disappear completely when the computer is turned off or when the computer devotes its memory to another task. A temporary copy also cannot be handed to another person, because it remains in the computer. Some argue that they are transitory and do not meet the definition of "fixed" under the copyright statute. Moreover, the argument continues, such temporary copies should not be treated as copies because that gives too much control to the copyright owner, effectively expanding the exclusive right to make copies into the exclusive right to use the work.

The counterargument is that a temporary copy in a computer can last as long as the user wishes and can easily be distributed to others. It should count as a copy both for the literal meaning of the statute (because it lasts more than a "transitory duration") and for policy reasons (because any other reading would permit the potential proliferation and distribution of copies). The issue has not been definitively settled. But several recent amendments to the copyright statute appear to assume that such temporary copies are copies. Section 117 now authorizes the owner of a computer to make a copy of a computer program, where the copying occurs automatically by activating the computer. Someone in rightful possession of a computer program may make a copy if that is necessary to activate the machine containing the program. Section 501 limits the liability of Internet service providers for transient storage of digital materials sent over computer networks. Both provisions would hardly be necessary if temporary copies were not potentially infringing copies. The Copyright Office (that persuasive if not binding authority on interpreting the Copyright Act) has also repeatedly taken the position that such temporary copies are sufficient to meet the fixation requirement. So it appears to be the law that a temporary copy in a computer is a copy for the purposes of copyright law—both for initial fixation of the work by the author and for potential infringement of the copyright by others.

Examples

1. *Rats*. The musical *Rats* is highly successful. The musical has a number of memorable characters drawn from a children's book about rats living under a restaurant. The musical has several popular songs and lots of funny banter. The Broadway production features creative makeup designs on the actors' faces. Part of the attraction is that Producer bans the publication of photos of the made-up actors—only those attending live performances see the makeup designs. Tabloid Photographer takes unauthorized photos of the actors by sneaking backstage. When Producer seeks an injunction against publication of the photos, Photographer argues that the makeup designs are not fixed and therefore are unprotected. Are the designs painted on the actors' faces sufficiently fixed to attain copyright protection?

2. *Double Rats*. Suppose that none of the songs and dialogue in *Rats* had ever been recorded or written down. Rather, they had all been improvised over time. Another production of the musical starts up. Producer argues

that the musical is fixed because the characters' makeup designs are painted on the actors' faces. Does that suffice?

3. *Screen display.* Omni creates a successful video game called *Scramble.* Omni sells the game in game cartridges. When a cartridge is put in a game console, on-screen cartoon characters perform various actions, subject to some control by the player. Competitor creates a strikingly similar game. Sued for copyright infringement, Competitor argues that *Scramble* is not copyrightable because it is not fixed but appears only in fleeting images on the screen. Is *Scramble* fixed?

4. *A room of her own.* Sitting thoughtfully through her payment systems class, Virginia decides to write a poem about the challenges of Reg. CC. She types the poem into her laptop over the course of an hour. The poem's wordplay and vivid imagery easily meet the minimal creativity requirement for copyright. Does she have a federal copyright in the poem? How can she ensure that she does?

Explanations

1. Copyright protection does not require the actor to wear the makeup permanently. Rather, fixation must be "sufficiently permanent or stable to permit it to be perceived, reproduced, or otherwise communicated for a period of more than transitory duration." 17 U.S.C. §101. The makeup on the actor's face is sufficiently stable to meet the fixation requirement. Cf. *Carell v. Shubert Org.*, 104 F. Supp. 2d 236 (S.D.N.Y. 2000).

2. Painting the actors' faces does fix the makeup designs. It does not fix the entire musical, which is a musical work (as well as a literary and a dramatic work). Fixation must embody the work in a tangible medium of expression, such that it may be "perceived, reproduced, or otherwise communicated." Simply showing the makeup designs on the actors' faces does not communicate the entire musical. Rather, Producer would have to write it down, videotape it, or otherwise fix the entire work. Once Producer did so, however, he could then exercise his exclusive rights and prevent the other production from publicly performing the work. Even if the other production fixed the work first, the other producers would have no copyright, because the musical was not original to them.

3. *Scramble* is fixed in the game cartridges, which are clearly sufficiently stable. Although the game is viewed on the screen, fixation can be in any form. Likewise, a musical work may be fixed on a CD even if it is usually

experienced only in the fleeting sounds from the speakers. The game is fixed even if the player can affect particular performances of the game. *See Stern Electronics v. Kaufman*, 669 F.2d 852 (2d Cir. 1982). Many types of works are affected by choices of the audience.

If the work did appear *only* on the screen, it probably would not qualify as fixed. Such a copy is not permanent or stable. The weight of authority now seems to be that temporary copies in computer memory are sufficiently stable, even though they are constantly renewed. A screen display is also refreshed many times a second (although not as frequently as memory), but the overall duration is much more fleeting than the temporary memory copy. The screen display changes in less than a second, while the memory copy sits there much longer.

4. As Virginia types her poem into her laptop computer, it is saved in the temporary working memory of the computer. Although the issue is unsettled, the trend of authority is that this is probably sufficiently permanent to qualify as fixing a copy of the poem and therefore giving her copyright protection. If she wants to be sure, she can simply save the poem in a file in a more permanent form (such as simply saving it on her hard drive, a network drive, or an external memory device). She will probably do this anyway if she wants to save the text for future use (and of course her computer may do this automatically for various reasons, such as making a backup).

BY OR UNDER AUTHORITY OF THE AUTHOR

The author of the work need not personally fix the work in tangible form to gain copyright protection. Rather, the work can be fixed "by or under the authority of the author." If Author dictates his novel to a stenographer, that suffices. By contrast, unauthorized fixation does not serve to trigger copyright. If Speaker gives her impromptu speech and is surreptitiously recorded by Bootlegger, copyright does not apply. But if Speaker writes the speech down, Bootlegger is potentially infringing if he made more copies or performed the work in public.

An open issue is whether authorization must be given before the fixation. If Bootlegger is the only one to record Musician's new song, can Musician meet the fixation requirement by subsequently ratifying the fixation, thereby authorizing it? The language of the statute seems to require that the fixation be authorized at the time. Moreover, courts generally consider issues of copyrightability as of the time of fixation. Subsequent authorization, then, may well be insufficient.

Examples

1. *Dance.* Choreographer works over several weeks to create an intricate dance. She then spends hours rehearsing the dance with her troupe. She does not write down the choreography, but rather remembers it and teaches it face-to-face to the dancers. They perform the dance to a large and appreciative audience. Choreographer then learns that another troupe surreptitiously recorded the performance and plans to perform it. Does she have a copyright in the choreography of the dance?

2. *Fixed?* Author prepares a lecture on literary theory, which sets forth her views in witty and incisive fashion. She does not write her remarks down. She delivers the lecture to an audience of two people. Author uses a tape recorder to record the lecture. Has she fixed an original work of authorship? Would it make a difference if the recording was never published or even played again?

3. *Authorized by author?* Poet composes a poem in his mind. He recites it privately to several friends, not realizing that one friend is videotaping the performance. When he is later informed of the taping, Poet says, "That's okay. You did me a favor by fixing it. Now I have copyright in the poem." Is he right?

4. *Unplugged.* Scribbler appears at a book signing to plug his latest collection of short stories. Before sitting down to sign copies of the book, he reads one story from the book aloud to the assembled throng. The store offers to tape the reading, but he declines. One audience member tape-records the reading without permission and sells copies to the public, advertising in various literary journals. Accused of copyright infringement, the entrepreneur argues that she tape-recorded an unfixed work (the reading) and cannot be infringing. Will that argument succeed?

Explanations

1. Choreographer does not have a federal copyright in the dance. Until the work is fixed under her authority, it is not protected by federal copyright. If a speaker gives a speech, or a songwriter creates a song, or a choreographer makes a dance, all without reducing the works to any tangible form, the work is uncopyrighted. Anyone else who sells copies of the speech, or sings the song in concert, or performs the dance publicly is not infringing copyright. The fixation requirement is not difficult to meet: The speaker could simply write the speech down or record it; the songwriter could put the music in sheet music form or use a tape recorder; the choreographer could make notations about or videotape or photograph the dance. Once the work is fixed, copyright protection attaches. Anyone who *subsequently* made copies (or did other things

within the exclusive rights of the copyright holder) would be potentially infringing.

Her choreography is an original work of authorship, but it has not been fixed by or under the authority of the author. Even though she and her troupe have committed it to memory and performed it in public, copyright does not attach without authorized fixation. The other troupe did videotape the dance, but that would have met the fixation requirement only if it had been authorized.

Choreographer is not out of luck. She can still fix the work (in notation, videotape, or any other tangible form), thereby receiving copyright protection. As later chapters discuss, the other troupe would be liable if it subsequently made copies or performed the work publicly (although it can keep the videotaped copy it made before protection attached).

2. Yes. By tape-recording the lecture, Author fixed a literary work. Fixation need take no particular form, so she need not transcribe the lecture or put it on paper in any way. The size of the audience is irrelevant. If she had simply tape-recorded the lecture with no one else present, it would have been fixed.

   Copyright no longer turns on publication, so whether a work is published or used in any other way does not affect whether it receives copyright protection. So if Author never publishes the recording, never plays it again, or promptly loses it, she is still entitled to copyright protection (although any of those would make it harder to prove infringement, which, as discussed in subsequent chapters, requires proof that defendant copied from the protected work).

3. The videotaping was initially unauthorized and hence did not fix the poem. Poet is seeking to subsequently ratify the fixation, thereby retroactively authorizing it. This argument seems to lack support in the statute. Poet would be well advised to simply write the poem down or otherwise fix it himself (or authorize someone to do so).

4. The short story was fixed in tangible form when Scribbler wrote it. (It is also being sold in fixed form in the books.) Upon fixation, Scribbler had a copyright in the story. Audience member is making copies (and distributing them to the public, which also falls within the copyright holder's exclusive rights) and therefore is infringing.

FIXATION AND TRANSMISSIONS

The definition of "fixed" also addresses a potential loophole. Suppose that a television or radio program is being broadcast live. If a work must be fully fixed before it is protected by copyright, then during the broadcast the work would be unprotected by copyright. Someone who made a contemporaneous copy or performed the work in public would not be infringing. The definition closes this loophole:

> A work consisting of sounds, images, or both, that are being transmitted, is "fixed" for purposes of this title if a fixation of the work is being made simultaneously with its transmission.

17 U.S.C. §101.

THE ANTI-BOOTLEGGING PROVISION

Another loophole for bootleggers is closed by protection for a category of unfixed works. Live musical performances receive special protection, even if the performance is not fixed under the authority of the author. The statute imposes liability for anyone who makes an unauthorized recording or transmission of a live musical performance or who thereafter distributes recordings. 17 U.S.C. §1101. Whether this provision is constitutional is unsettled. There are several arguments that it may exceed the powers of Congress under the Copyright Clause. Recall that Congress has the power to "promote the Progress of Science and useful Arts, by securing for limited Times to Authors and Inventors the exclusive Right to their respective Writings and Discoveries." U.S. Const. art. I, §8. The anti-bootlegging provisions give protection to works that have not been fixed in a tangible form. It may give protection to works that do not qualify as "Writings." Second, there is no period of protection specified in the anti-bootlegging provision, as opposed to copyrights, which have a specified term, such as life plus 70 years for works of individual authors. The anti-bootlegging provision may also fail to give exclusive rights "for limited Times." Last, it is not limited to protection of original works; rather, by its terms, it applies to all live musical performances. Recognizing these issues, Congress passed the provision under its Commerce Clause powers, rather than relying on the Copyright Clause. Some have argued that is insufficient to support the legislation, because otherwise the limits in the Copyright Clause would lose their effectiveness. The Second Circuit, however, has upheld the legislation against such a constitutional challenge. See *U.S. v. Martignon*, 492 F.3d 140 (2d Cir. 2007).

Examples

1. *Intercepted.* Butkus, a stand-up comedian, performs several times a week at various comedy clubs. His present act is a rambling account of his trip to Tibet and is filled with anecdotes and topical jokes. He has gradually honed the act over the past several months, and it is indelibly inscribed in his memory. Killing some idle time between performances, he googles his name. Much to his surprise, he finds that recordings of his recent show at the Kibble Kat Lounge are being auctioned on eBay. Can he take advantage of the anti-bootlegging provisions in the Copyright Act?

2. *Unprotected?* The *Weekly Gig*, a popular trade paper for musicians, reports that a federal district court has struck down the anti-bootlegging provision of the Copyright Act on the grounds that it is unconstitutional. First, it goes beyond protecting "Writings," because it protects unfixed works. Second, it goes beyond giving rights for "limited Times," because it has no specific period of protection. Copyright holders are aghast. If other courts follow the ruling, will concertgoers be free to record performances and sell the recordings?

Explanations

1. Unfortunately for Butkus, the anti-bootlegging provisions apply only to live musical performances. His comedy routine would not qualify. If he wants protection, he should fix his act in some way (e.g., write it down or record it).

2. Even if the anti-bootlegging provisions are held unconstitutional, that may not be too terrible for musicians. There would still be copyright protection in the musical works, so people who record concerts would be potentially infringing unless the songs were in the public domain.

CHAPTER 5

Ideas Are Not Subject to Copyright

Copyright does not protect ideas. That may be the easiest copyright rule to state and the hardest to apply. It is often difficult to distinguish noncopyrightable ideas from copyrightable creative expression of those ideas. The rule is also one of the most important rules in copyright. Because copyright does not protect ideas, copyright should not restrict the free flow of ideas. Indeed, the noncopyrightability of ideas is important in making copyright, which restricts many types of speech, consistent with the freedom of speech mandated by the First Amendment.

If an author has an idea for a short story, the idea is not protected by copyright—no matter how original the idea is. There is no copyright infringement if someone copies the unprotected idea. If the author confides her idea in a letter to a friend, and the friend uses the idea to write a story, there is no copyright infringement. If the author instead writes the short story, which is read by a famous author, who then takes the idea by using it in a short story, there is no copyright infringement. If a moviemaker steals the idea and uses it as for a blockbuster movie, there is no copyright infringement. Ideas are not copyrightable, and the copying of unprotected elements is not copyright infringement.

Copyright protects only the elements of the work that are creative expression, such as the particular ways an author expresses an idea. This central exclusion is set forth in 17 U.S.C. §102(b):

> In no case does copyright protection for an original work of authorship extend to any idea, procedure, process, system, method of operation, concept,

> principle, or discovery, regardless of the form in which it is described, explained, illustrated, or embodied in such work.

Ideas of all sorts are excluded from copyright protection. A paper in a biology journal may propose a new interpretation of some fossils. The author's theory would be an unprotected idea. A legal brief may argue for the application of a statute to a particular case—likewise an unprotected idea. A movie's premise, like the Chicago Cubs winning the World Series and thereby triggering a new ice age, is an unprotected idea. An idea for a new product (picnic tables configured to confuse wasps), the idea that makes a joke funny, the idea that makes a song memorable, and the idea to write a play about the kidnapping of heiress Patty Hearst are all unprotected by copyright.

A copyrighted work may contain many ideas. The overall idea for the movie may be "what happens when the Cubs finally win a championship," but the movie may be built with many more ideas, such as the return of Al Capone and the effect of Lake Michigan freezing solid. A book of science will likely be chock-full of ideas. None of the ideas are protected by copyright.

Copying ideas is not copyright infringement, even if the copying is deceitful, or in breach of a confidence, or otherwise underhanded. Stealing an idea is not copyright infringement. Even if the obscure short-story writer can prove that a famous author copied an idea from her story, she is not entitled to collect for copyright infringement. Plagiarism (presenting the work of others as one's own) is not necessarily copyright infringement.

Therefore, copyright does not protect the most valuable aspects of creative works. As Justice Brandeis famously said, "The general rule of law is that the noblest of human productions—knowledge, truths ascertained, conception, and ideas—become after voluntary communication to others, free as the air to common use." *Int'l News Serv. v. AP*, 248 U.S. 215, 250 (1918). At first blush, the nonprotection of ideas might seem contrary to the purpose of copyright. Copyright serves as an incentive to authors. By giving authors exclusive rights in their works, copyright gives the authors a reason to create and publish. An author need not fear that she will bear all the costs of creating the work while unscrupulous copiers garner the benefit. If others can freely copy the author's ideas, doesn't that decrease the incentive to produce ideas?

It might. There would arguably be a greater incentive to produce ideas if ideas were protectable by copyright. Or perhaps not, because there are many other incentives to produce ideas. Moreover, copyright protection has costs as well as benefits. If ideas were copyrighted, the flow of ideas would be greatly restricted. Anyone who wanted to use the ideas in a story, a scientific paper, a painting, or a computer program might need the permission of the copyright holder. The rule denying protection to ideas but granting protection to the particular way an author expresses her ideas reflects a balance between the benefits of copyright (providing incentives to authors and giving authors the right to control what they have created), and the costs of copyright (the increased costs on those who wish to use copyrighted works, the transaction costs of negotiating for agreements to use copyrighted works, and the deadweight costs where potential uses are not realized because of copyright concerns). The role of copyright, therefore, is not to provide the maximum incentive possible for authors. Rather, copyright protection is limited in order to balance the benefits to authors against the costs of copyright protection. By giving an author rights in her creative expression, copyright provides sufficient protection for the production of creative works. If an author can have the exclusive right to sell copies of her novel and to make a movie out of it, that may give her sufficient incentive to spend a year or two writing the book. Even if others can copy the idea behind a movie, the producers can prevent others from closely copying the movie. That is sufficient protection, evidently, for movie companies to spend millions of dollars on their works.

The reason ideas are not protected by copyright has nothing to do with ideas being less valuable than expression or with Congress not wishing to provide incentives for the production of ideas. Quite the opposite: Ideas are too valuable to be copyrighted. The free flow of ideas is too important to permit the exclusive rights of copyright to control ideas. Sufficient incentive for the production of works exists by giving authors exclusive rights limited to the expression in the works. The rule does not necessarily hurt authors, even if it provides them less copyright protection. Authors are also users. To some extent, every work uses ideas that have been created by others.

The freedom to copy ideas is central to the constitutional role of copyright. If copyright prohibited the copying of ideas, it would be difficult to square with the First Amendment's freedom of expression. The Supreme Court has recognized this. *Eldred v. Ashcroft* rejected a First Amendment challenge to extension of copyright terms. The plaintiffs had argued that adding 20 years to the terms of existing copyrights was an impermissible limitation on freedom of speech. The Court held, however, that copyright legislation was not normally subject to First Amendment scrutiny. Rather, copyright has "built-in First Amendment accommodations." Copyright does not prohibit the copying of ideas, and copyrighted works are subject to fair use for such purposes as education, criticism, news reporting, or research. The Court reasoned that copyright and the First Amendment actually serve the same goal. Copyright promotes freedom of expression by giving an incentive to produce works, while protecting freedom of expression by limiting protection to an author's expression, as opposed to the ideas in the work.

DISTINGUISHING PROTECTED EXPRESSION FROM NONPROTECTABLE IDEAS

Ideas are not protected by copyright, but the original way an author expresses the ideas is protected. The distinction between nonprotected ideas and protected expression is key to the scope of copyright protection. If an author writes a novel, her original expression is protected by copyright, but the ideas in the novel are not. The rule is simple to state but difficult to apply. Literal copying (such as word-for-word copying of a novel, or a recording of a copyrighted song) is copying protected expression and likely infringement. Copying only the basic idea behind the work (the premise of a movie or the big idea in a novel) is copying unprotected ideas and not infringement. The more difficult cases are where the copying lies between those extremes.

The distinction between protected ideas and unprotected expression arises frequently in both advising and litigation. Suppose the comedy about the Cubs winning is a hit movie. Other producers will consider following in its footsteps. How closely may they copy without infringing? Would a film infringe if it copied the overall structure, substituting elements from another city? In another context, a publisher wishes to create a new biology textbook to compete with an established work. The new book cannot copy word for word without infringing. But may it copy the overall organization? The specific way that the material is divided into chapters? The selection of topics to cover and to exclude?

Neither the statute nor the case law defines "idea" or "expression." In fact, there is no true distinction between ideas and expression. Rather, the idea-expression distinction in copyright law is really a policy-based distinction about which elements of a work should be subject to the copyright holder's exclusive rights and which elements should be free for others (other authors and other users of the work) to copy. If a bootlegger sells posters of a copyrighted painting, word-for-word copies of a novel, or bit-by-bit copies of a computer program, that clearly constitutes copying an author's expression of his ideas. But copyright must do more than protect against such literal copying. Otherwise, another author could simply change the wording and still free-ride on the first author's work. On the other hand, copyright must permit some copying. If it were infringement to copy any element of a work, regardless of how general, copyright would effectively grant protection to the ideas as well as to their expression. But if the protection against nonliteral copying is too strong, then it will effectively prohibit copying of ideas.

A leading treatise provides a helpful guide to the analysis. *See* Paul Goldstein, *Copyright*, §2.3.1. Ideas may be concepts, solutions, or building blocks. Copyright would not apply to such ideas as a parade with floats or a game show or contest, or the concept that items might be painted in rainbow colors. *Id.* Rather, such general concepts should be free for others to copy as long as they do not copy the particular expression of the concept in specific parade design or game show production. Ideas can be solutions, like the design of forms necessary to implement an accounting system, or rules for a game. *Id.* Ideas can also be "building blocks," such as the plot and theme of a novel, or colors and shapes in visual works, or rhythms and notes in musical works. *Id.* Such general elements are necessary for the creation of other works. By deeming them to be unprotected ideas, the law prevents a single author from controlling an entire genre of artistic expression. *Id.* Otherwise, the author of the first rap song or first situation comedy might claim the exclusive right to make works in that area. Seeing ideas as concepts, solutions, and building blocks is a useful way to see how the idea-expression distinction is really an exercise in balancing the author's rights against the costs of copyright protection on other authors, as well as consumers.

In deciding whether a defendant has copied protected expression, courts use the "abstractions test," formulated by Judge Learned Hand. The method is less a test or rule than it is a way of approaching the idea-expression question. Copying may be done at various levels of generality. For a literary work, such as a book, the lowest level would be word-for-word copying. One level up might be copying sentence by sentence, but changing the wording. Moving up slightly, the copier might copy the events and descriptions quite closely but use different words and sentences. At a more general level, the second author might copy in a more abstract way, such as retelling the story in a different time with different characters. Moving up again, the author might copy only the bare outline of the story. At the most general level, the second author might copy only the underlying concept, such as a love story involving a malfunctioning time machine.

Courts use the abstraction approach to first characterize how specifically the defendant copied, and then to try to decide whether the copying was too specific. Courts look to a number of factors in deciding whether the elements copied should be deemed protected expression, guided by the basic balance between giving authors protection and preventing authors from unduly restricting the expression of others. In short, the court asks, "How closely did the defendant copy?" and then, "Is that the sort of copying that copyright should permit?" In deciding how closely other authors may copy, courts consider many things, including such matters as the degree of originality in the copied work; whether the copied work has thick protection (such as a highly creative novel) or thin protection (such as a largely factual work like databases, or largely functional work like computer programs); whether permitting copying is necessary to allow the free flow of ideas, information, and other nonprotected elements; whether the copier appears to be free-riding on the efforts of the plaintiff; and other issues. Indeed, because the analysis is quite malleable, judges may be influenced by matters that properly should not count, such as the artistic or social merit of the parties' work.

Perhaps the key factor is whether giving protection to the copied element would reduce the ability of others to create works, or whether others are left with plenty of alternatives. As the following sections discuss, that depends largely on the nature of the works at issue. Some works have a higher degree of protection, because they contain more original, creative expression. Other works, composed largely of nonprotected material (for example, nonoriginal material like facts or material copied from earlier works), have less protection so that others have more ability to use the unprotected matter.

A nice example is *Educational Testing Services v. Katzman*, 793 F.2d 533 (3d Cir. 1986). ETS alleged copyright infringement by Princeton Review's copying from multiple-choice questions. Princeton Review made slight changes to the questions. For example, in a question on antonyms, it made this change:

SAT Question
9. REPROBATE: (A) predecessor (B) antagonist (C) virtuous person (D) temporary ruler (E) strict supervisor

Princeton Review Question
9. REPROBATE: (B) antagonist (A) predecessor (C) virtuous person (D) temporary ruler (E) strict supervisor

ETS would not have copyright protection in such ideas as the meaning of "reprobate," or whether the opposite of "reprobate" is a virtuous person or an evildoer, or even in the idea of writing a multiple-choice question about the word "reprobate." But Princeton Review copied much more specifically than that. Likewise, Princeton Review copied the ETS math questions, making only minor changes in the numbers that made no real difference to the question. ETS has no copyright in mathematical rules or their use, but was accorded copyright in the particular questions it formulated to test knowledge of math. The key with both is that ETS did not get exclusive rights in mathematical rules or in the meaning of words; rather, Princeton Review and others were left with many other ways to test the same ideas with multiple-choice questions.

Examples

1. *Staking a claim.* Nancy has a terrific idea for a children's book, *Heart's Bend* (the idea involves twins, salamanders, and pumping out a basement). She is concerned, first, that someone might copy her idea, and second, that someone might come up with a similar idea. Can she use copyright to protect her intellectual progeny?

2. *Suggestions.* A *New Yorker* cartoon shows a box with two slots, fixed on an office wall. The sign on the box reads, "Suggestions. Or toast." Esi, a designer at Wacky Products, sees the cartoon and uses it as the basis for a new novelty product: a toaster with "Suggestion Box" imprinted on the side. The toaster becomes a highly popular holiday gift that year. The cartoonist claims copyright infringement. Has Wacky Products infringed the copyright in the cartoon?

3. *Famillionaire. The Apprentice* is a "reality" television show. Each week, a team of aspiring businesspeople attempts an assigned business task, like marketing a new airline. The tasks are designed to test skills important in succeeding as entrepreneurs. Donald Trump, a quirky wealthy businessman, evaluates the team members. Some team members are summarily fired each week, until finally the remaining contestant is the winner. The show is highly successful.

   Imitation being the sincerest form of flattery, another network soon airs *The Rebel Billionaire.* In this show, team members attempt assigned tasks, like walking a tightrope between two hot air balloons. The tasks are designed to test such qualities as risk-taking and coolness under fire, qualities important for entrepreneurs. Richard Branson, a quirky wealthy businessman, evaluates the team members. Some team members are gently fired each week, until finally the remaining contestant is the winner. Does *Rebel Billionaire* infringe the copyright in *The Apprentice?*

4. *Ratz.* Mattel, the maker of Barbie dolls, develops an idea to follow up with a contrasting line of dolls—young and stylish, with exaggerated features, big heads, and attitude. A competitor learns the idea and markets Bratz dolls, with wild commercial success. Copyright infringement?

5. *An example from the Copyright Office.* "A toy manufacturer conceives a novel idea for a toy consisting of multicolored geometrical spheres, cubes, and cylinders of varying sizes. All of these parts or pieces are magnetized, and will adhere to one another when placed in close proximity. It is possible to construct an indefinite variety of shapes and figures by means of the magnetized parts or pieces. The manufacturer desires to protect the three-dimensional aspects of the toy before publication occurs. He applies to the Copyright Office for registration of a design for an unpublished sculptural work of art. His application Form VA is accompanied by one complete set of magnetized spheres, cubes, and cylinders arranged in a plain box according to size and color." Was his toy copyrightable?

Explanations

1. No. Copyright protection does not extend to ideas. §102(b). Even if she writes the book, registers the copyright, and puts "©2006 Nancy" on the copyright page (along with "All Rights Reserved" and "No Stealing My Ideas"), copyright does not apply to ideas.

   She may use contract law to get limited protection. She could have prospective publishers sign a nondisclosure agreement (they'll rarely agree). She could have readers sign nondisclosure agreements (hard to sell many books with conditions like that, though). But those contracts do not bind the rest of the world the way that copyright grants exclusive rights. Does this mean that coming up with good ideas for books is a waste of time? No. She can still write the book and have copyright protection in her particular expression of the idea. Moreover, commercial success (let alone artistic fulfillment, achievement, and recognition) does not depend on legal protection. Many aspects of commercially successful products are not protected. Anyone can write a book about schools for wizards, but *Harry Potter* still does quite well.

2. Wacky has not infringed the copyright in the cartoon. Wacky copied the basic idea of the cartoon: that a suggestion box might double as a toaster, implying that suggestions will be flamed. But Wacky did not copy the expression of the idea. Rather, Wacky expressed the idea in quite a different way.

3. *Rebel Billionaire* did not infringe the copyright in *The Apprentice*. Rather, it copied the unprotectable idea of a reality show in which contestants perform tasks assigned by a quirky rich person. *Rebel Billionaire* also copied some elements more specifically, such as eliminating contestants each week, but those elements would likely be unprotected as well, because they are necessary to implement the unprotected idea. If the second show had copied not just the idea but also more specific elements, such as scripted scenes or the specific tasks that were performed, the result might be different.

4. No copyright infringement. An idea for a line of dolls is not protected by copyright. *See Mattel Inc. v. MGA Entertainment Inc.*, 616 F.3d 904 (9th Cir. 2010).

5. The toy was not copyrightable: "We will refuse a registration in Class VA based solely upon the unassembled toy, even though its component parts or pieces are potentially capable of being arranged in copyrightable shapes and forms. The general idea of the toy is uncopyrightable, regardless of its novelty or uniqueness." Compendium II: Copyright Office Practices 503.02(b).

ELEMENTS THAT NECESSARILY FOLLOW FROM AN UNPROTECTED IDEA ARE UNPROTECTED

Elements that necessarily follow from unprotected ideas are also unprotected. If a play is set among immigrants in New York in the early 1900s, that setting largely determines such elements as dress, manners of speaking, elements of scenery, and so on. Likewise, if a detective story is set in a monastery, it likely will have several suspects who are monks. If such elements were protected, then other authors would have difficulty writing books with similar settings, which would effectively give protection to the idea of setting the book in 1900s New York or a detective story in a monastery. Accordingly, even specific copying will be permitted, if necessary to copy the unprotected idea.

The more original the idea, the more this rule will come into play. The science fiction work *Dune*, for example, had the original premise of a world in which water has become truly scarce and must be conserved with heroic means. That idea is not protected by copyright. Another author would be free to write her own science fiction novel set on a planet with very little water. Of necessity, specific elements of her book might be similar to elements of *Dune*. Water would be fought over, individuals would carry devices to minimize water usage and wastage, and the landscape would be more like a sandy desert than a lush rain forest. But even though such copying of specific elements would be at a relatively low level of abstraction, it would not be infringement. Otherwise, the idea underlying *Dune* would be effectively protected from copying.

A related doctrine results in less protection for less original ideas. Under the *scènes à faire* doctrine, elements of a work may be unprotected if they are commonly found in works of that genre. If a detective story has some fairly stock thug characters (who were nevertheless created by the author, if somewhat unimaginatively), another author may use such characters in her story without infringing. Otherwise, there would be some difficult factual determinations if similar stock characters cropped up in another book. There could be a dispute about whether they were copied from old public domain works or from some recent copyrighted works. In addition, the degree of originality in such stock elements is minimal, even if the author makes them sufficiently original for protection.

DISTINGUISHING IDEA FROM EXPRESSION IN CREATIVE WORKS

Judge Hand first formulated the abstractions approach in the case of fictional literary works. *See Nichols v. Universal Pictures*, 45 F.2d 119 (2d Cir. 1930).

Suppose a plaintiff's work is a popular play set in New York in the early 1900s. A young couple (one Jewish, one Irish Catholic) secretly marry. Their respective fathers become comically exercised and quarrel. The secretly married couple produces grandchildren. The fathers reconcile their differences. Such elements are unprotected ideas. Otherwise, the first playwright would be granted a virtual monopoly on a genre of works. One could express the same basic elements in innumerable ways. As Learned Hand put it, "A comedy based upon conflicts between Irish and Jews, into which the marriage of their children enters, is no more susceptible of copyright than the outline of *Romeo and Juliet*." *Id.* at 122. Therefore, no infringement results if a second author copies all those general elements but expresses them in a different form. The second author could write new dialogue, invent a new specific plot to follow the general outline, invent different characteristics to give the respective family members, change the neighborhood in which the story was set, and concoct a new scene that resolves the various conflicts. Provided the second author copies only the unprotected general ideas from the first work, she does not infringe.

By contrast, to copy at a much more specific level is taking protected expression. Another author might copy not just the general story but also the particular way it unfolded in the plaintiff's play: the sequence of scenes, the plot mechanisms for revealing information to the characters, the dramatic series of acts and exchanges leading to the resolution. Such copying is infringement because it takes not just the general ideas but also their expression. Copyright does not protect the outline of a play in which a woman poisons her lover but is acquitted because of the perjured testimony of a friend. But it is infringement to copy the main traits of the characters, much of the dialogue, and also the long series of detailed incidents and actions of the story, down to the level of gestures. *See Sheldon v. Metro-Goldwyn Pictures*, 81 F.2d 49 (2d Cir. 1936). In deciding whether certain elements are idea or expression, one essentially asks whether the copying is like that in *Nichols* or in *Sheldon*.

The same principles govern other types of creative works. For example, a famous cover from the *New Yorker* magazine shows the myopic worldview of a typical New Yorker. *See Steinberg v. Columbia Pictures*, 663 F. Supp. 706 (S.D.N.Y. 1987). The illustration showed Manhattan depicted in detail, a brown strip vaguely labeled "Jersey," and then an anonymous square, with only a few spots labeled "Las Vegas," "Los Angeles," and "Asia" off on the horizon. The picture captures how a New Yorker thinks of the world as comprising New York, with a few other places only vaguely on the horizon. Another artist could copy the idea by depicting a view that echoes the primacy of Manhattan in the world. That would be like *Nichols*, just copying the unprotected idea at a relatively high level of abstraction. But it would be copying of expression if the second artist depicts the same vantage point, colors the sky similarly, copies details of buildings originally invented by the first artist, and copies other specific expressive elements. Such specific copying, at a much lower level of abstraction, would constitute copying of protected expression.

The scope of protection is also affected by the degree of originality in the work in two ways. First, not all copying of specific elements is deemed copying of expression. Nonoriginal elements are not protected. If the copyrighted work contains material copied from other works (such as quotations from other books, or story elements copied from other works), then even literal copying of those elements would not be infringement.

Second, the more originality a work contains, the more protection it has. One novel might be written in highly creative form, with unique characters, an inventive plotline, and imaginative prose. Another novel might be original enough to meet the minimal requirements for protection, but composed of clichés, recycled plot turns, and derivative characters. Both are protected against word-for-word copying, but the first has greater protection against nonliteral copying. This means that the copyright in the first work might be infringed by copying at a relatively high level. Even though the second author did not copy word for word or scene by scene, she may still have copied the original inventive plotline and the unique characters. But copying at the same level might not infringe the copyright in the second, less creative work. An author who copies its recycled plotline or derivative characters would be copying little that originated with the author. The distinction between ideas and expression depends on how creative the work is.

One specific topic often discussed is copyright protection for characters. If an author places Superman or Harry Potter in her novel, has she infringed copyright? Learned Hand's language is often quoted:

> If *Twelfth Night* were copyrighted, it is quite possible that a second comer might so closely imitate Sir Toby Belch or Malvolio as to infringe, but it would not be enough that for one of his characters he cast a riotous knight who kept wassail to the discomfort of the household, or a vain and foppish steward who became amorous of his mistress. These would be no more than Shakespeare's "ideas" in the play, as little capable of monopoly as Einstein's Doctrine of Relativity, or Darwin's theory of the Origin of Species. It follows that the less developed the characters, the less they can be copyrighted; that is the penalty an author must bear for marking them too indistinctly.

Nichols v. Universal Pictures Corp., 45 F.2d 119, 121 (2d Cir. 1930).

Hand addresses two points in the passage. First, with respect to copyrightability, the elements of the work that delineate the character must constitute creative expression. If an author uses stock characters (like the ethnic stereotypes in *Nichols*), then there may be no protection for lack of originality. Second, even if the author uses sufficient creativity to meet the requirements for copyright protection, there is no infringement if the second author copies not the specific expression but rather the ideas of the characters. In claiming infringement, an author should identify as specifically as possible the creative elements of hers that were copied by the defendant.

Examples

1. *Fame*. Harvey's photograph "Leg Warmers" shows the legs of a ballerina, from the knees down, in the classic fifth position: "feet touching, one foot in front, heel to toe and toe to heel." The dancer wears torn leg warmers, stockings, and ballet shoes. Harvey has licensed the evocative photo for a number of uses, including a best-selling gallery art poster. Just as Harvey is negotiating to license the photo to a major greeting card publisher, another publisher comes out with a card featuring a suspiciously similar picture. Titled "Toe Shoes," the new image shows a ballerina in the fifth position, from just below the knee down, wearing intact leg warmers, stockings, and ballet shoes. The photo was taken from a slightly different angle, the clothing and shoes are different colors, and the lighting is a little brighter—but the impact on the viewer is quite similar. The image, showing the feet turned out, touching each toe to the other heel, the legs crossing and slightly bent, gives a feeling of expectancy. The second publisher at first completely denies copying Harvey's picture, but eventually admits copying after some clever investigation by Harvey. Is the second publisher liable for copyright infringement?

2. *Stolen idea*. Pixie Studio is in the midst of producing an animated movie, *Pumpkin*. The title character is adopted by a little boy, who finds the orange kitty sleeping on a warm jack-o'-lantern late one Halloween night. A month before the movie is ready to open, a rival studio suddenly comes out with *Tango*, an animated tale about a boy who finds a stray kitten one Thanksgiving, sleeping in the boy's furry boots. Like *Pumpkin*, the movie has various scenes of an outdoor cat adapting to indoor life, encountering various household appliances for the first time, and learning about the wonders of the food and water dishes. It turns out that the rival learned about the basic story line of *Pumpkin* through industry gossip. Pixie's executives are livid about the blatant theft of their intellectual work. Can they sue for copyright infringement?

3. *Zooperman*. A cartoonist starts a new comic book series, *Zooperman Comics*. She copies a number of elements from the popular Superman cartoons. Like Superman, Zooperman is a journalist who hides his identity beneath everyday clothing but periodically changes into a special costume and fights crime. Both costumes are tight-fitting acrobatic suits with flowing capes. Both cartoons show their heroes crushing guns in their powerful hands, stopping bullets with their bodies, ripping open

steel doors, and making building-size leaps in a city. Each is described as the strongest man in the world who uses his powers to fight "evil and injustice." Each is vulnerable to a rare substance (kryptonite for Superman, festonium for Zooperman). Each occasionally retreats to a refuge in the Arctic for contemplation. The specific depictions are different in many details. Their capes and costumes are different colors. One hero catches bullets; one lets them bounce off him. One leaps over buildings; one leaps from building to building. Superman's Arctic refuge is a fortress; Zooperman's is a whalebone tent. Cartoonist argues that she has simply copied an idea (the strongest man in the world who hides his identity whenever he is not fighting crime). Has she copied only unprotected ideas, or also protected expression?

4. *"I'll Fly Away."* Freelance Writer spends several weeks writing a short story, "I'll Fly Away," about a prisoner who seeks solace in music. Serving time for youthful crimes, the young man writes songs describing his life and expressing his frustrations and dreams. He works with other prisoners to develop his music. Over time, they help each other learn many other life lessons. The story ends as he reenters the outside world with the various possibilities in the balance.

   Writer submits the story to Magazine and receives a polite rejection. A few months later, Magazine publishes a story attributed to one of its editors. The basic story line is the same: A prisoner enters prison as a confused teenager, spends time writing music and songs, and emerges as a man. Other than the basic storyline, all the elements are different. Magazine admits that Editor was inspired by Freelancer's story. Has Magazine copied protected expression?

5. *"Wing Tips over the Edge."* Photographer creates "Wing Tips over the Edge," a photo taken from the point of view of a businessperson on the edge of a roof looking down on a city street. The photo is in a book distributed to local advertising agencies. An advertising agency has the photo in mind when it makes its ad for a financial news service. The similarities are the point of view—that of a potential jumper looking past his shoes, the business attire of the jumper, and a city street below. The street and buildings are quite different, and all other details such as the background, perspective, lighting, shading, and color of the photographs are dissimilar. Has the advertising agency copied protected expression?

6. *My corner.* Photographer poses a languid woman with a concertina in a booth of a jazz bar, using the angles of the roof and wall to create suggestive geometric shapes. Photographer places the camera and arranges the lighting very specifically to create a particular image, paying great attention to the interplay between the various shapes formed by the interior

of the building, its decor, and the lighting. The combination of elements creates a pleasing image for a number of reasons—the proportions of the basic elements, the play of the lighting, and the suggestive air from the slight view into the rest of the bar. Advertising Agency sees the photo and decides it captures the mood it seeks to sell a brand of vodka. Agency poses a chic celebrity with a vodka bottle, similarly relaxed, in the same booth. Agency takes a photo, framing the same area of the bar and using the same lighting and angles, carefully making sure that every detail from the first photo appears in the second (apart from replacing the model with the celebrity and the vodka bottle). Advertising Agency argues that it has copied only unprotected ideas: the languid mood of a jazz bar, with its vaguely suggestive atmosphere. Do you agree?

7. *One fine groundhog.* The novel *One Fine Day* is about a man trapped in a repeating day. The novel starts with an account of a typical day: He wakes up to his custom-rigged alarm saying, "Wake up, you lazy bustard"; he rides down the elevator with a redheaded woman; he sees a number of people and incidents on his way to work, where he has a number of contentious encounters; he then spends the evening listening to music and ignoring periodic phone calls. Before going to sleep, he changes the tape to a friendlier message. The next morning, however, he again hears, "Wake up, you lazy bustard." He sees the same woman in the elevator and the same people in the same places as he goes to work, and the same incidents occur over the course of the day in exactly the same way. The next day, everything repeats itself, with the exception of the changes that the man himself makes. The day repeats itself numerous times until it is fixed by a combination of witchcraft and divine intervention.

   The novel serves, without permission, as the basis for the film *Groundhog Day*. A self-centered weatherman becomes trapped in Punxsutawney, Pennsylvania, on Groundhog Day. He wakes up every day to the same song from his clock radio, runs into the same characters on his way to work (the groundhog's hole), and experiences the same incidents, except as changed by his actions. The repeating characters and incidents in the film are quite different from those in the novel. As the man realizes the day is endlessly repeating, he uses the time to better himself in various ways—learning music, becoming empathetic toward others, and finally falling in love. The final change breaks the spell, and he wakes to a new day. Does the script use unprotected ideas or protected expression?

8. *Greetings.* SentiMental sells a popular greeting card. The cover has the message "I Miss You," and inside reads, "and you haven't even left yet." There is an accompanying picture of a boy crying forlornly while sitting on a curb next to his dog. Another card publisher, Rival, copies the card using the same words and a rather different picture of a weeping

boy sitting on a curb next to his dog. Rival argues that it has simply copied the unprotected idea and that finding infringement gives SentiMental a monopoly over a rather mundane sentiment—a boy's doleful anticipation of the departure of a loved one. Has Rival copied protected expression or an unprotectable idea?

9. *I missed you*. Souvenirs sells a T-shirt to tourists in San Francisco. The shirt reads, "Someone went to San Francisco and got me this shirt because they love me very much." The shirt has simple illustrations of Bay Area staples: the Golden Gate Bridge, Chinatown, and Fisherman's Wharf. Seeing how popular the shirt is, another vendor comes out with a shirt reading, "Someone who loves me went to San Francisco and got me this shirt." The shirt also has several simple designs: the Golden Gate Bridge, Chinatown, cable cars, sea lions, and Nob Hill. The overall arrangement of the elements in the two shirts is completely different. Did the second vendor copy protected expression?

10. *Jellyfish*. Satava, an artist in California, is inspired one day by the jellyfish in a local aquarium. He sets to work to make glass-in-glass sculptures of jellyfish. Soon, he is selling several hundred a year. Another artist begins making glass-in-glass jellyfish sculptures. Satava seeks an injunction. He recognizes that he cannot protect the idea of a jellyfish sculpture but claims protection in his particular expression of that idea: "vertically oriented, colorful, fanciful jellyfish with tendril-like tentacles and a rounded bell encased in an outer layer of rounded clear glass that is bulbous at the top and tapering toward the bottom to form roughly a bullet shape, with the jellyfish portion of the sculpture filling almost the entire volume of the outer, clear-glass shroud." Should the court enjoin the copier from making jellyfish sculptures with those elements?

11. *Piracy?* Erickson's *Pi Symphony* assigns a musical note to each digit in pi from zero to nine. Blake likewise makes *What Pi Sounds Like*, with different rhythms and harmonies. Infringement?

Explanations

1. The second publisher is probably not liable. It copied the idea of a photo of a ballet dancer in the fifth position. Many of the specific elements would be the same, but that would be necessary to use the unprotected idea. *Edwards v. Ruffner*, 623 F. Supp. 511 (D.N.Y. 1985).

2. Pixie would not be entitled to remedies for copyright infringement, because the rival has copied only the unprotected idea of finding a stray kitten on a holiday together with elements that flow from that idea, such as various scenes of the outdoor cat adjusting to indoor life. This would be true regardless of how the rival learned of the idea, whether

through gossip or even espionage (although the latter could give rise to liability under other theories, such as misappropriation of trade secret if the project were subject to security measures, or breach of contract if a Pixie employee were involved).

3. Cartoonist has copied protected expression, as well as unprotected ideas. She is free to copy the idea of a crime-fighting superstrong man who hides his identity and secret powers. Some other elements necessarily follow from the unprotected ideas: He likely would dispose of bullets fired by criminals and might have to rip open a few doors to get at them. But there are many ways that such an idea could be expressed. The hero need not leap around city buildings, specifically battle "evil and injustice," be vulnerable to a rare substance, or have an Arctic refuge. All those details express ideas that could be expressed differently. Cf. *Detective Comics v. Bruns Publications*, 111 F.2d 432 (2d Cir. 1940). For example, the superstrong man could have a vulnerability, but it need not be to some rare substance.

4. Magazine has copied only unprotected ideas. The elements copied were very general and represented only the bare bones of the story: a prisoner coming of age through working in music. The fact that the story was submitted directly to Magazine does not affect its protectability under copyright. Offering unprotected ideas does not confer copyright protection to the ideas.

5. The author of the second photo probably did not copy protected expression. The idea of the first photo is of a businessperson looking down on the street contemplating a leap. That idea is not protected by copyright. There are also a number of quite specific similarities. In other cases, copying such specific elements would constitute protected elements. But here a court likely would hold that the similarities follow from the idea—the point of view, the business attire, the city street below. So the second photograph did not copy protected expression. Cf. *Kaplan v. Stock Market Photo Agency*, 133 F. Supp. 2d 317 (S.D.N.Y. 2001). A counterargument is that the idea is more general—the idea of a businessperson contemplating suicide. The view of a city street from the ledge of a building, including the feet of the businessperson, is only one way of expressing that unprotected idea. Under this view, the many specific elements in the photo are protected expression.

6. The author of the second photograph probably has copied protected expression. The mood of the first photo is not protected; nor is the idea of a languid musician sitting in a jazz bar. So there would have been no infringement if the second photo captured the same languorous mood or were set in the corner of some other jazz bar. But the second

photo goes beyond copying such unprotected ideas. Working from the first photo, this copyist chose the same unusual location, framed the photo identically, used the same lighting and angles, and included other visual elements such as items of decor. Cf. *Kisch v. Ammirati & Puris*, 657 F. Supp. 380 (S.D.N.Y. 1987). The photo necessarily captures many protected expressive elements from the first photo.

7. Despite the copying of a number of specific elements, the author of the film probably has copied only unprotected elements—ideas and elements that necessarily flow from the idea. The general idea is a man caught in a repeating day. The copied elements flow closely from that idea. There are a number of ways that a repeating day could unfold, but the basic outline likely would involve waking up, going to work, encountering a number of people, and experiencing various incidents. The film does not copy elements that do not flow from the idea, such as the specific characters and incidents that occur during the day. Cf. *Arden v. Columbia Pictures Indus.*, 908 F. Supp. 1248 (S.D.N.Y. 1995). A counterargument is that the copying was more specific than necessary. The day always has the central character woken up by an alarm, meeting people on his way to work to generate comic incidents, and changing the repetition of action only from the man's intervention. A repeating day could be portrayed in many other ways, for example, by losing its repeating character. But deeming such elements to be protected probably would give too broad protection to the first work because it would encompass many variations on the basic plot idea of a repeating day.

8. This case probably involves copying of protected expression. Copyright does not protect the idea of feeling someone's absence before the actual departure—or even the more specific idea of telling someone that you miss him before he goes. But Rival copied more specifically than that. It copied the exact words: "I Miss You . . . and you haven't even left yet," coupled with a picture of a weeping boy sitting on a curb by his dog. There are many other ways that a card maker could have expressed the same ideas. Cf. *Roth Greeting Cards v. United Card Co.*, 429 F.2d 1970 (9th Cir. 1970).

9. Only unprotected ideas were copied here. As in the preceding example, the second author copied a relatively mundane sentiment, coupled with appropriate images. But the second author did not literally copy the words of the message. The second author also did not use the same set of images. In addition, the various images likely would be treated as *scènes à faire*. When certain elements are commonly used in a particular genre, their copying is not deemed taking of protected expression. Icons of San Francisco on souvenir T-shirts are likely to fall into

that category. *Cf. Matthews v. Freedman*, 157 F.3d 25 (1st Cir. 1998). This example reflects the lower scope of protection for works with limited originality.

10. As the court aptly put it, "Satava's glass-in-glass jellyfish sculptures, though beautiful, combine several unprotectable ideas and standard elements. These elements are part of the public domain. They are the common property of all, and Satava may not use copyright law to seize them for his exclusive use." *Satava v. Lowry*, 323 F.3d 805, 811 (9th Cir. 2003). "Satava may not prevent others from copying aspects of his sculptures resulting from either jellyfish physiology or from their depiction in the glass-in-glass medium. Satava may not prevent others from depicting jellyfish with tendril-like tentacles or rounded bells, because many jellyfish possess those body parts. He may not prevent others from depicting jellyfish in bright colors, because many jellyfish are brightly colored. He may not prevent others from depicting jellyfish swimming vertically, because jellyfish swim vertically in nature and often are depicted swimming vertically. Satava may not prevent others from depicting jellyfish within a clear outer layer of glass, because clear glass is the most appropriate setting for an aquatic animal. He may not prevent others from depicting jellyfish 'almost filling the entire volume' of the outer glass shroud, because such proportion is standard in glass-in-glass sculpture. And he may not prevent others from tapering the shape of their shrouds, because that shape is standard in glass-in-glass sculpture." *Id.* at 810-811.

11. In the court's words, "Pi is a non-copyrightable fact, and the transcription of pi to music is a non-copyrightable idea. The resulting pattern of notes is an expression that merges with the non-copyrightable idea of putting pi to music: assigning digits to musical notes and playing those notes in the sequence of pi is an idea that can only be expressed in a finite number of ways." *Erickson v. Blake*, 839 F. Supp. 2d 1132 (D. Or. 2012).

DISTINGUISHING IDEA FROM EXPRESSION IN FACTUAL WORKS

The idea-expression analysis is often closely linked to the question of originality. A work that primarily conveys unprotected material (such as facts or theories) has more limited protection than a work that is principally creative expression. This follows from the principle that the scope of protection is affected by the degree of originality. Facts are not original. A book of history, then, may be copied more closely than a book of fiction.

5. Ideas Are Not Subject to Copyright

The classic case for this proposition is *Hoehling v. Universal City Studios*, 618 F.2d 972 (2d Cir. 1980). The work at issue, *Who Destroyed the Hindenburg?*, detailed the history of that famous zeppelin and set forth the theory that a particular member of the crew had sabotaged it. The book contained many elements that are nonprotected (facts or theories based on those facts). A disaster film was made (without permission of the book's copyright owner) that copied many specific elements from the book, such as the age and birthplace of the saboteur, various specific pertinent details about the airship and its crew, a warning letter from a Mrs. Rauch, Germany's ambassador discounting threats of sabotage, even the smuggling of monkeys aboard another zeppelin in the fleet. Such specific copying from a largely fictional novel would have likely been infringement. The copying here was similar to the copying deemed infringement in *Sheldon*, but in this case, the details were not the product of the plaintiff's creativity but rather facts and theories from his research. With factual works (and other works largely composed of nonprotected subject matter), copying of protected expression can occur only at a much lower level of abstraction, closer to verbatim copying.

Once again, the rule appears to give greater copyright protection to elements of less social value. A goofy comic novel would receive thicker copyright protection than a thoroughly researched and thought-out biography of Mahatma Gandhi. Again, the reason springs from the balancing role of the idea-expression dichotomy. Giving thick protection to the novelist imposes fewer restrictions on others. Other authors are still virtually unfettered in writing their comic novels, as long as they do not lift creative expression from our novelist. But other authors have a greater need to copy from the Lincoln biography—in order to build on its scholarship and criticize or propagate its theories. But the creative aspects of the work remain protected. Other authors do not need to copy the wording that the author chooses to relate the historical facts.

Examples

1. *History mystery*. Lucky Jim writes a scholarly article, the fruit of his months of research in the Fort Wayne archives. The article describes his research activity in detail, relates numerous interesting facts gleaned from his readings, and argues that those facts refute the accepted version of the history of Indiana. Kingsley Amiss, the editor of *History Journal*, reviews the manuscript and offers to publish it. Months pass without the article appearing. Finally, the article does appear—but it appears, word for word, in *Monthly History Revue*, with authorship attributed to Amiss. Sued for infringement, Amiss argues that he has stolen only ideas about history, which may be blameworthy but is not copyright infringement. Has Amiss copied protected expression? What if Amiss had written the essay

in his own bombastic prose, copying only Lucky Jim's theories and some of the supporting facts but still deceptively claiming credit for the work himself?

2. *Exam copying*. Each year, prospective college students take the Scholastic Aptitude Test. Its multiple-choice questions are intended to reflect the test takers' abilities in various verbal and mathematical tasks. Shady Prep Services registers a young employee to take the test and photograph each page with a hidden camera. Shady Prep then makes copies of the test and uses it in the SAT prep courses it sells to teenagers. Sued for infringement by the makers of the SAT test, Shady argues that it has copied only unprotectable ideas. The test, it argues, is simply a series of ideas. Is Shady liable? What if Shady had used the photos only to draft its own multiple-choice questions, which loosely followed the testing techniques of the SAT?

Explanations

1. Amiss copied protected expression, as well as unprotected ideas and facts. The article contained unprotectable ideas. But there are many ways in which such ideas could be expressed. A word-for-word copy captures the expression as well as the ideas. There is no infringement if Amiss copies only theories and facts. Taking unprotected material does not infringe the copyright, no matter how scurrilous the actions may be.
2. Shady has copied protected expression, as well as unprotected ideas. Cf. *Educational Testing Services v. Katzmann*, 793 F.2d 533 (3d Cir. 1986). The SAT test certainly contains ideas, but the questions also contain much creative expression. Indeed, the wrong answers may have more protection than the other answers, because they are not unprotected facts but instead originate with the makers of the test.

MERGER DOCTRINE

Sometimes an idea can be expressed only one or a few ways. To the extent that the idea constrains its expression, the expression is unprotected. Courts have called this rule the "merger doctrine." The illustrations on the label of a product, for example, are often creative drawings that qualify for copyright protection, but the nature of the product often constrains the nature of the illustrations. A box of cinnamon tea is likely to bear pictures of cinnamon sticks or cinnamon toast. Such depictions are not protected by copyright. *See Yankee Candle v. Bridgewater Candle*, 259 F.3d 25 (1st Cir. 2001). The merger doctrine only limits protection to the extent of the relevant idea. It does not authorize copying that goes beyond that necessary to use the idea. Another tea seller would infringe if, in addition to the cinnamon stick, she copied in minute detail the box's expressive elements such as shading, exact forms, and arrangement of elements.

The Fifth Circuit held that when a model code was enacted into law, it became unprotected by copyright under the merger doctrine. *See Veeck v. Southern Bldg. Code Congress*, 293 F.3d 791 (5th Cir. 2002) (en banc). In *Veeck*, a nonprofit entity had authored a model building code. It also sold copies of the code. Two towns in Texas adopted the model code as their municipal building codes. A local resident, after unsuccessfully seeking copies from the town offices, bought a copy from the nonprofit and posted it on a website. Such activity would be potential copyright infringement for making copies and for distributing copies to the public. The case raised the issue of copyright protection for privately authored codes that are adopted into law. The court held that once the codes had been adopted into law, they become uncopyrighted under the "merger doctrine." As first authored, codes represented original, creative expression (which would normally be copyrightable). But, the court reasoned, once adopted as law, the codes become "ideas" or "facts," which are not protectable (under the idea-expression dichotomy). "They are the unique, unalterable expression of the 'idea' that constitutes local law. Courts routinely emphasize the significance of the precise wording of laws presented for interpretation." To the extent the codes contained expression, it was inseparable from the unprotectable ideas and facts and therefore unprotected under the merger doctrine.

One could argue that application of the merger doctrine was too broad, and that a narrower approach, such as relying on fair use, may have been appropriate. Application of the merger doctrine is a blunt instrument, because it entails holding that the model code loses all copyright protection once adopted. Merger would permit not just nonprofit uses in areas where the code had been adopted but also free copying and use, even if for strictly commercial purposes in jurisdictions where the code was not the law. Fair use would permit a more nuanced approach.

A greater objection to application of the merger doctrine follows from the nature of the case law system. Copyrighted works can become part of the law in contexts well beyond adoption of model codes. For example, various leading copyright cases involve analysis of such works as the novel *Gone with the Wind*, the song "Pretty Woman," and President Gerald Ford's autobiography. In a real sense, such works have become part of copyright law. To determine whether fair use applies in a case, parties must determine whether the facts of those cases (including the copyrighted works) apply by analogy to the case at issue. Applying *Veeck* mechanically would lead to the absurd result that copyrighted works lose copyright status if they become part of the facts of precedential cases.

Examples

1. *Neologism.* Lingo coins the word "flugonym," to mean a particular type of homonym, one in which two words with different meanings are spelled the same way (like "bear" meaning "to carry" and "bear" meaning a big shaggy mammal). One can differentiate them from other homonyms, in which two words are spelled differently but sound the same (like "bear" and "bare"). For some reason, Lingo's term catches on, being more appealing than "homograph." As Lingo sees more and more people using "her" word, she wonders if, as its creator, she has some exclusive rights in it. She would like to control the use in various benign ways, such as to make sure it is used accurately. Does Lingo have a copyright in the word?

2. *Blues clues.* Punkt paints "Blue Moom," a four-by-five-foot painting, all basic blue. The painting is well received by critics and the public. Not long after, Vango paints "Aquatic," a painting exactly the same color and about 25 percent larger. Vango freely admits that he copied from Punkt's work but argues that he copied only the idea of a basic blue painting. Has Vango copied protected expression?

3. *My code.* The town of Plunger, Illinois, has little money to pay its local officials. The town decides it badly needs a municipal ordinance governing such matters as littering, refuse collection, and recycling. A good-hearted local resident, Augustus Gloop, volunteers to take on the task. Augustus spends much of his spare time over the course of the year talking to town workers and residents and writing the code. His code not only provides a detailed set of rules governing a number of town matters but does so in amusing fashion, with puns, limericks, and a few entertaining stories worked in. The town council warmly thanks Augustus and unanimously adopts his municipal code into law in its entirety. A year later, Augustus is reading a new post-modern novel and finds that it has copied many pages of his code verbatim. When he writes to complain, the publisher responds that the law belongs to the public domain. Has the publisher copied protected expression?

Explanations

1. This example revisits the question "Can a word or short phrase be protected by copyright?" The generally accepted rule is that they cannot be protected. In earlier chapters, we saw two good arguments for the rule: lack of originality and failure to qualify as a work of authorship. This chapter gives yet another possible justification: the merger doctrine. Because a word or short phrase is so brief, it likely cannot be separated from the idea it expresses. Under the merger doctrine, it would be unprotected. "Flugonym" would not be protected, so the idea it expressed could be copied. The same would be true of many creative short phrases.

2. Art can often present puzzles for copyright law. Sometimes, as here, the idea behind a work is very difficult to both define and separate from the expression of the idea. One could say that the idea of a work is a basic blue painting, and therefore Vango copied only the unprotected idea. Or one could say that the idea is a painting of one color, and that Vango copied the particular expression of the idea. On policy grounds, a court is likely to hold that one painter cannot have the exclusive right to make blue paintings and therefore that Vango copied only the unprotected idea.

3. Under the *Veeck* approach, the municipal code would lose copyright protection when it was enacted into law, on the theory that it is a statement of the law and therefore an unprotected idea (or that its expression merges with the unprotected ideas it expresses). For the reasons discussed in the text, other courts might differ. Rather, the code could remain under copyright but be subject to appropriate fair use. Under that approach, the publisher of the postmodern novel is potentially infringing. The publisher could still argue that it had made a noninfringing fair use. Fair use is discussed later in the book.

SO, THEN, HOW DO YOU PROTECT AN IDEA? TRY CONTRACT OR SECRECY OR NORMS OR ATTRIBUTION

An idea is not protected by copyright. An aspiring Spielberg or Edison or Gates has a great idea. How can she protect it from copying by others—especially if she needs help from others to realize the idea (make the movie, sell the invention, start the business)?

One device is contract. Before disclosing the idea, she can require others to sign a nondisclosure agreement (NDA). That contract will enforceable. But she may find others reluctant to sign. Movie studios, venture capitalists, and others often have a policy of not signing NDAs. They have legitimate concerns about signing an NDA and then hearing an idea that they have already heard (or is obvious, or would have come around anyway) or being subject to a claim later that is broader than the idea actually disclosed. Someone requiring an NDA before disclosure may find no one willing to hear the pitch at the price of signing.

Secrecy may work for some ideas. Some ideas can be exploited without disclosing them to others. Software, manufacturing processes, customer lists, and other trade secrets can be kept confidential. But other ideas—the idea for a movie or product—must be disclosed at some point to sell it to the public. But secrecy may help gain lead time over competitors.

Norms (rules of customary behavior, as opposed to rules of law) may also cut down on copying. A comedian's jokes may not be protected by copyright, but comedians may reduce copying through informal social sanctions. *See* Christopher Sprigman and Dotan Oliar, *There's No Free Laugh (Anymore): The Emergence of Intellectual Property Norms and the Transformation of Stand-Up Comedy*, 94 Va. L. Rev. 1787 (2008). Many professions and social networks have norms against copying.

Attribution may help for some authors. Ideas may not be protected, but the originator of an idea is often accorded public and professional respect. Artists, academics, scientists, and businesspeople often benefit from a reputation as an innovator.

Example

1. *Ratz again.* Bryant works for Mattel, designing fashion and hairstyles for high-end Barbie dolls. Bryant's contract provides the following: "I agree to communicate to the Company (Mattel) as promptly and fully as practicable all *inventions* (as defined below) conceived or reduced to practice by me (alone or jointly by others) at any time during my employment by the Company. I hereby assign to the Company . . . all my right, title and interest in such *inventions*, and all my right, title and interest in any patents, copyrights, patent applications or copyright applications based thereon" (emphasis added). The contract further provides: "[T]he term 'inventions' includes, but is not limited to, all discoveries, improvements, processes, developments, designs, knowhow, data computer programs and formulae, whether patentable or unpatentable." Bryant has an idea for a Bratz line of dolls and makes some sketches and models. Bryant later leaves Mattel for a competitor, who makes and sells the Bratz dolls, reaping millions of dollars. Is Bryant liable for breach of contract?

Explanation

1. Bryant is not liable for breach of contract. He agreed to communicate and assign his rights to "inventions," as defined in the contract. An idea for a line of dolls did not fall within the contract's definition of invention. *See Mattel Inc. v. MGA Entertainment Inc.*, 616 F.3d 904 (9th Cir. 2010). Mattel did not have the right to the multimillion-dollar deal. This example illustrates that one can use contracts to control the rights of noncopyrightable ideas—but those contracts must be carefully drafted.

CHAPTER 6

Copyright Does Not Protect Functional Aspects, Infringing Material, and Government Works

This chapter continues with subject matter that, like ideas, is excluded from copyright protection. Copyright would not apply to a method of cloning mice, the rules of a game, an unauthorized sequel to *WALL-E* (unless making the sequel was fair use), or the Copyright Act itself. Copyright does not apply to functional matter, infringing material, and government works. The first, functional matter, like the nonprotection of ideas, is a major boundary on copyrighted subject matter. The second, infringing material, prevents infringers from receiving copyright protection in the parts of their works that contain infringing material. The third, the exclusion for government works, shows a balance struck among several copyright policies.

FUNCTIONAL ASPECTS OF WORKS

Copyright applies to original creative expression. As the last chapter discusses, copyright protects only the elements of the work that are creative expression, such as the particular ways an author expresses an idea. Copyright does not protect ideas. Copyright also does not protect functional aspects of works, as opposed to their expressive aspect. The exclusion for functionality is closely related to the exclusion for ideas. Both are embodied in 17 U.S.C. §102(b):

> In no case does copyright protection for an original work of authorship extend to any idea, procedure, process, system, method of operation, concept,

> principle, or discovery, regardless of the form in which it is described, explained, illustrated, or embodied in such work.

Section 102(b) emphasizes the exclusion for functional aspects by specifically listing several types of functional elements, excluding protection for any "procedure, process, system, method of operation." 17 U.S.C. §102(b). There would be no copyright protection for an original safety *procedure* for scuba diving in caves, an original *process* for domesticating wild berries, an original *system* of operating a dental office, or an original *method of operation* for steering a rocket ship. The functional elements of software may be noncopyrighted under these provisions.

Many functional elements, such as procedures, systems, or methods of operation, could simply be viewed as noncopyrightable ideas. But the functionality issue differs in an important way from the exclusion of such ideas as the concept for a story or a mathematical principle. When the plot of a novel or the concept underlying an abstract painting is an uncopyrightable idea, the effect is likely to be that the idea is left in the public domain, free for others to copy. In general, the idea-expression question revolves around whether elements should be copyrightable or left in the public domain.

With functional elements, the dividing line is slightly different. Functional elements, such as manufacturing methods or designs of machines, are not copyrightable—but they may be patentable. Patent law, unlike copyright law, protects functional elements. Indeed, patents on inventions can apply only to new and useful products or processes. The basic issue in functionality is often whether an element is creative, and therefore belongs in the realm of copyright, or functional, and therefore belongs in the realm of patent. Some useful ideas are too abstract for patent protection. Like copyright, patent does not protect ideas. Rather, patent only applies to practical applications of ideas in useful inventions.

Different elements of the same work may be protected by both copyright and patent. The creative elements of a computer program are protected by copyright. The program may implement patentable inventions (such as methods of performing particular tasks). A company often has copyright and patent (not to mention trademark) protection on the same product, which all apply to different elements of the product.

The rule that copyright does not protect functional elements may play an increasing role in a world where everyday events and behavior are recorded by devices such as security cameras, personal video recorders, and gaming and virtual world software. Such collections of information may, in some cases, be regarded not as copyrightable works of authorship but rather simply functional and factual data.

Distinguishing Nonprotectable Functional Elements

Copyright does not protect functionality, but a work may be functional and still have protected creative expression. A lamp base functions to hold the lamp up, but a lamp base made of a dancer statuette is protectable by copyright. *Mazer v. Stein*, 347 U.S. 201 (1954). A map functions to help navigation but is protectable. Computer programs fulfill many functions but are protected literary works. In each case, the key is to differentiate the protected expressive aspects from the unprotected functional aspects.

Baker v. Selden, 101 U.S. 99 (1879), sets the standards for functionality analysis. The plaintiff held the copyright on a book explaining an accounting system. The book contained an essay that explained how the system worked. The book also provided forms to implement the accounting system. The accounting system was clearly unprotected (in the terms of the present statute, as a "process" or "system"). The essay explaining the system was protected expression because the essay was simply the way in which the author explained the system. Another author could explain it in quite different terms. The issue was whether there was copyright protection for the forms used to implement the system. The forms were held unprotected because use of such forms was necessary to use the system. To prevent copying of the forms would have the effect of protecting the system. Copyright does not protect elements that necessarily flow from unprotected ideas. *Baker* stands for the proposition that even expressive elements are unprotected when they are functional.

Even an explanation of a system could be unprotected. The lengthy essay in *Baker* could have been written quite differently. But some descriptions are largely dictated by the systems they describe. The rules of a sweepstakes competition, for example, set forth how the competition operates. Giving copyright protection to the explanation of the sweepstakes could, in effect, give one competitor exclusive rights to hold such competitions. There are only a few ways to clearly say, "Entrants should print name, address, and Social Security number on a boxtop or on plain paper." *See Morrissey v. Procter & Gamble*, 379 F.2d 675 (1st Cir. 1967). Likewise, documents used to implement the corporate reorganization of insurance companies have little, if any, protection. For others to copy the plan of the reorganization, it is necessary to use similar wording. *See Crume v. Pacific Mutual Life Insurance*, 140 F.2d 182 (7th Cir. 1944). Many legal documents have little or no protection because the use of particular words and phrases is necessary to comply with applicable legal requirements.

Although courts frequently state that copyright does not protect functional aspects of works, perhaps the more accurate phrase is elements with a *utilitarian* function. Almost every creative element of a work performs some function in a broad sense. Witty lines amuse, dramatic plots cause suspense, music stirs many emotional responses, beautiful forms inspire, but such elements are exactly the sorts of creative expression that receive protection.

Courts look to several guides in determining whether elements are functional. Courts consider whether it is necessary to copy the element to implement an unprotected idea. The scope of protection depends heavily on how broadly the unprotected idea is defined. Courts may also consider factors geared to the need for competitors to copy the element, such as whether the element in question increases the efficiency of the process, whether external factors favor adoption of the element in question, or whether the element has become a standard in the relevant industry or is necessary for compatibility with other works. Courts also look to the specific excluded categories listed in the statute: whether the elements constitute an unprotected procedure, process, system, or method of operation. Such words are subject themselves to broad or narrow interpretation.

With all the approaches, the underlying policy is determining whether the element at issue is one that is a solution or building block that others should have the ability to use. The functionality analysis often follows the approach of the abstractions test. The following sections show how courts look at functionality issues in particular subject matter areas.

Examples

1. *Fosbury flop.* In 1968, Dick Fosbury changed the sport of high-jumping. He introduced a radically new technique, jumping headfirst and facing the sky. The "Fosbury Flop" turned out to be the most efficient way for people to high-jump, both in terms of physics and physiology. It is now the standard technique. Could Fosbury have copyrighted the move?

2. *Theme song. The Flimpsons* is a weekly television show. Its catchy theme song, "Meet the Flimpsons," begins the show each week. The song wittily introduces the main characters and the premise of the show, and is also used to market the show. A local bar regularly plays the song without a license from the copyright owner, arguing that the song is functional and therefore not protected. Is the song an unprotected functional work?

3. *Kregos revisited.* Recall that Kregos sells a "pitching form," listing nine items of baseball statistics, for use by baseball fans. The purpose of the form is to provide information with which a baseball fan could use her own knowledge to predict the likely performance of a pitcher. We discussed earlier the fact that the form is sufficiently original to qualify for copyright protection, but should it be excluded from protection for another reason, namely functionality?

4. *Taxonomy*. The American Dental Association created the *Code on Dental Procedures and Nomenclature*. The code classifies all dental procedures into groups and gives each procedure a number, a short description, and a long description. One example would be #04267, classified among surgical periodontal services, with the short description "guided tissue regeneration—nonresorbable barrier, per site, per tooth (includes membrane removal)," and a longer, more detailed description of the procedure's steps. An insurer copies the numbering system and short descriptions into its own dental procedures manual. Sued for infringement, the insurer argues that it has copied only an unprotected system of classifying dental procedures.

5. *Stolen act*. Ved the Magician devises ingenious ways to make pigeons appear from his sleeve, mice disappear from boxes, and playing cards pop up on demand. Roman attends Ved's shows, figures out the tricks, and incorporates them in his own act. Copyright infringement?

Explanations

1. Fosbury could not have copyrighted the move, because it is functional: the most efficient way to high-jump. Copyright did not protect a sequence of yoga poses. The sequence was functional, as opposed to a creative arrangement such as the choreography of a ballet (which could include creative leaps).[1]

2. The theme song is not functional in the sense of copyright law. The theme song does perform several functions in a modest dramatic sense. It introduces characters and the premise of the show. It may put the viewer in a proper mood to enjoy the show. It serves a marketing role as a reminder of a popular product. But such aspects of a creative work are not functional for the purpose of limiting copyright protection. The song is not utilitarian, or an "idea, procedure, process, system, method of operation." Nor is it an element that has become an industry standard or is necessary for compatibility with other products (factors that some courts would consider). Protecting the theme song does not limit competitors in any substantial way: A rival TV producer can use its theme song to do whatever she pleases without fear of infringing the *Flimpsons'* theme song. Use of the song is not necessary to comply with industry standards or to efficiently create a television program. Therefore, none of the factors weighing toward functionality apply here.

3. The form is not denied copyright on the basis of functionality. It would be unprotected if it embodied a system for predicting the outcomes of

1. *Bikram's Yoga Coll. of India, L.P. v. Evolation Yoga, LLC*, 803 F.3d 1032 (9th Cir. 2015).

baseball games. If Kregos had devised a formula for using specific statistics to predict outcomes, then the form would probably be denied protection under *Baker v. Selden*, as something necessary to implement the system. But Kregos's form makes a more modest claim, simply suggesting that those nine statistics might be helpful to the fan in making her own predictions.

4. A taxonomy might embody a classification system, but the defendants copied more than the classification system. They also copied the specific numbers and the text of the individual entries. The court aptly described why the short descriptions require creative choices in description: "Number 04267 reads 'guided tissue regeneration—nonresorbable barrier, per site, per tooth' but could have read 'regeneration of tissue, guided by nonresorbable barrier, one site and tooth per entry.' Or 'use of barrier to guide regeneration of tissue, without regard to the number of sites per tooth and whether or not the barrier is resorbable.' Even the numbers arguably are original creative expression: 'The number assigned to any one of the three descriptions could have had four or six digits rather than five; guided tissue regeneration could have been placed in the 2500 series rather than the 4200 series; again any of these choices is original to the author of a taxonomy, and another author could do things differently. Every number in the ADA's Code begins with zero, assuring a large supply of unused numbers for procedures to be devised or reclassified in the future; an author could have elected instead to leave wide gaps inside the sequence. A catalog that initially assigns 04266, 04267, 04268 to three procedures will over time depart substantively from one that initially assigns 42660, 42670, and 42680 to the same three procedures.'"

5. No infringement if Roman has copied only Ved's methods. *See Rice v. Fox Broad. Co.*, 330 F.3d 1170 (9th Cir. 2003). A magic trick is functional, because it accomplishes a specific task. As long as Roman did not copy Ved's patter or creative elements not part of the workings of the tricks, he would not infringe.

Instructions and Rules

Words, pictures, and other symbols can be functional. The instructions for assembling a bicycle are utilitarian in that they are intended to be used to bring about a result: the assembled bicycle. Many literary works are functional in this sense: cooking recipes, operating manuals for electrical devices, instructions for games, how-to books for home maintenance, and so on. Rules can also be functional in nature. The rules for playing card games, or the rules for contests, or the safety rules for workers at a construction site are all functional, intended to be used to accomplish various goals.

The functional elements of such works are not protected, but their purely expressive elements are protected. In determining whether an element may be copied, a court is likely to rely heavily on *Baker v. Selden*. Suppose that defendant copied plaintiff's instructions for operating a digital camera. The court may first attempt to identify a clearly unprotectable functional element (the system for operating the camera). Then the court, in effect, will consider whether the elements that were copied were like the forms in *Baker v. Selden* (which were necessary to use the accounting system and therefore not protected) or like the essay explaining the system (which was protected, because there are many different ways that one could write an essay explaining the accounting system). In short, the question is whether there were alternative ways to implement the functional purpose of the work. If there were many different ways to write the instructions to operate the camera, then plaintiff's set of instructions would be deemed to be protected expression. But if there is only one or a few ways to efficiently give a set of instructions, then the instructions would likely be deemed to be nonprotected.

The level of creativity in the work is likely to affect the issue of functionality. If the instructions are set forth in a simple, straightforward way, then it is more likely that they will be deemed functional and hence nonprotected. If the instructions clearly contain elements that are not necessary for instruction but rather serve other purposes (such as creative phrasing, jokes, or historical information), then the instructions are more likely to be deemed protected by copyright. In that event, however, only the creative aspects are protected. A party that copies only functional aspects (such as copying the information necessary to operate the camera without copying the jokes and historical information) would not infringe. Instructions and rules, therefore, may be protected but would receive only thin protection.

Examples

1. *Shake well.* Baker Duval, after many experiments, perfects a recipe for squish-squash, a delicious concoction of sweet potato, squash, and marshmallows. She writes down the ingredients and a straightforward set of instructions for making the dish. In writing it down, she uses standard terms and styles for recipe writers. She e-mails the recipe to a small group of fellow chefs. Not long after, as often happens in copyright fact patterns, her recipe is swiped and included verbatim in a best-selling cookbook. Will she be entitled to a slice of the royalties?

2. *Running a tight ship.* Carnivore Cruises is the most profitable cruise company because of its ability to operate extremely efficient ships while spending

less than its competitors on salaries and other expenses. It owes its productivity to its founder, Efua the Efficient. She spent years thinking of better ways to serve cocktails, clean cabins, and amuse passengers. All of her instructions are detailed in the company's employee manual, a closely guarded book given to each employee.

A competitor, Caesar Sails, sends several employees incognito as passengers on a Carnivore cruise. Over two weeks, the spies carefully observe the operation of the boat and note as much as they can in great detail. In effect, they reverse engineer most of the content of the employee manual. Within months, Caesar has its employees adopt dozens of time- and money-saving instructions gleaned from its espionage. Can Carnivore sue for infringement of its employee manual?

3. *Voop*. Two kids invent Voop, a card game. They creatively combine various elements from card games like bridge, hearts, spades, and poker. Their combination results in a new game that is easy and fun to play. The kids write up the rules. Rather than a straightforward statement of the rules, however, the kids use many puns, puzzles, and tricks to state the rules. They also include a number of stories and pictures, springing from events during various Voop games. All of this material is included in their notebook, titled *Rules of Voop*. Is it copyrightable? Suppose Yoyle read *Rules of Voop*, figured out the basic rules of Voop, and wrote a concise statement of those rules. Would Yoyle infringe the kids' copyright?

4. *Rollerball*. Promoter invents rollerball, a new sport that combines various elements of hockey, speed skating, and lacrosse, together with a few new rules devised by Promoter. Promoter stages several matches, which turn out to be great spectacles as well as exciting athletic events. The number of fans increases quickly. Knowing that he cannot copyright the rules of play, Promoter writes detailed accounts of the matches. Another promoter stages a rollerball match after she reads some of Promoter's accounts. She simply uses the same rules without staging the same events during those games. Promoter then sues for copyright infringement, arguing that the match infringes the copyright in his written descriptions, which are protected literary works. Were protected elements copied?

5. *Draft evader*. The Law Society drafts a Model Right of Publicity Statute. The society is concerned that the right of publicity is a cause of action that varies widely from state to state, is created by statute in some states and common law in others (or both), and is subject to considerable differences in judicial application. To promote uniformity among states, the society drafts the model statute, which the society regards as a concise statement of the best view of the elements, defenses, and remedies of the cause of action. The drafters first agreed on the set of rules that should govern the right of publicity. They then agreed, after several drafts, on

how to express those rules. They also arranged the rules in a comprehensive fashion. Finally, they drafted commentary and examples to guide interpretation of the rules. Unlike drafters of some model statutes, the society does not urge states to adopt the model statute as drafted, but rather to use it only for guidance in drafting statutes. No jurisdiction has enacted the model statute into law. Is the model statute (including the rules as written by the drafters, the arrangement of the rules in the outline, the commentary, and all examples) protected by copyright?

Explanations

1. Baker Duval probably does not have a claim for copyright infringement. A set of instructions for making a dish is functional and therefore not protected by copyright. A recipe could have protection if it had creative, expressive elements additional to the functional elements. Duval's recipe was evidently written in a way that simply set down the steps to follow to make squish-squash, without adding any creative elements that were not necessary for implementing the unprotected functional aspects.

2. Caesar has not infringed the copyright in the employee manual. Caesar has copied only elements of an unprotected system described in the manual. (Indeed, Caesar arguably has not copied from the manual itself at all.) This example shows again that copying unprotected elements is not copyright infringement, regardless of how the copying is done.

3. *The Rules of Voop*, as written by the kids, is protected by copyright. To the extent the rules govern the play of the game, however, they are unprotectable functional elements. Even though a game is for recreation and playing the game serves no end in itself, the rules of a game are functional. They represent an unprotected idea, process, or system. If the kids had written the rules in a straightforward way, their description would have no protection. Because card games are described by a standard terminology, there is only one way (or only a few ways) to succinctly state the rules. Accordingly, such a statement is unprotected under the merger doctrine. Otherwise, giving protection to the description of the rules effectively protects the game itself. But the kids chose a creative way to express the rules of the game. Giving them exclusive rights to their particular description does not limit others from copying the functional aspects. For the very reason that the description is protected, its copyright is not infringed by Yoyle. Yoyle did not copy the creative, protected aspects of the description. Rather, Yoyle copied only unprotected functional aspects.

4. The rival promoter has not copied protected expression. Promoter does have copyright protection in his detailed descriptions of the rollerball

games. The rules of rollerball are not protected (as an idea, system, or process). His descriptions, however, capture much more than the rules. They describe the events in particular games of rollerball, as well as other details like descriptions of players and the crowd. The rival promoter, however, did not copy the protected expression. Rather, by staging her own rollerball games, she simply copied the unprotectable rules of play.

5. The rules of a game have been deemed unprotected because copying the rules is necessary to implement the game, an unprotected procedure. One might then expect that a model statute setting forth the rules governing the right of publicity would also be unprotected. However, although authority on the subject is sparse, copyright has been generally recognized in model statutes. The model statute sets forth proposed rules, which in themselves are unprotected as ideas, systems, or procedures. But the model statute also contains creative elements, such as the arrangement of the rules, the wording chosen to describe particular rules, and the commentary and examples chosen to illustrate the rules. Only if the rules could be expressed in one (or a few) forms of expression would the draft statute be denied protection. Here, that is not the case. The drafters found numerous possibilities to express individual rules. They arranged the rules for creative reasons, unconstrained by functional considerations. The examples would also be creative expression. An infinite number of examples could be devised to illustrate the application of broad-ranging rules.

Software

By their nature, computer programs (also known as software) are functional. The copyright statute defines "computer program" as "a set of statements or instructions to be used directly or indirectly in a computer in order to bring about a certain result." 17 U.S.C. §101. At one time, there was considerable debate about whether computer programs were subject to copyright at all, or rather were nonprotected functional works. The present statute, however, clearly implies that computer programs are eligible for protection as literary works. The question has shifted to determining the extent of protection for computer programs. In software infringement cases, the basic question is to identify which elements have been copied and determine whether those elements are protected.

A computer program performs intellectual work. It might operate a video game, predict the weather, monitor credit card transactions for possible fraud, create architectural drawings, or anything else. It will get input (information from databases of customer information, other programs that it interacts with, automatic sensors, users via a keyboard, mouse, or joystick, etc.). It produces output (the video game display, the weather predictions, the fraud warnings, the drawings—not to mention things like prompts for more input and error messages). The software engineer will design how the program will receive the input and produce output. She is likely to make an overall design (which would be an outline, or flowcharts, or scribbled notes, or ideas in her head). She will then implement that design by writing the program in source code. A compiler then translates the source code into machine code. In other words, a compiler takes the source code as its input and produces machine code as its output. The machine code is the form of the program that is executed by the computer. Once compiled, the program can be run. It won't work perfectly the first time. It will be tested and revised many times to remove bugs, to make other changes suggested by users, and to add other features. In general terms, a computer program is likely to start as a design, then be written out in source code, a portion of which might look like this:

```
#include <time.h>
#include <limits.h>
#ifndef ACOS4
#include.<sys.types.h>
#endif
```

It then will be compiled into machine code, which can look like this (except it would go on for many more lines):

```
F0F0F3F5 F0F0F0F0 F0F0F0F0 7B899583 93A48485
F0F0F3F6 F0F0F0F0 F0F0F0F0 7B859584 89864040
F0F0F3F7 F0F0F0F0 F0F0F0F0 40404040 40404040
F0F0F3F8 F0F0F0F0 F0F0F0F0 A3A89785 84858640
F0F0F3F9 F0F0F0F0 F0F0F0F0 A3A89785 84858640
F0F0F4F0 F0F0F0F0 F0F0F0F0 A3A89785 84858640
F0F0F4F1 F0F0F0F0 F0F0F0F0 40404040 40404040
F0F0F4F2 F0F0F0F0 F0F0F0F0 615C40E2 E8D4C1D7
```

That pattern (design, source code, machine code) is common, but programs may be created other ways. Novels are often outlined, written, and edited, but some writers may simply write without outlining. Likewise, some software engineers may simply write the source code without much of an overall design. Moreover, automated development tools often do much of the coding today. In some instances, an engineer may write the program in machine code.

Computer programs are quite different from things like novels because they are primarily functional. Programs do things. A program is a text that "behaves." Pamela Samuelson, Randall Davis, Mitchell D. Kapor, and J.D.

Reichman, *A Manifesto Concerning the Legal Protection of Computer Programs*, 94 Colum. L. Rev. 2308, 2316-2317 (1994) (proposing new legal regime more suited to software). A program is more like a machine than a poem in many ways. But programmers are also like poets in many ways. Just like other literary works, programs can be elegant, creative, clumsy, overlong, or terse. A program is functional, but there is always more than one way to skin a cat. The programmer is likely to have many choices about how to accomplish her goal, and some of her choices may be purely creative. The difficulty in applying copyright law to software has been to separate its functional (not copyrightable) aspects from its aesthetic (copyrightable) aspects. Copyright law must adapt to special concerns with software: functionality (software has creative aspects but is largely functional), interoperability (software must often be adapted to work together with other programs or with devices), and network effects (the more people use a program, the more useful it is to others). *See, e.g.*, Stacey L. Dogan and Joseph P. Liu, *Copyright Law and Subject Matter Specificity: The Case of Computer Software*, 61 N.Y.U. Ann. Surv. Am. L. 203 (2005).

A very helpful case to understand the issues is the much-criticized *Whelan Associates v. Jaslow Dental*, 797 F.2d 693 (3d Cir. 1986). In *Whelan*, the plaintiff held the copyright in a program used to administer a dental office. The defendant had not copied the program code line for line but rather had copied the structure of the program. The court, recognizing that computer programs are literary works, analyzed the case much like a case involving copying of a novel. The court reasoned that the computer program's unprotected idea was to efficiently administer a dental office. There are many different ways to implement that idea. Therefore, the court reasoned, the particular program structure chosen by the plaintiff was protected expression.

Courts and commentators have overwhelmingly rejected the *Whelan* approach, as based on a faulty analogy. A computer program is not like *Moby-Dick*. Computer programs are indeed literary works, but not all literary works receive the same level of protection. As Chapter 5 discusses, factual works receive a thinner level of protection than creative fictional works. Likewise, computer programs, which are largely functional, should receive thinner protection. In particular, the *Whelan* court erred in assuming that a program had a single unprotected idea. Rather, computer programs have an overall function (like administering a dental office), but implement that function through many less-abstract functions (such as performing accounting tasks, sorting through patient records, or keeping track of appointments). All of those elements make up the structure of the program, which *Whelan* had held protectable. In short, *Whelan* gave the plaintiff exclusive rights in its system for operating a dental office. This is exactly what *Baker v. Selden* warned against—using copyright to give patent-like protection to a system.

After *Whelan*, courts have accorded a much thinner level of protection to computer programs. Notably, the cases borrow considerably from the analysis of the idea-expression dichotomy in literary works, vindicating the first step *Whelan* took. But they use those tools to considerably decrease the scope of protection, as applied to computer programs.

The leading case for analyzing claims of infringement for nonliteral copying of a computer program is *Computer Associates International v. Altai*, 982 F.2d 693 (2d Cir. 1992). *Computer Associates* set forth an abstraction-filtration analysis, which focuses on identifying elements of a program that would not be protected. In this approach, the court first borrows from the abstractions test by identifying the structure of the program from its highest level (the program's ultimate function, such as running the accounting system for a business), through midlevel (such as modules that update inventory or sort the customers in alphabetical order), to its lowest level of abstraction (the literal code of the program).

The next step is to filter out nonprotected material. Such material would first include "elements dictated by efficiency." If there were only a limited number of ways to efficiently store the information or to update the financial records, then such methods would not be protected. The court also indicated that "elements dictated by external factors" would be functional and therefore nonprotected. It made analogy to the *scènes à faire* doctrine, which denies protection to stock characters in literary works. Likewise, many elements in the computing environment are standard, like the Windows operating system or the use of personal computers. Therefore, elements in the program used to meet such standards would not be protected. Note here that the extent of this exclusion is unclear. It would arguably remove protection for program features that became industry standards, even if the feature itself was just ornamental or aesthetic. The final step is to filter out elements that did not originate with the program's author, such as code or algorithms copied from others.

Computer Associates emphasizes filtering out all the unprotected functional or nonoriginal elements to see if any nugget of original, creative expression remains. In practice, this leads to a very thin level of protection. In general, the literal code of the program is likely to be held copyrightable because there are many different ways to write code to implement the various nonprotected functional features of the program. Elements any more general than that are likely to be identified as functional because they serve efficiency, or external factors, or borrow from the works of others.

Computer Associates analyzes software the way that courts analyze novels and plays—using the abstractions approach. *Computer Associates* has been widely followed by courts in the United States and even abroad as an imaginative guide to the problem of applying copyright to computer programs. Others see the software/literature analogy as "an abomination that has ravaged copyright like the Black Plague." *See Bill Gates and Software Copyright*, Patry Copyright Blog, August 3, 2005, http://williampatry.blogspot.com/ 2005/ 08/bill-gates-and-software-copyright.html.

An approach that might lead to greater protection is exemplified by *Softel v. Dragon Medical and Scientific Communications*, 118 F.3d 955 (2d Cir. 1997). *Softel* made a point missing from *Computer Associates*. It is not enough to go through the elements of a work individually and ask whether each element is protected expression, as *Computer Associates* seems to do in its filtration approach. Rather, individual unprotected elements may be put together in a way that is protected. The individual facts in a database are not protected, but an original selection or arrangement of those facts may be protected. The individual words in a poem are not protected, but the arrangement of those words in the poem is protected. Courts should also consider whether unprotected functional elements in a computer program were put together in an original, nonfunctional way. A computer program might qualify for protection as a *compilation* of unprotected elements.

Computer Associates stands for one approach—looking at the software and filtering out all unprotectable elements to see if a protectable nugget remains. *Softel*, on the other hand, suggests looking at what the software developers have done to see if they have shown originality in compiling unprotected elements. Courts need not choose between the two approaches. Rather, both can guide courts in trying to determine whether the program represents original, creative expression.

A factor in software cases is whether the defendant copied literally or nonliterally. *Computer Associates* and *Softel* dealt with nonliteral copying. The defendants did not literally copy the code of the program but wrote their own program that did similar things. Literal copying of the code will usually be infringement because there are usually many ways to write code that expresses the various functions of the program. However, the question may be more difficult when there is literal copying, not of the code but of other elements of the program, such as words or pictures that the user sees.

The leading case is *Lotus Development v. Borland International*, 49 F.3d 807 (1st Cir. 1995). Lotus 1-2-3 was an immensely popular spreadsheet program that allowed users to perform accounting functions and other finance tasks on a computer. The program was so popular that it fueled the popularity of early personal computers. Borland, seeking to lure Lotus users to Borland's less popular program, copied Lotus's "menu command hierarchy." In other words, Borland copied the exact commands (such as Copy, Print, or Quit) that 1-2-3 employed, as well its menu command hierarchy. Lotus had "469 commands arranged into more than 50 menus and submenus." *Lotus* presented a close call on the functionality/expression issue. Each command by itself was functional. Lotus could not claim protection in such functional (not to mention nonoriginal) commands as Copy or Print. But Borland also copied the intricate arrangement of those commands in various menus and submenus. That menu hierarchy would seem creative. There are millions of ways to arrange the commands into menus, and many would function just as well as the Lotus arrangement. The reason Borland copied those elements was to allow Lotus users to switch to Borland without learning a new set of menus (and to allow users to copy over their macros, which they could write themselves to implement series of commands). Lotus users could then use their old material with Borland's spreadsheet, and also with other compatible software.

The courts struggled with *Lotus*. The trial court held that the menu command hierarchy was protectable creative expression on the theory that Lotus had chosen just one of many ways of implementing the idea of a menu command hierarchy. On appeal, the First Circuit recognized first that the *Computer Associates* approach was not apt, because it was geared toward nonliteral copying. The court then took a narrow approach to the issue. Rather than approaching it in general terms, the court held that the menu command hierarchy was a "method of operation," one of the specific exclusions from copyright in section 102 of the Copyright Act. The menu command hierarchy, in this view, was the means by which users control and operate the Lotus program. When the Supreme Court decided to hear the case, the computer industry and copyright lawyers eagerly awaited guidance on applying the functionality doctrine to software. But the court split 4-4, thereby simply affirming the appellate court and without a written opinion. So *Lotus* leaves the extent of protection for software an open issue. As the Java example below shows, courts are now split on the issue.

Examples

1. *The examined life.* Bug is a very busy person. She works as an independent software developer, takes evening courses in law, and has a family with four kids. She uses some of her precious time to write a computer program that will give her more time. The program runs a calendar, maintains an updated contact list (friends, kids' friends, doctors, teachers, coaches), schedules a carpool, sends out thank-you and reminder e-mails, and performs various other mundane yet critical tasks. Bug uses the program herself, then sells copies to a few dozen people in town. She learns that one buyer, Abel, made several copies and sold them. Another buyer, Babel, watched Abel using the program a number of times and wrote another program that performed all of the same tasks. The overall structure of the program is similar, but the code written to implement that structure is quite different. Has Abel or Babel infringed Bug's copyright?

2. *An elegant solution.* At work one day, Bug takes on the task of writing a program that will use publicly available data from a weather satellite to calculate the amount of energy a particular area receives in the form of sunlight. Bug tries various approaches to the problem. Finally, she comes up with a brilliant solution and writes an extremely short program that

performs the task, ingeniously using only about six lines of code. Does Bug have a copyright in her short but powerful program?

3. *Let a thousand flowers bloom.* Blossom Software sells Wypo, a popular photo-processing program that consumers use to manipulate digitized pictures. Wypo presents a user with commands such as Stretch, Copy, Print, and Even Out Colors. The user can make sophisticated changes by using these rather simple commands. The commands are arranged in various menus, which pop up for different tasks. A competitor develops a new photo-processing program. To lure customers who are using Blossom's program, the competitor copies the commands and the pop-up menu structure. This way, a Blossom user can switch to the new program without learning a new set of commands and menus. By copying those elements, the new program is also compatible with other Blossom software products, making it more attractive to Blossom users. Has the competitor copied unprotected functional elements or protected creative expression?

4. *Mirroring Windows.* Commentators have raised the following puzzle: Copyright law protects Microsoft's Windows operating system. Copyright law, however, protects only the expressive aspect of works, not their functional aspects. Another software company could copy the unprotected functional aspects of Windows and sell the functionally equivalent program to a big market without violating the copyright. Why has this not been done by another mighty software company?

5. *Java.* Google wanted to make Android phones work with the widely used Java language so that developers could write apps in Java to run on Android phones. Unable to agree on a license with Oracle, which owns Java, Google decided instead to independently develop software that worked with Java. Google did not copy the code that runs Java but did copy the "structure, sequence, and organization" of the code that runs Java. To do that, Google also copied Java's application programming interfaces (APIs). To enable Android developers to use Java functions, Android copied the names and headers for the Java modules. For example, Google would copy the header for a method that compares numbers, "java.lang.Math.max," and then write code that does the comparison and returns a result. Did Google copy creative expression, which is protected by copyright, or functional matter, which is not copyrightable?

6. *Tetris.* In *Tetris*, developed in the USSR in the 1980s, players must align "falling geometric block pieces (called tetrominos)" to fill the horizontal lines. Mino wrote and sold code to reproduce *Tetris*. As the court described it, "[T]he style of the pieces is nearly indistinguishable, both in their look and in the manner they move, rotate, fall, and behave. Similar bright colors are used in each program, the pieces are composed of individually delineated bricks, each brick is given an interior border to suggest

texture, and shading and gradation of color are used in substantially similar ways to suggest light is being cast onto the pieces." *Tetris Holding, LLC v. Xio Interactive, Inc.*, 863 F. Supp. 2d 394 (D.N.J. 2012). Infringement, or permissible copying of a functional game?

Explanations

1. Babel is not liable for infringement. Babel copied only functional elements. Babel watched how the program worked and wrote one that performed the same functions. That is not infringement.

   Abel is potentially liable. Abel made several copies and sold them. Presumably, Abel copied not just the unprotected functional elements but also the protected expression of those elements in the literal lines of object code.

   The example does not ask about a more difficult case in which someone looked at the source code of the program in detail and copied it rather closely in writing her own code. Addressing that question would require more facts about the program itself and the specific elements that were copied. This example just shows that in general, wholesale literal copying of software is likely to infringe, but simply copying the function of a program does not.

2. Bug probably does not have a copyright. In general, computer programs are protected by copyright, but this program is so short and written so ingeniously that it is probably denied copyright under the merger doctrine. "Short programs may reveal high levels of creativity and may present simple, yet unique, solutions to programming quandaries. Just as a mathematician may develop an elegant proof, or an author may express ideas in a spare, simple, but creative manner, so a computer programmer may develop a program that is brief and eligible for protection. But unless a creative flair is shown, a very brief program is less likely to be copyrightable because it affords fewer opportunities for original expression." *Lexmark International v. Static Control Components*, 387 F.3d 522, 542-543 (6th Cir. 2004). The functional aspects of Bug's program are so closely identified with its short text that it is not copyrighted. Otherwise, Bug might effectively have exclusive rights in the functionality of the program. If, however, a program could easily be written that did the same thing using different code, the answer would be different.

3. This example is drawn from *Lotus Development v. Borland International*, discussed above. Courts have differed on whether such elements of software are protected by copyright. A narrow view of functionality would deem the menu command hierarchy to be protected expression. The unprotected idea is the use of a hierarchical set of commands to implement the photo-editing program. The particular set of commands and menus

chosen is only one possible expression of that idea. Another software developer could have achieved the same function with a completely different set of commands.

Another view, concentrating on interpreting the specific categories in 17 U.S.C. §102(b), could be that the set of commands is an unprotected "method of operation." The user uses the program by responding to the menus the program presents. Likewise, the set of commands could be deemed an unprotected "system": The set of commands function together to perform the functions of the program.

Yet another view would be to deem the set of commands to be functional simply because it is necessary to achieve compatibility with other Blossom products. Consumers have become accustomed to using Blossom's set of commands. Copying the elements also allows the new program to interact with other Blossom software products. A court could hold that such compatibility characteristics make the set of commands functional. Standing alone, this is probably the weakest argument for functionality.

4. Several reasons militate against such a strategy, as explained in Mark A. Lemley and David McGowan, *Legal Implications of Network Economic Effects*, 86 Cal. L. Rev. 479, 528-530 (1998). Although copyright does not protect functional aspects of the program, there remains legal uncertainty about which aspects are functional. Also, other intellectual property (such as patents or trade secrets) might protect some aspects of the program. More important than the legal uncertainties, perhaps, the market risks would be great deterrents to a commercial competitor. Reverse engineering the program is a time-consuming and uncertain enterprise, and Microsoft periodically upgrades the program, which means that a commercial competitor might have difficulty in selling an up-to-date product. Consumers might also be wary of whether the program was truly a functional substitute. Finally, and most dulling to the incentives, Microsoft presumably has the ability to lower the price of its program to compete with any new entrant, greatly reducing the potential payoff. All in all, it makes little sense for a commercial competitor to make the huge investments in development and marketing that would be required to compete when other avenues of investment are likely to be more fruitful. This may explain why no large-scale commercial software developer has taken on such a project.

   Others with different incentives have at least attempted parts of it. Some open source developers (who give their software away) have attempted such efforts for such purposes as honing their programming and reverse-engineering skills and adding to the free software movement. The WINE program allows computers running other operating systems, such as LINUX, to run Windows programs.

5. This case created a split among the Federal Circuits on the scope of copyright protection for software, which the Supreme Court has left unresolved. Under *Lotus*, this would seem like permitted copying of functional matter. The hierarchy of methods and wording of headers sounds like the hierarchy of menus and wording of menus that were held unprotected in *Lotus*. But the Federal Circuit took a different approach. *Oracle Am., Inc. v. Google Inc.*, 750 F.3d 1339 (Fed. Cir. 2014). Like the trial court in *Lotus*, it focused on whether there were other ways to accomplish the same function. In the court's view, there were: Google could have used a different taxonomy of methods and used different headers to have its own program to implement a programming language (although it would not have been compatible with Java). So the court held the Java headers were protected by copyright. The case eventually made it to the Supreme Court. But the Court did not decide whether the code was protected. Rather, it left the question open, deciding the case on the fair use issue, as we will discuss in a later chapter. Spoiler alert: *Google LLC v. Oracle America, Inc.*, 141 S. Ct. 1183 (2021)(holding that Google's use of Oracle's Java SE API packages in its Android operating system constituted fair use).
6. Infringement: Mino copied not just the functional elements of how the game worked but also its aesthetic elements. There "was no necessity for Mino to mimic Tetris's expression other than to avoid the difficult task of developing its own take on a known idea." *Tetris Holding, LLC v. Xio Interactive, Inc.*, 863 F. Supp. 2d 394 (D.N.J. 2012).

Useful Articles

One class of works has a specific test of functionality. If a "pictorial, graphic, or sculptural work" is a "useful article," it is protectable only if its aesthetic features are separable from its utilitarian aspects. In the words of the statute:

> the design of a useful article, as defined in this section, shall be considered a pictorial, graphic, or sculptural work only if, and only to the extent that, such design incorporates pictorial, graphic, or sculptural features that can be identified separately from, and are capable of existing independently of, the utilitarian aspects of the article.

17 U.S.C. §101.

This "separability" rule applies only to a "useful article," a narrow category: "an article having an intrinsic utilitarian function that is not merely to portray the appearance of the article or to convey information." A hammer, chair, or door would be useful articles. Each may "portray" its own appearance, and each may provide information (a door, for example, shows people that there is a way to get out of the room), but each serves other utilitarian purposes (banging nails, sitting, going through walls). By contrast, maps, computer programs, and clocks are all useful things but are not "useful articles." The utilitarian purpose of each is to provide information. A painting is not a "useful article," because its purpose is to portray its own appearance. Whether the work is a useful article can be important because the separability rule has been interpreted differently than the general exclusion of functionality from copyright. Computer programs, for example, raise issues of functionality, but are not useful articles.

Sometimes it is easy to determine whether something is a "useful article." The Copyright Office regulations give several clear examples: "automobiles, boats, household appliances, furniture, work tools, garments, and the like." Compendium II: Copyright Office Practices 503.03(a). There are borderline cases. One case held that a toy airplane is not a useful article because it serves to play the role of an airplane in child's play, which is intrinsically linked to its appearance. *See Gay Toys v. Buddy L. Corp.*, 703 F.2d 970 (6th Cir. 1983). The counterargument would be that the toy plays a purely functional role: something to play with.

Clothing would usually be a useful article. Even if it serves to portray its own appearance, it also serves the purely utilitarian functions of clothing (clothing the person wearing it, keeping them warm). Some clothing, however, might not go beyond portraying its appearance. A costume worn over other clothing might serve only to portray its own appearance.

Clothing design, then, is copyrightable only if its aesthetic elements are separable from its function. Generally, this bars copyright for clothing designs. A change in the design for aesthetic reasons (changing the hemline, narrowing the shoulders, making the pants wider) will affect the way the work functions as clothing. Function and form are generally so intertwined that copyright protection is negligible. As a result, copyright gives fashion designers little protection against copying (as long as the copier does not infringe the relevant *trademark*, as opposed to copyright). Knock-off designs are freely sold. Some have proposed changes in the copyright statute to give special protection for fashion designs. Others argue that the lack of legal protection has made the field more dynamic, because designers must rely on constant change and on building a reputation as a market advantage. For useful articles, there is protection only if it has aesthetic features that are "separable" from its utilitarian aspects, but separability can be understood several different ways. Courts have used several approaches to define separability.

Some courts require physical separability. Under this approach, a creative lamp design is not protectable because the shape of the lamp is not physically separate from its functional aspect. *See Esquire, Inc. v. Ringer*, 591 F.2d 796, 807 (D.C. Cir. 1978). The physical separability approach is the most difficult one for the author to meet because it requires that the work contain separable physical elements. A hood ornament, to use a classic example, might be protected, because it could be broken off the car. The rest of the car's design, however, would be nonprotected, no matter how fanciful and nonutilitarian it seemed. Under the physical separability approach, then, most useful articles will be held noncopyrightable. The requirement of physical separability is a plausible reading of the statute, which requires that the aesthetic features be "separable" for protection. But courts have sought a less demanding approach for two reasons. First, the test seems too demanding, barring protection for many works that have both functional and creative aspects. Second, it arguably is inconsistent with the landmark *Mazer* Supreme Court case, which held that a lamp base consisting of an angel statuette was protectable. The lamp base was likely not physically separable, because the lamp would have fallen down without it, but as a sculpture of an angel, it clearly had creative aspects that should be protected by copyright.

To avoid the high demands of physical separability, most courts now require "conceptual" separability. This can be understood several ways. There may be conceptual separability if the article has a useful function but is also shown to be appreciated for its aesthetic appeal. A belt buckle design could have separability if the buckles produced from it served to buckle belts but also were displayed as artworks in a museum, sold to art collectors, or featured in design magazines. *See Kieselstein-Cord v. Accessories by Pearl*, 632 F.2d 989 (2d Cir. 1980). Another approach is to ask whether an individual thinks of the aesthetic aspects of the work as being separate from its functional aspects. Yet another approach considers the design process: There is separability only if the designer is able to make aesthetic choices that are unaffected by functional considerations. A serpentine bicycle rack design is unprotected because every change in the shape made for aesthetic purposes affects the function of the bike rack. *See Brandir International v. Cascade Pacific Lumber*, 834 F.2d 1142 (2d Cir. 1985).

The conceptual approach seems to have been adopted by the Supreme Court. Is the header to a Java application programming interface similar to a cheerleading uniform? In *Star Athletica, L.L.C. v. Varsity Brands, Inc.*, 137 S. Ct. 1002 (2017), the Supreme Court increased the copyright protection for functional works, holding that cheerleader uniform designs were not precluded from protection as functional. The Court upheld copyright in the design of cheerleader uniforms, which consisted primarily of "combinations, positionings, and arrangements of elements" that include "chevrons. . ., lines, curves, stripes, angles, diagonals, inverted [chevrons], coloring, and shapes." *Varsity Brands* replaced a number of vague tests formulated by courts over the years with a single, if elusive, test: "In sum, a feature of the design of a useful article is eligible for copyright if, when identified and imagined apart from the useful article, it would qualify as a pictorial, graphic, or sculptural work either on its own or when fixed in some other tangible medium."

> Applying this test to the surface decorations on the cheerleading uniforms is straightforward. First, one can identify the decorations as features having pictorial, graphic, or sculptural qualities. Second, if the arrangement of colors, shapes, stripes, and chevrons on the surface of the cheerleading uniforms were separated from the uniform and applied in another medium — for example, on a painter's canvas — they would qualify as "two-dimensional . . . works of . . . art," §101. And imaginatively removing the surface decorations from the uniforms and applying them in another medium would not replicate the uniform itself. Indeed, respondents have applied the designs in this case to other media of expression — different types of clothing — without replicating the uniform. See App. 273-279. The decorations are therefore separable from the uniforms and eligible for copyright protection.

The direct effect is more protection for fashion design, until now ripe for knockoffs. A federal appellate court has applied the case to give copyright protection to sculptural aspects of a banana costume. *See Silvertop Assoc., Inc. v. Kangaroo Mfg. Inc.*, 931 F.3d 215 (3d Cir. 2019) ("Those sculptural features include the banana's combination of colors, lines, shape, and length. They do not include the cutout holes for the wearer's arms, legs, and face; the holes' dimensions; or the holes' locations on the costume, because those features are utilitarian."). *Star Athletica* could also be read broadly, to lead to more protection for other functional works, like computer programs.

To summarize the useful article analysis: The first question is whether the work is a useful article under the statutory definition. If it is a useful article, the next question is whether it has "pictorial, graphic, or sculptural features that can be identified separately from, and are capable of existing independently of, the utilitarian aspects." If it does have such separable aesthetic elements, it may be copyrightable. Otherwise, it is not. If the item does not fall within the definition of useful article, then it still must have original, creative elements to be protected, and its functional aspects will not be protected. A map, for example, is not a useful article. But whether a particular program is protectable depends on analyzing its elements to determine whether it has the necessary original, creative expression to qualify for protection.

The Copyright Office's regulations on the copyrightability of costume designs illustrate the analysis well, giving an example of the major variations on the theme:

> The examining practices with respect to masks will not treat masks as useful articles, but will instead determine registrability on the existence of minimum pictorial and/or sculptural authorship. Garment designs (excluding separately identifiable pictorial representations of designs imposed upon the garment) will not be registered even if they contain ornamental features, or are intended to be used as historical or period dress. Fanciful costumes will be treated as useful articles, and will be registered only upon a finding of separately identifiable pictorial and/or sculptural authorship.

Copyright Office, Library of Congress, Registrability of Costume Designs, 56 FR 56530 (1991). Under this view, masks are not useful articles, because they serve only to portray their own appearance. Garments are useful articles (worn to clothe the person), so they are subject to the separability rule—and generally will not have separable elements because each part of the garment usually plays a functional role. Fanciful costumes (like a Wookie costume) are also useful articles, subject to the separability analysis, but they will sometimes pass the separability test because they may have separable pictorial or sculptural elements.

Examples

1. *Useful articles?* Only "useful articles" are subject to the separability requirement to qualify for copyright protection. Which of the following are useful articles? Of those, which meet the separability requirement?
   a. Swiss Army knife
   b. Instruction manual for a car
   c. A human dummy used in anatomy classes
   d. A radiator cover with an ornate design
   e. A car engine
   f. Design of an automobile body

2. *Mannequin.* Pad designs a human torso form, which is used to display clothing. In designing the form, Pad attempts to make it both realistic-looking and well suited for draping clothing. The form works very well, and a number of stores and clothing designers seek to buy from Pad. Another designer, Sad, copies Pad's form exactly and offers a similar form at a lower price. Has Sad copied protected expression?

3. *Man again.* Tad creates a sculpture of a human torso. Tad's sculpture is quite realistic, capturing a form that is both lifelike and aesthetically appealing. Is the sculpture protected expression?

Explanations

1. A useful article is "an article having an intrinsic utilitarian function that is not merely to portray the appearance of the article or to convey information."
   a. The Swiss Army knife is a useful article. It has numerous utilitarian functions (cutting, opening bottles, unscrewing screws, opening cans) and does not merely portray its own appearance or convey information.
   b. A car's instruction manual is useful, but it is not a "useful article." It has a utilitarian purpose, but that is to convey information.

c. A human dummy designed for use in anatomy classes is not a useful article. It serves both to portray its own appearance and to convey information.
d. The radiator cover is a useful article. It is ornamental but does not serve to "merely" portray its own appearance. Rather, it has other, utilitarian functions (hiding the radiator and preventing burns).
e. A car engine is a useful article. It satisfies the statutory definition.
f. A car body is a useful article. Like the radiator cover, it has both aesthetic and utilitarian functions.

Of the useful articles, the designs of the Swiss Army knife and the car engine are very likely unprotected, because they lack utilitarian aspects separable from their aesthetic features. Whether the designs of the automobile body and radiator cover are protected depends on which test of separability the court employs. Both designs lack physical separability. The automobile body might also lack conceptual separability under the design process test, because any change in the design would affect the functional aspects—changing the shape, for example, would affect the aerodynamics. But if the broader approach were used, the aesthetic aspects would be shown by displays in museums and in magazines. The radiator cover likely passes all the conceptual separability tests. The variation in design does not affect its function. It also has aesthetic features that make one appreciate it separately as an artwork.

2. The torso form is a useful article. It has a utilitarian function (to drape clothes) and does not serve to convey information. Accordingly, it is protected only if its aesthetic features are separable from its utilitarian aspects. The design lacks physical separability, so a court using that test would hold it unprotected. Because its design is geared solely toward its utilitarian role, it probably also lacks conceptual separability. Under the design process test, none of the design choices are free of functional considerations. Even under the broader approaches, separability is lacking. The aesthetic features still are linked to the utilitarian aspects. There is no suggestion that it can be appreciated simply as a work of sculpture. *Cf. Carol Barnhart, Inc. v. Economy Cover Corp.*, 773 F.2d 411 (2d Cir. 1985). The result would be different if the mannequin also had purely expressive features, not affected by its functional role, such as sculptural elements designed to give it a "hungry look." *See Pivot Point Int'l, Inc. v. Charlene Prods.*, 372 F.3d 913, 931 (7th Cir. 2004).

3. Tad's sculpture of a human torso is probably protected. It is not a "useful article." As a sculpture, it has no utilitarian function. Therefore, it is not subject to the separability test. Rather, whether it is functional would be determined by the general functionality analysis (which varies from court to court, as discussed above). Under any approach, however, a pure sculpture likely is not functional.

INFRINGING WORKS

Infringing works are barred copyright. Sylvester Stallone wrote and starred in three movies about a plucky boxer, Rocky Balboa. Anderson wrote a 31-page treatment for a proposed *Rocky IV* and met with Stallone's movie company, but no deal developed. Later, Anderson claimed copyright infringement, alleging that Stallone used the treatment in making *Rocky IV*. But Anderson's treatment infringed, as an unauthorized derivative work of the Rocky movies. Anderson could not sue Stallone for copyright infringement, because Anderson had no copyright to infringe. *Anderson v. Stallone*, 1989 U.S. Dist. LEXIS 11109 (C.D. Cal. Apr. 25, 1989).

Copyright does not protect material created by infringing another copyright. Under 17 U.S.C. §103(a), "protection for a work employing preexisting material in which copyright subsists does not extend to any part of the work in which such material has been used unlawfully." In part, this rule reinforces the originality requirement. If Author's novel includes a chapter lifted word for word from another novel, Author has no copyright protection in that chapter because it was not original with her.

The rule is broader than simply barring copyright to the copied material. The rule bars copyright for "any part" of a work in which infringing material is used. It bars copyright for original expression that was created by unlawful use of other works. Suppose Author takes another's short story and expands it into a novel. If Author copies only the unprotected ideas, of course, there is no infringement. But if Author copies protected expression, there is no protection for any part that used material from the short story.

A copyright holder effectively controls the market for copies of the work and for derivative works (such as sequels, translations, movies made from novels). For example, in *Palladium Music v. EatSleepMusic*, 398 F.3d 1193, 1197 (10th Cir. 2005), a maker of recordings for karaoke music did not obtain permission to use the underlying musical works. Because the musical work was used in every part of the karaoke recording, the karaoke maker had no copyright in the sound recordings.

This is different from patent law, where anyone may seek a patent on an improvement on a patented invention. The second inventor may not be able to practice the improvement without infringing, but the first inventor likewise cannot practice the invention without infringing the improvement patent. In copyright, one who builds on an existing work has no copyright in the parts using infringing material, meaning the first author can use those parts without infringing.

What constitutes a "part" of a work remains an open question. For example, every chapter of a book might make unauthorized use of material from another copyrighted book. A court could reason that because each chapter makes unlawful use of material, each chapter is not protected, making the entire work unprotected even if Author adds much original expressive material. Likewise, if Author instead makes a film closely based on the story, a court could deny copyright to the entire film. Another approach is for the court to separate out portions that do not use protected material and to hold those portions to be copyrightable.

Examples

1. *While my guitar gently weeps.* The musician sometimes known as Prince often refers to himself with an elaborate, unpronounceable, copyrighted symbol of his own devising. He gives permission to various entities to use the symbol on T-shirts and other products. Without Prince's permission, an instrument maker fashions a guitar in the shape of the symbol and shows it to Prince. Soon, Prince appears in concert with a similar guitar. Is Prince liable for copyright infringement?

2. *Payback Day?* The makers of the film *Groundhog Day* used ideas copied without permission from the novel *One Fine Day*. That does not constitute copyright infringement because ideas are not protected by copyright. The writer of *One Fine Day* obtains a copy of *Groundhog Day* and starts making copies and selling them to the public. The writer argues that *Groundhog Day* is itself not protected by copyright because the complete film is based on ideas taken without permission from another work. Is *Groundhog Day* unprotected by copyright?

3. *Free for all?* Andre writes a novel, *My Birthday*. Bootles unscrupulously copies in wholesale fashion from *My Birthday* in writing his novel, *Bad Dog Day*. Every part of *Bad Dog Day* makes ample use of original creative expression from *My Birthday*. Clever then makes and sells copies of *Bad Dog Day* without permission from Andre or from Bootles. Clever contends that her actions are not copyright infringement. *Bad Dog Day* is unprotected by copyright because it copies so much from *My Birthday*. Accordingly, Clever argues, it is not infringement to copy or sell copies of *Bad Dog Day*. Has Clever copied protected expression—and if so, whose?

4. *Partial protection.* Dorrie publishes *Yippie*, a social history of the 1960s. Critics quickly point out that every chapter of the book contains paragraphs lifted verbatim from *Hippie*, a copyrighted book published several years back. The rest of the book is evidently Dorrie's original work. Dorrie's publishers retract the book, then republish a redacted version with all of the copied material removed. Zippy Press scans the book and starts printing and selling copies, arguing that there is no copyright in *Yippie* because it was an infringing work. Is Zippy right?

Explanations

1. Prince is not liable for infringement. The guitar design was based on the copyrighted symbol. Assuming it was infringement to copy the symbol, then there is no copyright in any part of the guitar design using the symbol. Assuming the entire design depended on the symbol, because it set the shape of the guitar, then the entire design of the guitar would be noncopyrightable. There would be no infringement for copying it. *See Pickett v. Prince*, 207 F.3d 402, 406 (7th Cir. 2000). Note also that some elements of a guitar's design would be functional and therefore noncopyrightable.

2. *Groundhog Day* is protected by copyright. The bar to copyright for works making unauthorized use of preexisting material applies only to "unlawful" use of such material. Copying of ideas is not unlawful. To the contrary, the nonprotection of ideas is intended to encourage the copying of ideas by authors. Copyright encourages the free flow of ideas by providing enough protection for the creation of works but not so much protection to discourage the free use of ideas.

3. Clever has copied protected expression—from *My Birthday*. Every part of *Bad Dog Day* makes unlawful use of infringing material copied from *My Birthday*, so *Bad Dog Day* is denied copyright entirely. Copying *Bad Dog Day* does not infringe any copyright in *Bad Dog Day*, but anyone who makes literal copies of *Bad Dog Day* does copy protected expression from *My Birthday* (because that expression had been copied into *Bad Dog Day*). Therefore, such a copier infringes the copyright in *My Birthday*. The fact that *Bad Dog Day* is not protected by copyright does not effectively put *My Birthday* into the public domain.

4. *Yippie* infringed the copyright in *Hippie*. Therefore, there is no copyright in "any part" of *Yippie* that used infringing material. This example raises the question: What is a "part" of a work? Each chapter contained paragraphs copied from *Hippie* but also many separate, original paragraphs. If a chapter is a "part" of a book, then one could conclude that each chapter is unprotected. If each paragraph is a separate "part," then only the infringing paragraphs are denied copyright.

   There is little case law on this issue. It would seem that one could best define "part" by looking at how the material was used. Perhaps copyright should be barred for all elements that depended on use of infringing material. Here, that would lead to the conclusion that the original paragraphs would be protected by copyright.

GOVERNMENT WORKS

The Copyright Act is not copyrighted. Copyright protection "is not available for any work of the United States Government." 17 U.S.C. §105. The statute defines a "work of the United States Government" as "a work prepared by an officer or employee of the United States Government as part of that person's official duties." 17 U.S.C. §101. This rule denies copyright to thousands of works produced by federal employees: court opinions, federal laws and regulations, administrative reports, official photographs, and much more. NASA, for example, produces many wonderful noncopyrighted photographs and videos.

The rule does not bar copyright if the author is an independent contractor, as opposed to a federal employee. Therefore, a photographer hired for a particular event would take copyrighted photographs. The bar also does not apply to work by federal employees that is not part of their official duties. Therefore, a senator's diary or the personal photos taken by a soldier are copyrighted. Moreover, the provision authorizes the federal government to acquire ownership of copyrights—even if the government funded and directed the work and required transfer of copyright as part of the contract. *See Schnapper v. Foley*, 667 F.2d 102 (D.C. Cir. 1981).

Several policies support the rule against copyright in U.S. government works. Copyright gives the copyright holder exclusive rights to copy, distribute, adapt, perform, and display the work. People need access to government works for many reasons: to obey the law, to participate in government programs, and so on. To permit the government to limit access to some official works would run contrary to the principles of due process. Moreover, copyright in government works would create a potential for censorship. Finally, the purpose of copyright is to provide an incentive to produce works. If the government is funding and directing the work, however, the incentive rationale has less force.

The statute by its term applies only to works of the federal government. The United States has three sets of sovereigns: the federal government, the states, and Indian tribes. Relying on the due process rationale, courts have extended the rule to other legal documents, such as state or tribal statutes and judicial opinions, that create legal obligations. Less settled is whether the rule applies to other government-produced documents, such as the reports of state or tribal administrative agencies, and governmental maps. In deciding whether copyright applies, courts can look to the basic purposes behind the bar: the notice required by due process of law, the incentive provided by copyright to create works, and issues of free speech.

The Copyright Office has taken the position that

> [e]dicts of government, such as judicial opinions, administrative rulings, legislative enactments, public ordinances, and similar official legal documents,

> are not copyrightable for reasons of public policy. This applies to such works whether they are Federal, State, or local as well as to those of foreign governments.

Compendium II: Copyright Office Practices 305.08(d).

The Supreme Court has held that, under the edicts of government doctrine, legislative annotations to state statutes are not protected by copyright:

> We have previously applied that doctrine to hold that non-binding, explanatory legal materials are not copyrightable when created by judges who possess the authority to make and interpret the law. See Banks v. Manchester, 128 U.S. 244, 9 S.Ct. 36, 32 L.Ed. 425 (1888). We now recognize that the same logic applies to non-binding, explanatory legal materials created by a legislative body vested with the authority to make law. Because Georgia's annotations are authored by an arm of the legislature in the course of its legislative duties, the government edicts doctrine puts them outside the reach of copyright protection.

Georgia v. Public.Resource.Org, Inc., 140 S. Ct. 1498, 1504 (2020).

Another issue arises when a work created by a private party becomes part of the law. For example, a private party could draft an ordinance that is adopted by a municipality. If Citizen made a copy of the ordinance, she would also be making a copy of the private party's draft code. Authority is split on whether adoption of the code by a government puts the text into the public domain. As discussed earlier, the Fifth Circuit held that when a model code was enacted into law, it became unprotected by copyright under the merger doctrine. *See Veeck v. Southern Bldg. Code Congress*, 293 F.3d 791 (5th Cir. 2002) (en banc). One could reach the same result by applying the rule of noncopyrightability of official governmental works. Alternately, the private works could remain under copyright but subject to considerable copying under the idea-expression rule and the fair use doctrine. *Am. Soc'y for Testing & Materials, et al. v. Public.Resource.Org, Inc.*, 896 F.3d 437, 441 (D.C. Cir. 2018) addressed technical standards, authored by private organizations, which have been incorporated into law. The court held that it could be fair use to post such standards online; the court did not decide "the far thornier question of whether standards retain their copyright after they are incorporated by reference into law."

Examples

1. *Entitled to my opinion.* Handy, a federal judge, writes a draft of a blistering dissent in the case of *Soda v. Pop.* The draft sets forth Handy's unorthodox views on the doctrine of equivalents, interspersed with ad hominem attacks on the other judges on the panel. After reconsideration, Handy decides not to submit the opinion but simply to join in the majority

opinion. She thinks she has destroyed every copy of the draft. Much to her dismay, she learns that the *National Jaw Journal* has obtained a copy and plans to publish it. She seeks to prevent publication, claiming the copyright in the opinion. A draft opinion that was never submitted, she argues, does not have the force of law and therefore should not be treated as a government work. Is the draft opinion copyrighted?

2. *Article of impeachment*. Dandy, another federal judge, drafts an article about ceramics. The article has nothing to do with Dandy's duties but is written for purely personal purposes. The article argues that ceramics have played a hitherto unappreciated role in historical developments. The article is based more on Dandy's imagination than on historical research. Is the article a nonprotected U.S. government work? Would it make a difference if the article were actually written by Dandy's law clerk, acting on Dandy's orders, working in his office during normal office hours?

3. *Brief encounter*. Advo submits an amicus brief in the case of *Soda v. Pop*. Advo, a beverage lawyer, is deeply interested in the issues raised by the case and submits the brief to suggest to the court a resolution that balances various competing policies. Months later, Advo is surprised to see her brief reprinted in *Vending Machine Law Journal*. The editors of the journal tell Advo that they did not ask her permission for publication because a brief submitted in a federal case is a U.S. government work, unprotected by copyright. Did Advo produce an uncopyrighted work?

4. *Animal farm*. The U.S. Department of Agriculture decides to make an entertaining documentary about methane as an alternative energy source, intended for instructional use in high schools. It has a number of employees in its film production department, but they are all booked on other projects. The department pays an independent contractor a lump sum to write and produce the film, leaving all the creative and production details up to the contractor. The contract stipulates that the copyright in the film belongs to the U.S. government. The film is completed, and copies are distributed to a number of teachers. Gadfly, an activist, obtains a copy, and then makes and sells copies. Gadfly argues that the film is not protected by copyright because it is really a product of the federal government. Otherwise, Gadfly contends, the U.S. government could engage in the sort of limits on distribution of publicly financed works that the statute seeks to prevent. Is the film a U.S. government work?

5. *Slowpoke County maps*. Slowpoke County prepares "info maps" that provide lots of information about Slowpoke County. Slowpoke prepares the maps by having employees sift through information from the county's public real estate and other records, as well as various sources of data in the local public library and online. The maps provide much information

about Slowpoke's economic and social makeup. Reading the map gives its viewer an overall picture of the businesses, schools, residences, farms, and other community-related organizations that make up the county. Slowpoke makes the maps to promote the county. Slowpoke sells the maps for a modest price to real estate agents, investors, tourists, historians, and various others interested in such data. Slowpoke's revenue from the maps almost exactly matches its costs. Indeed, without the revenue, Slowpoke's council well might not authorize the activity. Floyd, the local barber, makes a copy of one of the maps and begins selling them to Slowpoke's usual buyers for half the price. Floyd argues that Slowpoke cannot claim a copyright in a government-produced work. Are the maps copyrightable?

6. *Copyright a patent?* Christopher invents an automatic macaroni-and-cheese maker. He drafts a patent application. The application has two principal parts: the written description, which artfully describes the device and how to make it, and the claims, which set the boundaries of his claimed rights. The U.S. Patent and Trademark Office allows the claims and issues a patent. The patent contains the written description and claims, which taken together define the scope of Christopher's rights.

   Andy, writing a book on patent law, considers including portions of Christopher's patent in a book on software law. A patent office regulation permits facsimile reproduction of the entire patent (37 1.71(e)), but that would take up too much space in Andy's book. Does Andy need Christopher's permission? Would it be different if Andy were writing a book about food technology?

7. *Monumental.* The U.S. government is holding a competition seeking a design for a monument to the space shuttle. Frank submits the winning design. In negotiations, Frank declines to assign the copyright to the government. He still gets the contract and builds the monument. Is it copyrighted?

Explanations

1. The draft opinion is not subject to copyright. Handy is a federal employee, so any work she creates as part of her official duties is a noncopyrightable work of the U.S. government. The statute does not differentiate between categories of work but applies across the board. Whether the draft is submitted, has legal effect, or ever sees the light of day is irrelevant. The only question is whether Handy prepared it as part of her official duties. Had she vented her feelings in a personal diary, the result would be different, but preparation of draft opinions is well within the scope of a judge's official duties.

2. The article is not a U.S. government work, which is work prepared by a federal officer or employee within the scope of that person's official duties. A federal judge's official duties include presiding over cases, drafting opinions, and participating in the administration of the courts. An article on ceramics written for purely personal purposes does not qualify because it is a personal project.

   If the law clerk drafts it, the article is a nonprotected U.S. government work. The law clerk is a federal employee, and her duties probably include following the orders of her boss, including drafting the article. From her point of view (unlike Dandy), the writing is not a personal work but is a part of her job.

3. Advo is not a federal employee, so her brief is not a U.S. government work. Nor is it denied protection under the judicial doctrine denying protection to official legal documents. The brief may set forth Advo's view of the law, but it does not authoritatively establish law, unlike a judicial opinion or legislative edict. By custom, lawyers have rarely enforced copyright in briefs or other documents that are made part of the public record—and the fair use doctrine (discussed in Chapter 5) authorizes some uses of such works.

4. The film is not a U.S. government work. It is a copyrighted work, with the copyright owned by the U.S. government. The statute, by its terms, applies only to works prepared by U.S. officials or employees. An independent contractor, who is neither an official nor an employee, prepared the film. The statute also specifically permits the United States to acquire ownership of copyrights. The statute contemplates that the United States will indeed have exclusive rights in some works, with the attendant ability to restrict their reproduction, distribution, and performance by others. Moreover, the work at issue does not raise the sort of censorship or due process issues that might arise if, for example, the United States commissioned contractors to prepare judicial opinions and then sought to restrict their distribution.

5. The maps probably would not be denied copyright, although they are government works. In deciding whether official legal documents should be noncopyrightable, courts look to whether individuals require access to the works to have knowledge of the law and to the incentive rationale behind copyright. The maps contain much information, but nobody requires access to the maps to comply with the law. The information is available in publicly accessible sources. In addition, the incentive rationale applies here. If not for the ability to raise revenue from the maps, Slowpoke might not produce them at all. Making such maps is not necessary for fulfillment of the county's basic governmental activities, so it is not an activity that would occur with or without copyright in the

maps. A court might also consider whether granting copyright creates a risk of government censorship. When the information is freely available elsewhere (if in a less handy form), censorship would not appear to be a risk.

6. The patent is a U.S. government work, so is not copyrighted, but it includes material from a preexisting work—Christopher's patent application. The question would be whether Andy would potentially infringe the copyright (if any) in Christopher's patent application. Presumably, the patent application would be copyrightable as an original work of authorship. It would contain many functional elements but would likely easily meet the low standard of creativity required. The issue is what effect it has when the application is then largely copied into a patent issued by the U.S. government, a document that has the legal effect of defining legal rights. There are several possible approaches a court might take.

   Merger. Under *Veeck*, a court might reason that, like a privately drafted code adopted into law, the text is now inseparable from the law (an idea) and therefore unprotected. But that seems to take the *Veeck* approach too far, to strip copyright from every document with legal effect.

   Official government work. A court might consider several policies: the notice required by due process of law, the incentive provided by copyright to create works, and issues of free speech. The court could reason that the public needs access to patents (to avoid infringement, etc.), that the patent right is plenty of incentive to draft patents, and that free discussion of patent rights requires they be uncopyrighted.

   Fair use. The best result would allow a balancing of interests. A court might hold that Christopher does not lose his copyright, but the patent text is subject to broad fair use (discussed later in the book), such as inclusion in a patent law text. One might argue that using the description in a technology book is not a fair use, because it does not depend on the legal nature of the patent but rather is simply using Christopher's description. But one factor in fair use (to jump ahead a little) is the nature of the work. Christopher drafted the application hoping his text would wind up in a U.S. patent, so he might have expected to be subject to use of the text by others. This case would differ from a case where a novel became evidence in a precedential case (defamation, copyright infringement). In that case, the relevant portions of the novel would be fair use for legal discussion, but the author would not lose her entire copyright.

   Estoppel. To throw in some more review: Just as one forfeits copyright protection by representing creative expression as facts, so too one might forfeit copyright by drafting something with the expectation that it be included in an official legal document. A party could implicitly consent to that by filing its application with the USPTO.

The USPTO allows an applicant to include a copyright notice, provided the applicant includes the following authorization:

> A portion of the disclosure of this patent document contains material which is subject to copyright protection. The copyright owner has no objection to the facsimile reproduction by anyone of the patent document or the patent disclosure, as it appears in the Patent and Trademark Office patent file or records, but otherwise reserves all copyright rights whatsoever.

7. The monument is copyrighted. It was created not by a federal employee but by an independent contractor. For the same reason (Frank is not an employee), the work made for hire doctrine does not apply. Frank owns the copyright. *See Gaylord v. United States*, 595 F.3d 1364 (Fed. Cir. 2010).

PART II

Ownership and Transactions

Chapter 7

Initial Ownership of Copyright

Copywriters may not get copyrights. If an advertising agency's employee writes copy or draws graphics for an ad campaign, the copyright in the work will belong to the employer agency, not the employee—unless the agency has agreed in writing that the copyright will belong to the employee (unlikely) or to the client who paid for it (quite likely). When several parties are involved in creating a work (whether paying for it, physically creating it, or contributing material), we may ask which one owns the copyright. If the parties have agreed in writing as to who will own the copyright, then it will be assigned however they agreed. Well-advised parties always do this, but in many cases, creative works are made without alerting lawyers. In the absence of agreement, copyright provides default rules that assign ownership.

Copyright subsists from the first time the work is fixed in tangible form. *See* 17 U.S.C. §302(a). The author initially owns the copyright. She may transfer any or all of her rights or grant licenses to allow others to exercise those rights. To determine ownership of a copyright (or of some of the exclusive rights of the copyright), one needs to determine two things: Who is the author or authors (and therefore the initial owner of the copyright), and has ownership of the copyright (or some of the rights of the copyright holder) been effectively transferred to someone else (and if so, was such transfer subsequently terminated pursuant to contract or a statutory right)? This chapter deals with the first of those questions: Who owns the copyright to begin with?

Suppose Writer writes a story. The copyright vests initially in the author or authors of the work. 17 U.S.C. §201(a). The general rule is that the actual creator of the work is the author. If, however, Writer is an employee creating a "work made for hire," her employer is deemed to be the author and owns the copyright. For example, if Writer is a reporter employed by a newspaper company, the newspaper company is the author of the stories written by Writer. Likewise, for some specially ordered or commissioned works, the parties may agree that the work is a work made for hire, with the hiring party deemed the author. By contrast, if Writer is an independent contractor and has not made a valid agreement that the work is a work made for hire, Writer is the author and initially owns the copyright. If a newspaper hires her as a freelancer to write a single story, Writer owns the copyright in the story.

If she is a joint author, she is a co-owner of the copyright. If the work is a collective work, then the various copyright holders retain the copyright to their respective contributions, and the author of the collective work has a copyright limited to reproducing the entire work and its revisions. If the freelancer's story is included in an edition of the newspaper, the newspaper owns the copyright in the collective work (the edition of the newspaper), but Writer retains her copyright in the story.

Note that all these rules matter only if there is not a contract assigning copyright ownership. These days, most employees sign contracts assigning to their employer copyright in their works. Ownership of copyright should likewise be specified in contracts with consultants, freelancers, architects, actors, software consultants, and joint venture partners. If the question is, Who owns the copyright?, the answer should be in the contract. If it is not, then we look to rules such as work-made-for-hire and joint author.

Ownership of the copyright has important consequences. Suppose Business hires Software Developer to write a program that performs the accounting, inventory, and other functions for the business. The parties say nothing in the contract about ownership of the copyright. The copyright owner has the exclusive rights to copy, adapt, distribute, publicly perform, and publicly display the work. If it is a work for hire, Business owns the copyright. If it is not a work for hire, Software Developer owns the copyright. Business would presumably get implicit permission to make copies or adapt the program for the purposes of the contract. But Software Developer, not the business, owns the exclusive rights to sell copies to any similar business, or adapt the program to other uses, and so on. If it is a joint work, they are co-owners of the copyright and both can exercise the exclusive rights.

The rules assigning ownership are only gap-filling rules. The parties can and should agree among themselves as to who will own the copyright. A party hiring an independent contractor can secure an assignment of the copyright in the contract. An employer can agree that an employee will own the copyright to works she creates. Joint authors can agree that the copyright in the work will belong to a single author or to a third party (such as a corporation formed by the joint authors). The ownership assignment rules come into play only if the parties have not effectively addressed the issue.

WHO IS THE AUTHOR?

17 U.S.C. §201. Ownership of copyright

(a) INITIAL OWNERSHIP.—Copyright in a work protected under this title vests initially in the author or authors of the work. The authors of a joint work are co-owners of copyright in the work.

(b) WORKS MADE FOR HIRE.—In the case of a work made for hire, the employer or other person for whom the work was prepared is considered the author for purposes of this title, and, unless the parties have expressly agreed otherwise in a written instrument signed by them, owns all of the rights comprised in the copyright.

(c) CONTRIBUTIONS TO COLLECTIVE WORKS.—Copyright in each separate contribution to a collective work is distinct from copyright in the collective work as a whole, and vests initially in the author of the contribution. In the absence of an express transfer of the copyright or of any rights under it, the owner of copyright in the collective work is presumed to have acquired only the privilege of reproducing and distributing the contribution as part of that particular collective work, any revision of that collective work, and any later collective work in the same series.

The copyright initially belongs to the author or authors of the work. When a work is created, one of the following situations will apply:

- *The author is an individual*: If the author is an individual, she initially owns the copyright.
- *The work is a work made for hire*: In this case, the hiring party owns the copyright. There are two types of works made for hire:
  1. works by employees within the scope of their employment
  2. certain specially ordered or commissioned works, where the parties expressly agree in writing that it is a work made for hire
- *The work is by joint authors*: The joint authors are co-owners, with equal, undivided interests in the copyright.
- *The work is a collective work*: The author of the collective work will have a thin copyright in the work as a whole, but authors of individual portions may retain their separate copyrights.

Typical disputes over ownership include disputes between a hiring party and a hired creator, disputes over whether the work was a work made for hire, and disputes between the primary author of a work and another who contributed to the work over whether the work was a joint work.

The ownership-assignment rules above are subject to transfers of the copyright. For example, if Scribbler has signed an agreement transferring copyright in her novels to Publisher, then Publisher will own the copyrights even though Scribbler is the author of the novels. The copyright will initially vest in Scribbler and then be transferred to Publisher.

Note that courts have held that an AI cannot be an author, for the purpose of copyright law. So an AI will not be an author if it alone creates the work, nor would it qualify as a joint author or create a work made for hire. At least for now, copyright is for human authors (although fictional persons like corporations may own copyrights by transfer, or be deemed authors by the work-made-for-hire doctrine).

Individual Works

The statute does not define "author." Usually, there is no question as to who could claim authorship. The person who creates the work is generally the author. If Poet pens an ode, Mime choreographs a pantomime, or Crooner doodles a ditty, each owns the respective copyright (assuming none is working as an employee). Where more than one person produces the work, a single person may nevertheless be deemed the author of the work even if he did not actually perform any of the hands-on labor in fixing the work. If more than one person claims to be the author, courts look to such factors as who initiated the work, who contributed original creative expression, who controlled the production of the work, whom the parties considered to be the author, and whom third parties recognized as the author. For example, the undersea filming of the wreck of the *Titanic* required the participation of many people who could man the surface ship and the submarine filming unit. But a single person could be the author if he did the following: directed the filming, specified the camera angles and shooting sequences, held daily planning sessions with the film crew to give them detailed instructions for filming, directed the crew's work from the surface, and screened the footage each day to see that it was satisfactory to him. *Lindsay v. The Wrecked and Abandoned Vessel* Titanic, 52 U.S.P.Q. 2d 1609 (S.D.N.Y. 1999).

The author need not be identified, because the statute contemplates anonymous and pseudonymous works. A nice example was the novel *Primary Colors*, written by "Anonymous." Whether one considered it an anonymous work (because the author was not named) or a pseudonymous work (under the name "Anonymous"), there was still a valid copyright, initially belonging to the author.

Example

1. *Image conscious.* Paparazzi, a self-employed photographer, lingers outside the entrance to Celebrity's apartment building. When Celebrity emerges, Paparazzi takes a photo of Celebrity walking by a garbage can. When Paparazzi seeks to license the photo to various tabloids, Celebrity claims copyright in the photo. Celebrity argues that the photo has value only because of her hard work in establishing her fame, and therefore the right to exploit that fame belongs to Celebrity. Who owns the copyright in the photo?

Explanation

1. Paparazzi owns the copyright in the photo. Celebrity may have done all the work to establish the public interest in Celebrity, but the copyrighted work at issue is simply the photograph, with its image of Celebrity. Paparazzi is clearly the author of the photo. In deciding authorship, courts consider such factors as who initiated the work, who contributes creative expression, who controls the creation of the work, who makes the creative decisions, and who third parties would consider the author. All of those factors weigh toward Paparazzi being the author. The photo also is not a joint work (discussed below), which requires that (1) each author contribute copyrightable expression and (2) each author intend to be a joint author when the work is created. Celebrity would not meet either of those requirements. Note that Paparazzi's copyright does not give unlimited rights to use the photo; it confers only the exclusive rights of a copyright owner. Certain commercial uses of the photo would make Paparazzi liable under trademark law or right of publicity law.

Works Made for Hire

Suppose a hired party creates a sculpture, dance, book, software program, movie. . . . The contract between the parties should spell out who owns the copyright. If not, we first ask if it is a work made for hire. The work-made-for-hire doctrine can be a real trap for the unwary. Just because a party pays for a work does not mean she owns the copyright (where the author is an independent contractor, as opposed to an employee). Similarly, an employee may not realize that she does not own the copyright in the very works she creates. Ideally, affected parties will agree among themselves as to who owns the copyright. If they do not, the statute assigns ownership.

If the work is a work made for hire, the employer is deemed to be the author and, unless the parties agree otherwise, owns the copyright.

According to 17 U.S.C. §101, two types of a work may qualify as a work made for hire: works by employees or certain specially commissioned works:

1. The work was prepared by an employee within the scope of her employment.
2. The work was specially ordered and commissioned, it falls into one of several specific categories, and the parties expressly agree in writing it is a work made for hire.

Works by Employees Within the Scope of Employment

The first category applies to many works vesting the copyright in the employer: manuals written by technical writers employed by a software company; advertisements (copy, visuals, and editing) created by employees of an advertising agency; a brief written by an associate at a law firm. The second category applies more narrowly because it requires a specific agreement and only applies to the specific categories. It applies when a newspaper agrees with a freelancer that a story constitutes a work made for hire or if a movie producer hires a freelance scriptwriter and the parties agree that the script is a work made for hire.

As in tax law and employment law, it is not always clear whether someone is an employee or an independent contractor. Courts had applied several different tests, such as the actual control test or the right to control test. The Supreme Court set forth the applicable test in *Community for Creative Non-Violence v. Reid*, 490 U.S. 730 (1989). In *CCNV*, a nonprofit organization hired a sculptor to create a sculpture of a homeless family. After the sculpture was complete, the parties disputed ownership of the copyright. The Supreme Court held that the classification of the hired party follows the common law of agency, looking to such factors as the following:

- the hiring party's right to control the manner and means by which the product is accomplished
- the source of the instrumentalities and tools
- the location of the work (such as the hiring party's place of business or the hired party's home)
- the duration of the relationship between the parties
- whether the hiring party has the right to assign additional projects to the hired party
- the extent of the hired party's discretion over when and how long to work
- the method of payment
- the hired party's role in hiring and paying assistants
- whether the work is part of the regular business of the hiring party

- whether the hiring party is in business
- the provision of employee benefits
- the tax treatment of the hired party

The *CCNV* court held that the work was not a work made for hire. CCNV did direct the work to some extent, suggesting that the family be portrayed reclining on a steam grate and ensuring in other ways that the sculpture met their specifications, but the other factors weighed heavily in favor of holding that the sculptor was an independent contractor and not an employee. Working as a sculptor is a "skilled occupation." He supplied his own tools and worked in his own studio without daily supervision by CCNV. The contract was for only two months. CCNV had no right to assign other tasks to him. He had complete freedom in deciding "when and how long to work." The contract price was payable upon completion of the job, a typical way to pay independent contractors, as opposed to a typical employee's salary. CCNV did not "pay payroll or social security taxes, provide any employee benefits, or contribute to unemployment insurance or workers' compensation funds."

CCNV is the touchstone when the issue is whether a work was created by an employee or by an independent contractor. Note that the factors are relatively concrete (such as asking where the work occurred and whether the hired party was listed as an employee for tax and other payroll purposes). The analysis does not turn on the more difficult questions of creative contributions to the work.

Not everything an employee creates is a work made for hire. If a police officer paints landscapes in her spare time, the copyright in her paintings will not belong to the police department. Rather, to be a work made for hire, the work must also be created within the scope of her employment. Courts also follow agency law here, considering several factors:

1. whether the work is of the type that the employee is employed to perform
2. whether the work occurs substantially within authorized work hours
3. whether its purpose, at least in part, is to serve the employer

A writer who writes an article at home outside office hours may nevertheless create a work for hire if he wrote on topics within his job description, coauthored and discussed the article with a fellow employee, and received reimbursement to present the paper at a symposium. *See Marshall v. Miles Laboratories*, 647 F. Supp. 1326, 1331 (N.D. Ind. 1986). Likewise, software may be a work made for hire, even though written by a chemist, if it performed functions within his general work responsibilities. *See Miller v. EP Chemicals*, 808 F. Supp. 1238 (D.S.C. 1992).

A somewhat different test applies if the work was under copyright before 1978. Under the 1909 Act, the test is whether the work was created "at the instance and expense" of the hiring party—which turns mainly on whether the hiring party motivated and financed the creation of the work. In *Twentieth Century Fox Film Corp. v. Entmt. Distrib.*, 429 F.3d 869 (9th Cir. 2005), the issue was whether *Crusader in Europe*, an account of World War II by then General and later President Dwight Eisenhower, was a work made for hire. The publisher had persuaded Eisenhower to write the book, had significant supervisory control over its writing, and paid him a lump sum (thereby taking the financial risk of the project). Those factors led the court to conclude that the book had been written "at the instance and expense" of the publisher and was therefore a work made for hire.

To repeat the point: parties are well advised to agree between themselves who owns the copyright, not leave it to the default rules. For example, universities (especially research-heavy institutions like Duke, Michigan, and Carnegie Mellon) often set policies about ownership of copyright in materials. This is clearer than trying to figure out whether academic articles, online classes, graduate student papers, self-driving car software built in a university lab, and so on are works made for hire by employees within the scope of their employment.

Examples

1. *Go-getter*. Snaps has been a full-time employee of Tabloid for many years. Snaps's job is to take pictures of celebrities. Tabloid pays Snaps a regular paycheck (subject to withholding all relevant employee taxes, such as Social Security and income taxes) and offers participation in the company employee retirement plan. Tabloid assigns Snaps to photograph specified celebrities and also instructs Snaps to photograph celebrities if the opportunity arises by chance during another assignment. Tabloid also provides considerable support, including equipment, reimbursement of expenses, and help with logistics. Snaps discusses various matters with editors in general terms but has great discretion in fulfilling his duties. Snaps's work hours are largely set by Tabloid, although Snaps sometimes fits in jobs before or after the assigned hours. Snaps has signed a multiyear employment contract, which does not contain a clause assigning copyright in Snaps's photos to Tabloid. One photo target is Celebrity. Snaps, using considerable creativity, captures a great photo of Celebrity pushing aside a nonentity to get a taxicab. Who owns the copyright in the photo?

2. *Multitasker*. Tabloid requires Snaps to spend Monday mornings in his office at Tabloid to be available for meeting with editors. While sitting at his desk, Snaps borrows a pad of paper from a secretary and writes a short

story about an adventurous celebrity photographer. Snaps writes the story purely for personal purposes, hoping vaguely to use it one day in a book. Just after finishing the story, Snaps learns that Laura Lawyer, a famous defense attorney, is having lunch in a nearby park. Snaps hurries off, camera in hand, and leaves his new manuscript sitting on the desk. An editor picks it up and decides to publish it in Tabloid's *Sunday Magazine*. Snaps learns of this and demands an extra bonus. Who owns the copyright in the story?

3. *Opportunity knocks*. Snaps leaves his camera gear in the office one Monday while he goes for a stroll. Suddenly, he notices that Wobbly Allen, a reclusive filmmaker, is ambling toward him, hiding behind big sunglasses and a sombrero. Snaps grabs a camera out of the hands of Terry Tourist and quickly takes six pictures of Allen. Tourist then grabs back the camera and vanishes. Snaps learns that Tourist is peddling the photos to other tabloids. Tourist argues that because the photo was made with Tourist's camera, the copyright belongs to Tourist. Who owns the copyright in the photos?

4. *The new guys*. Foodko hires two eager employees to work in its meat packing area. They sign detailed employment contracts, are put on the payroll, and are subject to supervision by various bosses. The employees are actually television producers, full-time employees of Network, making an undercover investigation of food industry practices. The two producers covertly videotape their workplace, recording various unsavory and unsafe things done with meat intended for consumers. To suppress the making and distribution of the video, Foodko claims that Foodko owns the copyright because it was made by Foodko employees while working at their jobs in the meat packing area. Who owns the copyright in the video?

5. *The occasionals*. Two photographers work sporadically on the set of the *Harpoon* television talk show. The producers hire them for a few days a month to capture still photographs of the lively program. When not working at the *Harpoon* show, the photographers take other freelance assignments. The *Harpoon* producers pay them cash and do not treat them as employees for payroll, tax, benefits, or other purposes. The producers set up the set, select guests, and largely control the proceedings. The producers do not pay any attention to the photographers and do not consider the photographers when making various choices about how to stage the show. The photographers decide when and how to take photos, under no supervision by the producers (other than to stay out of the way). Who owns the copyright in the photographs?

6. *Informality*. A software developer takes on various projects for a start-up company. He works under the supervision and direction of the company,

takes on additional tasks when assigned, and regards himself as an employee in his dealings with the company. But he is relatively independent. He works at home, not at the office. He sets his own hours and working conditions. He does not receive a salary but is paid in stock. The company does not list him as an employee for tax purposes or employee benefits. Is the software he writes a work made for hire?

7. *Terms of employment.* Stallman does occasional freelance consulting for Softco. The terms of their contract provide that Softco owns copyright in all the code Stallman writes for each project. But Stallman later contends he owns the copyright. He was an independent contractor working sporadically; hired and paid for specific projects; completely in control of how, when, and where he worked; and not listed as an employee for taxes or any other purpose. The contracts even listed him as Stallman Contracting. Who owns the copyright?

Explanations

1. The copyright in the photo belongs to Tabloid. A work is a work made for hire if it is made by an employee within the scope of his employment. Whether the hired party is an employee or is an independent contractor is governed by the factors listed in the text above. Almost every factor favors finding an employment relationship here. Snaps receives a regular paycheck; Tabloid withholds taxes consistent with an employment relationship; Tabloid provides Snaps employee benefits; Tabloid assigns jobs to Snaps and sets Snaps's hours; Tabloid also provides other support, such as reimbursing expenses and helping with logistics. The only factors at all tending toward a finding that Snaps is an independent contractor are that Snaps has considerable discretion in carrying out assignments and that he took the initiative in snapping the particular photo. But the weight of the other factors shows that Snaps is an employee, albeit one with some discretion.

   For the photo to be a work made for hire, it must also have been within the scope of the employee's employment. That is clearly met here; Snaps's job is to take pictures of celebrities, and here he did exactly that.

2. Snaps owns the copyright in the story. He is an employee, but the work is only made for hire if it is created within the scope of his employment—in this case, to take photos of celebrities. As the text above states, the relevant factors are
   a. whether the work is of the type that the employee is employed to perform
   b. whether the work occurs substantially within authorized work hours
   c. whether its purpose, at least in part, is to serve the employer

Here, only the second factor weighs in favor of its being within the scope of his employment—and very weakly so because he was simply biding time. Writing a story is well outside his job of taking pictures, and the purpose was purely personal, so the work is outside the scope of Snaps's employment and therefore not a work made for hire.

3. The copyright belongs to Tabloid. Snaps created the photo. Snaps made all the relevant creative decisions and controlled the production of the photo. He did make unauthorized use of Tourist's camera, but those are not relevant factors here. Snaps is an employee of Tabloid, working within the scope of his employment, so the copyright belongs to Tabloid.

   The foregoing applies only to the copyright. If Tabloid wishes to exploit its copyright, it may need access to the camera (or at least the card with the pictures). Personal property law would determine the ownership of the camera and card—and they presumably still belong to Tourist. So Tabloid owns the copyright, but Tourist owns the physical embodiment of the pictures. Neither can exploit their property without the other, which would encourage a mutual agreement.

4. Network owns the copyright. The producers were indeed employees of the food company—but the video was not made within the scope of their employment. It was made on Foodko premises on Foodko time, but the nature of their employment was far removed from making revelatory videos. The video was made by employees of Network within the scope of their employment. Network accordingly owns the copyright. *Cf. Food Lion v. Capital Cities/ABC*, 946 F. Supp. 420 (M.D.N.C. 1996).

5. The photographers own the copyrights in the photos. The photographers are not employees. Although they are paid by the producers, all the other factors weigh in favor of their being independent contractors rather than employees. They work only sporadically, are not paid out of the payroll, and are not treated as employees for purposes of benefits or other employment arrangements. The producers do control the set and proceedings of the show but do not exercise control over the making of the photographs.

   Producers might also argue that the photos are joint works. Arguably, the producers meet the first requirement, contribution of copyrightable expression. The producers control the staging of the set and the proceedings, so their creative decisions would contribute to the content of the photographs. But there must also be intent on the part of all parties to be joint authors, and that is not shown here. *Cf. Natkin v. Winfrey*, 111 F. Supp. 2d 1003 (N.D. Ill. 2000).

6. Courts are very leery when a company fails to treat a person as an employee for tax and other filing purposes and then claims the person

as an employee to claim ownership of copyright. *JustMed, Inc. v. Byce*, 600 F.3d 1118 (9th Cir. 2010) took a more practical approach. The court emphasized that the dispute arose in a small start-up company, where there is often insufficient attention to formalities. The substance of the relationship was an employment relationship, and so the software was a work made for hire. *JustMed* shows that courts approach the issue with flexibility. It also emphasizes the practical point: the company should have had a signed writing agreeing that it would own the copyright in the software. Then there would be no need to deal with the uncertainty of the work made for hire doctrine.

7. This example reminds us that the parties can (and generally should) assign ownership of the copyright by agreement. The copyright was not a work made for hire. The copyright vested initially in Stallman—and instantly transferred to Softco, per the agreement. Ownership of the copyright depends on the work-made-for-hire doctrine only when the parties have not already settled the matter.

Specially Made or Commissioned Works

Even works made by nonemployees may qualify as works made for hire. Usually, if an independent contractor creates the work, it is not a work made for hire, but the statute does permit the parties to effectively agree that some such works will be treated as works made for hire. A work will be a work made for hire if it:

a. is specially ordered or commissioned; *and*
b. falls into one of nine specific categories (a contribution to a collective work, a part of a motion picture or other audiovisual work, a translation, a supplementary work, a compilation, an instructional text, a test, answer material for a test, or an atlas); *and*
c. the parties sign an agreement designating it to be a work made for hire.

If Publisher commissions Scholar to make a translation of a book, the parties can effectively agree that the translation will be a work made for hire. Publisher will therefore be the author and own the copyright.

Mere assignment of ownership is not the reason for the rule. The parties can always agree to a transfer of ownership of the copyright, so Publisher and Scholar could simply have agreed that Publisher would own the copyright. Likewise, for works that do not fall within the specific categories, the parties can still agree that the hiring party will own the copyright. Indeed, if they agree that it is a work made for hire, a court may simply treat that as an assignment of ownership.

But work made for hire status has other effects (discussed later in the book): the duration of copyright is different; for works of visual art, there are no moral rights under 17 U.S.C. §106A; and there are no rights of termination of transfers. The latter is of particular importance, because termination rights are not subject to change by agreement of the parties. When Scholar agrees that the translation will be a work made for hire, Scholar effectively gives up any rights to terminate the transfer. Likewise, if the screenwriter, soundtrack composer, and director of a film all agree that their contributions will be works made for hire, they will have no rights to terminate the transfers.

Example

1. *Stipulation.* Shudderbug has long worked as a freelance fashion photographer. Tabloid contacts Shudderbug, offering to hire her to take some photos of Designer to accompany a tell-all interview to be published in *Tabloid*. The parties agree that Shudderbug will receive $3,000 to spend the morning taking photos of Designer at Shudderbug's studio. They also agree in writing that the photos will be works made for hire. Shudderbug has never worked for Tabloid before. After seeing how well the photos come out, Shudderbug wants to be the author. Shudderbug argues that the photos cannot be works made for hire because Shudderbug was never an employee. Are the photos works made for hire? Would it make a difference if Designer had simply commissioned the photos to hang in Designer's living room with a similar agreement that the photos will be works made for hire?

Explanation

1. The photos are works made for hire. They do not fall into the first category of works made for hire (works by employees within the scope of employment), but some parties may effectively stipulate that a work is made for hire. The work must be specially commissioned or ordered, fall into one of the specified categories, and be subject to a written agreement that it will be a work made for hire. All three requirements are met here. Tabloid specially commissioned the work. The work falls within one of the categories: a contribution to a collective work (as a photo to be included in an edition of *Tabloid*). The parties signed the requisite agreement.

   It would not be a work made for hire if it had been commissioned by Designer to hang on the wall. Even though the first and third requirements would have been met (specially commissioned and subject to a signed stipulation), the photo would not fall into any of the nine specific categories. It would not be a work made for hire. A court, however, might construe the agreement as transferring ownership of the copyright to Designer.

Implied License, Where Contract Does Not Address Copyright

Family business hires software consultant to write some software to handle accounting and inventory tracking. The contract between the parties does not address the question of who will own the copyright in the software. The consultant finishes the job, installs the software, and takes the agreed fee. The consultant is not an employee (the business does not pay her a salary, supervise her work, or treat her as an employee for tax or benefits). The software is not a work made for hire. The software consultant is the author and owns the copyright—including the exclusive right to make copies and adapt the work. Does that mean that the business now needs permission to use the software (which would involve making copies) or adapt it (which could involve preparing a derivative work)?

Courts hold that if a party is hired to create a work and the parties do not address the copyright issue in the contract, there will be an implied, nonexclusive license for the hired party to use the work as contemplated by the parties' transaction. *See, e.g., Asset Marketing Systems Inc. v. Gagnon*, No. 07-55217 (9th Cir. 2008). The family business would have an implied license to make copies and adapt the work to the extent the parties expected family business to use the work.

But software consultant still owns the copyright, and the implied license is nonexclusive, so uses beyond the original plan would not be permitted. Software consultant would be able to market the software to other businesses, or sell the copyright to a big software company, or adapt the software to other uses.

Whenever a party is hired to create a work, the parties should address the ownership of the copyright in the contract. Otherwise, the hiring party may end up with limited rights in the work they paid to have made.

Example

1. *"Hollywood is a place where a man can get stabbed in the back while climbing a ladder."* Studio commissions Faulkner to write a screenplay for *Meet the Snopes*. The agreement is informal and oral. Before too long, Faulkner hands over the text and Studio hands over the check. Just as production is to begin on the film, Faulkner's attorney contacts Studio. Faulker was not an employee. The screenplay was not a work made for hire. Faulkner, as author, owns the copyright, and is offering to grant permission for Studio to make the

film and distribute it—for a fee. Has Studio bought nothing more than a piece of paper because they did not get the copyright?

Explanation

1. Faulkner does own the copyright, but Studio will have an implied license to use the screenplay as contemplated by the parties. Where the parties neglect to address copyright ownership in the written agreement, the hiring party will get an implied, nonexclusive license to use the work. Studio can make the film and distribute it without permission from Faulkner.

   Uses beyond the parties' implied agreement, however, would infringe the copyright. This would depend on a showing of what the parties intended. Faulkner could argue that Studio would infringe if it made a sequel, or a novelization, or a Broadway musical. In addition, Faulkner would have the right to grant licenses to others. Studio should have addressed the ownership of copyright in the contract. The implied license rule will help it, but getting a clear assignment of copyright in the contract is much better.

Joint Authors

More than one person may qualify as the author. Authors of a joint work are co-owners of the copyright in the work. 17 U.S.C. §201(a). Joint authors have equal undivided interests in the copyright. Each has the right to use or to license the work without requiring permission from the other. The one obligation is to share any profits made. If Poe and Doe are joint authors of a novel, either one could authorize a publisher to print and distribute it or a moviemaker to film it. She would then be accountable to her joint author to share the profits, if any.

One joint author may grant permission to use a work, but the permission must come before the work is used. If one infringes a joint work, either joint author may sue for infringement, and a settlement or license from one still leaves liability to the other. *See Davis v. Blige*, 505 F.3d 90 (2d Cir. 2007).

A work is not a joint work simply because more than one person has input. A joint work is defined as "a work prepared by two or more authors with the intention that their contributions be merged into inseparable or interdependent parts of a unitary whole." 17 U.S.C. §101. Courts read that definition to set a high standard for showing joint authorship, requiring (1) that each author contribute copyrightable expression, and (2) that each author intend to be a joint author when the work is created. *See, e.g., Thomson v. Larson*, 147 F.3d 195 (2d Cir. 1998). A person may contribute a considerable amount to a work without qualifying as a joint author. For example, in *Thomson v. Larson*, the author of the musical *Rent* worked with a dramaturge in revising the musical. The two worked together intensively on revising the work, which later became a commercial success. Larson had the sole decision-making authority, was consistently billed as the author (with credit to Thomson as dramaturge), and showed through other conduct and statements that he viewed himself as the sole author. In addition, all agreements with third parties characterized Larson as the author. Accordingly, there was no showing that he had the necessary intent for joint authorship. This rule avoids making a joint author of everyone who contributes to a work, which would result in numerous authors for works. Rather, to be a joint author, one must generally bargain for that status.

Examples

1. *When I nod my head, hit it*. Celebrity decides to enter the market for photos of Celebrity. She meticulously dresses herself and arranges furniture and artwork for a backdrop. She sets a camera on a tripod, picks a filter, sets the lighting, frames a shot, and focuses the camera. She asks Friendly Neighbor to help. Celebrity poses and gives a signal to Neighbor, who pushes the button to take the picture. Neighbor subsequently becomes less friendly and claims that the photo's copyright belongs to Neighbor or that both Neighbor and Celebrity are joint authors. Who owns the copyright?
2. *Muses*. Poet writes a series of poems about spring. Poet assigns the copyrights in the poems to Publisher for an agreed sum. Publisher commissions Musician to set the poems to music. Musician does so, resulting in a number of popular songs. When Poet hears how much revenue the songs are earning, she demands a share. She argues that the songs are joint works and that Poet is a joint author, entitled to a share of the profits. Are the songs joint works?
3. *Second thoughts*. Serving a lengthy sentence for stock fraud, Aaron decides to tell his story to the public. He contacts a friendly journalist, Roswell. They decide to have Aaron do a tell-all interview. They discuss the points they want to make and the effect they seek on the audience. They also discuss the role each will play, both in planning and execution. Aaron thinks of a sympathetic way to present his tale. Roswell thinks up lengthy questions that both serve as background and paint Aaron in a good light. They meet to discuss and revise their respective contributions. They then conduct the interview, recorded by a video recorder set up by Roswell. Everything goes according to plan, and they get precisely the interview they sought. But Aaron then rethinks his original plan and decides he would be better off remaining silent. Aaron claims authorship of the

work and forbids Roswell from making copies, broadcasting the interview, or doing anything else that falls within the copyright holder's exclusive rights. Does Aaron have the exclusive rights in the work?

4. *Separate ways.* Zach and Cody write a musical together, hoping for a Broadway hit. Their relationship sours. Zach is still seeking investors when he learns that Cody has freely permitted various troupes to perform the work. Commercial opportunities fade for a work that is no longer new. Are the troupes liable for performing the work without Zach's permission? Is Cody liable to Zach for infringement?

Explanations

1. The copyright belongs to Celebrity. In deciding authorship, courts consider such factors as who contributes creative expression, who controls the creation of the work, who makes the creative decisions, and who third parties would consider the author. Celebrity made all the artistic and technical decisions in producing the image. Neighbor played a purely mechanical role, hitting the button on cue from Celebrity.

   For the same reason, Neighbor does not qualify as a joint author. Under the standards most courts apply, joint authorship requires (1) that each author contribute copyrightable expression and (2) that the joint authors intend to be joint authors. Neighbor meets neither requirement. Neighbor simply pushed a button on cue, without contributing any original creative expression. Celebrity did not show any intent to make Neighbor a joint author. So Celebrity alone owns the copyright.

2. The songs are not joint works, even though they use Poet's creative expression. As courts now apply the rule, joint work status requires intent on the part of all authors, at the time of their respective contributions, to create a joint work. When Poet wrote her poems, she intended to create poems. The songs are musical works, incorporating preexisting material from Poet's poems. Had Poet not sold the copyright, making the songs, selling them, or performing them publicly would have infringed her copyright. But she sold the copyright to Publisher, who accordingly has the exclusive rights to make copies of the poems, adapt them, or perform them publicly.

3. Aaron is an author, but not the only one. Aaron and Roswell are joint authors. Each had the requisite intent to be a joint author and contributed copyrightable expression. They are co-owners of the copyright. Either can exercise the exclusive rights of the copyright owner without the permission of the other. Accordingly, Roswell can make copies, broadcast the tape, or do anything else without infringing Aaron's copyright.

Not every interview would be a joint work. There are several possible permutations. Depending on the roles the parties played, one or the other could be the author. An interview could even be a compilation of separate individual works.

4. With a joint work, either joint author may authorize others to use the work. The joint author need only account to the other joint authors for a share of the profits. So Cody could independently authorize the troupes to perform the work. Zach's permission is not necessary. Neither the troupes nor Cody is liable for infringement. Cody must account to Zach for a share of the profits, but there were none to share. Failing to protect a joint author's ability to exploit a work is not copyright infringement. *See Severe Records LLC v. Rich*, No. 09-6175 (6th Cir. 2011). Joint authors are well advised to have a contract covering their relationship. Otherwise, each may be at the mercy of the other.

Collective Works

Collective works are distinguished from joint works. A collective work is "a work, such as a periodical issue, anthology, or encyclopedia, in which a number of contributions, constituting separate and independent works in themselves, are assembled into a collective whole." 17 U.S.C. §101. Newspapers, magazines, encyclopedias, and collections of literary works are often collective works. A CD with various songs could be a collective work, with the author of each separate contribution retaining copyright in that individual work. The author of the collective work acquires only "the privilege of reproducing and distributing the contribution as part of that particular collective work, any revision of that collective work, and any later collective work in the same series." 17 U.S.C. §201(c).

Suppose Editor puts together a book of poems for children with the permission of the various copyright holders. The parties could arrange ownership interests between them. For example, Editor could acquire all the copyrights or acquire exclusive rights to publish all the poems. If the parties do not specify, then each copyright holder retains the copyright in his or her poem, while Editor has the copyright in the collective work. Editor has the right to make and distribute copies (sell, give away, rent, and so on) of the collective work.

Editor also has the right to make and distribute copies of a revision of the work or of a "later collective work in the same series." In *New York Times v. Tasini*, 533 U.S. 483 (2001), the Supreme Court rejected the argument that a newspaper's right to use contributions (written by freelancers) in "revisions" of the newspaper extended to putting the articles on Lexis, an online periodical database. In deciding whether a work was a revision of a collective work, the Court focused on how the work is presented to and perceptible by a user. Online databases "present articles to users clear of the context provided either by the original periodical editions or by any revision of those editions." *Id.* at 516. A user searches thousands of files for articles from thousands of collective works and then receives separate items as search results. Articles appear "without the graphics, formatting, or other articles with which the article was initially published," or without the other pages in the original work. *Id.* at 500. Such presentation was quite different from the presentation in a newspaper, so the online database did not qualify as a revision of the newspaper.

Examples

1. *Collective work or derivative work?* Jarvis provides a group of photographic images that K2 uses in advertising. After the parties fall out, K2 continues to use the images in making a collage. The collage shrinks, expands, and overlays the images in creative ways. K2 argues that it has the right to do so as the holder of the copyright in the collective work, the group of images (even if Jarvis has the copyright in the individual images). Does K2 have that right?

2. *Shorties.* Here's a roundup of all the rules. Who owns the copyright?
   a. Jada, a freelance writer, writes a history of Gown Town, using the computer and historical records in the town library.
   b. Same, except Jada is a historian employed by Gown Town, assigned to write the book.
   c. Same, except Jada is a freelance historian, commissioned by Gown Town to write its history for a lump sum, with free rein on how, when, and where to proceed (and no health or pension benefits). To everyone's surprise, Edur Studio offers millions for the movie rights to the book.
   d. Same, except Jada and Gown Town sign a contract providing that the copyright will belong to Gown Town.
   e. Davion, a freelance composer working in Hawaii, writes the score for the movie. His contract with Edur Studio provides that the score will be a work made for hire, but Davion is his own boss, not an employee of Edur Studio.
   f. Edi compiles *Best Short Stories of 2006*, with the permission of the copyright holders in the various stories.
   g. Bim and Bam, independent researchers, work closely together as equals in writing a study of the U.S. National Park system.
   h. Same, except Bim and Bam are employees of Gorp Incorporated.
   i. Same, except Bim and Bam do the work as employees of the U.S. Park Service, a federal agency.

Explanations

1. The collage is a derivative work, not a collective work, so the collective work right to make a revision of the work does not apply. *See Jarvis v. K2*, 486 F.3d 526 (9th Cir. 2007). A work is only a collective work if the individual works remain "unintegrated and disparate," and here they were combined together into a new work. The author of a collective work does not have the right to prepare derivative works based on the individual works.

2. a. Jada, as the author, would own the copyright. Whether she used facilities of others to create the work is irrelevant.
   b. Gown Town is deemed the author and owns the copyright, where Jada created the work as an employee within the scope of her employment. Note that Jada would own the copyright if the work was outside the scope of her employment, such as if she was a judge employed by the town and completed the project on her own time and initiative.
   c. Jada would be the author. She is not an employee of Gown Town, so it is not a work made for hire, even though Gown Town commissioned it and paid for it. Gown Town would presumably get an implied license to make contemplated uses of the work, such as printing copies for local distribution, but Jada would own the copyright, including the ability to sell the movie rights.
   d. The copyright would initially belong to the author, Jada, but it would transfer as agreed to Gown Town. This illustrates the practical point that parties are well advised to expressly address copyright ownership in the contract.
   e. It will be a work made for hire, so Edur Studio is the author and owns the copyright. This illustrates the second category of works made for hire: specially commissioned works that fall into specified categories (one of which is "a part of a motion picture or other audiovisual work," applicable here), where the parties sign an agreement designating it to be a work made for hire, as they did here. There need be no employee relationship for this category to apply.
   f. Edi holds the copyright in *Best Short Stories of* 2006, even though Edi did not write any of the stories. It is a collective work: "a work, such as a periodical issue, anthology, or encyclopedia, in which a number of contributions, constituting separate and independent works in themselves, are assembled into a collective whole." 17 U.S.C. §101. But that does not give Edi the copyright in the various stories. Rather, Edi's copyright in the collective work comprises "the privilege of reproducing and distributing the contribution as part of that particular collective work, any revision of that collective work, and any later collective work in the same series." 17 U.S.C. §201(c).

g. Bim and Bam are joint authors. Each may license the work independently but must account to the other for profits. Bim could authorize the sale of the book. Bim would have to pay a share of the profits (if any) to Bam.
h. If they created the work as employees working within the scope of their employment, the author and copyright owner would be the employer, Gorp Incorporated.
i. Thrown in for review: No one would own the copyright. There is no copyright in a work created by an employee of the U.S. government working within the scope of employment.

OWNERSHIP OF COPYRIGHT DISTINGUISHED FROM OWNERSHIP OF MATERIAL OBJECT

Collector purchases a painting. A year later, she is disturbed to see that a local gift shop is selling posters of the painting. But she owns the painting—doesn't the shop owner need her permission to make copies? If not, can she at least set up in competition and sell her own posters? No and no:

> Ownership of a copyright, or of any of the exclusive rights under a copyright, is distinct from ownership of any material object in which the work is embodied. Transfer of ownership of any material object, including the copy or phonorecord in which the work is first fixed, does not of itself convey any rights in the copyrighted work embodied in the object; nor, in the absence of an agreement, does transfer of ownership of a copyright or of any exclusive rights under a copyright convey property rights in any material object.

17 U.S.C. §202. Painter created the painting, so Painter owns the painting (under property law) and the copyright (under copyright law). Collector bought the painting. A sale of the painting does not implicitly include the copyright. Likewise, if Painter had sold Collector the copyright, that transaction would not have automatically included the painting. Indeed, if Collector bought the copyright without buying a copy of the work, she would have the exclusive right to make copies but be unable to exercise it, since she owned no copy to work from.

Painter could own the copyright to a painting while Collector owns the painting. Their rights could block each other. If Painter wanted to make posters, she might need Collector's permission to have access to the painting. Collector could not make posters without Painter's permission. Unless they can come to an agreement, there could be a stalemate.

Separation of the two rights is the rule under the present statute. A slightly different rule might govern works that were created before 1978. At that time, the federal statute did not address the distinction between ownership of the physical object, where the work had not been published. Rather, for unpublished works, the rule was left to state law. Some states appeared to take the position that unconditional sale of the work included sale of the copyright. *See Pushman v. New York Graphic*, 287 N.Y. 302 (1942). Under *Pushman*, whether the copyright is conveyed is simply a matter of the intent of the parties. If the author sells the work without reserving rights, the court may decide that the parties intended the sale to include the copyright.

Examples

1. *Scarlet's letter*. Scarlet writes a letter to Red, musing at length about philosophy and relating a number of amusing incidents, using her considerable wit and wisdom. Red then offers to sell the letter to Ashy. Ashy is aware that sale of an object does not convey the copyright in a work. Ashy decides to make sure that the contract clearly conveys the copyright. Ashy and Red sign a sales contract, agreeing that Red conveys ownership of both the letter and the copyright in the letter. Ashy pays the agreed price. Who owns the copyright in the letter? What if all this occurred in 1966?

2. *Services rendered*. Sculptor, a self-employed artist, agrees to create a sculpture for Mogul's garden. Mogul supplies a large block of stone. Sculptor, over several days, uses various tools to fashion various abstract geometric forms in the stone. Mogul is delighted with the result and hands over the agreed fee. Sculptor then prepares to load the sculpture into a truck, much to Mogul's dismay. Sculptor claims ownership of the sculpture, on the grounds that the sculpture was not a work made for hire and they did not agree that the copyright would belong to Mogul. Who owns the sculpture?

3. *My music*. Boutique Owner purchases a CD of songs written and performed by the group Dansel. Boutique Owner likes the CD so much that she plays it several times a day in her boutique. She then hears from the owner of the copyright in the songs, who claims that Boutique Owner is infringing the copyright owner's exclusive right to perform the songs in public. Boutique Owner is dumbfounded. Does she need permission to play a CD she owns?

4. *Your tape, my music*. Forward, a music enthusiast, hears the Destroyers play at a blues bar. Impressed, he invites them to record a demo tape of their songs at a studio, all expenses paid. The demo helps the Destroyers get a record deal, and they agree to let Forward keep the tape for his own enjoyment. Years later, the Destroyers now famous, Forward decides to reproduce his tape and sell copies to the public. May he?

5. *Ambiguous question.* If the Pink Panther stole the demo tape and sold it, would the Pink Panther be liable to Forward or to the Destroyers?

Explanations

1. Scarlet owns the copyright in the letter. Scarlet gave Red the letter but did not give Red the copyright in the letter. Transfer of ownership of a copy of a work (even when the copy is the original form of the work) does not convey the copyright in the work. Scarlet did not convey the copyright to Red, so Scarlet retains the copyright. The fact that Red agreed to convey the copyright to Ashy does not help Ashy; Red cannot convey something Red does not own or have power to transfer. Scarlet owns the copyright, and Ashy is left with a breach of contract action against Red for failing to convey the copyright Red promised to Ashy.

   Had this occurred in 1966, the result might be different. Before 1978, state law governed copyright in unpublished works. Some state courts would hold that transfer of the work might include an implicit transfer of the copyright (depending on the intent and conduct of the parties). A court might hold that in sending the letter, the author implicitly transferred the copyright. Other courts might well hold that the author intended to keep the copyright, because there was no expectation that the recipient would publish the letter.

2. The sculpture belongs to Mogul. The copyright belongs to Sculptor because the work was not a work made for hire and the parties did not agree to a transfer of the copyright. But ownership of the sculpture, a physical object, is entirely separate. Since Sculptor agreed to make it for Mogul's garden, using materials supplied by Mogul, property and contract law likely would deem the sculpture to belong to Mogul, so Sculptor does not have the right to take the sculpture away.

3. This problem contains some preview of material later in the book. Boutique Owner does need authorization from the copyright holder (or from some provision of the Copyright Act, as the next chapter discusses) to play the CD publicly. Boutique Owner bought the CD; she did not buy the copyright or receive a license of any of the exclusive rights. The copyright owner in the musical work has the exclusive right to perform the work publicly, which includes playing the songs publicly on a CD player. Boutique Owner can, however, play the songs privately without permission. Ownership of a copy of the work does not give the owner unlimited rights to use that copy (as the other chapters discuss in more detail), in particular under the first sale and fair use provisions.

4. Forward owns the tape, but the Destroyers own the copyright to their music and, assuming they controlled the session, to the sound recording. If Forward makes copies and distributes them, he would infringe both copyrights. *See Forward v. Thorogood*, 985 F.2d 604 (1st Cir. 1993).

5. Both. Pink Panther would be liable to Forward for stealing his physical property and selling it (conversion) and to the Destroyers for distributing a copy (that he does not own, so first sale does not apply, as discussed later in the book) of their copyrighted work to the public (copyright infringement).

CHAPTER 8

Formalities

Copyright Notice, Registration, and Deposit

Until 1989: No "©", no copyright. Until 1992: no renewal, bye-bye copyright. This chapter tells how Picasso lost his copyrights—and got them back, decades later.

Nowadays, copyright arises automatically. To have her copyright, an author need not register the work, publish with a copyright notice, or deposit a copy with the Library of Congress. Registration is very useful, however. The biggest advantage—especially for works of low commercial value—is that infringement of a registered copyright gives a right to statutory damages. Even if there are no actual damages, statutory damages are $750 to $150,000 per work infringed.

Until 1989, authors, especially foreign authors and publishers less familiar with U.S. copyright law, often lost their U.S. copyright by failing to publish with a copyright notice or failing to file a renewal application for the second 28-year term. Such has been the fate of works by, among others, George Orwell, Igor Stravinsky, J.R.R. Tolkien, and Virginia Woolf.

At one time, formalities represented a great risk to authors. The greatest hazard, until 1989, was the requirement of a copyright notice ("© 1936 Nora Huston") on published copies. If a work was published without a copyright notice, the work lost copyright protection in the United States (subject to some narrow exceptions in force until 1978 and broad exceptions in force until 1989). Suppose Allie Author published her novel in 1966 and omitted to put a copyright notice on it. A simple "© 1966 Allie Author" on the copyright page would have been sufficient, but Allie simply did not know of the legal requirement of a copyright notice. Because she published without the notice, Allie's book would go into the public domain.

She would have no copyright in her book under the federal copyright statute or state common law. She would not have the basket of exclusive rights (to make copies, adapt the work, distribute copies to the public, publicly perform the work, and publicly display the work). Anyone would be free to make and sell copies, or to copy elements of her novel into their works, or to make a movie from her novel.

Another hazard, until 1992, was the need to file for the renewal term. Registration of copyright with the Copyright Office was not a condition to copyright. But until 1978, copyright lasted 28 years, with an additional 28 years of protection only if the copyright owner registered and filed for the renewal term. Even until 1992, it was necessary to file for renewal for pre-1976 works to receive the entire term of copyright. Failure to file for renewal also caused many works to go into the public domain, including many paintings by Picasso and the *Lord of the Rings* trilogy.

Such formalities are no longer a condition of copyright. The old rules are still important, because they often control whether works published between 1923 and 1989 are under copyright or not. In particular, from 1909 to 1989, publication of the work without a copyright notice could mean loss of copyright. Until 1992, renewal of registration was also required to secure the full term of copyright. Many works went into the public domain for failure to comply with such formalities, especially works by foreign authors or authors without timely legal advice.

Today, an author no longer risks losing her copyright for failure to include a copyright notice or register the work. However, many practical advantages remain for notice, registration, and deposit.

COPYRIGHT NOTICE

A copyright notice is simple: © 1926 Fitzgerald. For works published before March 1, 1989, however, the notice was essential to copyright protection.

In considering copyright notice, three time periods are key:

1909 to December 31, 1977. Under the 1909 Act, federal copyright generally began on publication with proper notice (or for some works, upon registration). State common law generally gave copyright in unpublished works. Copyright (federal and state) was generally forfeited for works first published without proper notice, although there were narrow savings provisions.

January 1, 1978, to February 28, 1989. Under the 1976 Act, federal copyright began upon fixation of the work in tangible form, so federal copyright law governed both published and unpublished works. Copyright could be lost by first publication without effective notice, but there were generous savings provisions.

March 1, 1989, and after. The 1976 Act is still in effect but amended to conform to international treaties. Formalities are no longer required for copyright. No "©", no problem.

Works Published Between 1909 and December 31, 1977

Before 1978, when the 1909 Act was in effect, federal copyright applied primarily to published works. State copyright could potentially apply to unpublished works. Federal copyright protection was generally secured by placing a proper copyright notice on copies of the work when it was first published (some unpublished works could also receive copyright by registration). Allie Author could get a federal copyright simply by including "© 1966 Allie Author" on the copyright page (the back of the title page) of the first published copies of her book. If she published without that simple notice or included a defective notice, however, it was a divestive publication—meaning her book was not under copyright, and she lost the ability to claim copyright.

An unsettled question is whether publication without proper notice outside the United States divested U.S. copyright. Courts split on that question, so it is not certain whether the many works published without notice outside the United States, but not published in the United States, between 1909 and 1978 were divested of U.S. copyright protection. Because of restoration (discussed below) and the fact that older foreign works tend to have less commercial importance, the practical importance of that uncertainty has lessened.

Several reasons have been offered for the notice requirement. *See, e.g.*, House Report 94-1476 (legislative history to the 1976 Act). The rule put works into the public domain unless the copyright holder took a relatively easy step to preserve her rights. Copyright would not apply to works that were unclaimed, meaning that others could use works where the copyright owner had not reserved her rights. Notice of a claim of copyright also put others on notice that a work was copyrighted, like a No Trespassing sign. The notice also identified the copyright holder, so potential users could seek permission to use the work, where permission was required. It provided the date of publication, from which one could determine the duration of copyright. The notice requirement provided an incentive for authors to claim copyright if they wished, but it also created a harsh forfeiture for authors who failed to meet the requirement.

The form of notice required by the 1909 Act was generally as follows: a copyright symbol (©, Copr., or Copyright) and the name of the "copyright proprietor." Copyright Act of 1909, §19. The year of first publication was also required for "printed literary, musical, or dramatic works." For some works, such as maps, artworks, drawings, photographs, and labels, the statute permitted a shortened form, consisting of the © symbol with the initials or other symbol of the copyright proprietor. For some types of works, such as books, periodicals, and musical works, the statute specified the required location. Copyright Act of 1909, §20. For such works, notice generally had to be on the title page or the following page. One copyright notice would be sufficient for a volume, even if it contained multiple works.

The 1909 Act excused some failures to comply with the notice requirement. The Copyright Act of 1909, §21. Where the copyright owner sought to comply, "the omission by accident or mistake of the prescribed notice from a particular copy or copies" did not invalidate the copyright. Copyright Act of 1909, §21. To come within the provision, the proprietor must have attempted to comply; it would not excuse one who did not know of the requirement or its dire consequences. It also excused only a relatively small failure ("a particular copy or copies"). In addition, the copyright owner could not recover damages from an innocent infringer who relied on the lack of notice.

A common issue was whether the work had been published or not. Because publication without notice resulted in such a harsh forfeiture, courts sometimes seemed to reach to find that no publication occurred. Some courts even applied different standards for publication, reasoning that to get copyright (an investive publication with notice), a lower standard applied; to lose copyright (a divestive publication without notice), a higher standard applied.

Courts held forfeiture required a "general publication," meaning that the work be made available to members of the public "without regard to their identity or what they intended to do with the work." By contrast, there was no forfeit by a "limited publication" when the work was made available to only selected persons for limited purposes, such as circulation of an academic paper for comments from chosen colleagues. In deciding whether a publication was general, courts looked at such factors as the number of recipients, how they were chosen, what restrictions were placed on the work, and whether the work became disseminated further. If an author sold copies of her short story to the public without affixing a copyright notice, the book would go into the public domain. If the author merely distributed some copies to members of a writing class for criticism, with instructions not to show the story to anyone else, then there would be no publication and no forfeit. She would not yet have a federal copyright but could still obtain copyright by publishing with the proper notice of copyright.

Public display of a work could also constitute publication. If the work was displayed in such a way to permit unrestricted copying by the general public, then the work was deemed to be published. If restrictions were imposed, such as prohibitions against making pictures of the work, there would be no publication. By contrast, courts held that performance of a work, no matter how public, was not publication. A performance of a play or a musical work before a paying public audience would not constitute publication. The distinction between display and performance of a work makes sense. If a work is displayed, then it would not be difficult to provide a copyright notice. (The statute even provides for a shortened form of notice for artworks, so the notice need not interfere with the display.) A copyright notice is harder to integrate with a performance. It would be burdensome to hand out copyright notices to every audience member—and impossible when the performance is in an open public place. The alternatives, such as having the performers wear T-shirts with the © symbol, would likely interfere with the performance.

The leading case on publication under the 1909 Act is *Estate of Martin Luther King, Jr. v. CBS*, 194 F.3d 1211 (11th Cir. 1999). The result at first seems counterintuitive: Dr. King's famous speech using the phrase "I have a dream" was held not to be published, even though it was delivered before some 200,000 people and a nationwide television and radio audience, and copies of the speech were distributed to journalists. But the case invoked two of the long-standing rules on publication. First, a limited distribution for limited purposes is not a distribution, so distributing copies of the text to journalists was not publication (as opposed to distributing copies of the text to the public). Second, Dr. King delivering the speech was a performance of the work, and a performance (as opposed to a distribution or a display) has been consistently held not to be publication.

Courts differed on the question of whether a work was published when a derivative work based on the work was published subsequently. Suppose an author had not published her short story, but she permitted a playwright to write a play based on the short story. The play used large portions of the short story—its detailed plot, its characters, and most of its dialogue. The playwright next published the play without a copyright notice. The play would go into the public domain. Courts were split on whether publication of the play also constituted publication of the underlying work, which would put the underlying work into the public domain.

Another protection for authors was in the rule that publication divested copyright only if it was authorized. If a publisher published Author's book without her permission, the publication would not divest copyright. Some courts went further and would hold that no divesting publication occurred even when the publisher had permission if the publisher had promised to include a copyright notice. Otherwise, putting the work into the public domain would be inconsistent with the author's requirements and best efforts.

Finally, there is once again a special rule for sound recordings. One unsettled question was whether distribution of recordings constituted publication of works. Some believed it did not because a phonorecord is not a copy. Others held that there was no functional difference, so selling recordings of a song without a copyright notice would divest copyright in the song. Congress settled the question in 1997, amending the statute to provide that distribution of phonorecords before the effective date of the 1976 Act did not constitute publication of musical works embodied in them. *See* 17 U.S.C. §303(b). Courts have applied this particular rule retroactively (otherwise, it would have little applicability).

Works Published Between January 1, 1978, and February 28, 1989

In 1978 (upon the effective date of the 1976 Copyright Act), several things changed. First, the subject matter of federal copyright was expanded to include both published and unpublished material. Federal copyright no longer began upon publication. Rather, copyright began as soon as the work was fixed in tangible form. If Abby Author wrote a book in 1981, she had copyright as soon as she wrote it.

The 1976 Act continued the rule requiring copyright notice on publication, but made it much less harsh. If Abby published her book without including a copyright notice ("© 1981 Abby Author"), she could still lose her copyright, but the 1976 Act provided several ways to cure the defect. The required notice had three elements:

1. for copies: the familiar "©," or "Copyright," or "Copr."; for phonorecords: ℗
2. the year of the work's publication (with special rules for compilations and derivative works), which could be omitted for certain works such as artwork on greeting cards, jewelry, dolls, toys, or useful articles
3. the name of the copyright owner (or recognizable abbreviation or alternative designation).

17 U.S.C. §401(b). Omission of the name or date meant that the work was published without the required notice. 17 U.S.C. §406. If the name was incorrect, the notice was valid (but there were protections for innocent infringers misled by the notice). If the date was earlier than actual publication, that could shorten the term (if calculated from date of publication). If the date was later, then again the work was treated as published without notice.

The location requirement was more flexible than under the 1909 Act. The notice had to be placed "in such manner and location as to give reasonable notice of the claim of copyright." 17 U.S.C. §§401(c), 402(c). A single copyright notice would suffice for collective works, such as a book of short stories or a law review volume.

The 1976 Act also specifically defined "publication" as

> the distribution of copies or phonorecords of a work to the public by sale or other transfer of ownership, or by rental, lease, or lending. The offering to dis-tribute copies or phonorecords to a group of persons for purposes of further distribution, public performance, or public display, constitutes publication. A public performance or display of a work does not of itself constitute publication.

Most important, the consequence of publication with omitted or defective notice was much less severe. The drafters of the 1976 Act chose to continue the notice requirement, but omission of the copyright notice did not invalidate the copyright if:

1. notice was omitted "from no more than a relatively small number of copies or phonorecords distributed to the public"; or
2. the work was registered no later than five years after publication without notice, and "a reasonable effort is made to add notice to all copies or phonorecords that are distributed to the public in the United States after the omission has been discovered"; or
3. notice was omitted by a licensee in violation of an express written requirement in a licensing agreement.

If Author's story was published without the required notice, she would not lose her copyright if only a few copies were published without notice, or she registered within five years (while attempting to add notice to existing copies), or the publisher had omitted the notice despite a clause in the publishing contract. Although Author would not lose copyright, she would not be able to collect damages from an innocent infringer who relied on a copy with no copyright notice. 17 U.S.C. §405(b).

Works Published After March 1, 1989

Effective March 1, 1989, Congress did away with the requirement of notice as a condition for copyright. The United States removed the requirements of formalities because they were inconsistent with the Berne Convention, the leading international copyright treaty. Berne provides that "the enjoyment and the exercise" of copyright "shall not be subject to any formality." Berne Convention for the Protection of Literary and Artistic Works 5(2). One can see the difference between Berne (no formalities allowed) and the pre-1989 U.S. law (must publish with notice to keep copyright) as rooted in two different views of copyright. Copyright in the United States is often seen as providing an incentive for authors. To encourage authors to produce works, they are entitled to claim exclusive rights in their works. If copyright is an incentive to produce, then requiring authors to meet formalities helps limit copyright to those authors who really had copyright in mind when creating the work. By contrast, Berne is often seen as representing the view that copyright is a moral right. An author, as the creator of the work, has a natural entitlement to control uses of the work. Such natural rights should not be conditioned on complying with legal formalities.

Accession by the United States to Berne represented a long, gradual change in U.S. policies toward intellectual property rights. In its first century, the United States was often regarded as a pirate nation with regard to copyright. In the nineteenth century, it was very difficult for foreign authors to get effective copyright protection in the United States. U.S. law had requirements of formalities, including notice, registration, and even the manufacturing clause, which required that works be printed in the United States. As a result, foreign works were generally not protected under U.S. law. This meant that U.S. publishers could freely publish the works of foreign authors without paying royalties. U.S. publishers did so, especially making use of English authors, because of the common language. This may have benefited U.S. publishers (by reducing their costs) and perhaps U.S. consumers (by reducing the price they paid), but it hurt U.S. authors. All things being equal, a U.S. publisher might prefer to publish the work of an English author over an American, because the English author's work would be published without paying royalties. Abroad, U.S. authors found they would not get copyright protection because of the failure of the United States to provide protection for foreign authors.

During the twentieth century, the United States gradually reduced obstacles to foreign authors by joining international treaties, reducing the consequences of the manufacturing clause, and softening the notice requirement. But the United States could not adhere to Berne if U.S. law imposed formalities on foreign authors. As intellectual property became more important to the U.S. economy, the pressure increased on the United States to conform to international standards (and more credibly demand that others respect intellectual property rights of U.S. authors). Finally, as of May 1989, U.S. law was amended to provide that an author no longer faced forfeiture of copyright for failure to comply with the notice requirement.

The actual change in the U.S. copyright statute dealing with copyright notice was small. Where pre-1989 law provided that a copyright holder *shall* use a copyright notice (at the risk of forfeiting copyright), the statute now provides that the copyright holder *may* use a copyright notice. The Copyright Act no longer requires copyright holders to use copyright notices, but it continues to authorize the practice.

Although notice is not required, copyright owners continue to use copyright notices as a matter of course. The cost of including a notice is small, and there are considerable legal and practical advantages. If a defendant has access to a copy or phonorecord with a proper copyright notice, she cannot generally raise the "innocent infringement" defense, which may reduce damages. The copyright notice both identifies the owner (or purports to) and makes clear that the person claims those rights. The notice serves as a warning to potential infringers but also as a guide to potential licensees: "This is the person to contact if you wish to make a use of this work within the rights of the copyright owner."

Examples

1. *First folio*. In 1966, Esen self-published a thriller, *The Confounded*. She had 100 copies printed and sold them through a bookstore in Denver. Because Esen knew nothing of copyright law, she did not include a copyright notice on any copies. The issue was never raised until 2006. That year, the movie *Confabulated* was released. Esen saw it and immediately realized that the script was taken practically verbatim from her book. The producers admit the copying but claim the book was not under copyright. Esen now has several arguments. Esen argues that she did not intend to put the book into the public domain and that the requirement of formalities was abolished in 1989. Finally, at the least, she can use restoration to get her copyright back. Will these arguments work?
2. *Second folio*. In 1986, Esen self-published her second thriller, *Children of the Confounded*. Again, she published a mere 100 copies without a copyright notice and sold them through a Denver bookstore. Now it is 2006. Given the success of *Confabulated*, publishers and producers are quite interested in the rights to *Children of the Confounded*. Does Esen have a copyright?
3. *Third folio*. In 1996, Esen self-published *Grandchildren of the Confounded*. 100 copies, no copyright notice, sold in Denver. Does Esen have a copyright?
4. *Published by another*. In 1966, Noah wrote his thriller, *The Unpublished*. Sure enough, Noah was unable to find a publisher for the book, and his efforts at self-publishing failed, but he managed to sell the movie rights. The moviemakers promised to include proper notices of copyright on the work when distributed—but did not. The film was very true to Noah's book. It had wide distribution in 1968. Noah contends that the book was not published, on several grounds. First, the showing of the movie is a performance, which is not a publication. Second, the distribution without notice violated the contract. Third, the movie was made public, not the book. What result? What result if this had occurred in 1986? In 1999?

5. *And the copyright goes to. . . .* Each year, the Academy of Motion Picture Arts and Sciences awards various Academy Awards (Best Picture, Best Director, etc.). The awards are given at a public ceremony, and each winner gets an Oscar statuette. The winners frequently hold them up to be viewed by photographers, the admiring public, and their envious colleagues. From 1929 to 1941, the Oscars were handed out without a copyright notice. After that, a notice was put on every statuette. The happy recipients generally kept their Oscars. The estate of one winner sold his, but it was eventually bought by the Academy.

   Creative Choices has the clever idea to make Oscar statuettes for companies to give to Best Salesman and Best In-House Attorney in a Supporting Role. When the Academy sues, Creative contends that Oscar went into the public domain by publication without notice. He has been on TV, has appeared in many newspaper photos, and was handed out year after year from 1929 to 1941. What result?

6. *The chosen.* The Church of the Notion was a small, cohesive group, trying to grow. In 1966, the group's leader wrote a pamphlet explaining some of their beliefs. The members spent much time combing the streets of Los Angeles for sympathetic souls. After engaging thousands of passers-by, members distributed copies of the pamphlet to about 100. The members tried to select people who seemed open to their beliefs and willing to look at the pamphlet.

   Some of the members split from the church and formed a rival group. They took a copy of the pamphlet. After editing it to reflect some philosophical differences, the splinter group printed hundreds of copies to use in their own efforts. They contend that there was no copyright in the pamphlet because it had not been published. Had it?

7. *Proper form.* Allie wrote a play, *Ultimate Effect, in* 1965. She was working as an employee of the Theater Theater, so the play was a work made for hire. Theater Theater published the play that year with a copyright notice reading "© 1965 Allie." Was the copyright notice correct?

8. *Bad date.* In 1980, Allie was working as a freelance playwright. She wrote *Affect* and had several hundred copies printed. Modestly thinking she would not undertake publication for a year or two, she had the copyright notice read "© 1982 Allie." But word of the play spread. At the urging of friends, she sold the copies to a local bookstore, which quickly sold them to the public. Was the copyright notice correct? Is there anything she could have done around that time?

9. *Type A sees typo?* The perfectionist Boss of Squarer Records personally examines a CD from his company's most popular singer, Rhoda Rooner. Rooner wrote all the music and supervised the recordings. The CD case includes the CD embodying the recording, along with a booklet with

artwork, the lyrics to the music, and information about Rooner. Under Rooner's contract, the copyrights in all her work transfer to Squarer Records. The copyright notice on the CD and on the booklet reads: "©℗2002 Squarer Records." First, Boss wonders, shouldn't Rooner's name be included? Second, why does the notice have both © and ℗?

10. *All together now.* In 2006, Otter remembers a story she had published back in 1964. She had submitted the story to *Trail Tales* magazine, which agreed to publish it. Now she wonders if she owns the copyright to the story. She digs out her copy of the magazine and is horrified to see that the story was printed without an accompanying copyright notice. There was a copyright notice on the title page of the magazine but none on the individual pieces. Has her story been in the public domain ever since?

Explanations

1. Esen's book is not under copyright because she published without copyright notice during the time the harsh provisions of the 1909 Act were in effect. Her intent is irrelevant. No intent to put the work in the public domain is required. The fact that she published only 100 copies will not save her. Under the 1909 Act, where the proprietor sought to comply, "the omission by accident or mistake of the prescribed notice from a particular copy or copies" did not invalidate the copyright, but she had made no attempt to comply, so the provision does not apply to her case. Even if she had, omission of the notice from 100 copies may be too much to qualify as "particular copy or copies."

   The abolition of the formality requirement in 1989 does not affect her, because it did not apply retroactively to works published before that time. Nor does restoration help her, because it applies only to copyrights owned by foreign authors.

2. This time, Esen published without notice during the decennial period governed by the 1976 Act's initial notice provisions. Under the 1976 Act, there is no loss of copyright if notice was omitted "from no more than a relatively small number of copies or phonorecords distributed to the public." The question here is whether the 100 copies were a relatively small number. As compared to books generally, 100 copies are not too many, so a court might hold that it was "relatively small." On the other hand, it was *all* the copies she had printed, so a court might hold that it was not *relatively* small.

   The other savings provisions would not help her. She did not register and try to fix the missing notices. Nor did a licensee omit the notice in violation of instructions from her.

3. This time, Esen published without notice during the time governed by the post-March 1, 1989, rules. Copyright notice on published copies is no longer a condition for copyright protection, so she has her copyright. She may be subject to the innocent infringer defense, but her rights generally are not affected.

4. Noah did not publish his novel as such, but a movie was published with his permission that contained much of the creative expression in Noah's novel. Most courts would hold that constitutes publication of Noah's novel. Because this occurred in 1966, he would potentially lose his copyright.

   One wrinkle is that the agreement required the moviemakers to include a proper copyright notice, and they failed to do that. The law before the 1976 Act was unclear. Some courts may hold in Noah's favor. The publication was unauthorized and therefore would not divest his copyright. Had it occurred in 1986, the rule would be clear that there was no divestiture, under 17 U.S.C. §405. In 1999, there was no loss of copyright by publication in any case, so it would not matter.

5. The court held that there was no divesting publication. *See Academy of Motion Picture Arts & Sciences v. Creative House Promotions*, 944 F.2d 1446 (9th Cir. 1991). The Oscars were distributed to the winners and shown to news photographers without a copyright notice, but the distribution was a limited distribution, not to the general public. They were given to winners of the Academy Awards. When one went on auction, the Academy eventually managed to buy it. The display was also somewhat limited. Unlike public display of a sculpture, with no limits on copying, the three-dimensional statuettes were made available to photographers, who made two-dimensional photos. The court held that did not permit unrestricted copying (although one wonders how the defendant could then have made the allegedly infringing statuettes).

6. There was probably publication without notice here and loss of copyright under the 1909 Act rule. The copyright owners would argue that it was a limited publication, which would not divest copyright. Rather than unrestricted public distribution, they made the work available only to selected members of the public, for the specific purpose of interesting them in the pamphlet. When copies of the pamphlet were given to any member of the public who seemed receptive, however, that would go well beyond a limited publication.

7. The notice was not correct. Allie was the author, but the copyright notice was required to show the name of the copyright owner. She had been an employee of Theater Theater, so it owned the copyright. A court could hold that the invalid notice meant the work was published

without notice and therefore was not under copyright. Note that under the 1976 Act, an error in the name did not invalidate the copyright.

8. Here Allie published without notice under the 1976 Act's original rules. She had several hundred copies printed and sold, which was probably too many to qualify as a "relatively" small number, but she could have used the other savings provision by registering the work within five years and taking reasonable steps to correct the omission.
9. The compact disc is a phonorecord embodying both the musical work and the sound recording. The booklet is a copy of the musical work (at least the lyrics of the music), as well as the artwork, and perhaps a literary work (the other info). So use of both symbols is appropriate, © for copy and ℗ for phonorecord.
10. Otter still has her copyright. For collective works, a single copyright notice on the copyright page was sufficient.

Limited Information in a Copyright Notice

A copyright notice provides little information: © 1959 Dinsdale Piranha. A named person claims copyright in the work, along with a publication date. There may be much in the work that is not protected by copyright. Ideas, facts, preexisting material, functional matter, and other elements are not protected by the copyright. Someone who wishes to copy from the work does not receive direct information about which particular elements are subject to the copyright claim. One exception is that where a work consists predominantly of works of the U.S. government (which are noncopyrightable), the copyright notice must identify the portions that embody protected material. 17 U.S.C. §403.

Copyright notices may be wrongly used to claim protection in works that are in the public domain. It is common to find a copyright notice on an edition of a noncopyrighted work, such as a symphony by Beethoven or a play by Shakespeare. *See* Paul J. Heald, *Payment Demands for Spurious Copyrights: Four Causes of Action*, 1 J. Intell. Prop. L. 259 (1994). If the claimant added new material, the copyright claim may have some basis to it, but if the claimant simply copied existing public domain material and put a copyright notice on it, the claim would be spurious. Federal copyright law does not provide a civil cause of action for such spurious claims, but when the claim lacks any basis, there could be liability under various state law theories, such as fraud, unjust enrichment, consumer protection, or breach of warranty. *Id.* There may be criminal liability, with a fine up to $2,500 for fraudulent copyright notices. That is rarely prosecuted beyond counterfeiting cases. Someone who wishes to use the work, however, may file an action for a declaratory judgment that the material is not under copyright (or that a proposed use would be fair use). Cf. Karen Sloan, *James Joyce Estate Agrees to Pay Plaintiff's Fees in Fair Use Dispute*, Nat'l L.J., September 30, 2009.

Restoration of Lost Copyrights for Foreign Authors

Many foreign copyright holders lost their U.S. copyrights because of failure to comply with requirements of formalities. Copyright could be lost by publication without a copyright notice during the years that U.S. law had such a requirement. If Zondag published in the United States without "© 1945 Zondag", she would lose her U.S. copyright. Even if the work was published with a copyright notice, the owner could lose part of the copyright term by failing to file for renewal of the copyright. So if Zondag published with "© 1945 Zondag", but did not file a renewal, her U.S. copyright would expire in 1974, instead of 1992 (and lost the benefit of the extension to 1931, under the extension in 1976 and 1998). U.S. authors rarely suffered such losses in other countries, because few countries required such formalities as a condition to copyright. Indeed, the leading international copyright treaty, Berne, forbade imposing such requirements on foreign authors.

As intellectual property became part of international trade negotiations, the United States agreed to restore some of the foreign copyrights lost because of failure to comply with U.S. formalities requirements. Under legislation implementing U.S. adherence to the Agreement on Trade-Related Aspects of Intellectual Property Rights (TRIPS) 1994, certain copyrights of foreign authors were restored, effective January 1, 1996. *See* 17 U.S.C. §104A—meaning Zondag could get her copyright restored. Restoration applies if several conditions are met:

- The work was first published in an eligible country (a country other than the United States that adheres to Berne, the WIPO Copyright, and the WIPO Performances and Phonograms Treaty; is a member of the World Trade Organization; or is subject to a special presidential proclamation) at least 30 days before U.S. publication.
- The work has not passed into the public domain in its source country because of expiration of the period of protection.
- The work is in the public domain in the United States because of failure to comply with formalities (such as publication without a copyright notice or failure to file for the renewal term), because of lack of protection before 1972 in the United States for sound recordings, or because of lack of national eligibility.
- The author was a national of an eligible country.

The foreign copyright holder is entitled to the remainder of the term that the copyright would have had but for the loss of protection. The copyright holder need not file any form to have the copyright restored—restoration is automatic—but the copyright holder may file a Notice of Intent to Enforce (NIE) a restored copyright with the Copyright Office. In addition, the copyright holder may serve notice of intent to enforce upon "reliance parties," persons who used the work while it was in the public domain.

The owner of a restored copyright generally has the right to enforce the copyright like other copyrights against infringement that occurs after the date of restoration, but reliance parties have limited protection. They are not liable for acts that occur before the claimant files with the Copyright Office or serves notice on the reliance party. The reliance party then gets a grace period (about one year) after filing or service. The reliance party may not make new copies during the grace period, but may sell existing copies and exploit derivative works. After the grace period, a reliance party may continue to exploit a derivative work prepared outside the United States, provided it pays reasonable compensation to the owner of the restored copyright.

Golan v. Holder, 132 S. Ct. 873 (2012), rejected the argument that taking works out of the public domain was unconstitutional, either because Congress exceeded its powers to grant copyrights or because it offended the First Amendment. Golan held that the Progress Clause gave considerable latitude to Congress in addressing copyright and was not strictly limited to provisions that gave an incentive to created works, as opposed to provisions like the restoration provisions, which gave more general support to the distribution of works. Golan interpreted its earlier decision in *Eldred* very narrowly. Under *Eldred*, as long as Congress continued to maintain the "traditional contours" of copyright, First Amendment scrutiny is unnecessary. *Golan* interpreted this to mean the "traditional contours" to only the doctrine of fair use and the nonprotection of ideas (as opposed the more general shape of copyright, such as the practice of generally not taking works out of the public domain). As long as Congress did not do away with fair use and the nonprotection of ideas, First Amendment scrutiny will not apply. Even large changes, such as putting material under copyright that was in the public domain, will not be scrutinized under the First Amendment.

Example

1. *Restoration*. Gen's dissertation was published in Japan in 1965, and in the United States in 1968, both without a copyright notice. Gen's dissertation is still under copyright in Japan. Is there anything Gen can do to recover his U.S. copyright? What if the dissertation had been first published in the United States without the requisite notice? Or what if it had been published without notice in 1920?

Explanation

1. The restoration provisions would give Gen his copyright back. To maximize his ability to enforce the copyright, Gen could file a Notice of Intent to Enforce with the Copyright Office, which would limit the ability of reliance parties to continue acts that would infringe Gen's copyright.

   Had it been first published in the United States, restoration would not apply. It applies only if the work is first published in an eligible country (a country other than the United States that is party to one of various copyright-related treaties). Had it been published in 1920, restoration would also be inapplicable. Restoration gives the work only the term it would have had. Works published before 1923 are out of copyright.

REGISTRATION

The United States is unique in having a Copyright Office for registration of copyrights, for deposit of copies of works, for recording various documents relating to copyrights, and for maintaining records and permitting public searches of the records. Some other countries have copyright offices, but none with such a range of services. The copyright owner (or owner of any of the exclusive rights) may register the work at any time during the copyright term. 17 U.S.C. §408. Both published and unpublished works may be registered. Registration is not a condition of copyright but has several practical advantages, discussed below. In particular, the remedies of statutory damages and attorney's fees are available only where the infringed work was registered, a strong incentive for registering any copyright that the owner intends to enforce or even license. Registration requires filling out an application form, paying a modest fee, and meeting the deposit requirement (two copies of the best edition for works published in the United States; one copy for unpublished works, works published outside the United States, or works included in a collective work). 17 U.S.C. §408.

There are several different application forms, depending on the category of work. The information required is relatively straightforward, bearing on the ownership and existence of copyright. The applicant must identify the author (unless the work is anonymous or pseudonymous), the author's nationality or domicile, and whether the work was made for hire (meaning it was created by an employee and the employer is deemed the author). 17 U.S.C. §409. If the copyright claimant is not the author, she must state how she obtained ownership of the copyright. The applicant must provide the title of the work (and any previous or alternate titles), its year of creation, and date and location of first publication (if published). Such facts may determine the duration of copyright. In the case of a compilation or derivative work, the applicant must identify any preexisting works on which the present work is based and briefly state the additional material covered by the copyright claim being registered. If a screenwriter adapted a novel into a screenplay, she would have to identify the novel as a preexisting work and briefly state the material added by the screenplay. Her copyright in the screenplay would extend only to new, creative expression, not to any elements taken from the novel. Note that knowing falsities in the application may void the registration.[1]

An examiner makes a limited examination. Under the Copyright Office's "Rule of Doubt," registration is allowed unless it is clear that the material is not copyrightable or that other requirements (including ownership) are not met. If registration is refused, the applicant may appeal. If registration is allowed, the Copyright Office issues a certificate of registration to the applicant. The Copyright Office maintains records and indexes of registered works. Anyone interested in the status of a work may search the Copyright Office. Online searches may be performed at www.loc.gov/copyright to get information on registrations and recorded documents dating back to 1978 (it may take a few months for recent filings to appear in the database). One may also visit the Copyright Office and search the records in person or, for a fee, have the Copyright Office perform a search.

Copyright registration has several advantages. An action for infringement (other than infringement of 17 U.S.C. §106A moral rights) of the copyright in a "United States work" cannot be brought until the copyright holder registers the copyright (or, if the U.S. Copyright Office refuses registration, until the copyright owner files the application, tenders the fee, and meets the deposit requirement). 17 U.S.C. §411. This requirement is limited to "United States works"—that is, works first published in the United States, unpublished works by U.S. residents, or works originating in a country that is not party with the United States to a copyright treaty. *See* 17 U.S.C. §101. In short, the copyright owner must register before filing an infringement

1. *Gold Value Int'l Textile, Inc. v. Sanctuary Clothing, Ltd. Liab. Co.*, 925 F.3d 1140, 1146 (9th Cir. 2019).

An inaccuracy in the application does not necessarily invalidate a copyright registration, however. *See* 17 U.S.C. § 411(b)(1). Rather, the inaccurate information must have been included in the application for copyright registration "with knowledge that it was inaccurate" and "the inaccuracy of the information, if known, would have caused the Register of Copyrights to refuse registration." *Id.; see also L.A. Printex*, 676 F.3d at 852-853. The district court found that Fiesta knew the information in the application was inaccurate because it knew that it had previously sold fabric bearing the 1461 Design to customers when it applied for the '509 Registration. Fiesta argues that it did not know that the sale of samples to its customers constituted publication as a matter of law under the Copyright Act, and therefore, it did not have the requisite knowledge or fraudulent intent. The district court characterized Fiesta's position as one of "ignorance of the law," which is "no excuse," and determined that a showing of fraudulent intent is not required to invalidate a copyright registration under § 411(b).

action, unless the work was created and first published in a foreign country that is party with the United States to a copyright treaty.

Registration is also a prerequisite for certain remedies for infringement. Statutory damages and attorney's fees are generally available only for infringement of registered works (unless the work is unpublished or is registered no later than three months after publication). 17 U.S.C. §412. The limitation does not apply to actions for infringement of §106A moral rights. Note a distinction here. Copyright registration is a condition for filing an infringement action, but it need not precede the infringement, only the filing of the subsequent lawsuit. Registration, however, must precede the infringement (or registration must occur no later than three months after publication) for statutory damages or attorney's fees to be awarded. In practical terms, infringement of an unregistered work may lead to a lawsuit but not to an award of statutory damages or attorney's fees. This is an important consideration, as statutory damages often greatly exceed actual damages (discussed in Chapter 19, on remedies).

The certificate of registration is prima facie evidence of the validity of the copyright, provided the work is registered no later than five years after first publication. 17 U.S.C. §410(c). The court, however, has discretion as to the weight to give that evidence, and courts will hold registered works to be noncopyrightable if other evidence shows lack of originality or other requirements.

Registration also has the practical advantage of making a public record of the copyright ownership, available to anyone who searches the U.S. Copyright Office records. In addition to registering the copyright, one may record transfers of copyright ownership or other documents relating to a copyright. *See* 17 U.S.C. §205. Such recordation provides constructive notice of the documents to others, but only if the copyright has been recorded. 17 U.S.C. §205(c).

In addition, registration was necessary in order to file for renewal. Until renewal was made automatic in 1992, it was a condition to obtain the renewal term after the initial 28-year term. Works published before 1964 went into the public domain unless they were registered and a renewal filed in the 28th year. Registration could also be necessary to preserve copyright for works published without the necessary copyright notice between January 1, 1978, and March 1, 1989. During that period, failure to publish with the required notice could be cured by registration within five years.

The advantages of copyright registration (statutory damages and attorney's fees in case of infringement, presumption of validity and ownership of copyright; constructive notice of recorded documents) are dependent on a valid copyright registration. In addition, registration is a prerequisite for bringing an infringement action (for U.S. authors). An applicant should be careful not to make a mistake in the registration process that could invalidate the registration. Errors such as mistakenly identifying a work as a work made for hire or failing to identify preexisting works from which the work was adapted can invalidate the registration. But not every mistake will void registration. The Supreme Court, in *Unicolors, Inc. v. H&M Hennes & Mauritz, L.P.*, 142 S. Ct. 941 (2022), held that a copyright registration with inaccurate information is nevertheless valid if the registrant did not know of the inaccuracy. The Court reasoned that authors are musicians and novelists and the like, not lawyers, and should not forfeit rights for innocent mistakes.

Example

1. *Keeping a lid on it.* Spakester writes a humorous five-act play. He distributes copies to a number of local writers. They all agree that the play will be a huge hit. One friend suggests that Spakester register the copyright in the play. Spakester responds that he will wait until the play is published. Spakester believes that he has no copyright until the play is published and that registering before then would not give him any benefits. Moreover, he figures, until the play is published or produced on stage, no one could possibly infringe. Would Spakester get any benefit from registering the copyright?

Explanation

1. Spakester would benefit from registering the copyright. He had a copyright as soon as the work was fixed in tangible form. Works may be registered whether published or not. His copyright could certainly be infringed before publication or production. Several copies are already circulating among writers, who may pass them on to others. The benefit of registration would be that if the copyright is infringed, the remedies available may be greater. Statutory damages and attorney's fees may be awarded only for infringement of registered copyrights. In addition, registration and deposit provide some evidence that he wrote the work by the date of registration, which would compare favorably against an infringing author who denies copying the work.

RENEWAL

If a work was published before 1964, it went into the public domain after 28 years unless an application for renewal was filed, which resulted in an additional 28-year renewal term.

Under the 1909 Act, the term of copyright was divided. Upon publication with notice, the copyright owner was entitled to a 28-year initial term. The owner could also have an additional 28-year term, provided she had registered the copyright and also filed for a renewal certificate during the 28th year of the initial term. Failure to file for renewal meant that the copyright ended after the initial term. Many copyrights went into the public domain under this provision.

The 1976 Act changed the term of copyright to a single term: for individual works, life plus 50 years; for works made for hire and for anonymous or pseudonymous works, a fixed term of 75 years. The 1976 Act also potentially tacked on 19 years to the renewal term of works published before 1978, giving them a total of 75 years (28-year initial term, 28-year renewal, 19 years added by the 1976 Act). But the right to the renewal term still depended on filing for renewal during the 28th year, so works published before 1978 would still go into copyright after 28 years. Eventually, effective 1992, the statute was amended to provide for automatic renewal for works published after 1963. Finally, in 1998, the Copyright Term Extension Act added another 20 years to the copyright term, which was added to the renewal term for pre-1978 works.

When dealing with a work published before 1964, two things must be checked. First, whether the work was first published without a proper copyright notice, sending it into the public domain. Second, whether the copyright owner failed to file for renewal in the 28th year (if that occurred before 1992), which likewise would send it into the public domain. In addition, for works published between 1963 and March 1, 1989, publication without notice may have divested copyright.

DEPOSIT

There are technically two separate deposit requirements. Copyright owners who register works must make a deposit (of one or two copies or phonorecords, depending on the type of work) with the U.S. Copyright Office. Copyright owners of published works are required to deposit two copies or phonorecords with the Library of Congress. Within three months of publication, a copyright owner must deposit two copies or phonorecords with the U.S. Copyright Office, "for the use or disposition of the Library of Congress." 17 U.S.C. §407(a). The Library of Congress deposit requirement applies only to works published in the United States (not to unpublished works or works published only abroad), but a copyright owner is permitted to use the Library of Congress deposit to also fulfill the registration deposit requirement. Copyright owners who neither register nor publish have no deposit requirement to meet.

All copies and phonorecords that are deposited become the property of the U.S. Government. 17 U.S.C. §704(a). The deposited material is available to the Library of Congress for its collections (subject to narrow exceptions for some unpublished works). 17 U.S.C. §704(b). The deposit requirement has helped the Library of Congress amass a huge collection of works. Not all works deposited, however, are retained. Rather, the Library of Congress chooses which works to retain and which to discard. Not every ketchup bottle label registered for copyright will remain as part of the country's storehouse of creative works. In addition, the deposit requirements are relaxed or excluded for many categories of works. For software, parties may exclude large portions, especially any code claimed as a trade secret. The rules are expanding to accommodate the increase in number of works and the changing nature of works. For example, Copyright Office temporary regulations both limit the need to deposit electronic works if they are published in the United States and available online and provide that any electronic deposits shall not be made generally available to the public. *See Mandatory Deposit of Published Electronic Works Available Only Online*, 75 Fed. Reg. 3863 (2010).

The regulations of the U.S. Copyright Office exempt many works from the deposit requirements, in whole or in part. For example, it is necessary to deposit only the first and last 25 pages of a computer program's source code. In addition, if the program contains trade secrets, the copyright owner may omit portions of the code and thereby avoid disclosing the code to competitors or others. For secure tests (like the LSAT), the Copyright Office returns the copy after examination. Compendium II: Copyright Office Practices 315.

The penalties for failing to deposit are modest and do not affect the validity of the copyright. If deposit is not made for a published work within three months of publication, then the Register of Copyrights may demand that it be made. If deposit still is not made, fines of up to $2,500 may be imposed, together with paying for the Register to buy copies. 17 U.S.C. §407.

There can be greater risks in connection with deposit. Deposit is required as part of registration. If deposit is done incorrectly, that may invalidate the registration. In addition, if the copy deposited does not match the copy allegedly infringed, that could likewise invalidate registration. This could mean that there is no claim for statutory damages. Copyright owners in works that are frequently revised, like computer programs, must be careful to register succeeding versions of the work. In addition, the copyright holder should be careful to maintain its own copies of each version registered to prove any alleged infringement. She cannot rely on retrieving copies from the Copyright Office if necessary. As noted, the copies deposited with the Copyright Office may not be complete copies, and the Copyright Office may discard those copies.

One key aspect of deposit: If the copyright owner later sues for infringement, there must be infringement of the work as it appears in the deposited copy. So where Led Zeppelin allegedly infringed copyright with "Stairway to Heaven," Zeppelin's version was compared to the sheet music on deposit in the Library of Congress, not the version as performed by plaintiff in concerts opening for Led Zeppelin. Skidmore v. Led Zeppelin, 952 F.3d 1051 (9th Cir. 2020) (en banc). On the flip side, registration of a derivative work may suffice as registration of the underlying work, at least for common elements.[2]

What if there is no copy of the work to deposit? In *Kodadek v. MTV Networks*, 152 F.3d 1209, 1210 (9th Cir. 1998), the plaintiff contended that he had made drawings of two characters called Beavis and Butthead in 1991. He allegedly gave one to Mike Judge, who subsequently was a creative force behind the MTV animated show *Beavis and Butthead*. To bring an infringement action, Kodadek had to register the works. To register the works, he had to deposit a copy of the work. Because he had no more copies of the drawings, he made new versions in 1993 and deposited them with his registration. The Ninth Circuit held that such copies did not meet the deposit requirement, and the registration was invalid. Rather, the registrant must deposit "bona fide copies of the original work only." Such copies must be "virtually identical to the original and must have been produced by directly referring to the original." Reconstructions of drawings made from memory years after the fact did not qualify, the court held, as copies of the work for the purposes of registration.

Example

1. *Smitten with code.* Alga registers the copyright in her computer program, a useful piece of software for designing buildings. Over the next few years, she continues to test and adapt the program. A copy of the latest version is somehow purloined from her laptop and passed on to Smite Architects, which makes more copies and permits several of its architects to make use of the software. Alga is pleased that she took the step of registering the program. Because it was registered at the time of the infringement, she may get attorney's fees and statutory damages. In addition, she need not wait to register before filing her infringement action. Any problem?

2. *Enter. Mgmt. Ltd., Inc. v. Construx Software Builders, Inc.*, 73 F.4th 1048, 1050 (9th Cir. 2023) ("We also hold, as a matter of first impression, that by registering a derivative work, an author registers all of the material included in the derivative work, including that which previously appeared in an unregistered, original work created by the author.").

Explanation

1. Alga may have a problem. She registered and deposited one version of the computer program. She then continued to test and adapt the program. It may well be that the version that was infringed was sufficiently different that it was a separate derivative work not registered by Alga.

   The effect would be that Alga could still sue for infringement, but infringement of an unregistered work. She would have to register before suing and would not be eligible for attorney's fees and statutory damages.

   One twist here is that the work was a computer program. The deposit rules permit deposit of limited portions of computer programs, so maybe the portions deposited were not changed. The question would then be whether the original registration would be sufficient.

BRING BACK FORMALITY REQUIREMENTS?

Recent years have seen several proposals to reinstitute requirements of formalities. As of 1989, formalities were no longer a condition for copyright in the United States. But other trends in copyright law, as commentators have noted, actually strengthened the argument for some formality requirements. The 1976 Act broadened the scope of copyright to include unpublished works. Computer software has become an increasingly important category of copyrighted material, although its functional nature makes it something of an awkward fit into copyright. The term of copyright has been repeatedly extended. The notice requirements did have the advantage of putting works into the public domain unless the copyright claimant took affirmative steps to claim copyright (by using a copyright notice or registering the work).

One suggestion has been to condition copyright protection on registration, with periodic renewal. *See* Lawrence Lessig, *The Future of Ideas* 249 (2001) (proposing five-year copyright term, renewable 14 times); William M. Landes and Richard A. Posner, *Indefinitely Renewable Copyright*, 70 U. Chi. L. Rev. 471 (2003) (proposing 20-year terms, renewable indefinitely). Landes and Posner propose a trade-off: permitting indefinitely renewable copyright in exchange for requiring renewal. Their empirical analysis showed that when renewal was required for the second 28-year term, fewer than 11 percent of copyrights were renewed. In addition, most copyrighted works have a relatively short economic life expectancy. Moreover, copyright owners are sensitive to fees, meaning renewals would not be numerous if even modest fees were required. Therefore, few works would remain under copyright beyond the initial term. Owners of valuable copyrights would renew as long as permitted, but Landes and Posner see that as beneficial, because keeping copyrights as private property provides incentives for efficiently exploiting them (though others might differ on that). Landes and Posner even suggest an interesting side benefit of permitting indefinitely renewable copyright: around 2015, when the 20-year term extension in 1998 would otherwise be soon to run out, there would be fewer resources wasted in attempting to convince Congress to once again extend the term.

One could have a formality regime that was less harsh than the old version. Until 1989, an author could lose copyright by failing to publish with a copyright notice. A kinder rule would provide that a work would not be copyrighted until publication with notice, or perhaps when a registration was filed, but failure to carry out such formalities would not forfeit copyright completely; rather, the author would not have copyright until she eventually complied.

The greatest legal obstacle to bringing back formalities as a condition to copyright would be that it might violate U.S. treaty obligations, unless the rule applied only to U.S. authors. One proposal avoids that problem. The DMCA (discussed in subsequent chapters) gives legal protection for anti-copying and anti-access technology used on copyrighted works, but those protections are distinct from copyright itself, so it may be permissible to require formalities as a prerequisite for such legal protection. *See* Pamela Samuelson and Jason Schultz, *Should Copyright Owners Have to Give Notice About Their Use of Technical Protection Measure?*, 6 J. Telecom. & High Tech. L. 41 (2007). If a copyright owner wished to have legal protection for anticopying or anti-access technology (such as scrambling cable TV signals or putting anti-copying code on music files), she might be required to put some kind of notice on the work.

CHAPTER 9

Duration of Copyright

Copyright lasts a long time. Mark Twain argued that copyright should last forever, like most property rights. Some argue that copyright should last just a few years, which would be sufficient to provide an incentive to authors but would also put works into the public domain quickly. Copyright law takes a position closer to Twain's. The duration of copyright is long. *The Great Gatsby* (published in 1925) only saw its copyright expire in 2021. Works published before 1923 are no longer under copyright in the United States. Works copyrighted from 1923 until 1977, however, may have an effective term of 95 years. Therefore, 1923 works were under copyright through 2018. Works created after 1978 have a term of at least 70 years (and generally much more), so they will remain under copyright until at least 2048. The duration rules infrequently come into play by a work reaching the end of its copyright term, but the duration rules are also linked to important rules affecting formalities (such as renewal of copyright) and ownership (especially termination of transfers). Understanding the duration rules (under both the 1909 Act and the 1976 Act) is necessary to understand formalities and ownership completely. Copyright lawyers must get used to adding 28, 75, and 95 to various dates (to add 95, add 100 and subtract 5).

The first U.S. copyright statute in 1790 provided a potential term of 28 years (14 years from publication, plus a renewal term of 14 years). *See Eldred v. Ashcroft*, 537 U.S. 186 (2003). In 1831, Congress increased the potential duration of copyright to 42 years (28-year initial term, 14-year renewal term). All works copyrighted under those statutes have long passed into the public domain.

In 1909, Congress changed the potential term to 56 years (initial term of 28 years from publication, or registration for some unpublished works, plus renewal term of 28 years). *The Great Gatsby*, published in 1925, had a copyright that would last until 1982. Effective 1978, Congress made the term of copyright yet longer (for most works). The general rule was that copyright would begin at creation of the work and endure for the life of the author plus 50 years. For anonymous works, pseudonymous works, and works made for hire, the term was 75 years (a set number, not dependent on the life of the author). Works that were already under copyright before 1978 were also given the 75-year term by adding 19 years to the renewal term (75 = 28 + 28 + 19 more years). Copyrights in works published in 1922 or before had expired by then (1922 + 56 = 1977). But works from 1923 and after would now remain under copyright until at least until 1998 (1922 + 75 = 1998). So now the copyright in *The Great Gatsby* was extended until 2002.

In 1998, Congress added yet 20 more years to the copyright term. Post-1977 individual works now have a term of life of the author plus 70 years (50 + 20), while the other categories have 95 years (75 + 20). Works under copyright before 1978 now have a term of 95 years (28 + 28 + 19 + 20). When 2018 rolled around, Congress did not add 20 more years to the copyright term. So works from 1923, which had remained under copyright due to the extensions in 1976 and 1998, finally had their copyrights expire in 2019. Works from 2024 followed in 2020. The copyright of *The Great Gatsby*, published 1925, expired January 1, 2021, meaning that anyone could, without permission, write a sequel, make a movie, or translate it into Yoruba.

To preview the interaction between duration and other topics: Suppose Author wrote a book and sold the copyright (along with renewal rights) to Publisher, which published the book in 1930. Publisher may retain copyright until 2025, but only if certain events marked by those numbers did not occur. There would be no copyright if the work was published without sufficient notice in 1930. The work would also go into the public domain by 1959 if Publisher did not file for renewal in 1958 (1930 + 28). Moreover, if Author died before 1958, the right to file for renewal would belong to Author's heirs, not Publisher. Even if Publisher retained the renewal term, there could be termination of the transfer (meaning Author or her heirs would get the copyright back) in 1988 (1930 + 28 + 28) or 2007 (1930 + 28 + 28 + 19). The duration rules are important both in determining the length of copyright and in applying other rules affecting copyright ownership.

For a comprehensive table summarizing those rules (and more!), see Cornell University, Copyright Services: Copyright Term and the Public Domain, https://guides.library.cornell.edu/copyright/publicdomain.

WORKS CREATED AFTER 1977

Under the 1909 Act, copyright lasted from publication with notice (or registration for some unpublished works) for 56 years (28-year initial term, plus 28-year renewal term, provided copyright owner filed for renewal during the 28th year of the initial term). The 1976 Act changed several things about the copyright term: when it started (upon fixation, not publication), whether it included two separate terms (for post-1977 works, a single term), and how long it lasted (generally much longer).

The general rule for copyright duration is:

> Copyright in a work created on or after January 1, 1978, subsists from its creation and, except as provided by the following subsections, endures for a term consisting of the life of the author and 70 years after the author's death.

17 U.S.C. §302(a). Copyright begins when the work is fixed in a tangible form and lasts for the rest of the author's life and then for another 70 years. If there are joint authors, the copyright lasts until 70 years after the last surviving author's death.

What if it is unknown whether an author has died? The statute provides for that:

> (e) Presumption as to author's death. After a period of 95 years from the year of first publication of a work, or a period of 120 years from the year of its creation, whichever expires first, any person who obtains from the Copyright Office a certified report that the records provided by subsection (d) disclose nothing to indicate that the author of the work is living, or died less than 70 years before, is entitled to the benefit of a presumption that the author has been dead for at least 70 years. Reliance in good faith upon this presumption shall be a complete defense to any action for infringement under this title.

17 U.S.C. §302(e).

For some works, measuring duration by the life of the author would not work. For works made for hire, the employer is the author. If the employer was a corporation, that life is potentially unlimited. For anonymous and pseudonymous works, the identity of the author might be unknown. For such works, Congress uses a fixed term of years.

> In the case of an anonymous work, a pseudonymous work, or a work made for hire, the copyright endures for a term of 95 years from the year of its first publication, or a term of 120 years from the year of its creation, whichever expires first.

17 U.S.C. §303(c). If the identity of the author of "an anonymous or pseudonymous work is revealed in the records of a registration" or related records, the copyright is measured by the life of that author plus 70 years. Works made for hire always have a fixed term of 95 years. Works authored by an artificial intelligence are not under copyright, making moot the question of how to measure the duration (life of the software plus 70?).

WORKS UNDER COPYRIGHT BEFORE 1978

Under the 1909 Act, the maximum federal copyright term was 56 years (28-year initial term, renewable for another 28 years). In enacting the 1976 Act, Congress could simply have left the term for pre-1978 copyrights as it was and used the longer terms only for post-1977 works. Congress chose to give pre-1978 copyrights the same 75-year term given for post-1977 works made for hire. It did not simply switch the term to 75 years. Rather, it did so by adding 19 years to the renewal term (28 + 28 + 19 = 75). When Congress extended copyright term by 20 years in 1998, it did so by adding another 20 years to the renewal term, for a total of 95 years for pre-1978 works (28-year initial term, 28-year renewal under 1909 Act, 19 years added by the 1976 Act, and 20 years added by the 1998 CTEA). It may seem a mere technicality that the term is calculated by using the initial term of 28 years and then an extended renewal term of 67 years. But the role of renewal can raise key issues as to who had the right to the renewal term and whether a proper renewal filing was made.

Filing for Renewal

Under the 1909 Act, it was necessary to file a renewal certificate during the last year of the initial 28-year term to secure the 28-year renewal term. To file a renewal certificate, it was necessary to register the work. If no valid renewal certificate was filed, the work went into the public domain after the initial 28-year period.

The 1976 Act did not change that requirement. For works copyrighted (i.e., published with notice or registered) before 1978, it remained necessary to file for renewal in the 28th year to get the renewal term. In 1992, Congress made renewal automatic, so renewal is automatic for works copyrighted from 1964 to 1977. Filing for renewal was still permitted and did give some benefits. The main effect is that, for such works, the *Stewart v. Abend* rule discussed below applies only if a renewal certificate is filed.

Ownership of Renewal Rights

One rationale for dividing copyright term into an initial 28-year term and a 28-year renewal term was that it gave authors a second bite at the apple. If an author sold her copyright during the initial term, she retained the right to the renewal term. So if a young author sold her novel, which turned into a blockbuster for the publisher, the author might reap the benefits when the initial term ended and the author enjoyed the renewal term. Publishers and other purchasers of copyrights routinely avoided this by buying both the author's copyright and the author's renewal rights.

Some argued that an assignment of renewal rights should not be effective, because this vitiated the protection for authors. *Fred Fisher Music Co. v. M. Witmark & Sons*, 318 U.S. 643 (1943), however, held that an assignment of renewal rights was enforceable. The Court subsequently put an interesting limit on *Fred Fisher*. *Miller Music v. Charles N. Daniels, Inc.*, 362 U.S. 373 (1960), held that the assignment would not be effective if the author died before the time came for filing for renewal. Rather, the right to renew would pass to the author's heirs.

The next question was what about derivative works prepared by the assignee? For example, in *Stewart v. Abend*, 495 U.S. 207 (1990), the author of a short story assigned motion picture rights to a production company, along with the motion picture rights during the renewal term. The production company made a film, *Rear Window* (directed by Alfred Hitchcock and starring Jimmy Stewart and Grace Kelly). The short-story author died before the renewal term, so under *Miller Music*, the assignment of renewal rights was ineffective. The production company argued that it should at least retain the right to show a film that it made during the initial term. The Court rejected that argument, holding that all rights reverted to the author's heirs.

Taken together, the cases meant that assignments of renewal rights were effective, provided that the author survived until the time of renewal. If the author died, all rights reverted to the author's heirs, and even derivative works prepared during the initial term could not be distributed or performed without infringing copyright.

Examples

1. *No starter*. Azure wrote *False Start*, a novel, in 1960. She quickly published, not even pausing to put "© 1960 Azure" on published copies. When does her copyright begin and end?

2. *A little more careful*. Azra wrote *Twenty-Eight Years of Solitude*, an epic poem, in 1960. He meticulously put "© 1960 Azra" on every published copy. Then he went into advertising and forgot about the work. When does his copyright begin and end? What result if he had published the work in 1970?

3. *Belt and suspenders.* Nevaeh wrote "Four Score and Fifteen Years Ago," a ballad, in 1960. She made sure copyright notices appeared where required. She registered the work and duly filed a renewal certificate in 1988. When does her copyright term begin and end?

4. *Portrait of the artist as a young man.* In 1960, Ellis published a superhero comic book, *Invisible Man*. He included a copyright notice, thereby securing federal copyright in the work. He then sold the copyright to Chilton Publishing, along with an assignment of the renewal rights. During the last year of the initial 28-year term, Chilton is about to file a renewal certificate when Ellis objects. The assignment of renewal rights is not enforceable, he argues, because the whole purpose of renewal is to give the author his copyright back—and prevent struggling young artists from irrevocably signing away their rights.
   a. Who owns the rights to the renewal term?
   b. What if Ellis had died and his heirs were seeking the rights? If Chilton had made a movie based on the book, would it retain the right to keep showing the movie?

5. *Life is short; copyright is long.* In 2000, Miranda wrote down the choreography of her dance, *Trailer*. She published the work without including a notice of copyright. She never registered the copyright or filed a renewal certificate.
   a. When would her copyright begin and end? Would it make a difference if the work was never published? Would it make a difference if the author was not identified, making it an anonymous or pseudonymous work?
   b. Suppose the dance was a work made for hire, so that the author and copyright owner was her employer, *Hurricane Dance Co.* When would the copyright expire?

6. *Alternate universe.* Suppose that, rather than life plus 70, the basic term of copyright was life of the author. How would that change things?

7. *The dog that did not bark.* Arthur Conan Doyle's stories featuring Sherlock Holmes were variously published from 1887 to 1927. The last ten were published after 1922 and are therefore still under copyright. The earlier stories are no longer under copyright. Would someone need permission from the copyright owner to create new works with the character of Sherlock Holmes? Would it matter if the character changed somewhat in the final ten stories?

8. *Yes we have no more copyright.* The immortal song "Yes! We Have No Bananas" was published with a proper copyright notice in 1923 and properly renewed. How long did its copyright last? It got a copyright term of 28 years, until 1951. A renewal would extend the term by another 28 years, until 1979. Then the 1976 Copyright Act extended

the terms of such copyrights by 19 years, until 1998 in this case. In 1998, Congress once again extended copyright by 20 years, giving "Yes! We Have No Bananas" a term expiring in 2019. Other works will gradually follow.

Explanations

1. Under the 1909 Act in effect in 1960, when she created the work, she had state law copyright protection. When she published without notice, however, she put the work into the public domain, meaning she had neither state nor copyright protection. This example shows how the subject of this chapter, duration of copyright, often depends on the formalities rules discussed earlier.

2. Under the 1909 Act in effect in 1960, Azra secured the initial 28-year term by publishing with notice. But he did not file for a renewal certificate, which was necessary to get the renewal term, so his copyright term began in 1960 and ended in 1988.

   Had he published in 1970, the result would be different. As a result of the 1992 amendments, filing for renewal is not necessary for works copyrighted after 1963. So he would get an effective term of 95 years (28-year initial term plus 67-year renewal term, comprised of 28 years under 1909 Act, extended by 19 years in 1976, and another 20 years in 1998). 1970 + 95 = 2065.

3. Neveah got her copyright in 1960 by publishing with notice and duly renewed, so she would get an effective term of 95 years (28-year initial term plus 67-year extended renewal term). 1960 + 95 = 2055.

4. a. Ellis cannot get the renewal term back. Notwithstanding the policy underlying renewal, *Fred Fisher Music* held that assignments of renewal rights are enforceable.

      But all is not lost. As discussed later in the book, Ellis would have rights under §304 to terminate the transfer and get his copyright back, effective 56 years into the term of the copyright. 1960 + 56 = 2016. He would then get the last 39 years of the extended renewal term. (If he missed in 2016, he could terminate effective 2035.)

   b. Had Ellis died, the result would be different. Under *Miller Music*, if the author dies before the renewal term vests, an assignment of rights is not effective and the heirs have the right to the renewal term. All rights under the copyright would belong to Ellis's heirs. Had Chilton made a movie based on the book, it would no longer be able to show the movie (which would infringe the public performance right) or make copies of it (which would infringe the reproduction right) or do anything else that would infringe the copyright.

5. a. The §302 rules for post-1977 works would apply. Miranda's copyright term begins when the work is fixed in tangible form and would last for her life plus 70 years. If she died in 2040, for example, the copyright would endure until 2130. Whether the work was published or not makes no difference. Were it an anonymous or pseudonymous work, the term would be 95 years, lasting until 2095.
   b. If it were a work made for hire, her employer would own the copyright, with a term of 95 years.

6. Under existing rules, works published after 1922 are likely to remain under copyright. Works later than 1950, for example, may be under copyright until 2045. Under the copyright-for-life rule, works would frequently pass into the public domain. Authors, unlike copyright, reach the end of their term with regularity. Such a rule would also yield quite dramatic results. Each time a noted author passed away, her works would become free for all, sort of an impromptu copyright amnesty—but it would also introduce considerable uncertainty. It would add risk to making films, for example, because the author of an underlying work might die during production, opening the door to other filmmakers.

7. Because the earlier stories are no longer under copyright, anyone is free to copy them or adapt them, such as using Sherlock Holmes or his sidekick, Dr. Watson. There might be infringement if someone copied creative expression from the stories that are still under copyright. In those stories, Holmes has grown to like dogs, and Watson has been twice married. Copying such later-added elements could be infringement, provided they qualified as protected creative expression. But there is no longer copyright protection in elements from the earlier stories, such as the characters or plots. *See Klinger v. Conan Doyle Estate, Ltd.*, 755 F.3d 496 (7th Cir. Ill. 2014).

8. 1923 + 28 + 28 + 19 + 20 = 2018. In short, 1923 + 95 = 2018. The copyright expired at the end of 2018. After the extensions in 1976 and 1998, Congress did not add 20 more years in 2018. So finally works from 1923 and after are starting to enter the public domain as their copyrights will expire.

WORKS CREATED BUT NOT PUBLISHED OR COPYRIGHTED BEFORE JANUARY 1, 1978

Before the 1976 Act, copyright generally began upon publication of the work with the proper notice. Some unpublished works received federal copyright protection by registration, but generally, the federal copyright statute did not cover unpublished works. The 1976 Act changed that, providing that copyright began upon creation of the work, so now unpublished works had federal copyright. The act provided a specific rule providing for the duration of copyrights in unpublished works created before 1978:

> (a) Copyright in a work created before January 1, 1978, but not theretofore in the public domain or copyrighted, subsists from January 1, 1978, and endures for the term provided by section 302. In no case, however, shall the term of copyright in such a work expire before December 31, 2002; and, if the work is published on or before December 31, 2002, the term of copyright shall not expire before December 31, 2047.

17 U.S.C. §303(a).

Congress tried to balance removing common-law protection with its perpetual term, with a reasonable period of federal protection. Works unpublished as of 1978 get at least the §302 term for post-1977 works (life plus 70, or 95 years for works made for hire, etc.). In addition, by providing for a potentially longer term if the work became published, Congress also provided an incentive to disclose works to the public.

Example

1. *Private correspondence.* In 1970, Baz wrote a long letter to his parents, telling the tale of his first year at college. His parents left the letter in a desk drawer. When would the copyright term begin and end? Would it make a difference if Baz published the letter in 2002?

Explanation

1. This one implicates the special rule for works created but not published as of January 1, 1978. Such works get at least the §302 term for post-1977 works, so the copyright would last until at least the life of Baz plus 70. Moreover, such copyrights last until at least December 31, 2002. If published before December 31, 2002, the term lasts until at least December 31, 2047. In this case, those rules would give few, if any, extra years. If Baz survived until 1978, then his copyright would last until at least 2048 (1978 + 70).

SPECIAL RULE FOR SOUND RECORDINGS

With respect to duration, there is a special rule for sound recordings made prior to 1972. In 1971, Congress amended the 1909 Act to extend federal copyright protection to sound recordings. However, Congress made federal copyright law applicable only to sound recordings fixed on or after February 15, 1972. Sound recordings fixed before that date are still not subject to federal copyright law. *See* §301(c). Rather, they are protected, if at all, by state copyright law (at least until the year 2067! *Id.*). New York law, for example, gives perpetual protection to pre-1972 sound recordings when the alleged act of infringement occurs in New York. *See Capitol Records, Inc. v. Naxos of Am.*, 4 N.Y.3d 540 (N.Y. 2005). Special attention must be paid to pre-1972 sound recordings, which are not subject to the rules governing other works.

HOW LONG CAN COPYRIGHT PROTECTION LAST?

In 1998, Congress added 20 years to the term of all copyrights, both existing and future, but for this term extension, works created during the 1920s and 1930s would be entering the public domain. Now such works will remain under copyright until 2018 and beyond. *Eldred v. Ashcroft* rejected two challenges to the constitutionality of the copyright extension.

The free speech issue in *Eldred* was whether extending the term of existing copyrights by 20 years violated the First Amendment. Copyright, by nature, restricts expression. A copyright holder generally has the exclusive rights to make copies of the work, distribute copies to the public, adapt the work, perform the work publicly, and display the work publicly. The *Eldred* plaintiffs contended that copyright is a content-neutral restriction on speech, subject to an intermediate level of scrutiny, under which the restriction would be constitutional only "if it advances important governmental interests unrelated to the suppression of free speech and does not burden substantially more speech than necessary to further those interests."

The Court held that copyright protection is generally not subject to First Amendment scrutiny, relying on several grounds. First, the Copyright Clause and First Amendment were adopted close together in time. This indicated that the Framers regarded copyright as consistent with the First Amendment. Second, the Court considered copyright and the First Amendment consistent in effect. Copyright is a restriction on speech, but its purpose is the same as the First Amendment: to promote speech. By giving authors exclusive rights, copyright provides a strong incentive for the creation and dissemination of works. Copyright law also has "built-in First Amendment accommodations." Copyright protects only creative expression. It is not copyright infringement to copy ideas from a copyrighted work or make fair use of copyright works for such purposes as education, criticism, news reporting, or research. Relying on these "traditional First Amendment safeguards" contained within copyright law, the Court held that First Amendment scrutiny is unnecessary where "Congress has not altered the traditional contours of copyright protection."

After *Eldred*, fair use and the idea-expression dichotomy appear to attain constitutional status because they are central to the constitutional basis of copyright protection. *See* Stephen M. McJohn, *Eldred's Aftermath: Tradition, the Copyright Clause, and the Constitutionalization of Fair Use*, 10 Mich. Telecommun. Tech. L. Rev. 95 (2003). The fair use doctrine can now also be more explicitly used to protect First Amendment values. Courts may be more likely to go beyond the specific factors listed in the statute. Fair use is a flexible doctrine well suited to addressing the many factors that affect issues of free expression.

The other constitutional issue in *Eldred* was whether the copyright extension exceeded the powers of Congress under the Copyright Clause. The plaintiffs argued that Congress's power to grant copyright for limited times to promote creativity could not be stretched to granting copyrights with no real time limit on works that had been created decades ago. The Court did not read the Copyright Clause itself to impose limits on the intellectual property regime chosen by Congress. Copyright legislation would not be subject to scrutiny to see whether it indeed served the avowed purpose of the clause, to further the Progress of Science. Rather, *Eldred* largely left it to Congress to choose how to regulate in the area of intellectual property: "As we read the Framers' instruction, the Copyright Clause empowers Congress to determine the intellectual property regimes that, overall, in that body's judgment, will serve the ends of the Clause."

Congress needed only a rational basis for the copyright extension. Various justifications were made for extending the term of existing copyrights. By consistently making all extensions retroactive, Congress could assure authors of the benefit of extensions that occurred after creation. This assurance would add to the initial incentive to create the work. The extension also was thought to harmonize U.S. law with the longer copyright terms in some jurisdictions, assuring U.S. authors of equal treatment abroad, permitting the United States to play a strong role in shaping international intellectual property regimes, and creating more incentives for foreign works to be distributed in the United States. Another rationale was that longer copyright terms would encourage copyright holders to invest in the "restoration and public distribution of their works." There were colorable arguments served by the term extension. Such reasons were sufficient to show a rational basis for the retrospective copyright term extension, *Eldred* held.

Example

1. *Copyright futures*. Suppose that in 2018 Congress again adds 20 years to the term of copyright. Pre-1978 works would then have a term of 115 years, and works dating back to 1922 would remain under copyright (assuming that formalities such as publication with notice and renewal had been met). Would that be constitutional under *Eldred?* Suppose instead of lengthening copyright, Congress broadened it by abolishing fair use

or by prohibiting copying ideas from copyrighted works. Would that be constitutional under *Eldred?*

Explanation

1. The reasons *Eldred* gave for upholding the 20-year extension of 1998 would probably apply equally to another 20-year extension in 2018. As to the Copyright Clause, *Eldred* essentially held that Congress's reasons met the low requirements of a rational basis. One reason (harmonization with other countries) might not apply to a 115-year term, but the others would still obtain. The First Amendment argument would likewise seem similar, where Congress retained the traditional contours of copyright while extending the term. In short, *Eldred* did not require much of Congress in 1998 and likely would not in 2018.

   Abolishing fair use or prohibiting the copying of ideas would be different. *Eldred* held that copyright's restrictions on speech are consistent with the First Amendment because of copyright's built-in First Amendment protections, in particular fair use and the idea-expression dichotomy. If those safeguards were removed, then stricter scrutiny under the First Amendment would apply. It is hard to think of any policies that would support such broad restrictions on speech.

CAN TRADEMARK LAW EFFECTIVELY EXTEND COPYRIGHTS?

In *Dastar Corp. v. Twentieth Century Fox Film Corp.*, 123 S. Ct. 2041, 2047-2049 (2003), the Supreme Court carefully maintained the distinction between copyright protection and protection under the Trademark Act. Twentieth Century Fox had held copyrights in videos about World War II, but the copyrights had expired because of failure to renew. Dastar subsequently republished the videos after removing credits to the original producers. Fox could not sue for copyright infringement, but Fox contended that by failing to properly attribute authorship, Dastar falsely attributed the "origin" of the goods in violation of trademark law. But "origin of goods," the court held, "refers to the producer of the tangible goods that are offered for sale, and not to the author of any idea, concept, or communication embodied in those goods." Trademark law would not provide a cause of action for failing to attribute authorship. In so holding, the court sought to maintain the distinction between the proper domains of copyright and trademark: "To hold otherwise would be akin to finding that §43(a) created a species of perpetual patent and copyright, which Congress may not do." Under *Dastar*, once a work falls into the public domain, the former copyright holder may not use trademark law to prevent its use by others.

CHAPTER 10

Copyright Transactions

Author writes her brilliant novel. She owns the copyright, with its bundle of exclusive rights: the right to make copies, sell them, make a movie out of her book, distribute and exhibit the movie, translate the book into Swedish, and so on. She may wish to do those things for various reasons—to make money, to deliver her work to audiences, to gain the esteem of the public and her peers. But she need not do those things personally. Rather, she could enter into contracts with publishers, movie studios, translators—or simply sell the entire copyright and leave it to the buyer to exploit the rights (but what if she wants to write a sequel?). She can transfer the copyright or license the novel for various purposes. Such agreements allow her to do various things: get licensing fees and control how the work is distributed, adapted, and disseminated. She can even use the copyright as collateral to get a loan. Copyright transactions serve both the incentive purpose of copyright (by providing an avenue to receive income, which is an incentive to create in the first place) and the author's rights purpose (by allowing authors a measure of control over how the work appears to the public—how it is distributed, adapted, and performed).

There are several mechanisms by which copyright owners can grant some or all of their rights to others. The author can simply sell the copyright outright. She may sell it for cash, for a promissory note, for a percentage of the buyer's revenue. She might sell it along with other assets in the sale of a business, or she might sell it along with a promise to perform services for the buyer (such as promoting, adapting, or updating the work). Authors can sell their copyrights before the work is even created. Employees and independent contractors, for example, often sign contracts providing that copyright in works they create will belong to the hiring party. Copyrights may also be conveyed for noncommercial reasons, such as donating to a museum or foundation the copyright in a work.

Other transactions allow the copyright owner to retain some rights while granting some rights to others. An exclusive license allows Author to grant a chunk of her rights to another. For example, Author might sell publication rights to Publisher. She might sell to Publisher an exclusive license to make copies and distribute copies of the work in book form. She would retain all other rights, such as the right to make a movie out of the book and to write a sequel. Through a contract, Author can carve out the rights conveyed quite specifically. Publisher might get the exclusive right to publish the book in hardcover form in English in the United States for a limited number of years. Copyrights, in a word, are divisible, meaning that rights may be parceled out to different licensees. To see the importance of divisibility in licensing, one need only look to Broadway. A musical may be just one of many works licensed under the original work. Works like *Harry Potter* and *The Lion King* have generated a broad range of derivative works (copyright) not to mention associated goods and services (trademark)—which would be more difficult in a world where copyright was indivisible and trademarks could not be licensed (if an overly strict view of source indicator was applied).

Copyright owners also use nonexclusive licenses, both for commercial and noncommercial purposes. An exclusive license does two things: It grants permission and makes that permission exclusive (meaning the grantor cannot give the same permission to someone else). A nonexclusive license does only the first—grants permission. Software companies that "sell" software typically grant nonexclusive licenses. Someone who purchases the software may use it (because they get a license), but cannot exclude others from using it (because the license is nonexclusive). Two competitors might settle a copyright infringement suit by granting each other nonexclusive licenses (thereby freeing each other of their respective infringement claims). An author might give permission for an anthology to include large portions of the novel, or a filmmaker might agree to let her footage be used in another's documentary. The permissions would likely take the form of a nonexclusive license. Universities are increasingly involved in intellectual property licensing, both licensing their own works and getting licenses to use material. Hence such tech transfer offices as the Innovation and New Ventures Office (INVO) (Northwestern University), the Center for Technology Transfer and Enterprise Creation (CTTEC) (Carnegie Mellon), the Office of Licensing and Ventures (Duke), and the Office of Industry Engagement (OIE) (Georgia Tech).

The author may also wish to allow others to use her work freely. Copyright licensing is used to make works available to the public for free.

Software, for example, may be distributed subject to an open source license. The license may provide that anyone may freely use, copy, adapt, improve, or do anything they like with the software—provided that they do not impose any legal restrictions on use of the software or on the changes they make. Some writers, musicians, and other creators are following this practice. An author may use a Creative Commons license to permit others to use her work, subject to conditions of the author's choosing (such as giving proper attribution or use for nonprofit purposes).

As AI starts to handle many transactions, the power of AI to make binding agreements on the behalf of people may become an issue. Related to that is the issue of smart contracts, where the formation and execution may all be done by software, which raises contract issues as well.

In short, licensing has become a substantial practice area among copyright lawyers. This chapter lays out some of the fundamental rules and issues.

TRANSFERS AND LICENSING: FORMALITIES REQUIRED

For many grants to be effective, there must be a writing signed by the copyright owners:

> A transfer of copyright ownership, other than by operation of law, is not valid unless an instrument of conveyance, or a note or memorandum of the transfer is in writing and signed by the owner of the rights conveyed.

17 U.S.C. §204(a). A transfer of copyright ownership is not valid without a signed writing. The rule sounds relatively narrow, as though a signed writing is required if the author sells the copyright, but not for other transactions. The term "transfer of copyright ownership," however, is broadly defined to include even partial or contingent transfers of ownership:

> assignment, mortgage, exclusive license, or any other conveyance, alienation, or hypothecation of a copyright or of any of the exclusive rights comprised in a copyright, whether or not it is limited in time or place of effect, but not including a nonexclusive license.

17 U.S.C. §101.

Many transactions involving a copyright must be reflected by a writing signed by the transferor. Validity requires a signed writing if the author sells his copyright, grants a studio an exclusive right to make a movie, uses the copyright as collateral for a loan ("hypothecation," as the statute quaintly puts it), gives a bookstore the exclusive right to sell the book in Boston, or gives another author exclusive rights to write a sequel to the book. Judge Kozinski has nicely summarized the rationale:

> Common sense tells us that agreements should routinely be put in writing. This simple practice prevents misunderstandings by spelling out the terms of a deal in black and white, forces parties to clarify their thinking and consider problems that could potentially arise, and encourages them to take their promises seriously because it's harder to backtrack on a written contract than on an oral one.

Effects Associates v. Cohen, 908 F.2d 555, 557 (9th Cir. 1990).

The statute requires no special form. It requires "an instrument of conveyance, or a note or memorandum of the transfer" signed by the transferor. The statute does not require any particular wording. A "transfer of copyright" need not use the word "transfer" or "copyright" or any other particular word, but the writing must be sufficient to show that the parties actually agreed to convey rights in the copyright. An agreement to sell an author's "ownership rights" to a book would not suffice if it was not clear that the agreement covered the copyright in the work, as opposed to other rights, such as ownership of the manuscript or contractual royalty rights. *See Saxon v. Blann*, 968 F.2d 676 (8th Cir. 1992). The writing must also be sufficient to show which rights the parties agreed on.

The actual agreement between the parties need not be set forth in a writing signed by the transferor. Rather, a "note or memorandum" would be sufficient, meaning that not all the terms of the agreement need be reflected in the writing. The memorandum could be signed after the fact. Some courts have even held that if a writing is signed sometime after an oral agreement, it makes the transfer effective as of the date of the oral agreement. Other courts have held the transfer would be effective only when the writing is signed. It could make a big difference, such as where a party went into bankruptcy or signed an agreement with another party during the interval between the oral agreement and the written memorandum.

An electronic "writing" could also suffice. Under the federal E-Sign statute, "a signature, contract, or other record relating to such transaction may not be denied legal effect, validity, or enforceability solely because it is in electronic form." 15 U.S.C. §7001. The mere fact that the agreement or signature was in electronic form would not prevent validity.

Not every writing will qualify as "instrument of conveyance, or a note or memorandum." A fax that simply references a deal without specifying even the general terms of the deal is insufficient. *See Radio Television Espanola v. New World Entertainment*, 183 F.3d 922 (9th Cir. 1999). Likewise, a writing that refers to contracts which are not yet finalized is insufficient. *Id.* Rather, the writing must show that there was an agreement and show the key terms of the agreement.

Courts have not been amenable to arguments that exceptions should be read into the statute. In state contract law, no signed writing may be required for various reasons (if one party has performed, or if the parties do not deny the existence of a contract, or if the amount at stake is small, or if the goods are specially manufactured). Under the federal copyright statute, however, courts have rejected arguments that no writing should be required where industry practices are to use oral agreements or where one party has paid the agreed-on price. Rather, courts generally apply the unconditional language of section 204 according to its terms.

NO WRITING REQUIRED FOR NONEXCLUSIVE LICENSE (MAY BE WRITTEN, ORAL, OR IMPLIED LICENSES)

A "transfer of copyright ownership" is invalid without a signed writing. The definition is very broad, covering any transfer of rights or exclusive license. But a *nonexclusive* license need not be reflected by a writing. One must therefore distinguish between exclusive and nonexclusive licenses. A license is exclusive if the author cannot then grant the same rights to someone else. An exclusive license could be broad (the exclusive right to make copies of author's book) or narrow (the exclusive right to sell copies of the book in Dubuque, Iowa). An exclusive license effectively conveys parts of the copyright holder's rights to the licensee, so it is treated as a transfer of ownership. By contrast, a nonexclusive license effectively says, "I authorize you to do the following, but I can turn around and authorize someone else to do it as well." If an author gives a nonexclusive license to Publisher 1 to print and sell the book, the author could authorize Publisher 2 to do so as well. Some examples of nonexclusive licenses are a playwright who authorizes a theater troupe to perform her play publicly; an author who gives permission to publisher to reprint excerpts of his novel in a book on creative writing; a software developer who allows others to freely use, copy, and adapt her computer program, provided they abide by certain conditions; a software company that allows users to use its software, for a fee. Provided each copyright owner retains the ability to grant similar licenses to others, all would be nonexclusive licenses.

No writing is required for a nonexclusive license. The grant of permission may be oral. It need not even be explicit. A nonexclusive license may be implied from the conduct of the parties. Where one party could reasonably conclude that the copyright owner has agreed to allow certain conduct without claiming infringement, there will be an implied nonexclusive license. For example, if an author and an investor form a partnership to publish a book on how to restore Ford F-100 pickup trucks, the investor supplies the capital, and the author hands over a manuscript, there is an implied license from the author to the partnership to use the manuscript. *See Oddo v. Ries*, 743 F.2d 630 (9th Cir. 1984). The implied nonexclusive license often acts as a gap filler when the parties fail to address the copyright issue in a signed writing.

There is often interplay between the requirement of a writing and the work-made-for-hire doctrine. If one party hires an independent contractor to create a work, the contractor owns the copyright unless the parties agree otherwise in writing. If a newspaper hires a freelancer to write a story about winter sports in Buffalo, the freelancer would own the copyright to the story (unless the parties agree otherwise in writing, which newspapers and writers usually do), but the parties' conduct implies that they expect the newspaper to print the story. That was the purpose of the transaction. The newspaper would have an implied, nonexclusive license to print the story. The scope of the license would be limited. The newspaper may not have the right to reprint the story in a book, and the license would be nonexclusive—meaning that the freelancer would retain the entire copyright, with the ability to grant licenses to others (such as permitting other newspapers to print the story or authorizing publication of the story in a book). Note that the implied contract theory is only a gap filler for when the parties simply do not address the copyright issue. It would not override an agreed term in the contract.

Is There a Contract?

A key contract law issue for nonexclusive licenses: Under contract law, what does it take to get binding consent to the conditions in a copyright license? The formalities of a signature and a signed writing may not be necessary, but some agreement (express or implied) is necessary before a court will enforce the terms against the purported licensee. This can be especially important when the licensor uses the license not just to convey rights but also to condition use of the material on various restrictions, which may well go beyond what copyright alone gives the rights holder. Copyrighted content is increasingly provided online with click-through licenses that seek to protect the copyright holder and to limit the use of information. The limited case law has generally proved favorable for licensors. *Register.com, Inc. v. Verio, Inc.*, 356 F.3d 393 (2d Cir. 2004), for example, held a license binding even when the user would not encounter it before using the material. The defendant was a repeat visitor to a database. The contractual restrictions would not appear until sent with a response to each request for information. Such restrictions may not have bound a onetime visitor, but since the defendant used the database numerous times, it was well aware of the practice of providing information subject to restrictions. By continuing to use the database, it was deemed to manifest assent.

Examples

1. *Unpermit.* The PolCon convention brings together politicians from all parties for nonpartisan panels discussing matters from campaign strategy to fundraising to relocation of families. At one public panel, Senator Stinton discusses her recently released autobiography. Mower, a filmmaker on the panel, requests the exclusive right to make a film adapted from the book, promising any profits to go to charity. Stinton publicly and clearly agrees to Mower's offer. Mower starts work on a screenplay but soon learns that Stinton has authorized another film. Mower complains, arguing that the film would violate the exclusive rights granted by Stinton. The transfer of exclusive rights was invalid, Stinton contends, because there was no signed writing. Mower responds that the lack of writing is irrelevant. No one denies that Stinton gave permission, he argues, so the usual need for a writing as evidence of the agreement is unnecessary. What result?

2. *Change of heart.* Gray phones Leonardo, a gifted artist. Gray requests permission to include Leonardo's drawings of human figures in Gray's anatomy text. Leonardo tells her to go right ahead. After Gray's book becomes a fixture on every medical student's bookshelf, Leonardo demands royalties and threatens to sue. Leonardo does not deny that he gave permission. Oral permission, he contends, is insufficient. Since there is no signed writing, the permission is invalid. Is Leonardo correct?

3. *Not worth the paper it's not written on.* Palette shows her latest painting to Baron, who is immediately enthralled. The two orally agree that Palette will sell both the painting and its copyright to Baron for an agreed sum, immediately paid by Baron. Baron's art collection is included in a show that tours the country. Palette's painting becomes renowned. Baron decides to market posters with reproductions of the painting. Palette's lawyer contacts Baron, contending that the copyright was not validly conveyed to Baron. Was there a valid transfer of copyright ownership?

   Suppose instead that Baron purchased the painting and Palette orally gave him permission to make and distribute posters that reproduced the painting. Is such oral permission valid?

4. *Transfer of copyright ownership?* As the statute states, a "transfer of copyright ownership, other than by operation of law, is not valid unless an instrument of conveyance, or a note or memorandum of the transfer, is in writing and signed by the owner of the rights conveyed." Which of the following would require a signed writing?
   a. Jot sells Print the copyright to Jot's new novel.
   b. Print sells Press the copyright to Jot's novel.
   c. Press sells Mag the exclusive right to reprint a chapter from the novel, with such right limited to publication in a magazine during December of that year.

d. Editor phones Potaster and receives permission to include one of Potaster's sonnets in a collection of poetry.
e. Jute sells Museum the manuscript to Jute's new novel.
f. Jape gets a loan from Bank, putting up the copyright in a software package as collateral.
g. Publisher agrees to print 1,000 copies of Potaster's book of poetry in exchange for 10 percent of Potaster's sales.
h. Condi gets permission from Ringo to sample one of his recordings in a song she is recording. She intends to take a three-second snippet from Ringo's recording and use it repeatedly as part of her work—and hopes to sell millions of copies.

5. *Sign-off.* Newfie Museum purchases a painting from Artist. Newfie writes a check payable to Artist. The back of the check reads, "By signing this, you acknowledge that rights to the painting belong to Newfie." Artist signs the back of the check and deposits it in his account. Does Newfie now hold the copyright in the painting (including, for example, the exclusive right to publish a copy of the painting in a magazine)?

6. *Hypothecation situation.* Bank agrees to finance Houston's new animated film. The parties sign a loan agreement, in which Houston grants Bank a security interest in all her "equipment, accounts, and general intangibles, now owned or after-acquired." The legal definition of "general intangibles" would include copyrights. Houston subsequently denies that Bank has a security interest in the copyrights of a screenplay and film authored by Houston. The bank, Houston contends, would have needed a separate transfer of copyright, specifically identifying the copyrights, using such words as "I hereby transfer ownership of my copyright, as collateral for the loan." Are the copyrights collateral for the loan?

7. *E-writing?* Shiva reads a new play by Russ, *Motion to Remove File from Pile with Forklift*, a saga of wily debtors and ruthless creditors. Shiva e-mails Russ, clearly requesting exclusive rights to stage the play in Illinois, promising Russ that her troupe will do the work justice (and pay him 25 percent of the ticket sales). He e-mails back: "Agreed! Best, Russ." The play opens in Peoria to rave reviews and full houses. Just as Shiva is negotiating for a run in Chicago, she learns that Russ has authorized a production by a Chicago company, Steppenwolf. When she threatens to sue, Russ denies that he ever put the permission in a signed writing, as required for validity. Shiva offers to show printouts of the e-mail. She further points out that copies of the e-mail have been saved on her and Russ's computers and likely elsewhere, which would be more than sufficient to fix a work in tangible form. If that's sufficient for the Constitution (which treats them as "Writings" of an author), that should be enough for section 204, she argues. Will she succeed?

8. *Invitation withdrawn*. The copyright page of *Fitz's Guide to Linux* reads, "To help spread the word about Linux, the author hereby grants permission to anyone to republish the contents of this book." Fitz had orally instructed the publisher to include that statement but never put anything in writing. Thusi takes Fitz at his word and prints and sells thousands of copies of the book. Fitz, who retained the copyright, is enraged that Thusi is profiting from his generosity and sues Thusi for copyright infringement. The permission is not valid, Fitz contends, because it was not signed by Fitz.

9. *Policy*. Foraste works as a photographer for Brown University, taking photos that are used in various Brown publications. Brown has adopted a copyright policy:

   > Ownership: It is the University's position that, as a general premise, ownership of copyrightable property which results from performance of one's University duties and activities will belong to the author or originator. This applies to books, art works, software, etc.

   After Foraste leaves his job at Brown, he claims copyright in all the photos he took. Is the university policy sufficient to transfer copyright to him?

10. *Implied exclusive license?* Freelancer orally agrees to shoot some wildlife footage for Auteur's feature film. Freelancer spends a couple of weeks camping and shooting digital video in Alaska, returning with some great grizzly footage. In exchange for $100,000, Freelancer hands over several storage discs with the best footage, which Auteur incorporates into the film. Auteur is then enraged several months later when she sees the same footage used in a competing film with permission of Freelancer. Auteur argues that the generous fee gave her an implied transfer of the exclusive right to use the footage in a film. Was there an implied exclusive license?

11. *Hidden masterpiece*. Taeto creates a phantasmic tattoo, stitching a sketch of a snow leopard onto Becket's forearm. Becket is pleased and hands over the agreed fee of $400. Taeto then tells Becket, "Now remember not to let anyone take your picture. I hold the copyright in that tattoo and don't want anyone making copies of it." Does Taeto own the copyright? Must Becket cover up when a camera comes out to protect his family and friends from infringement?

12. *Who owns Bob the Tomato?* Lyrick Studios and Big Idea Productions negotiate over a distribution deal for videos of Big Idea's *Veggie Tales*, a cartoon featuring Bob the Tomato and Larry the Cucumber. The parties exchange faxes, listing both agreed terms and terms still under discussion. They strike an oral agreement, under which Lyrick will have

the exclusive license to distribute *Veggie Tales*. Lyrick distributes *Veggie Tales* for some time, until the relationship deteriorates. Big Idea authorizes another distributor to take over, whereupon Lyrick sues for breach of the exclusive license agreement. Is there an enforceable agreement? If not, is Lyrick itself liable, for distributing *Veggie Tales* without authority?

13. *Or not to tweet*. Twitter's terms of service, which grant Twitter a nonexclusive license to photographs uploaded by users. Would that authorize Twitter's users to reproduce the photos, such as by other media outlets using them for news reporting?

14. *All for one*. Under and Ground are joint authors of the novel *Railroad*. Could either one effectively grant exclusive movie rights to studio?

Explanations

1. The transfer of exclusive rights was invalid, for lack of a signed writing. The rule is quite plain: "A transfer of copyright ownership, other than by operation of law, is not valid unless an instrument of conveyance, or a note or memorandum of the transfer is in writing and signed by the owner of the rights conveyed." Its text includes no exceptions, and courts have not read any into the statute, so Mower would not have exclusive rights to make the movie.

2. No writing was necessary, because Gray is not claiming that there was a transfer of copyright ownership. If she claimed to have exclusive rights to use the drawings, that would be a transfer of copyright ownership (as an exclusive license), requiring a signed license. But Gray claims only that Leonardo gave her permission to use the drawings. That would be a nonexclusive writing, which may be oral (or even implied). So oral permission is sufficient. The court must also determine, as a matter of state contract law, whether the agreement is valid.

3. No valid transfer of copyright ownership occurred. A transfer of copyright ownership is not valid without a writing signed by the transferor. Here the parties had only an oral agreement, so the necessary writing is absent. Palette still owns the copyright, and Baron would potentially infringe if he started making and selling copies of the painting.

   The result would be different if Palette had given Baron oral permission to make and sell copies. If she did not give him the exclusive right to do so, such permission would be a nonexclusive license. A nonexclusive license need not be in writing to be valid.

4. a. A conveyance of the copyright is a transfer of copyright ownership and requires a signed writing for validity.

b. This is also a conveyance of the copyright and likewise requires a signed writing. The rule is not limited to a conveyance by the initial author but applies to any transfer of copyright ownership.
c. The exclusive license is a transfer of copyright ownership and requires a signed writing for validity. The definition of "transfer of copyright ownership" explicitly includes the transfer of an exclusive right, even if there are limits as to time and place (such as the limits to publication in a magazine during December).
d. Permission to reprint the sonnet in a collection of poetry is not a transfer of copyright ownership; rather, it is a nonexclusive license, which does not require a writing for validity. The permission is nonexclusive because Potaster could give permission to someone else to likewise include the sonnet in a collection of poetry. It would be exclusive only if Potaster granted permission to publish and agreed that Potaster could not authorize others to do the same thing. In other words, the license is exclusive if it excludes others from the rights at issue.
e. Here there was a sale of the manuscript, not of the copyright. Sale of the manuscript is not a transfer of copyright ownership. Sale of the manuscript is not a transaction involving the copyright at all but simply the sale of an object, so copyright law does not apply. Rather, contract law governs whether a signed writing is required (and, under the U.C.C., if the price is paid, no writing is required for enforcement of the contract).
f. Putting a copyright up as collateral falls within the definition of "transfer of copyright ownership" as a "hypothecation" of a copyright. Accordingly, a signed writing is required for validity.
g. This is simply a nonexclusive license, requiring no signed writing. Mainly it is a contract for printing services, but there is also a license permitting Publisher to make copies without infringing.
h. This permission is not exclusive, so it would not require a signed writing. Of course, Condi may still have to prove that Ringo agreed, so a signed writing is a good idea.

5. Newfie probably does not hold the copyright on the grounds that there was not a sufficient signed writing. This case is really a matter of contract law and of interpreting the parties' writing. A note or memorandum of transfer of copyright need be in no special form. If the check had read, "By signing this, you acknowledge that the copyright in the painting is transferred to Newfie," and the author signed it, it would have been sufficient. But the note or memorandum must show the parties' intent to transfer the copyright. "Rights to the painting" does not clearly do so; rather, it seems to refer to ownership of the painting itself. A court likely would not hold it to be a note or memorandum of transfer of ownership. *Compare Playboy Enters. v. Dumas*, 53 F.3d 549 (2d Cir. 1995).

6. The copyrights are collateral for the loan. Use of copyrights as collateral is a transfer of copyright ownership ("hypothecation" is included in the definition of "transfer of copyright ownership"). The transaction requires a signed writing. The statute does not require the use of any particular words, however, but rather a writing sufficient to show the specific grant of rights claimed. If the parties used a term ("general intangibles") commonly understood to include copyright, that would likely be sufficient. This is not a case where the parties' writing was too vague to show that the claimed rights were not transferred.

7. The case involves a claimed exclusive license, so there must be a writing signed by Russ for it to be valid. The question would be whether the e-mails would be sufficient. Shiva's e-mail clearly set out the terms of the exclusive license (exclusive rights to perform the play in Illinois in exchange for 25 percent of the ticket sales). Russ's e-mail shows clear acceptance ("Agreed! Best, Russ."). Is an e-mail a "writing" for the purposes of section 204? And did Russ "sign" it? The copyright statute does not define writing. E-mail was not in widespread use when the provision was enacted in 1976, but the federal E-Sign statute provides that "a signature, contract, or other record relating to such transaction may not be denied legal effect, validity, or enforceability solely because it is in electronic form." So, provided that the e-mails otherwise meet the requirements of section 204, the fact that they are in electronic form will not deny validity.

8. The permission did not need to be signed. Fitz granted "permission to anyone to republish the contents of this book." He did not grant exclusive rights to anyone, so it was a nonexclusive license, which does not require a signed writing. It was therefore effective.

9. The court held that the policy was insufficient to convey the copyright to Foraste. It held that the policy was not sufficiently clear to show specifically which rights had been conveyed, because it spoke only of a general policy, and the specific works referred to were books, artworks, and software, quite different from the catalog photographs taken by Foraste. *See Foraste v. Brown Univ.*, 290 F. Supp. 2d 234, 236 (D.R.I. 2003). It lacked the requisite specificity to meet the requirements of section 204.

   With respect to university copyright policies generally, another problem for employees may be the requirement of a signature. If, for example, the policy is adopted by vote of the faculty or by inclusion in an employee handbook, there may be no actual signature by the university. Rather, the employee may need to find a writing signed by the university (such as an employment contract that incorporates the employee handbook by reference). A careful employee may have it spelled out in writing in the employment contract.

10. Auteur cannot get an implied exclusive license. *Cf. Effects Associates v. Cohen*, 908 F.2d 555, 557 (9th Cir. 1990). A transfer of copyright ownership (which includes an exclusive license) must be evidenced by a signed writing to be valid. So such a transfer cannot be implied from the conduct of the parties. A nonexclusive license need not be in writing, so courts can infer a nonexclusive license from conduct. If Auteur used the footage, a court likely would hold that Auteur did not infringe because, under the circumstances, Auteur received implied permission to use it, but such implied permission would not be exclusive.

11. This example serves to point out some other rules that interplay with the writing requirement. Taeto does own the copyright. The tattoo was not a work made for hire, and the parties did not assign ownership, so Taeto is the author and owner of the copyright. When one party creates the work for another but retains the copyright, courts are likely to hold that the hiring party has an implied license to utilize the work. But that may make little difference here. Becket does not need Taeto's permission to wear the tattoo. Under the first sale doctrine (discussed later in the book), he may publicly display the work because he is the owner of a lawfully made copy. He might be concerned that infringement may occur if others take pictures of the tattoo. A court could decide that Taeto gave an implied license for some photos (such as typical family or news photos). That would be most appropriate if the parties discussed likely uses of the tattoo before having it done, but generally speaking, the issue would be addressed under such doctrines as fair use or de minimis infringement (both discussed later in the book). For a discussion of such issues, *see* Thomas F. Cotter and Angela M. Mirabole, *Written on the Body: Intellectual Property Rights in Tattoos, Makeup, and Other Body Art*, 10 UCLA Ent. L. Rev. 97 (2003).

12. If this were a contract case, there would probably be an enforceable contract in which the parties have an oral agreement and have performed it for a period of time. But federal copyright law requires a signed writing for an exclusive license (or other transfer of copyright ownership) to be effective, so Lyrick would not have an enforceable exclusive license agreement. *See Lyrick Studios, Inc. v. Big Idea Prods.*, 420 F.3d 388 (5th Cir. 2005).

    Lyrick would not succeed in enforcing the agreement. On the next issue, however, Lyrick would not be liable for unauthorized distribution. From their oral agreement and conduct, a court would likely find an implied, *nonexclusive* license to distribute *Veggie Tales*.

13. Permission to Twitter does not give permission to Twitter's users. If others make use of the photos, they could be liable for infringement. *See Agence France Presse v. Morel*, 769 F. Supp. 2d 295 (S.D.N.Y. 2011).

14. No. Joint authors each have independent rights to grant licenses, subject to the requirement to share profits. One joint author could not effectively grant exclusive rights, because the other joint author could grant similar rights to someone else. *See Tresóna Multimedia, LLC v. Burbank High School Vocal Music Ass'n*, 953 F.3d 638 (2020).

OPEN SOURCE LICENSES AND FREE SOFTWARE ("THINK FREE SPEECH, NOT FREE BEER")

Someone who writes software can give the world permission to use it for free, subject to certain restrictions, by using an open source license (also known as a free software license). Open source software is not in the public domain. The software is kept under copyright but freely licensed under one of various open source licenses, such as the General Public License ("GPL," used as verb, noun, adjective, and every other part of speech), the certification mark "OSI Certified," or the Artistic License. *See* Stephen McJohn, *The Paradoxes of Free Software*, 9 Geo. Mason L. Rev. 25 (2000).

Ariel develops a computer program that translates text from Swedish to Finnish. She could make it freely available to others under an open source license. Such licenses state that anyone who gets a copy of the software can use it, change it, make and distribute more copies, and even sell copies or adaptations without paying royalties to the original author. The open source license requires little—but it does not abandon the copyright. It may restrict uses, such as not permitting commercial applications or certain adaptations. It may require attribution—meaning that the author must be given credit. Most open source licenses seek to ensure the software remains free by providing that anyone who incorporates it into software must make that software available under an open source license.

The idea spread from software to other creative fields. Creative Commons (CC) licenses are often used with works (literary works, music, film, and beyond). A CC license allows others to use this work, subject to the author's choice of restrictions:

- **Noncommercial:** You let others copy, distribute, display, and perform your work—and derivative works based on it—but for noncommercial purposes only.
- **No Derivative Works:** You let others copy, distribute, display, and perform only verbatim copies of your work, not derivative works based on it.
- **Share Alike:** You allow others to distribute derivative works only under a license identical to the license that governs your work.

Others may use the work, provided they abide by whatever restrictions the author chose, such as not making a commercial use, or not making derivative works, or allowing others to likewise use the user's work. The use must also give proper attribution to the copyright holder—meaning that the user must give credit to the copyright holder. CC used to provide an option of whether attribution was required—but no one ever chose to make their work available without requiring attribution. Even when people give their work away, they feel credit should be given, suggesting that attribution is a core value of intellectual property generally.

Example

1. *Abandoned?* Model railroad enthusiasts use Jacobsen's copyrighted software to control model trains. One can visit Jacobsen's website and download the code by agreeing to the terms of the Artistic License, which allows most uses but conditions that permission on proper attribution. A company downloads the code and incorporates it into a commercial product without giving any credit to Jacobsen. The company argues that Jacobsen cannot sue for copyright infringement, because he has agreed that anyone can make copies and otherwise use the software. They may have failed to give attribution, but that would merely be a breach of the licensing contract, not copyright infringement. Has Jacobsen given up his right to sue for copyright infringement by allowing the world to freely use the code?
2. *Commercial use?* Timor writes a play satirizing the political events of the year and releases it under a Creative Commons Noncommercial license. Nonprofit loves the play and decides to distribute hundreds of copies across the nation's capital. Nonprofit has a commercial copy shop make 500 copies of the play, for which the copy shop makes a nice profit. Is the copy shop liable for breaching the "noncommercial" condition of the license?

Explanation

1. Jacobsen can sue for copyright infringement, because the permission to use the code is conditioned on compliance with the license. *Jacobsen v. Katzer*, 535 F.3d 1373 (2008). The copyright holder can sue for copyright infringement (on the theory that unauthorized use beyond the conditions in the license took the licensee beyond the scope of the nonexclusive license), and is not limited to an action for breach of license. Open source licenses are enforceable contracts, not gifts. They can be a tool to encourage the use of the subject matter but control the manner in which it is used.

2. One court has held that a party making a nonprofit use may use the services of profit-making entity, such as a for-profit copy shop, to achieve its permitted use.[1]

RECORDATION

Transfers of copyright ownership and other documents pertaining to a copyright may (not must) be recorded in the U.S. Copyright Office. 17 U.S.C. §205. Suppose Electra has the copyright in a song she wrote. She could sell the copyright, or give permission to use the song in a film, or use her copyright as collateral for a loan, or sign any other document pertaining to the copyright. Any of the documents could be recorded in the Copyright Office.

The person who directly benefits from recording is not Elektra but the recipient of the grant. By recording the document, the recipient gets protection against subsequent, inconsistent grants by Elektra. If Elektra sells her guitar to Jimi, it would likely be difficult for her to sell the same guitar again to Eric. Jimi has the guitar now, so Elektra has nothing to deliver. But if she sells her copyright, that is simply an agreement to transfer an intangible right, not bound up in any object, so if Jimi pays her for it, she could still get Eric to pay her for it. Recordation provides a mechanism for parties to protect their rights.

Recordation gives other persons constructive notice of the facts within, provided the work has been registered and the document so identifies the relevant copyright that a reasonable search of the records would disclose it. 17 U.S.C. §205(c). As between two conflicting transfers, the first to be executed has priority if it is recorded within a month of execution (two months if executed abroad). Otherwise, the first to be recorded takes priority if the transferee took it in good faith, for consideration, and without notice. 17 U.S.C. §205(d). If Jimi buys Electra's copyright and promptly records the transfer agreement, he has priority against Eric, a subsequent transferee. By

1. Nor can the reservation of rights contained in the License be read to preclude a licensee from hiring someone to make copies of the Materials so the licensee can use them for a "non-Commercial" purpose. The applicable provision states in relevant part: "To the extent possible, Licensor waives any right to collect royalties from You for the exercise of the Licensed Rights. . . . In all other cases the Licensor expressly reserves any right to collect such royalties, including when the Licensed Material is used other than for NonCommerical Purposes." Rather, the unambiguous import of this provision is to reserve GM's right to collect royalties from a licensee if the *licensee* exceeds the scope of the license by, for example, selling copies of the Materials. *Great Minds v. Fedex Office and Print Services, Inc.*, 886 F.3d 91 (2d Cir. 2018).

contrast, if an author sells his copyright twice, the second buyer may take priority if she records first. Someone who receives a grant of copyright is well advised to record it to protect against subsequent claimants.

A buyer can also get protection from searching the records. The first transferee gets priority only by recording first or by recording within a month of the transfer (two months for transfers executed abroad). The buyer can condition payment on recording and searching to ensure no prior transfers were recorded. A careful buyer could file and then wait long enough to make sure that no competing transferee had filed within a month of their transfer.

COPYRIGHTS AS COLLATERAL

One important question remains open. A software company might put up the copyright in its software as collateral to get a loan. A songwriter could use the copyrights in her songs as collateral for a loan. If a creditor agrees to take an interest in a copyright as collateral, she will wish to perfect her security interest. An unperfected security interest is likely to be nullified if the debtor goes into bankruptcy or if other creditors perfect first. It is quite unsettled whether a security interest in a copyright is perfected by filing in the state U.C.C. office (as for many types of personal property) or in the U.S. Copyright Office. The question is whether the federal system for recording documents related to copyrights preempts the state system for recording security interests. At least one court has concluded that the creditor must file in the Copyright Office if the copyright is registered, and in the state U.C.C. office if the copyright is unregistered.

Requiring federal filing is less efficient. Rather than a single U.C.C. filing, the creditor must file for each copyright that debtor owns. If the debtor owns many copyrights (like a publisher or music company), that could mean thousands of filings. On the other hand, where the federal statute provides a system for recording interests and a rule governing priority, there is a good argument that it preempts the state system for recording creditors' claims and resolving their respective priority. Local recording systems are subject to their own hazards. The filing system in the U.S. Virgin Islands was by paper and not yet online when Hurricane Irma hit, meaning that filings were on hold while the government dealt with more urgent matters.

Although the rule is quite unclear, a careful creditor can simply file in both offices. There is no rule against filing in both offices, and the fees are not too great. The lack of clarity is more of a trap for the unwary creditor than an obstacle to using copyrights as collateral.

Things get more complicated if foreign copyrights are collateral. For example, for a Bermuda debtor, it could be necessary to first assess whether filing in a copyright office was required. As in many jurisdictions that do not have the formalities of U.S. copyright law, Bermuda does not maintain a copyright office for registration and recording. So then the question would be whether Bermuda has the equivalent of a U.C.C. filing system: "a jurisdiction whose law generally requires information concerning the existence of a nonpossessory security interest to be made generally available in a filing, recording, or registration system as a condition or result of the security interest's obtaining priority over the rights of a lien creditor with respect to the collateral." U.C.C. §9-307(c). If not, a U.C.C. filing would be made in the District of Columbia.

Examples

1. *Stake your claim*. Author writes her brilliant novel and registers her copyright. She signs a contract with Publisher, transferring the copyright for a payment of $1 million. A year later, Author signs a contract with Studio, granting Studio the exclusive right to make a movie from the book. Studio knows nothing of Author's agreement with Publisher. Studio records the contract with the U.S. Copyright Office. Publisher did not record. Studio makes the film and begins showing it nationwide. Publisher claims copyright infringement. Studio claims that it owns the copyright, having bought it from Author. Publisher responds that Author had no copyright to sell, having already sold it to Publisher. Who owns the copyright?

2. *File under "bogus claims."* Entrepreneur holds the copyright to Soft Granite, a new computer game. Entrepreneur signs a sales contract with Bolly, selling the copyright for $200,000. Bolly does not record the sales contract with the U.S. Copyright Office. A year later, Soft Granite has become wildly popular. Entrepreneur delivers a check to Bolly for $200,000 and states that the copyright still belongs to Entrepreneur because of Bolly's failure to record the transfer. Who owns the copyright?

3. *Security*. Bank is lending $1,000,000 to Music Licensing, which will put up as collateral its registered copyrights in some 5,000 songs. Bank fills out a UCC-1 statement, listing the collateral as "all copyrights owned by Music Licensing." It will cost Bank a $30 fee to file in the relevant state U.C.C. office. Bank's lawyer advises that because the rule is unclear, Bank should also file in the Copyright Office. On learning that the fees for filing for 5,000 songs will be more than $10,000 dollars, Bank resists. What risk does it have if it does not file in the Copyright Office?

Explanations

1. Because Studio recorded before Publisher, Studio takes priority. This is true even though Publisher's agreement came first in time. Publisher should have recorded its agreement, thereby putting others on constructive notice of the transfer of copyright. Publisher has a cause of action against Author but not against Studio.

2. The copyright belongs to Bolly, pursuant to the agreement between the parties. Recordation is not necessary to have a valid transfer of copyright ownership. Rather, recordation provides protection against the claims of a subsequent good-faith purchaser. Here, there is no subsequent good-faith purchaser. The dispute is between the seller and the buyer—and the seller is bound by their valid agreement.

3. It is unsettled whether the Bank can perfect its security interest by filing in the state U.C.C. office or the federal Copyright Office. Its risk of not filing in the Copyright Office is that it will not have a perfected security interest (if the court follows the rule requiring federal filing for registered copyrights). That would mean that it would be second in line if Music Licensing used the copyrights as collateral for another loan (or simply sold the copyrights). Moreover, if Music Licensing went into bankruptcy, Bank's security interest would be wiped out. This is a risk to consider.

AUTHOR'S RIGHT TO TERMINATE TRANSFERS AND LICENSES

In 1938, the creators of Superman sold their rights in the comic for $130—rights that later proved to be worth millions. In 1997, however, the heirs of one author were entitled to terminate the transfer and get the rights back. The 1976 Copyright Act created two statutory rights to terminate grants of transfer or license of copyright. The two termination rights, in section 304(c) and section 203, have different rationales. Section 304(c) deals with this issue: Suppose in 1966, Author transferred her copyright to Publisher. The copyright was due to expire in 1980, but in 1976, Congress extended the copyright term by 19 years (and by another 20 years in 1998). Should Publisher get the extra 39 years, or should Author get them back? Section 203 deals with a much different issue. In 1986, struggling Author sells the manuscript to her first novel to Publisher for a few months' rent and groceries. The novel is a huge hit. Thirty-five years later, it is still selling millions and generating movies and sequels. Should Author get the rights back? Congress came out in favor of Author on both questions. Transfers and licenses of copyright do not terminate automatically. Rather, in some instances, authors have the right to terminate transfers and get their copyrights back. By failing to act in time, authors may lose the right to terminate.

Section 304(c) gives authors the right to the extra 19 years of copyright protection, even when the author had sold the copyright. In the 1976 Act, Congress extended copyright terms of existing works by 19 years, effectively changing the potential copyright term from 56 to 75 years. The termination rule for pre-1978 grants gives the author the benefit of the extra 19-year copyright term extension, rather than letting transferees get the extra 19 years. The author can terminate any transfer, effective during the five-year period after 56 years, by giving notice at least two years before the effective date. The copyright term was extended by 20 more years in 1998, and the present statute allows termination for the author to get that period as well. Many pre-1978 grants have been terminated, giving rights back to authors (or their heirs) that were transferred some 56 years in the past. Because so few works have importance after that much time, the commercial impact has been limited.

The other termination right under section 203 applies to post-1977 grants. It allows authors to terminate grants after 35 years. Section 203 is somewhat paternalistic. It limits the ability of authors to sell their copyrights. Rather, it effectively limits a conveyance of rights to 35 years. A starving artist or struggling novelist who sells his or her work will be able to get rights back in 35 years. The author can terminate any grant, with an effective date any time during the five-year period starting 35 years after the grant, by giving notice two years before the effective date. In other words, after 1977, an author cannot sell her copyright; she can only sell the next 35 years of her copyright.

Termageddon is upon us. Grants made after 1977 may be terminated after 35 years. The first terminations took effect in 2013. Parties relying on rights transferred from 1978 and after will face a possible wave of terminations each year. Music companies in particular must address the issue, because many works from around 1978 are commercially significant.

Termination rights do not apply to works made for hire. In addition, if joint authors made the grant, a majority of the grantors must join in the termination. An issue in many cases will be whether the work was an individual work (where termination applies), joint work (multiple grantors must join), or work made for hire (termination not applicable). This may require resolving questions of fact based on works created decades ago. A work made for hire is one made by an employee, as opposed to a freelancer. Courts may be asked, for example, to determine the precise working arrangement of rock bands working in the 1970s in cases in which the memories of key witnesses are likely to be affected by narcissism, narcotics, or necromancy (especially with drummers, as noted in the film *Spinal Tap*).

In general terms, sections 304(c) and 203 may allocate an unexpected benefit. The parties to a pre-1978 grant may not have anticipated the subsequent extension of copyright term. Likewise, parties to a post-1977 copyright transaction may have had little reason to think that the copyright would be valuable in 35 years—not many works have such lasting value. Both termination rights give the author the benefit of the unexpected value. One can see the rules as contrary to the general, economic basis of U.S. copyright law. Someone who purchases an asset usually gets the benefit of an unexpected increase in price. If real estate or stock prices shoot up, homeowners and shareholders do not have to split the increase with former sellers. Rather, the termination provisions are more in accord with the natural rights view of copyright. Indeed, they are quite similar to the type of moral right known as droite de suite (following right). If an artwork is sold, the original author may be entitled to a share of the price, even if she has not owned it for decades.

Section 304(c) Termination (Grants Made Before January 1, 1978)

Before 1978, the term of copyright was 56 years: an initial 28-year term and a 28-year renewal term. The 1976 Act added 19 years to the renewal term. In 1998, Congress added a further 20 years. Works under copyright before 1978 now may have a total of 95 years: the 28-year initial term and a renewal term of 67 years (28 + 19 + 20 years). If the extensions simply added 39 years to the copyright term, that arguably would be a windfall for transferees. Section 304(c) provides a mechanism that allows authors (or their successors) to get the benefit of the extra 39 years by terminating the grant.

A grant made by the author (or renewal beneficiary) before 1978 may be terminated, subject to certain conditions. Works made for hire are not covered, nor are grants by will. Termination may be made by the author or, if the author is dead, the author's successors. Written notice must be served on the grantee or its successor specifying the effective date of termination. A copy of the notice must be recorded in the Copyright Office before the effective date. The grant may be terminated within five years after the original 56-year total term. If the author misses that deadline, she has another opportunity to terminate during the five years after the 75-year period (i.e., the 1976 Act term). Special provisions govern such contingencies as termination where there are joint authors and specifying the successors for deceased authors.

The effect of termination is that the copyright reverts to the author (or renewal beneficiary). The statute does permit the grantee to retain rights in some derivative works: "A derivative work prepared under authority of the grant before its termination may continue to be utilized under the terms of the grant after its termination." 17 U.S.C. §304(c)(6)(A). If a songwriter terminated the transfer of the copyright in a song, the music company would retain the right to use derivative works, such as sound recordings embodying the song, but it could use them only "under the terms of the grant." If the grant required payment of royalties, that obligation would continue. *Cf. Mills Music v. Snyder*, 469 U.S. 153 (1985). In addition, the grantee may utilize existing derivative works but may not prepare other derivative works after termination. So the music company could not make new versions of the song.

The right of termination may not be waived: "Termination of the grant may be effected notwithstanding any agreement to the contrary, including an agreement to make a will or to make any future grant." 17 U.S.C. §304(c)(5).

Section 203 Termination (Grants Made After January 1, 1978)

The section 203 termination provision has the effect of limiting many transfers to 35 years, rather than permitting complete conveyances. An author has the inalienable right to terminate any exclusive or nonexclusive grant of a transfer or license of any or all of the rights under a copyright. 17 U.S.C. §203. The right of termination does not apply to works made for hire. Under section 203, termination may be effected during the five-year period after 35 years from the date of the grant. There must be written notice to the grantee or successor within certain time limits, and a copy of the notice must be recorded in the U.S. Copyright Office. The effect of termination is that all rights under the grant revert to the author (or her heirs or estate). The grantees may continue to utilize derivative works prepared pursuant to the grant but do not have the right to prepare new derivative works.

The right of termination may not be waived: "Termination of the grant may be effected notwithstanding any agreement to the contrary, including an agreement to make a will or to make any future grant." 17 U.S.C. §203(a)(5). This is consistent with the protective aspect of section 203 termination rights. They prevent the author from selling more than 35 years of her copyright. If she could waive her termination rights, then the buyer would simply include a waiver clause in the contract as a matter of course.

Suppose that Author writes her children's novel in 2001 and assigns the copyright to Megacorp on January 1, 2002. The book becomes an enduring commercial success. Over the next decades, Megacorp sells thousands of copies every year. Megacorp also makes a successful movie, which is a long-running success. Author (or her heirs or estate) may terminate the transfer of the copyright, effective anytime from January 1, 2037 (35 years from the grant, not from the beginning of the copyright) for the next five years. The same would be true if she had made a lesser grant, such as a license of the publication rights. She must give at least two years' prior notice and record a copy for termination to be effective. The copyright would revert to Author, who could now sell the book or make another movie. She would not get the copyright to the movie made by Megacorp, which could continue to utilize the movie. Megacorp could not make another movie that was a derivative work of the book. If Author did not terminate the transfer, then Megacorp would continue to own the copyright for its entire term (Author's life plus 70 years).

Termination Rights Do Not Apply to Works Made for Hire

Note that if Author had written the book as an employee of Megacorp, there would be no right of termination. The termination right (for both rules, governing pre-1978 works and post-1977 works) does not apply to works made for hire. As a work made for hire, the copyright would belong to the employer, Megacorp. Neither Megacorp nor Author would have termination rights. Author would have no right to get it "back" after 35 years. Similarly, if Megacorp sold the copyright (or granted a license), Megacorp would have no statutory right of termination. Note that there are different tests for pre-1978 and post-1977 works to determine whether a work is made for hire. For pre-1978 works, under the 1909 Act, the test that most courts apply is whether the work was made at the instance and expense of the hiring party. For post-1977 works, under the Supreme Court's decision in *CCNV*, the test is whether there was an employment relationship under the various factors used in agency law.

Examples

1. *Yo-yo*. In 1946, Hermana wrote a love song called "Hesse." She published with the required notice in 1946. She sold the copyright to Robert Records in 1950 (along with renewal rights, which Robert subsequently secured). In 2000, "Hesse" still generates a nice income. Robert Records gets royalties from past recordings of the song. It also gets royalties from sales of sheet music containing Hermana's original arrangement of the music and lyrics. Hermana wonders whether she can somehow get the copyright back, along with the rights to royalties. Can she?

2. *Back story*. In 1940, a freelance writer wrote a screenplay, *Nothing New in the West*, and sold it to a movie studio. The resulting movie, released in 1940,

was a landmark in cinema and is still regularly shown. The freelancer has learned that plans are being made to release the movie again. The freelancer would like to know what his rights are.

3. *Go ahead and take it back*. In 1955, Terra sold the copyright to her play, *Earth Day*, to Green Productions. Their agreement provided that Terra would receive 50 percent of all revenue that Green received from the work. Green made various uses of the work, including the production of a huge hit film, *Global Crossing*. Terra recently terminated the transfer in accordance with section 304. Green's reply was, "Fine. You can have the copyright back, but the statute allows us to continue to utilize derivative works, so we are going to keep showing *Global Crossing* and make a sequel that will make even more money. Since you have terminated our agreement, we no longer have to pay you 50 percent. Thanks!" Did Terra do them a favor?

4. *Where there's a will*. W.W. published his first book of poetry in 1939. He properly renewed the copyright in 1967. In 1974, he died. In his will, he left the copyright to *Poetry Magazine*. In 1995, W.W.'s children realized that it was time to exercise termination rights, because it was 56 years from the beginning of copyright. They notified *Poetry Magazine* that they were terminating the transfer of the copyright. Can they? Would the result be different if while still alive, W.W. had given the copyright to *Poetry Magazine* as a charitable gift?

5. *Home is where the art is*. In 2006, Starving Artist sells a painting titled *Goth with the Twin* and the copyright in the painting to Investor. Their contract provides that the transfers of ownership of the painting and the copyright "shall be permanent, irrevocable, and apply to all rights under personal property law and under copyright law that Artist has now, or shall have in the future, in the works." Investor pays the agreed contract price.

   Investor hangs the paintings in a local museum. Over the succeeding years, Investor makes quite a lot of money by licensing the copyright for various uses: The image appears on posters, coffee cups, and window shades. Investor also has an employee paint an adaptation of the work, *Goth Triplets*. Investor has plans for several more paintings, starting with *Goth Quadruplets*.

   Some 35 years later, Starving Artist sends written notice to Investor that Starving Artist is exercising his right of termination. The notice demands that Investor do all of the following:

   - cease exercising any of the exclusive rights of the copyright holder
   - return the painting to Starving Artist
   - hand over all revenues earned from licensing the copyright
   - cease utilizing *Goth Triplets* and hand it over
   - cease the planned preparation of *Goth Quadruplets*

Which of Artist's demands are legally his right to make? Would it be any different if Starving Artist had made the painting as an employee of Artsy Facts, which then sold the painting and the copyright to Investor?

6. *Lassie, come home.* In 1938, Eric Knight sells to Lassie Television the motion picture and television rights to his story that introduces Lassie. In 1978 (after the copyright has been duly renewed and the 1978 statute extends its term by 19 years), Knight's heirs sign over all motion picture and television rights in the Lassie story to Lassie Television. In 1996, the heirs seek to terminate the original grant of rights. Lassie Television contends that the 1978 agreement prevents them from doing so. Can the heirs get Lassie back?

Explanations

1. The grant was made pre-1978, so section 304(c) governs. Hermana may terminate within the five years after the 56-year total term. Note that the starting date is the beginning of the copyright, not the date of the grant; 1946 plus 56 is 2002, so the five-year period will end in 2007. It is 2000, so Hermana can terminate the grant effective 2002, by giving notice at least two years before the effective date.

   Termination will give her back the copyright, but Robert Records may still use derivative works under the terms of the grant. It will continue to receive royalties for the sound recordings. Unlike *Mills Music*, the agreement does not require Robert Records to pay a percentage to Hermana. The sheet music is Hermana's original arrangement, not a derivative work, so Robert Records has no rights to that.

   Note also that, to make money, Hermana might need the master recording or sheet music or other physical material. Termination of the copyright will not affect rights to that physical property. It may well be in Hermana's interest to negotiate a deal with Robert Records (as many songwriters and musicians have done, as opposed to simply terminating the grant). The same goes for movies, television shows, and many other works that rely on both copyright and other rights.

2. This is also a pre-1978 grant, governed by section 304(c). The freelancer had a right of termination beginning 56 years into the copyright, lasting five years: 1940 plus 56 is 1996; five more years is 2001. The freelancer missed the opportunity to terminate, but section 304(d) gives a second chance, beginning 75 years into the copyright and lasting five years: 1940 plus 75 is 2015, so the freelancer has a termination right until 2020. Upon termination, the freelancer would get the copyright back, but the studio could continue to use derivative works prepared under the terms of the grant. It could continue to show the film.

3. Terra did not do them a favor. After termination, the grantee may still use a derivative work but only under the terms of the grant. Here, such terms require Green Productions to pay Terra 50 percent of all revenue. Green may continue to use the film but subject to the continuing obligation to pay Terra royalties. Moreover, once the grant has been terminated, Green cannot make another film based on the book.

4. Termination rights do not apply to transfers by will, so W.W.'s children could not terminate the transfer to *Poetry Magazine*. If it had been a gift while he was still alive, then it would be a terminable transfer.

5. Even though Starving Artist agreed that the copyright would pass permanently to Investor, Starving Artist may still terminate the transfer after 35 years. Termination rights may not be effectively waived.

   The question then becomes what is the effect of termination? Termination causes all rights to revert to the author. One exception is that the licensee may continue to utilize derivative rights prepared pursuant to the grant but may not prepare new derivative works. Accordingly, the termination right supports only some of the demands. Investor must cease exercising the rights of the copyright holder because those rights revert to Author. The exception for derivative works applies, however, to *Goth Triplets*. Investor is entitled to continue utilizing that derivative work but is not authorized to prepare *Goth Quadruplets*, a new derivative work. The termination rights only cause copyright rights to revert. They do not apply to ownership of physical copies or retroactively apply to pretermination exploitation of the work. So Investor is not required to return the painting to Artist or hand over revenues earned from licensing the copyright.

6. They can. *Classic Media Inc. v. Mewborn*, No. 06-55385 (9th Cir. 2008). Even if the 1978 agreement were a waiver or transfer of the termination right, it would not be effective. Termination "may be effected notwithstanding any agreement to the contrary." 17 U.S.C. §304(c)(5). *See also Siegel v. Warner Bros. Entertainment*, 542 F. Supp. 2d 1098 (C.D. Cal. 2008) (upholding 1997 termination of 1938 grant of rights in *Superman* comics despite grants of rights subsequent to the 1938 grant).

   Another author's heirs were less successful in seeking return of rights to famous works. *Penguin Group v. Steinbeck*, No. 06-3226 (2d Cir. 2008). John Steinbeck's widow, during the time when she could exercise termination rights, signed a contract with Penguin continuing and expanding the original publishing contract. In that case, the court held that the second agreement was an effective waiver of termination rights. The difference between the two cases was that Lassie's heirs agreed to a second contract years before they could terminate the first, so they never had a right of termination. That sort of agreement cannot overcome the right to terminate. By contrast, Steinbeck's heirs could have terminated the original grant but chose not to and indeed signed an expanded contract. In that case, they had a present option to terminate and agreed to a new contract (as opposed to waiving a future option to terminate). The new contract was an effective grant of rights. *Accord Milne v. Stephen Slesinger, Inc.*, 430 F.3d 1036 (9th Cir. 2005).

COPYRIGHT AND CONTRACT INTERPRETATION

Beyond the Copyright Act, copyrights are governed by common-law property and contract principles (provided that such state law rules are not preempted by specific provisions or by general policies of the Copyright Act, as discussed in Chapter 20, on state law theories and preemption). So in determining the enforceability and effect of copyright agreements, courts must consider both the rules of the statute and any applicable rules of contract or property law. For example, property law would likely govern the effectiveness of transfers if no specific statutory rule applied.

Contract law often comes into play. License agreements, like other agreements, must often be interpreted to determine the parties' respective rights and duties. For example, a copyright owner might grant permission to make use of a work without making clear whether the permission was limited in time. Courts must also determine how broad the rights granted are.

One much-litigated issue has been interpreting agreements to apply to new technologies. Such issues have included whether a circa-1900 grant to utilize a work in dramatic works applied to making films, whether permission to distribute a film applied to distribution of videotapes, and whether the right to publish a work included the right to post it on a website. Courts determine the likely intent of the parties, based on the words of the agreement and other relevant evidence. Courts also apply other canons of interpretation, such as construing the contract against its drafter in some circumstances.

Examples

1. *A book by any other name.* In 1974, the successful author Monarch signed a contract with a publisher, Hidebound. The contract provided that Hidebound would receive the "exclusive right to publish the novel *Scarrie* in book form." The contract further stated that "Monarch retains all other rights, including without limitation the right to publish the novel in magazine or any other form other than books." By 2001, Hidebound had adopted a new form of distributing fiction, the "e-book." For a set price, consumers could download text files containing various works

sold by Hidebound. E-books did not exist in 1974, when the contract was signed. Does Hidebound have the right to sell *Scarrie* as an e-book?

2. *Debts included?* Prather signs an agreement assigning all "rights, title, and interest" in a copyright. Would that include the right to collect for infringement of the copyright when the infringing acts occurred before the date of the transfer?

Explanations

1. Hidebound does not have the right to sell *Scarrie* as an e-book. Although this case involves a copyright, it is really a contract law issue: Did the agreement convey the right at issue? The court would try to determine the intent of the parties, looking primarily to the words of the contract, but also considering other relevant factors. The narrow issue, then, is whether an e-book is a book, as the parties used the word. The rights were narrowly limited to publication in the form of a "book," and all other rights carefully reserved to Monarch. The court would likely hold that distributing the text using a computer network falls into the category of "all other rights." *Cf. Random House v. Rosetta LLC*, 283 F.3d 490 (2d Cir. 2002).

2. A court would likely hold that the assignment did not include the right to enforce for pretransfer infringement. *See Prather v. Neva Paperbacks*, 410 F.2d 698 (5th Cir. 1969). It is a question of contractual interpretation of the terms "rights, title, and interest" in the copyright. That sounds like ownership of the copyright itself, as opposed to rights previously arising out of such ownership. By analogy, if someone sells a house, the buyer probably could not claim unpaid rents that accrued before the house was sold. Of course, this is all interpretation of the terms. If the parties spelled it out clearly, there would be no need for the court to fill the gap.

PART III

Statutory Rights

CHAPTER 11

The Section 106 Exclusive Rights

"Copyright law" might be called "Copyadaptdistributeperformdisplayrights law." The copyright owner generally has the exclusive rights to do or authorize the following:

1. reproduce the copyrighted work in copies or phonorecords (often called the *reproduction right* or the *right to make copies*)
2. prepare derivative works based on the copyrighted work (*adaptation right*)
3. distribute copies or phonorecords of the copyrighted work to the public by sale or other transfer of ownership, or by rental, lease, or lending (*public distribution right*)
4. perform the copyrighted work publicly (*public performance right*)
5. display the copyrighted work publicly (*public display right*)

17 U.S.C. §106.

This chapter looks in more detail at the copyright owner's exclusive rights. The copyright owner does not have unlimited ownership of the copyrighted work. Rather, she has a set of exclusive rights. People can do all sorts of things with the work that she may not like. Copyright infringement occurs only if their actions fall within one of the exclusive rights.

Several principles are applicable to all the exclusive rights. Use of non-copyrighted elements (such as copying ideas) does not infringe an exclusive right. The rights extend to nonliteral copies and partial copies. Infringement requires "volition or causation." Independent creation is not infringement.

It may be that simply authorizing someone else to perform one of the protected rights is infringement. *Banco Popular de Puerto Rico v. Asociacion de Compositores y Editores de Musica Latinoamericana*, 678 F.3d 102 (1st Cir. 2012), held, without much discussion, that a party that licenses copyrights which it does not own is liable for copyright infringement. In any case, that would probably give rise to secondary liability (discussed in Chapter 18).

Each exclusive right also has rules specific to it (such as the definitions of "derivative work," "display," and "perform"). In addition, these exclusive rights are subject to a number of limitations discussed here and in subsequent chapters (such as the fair use doctrine, the first sale doctrine, and more specific limitations).

A key limitation is that intellectual property is territorial. If infringing conduct occurs outside the United States, then the mere fact that it was supported by some conduct within the United States will not trigger liability under the U.S. copyright statute (although it may be infringement under the laws of that country).[1] Allowing downloads from abroad was held not to infringe.[2] Unauthorized streaming of copyrighted televisions programs into the United States was held to infringe under U.S. law, on the theory that it caused performance of the programs to occur on users' computers in the United States.[3]

REPRODUCTION RIGHT

Copyright takes its name from the exclusive right to make copies of the copyrighted work. The owner of the copyright has the exclusive right "to reproduce the copyrighted work in copies or phonorecords." 17 U.S.C. §106(1). Copies are "material objects, other than phonorecords, in which a work is fixed by any method now known or later developed, and from which the work can be perceived, reproduced, or otherwise communicated, either directly or with the aid of a machine or device." 17 U.S.C. §101. The definition is very broad. It includes a material object in which the work is fixed "by any method" and therefore any type of medium (from paper to vinyl to DVD to ice sculpture, ad infinitum). It includes future technologies ("any method now known or later developed"). It includes objects used for

1. *Geophysical Serv., Inc. v. TGS-NOPEC Geophysical Co.*, 850 F.3d 785 (5th Cir. 2017).
2. *Motorola Sols., Inc. v. Hytera Commc'ns Corp. Ltd.*, 108 F.4th 458, 475 (7th Cir. 2024) ("Downloads of copyrighted data from mirrored servers located abroad cannot serve as predicate acts of domestic infringement even if the 'main' instance of those databases is stored on a U.S.-based server. A contrary rule would stretch U.S. copyright law far beyond its proper borders, giving global businesses an incentive to store local copies of copyrighted files in the United States as insurance against intellectual property theft worldwide.").
3. *Spanski Enters. v. Telewizja Polska, S.A.*, 883 F.3d 904, 915 (D.C. Cir. 2018).

various purposes ("from which the work can be perceived, reproduced, or otherwise communicated"). It includes the first embodiment of the work: "The term 'copies' includes the material object, other than a phonorecord, in which the work is first fixed." 17 U.S.C. §101.

The work may be perceptible either "directly or with the aid of a machine or device." This means the right encompasses forms perceptible to humans (such as paintings) and forms requiring the use of technology (such as DVDs). The statute emphatically rejects the reasoning of the piano roll cases. Courts had reasoned that a piano roll (a roll inserted into a player piano, with bumps encoding a musical work) was not an infringing copy, because it was not directly read by a human. But now a copy can be any form that fixes a work, so the text of a poem saved on a disc is a copy of the poem, even if a person could not look at the disc and read the poem directly.

Suppose Klink put together an abstract sculpture out of large steel beams. Her copyright would potentially be infringed by anyone who made a copy of the work. Possible examples: another sculptor who copied her work into a similar outsize steel work; another sculptor who made a tiny version of the sculpture with toothpicks; an artist who made a detailed drawing of the sculpture; a photographer who shot a picture of the sculpture. All would be copies and potentially infringe ("potentially" because they might be protected by fair use or other limitations on Klink's copyright). Note that the copy could be in any form. The photographer could make infringing copies on film, on paper, in negatives, in the memory of a digital camera, on the hard drive of a PC, or in the pages of a book.

The same would be true for other works. Suppose Dylan writes a short story, giving him the copyright in that literary work. He would have the exclusive right to make copies. He would have the exclusive right to make copies in paper form, on magnetic tape, on CD, on the hard drive of a personal computer, on an iPod, or any other form. Anyone who made such a copy would potentially infringe Dylan's copyright ("potentially" because they might be protected by fair use or by other limitations on the exclusive rights).

Likewise, the owner of copyright in a computer program has the right to make copies in the many forms available: as source code (the form in which a developer writes the program) or in object code (the set of binary instructions and data in which the program runs on a computer). An infringing copy could be saved on someone's computer, embedded on a chip, or carried on a keychain storage device.

The reproduction right, unlike the performance, distribution, and display rights, is not limited to public acts. A defendant can infringe by making a copy alone in her office. To infringe the reproduction right, a defendant need not distribute the copy or make it for commercial distribution. Simply making the copy potentially infringes the copyright. There may be potential infringement where copies are made for various purposes, such as studying the work, or preserving a backup or archival copy, or simply making a copy to practice a technique (such as copying a painting). Copyright holders sometimes claim copyright as a means to find a legal theory against a particular defendant. An employee who copies the employer's customer list may be subject to a trade secret case, but may also be the subject of a claim for copyright infringement (for making a copy of allegedly copyrighted list). In such cases, the issue is often whether fair use authorized making the copy.

Infringement cases involving AI are in their early days. Issues will include, whether the output of the AI is similar to copyrighted material used to train the AI, whether it is fair use to make copies to compile sets of data to train AI, and whether deliberate attempts to copy the style of an author (be it a novelist or musician) affect that analysis.

Independent Creation Is Not Infringement

The copyright owner has the right to make copies of the work. Someone else potentially infringes if they copy the work, even if they do not copy the entire work and even if they make a copy that is similar but not identical. But independent creation is not infringement. If someone makes a similar work without copying from the copyrighted work, there is no infringement—no matter how similar the works are. If Composer writes "Ode to Glee," she holds the copyright. If Composer hears a subsequent composition by someone else that sounds extremely similar, she may claim copyright infringement, but the second comer is liable only if she copied from Composer's work (directly or indirectly, such as by copying from a work that copied from the copyrighted work). If she simply happened to come up with a similar work or copied elements in the public domain from another work, she is not liable. This rule often leads to factual disputes—the plaintiff claiming copying and the defendant arguing independent creation. In deciding whether defendant copied from the copyrighted work, the fact finder will look for several factors: how similar the works are, how much access defendant had to the copyrighted work, and evidence of independent creation. That analysis is discussed in more detail in Part IV.

The Right to Make Copies Extends to Nonliteral Copies and Partial Copies

In everyday life, making a copy of something usually means making a literal copy: copying a newspaper article with a photocopy machine, copying some text or pictures on a computer. The meaning of copy in copyright law is much broader. A "copy" of a work may be any object into which protected elements of the copyrighted work have been copied. So the exclusive right to make copies is not limited to making exact or literal copies of the work. Rather, it extends to copying protected elements of the work. Protected elements of a work go well beyond the exact form of the copyrighted work. A writer who paraphrases another novel, or a photographer who closely models her photo on another may be liable. A copy of a work may also be in another medium or another category of work. Suppose Able wrote a compelling short story, which Baker filched and made into a novel. The novel would be a "copy" of the short story, infringing Able's copyright. Many noted copyright cases involve such nonliteral copying. The issue is often whether the defendant took protected expression or unprotected elements (such as ideas, functional aspects, and nonoriginal elements).

The right to make copies extends also to partial copies. Suppose Author has the copyright in a book. Anthologist copies a chapter without permission into her book. Anthologist might think that she has not infringed by making a copy of the book, because she only copied a portion. To the contrary, potential infringement requires only copying some original creative expression from the copyrighted work. Infringement has been found for copying a few hundred words from a lengthy autobiography or for copying a few seconds from the recording of a song, but such doctrines as fair use or de minimis infringement may protect the use.

The DRAM Issue: Is a Temporary Copy Inside a Computer a Potentially Infringing Copy?

Creative works now often come in digital form, as strings of zeros and ones. Texts were once typewritten or manually typeset; now they are likely to be created and stored using word-processing programs. VHS is joining Betamax in the format graveyard. CDs and MP3 files generally have supplanted tapes and records. Digital cameras are eclipsing film cameras.

The increasing use of digital technologies broadens the potential applicability of the right to make copies. Digital copies can be easy to duplicate and are the same as the original (as opposed to copies of other products, which are often inferior in quality to the original). Digital technology has made possible all sorts of innovations in creating and distributing works, but it has also led to increased fears of copyright piracy.

The process of using digital works often involves making additional copies. Suppose someone has access to a digital copy of a copyrighted work, such as a computer program, an image, or the text of a short story. He could have the copy on a disc or on a hard drive, or download it from a website. For his computer to run the program (or view the image or text), it must copy part of the program into its DRAM (the temporary, high-speed memory that constitutes the computer's working memory). A temporary copy of a work is often made when using software, playing a video game, or looking at text or pictures onscreen. When works are transmitted over the Internet, many temporary copies may be made along the way. The question is often moot, whether making a temporary copy within a computer counts as making a copy, for copyright law purposes.

The statute does not clearly state whether such a temporary copy is a copy. Good policy arguments have been made against the application of the exclusive rights to such fleeting copies. But the trend among the few courts to consider the issue is to hold that making a DRAM copy is indeed making a copy for the purposes of copyright law. *See, e.g., MAI Systems v. Peak Computer*, 991 F.2d 511 (9th Cir. 1993). Moreover, some recent amendments to the copyright statute indirectly indicate that a temporary copy is a copy for the purposes of copyright law. Section 117(c) protects against liability for making copies of a computer program by activating a computer. Section 512(a) now protects Internet service providers from liability for making "transient" storage of material during transmission. Such provisions would be unnecessary if temporary copies were not considered copies (and therefore potentially infringing). So the weight of authority now seems to be that a temporary copy made within a computer (such as a DRAM copy) is a copy and can potentially infringe if made without authorization from the copyright owner or some provision of the copyright statute (such as fair use, section 117 or 512, or some other provision). Some courts have held that copies that last for only a second or less would not constitute copies for the purpose of infringement.

If a temporary copy counts as a copy, then someone could potentially infringe copyright by using the program (or viewing the image or text on a computer) without authorization of the copyright owner. This is quite different from works such as books or paintings. Reading a book (or using processes described in it) or viewing a painting does not touch on the exclusive rights of the copyright owner. For electronic digital works, the copyright comes closer to giving an exclusive right to "use" the work.

Infringement Requires "Volition or Causation"

The copyright owner has the exclusive right to make copies of the work. Someone who makes copies potentially infringes. The statute does not require additional elements such as knowledge of the copyright, or intent to infringe, or motive of commercial gain. Copyright is often described as a type of strict liability, but courts have required a minimal showing of "volition or causation" by the defendant.

Suppose Business allows a customer to use one of Business's photocopy machines. Unbeknownst to Business, the customer uses the machine to make unauthorized copies of various poems. Courts agree that although Business owns and controls the copy machine, Business has not made copies and therefore is not an infringer. Likewise, courts have held that when customers of an Internet service provider (ISP) use their access to post copyrighted photos, the ISP has not made copies. Provided that the ISP did not play an active role, the fact that its network was used did not mean that it made copies. "[W]e hold that ISPs, when passively storing material at the direction of users in order to make that material available to other users upon their request, do not copy" the material in direct violation of section 106 of the Copyright Act. *CoStar Group v. LoopNet*, 373 F.3d 544, 555 (4th Cir. 2004). Providing a software tool that users can use to clip images whether copyrighted or not would not meet the volition requirement. *See BWP Media USA Inc. v. Polyvore, Inc.*, 922 F.3d 42 (2d Cir. 2019). If the ISP went beyond merely providing the use of a network and general tools, however, it could be held to make copies (or be liable as a secondary infringer, discussed later in the book).

Example

1. *Volition, volition.* Giganews allows users to download a browser app, Mimo. Using Mimo, users can view material that they access through USENET, a network of users that share messages and content. Is Giganews liable for infringement of the display right if the browser app it provided is used to view copyrighted images?

Explanation

1. The court reasoned that although users may use Giganews's reader to display infringing images, that does not constitute volitional conduct by Giganews. "'Mimo is just a reader, a piece of software that allows a user to view an image,' and therefore, '[t]o the extent that Mimo is used to view infringing images, this is done by the user.'" *Perfect 10, Inc. v. Giganews, Inc.*, 847 F.3d 657, 668 (9th Cir. 2017) (quoting trial court with approval).

Sound Recordings: Special Rules

Sound recordings are a category of works with a tailored set of exclusive rights. They are "works that result from the fixation of a series of musical, spoken, or other sounds, but not including the sounds accompanying a motion picture or other audiovisual work, regardless of the nature of the material objects, such as disks, tapes, or other phonorecords, in which they are embodied." 17 U.S.C. §101. For sound recordings, the terminology is a little different and the scope of exclusive rights is slightly narrower.

Most works are fixed in "copies"; sounds are fixed in "phonorecords." The copyright owner has the exclusive right to reproduce the work in copies or "phonorecords." The definition of "phonorecord" tracks the definition of copy. "Phonorecords" are "material objects in which sounds, other than those accompanying a motion picture or other audiovisual work, are fixed by any method now known or later developed, and from which the sounds can be perceived, reproduced, or otherwise communicated, either directly or with the aid of a machine or device." 17 U.S.C. §101. The statute differentiates between copies and phonorecords because (as discussed below) the exclusive rights in sound recordings are limited in some ways.

Sound recordings are an exception to the rule that nonliteral copies may infringe. The reproduction right in a sound recording is infringed only by a literal copy, one that recaptures the actual sounds fixed in the sound recording. 17 U.S.C. §114(b). Suppose Gilbert creatively makes a sound recording of the goings-on in a typical corporate office. If Sullivan gets hold of the sound recording and copies it into his own sound recording, Sullivan potentially infringes Gilbert's copyright. But if Sullivan listens to Gilbert's recording and then makes his own recording, making sounds very similar to Gilbert's recording, Sullivan will not infringe. He did not capture the actual sounds from Gilbert's recording. Sound recordings have a much narrower reproduction right than other categories of works. Had Sullivan copied so closely from a short story written by Gilbert (not word for word but copying every occurrence and description), he would very likely have infringed.

Examples

Copy parade. Dainter paints *Blue Bayube*, a crazy concoction of landscapes. Which of the following would constitute making a copy of *Blue Bayube*, potentially infringing the copyright ("potentially," because fair use or some other provision might authorize the making of the copy)?

1. Snaps takes a picture of the painting and prints it on four-by-six-foot paper.
2. Daubs sets up her easel and does her best to duplicate the painting. Daubs's final product is quite similar but also easily distinguishable from *Blue Bayube*.
3. Snaps takes and prints a close-up picture of about 1/10th of the surface of *Blue Bayube*.
4. Snaps takes a picture but does not print it. Rather, Snaps simply has a file saved on his digital camera.

5. At home that night, working from memory, Daubs tries again to duplicate *Blue Bayube*. She again produces a pretty similar painting. She then feeds the painting to her ostrich, and it is never seen again.
6. Snaps plugs his camera into his laptop computer and views the picture on the screen.
7. Snaps plugs his camera into a computer at the local library and uses the computer to upload the picture to Snaps's website. Has the library made a picture, where its network was used to upload the picture, making several transitory copies in the process?
8. A year later, Reinha paints a landscape. By sheer coincidence, her painting is practically identical to *Blue Bayube*.
9. Cablevision's customers can use its Remote Service DVR System to record cable television shows. The computer files with the recorded programs are saved not on consumers' machines (as occurs with TiVo or a home recorder), but are recorded first in a temporary buffer (for about one second) and then saved onto central hard drives housed and maintained by Cablevision in an undisclosed location. Has Cablevision made copies of the copyrighted programs (either by making copies in the temporary buffer or by saving copies on the hard drives)?

Explanations

They are all copies, except the last two, illustrating the broad range of ways to infringe the reproduction right. Although each made a copy, they may not have infringed because of such rules as fair use and de minimis infringement. Nor would the remedies for infringement necessarily be great.

1. A copy may take a different form or medium than the copyrighted work.
2. A copy need not be identical. One need only copy original creative expression from the copyrighted work.
3. A copy need not copy the entire work as long as it copies some protected creative expression.
4. A copy need not be in a form that a human can directly view. A copy in machine-readable form is still a copy.
5. A privately made copy is still a copy. Unlike some of the other exclusive rights, it is not limited to public acts.
6. When Snaps viewed the picture, his computer made a temporary copy in its working memory (and arguably another on the screen). Such temporary copies, the trend of authority holds, count as potentially infringing copies.

7. No copying by the library, because it did not exercise volition or causation in the making of the copy.
8. No copy. Independent creation is not copyright infringement.
9. The Second Circuit held that Cablevision did not make copies and therefore did not infringe the copyrights in the recorded programs. *The Cartoon Network LP v. CSC Holdings, Inc.* (2d Cir. 2008). The court first held that the buffer copies were not copies for the purpose of infringement, because they were not "for a period of more than transitory duration." If other courts follow this reasoning, this could limit the otherwise gigantic scope of copyright in the online age. Temporary copies of works are made constantly on devices ranging from handhelds to laptops to the various computers linked by the Internet and other networks.

   The court also held that Cablevision did not make the permanent copies. The customer, not Cablevision, entered the instructions that caused the copies to be made. Cablevision merely supplied access to the equipment used. That could make Cablevision liable as a secondary infringer (such as inducement liability), but that issue was not raised in the case.

ADAPTATION RIGHT

The copyright owner has the exclusive right "to prepare derivative works based upon the copyrighted work." 17 U.S.C. §106(2). A derivative work is

> a work based upon one or more preexisting works, such as a translation, musical arrangement, dramatization, fictionalization, motion picture version, sound recording, art reproduction, abridgment, condensation, or any other form in which a work may be recast, transformed, or adapted. A work consisting of editorial revisions, annotations, elaborations, or other modifications which, as a whole, represent an original work of scholarship, is a "derivative work."

17 U.S.C. §101. If an author owns the copyright on a novel, potential derivative works include a translation into French, a movie based on the novel, a sequel, and an annotated version for scholars. *Star Trek*, to use one copyright teacher's example, has boldly gone into any number of derivative works based on the original TV script: spin-off TV series, films, novels, theatrical productions, action figures, video games, and so on, ad infinitum and beyond.

One could ask whether copyright should be so broad. The author of a novel has the exclusive right not just to sell the novel in various forms but also to prevent others from writing sequels, making translations, or adapting the novel into a movie or play. The right to publish the novel itself might be sufficient incentive for the book to be written. One theory is that the derivative right avoids waste, because without exclusive rights, there might not be enough incentive to invest in creating the sequel or movie. But certainly plenty of books are written without such rights, and films are often based on public domain works (such as the many films based on works by Shakespeare and Jane Austen). Another theory links the right to author's moral rights: The creator should be able to control—and commercialize—the continuing fate of her fictional world or artistic work.

The derivative right often comes into play in licensing cases. Author might grant a license to Theater to perform her play. The licensing agreement may authorize Theater to perform the play but prohibit creation of derivative works. Likewise, authors may license Publisher to make copies of books but provide that the agreement does not authorize creation of derivative works. If Theater substantially adapts the play before performing it, or if Publisher changes the book, that could exceed the scope of the permission, meaning there was infringement of the copyright.

Boundaries of the Adaptation Right: Fixation, Creativity, and Substantial Similarity

Some regard the adaptation right as redundant. If Producer makes an unauthorized film that copies protected material from a copyrighted novel, that would infringe the adaptation right (by making an unauthorized derivative work). It would also infringe the reproduction right, because of the broad understanding of "copy." The film would be an infringing, unauthorized copy of the novel. So the question arises: In what respects is the adaptation right different from the right to make copies? There are several possible ways:

1. One may adapt a work without fixing it, such as changing a song or play during its performance (whether rehearsed or improvised).
2. One could adapt the work by changing the original (without making a copy), such as by painting an additional character into a family portrait, or a windmill on landscape—perhaps even by annotating a casebook.
3. One could make a derivative work that exceeded the scope of a license, such as by performing a serious play as a farce, contrary to stern licensing terms.

One way in which the adaptation right appears broader than the reproduction right is the need for a fixed copy to infringe the latter right. The definition of "derivative work" does not require it to be "fixed," unlike a copy. It could infringe the derivative right to orally translate a copyrighted play into Swedish, but that would not infringe the reproduction right (because no fixed copy was made). A musician might improvise an adaptation of a copyrighted work during a performance. It would not infringe the reproduction right if no fixed copy were made, but it could infringe the adaptation right (usual disclaimer: "could" infringe, because it might be fair use).

Another way the adaptation right could be broader than the reproduction right is that a work could be adapted by changing an existing copy of the work. Suppose another sculptor made big changes to Klink's sculpture without her authorization. The changes would not infringe the reproduction right because the second sculpture did not make a copy. But she could have infringed the adaptation right if she made sufficient changes to make a derivative work.

This brings us to the flip side of the issue: Read too broadly, the adaptation right would give the copyright owner control over almost any use of the work. But copyright is intended to permit free flow of ideas and other unprotected elements.

Two rules limit the scope of the adaptation right. First, the better view is that a derivative work is not created unless there is material added with sufficient creativity to have a new copyrightable work. Simply gluing reproductions of artworks on ceramic tiles is not making derivative works of the artworks. *Contra Mirage Editions v. Albuquerque A.R.T.*, 856 F.2d 1341 (9th Cir. 1988). *See also Lee v. A.R.T.*, 125 F.3d 580 (7th Cir. 1997)(rejecting *Mirage Editions* on narrower grounds). Simply speeding up the play of a video game does not create a derivative work. *But see Midway Mfg. v. Artic Intl.*, 704 F.2d 1009 (7th Cir. 1983). Note that gluing a reproduction on a plate or changing the speed of a video game might constitute a derivative work even under the "new copyrightable work" requirement if done in such a creative way that the new version was a parody of the original or was otherwise a new work.

The derivative right is also limited by the rule that no infringement occurs unless the alleged derivative work is substantially similar to the copyrighted work. This flows from the basic rule that infringement requires copying of protected elements of the work. Suppose the song "*Happy*" gives Playwright an idea for a comedy. Playwright does not copy any of the creative expression from the song. The play would not be an infringing copy, even though one could argue that it was "based on" the song or was a "dramatization" of the song. By the same token, a movie not substantially similar to a screenplay does not infringe, even if the movie is made with the screenplay in mind. *See Litchfield v. Spielberg*, 736 F.2d 1352 (9th Cir. 1984).

Micro Star v. FormGen raised issues about how far the adaptation right extends with digital works, an issue that will crop up more and more. Plaintiff FormGen had the copyright in *Duke Nukem 3D*, a computer game. In the game, players wandered a science fiction city and zapped "evil aliens and other hazard." *Duke Nukem 3D* consisted of a game engine (the program that ran the game), the source art library (the repository of the various images used in the game, from aliens to scuba gear), and MAP files (sets of instructions to compose scenes for the games). To run the game, the game engine would take images from the source art library and arrange them per a MAP file. Users could create more MAP files using a "Build Editor" and run the game in customized versions. Defendant Micro Star compiled and distributed these user-created MAP files.

Micro Star argued that the user-created MAP files were not derivative works because they did not contain protected elements of the *Duke Nukem* game. The MAP files did not contain any of the images from the game, but rather only instructions about how to rearrange those images. The court, however, held that MAP files were derivative works, in the same sense that a sequel or parody of a novel is a derivative work: "The work that Micro Star infringes is the *Duke Nukem 3D* story itself—a beefy commando type named Duke who wanders around post-Apocalypse Los Angeles, shooting Pig Cops with a gun, lobbing hand grenades, searching for medkits and steroids, using a jetpack to leap over obstacles, blowing up gas tanks, avoiding radioactive slime. A copyright owner has the right to create sequels and the stories told in the *Duke Nukem 3D* MAP files are surely sequels, telling new (though somewhat repetitive) tales of Duke's fabulous adventures." Another court may have held that the MAP files simply were functional works (affecting how a game was played) that did not copy creative expression. How broadly the courts construe the adaptation right for digital works, then, may well be influenced by how they categorize the work.

Use of a Derivative Work May Infringe the Underlying Work

A derivative work may have its own copyright. It may also contain copyrighted expression copied from the underlying work. Someone who uses the derivative work may therefore infringe the copyright in the derivative work and in the underlying work. Suppose Balbert writes a history of Newfoundland in French. Balbert authorizes Thickens to make an English translation of the book. Copyright in the derivative work applies to creative expression contributed by the author of the derivative work. 17 U.S.C. §103(b). Material taken from the original work is protected by the copyright in the original work (if any). Accordingly, use of the derivative work could potentially infringe both copyrights. Pirate gets hold of a copy of the translation and makes several hundred unauthorized copies. Pirate would infringe the copy in the derivative work (the English translation) and in the underlying work (the French language history of Newfoundland).

Different people may hold copyright in the derivative work and the underlying work. For example, it came to pass that one party held the copyright in the film *Rear Window*, and another held the copyright in the underlying short story, "It Had to Be Murder." *See Stewart v. Abend*, 495 U.S. 207 (1990). The story copyright owner had granted motion picture rights to the film's producers, along with a promise to extend the rights to the renewal term, but the author died before the renewal term began, meaning that all rights reverted to the author's heirs for the renewal term. Publicly showing a film would be performing both the story and the film. In that case, neither copyright owner could use the derivative work without the other's permission. The *Stewart* court rejected the argument that because the film had been made with the permission of the copyright owner, it should not be infringement to utilize it after the rights had reverted to the author's heirs. After *Stewart*, people who make a derivative work must ensure that they get the permission necessary not just to create the work but also to continue to use it.

Other variations occur. In the first, the underlying work is in the public domain. Therefore, anyone may adapt the work without infringing its copyright because it has no copyright. If some folk songs are so old that they are not under copyright, it is not infringement to make new musical arrangements of them, but the new musical arrangements themselves are copyrighted, assuming the author has contributed new creative expression. Someone who copies the new arrangements may be liable for infringement of the copyright in the derivative work.

Another variation is where the underlying work is under copyright, but the derivative work is in the public domain. It occurs less often, because the copyright in the underlying work would normally expire before the derivative work's copyright. But the copyright in the derivative work may have been lost because of failure to comply with formalities, such as copyright notice or renewal. For example, the film *It's A Wonderful Life* lost its copyright in 1974 because of failure to file for renewal. Assuming the film was in the public domain, many television stations aired it without seeking permission or paying licensing fees, but (inspired by the holding in *Stewart*) the holders of the copyright in the underlying story began to enforce their rights.

Finally, copyright does not apply to any portion of a derivative work in which material is used unlawfully. 17 U.S.C. §103(a). So the author of an infringing derivative work may have no copyright protection.

Examples

1. *If it ain't fixed.* Martha licenses F Troupe to perform her copyrighted choreographic work, *Febrile Convulsions*. The agreement provides that F Troupe may perform the work but may not make copies or create derivative works. F Troupe stages its production. Martha watches from the balcony and is horrified that F Troupe's performance has altered the work in many ways.

By changing the composition and arrangement of bodily movements, F Troupe produces an entirely different dance. Martha sues for unauthorized preparation of a derivative work. F Troupe responds that they are not liable because there is no new physical work. They did not write anything down or videotape it. Did they prepare a derivative work?

2. *Stick-ons*. Dragoon sells stick-on tattoos intended for use by kids. It gets a big order from Sporty Goods and sends out several hundred boxes. It then learns that Sporty Goods sticks the tattoos onto the basketballs it sells, making them appealing to kids. Sporty Goods sells the basketballs at a nice premium. The idea to stick the tattoos on the balls was not Sporty's; rather, it learned the idea from kids. Dragoon, perturbed that it has missed this marketing opportunity, sues Sporty Goods for copyright infringement. Is Sporty Goods liable?

3. *Stolen idea*. "*Qualia*," an original short story written by Rico, tells the story of the doomed civilization of Vroom, which unknowingly used up all of its mineral resources. The plotline inspires a filmmaker in a general way to make a film about the collapse of a myopic civilization. The resulting film does not copy any of the expressive elements of "*Qualia*." Rico sues for unauthorized preparation of a derivative work, arguing that the film would not have been made without "*Qualia*." Infringement?

4. *Underlying rights*. Broadway loves musicals adapted from films, like *The Producers*, *The Lion King*, and *Spamalot*. Suppose a Broadway producer decides to stage a musical called 2001. The production will be based on the movie. None of the people involved has even heard of the underlying science fiction story, let alone read it, but many original, creative elements of the story were used in the film and will be used again in the musical. The musical's producer will need permission from the holder of the film copyright. Will she need permission from the holder of the copyright in the science fiction story the movie was made from?

5. *Framed*. When returning results of image searches, Google shows the user, "Below is the image in its original context on the page." To do so, Google's computers send HTML code to the user's computer, which then sends a request to the page with the image. By "framing" the image in this way, is Google creating a derivative work based on the image?

6. *Checksheets*. The book *Big League Sales* describes techniques and case histories for salespeople to help prospective customers overcome their "brick overcoat" of fear. The Church of Scientology develops "checksheets" and "drill sheets," which it sells to be used with the book. Students (paired as "twins") can use the sheets to track completion of reading assignments and practical exercises. The holder of the copyright in *Big League Sales* claims that the checksheets and drill sheets are infringing derivative works. Are they?

Explanations

1. F Troupe did prepare a derivative work. The better view is that there is no fixation requirement for derivative works. It transformed the work into a new creative work, thereby creating a derivative work, without authority of the copyright owner.

2. Dragoon's argument is that sticking the tattoos on the basketballs constitutes preparation of a derivative work because they are "recast, transformed, or adapted" into another form. This raises a split between courts. Some courts have held that mounting a picture on a ceramic tile would be preparation of a derivative work. Others (probably the better view) hold it does not, because preparation of a derivative work requires sufficient creativity to qualify for copyright protection. Sporty did not meet the creativity requirement but simply mounted stickers in an unoriginal manner.

   The better view is no infringement.

3. No infringement. As with all the exclusive rights, there is no infringement unless the defendant has used protected creative elements from the copyrighted work. Copying ideas is not infringement of any of the exclusive rights.

4. She will need permission from the story's copyright owner. Copying from a derivative work can potentially infringe the copyright in the underlying work. The film was a derivative work based on the story. The film's copyright applied only to creative elements that originated with the authors of the film. Any creative elements that were copied from the story are subject to the copyright in the story, so if elements from the story are copied into the musical (via the movie), that could potentially infringe the copyright in the story. To avoid infringement, she needs permission from the story's copyright owner. Practical note: that requires identifying the copyright owner. The original author may well have transferred the relevant rights.

5. No derivative work is created here. Note that Google did not infringe by making a copy, because a copy was sent from the original image page to the user's page—Google just supplied the address. Framing the image on the user's computer would be no more a derivative work than putting a frame on a printed photograph. The better view is that such mounting of a work is not creating a new derivative work.

6. The court soundly rejected the infringement claim. *Peter Letterese & Associates v. World Institute of Scientology Enterprises*, 533 F.3d 1287 (11th Cir. Fla. 2008). The sheets do not copy creative expression from the book but rather at most copy only functional elements. Not every work that is based on a copyrighted work is a derivative work. It must copy protected expression.

PUBLIC DISTRIBUTION RIGHT

The copyright owner has the exclusive right "to distribute copies or phonorecords of the copyrighted work to the public by sale or other transfer of ownership, or by rental, lease, or lending." 17 U.S.C. §106(3). If a bookseller sells unauthorized copies of a copyrighted novel, the bookseller potentially infringes the distribution right. This is true even if bookseller had not made the copies. The distribution right is a separate right.

The statute does not define distribution but gives the examples of "sale or other transfer of ownership, or by rental, lease, or lending." Distribution may be a transfer of ownership (such as a sale or gift) or a temporary transfer (such as rental or lending). The right applies only to distribution to the public; a private sale or gift would not infringe.

At least one court has held that making copies available to the public may be distribution, even without a showing that a member of the public received a copy:

> When a public library adds a work to its collection, lists the work in its index or catalog system, and makes the work available to the borrowing or browsing public, it has completed all the steps necessary for distribution to the public. At that point, members of the public can visit the library and use the work. Were this not to be considered distribution within the meaning of section 106(3), a copyright holder would be prejudiced by a library that does not keep records of public use, and the library would unjustly profit by its own omission.

Hotaling v. Church of Jesus Christ of Latter-Day Saints, 118 F.3d 199, 203 (4th Cir. 1997). Other courts, however, are likely to hold that infringement requires distribution of copies. Unlike the patent statute, the copyright statute does not provide that offering for sale constitutes infringement. Rather, *Hotaling* may be narrowly read as a case about the burden of proof in showing that distribution to the public has actually occurred.

As with the other rights, digital technologies also raise questions about the extent of the exclusive rights. If a website allows browsers to download works (such as pictures or songs), does that constitute distribution of copies? How about peer-to-peer file sharing? One could hold that it is distribution on the theory that copies of the work have been given to the public. Others might hold that one did not "distribute copies or phonorecords" by such electronic dissemination of the work. When a web user downloads a work from a website or gets it from a file-sharing network, one could argue that the defendant does not distribute a copy to her. Rather, her computer receives an electronic signal that causes it to make a copy. Some would limit the distribution right to distribution of discrete copies, like books or CDs, which are themselves delivered to the public.

The statute also brings importation within the distribution right, providing that importation of a copy acquired outside the United States without the authorization of the copyright owner is infringement of the distribution right. 17 U.S.C. §602(a). If Importer buys 500 copies of Author's book abroad and ships them back into the United States, she potentially infringes the distribution right (although she may be protected by the first sale doctrine, discussed below). Section 602(a) exempts copies brought in as personal baggage, single copies imported for personal use, and certain governmental or nonprofit entities.

The first sale doctrine, discussed in detail in Chapter 12, is a key limitation on the distribution and display rights. The owner of an authorized copy may distribute or display that copy without infringing the copyright. Someone who purchases an authorized copy of a book may resell it.

Examples

1. *Pass it around.* Em, a typesetter at Oldstyle Publishing, steals a prepublication copy of a forthcoming book, the autobiography of a former president. After offering the book for sale on eBay, Em sends the copy to the highest bidder, a magazine called *Imagination*, which prints selected excerpts. Is Em liable for copyright infringement without even making a copy?

2. *Making available.* Suppose that Em had given the copy to a local library, which shelved it in the biography section and listed the book in its index. There is no record of anyone checking the book out, because this particular library simply does not keep records of user activity. Is the library liable for copyright infringement?

3. *No sale.* In addition to selling its own goods, Amazon provides third-party sellers the use of Amazon's logistical network. Amazon stores the goods for the seller, then ships them off when sold on the Amazon site. Does Amazon infringe the distribution right if goods are bootlegs?

Explanations

1. Em is potentially liable for copyright infringement. Em did not make a copy, but she did distribute a copy to the public. Note that it was not a private transaction but a distribution to the highest bidding member of the public. Em might argue fair use but would have a tough time, as discussed in Chapter 14.

2. The library has not made a copy, adapted the work, performed it publicly, or displayed the work publicly (putting a book on a shelf does not display its contents). There is no record that the library actually distributed

a copy to the public. Under *Hotaling*, there would be distribution: "When a public library adds a work to its collection, lists the work in its index or catalog system, and makes the work available to the borrowing or browsing public, it has completed all the steps necessary for distribution to the public." But *Hotaling* really stretched to find distribution. A more literal reading would require the plaintiff to show actual distribution.

3. Amazon did not distribute the goods by "sale or other transfer of ownership, or by rental, lease, or lending." Title to the goods did not pass from Amazon to the buyer. The court rejected arguments that Amazon was akin to a consignee and so should be treated as selling the goods. *Milo & Gabby LLC v. Amazon.com, Inc.*, 693 F. App'x 879 (Fed. Cir. 2017). Note that there could be possible liability for contributory or vicarious infringement, discussed in Chapter 18.

PUBLIC PERFORMANCE RIGHT

The copyright owner has the exclusive right to perform the work publicly. 17 U.S.C. §106(4). The performance right applies to "literary, musical, dramatic, and choreographic works, pantomimes, and motion pictures and other audiovisual works." 17 U.S.C. §106(4). It does not apply to architectural, pictorial, graphic, or sculptural works. It is hard to imagine how one might have performed an architectural or sculptural work. The notion brings to mind Elvis Costello's remark that writing about music is like dancing about architecture. For sound recordings, the performance right is limited to public performances via digital audio transmissions. 17 U.S.C. §106(6).

The copyright statute defines "perform" much more broadly than the word's everyday meaning. To "perform" in copyright law means "to recite, render, play, dance, or act it, either directly or by means of any device or process or, in the case of a motion picture, or other audiovisual work, to show its images in any sequence or to make the sounds accompanying it audible." 17 U.S.C. §101. To play a CD of music, watch television, or have the radio on is "performing" the music or show. Anyone can "perform" a Beethoven piano concerto simply by playing a recording of someone else actually playing the piano. Moreover, the performance right applies to most categories of works, not just to works in the performing arts. For example, reading a letter aloud publicly constitutes a public performance, although we do not usually speak of "performing" such texts.

The performance right applies only to *public* performances. A fan can sing a copyrighted song at home with his family without infringing copyright. What makes a performance public?

To perform or display a work "publicly" means:

1. to perform or display it at a place open to the public or at any place where a substantial number of persons outside of a normal circle of a family and its social acquaintances is gathered or
2. to transmit or otherwise communicate a performance or display of the work to a place specified by clause (1) or to the public, by means of any device or process, whether the members of the public capable of receiving the performance or display receive it in the same place or in separate places and at the same time or at different times.

A performance is public if the location is open to the public, if there are more people present than family and social acquaintances, or if the work is transmitted to such a public location or to the public (even if members of the public receive it at separate places and times). 17 U.S.C. §101.

The performance right in sound recordings is limited to the right to "perform the copyrighted work publicly by means of a digital audio transmission." 17 U.S.C. §106(6). Recall, for example, that when a song is recorded, there are potential copyrights in the musical work and the sound recording. A performance of a sound recording that involves no transmission or that uses analog format does not infringe. A business playing a CD of music on a stereo, or a radio station playing music over an analog radio transmission does not infringe the sound recording copyright. The former is not a transmission, and the latter is not in digital format, but both are publicly performing the musical works in question.

When people watch a broadcast television show at home, they "perform" the work, as copyright law understands it. They do not infringe, however, because it is not a public performance. The second paragraph of the definition of public performance (called the "transmission clause") was added to the statute to cover rebroadcasting by cable companies. In early days, cable companies would capture broadcast television shows on antennas and rebroadcast the shows over their cable networks. Courts had held that this was not a public performance, and therefore the cable company did not need permission from the television show copyright holder. Those copyright holders promptly convinced Congress to include such rebroadcasting in their exclusive rights (although Congress also permitted cable companies to get compulsory license to retransmit broadcasts). In 2008, the Second Circuit narrowly interpreted the clause. *Cartoon Network LP, LLLP v. CSC Holdings, Inc.*, 536 F. 3d 121 (2d Cir 2008), held that there was no public performance where customers of Cablevision used remote storage provided by Cablevision to record programs and watch them at their leisure. The court noted the broad scope of the transmission clause, applying where members of the public receive the transmission "in the same place or in separate places and at the same time or at different times," but the clause applies only to members of the public "capable of receiving the performance." Because the performance is the single copy transmitted, the court reasoned, only the single customer was capable of receiving it, meaning that it was not a public performance. Rather, many Cablevision customers could make private performances of the same program from their individual remote storage devices provided by Cablevision.

American Broadcasting Companies v. Aereo, Inc., 134 S. Ct. 2498 (2014), involved a convoluted rebroadcasting system designed specifically to piggyback on the *Cablevision* decision. Aereo's system had thousands of tiny antennas, each coupled with a small storage device. An Aereo customer could control their antenna and storage to record programs or rebroadcast them to the customer. The Second Circuit again held that meant that each customer had a private performance, even if thousands of customers were watching the same broadcast show. The Supreme Court reversed, looking both to the broader language ("in the same place or in separate places and at the same time or at different times") and to the purpose of the statute. In the Court's view, Aereo was doing the same sort of rebroadcasting that the definition was designed to target:

> Aereo sells a service that allows subscribers to watch television programs, many of which are copyrighted, almost as they are being broadcast. In providing this service, Aereo uses its own equipment, housed in a centralized warehouse, outside of its users' homes. By means of its technology (antennas, transcoders, and servers), Aereo's system "receive[s] programs that have been released to the public and carr[ies] them by private channels to additional viewers." Fortnightly, 392 U.S., at 400, 88 S. Ct. 2084, 20 L. Ed. 2d 1176.

The question after *Aereo* is how broadly it would apply. The Court took care not to cast a cloud on technological development, stating that it was not ruling on issues of cloud computing, remote storage DVRs, and other novel issues to arise in other cases.

Collective Rights Organizations

Suppose Little Music Company holds the copyright in the musical work "Just Another Song." Little Music released a recording of the song in 1995, and it is still often played on the radio. Various bands perform the song live. Bars and other businesses often play the recording over their sound systems. All those public performances are subject to Little Music's copyright, but enforcing that copyright would be quite difficult for Little Music, operating alone. To locate every potential use and reach a licensing agreement would be more trouble than it is worth.

Over decades, collective rights organizations like the American Society of Composers, Authors, and Publishers (ASCAP) and Broadcast Music Inc.

(BMI) have made the enforcement of musical copyrights more efficient. Rather than every copyright owner trying to go around locating users (and infringers) and negotiating license agreements, ASCAP, BMI, and the like do much of the work. ASCAP and BMI represent the owners of millions of copyrighted musical works. They offer a range of licenses to potential users. A bar that plays recorded music as well as hosts bands performing music could find a single license that would get the necessary permissions. These organizations also enforce the copyrights. Representatives of ASCAP and BMI regularly visit public establishments, monitor broadcasts, and browse the Internet to find unauthorized users. Software searches the Internet (especially places like YouTube) and sends automated takedown notices, cease-and-desist letters, and demands for payment.

When many sellers in a market band together, there is a risk of anticompetitive behavior. Both ASCAP and BMI have been subject to antitrust suits and operate under consent decrees that limit the sort of licenses and terms they can offer.

Examples

1. *Laundry list.* Bard holds the copyright in the music and words of the song "Farmhouse." Which of the following would be a public performance of the work?
   a. Alex sings the song on stage during a school talent contest.
   b. Bertha plays a recording of the song over the sound system in her restaurant.
   c. Cable transmits a recording of the song over its cable TV system as background music.
   d. The waiters at a restaurant sing the song to the diners.
   e. Frank sings the song in his secluded backyard.
   f. Gertrude prints the words and music of the song as part of a collection.

2. *Public performance?* Cablevision, at the request of customers, records cable programs for them and replays the shows on demand. Has Cablevision infringed the public performance right of the copyrights in the programs?

Explanations

1. All of the above, except *e* and f. "Perform" is defined very broadly:

   > to recite, render, play, dance, or act it, either directly or by means of any device or process or, in the case of a motion picture, or other audiovisual work, to show its images in any sequence or to make the sounds accompanying it audible.

   17 U.S.C. §101. To perform a work publicly is likewise broad, encompassing performance at any place open to the public or where a substantial

number of persons outside of the normal circle of a family and its social acquaintances is gathered, or a transmission to such a place.

a. Classic public performance.
b. Playing a work with a device is a performance, and this was in a public restaurant.
c. Transmission to the public is a public performance.
d. Singing the song in public is a public performance, even if the performers are not professional musicians. For this reason, restaurants often instruct their staff not to sing "Happy Birthday to You," that early twentieth-century song in which copyright was still claimed and enforced—until 2017, when those claims were held unfounded.
e. Not a public performance.
f. Not a performance.

All of *a* through *d* are public performances but may not infringe the copyright. Section 110, discussed in part in Chapter 12, specifically allows certain uses, such as nonprofit performances (a school talent show might qualify), face-to-face teaching, and small-business reception of transmissions (such as a newsstand playing the radio).

2. The *Cablevision* court, discussed in the reproduction right above, also rejected the theory of infringement of the public performance right. Each program is performed for a different subscriber at a different time, in their private home. Such performances, the court reasoned, are not public performances, even though the service is one that Cablevision offers to the public.

PUBLIC DISPLAY RIGHT

The copyright owner has the exclusive right "to display the copyrighted work publicly." 17 U.S.C. §106(5). The display right applies to "literary, musical, dramatic, and choreographic works, pantomimes, and pictorial, graphic, or sculptural works, including the individual images of a motion picture or other audiovisual work." It does not apply to sound recordings or architectural works, and for motion pictures and other audiovisual works is limited to individual images. 17 U.S.C. §106(5).

Copyright law also has a broad definition of "display":

> to show a copy of it, either directly or by means of a film, slide, television image, or any other device or process or, in the case of a motion picture or other audiovisual work, to show individual images nonsequentially.

17 U.S.C. §101. The broad definition of the right goes well beyond putting a copy of the work on exhibit. Wearing a T-shirt bearing a copy of a

copyrighted work could constitute a public display. Projecting an image of the work also constitutes display.

The display right applies only to public displays. The applicable definition of "publicly" is the same one as for performance. A display is public if the location is open to the public, if there are more people present than family and social acquaintances, or if the work is transmitted to such a public location. 17 U.S.C. §101. A website that allows users to browse pictures has been held to "display" those pictures to the public.

The increasing use of the Internet and other networks has considerably increased the importance of the display right. *See* Robert A. Gorman and Jane C. Ginsburg, *Copyright* 580 (6th ed. 2002). The display right was of less practical consequence than other rights in the days before electronic distribution of pictures. Under first sale (discussed later in the book), the owner of an authorized copy is entitled to display it. Under the definition of display, showing a film (as opposed to individual frames) was not a display, so there were fewer instances where the display right was of much importance, compared to the more frequently infringed rights to make copies, publicly distribute, or publicly perform works. But now that the Internet makes it so easy to show infringing copies to others (simply by putting up a website), the right is more likely to be litigated. *Id.*

Example

1. *Framed and displayed.* When returning results of image searches, Google arguably displays thumbnail images to the public, but that likely qualifies as fair use. Google also allows the user to see the full-size image, indirectly, under the wording "Below is the image in its original context on the page." To do so, Google's computers send HTML code to the user's computer, which then sends a request to the page with the image. By so "framing" the image, is Google displaying a copy of the work to the public?

Explanation

1. The Ninth Circuit held that Google was not displaying a copy of the work to the public. *Perfect 10 v. Amazon*, 508 F.3d 1146 (9th Cir. 2007). Google did not send a copy but rather sent the address of the original page. The user's computer could request a copy from the original page and display that copy if sent. Google would not be liable for infringing the public display right. Google might be liable on other theories (such as contributory infringement, discussed later in the book), but those would require showing other elements, such as knowledge of the infringing activity. Other courts have followed,

holding there was not infringement in linking to copyrighted content, such as embedding.[4]

The Southern District of New York, however, reached the opposite result in a somewhat similar case. Someone tweeted a copyrighted photo of quarterback Tom Brady. Many news organizations embedded the tweet on their own pages in reporting, meaning that they did not reproduce the photo, but had code that would make the photo appear on a user's browser in the midst of the news article. The court held that this did constitute a public display of the photo by the news organization. It first held that physical possession of a copy is not necessary to infringe the display right. It then distinguished Perfect Ten: "In Perfect 10, Google's search engine provided a service whereby the user navigated from webpage to webpage, with Google's assistance. This is manifestly not the same as opening up a favorite blog or website to find a full color image awaiting the user, whether he or she asked for it, looked for it, clicked on it, or not. Both the nature of Google Search Engine, as compared to the defendant websites, and the volitional act taken by users of the services, provide a sharp contrast to the facts at hand." *Goldman v. Breitbart News Network, LLC*, 302 F. Supp. 3d 585, 592 (S.D.N.Y. 2018).

The bounds of the display right online are under construction.

WALTER'S GRAND SLAM: A QUICK REVIEW OF THE EXCLUSIVE RIGHTS

The Internet provides a good example for application of the various exclusive rights because it can be seen as a global machine for making, transforming, distributing, performing, and displaying copies of works. *See* Mark A. Lemley, *Copyright Owners' Rights and Users' Privileges on the Internet: Dealing with Overlapping Copyrights on the Internet*, 22 Dayton L. Rev. 547 (1997). Suppose that Walter runs a website devoted to a pop star. Visitors to the website can view pictures of the singer, listen to her songs over streaming audio, and download Walter's own recordings of her songs, which he has rewritten from sappy ballads into political satire. Suppose also that Walter is using copyrighted pictures and music without authorization. He could potentially

---

4. *Hunley v. Instagram, LLC*, 73 F.4th 1060, 1071 (9th Cir. 2023):

> "We have not limited *Perfect 10* to search engines, and it is too late to argue that it is so limited. The application of the Server Test depends on the *method used* for displaying a photo—not the *context* in which the photo is displayed. And the process used by *BuzzFeed* and *Time* to show users third-party Instagram content is the same process used by Google to show users third-party images: embedding. Nothing in *Perfect 10* or the cases following it limits its application to search engines."

infringe all the exclusive rights in section 106 (but not the moral rights in section 106A), although the application of the exclusive rights in the Internet context is still being hashed out in the courts. Here is a quick review of exclusive rights as they pertain to Walter's situation:

1. *Reproduction right*: He made copies by loading copies of the works onto his server.
2. *Adaptation right*: He prepared derivative works by rewriting the songs.
3. *Distribution right*: He arguably distributes copies and phonorecords to the public by sending copies to visitors who download material. Some would not extend the distribution right so far, limiting it to distribution of more tangible copies, like books or CDs.
4. *Performance right*: He publicly performs the musical works by enabling visitors to listen to streaming audio versions of the music. He also violates the narrow performance right in the sound recordings because the streaming audio qualifies as a "digital audio transmission."
5. *Display right*: He displays copies to the public by causing the images to be viewed on the visitors' screens.
6. *Section 106A moral rights* (preview of a coming chapter): Even if Walter grossly distorts the songs with his revisions, he does not violate the rights of integrity and attribution afforded by section 106A because section 106A protects only the narrow category of works of visual art.

Examples

1. *Practice with 106*. After years of painstaking research, Arthur Author writes a book of history. The work describes the lives of several generations of Illinois farmers. Arthur draws most of the details from his personal research, which ranges from village records to estate sales to long interviews with various Illinoisians. But Arthur contributes a great deal of original expression to the work through his selection and arrangement of facts, his graceful and concise prose, and his vivid descriptions. The book sells very well. Two years after the book is published, Arthur visits his attorney. Arthur has learned of various activities related to his work and wonders if any fall within his exclusive rights. Of the following, which fall within the exclusive rights of the copyright holder?
   a. Knockoff copies large parts of Arthur's book verbatim into Knockoff's own book about Midwestern life. Knockoff proudly shows the manuscript to several friends. Knockoff has not yet offered the manuscript to a publisher or made any commercial use of the manuscript.
   b. Fan borrows a copy of the book, digitizes the text with a scanner, and saves the text in a file on the hard drive of her computer. Fan returns the book and reads the book at her leisure from the computer.

c. Nemesis purchases and promptly burns a copy of the book.
d. Critic writes a scathing review of the book. Critic does not copy any of Arthur's original expression. Critic makes several factual statements about the work that he knows are false and that are very likely to harm sales of the book.
e. Plago publishes a historical novel set in the time and place covered in Arthur's book. Plago copies a number of facts and ideas from Arthur's book but does not copy any original expression.
f. Scribbler buys a copy of the book and writes a screenplay based on the novel. The screenplay follows the book very closely, copying not just facts and ideas but also much original creative expression. Producer, with Scribbler's permission, makes a movie based on the screenplay. The movie, like the screenplay, uses much original creative expression from the book. Cinepeps, a local movie house, shows the movie to the public for several weeks.
g. Every week, Fan holds Arthur Appreciation Night at a local bar, charging a small admission. Fan and other adherents of Arthur take turns reading portions of the novel aloud to the crowd.
h. Fan holds Arthur Appreciation Night in her home instead and reads the book aloud to her family and friends.
i. Baton runs an advertisement and offers copies of Arthur's book at a huge discount. Baton receives payment from hundreds of buyers but never ships them any copies. Indeed, Baton had never acquired even a single copy.
j. Veb borrows Fan's scanned copy of the book. Veb then sets up a website, which permits viewers to read the book one page at a time.

2. *Artist's rights*. Vincent paints a portrait of himself wearing a straw hat. George buys the painting from Vincent and makes a poster featuring reproductions of the painting. George sells many copies of the poster to the public. When Vincent objects, George crudely draws horns on the portrait, purely out of spite toward Vincent. Do George's actions fall within any of Vincent's exclusive rights?

3. *What goes around*. Songs writes a hit song called "Edsel Medley." Songs sells the copyright in the song to Music Co. Songs continues to perform "Edsel Medley" in concert. Songs also records a follow-up song, which copies much of the original creative expression from "Edsel Medley." Music Co. writes to Songs, demanding that she cease and desist from performing "Edsel Medley" and from making any copies of the follow-up. Songs laughs at the idea that she could be accused of stealing her own work. Has she done anything within the exclusive rights of the copyright holder?

4. *Souvenir*. Lines, a software developer, works for Microfuzzy. Lines has worked for several years on Dindles, a strong-selling video graphics

program. Because Lines is a key developer, Microfuzzy provides her with a laptop loaded with the source code version of Dindles. Dindles is sold to the public in object code, and only a very limited number of people are given access to the source code version, which Microfuzzy considers to be a key competitive asset. Lines decides to give up the software business and become a songwriter. She resigns from Microfuzzy and moves to the mountains of Montana, taking the laptop with her. She has never so much as turned the laptop on. By leaving with a valuable copy of an unpublished version of a copyrighted work, has Lines done anything within the exclusive rights of the copyright holder? What if, on arriving in Montana, she prints out the source code so she can read it in the great outdoors?

5. *Matinee.* Bones operates a used clothing store. Bones enjoys listening to the music of Texas, a country singer. Early one afternoon, several customers are browsing in the store. Bones is playing Texas's most recent CD. A woman walks in with a clipboard, listens for a few minutes, and then asks to speak to the manager. She informs Bones that he is infringing the copyright in the musical works on the CD. Bones protests that he has not sold any copies of the CD or charged anyone for admission to the store. She informs Bones that he has nonetheless publicly performed the music. Has he?

6. *Thinner copyright.* Skins is devoted to classical music and pursues her interest with new technology. She obtains the music to Smaller's Third Symphony. She knows that the music is not under copyright because it was published in 1818. Skins records her audio synthesizer performing the symphony. In making the recording, Skins makes a number of creative decisions, so she has a copyright in the sound recording. She sells several copies of the recording on CDs. Among the buyers are Bones and Akimbo. Skins then learns that Bones has taken to playing the recording in his used clothing store. She also learns that Akimbo has made a recording of the same symphony. Akimbo does not copy any of the actual sounds of Skins's recording but does imitate her recording in a number of ways. Has Bones or Akimbo come within Skins's exclusive rights in the sound recording?

Explanations

1. a. Knockoff potentially infringes the reproduction right by copying protected expression from Arthur's book. Knockoff has not yet commercially exploited the book. Commercial exploitation, however, is not required for infringement.

   Knockoff's showing his manuscript to several friends does not infringe the display right because that exclusive right extends only to public displays.

   b. When Fan scans and saves a digitized version of the novel, she is making a copy. By doing so, she potentially infringes the reproduction right.

Every time she reads the book on her computer, a portion is copied from the computer's permanent memory (the hard drive) into its fast, temporary memory (the DRAM). This DRAM copying probably constitutes making an infringing copy as well. As noted in the text, whether making a copy in DRAM infringes the reproduction right is not definitively addressed in the statute, but such a reading is supported by most of the few cases on point, read together with recent statutory amendments.

c. By burning the novel, Nemesis might offend Arthur but does not infringe copyright. Section 106 grants five exclusive rights: to make copies, distribute copies to the public, prepare derivative works, perform the work in public, and display the work in public. None of those is triggered by burning a copy of the work—even if it is the only copy. Copyright does not grant a general property right in the protected work; it grants only the specific rights in the statute. Author might think Nemesis's actions are an infringement of his rights of integrity and attribution under section 106A, but section 106A applies only to works of visual art (paintings, sculpture, and the like), not to novels.

d. Simply writing a scathing review, even or an untrue one, is not copyright infringement because it does not implicate any of the exclusive rights.

   Critic does not copy any protected expression and therefore does not infringe. A sophistic argument for Arthur might be that Critic's false calumny reduced the sales of Arthur's book and therefore impinged on Arthur's exclusive right to distribute copies to the public. But copyright is infringed by those who wrongfully exercise one of the copyright owner's exclusive rights. There is no secondary layer of rights protecting the copyright owner's ability to ply his trade.

e. Plago does not infringe any of the exclusive rights. Copying from a copyrighted work is not infringement as long as protected expression is not copied. Plago copies but only unprotectable facts and ideas.

   Arthur might argue that Plago infringes the adaptation right (the right to prepare derivative works) by adapting Arthur's book of history into a historical novel, but none of the exclusive rights is infringed unless protected expression is used.

f. By writing the screenplay that copies much protected expression, Scribbler infringes both the reproduction right and the adaptation right. By making the movie that likewise copies much of Arthur's protected expression, Producer likewise infringes those rights. By showing the movie to the public, Cinepeps infringes the right of public performance. Note that this is true even if Producer and Cinepeps are unaware of the fact that the screenplay is copied from Arthur's book. The plaintiff need make no showing of negligence or knowledge.

Plaintiff need simply show that defendant did something that fell within plaintiff's exclusive rights.

g. By reading the book aloud to the crowd, Fan and the others potentially infringe the right of public performance. Infringement does not require a showing that the infringer acts for commercial purposes or gains money from the acts. Note also how broad the performance right is—simply reading a book aloud probably would not be thought of as a performance in the everyday use of the word.

h. If Fan simply reads the book aloud to her family and friends, there is no infringement. The copyright owner's exclusive rights extend only to public performance.

i. Baton does not infringe. Offering to sell the copyrighted work does not fall within the exclusive rights. Baton has not distributed or made copies. She would not be liable for copyright infringement, although presumably other legal theories such as fraud would apply.

j. Veb potentially infringes the right of public display. Veb does not infringe copyright by acquiring the copy that Fan made. Acquisition and possession of a copy do not fall within the exclusive rights of the copyright holder, even if the copy is made through infringement. But by showing the book page by page to visitors to the website, Veb is displaying the work publicly. A public display includes a transmission to the public. If the members of the public are enabled to view the work on the website, that constitutes a transmission, even if the people view it at separate times in different locations.

2. George has infringed Vincent's reproduction right (by making copies of the painting) and distribution right (by distributing copies to the public). George bought the painting, not the copyright on the painting. George may have also infringed Vincent's adaptation right by preparing a derivative work. That depends on whether drawing the horns on the painting had the requisite originality to create a new work, based on Vincent's painting. Some courts do not require that a derivative work be separately copyrightable, but rather that any adaptation is potentially infringing. Under that approach, drawing the horns would presumably suffice to create a derivative work. The better view, however, is that no derivative work is created unless the work meets the standards for being an original work of authorship.

   Beyond the section 106 rights, George may have infringed Vincent's right of integrity under section 106A, as discussed later in the book. Liability requires a showing that the modification is prejudicial to Vincent's honor or reputation. The offensive change to the portrait appears to meet that standard.

3. Songs may be liable for infringing the copyright in her own work. The copyright owner has the exclusive rights of section 106. Songs owned

those rights but sold them to Music Co., so Songs is infringing Music Co.'s exclusive right to perform "Edsel Medley" in public. By making the follow-up, which copies her own original creative expression, she potentially infringes both the reproduction and adaptation rights.

4. Lines is not infringing the copyright in Dindles (though she may be in possession of a copy without authority). Ownership of particular copies of works is largely governed not by copyright but by property law. Lines has not done anything that falls within the copyright owner's exclusive rights. She did not make a copy, adapt the work, distribute a copy to the public, perform the work publicly, or display it publicly.

   If Lines prints out the source code from the laptop, she is potentially infringing the reproduction right. Printing the code constitutes making a copy. Although the copy of the program is not one that could be run on a computer, the reproduction right can encompass making a copy in any medium.

5. Bones has made a public performance of the work, potentially infringing the copyright in the work. Bones might reasonably think that performing a song means singing it aloud. He might also wonder whether one performs "publicly" in a store with only a few customers present whose attention is on the merchandise they are browsing. But the right to public performance is very broad. "Performance" includes playing the work using a device. "Publicly" encompasses a place open to the public. Beyond the requirement that the performance be public, the statute does not require that it be before a paying audience or serve any commercial purpose. So Bones has made a public performance of the musical work. As discussed later in the book, section 110 does protect some not-for-profit public performances, but it would not apply here.

6. Neither Bones nor Akimbo has infringed Skins's copyright in the sound recording. The reproduction right and the right of public performance are both limited for sound recordings. The performance right in a sound recording extends only to a performance via a "digital audio transmission." Bones did not transmit the recording; he only played it aloud in his store. The reproduction right is infringed only by making a duplication that captures the actual sounds in the sound recording. Akimbo imitated Skins's recording but did not capture the actual sounds. Akimbo did not mechanically duplicate Skins's actual recording but only imitated the recording.

   Both results would be different if the work at issue were a musical work, as opposed to a sound recording. Bones could potentially infringe by a public performance. Akimbo would infringe by making a duplication that was substantially similar and copied protected expression.

CHAPTER 12

First Sale

The copyright holder has the exclusive rights to distribute copies of the copyrighted work to the public and to publicly display the work. But used bookstores sell copyrighted books. Video rental services rent copyrighted movies. Museums display copyrighted painting and sculptures to the public. Resellers recirculate copies of copyrighted software. Libraries lend copyrighted books. None need permission from the copyright owner as long as they own a copy that was made lawfully, such as a copy that was made by or licensed by the copyright owner. A copyright owner's exclusive right to distribute copies and display copies to the public is subject to the first sale doctrine. Once the copyright owner sells a copy, her rights with respect to that particular copy are limited. The owner may distribute it or display it (but not copy, adapt, or publicly perform it, unless protected by fair use, permission, or something else).

The first sale doctrine is an important limit on a copyright holder's exclusive rights of public distribution and display. Copyright law distinguishes between ownership of a physical copy of the work and ownership of the copyright. Sale of the physical object does not include transfer of the copyright. If Painter sells her latest landscape to Collector, Collector owns the painting, but Painter still owns the copyright. If Collector makes copies of the work or makes derivative works, Collector potentially infringes the copyright. But section 109, often called "the first sale doctrine," does give the transferee some rights. Under 17 U.S.C. §109(a), the owner of a lawfully made copy or phonorecord may sell or otherwise dispose of that copy or phonorecord. Under section 109(c), the owner of a lawfully made copy may display the copy to the public. Collector may sell, rent, or donate the painting (even though that is distributing a copy to the public) or put the painting on display (even if that means displaying the painting publicly).

FIRST SALE AND THE DISTRIBUTION RIGHT

Section 109 carves out a limitation to the copyright owner's right of public distribution:

> Notwithstanding the provisions of section 106(3), the owner of a particular copy or phonorecord lawfully made under this title, or any person authorized by such owner, is entitled, without the authority of the copyright owner, to sell or otherwise dispose of the possession of that copy or phonorecord.

17 U.S.C. §109(a).

In short, the owner of a book or painting or video game or sculpture may sell it (unless that copy was a bootleg, knockoff, or otherwise infringing copy). The first sale doctrine has distinct limits. The fair use doctrine, discussed later in the book, can apply to any of the five exclusive rights, but the first sale doctrine limits only the distribution right and the display right. It does not limit the copyright owner's exclusive rights to make copies, adapt the work, or publicly perform the work. If the owner of a copy makes copies, makes derivative works, or performs the work in public, first sale cannot protect her (although fair use or some other limitation might apply). If Collector owns a copy of the painting, she may display it or sell it without infringing. But first sale does not authorize her to make copies or adapt it (such as making a velvet version).

The first sale doctrine protects only the *owner* of a particular copy or phonorecord that was lawfully made under the copyright statute. Had Collector stolen the painting, Collector would not be the owner and would not be protected by first sale. Collector might rightfully have the copy yet fail to qualify for first sale. If the copy was loaned, rented, or otherwise transferred to Collector without transferring ownership, Collector would have no rights under first sale (unless the owner also authorized further distribution). Someone who rented a video might not be authorized to rent it to someone else.

The first sale protections apply only to the particular copy owned. It would not authorize the distribution of other copies. If Collector makes and sells a copy of the painting, Collector would potentially infringe both the right to make copies and the distribution right.

First sale applies only if the copy is *lawfully made*. Had the painting itself been an infringing copy, it would not be lawfully made, and Collector would have no rights under first sale. Note that the statute does not require that the copyright owner authorized the making of the copy, but rather that the copy was "lawfully made." As the legislative history puts it:

> To come within the scope of section 109(a), a copy or phonorecord must have been "lawfully made under this title," though not necessarily with the copyright owner's authorization. For example, any resale of an illegally "pirated" phonorecord would be an infringement, but the disposition of a phonorecord legally made under the compulsory licensing provisions of section 115 would not.

House Report No. 94-1476. A copy that was made under fair use or some other provision could qualify.

Examples

1. *The play's the thing*. Alec decides to mount a production of *Death of a Salesman*. Alex purchases a copy of the play at a local bookstore.
   - He scans the text of the play from the book into his laptop and prints 100 copies.
   - He gives 10 copies to members of his troupe, who use them during rehearsal.
   - The troupe, under Alec's direction, then gives several public performances at a local theater.
   - Alec sells 50 of the copies he made to members of the audience.
   - The next day, Alec visits a used bookstore and sells it the first copy he had originally bought.

   Does first sale authorize the various uses of the play?

2. *The little store*. Thatcher operates a used bookstore. He buys books from customers, at garage sales, at estate sales, and anywhere else he can find them. He often gets donations from people cleaning out their homes. Idly browsing through his inventory, he reads about the potentially severe remedies for copyright infringement. Thatcher wonders if he is infringing the various copyrights in books he sells. He is distributing copies to the public—isn't that one of the exclusive rights of the copyright holder? Should he limit his service to out-of-copyright books, such as nineteenth-century rare books?

3. *Clips*. Snippy runs a clipping service. Snippy reads several papers a day and clips stories that may be of interest to one client or another. A story might mention a client, a competitor of a client, or a topic of special interest to a client. She pops the stories in the mail. The stories are all copyrighted. Is Snippy infringing? Would it be different if she read the stories online and then cut and pasted them into e-mails to her clients?

4. *Wet blanket*. Becky purchases a CD of tunes by her favorite singer, Dee Vee Dee. Becky brings the CD to her job at the university library reference desk. Becky proceeds to play the CD over the public address system, to the surprise of the patrons and staff. The library director suggests that Becky has violated not just library rules but also copyright law by publicly performing the copyrighted musical works. Becky contends that she is protected by first sale because the sale of the CD to her eliminated the copyright owner's interest in that particular copy. Does first sale protect Becky? Would it make a difference if Becky had bought an authorized copy of sheet music and sung it over the PA system?

5. *First sale?* Imagick sells 700 copies of his copyrighted illustration, *Bikealot*. Imagick assures the buyers that the work is a limited edition, so they are buying a relatively scarce commodity. The illustration, in Imagick's distinctive hand, shows what the Knights of the Round Table might have looked like had they been members of the Hell's Angels. The purchasers of several copies do things that seem to fall within Imagick's exclusive rights as a copyright owner. State which of the following are protected by the first sale doctrine:
   a. Sleepy advertises his copy for sale and sells it to a collector for a premium price of three times what Sleepy paid to Imagick.
   b. Grumpy decides he does not like the illustration. Grumpy skillfully uses charcoal to change the expressions of the riders depicted by Imagick, changing them from fierce bikers to snooty tourists.
   c. Sneezy puts his copy on display in his gallery, admitting members of the public for a fee.
   d. Doc makes several copies of his copy and sells them outside Sneezy's gallery.
   e. Arb buys a copy from Doc and sells it online to a buyer for a nice profit.
   f. Dopey sets up a webcam that allows visitors to Dopey's website to view Dopey's copy.
   g. Imagick gives one copy to Ingrate as a birthday present. Ingrate promptly turns around and sells the copy for a nice price.

6. *Fair use and first sale.* Teacher makes 17 copies of a poem and hands them out to her class. Assume that making the copies and distributing them was fair use and not copyright infringement. One student sells her copy on eBay, mailing it to a complete stranger for $10. Copyright infringement?

7. *Photo Ops*. Prince purchases a book of photographs. He paints over portions of the photos and puts up an exhibit titled *Canal Zone*. Does copyright even matter when he did not make copies of the work? Is he protected by first sale?

8. *First sale in the cloud?* PJ signs up for Sinfony, an online music service. PJ can buy up to 100 songs a month and save them on the Sinfony Cloud Drive. In addition, PJ can listen to streaming audio of any one of thousands of songs in Sinfony's library. Does first sale protect PJ if he sells one of his songs on the Sinfony Cloud Drive on eBay? Does first sale protect him from infringement if he sells the entire Sinfony music library after adroitly copying the streaming versions?

Explanations

1. First sale authorizes Alec to sell his copy or to display his copy, but he went beyond the bounds of first sale.
   - By scanning the text, he potentially infringed the reproduction right.
   - By printing 100 copies, he likewise potentially infringed the reproduction right.
   - He potentially infringed the right of public distribution by distributing 10 copies to members of his troupe and by selling 50 copies to members of the audience (he had no first sale right in the copies he made because they were not lawfully made, assuming he infringed by making them).
   - By performing the play, the troupe potentially infringed the public performance right.

2. Thatcher is not infringing copyright. The copyright owner does have the right of public distribution, but that is subject to first sale. Under first sale, the owner of a lawfully made copy may sell it or otherwise dispose of it without infringing copyright.

   Thatcher could be infringing if he is not the owner or if the copies were not lawfully made. If he unknowingly received a stolen copy (or simply a borrowed copy that was never returned) or a copy that was made without permission, he could be infringing. But those risks are pretty small (and the remedy for such innocent infringement, as we will see, is likely to be so small that he would not be sued).

3. Snippy is not infringing. She owns the copies of the copyrighted stories and may distribute them as she wishes.

   It would be different if she made copies of the stories. It would also be different if she read the stories online, made copies, and e-mailed them to her clients. First sale does not authorize the making of copies, only their distribution (and display). By making copies, she would potentially infringe. (She might argue fair use, but such reproductive commercial use would probably not qualify, as later chapters discuss. Better that she simply e-mail links to her clients.)

4. Becky is not protected by first sale. First sale limits only the distribution and display rights. Becky has potentially infringed the performance right. She performed the musical works publicly by playing them over the PA system. The same would be true if she had bought the sheet music and performed it herself.

5. a. Sleepy is protected by first sale. He owns the copy, so section 109 authorizes him to sell the copy.
   b. Grumpy is not protected by the first sale doctrine. He has potentially infringed the adaptation right by transforming the work into a new creative work. He owns the copy, but ownership is not a general defense to copyright infringement. Rather, first sale protects the owner from infringement of the distribution or display rights. It is not a limitation on the copyright owner's exclusive rights of reproduction, adaptation, and performance.
   c. Sneezy is protected by first sale. As the owner of a lawfully made copy, Sneezy may display it.
   d. Doc is not protected by first sale. Doc made copies of the work without permission. First sale does not apply to infringement of the reproduction right. Nor does it protect Doc's distribution of the copies he made because it authorizes distribution only of lawfully made copies.
   e. Arb is likewise not protected by first sale. He is the owner of a copy but not a lawfully made copy, so Arb had no first sale protection at all. He infringes the distribution right by selling the copy to a member of the public.
   f. Dopey is not protected by first sale. He has made a potentially infringing public display. First sale authorizes the owner to display the copy only at the place where the copy is located. It is narrower than the display right, which encompasses display via a transmission to other places.
   g. Ingrate is protected by first sale. The owner of a lawfully made copy is protected by the first sale doctrine, and Ingrate received a lawfully made copy from Imagick as a gift. The owner need not have purchased the copy to acquire first sale rights.

6. Under section 109(a), "the owner of a particular copy . . . lawfully made under this title, . . . is entitled . . . to sell or otherwise dispose of the possession of that copy or phonorecord." The student would appear to fall within the provision. The copy was lawfully made because the teacher was protected by fair use. The teacher gave the copy to the student, so the student owned the copy. Under section 109, the student could dispose of it any way the student chose, including selling it. For first sale to apply, as the legislative history notes, the copy must be "lawfully made" but not necessarily with the authorization of the copyright owner.

7. This example reminds us that first sale limits only distribution and display rights. Prince potentially infringed the copyright owner's exclusive right to adapt the work (the right to prepare derivative works), so copyright does matter (even though he did not make copies), and first sale does not protect (it does not apply to allegations of infringement of the right to make derivative works, perform the work, or make copies). The next question is whether fair use applies, as discussed later in the book.

8. First sale applies awkwardly to works in digital form, which require copying to pass on. First sale protects PJ from copyright infringement for selling a copy if he is the owner of that particular lawfully made copy. If he downloads a copy from the Cloud Drive, maybe he is the owner of that particular copy, and it is likely lawfully made. But to sell it, he'd have to slice out a little section of his computer's hard drive (or maybe download it onto some smaller USB storage device). Meanwhile, he still "has" a copy on the Cloud Drive. Where copies are multiplying, it seems that first sale would not apply. In addition, it may be tricky to try to identify any actual stored copy on the Cloud Drive. For example, to save space, Sinfony may well store a single copy of a popular song and make it available to many users who believe they each have a copy on their individual Cloud Drive.

   First sale would probably not apply to streaming audio. PJ is probably not the owner of a copy, where portions are being sent to his computer simply to be played. Final note: Even if first sale did apply, the next question would be whether Sinfony or the copyright holders effectively limit first sale rights by agreement in its user agreement (also known as "terms of use," or "end user license agreement"). That issue is discussed in the next section.

   Some have argued that even if first sale did not allow sale by sending a copy of a digital work (because the owner is not selling their copy), that fair use should authorize the practice, especially if the owner promises to get rid of the original copy. But courts have consistently rejected that argument.

Copyright Holders May Seek to Limit First Sale Rights

Because first sale protects only the "owner" of a copy (or someone authorized by the owner), some copyright owners seek to avoid first sale by characterizing transactions in such a way that ownership of the copy does not pass to the recipient. Computer software, for example, is often "sold" pursuant to a license. If User downloads some software or purchases it at a store and walks out with it, she may often find that the seller has characterized the transaction as a licensing transaction. The terms will provide that User does not own the copy that she possesses. Rather, ownership of that copy remains with the software company. The company simply grants User a license to use the software, subject to various restrictions set forth in seller's forms.

If User claims the protections of the first sale doctrine, the software company may contend that first sale does not apply because User does not own the copy. Several issues may arise. The first would be, as a matter of contract law, whether User agreed to the terms in the form. One party may not unilaterally characterize the transaction. The restriction would apply only if the other party did something to become bound by the restriction. Usually this would be by agreeing to the license agreement. In some cases, agreement might be inferred from the conduct of the parties.

The next question would be whether the contract terms control, or whether courts will look to the substance of the transaction. Section 109 expressly limits first sale rights to one who owns a lawfully made copy: First sale does not apply "to any person who has acquired possession of the copy or phonorecord from the copyright owner, by rental, lease, loan, or otherwise, without acquiring ownership of it." 17 U.S.C. §109(d). A number of decisions have held that the agreement will control when the parties agree that the recipient does not own the copy. *See, e.g., Vernor v. Autodesk, Inc.*, 621 F.3d 1102 (9th Cir. 2010); Stephen McJohn, *Top Tens in 2010: Copyright and Trade Secret Cases*, 9 N.W. J. Tech. & Intell. Prop. 325 (2011). This approach allows the parties to allocate rights and risks between them. If User pays the agreed price in exchange, in part, for giving up first sale rights, then it might be unfair to override the agreed terms to give User first sale rights. In the leading case, Vernor bought copies of AutoCAD, a sophisticated piece of computer-aided design software, and sold them on eBay. Autodesk objected on the grounds that such sales infringed its exclusive right to distribute copies of the software to the public. The court looked at three factors in deciding whether a software user should be classified as a licensee, rather than the owner of a copy:

- whether the copyright owner specifies that a user is granted a license
- whether the copyright owner significantly restricts the user's ability to transfer the software
- whether the copyright owner imposes notable use restrictions

All three factors, in the court's view, indicated a license rather than a sale. Autodesk's license stated that the transaction was a license, not a sale of the software and that Autodesk retained title to the software. There were transfer restrictions: the license was nontransferable without Autodesk's written consent and could not be transferred outside the Western Hemisphere. There were use restrictions: It prohibited use outside the Western Hemisphere; prohibited modifying, translating, or reverse engineering the software; and prohibited removing trademarks or copy protection devices. In short, *Vernor* appears to hold that a software transaction characterized as a license will be treated only as a license if the seller so chooses and provides significant restrictive clauses.

By contrast, some courts will hold that User owns the copy when User has paid the price, received transfer of the copy, and is entitled to retain that copy forever. This is consistent with commercial law, where economic reality rather than the parties' description controls whether a transaction is treated as a sale, lease, or secured loan. This approach could get some support from patent law. The Supreme Court has applied first sale broadly in the patent context. *See Quanta Computer, Inc. v. LG Electronics, Inc.*, 128 S. Ct. 2109 (2008). Where the holder of several chipset patents licensed the patents to a chipset manufacturer, the patent holder was barred by patent exhaustion from pursuing infringement claims against the licensee's customers. The sale of authorized products embodying the patents terminated the patent rights in those products, meaning that the purchasers were free to incorporate them into otherwise infringing products. *Quanta* is a patent case, but its broad application of first sale may affect the first sale analysis in copyright, which shares underlying policy considerations. This suggests that some contract provisions that purport to override first sale will be ineffective. The provisions may be effective as a matter of contract law (as opposed to limiting copyright's first sale rights), but that would not bind future buyers who were not party to the contract.

First Sale and Digital Works

The owner of a lawfully made copy of a work (a book, a song, a picture, etc.) may distribute or display *that* copy. With digital works, however, distributing a copy (such as sending the copy to a friend) or displaying a copy (putting it online) involves making more copies. First sale authorized display and distribution of the lawfully owned copy. It does not authorize making copies or distributing or displaying additional copies. The owner of a digital copy can utilize first sale—by hand-delivering that particular copy (or mailing it, etc.), but first sale fits awkwardly with the usual means of distributing or displaying digital works.

Examples

1. *Owner?* Ada purchased a copy of some music software, *Mister Moon*. She clicked to agree to the standard purchase contract, which provided that she would get permanent possession of a copy of the software but that the software company would retain ownership of the copy. After using the software for a year, she decided to sell her copy on eBay. Would a sale violate the copyright owner's exclusive right to distribute copies?

2. *Nongift*. UMG Recordings mails promotional CDs of copyrighted music. Each CD bears this notice: "This CD is the property of the record company and is licensed to the intended recipient for personal use only. Acceptance of this CD shall constitute an agreement to comply with the terms of the license. Resale or transfer of possession is not allowed and may be punishable under federal and state laws." There was no provision for response by the recipient, such as clicking to agree to the terms of use. If a recipient sells the CD, is that copyright infringement?

3. *Peasgood's Nonsuch*. Psystar buys a copy of a Mac operating system, Mac OS X Snow Leopard, and then adapts it to run on non-Apple computers and loads copies on the computers built and sold by Psystar. With each computer, Psystar included an unopened copy of Snow Leopard, purchased from Apple. The Snow Leopard license provides:

   > This License allows you to install, use and run one (1) copy of the Apple Software on a single-Apple labeled computer at a time. You agree not to install, use or run the Apple Software on any non-Apple labeled computer, or to enable others to do so.

   Does first sale protect Psystar from copyright infringement?

4. *Redigi or not*. Redigi allowed users to sell its authorized music files. The user would upload the file to Redigi, which would sell it. Does first sale apply to such digital resales?

Explanations

1. Under the first sale doctrine, the owner of a lawfully made copy may sell that copy without infringing the copyright holder's exclusive right to distribute copies. The software company, however, might argue that Ada has no first sale rights, because she is not the owner of a copy. Rather, she has possession of a copy that belongs to the software company, delivered along with a license to use it. A number of courts have accepted this argument, allowing parties to limit first sale rights by agreement. Some other courts regard it as a formalism and would hold that where Ada has paid the price and is entitled to keep the copy forever, she owns it and is therefore protected by first sale.

2. In this case, the attempt to limit first sale rights would not succeed. The recipients did not agree to the terms and so were not bound by them. The CD was simply a gift, and the owner, under first sale, could sell it. *See UMG Recordings Inc. v. Augusto*, 628 F.3d 1175 (9th Cir. 2011).

3. First sale did not protect Psystar. The transaction was not deemed a sale, but rather a license. Psystar did not have an unrestricted right to redistribute the copies that it had acquired. In addition, Psystar made copies

and arguably adapted the work, neither of which would be authorized by first sale.

4. The court held first sale inapplicable. *Capitol Records, LLC v. ReDigi Inc.*, 910 F.3d 649 (2d Cir. 2018). First sale, as the statute says, applies only to a "particular copy or phonorecord lawfully made under this title." Redigi's service might offer the functional equivalent of resale, but customers were not selling their copy; they were instead sending another copy. The court declined to judicially rewrite the statute to extend first sale to fit the digital age, reasoning that the first sale doctrine was enacted in a world where the ease and speed of data transfer could not have been imagined. The court also declined to apply fair use to protect the service.

LIMITS ON FIRST SALE RIGHTS IN SOUND RECORDINGS AND COMPUTER PROGRAMS

Under first sale, the owner of a copy of a work may lease out the copy without infringing the copyright holder's distribution right. For some works, this could lead to infringement. Someone could open up a music or computer program rental store where customers rented musical recordings or computer programs for an hour or two to make copies and avoid having to buy authorized copies. At the urging of affected copyright holders, special protections for music and software copyrights limit the scope of first sale.

> Notwithstanding the provisions of subsection (a), unless authorized by the owners of copyright in the sound recording or the owner of copyright in a computer program (including any tape, disk, or other medium embodying such program), and in the case of a sound recording in the musical works embodied therein, neither the owner of a particular phonorecord nor any person in possession of a particular copy of a computer program (including any tape, disk, or other medium embodying such program), may, for the purposes of direct or indirect commercial advantage, dispose of, or authorize the disposal of, the possession of that phonorecord or computer program (including any tape, disk, or other medium embodying such program) by rental, lease, or lending, or by any other act or practice in the nature of rental, lease, or lending. Nothing in the preceding sentence shall apply to the rental, lease, or lending of a phonorecord for nonprofit purposes by a nonprofit library or nonprofit educational institution.

17 U.S.C. §109(b)(1)(A). In short, no rentals of software or music.

Section 109 does not authorize the owner of a phonorecord or a person in possession of a copy of a computer program to rent or lend the phonorecord or computer program for commercial advantage. In short, first sale does not protect rental of sound recordings or of software. This restriction applies only to rental or lending for commercial advantage, so people may still loan out their music or software gratis. The provision also specifically excludes non-profit schools and libraries. Public libraries can loan out music and software.

Note that first sale still protects other types of rental, such as video rentals. Presumably Congress did not consider the danger of unauthorized copying of rented movies to be as risky to copyright owners as with music or software. Movies are often watched just once, as opposed to music or software, which may be used many times. Copying and distributing copies of movies was also more cumbersome than with music and software, although that is rapidly changing.

There is also an exception to the exception. It does not apply to computer programs embodied in machines (where the program cannot be copied in ordinary operation) or in computers specially designed for playing video games. Many products, from cars to microwave ovens, have embedded computer programs. Video game players likewise contain software that runs them. This provision means that such products may be rented without infringing the copyright in the software they carry.

Examples

1. *Tunes to let.* Becky is looking for new employment. She decides to take advantage of the first sale doctrine. She buys dozens of popular CDs and goes into business from her apartment, renting out the CDs by the day. Does first sale authorize Becky's activity?

2. *Going out of business sale.* Becky decides to simply sell all her CDs to the public. Can she do so without infringing?

3. *Audiobook—a book or a record?* Local Bookie rents movies and audiobooks, such as a recording of Stephen Fry reading a *Harry Potter* book. First sale authorizes the rental of movies, but with respect to audiobooks, is Local Bookie covered by first sale, which does not authorize rental of phonorecords or computer programs?

Explanations

1. First sale does not authorize Becky to rent out the CDs. First sale generally does authorize the owner of a lawfully made copy to dispose of it by sale or otherwise, which includes rental. But there is an exception for sound recordings, computer programs, and musical works: Rental is not authorized. Otherwise, customers could simply rent the works, take them home, and make copies without buying the author's work.

2. Becky can freely sell her copies. The exception to first sale rights for sound recordings, computer programs, and musical works applies only

to rental. It does not make first sale inapplicable to sound recordings, computer programs, and musical works. If Becky sells her CDs rather than renting them, she is protected by first sale. People can sell, lend (for free, so it is not rental), and give away sound recordings, computer programs, and musical works, despite the limited first sale rights in such works.

3. The Sixth Circuit held that the record rental exception does not apply to audiobooks. *See Brilliance Audio, Inc. v. Haights Cross Communications, Inc.*, 474 F.3d 365 (6th Cir. 2007). The court viewed the question as whether the exception to first sale "applies to all sound recordings, or only sound recordings of musical works." From a policy point of view, one could argue that the same exception should apply because audiobooks are subject to the same risk of unauthorized copying as audio recordings of music. On the other hand, one could argue that consumers are less likely to compile and trade copies of stories than music, because stories are more likely to be listened to just once (though children's books are a different story). In addition, applying the exception to all sound recordings would take it beyond the commercial arena. Rather than trying to resolve such policy matters, the court relied on the language of the statute, which refers to "the musical works embodied therein." The court held that the first sale doctrine applies without triggering the exception for sound recordings, so businesses may rent audiobooks without infringing

FIRST SALE AND IMPORTATION

Supap Kirtsaeng came from Thailand to study in the United States. Observing that the same textbook was much more expensive in the United States, he started a nice business in arbitrage, having relatives purchase books at a low price in Thailand and ship them to him to resell at a higher price in the United States. Recall that section 602 provides that unauthorized importation of copies or phonorecords infringes the public distribution right. If first sale permits the owner of a copy to distribute the copy, does that mean she may import it? The Supreme Court has held that because first sale limits the right to distribute copies, first sale authorizes the owner of a lawfully made copy to import that copy. *See Quality King Distributors v. L'Anza Research International*, 523 U.S. 135 (1998). But because first sale applies only to a copy or phonorecord "lawfully made under this title," the holding was limited to reimportation of copies lawfully made in the United States. Whether first sale protected importation of an authorized copy made outside the United States remained an open question, answered in *Kirtsaeng v. John Wiley & Sons, Inc.*, 133 S. Ct. 1351 (2013). *Kirtsaeng* held that "lawfully made under this title" meant simply that making the book was not unlawful under U.S. copyright law. Publishers argued that first sale should not apply to imported books, which would allow publishers to safely publish less expensive editions in other countries, for the benefit of all. But *Kirtsaeng* put great weight on the fact that "reliance upon the 'first sale' doctrine is deeply embedded in the practices of those, such as booksellers, libraries, museums, and retailers." So Kirtsaeng can purchase authorized books abroad and import them into the United States and resell them. If first sale were limited to works sold in the United States, then it could be infringement to resell an imported book, for a library to lend an imported book, or a museum to exhibit a Picasso.

Example

1. *Neither lawfully nor unlawfully made?* Murky Glurky's heroic adventures amuse children everywhere. Murky Glurky appears in best-selling books, movies on DVD, and music CDs. Children love them, so parents buy them. If anyone tries to distribute a used copy of any Murky Glurky product (selling on eBay, Craigslist, or in a used bookstore—or even renting from a video store), the copyright holder in Murky Glurky products claims infringement. If the defendant argues fair use ("I bought this copy, so first sale allows me to sell this copy, rent it, or give it away"), the plaintiff responds that first sale does not apply because all Murky Glurky products are made overseas and shipped to the United States. Is Murky Glurky clear of first sale?

Explanation

1. Some courts had held that first sale does not apply to copies made overseas because they are not "lawfully made under this title"—that is, they are not lawfully made under U.S. copyright law, which has no applicability overseas. Such courts viewed such copies as neither lawfully nor unlawfully made under U.S. copyright law but rather made beyond the reach of U.S. copyright law. This would also permit the copyright holder to control the work in various markets. But the Supreme Court rejected that argument in *Kirtsaeng*, holding that first sale does apply to works printed overseas with authority of the copyright owner and imported to the United States. So it does not infringe copyright to purchase authorized copies abroad, import them to the United States, and sell them there (also known as "gray market" sales).

FIRST SALE AND THE DISPLAY RIGHT

Section 109(c) also authorizes the owner of a copy to display the work:

> Notwithstanding the provisions of section 106(5), the owner of a particular copy lawfully made under this title, or any person authorized by such owner, is entitled, without the authority of the copyright owner, to display that copy publicly, either directly or by the projection of no more than one image at a time, to viewers present at the place where the copy is located.

17 U.S.C. §109(c). Without this provision, the owner of a painting, by displaying it publicly, could infringe the copyright owner's right to publicly display the work.

There are limits to the authorization. It applies only to the owner of a lawfully made copy (as with first sale and the distribution right). In addition, it does not extend to all displays. Recall that the copyright owner's right to display the work extends the display in any public place and also to display by transmissions. Section 109 authorizes the owner of a copy only to engage in the first type: "to display that copy publicly, directly or by the projection of no more than one image at a time, to viewers present at the place where the copy is located." 17 U.S.C. §109(c). A display over the Internet, for example, would not be authorized by section 109.

The provision applies only to the display right. It would not authorize a public performance. This has particular relevance to films and other audiovisual works. Showing a film is considered a performance of the work. 17 U.S.C. §101. Section 109 does not authorize the owner of a copy of a film to show the film to the public.

CHAPTER 13

Some Other Limits on the Exclusive Rights

Copyright has quite a few rather specific limits on the exclusive rights of the copyright owner. A criminal law teacher would like to show her class the film *Minority Report*. She thinks back to her copyright course in law school. Showing the film would be a public performance, so potentially infringement. She owns a DVD copy of the film, so she has first sale rights, but that authorizes her only to distribute or display a work, not perform (or copy or adapt) the work. Fair use might well apply—the purpose is educational, she will not charge admission, and the use would not seem to hurt the market for the work. On the other hand, the students pay tuition, and she wants to show the entire work, both of which might weigh against fair use. But section 110(a) provides a specific answer. Section 110(a) authorizes "performance or display of a work by instructors or pupils in the course of face-to-face teaching activities of a nonprofit educational institution." She can definitely show the film without infringing or even worrying about the fact-specific, never-entirely-certain doctrine of fair use.

In addition to the relatively general doctrines of fair use and first sale, there are a good number of very specific limitations. In deciding whether there is infringement in any case, one should always check to see whether any of the specific limitations apply. This is not always easy. They are not grouped together in one place but are sprinkled throughout the copyright statute.

This chapter discusses some of those specific limitations on the exclusive rights of the copyright owner. For each limitation, scope is important. A limitation often only applies to one or two of the exclusive rights. The copyright owner generally has five exclusive rights under section 106, which bear repeating: the reproduction right (the right to make copies or phonorecords of the work); the right to prepare derivative works (adaptation right); the right to distribute copies to the public; the right to perform the copyrighted work publicly; and the right to display the copyrighted work publicly. The limitations discussed below protect users of the work only with respect to the rights specified in each limitation. For example, the face-to-face teaching provision applies to "performance or display" of certain works in teaching. It limits only the public performance and display rights. It would not literally protect a teacher who made a copy of a work (such as to display it in class) or distributed copies of a work to the class, because those would be possible infringements of the reproduction right and the distribution right. But of course, those might qualify for protection under fair use (discussed later in the book). The limitations may also only apply to specified works and specified uses.

PERFORMANCE AND DISPLAY DURING TEACHING

Face-to-Face

"Performance or display of a work by instructors or pupils in the course of face-to-face teaching activities of a nonprofit educational institution, in a classroom or similar place devoted to instruction" is not infringement. 17 U.S.C. §110(1). A teacher may show a copyrighted film to the class without infringing the performance right, or a pupil may show a copyrighted art work without infringing the display right.

The rule does not apply to all face-to-face teaching. It applies only to performance or display by instructors or pupils, so someone else would not qualify. It must be "in the course of face-to-face teaching activities," so a film shown as part of a fundraiser or a movie series might not qualify. It applies to activity within "a nonprofit educational institution," so instruction for corporate employees or government workers would not be protected, or even instruction by nonprofit institutions such as charities or human rights groups.

To perform or display the work, the teacher will need a copy. Section 110 does not authorize her to make a copy, so she could infringe if she made a copy to perform or display it to the class (although fair use might well protect her). In addition, section 110 specifically provides that its protections are inapplicable to performance or display of a motion picture or other audiovisual work if the copy was not lawfully made and the teacher knew it. It applies only if the activity is "in a classroom or similar place devoted to instruction," so if the instructor took her class to the movie theater, she would fall outside the terms of the provision.

Distance Learning

Section 110(2) provides similar protection for distance learning. There is not infringement by performance or display of a work through transmission to students enrolled in a course (or government employees as part of their duties). The protection is limited by a number of conditions. It does not apply to all works. It does not apply at all to "a work produced or marketed primarily for performance or display as part of mediated instructional activities transmitted via digital networks." In short, it does not apply to products sold for online distance learning; rather, it applies to online distance learning use of other works. It also does not apply if the copy or phonorecord was not lawfully made and acquired.

The provision permits only "the performance of a nondramatic literary or musical work or reasonable and limited portions of any other work, or display of a work in an amount comparable to that which is typically displayed in the course of a live classroom session." Nondramatic literary or musical works may be performed in their entirety. For other works, a performance must be reasonable and limited, while a display must be comparable to normal classroom use.

The use must be controlled by an instructor as part of a regular class session. It applies only to distance learning in conjunction with scheduled classes. Web-based courses where material was simply posted for students to view according to their own schedules would not be protected.

The performance or display must be directly related to and of material assistance to the teaching content of the transmission, meaning that the distance learning provision cannot be used as a pretext for transmission of works for other purposes.

The school must also provide "informational materials to faculty, students, and relevant staff members that accurately describe, and promote compliance with, the laws of the United States relating to copyright, and provide notice to students that materials used in connection with the course may be subject to copyright protection." It must, for digital transmissions, also take reasonable steps to avoid unauthorized retention or distribution of copies of the work, including not interfering with technological means used by the copyright owner to prevent copying and distribution.

Examples

Which of the following would be protected uses under section 110(1) or (2)?

1. Teacher reads a few pages from a novel to her class at a public university.

2. The students sing "Happy" to celebrate the teacher's birthday.

3. The students sing "Happy" as an exercise during music class.
4. Teacher makes 30 copies of a poem and hands them out to the class.
5. Teacher shows the movie *Gladiator* as part of a history class.
6. Teacher borrows a DVD of another movie, *The Lord of the Rings*, and makes a copy to show it to her literature class.
7. Teacher does some freelance instruction. She teaches an English class at Megacorp. She shows the film *Julius Caesar* to the class of young executives.
8. During a distance learning course at the university, students perform the entire play *Death of a Salesman*.

Explanations

1. This would be protected by section 110(1), as "performance or display of a work by instructors or pupils in the course of face-to-face teaching activities of a nonprofit educational institution, in a classroom or similar place devoted to instruction," and as meeting the other conditions.
2. This would arguably fall outside section 110(1) because it was not "in the course of face-to-face teaching activities." But celebrating a birthday is part of the teacher-student relationship—and educational in many senses.
3. Clearly within the "course of face-to-face teaching activities." Performances by both teachers and students are protected.
4. Not protected by section 110(4), which applies only to performances and displays (not to making copies, distributing copies, or preparing derivative works). But of course this would likely be protected by fair use (discussed in a later chapter).
5. Showing a movie is performing the movie, protected by section 110(1).
6. Making copies is not authorized by section 110(1), although again it might qualify as fair use.
7. This would not qualify. It was performance by an instructor in the course of face-to-face teaching activities, but it was not a nonprofit educational institution. For-profit entities do not qualify.
8. This would likely not qualify. Nondramatic literary or musical works may be performed in their entirety, but for other works only "reasonable and limited portions."

NONPROFIT PERFORMANCES

Nonprofit performances may use copyrighted works without permission and without payment, subject to various conditions. The statute prevents infringement claims for

> performance of a nondramatic literary or musical work otherwise than in a transmission to the public, without any purpose of direct or indirect commercial advantage and without payment of any fee or other compensation for the performance to any of its performers, promoters, or organizers, if—
>
> (A) there is no direct or indirect admission charge; or
>
> (B) the proceeds, after deducting the reasonable costs of producing the performance, are used exclusively for educational, religious, or charitable purposes and not for private financial gain.

17 U.S.C. §110(4).

As with all the limitations, the scope is key. It applies only to use of a "nondramatic literary or musical work." Use of dramatic literary or musical works is not authorized, so it could not be a performance of a play or an opera. An event will not qualify if there is an admission charge; if the performers, promoters, or organizers are paid for the performance; or if it is transmitted. Performances will not qualify if there is a commercial advantage (direct or indirect). Any proceeds, after costs of production, must be used not only for nonprofit purposes but also specifically "educational, religious, or charitable purposes." Note that the provision does not require that the event itself be for educational, religious, or charitable purposes, but that proceeds, if any, go to such purposes. The event itself need meet only the more general requirement that it be "without any purpose of direct or indirect commercial advantage."

Finally, the copyright owner has the right to prohibit planned uses. The exemption does not apply where the copyright owner gives signed, written notice at least seven days before the date of the performance, stating the reasons for the objection. 17 U.S.C. §110(4)(B). The procedure, as one commentator notes, is a little perplexing. *See* Marshall Leaffer, *Understanding Copyright Law* 328 (3d ed. 1999). To use this veto power, the copyright owner must know of the planned performance, but nothing in the statute requires the user to give prior notice. The copyright owner may find out, if at all, when it is too late. But the statute could be employed where a work is used repeatedly, as in a political campaign. The statute also requires the copyright owner to state a reason. Presumably any stated reason would be sufficient, so this requirement seems pointless.

Examples

1. *Good cause.* To raise money for care of homeless pets, a theater group stages a benefit performance of the musical *Cats*. The performers all work for scale, which for some is a mere fraction of their normal fee. The organizers, director, stagehands, and others all work for minimum wage (less than the governing union rate). The admission fee is $20 per person, with the proceeds (after the costs of production) going to a pet rescue charity. An additional $5,000 comes from selling naming rights to a local pet store, whose name is prominently advertised. Permission is not sought from the *Cats* copyright holder because the group believes that the nonprofit performance is authorized by section 110(a). Is it?

2. *Objection!* Bruce Springsteen learns that a candidate for political office has been playing a Springsteen song, "Born in the USA," at her rallies. Campaign staff have been careful to scrupulously observe all the requirements of section 110(a). Springsteen happens to have considerably different political views. The candidate has big rally scheduled three days from now. Can Springsteen order her campaign to cease and desist?

3. *Clearance needed?* At a campaign rally, someone sings "God Bless America." We will assume that the performance is authorized as a not-for-profit performance, under section 110(2). Suppose a filmmaker was there making a documentary about the campaign. If the filmmaker captures the performance, can he rely on section 110(a)?

Explanations

1. Section 110(a) did not authorize the performance, on several counts. There can be no payment of a fee to performers, promoters, or organizers. Here, the performers and organizers were paid. There can be no admission fee, but a $20 fee was charged. There can be no purpose of direct or indirect commercial advantage, but the advertising for the pet shop may have violated that requirement.

2. A copyright holder does have the right to withdraw the authorization of section 110(a), but he must serve written notice stating the reasons for objection at least seven days prior to the event. Here, the event is in three days, so it would be too late. Presumably, he could serve a general notice, which would bar further performances after seven days, so the rest of the campaign would require a different song. However, in addition to section 110(a), a campaign could argue fair use (difficult when the copyright owner is in contact and has objected, but there could be compelling reasons such as use of a particular song as criticism, commentary, or other expression)—or it might already have permission if the venue had a blanket copyright license with ASCAP or BMI. *See* Eugene Volokh, *May*

Singers and Composers Stop Campaigns from Using Their Songs?, Volokh Conspiracy, February 15, 2008, http://www.volokh.com/posts/1203103695.shtml.

Legal rights are not everything. If the musician objected, the campaign might well stop using the song as a matter of courtesy or strategy. In 2008, the McCain campaign stopped playing "Our Country" at events at the request of singer John Mellencamp.

3. Section 110(a) authorizes only the performance of a work. The filmmaker would make a copy and would like to distribute copies, which goes beyond the scope of section 110. Moreover, in showing the film (i.e., performing the song), the filmmaker would likely not be able to comply with all the conditions of section 110(a), such as not charging admission or seeking any commercial advantage. The filmmaker might qualify for fair use, but that is hard to predict and uncertain to rely on. In the actual case, the filmmaker obtained permission from the copyright holder and was relieved they did not refuse or charge a prohibitive licensing fee.

COMPULSORY LICENSE FOR NONDRAMATIC MUSICAL WORKS

Copyright law allows the making of covers of songs, without getting permission from the copyright owner. We hear many cover versions of songs. Dozens of musicians have released covers of "Dust My Broom." But dozens of authors do not release their own versions of *Harry Potter*—and there are not dozens of competing versions of movies. A special provision allows musical works to be recorded and distributed without permission of the copyright owner as long as statutory procedures are followed and statutory royalties paid. Nondramatic musical works are subject to the compulsory license of section 115. Once authorized phonorecords of the work have been distributed in the United States, anyone else may obtain a compulsory license to make and distribute phonorecords of the work. One must promptly serve notice of intention to obtain the license on the copyright owner. The copyright owner is entitled to royalties, set by statute. The rationale for the compulsory license is to keep musical compositions available to the public while assuring the copyright holder of licensing fees.

The compulsory license is subject to several limitations. It is available only if the primary purpose is to make and distribute copies for private use. It authorizes the making of a new recording, not simply duplication of the publicly released recording. It authorizes making a musical arrangement of the work to adapt it to another performance, but the arrangement may not change the "basic melody or fundamental character of the work." The new arrangement "shall not be subject to protection as a derivative work under this title." So a musician may record and sell a cover version of a copyrighted song but could infringe if he radically alters the song. He also does not have a copyright in his new arrangement (although he may have one in his new sound recording).

The license authorizes making and distributing phonorecords but not other uses, such as publicly performing the work. A musician may use the compulsory license to make a cover version of a song but will need permission to perform the song in concert.

Many cover versions of songs are recorded each year. Although the producers could use the compulsory license under section 115, they usually get permission from the copyright owner (usually through a "Harry Fox" license, named after the entity that handles the majority of such licenses). Not that section 115 does not have force, but since copyright owners are subject to the compulsory license, they have a great incentive to make their works available by agreement, which can be more efficient and permit some tailoring of licensing terms.

Example

1. *New wine in old bottles.* Lofty composes "My New Minuet" and records a version with her string quintet. The recording succeeds with critics and fans alike and becomes a best seller in its genre. Lofty then receives notices from several people, each stating that the sender intends to use the compulsory license under section 115 to utilize the work. State which of the following people could use the compulsory license (subject to compliance with the notice and fee requirements):
   a. Producer intends to assemble her own quintet and then record and sell a version of "My New Minuet."
   b. Low Budget intends to record directly from Lofty's recording and sell low-priced copies in supermarkets.
   c. Spieler intends to record another version with another quintet and use the music as the background music to a new movie.
   d. Smiling Al intends to record and sell a parody version that uses tin cans rather than violins to great comic effect.
   e. Viola intends to perform the work at Carnegie Hall.

Explanation

1. a. Producer could use the compulsory license. This is the typical-example—making a new version of a previously released, copyrighted musical work. Provided Producer complies with the statutory procedures, Producer does not infringe by making and distributing the recording, even without Lofty's permission (or even if Lofty specifically objected).
   b. Low Budget could not use the compulsory license. The compulsory license does not authorize duplicating the sound recording itself, as Low Budget plans. Record companies cannot use compulsory licenses

to copy and sell each other's recordings. Rather, the license authorizes the making of a new recording.

c. Spieler could not use the compulsory license. The compulsory license authorizes only the making of recordings to distribute to the public for private use—such as making CDs to sell in music stores. It does not authorize other uses, such as using the song in a movie soundtrack, in commercials, and so on.
d. Smiling Al could not use the compulsory license. The compulsory license does not authorize an arrangement that changes the fundamental character of the work. Smiling Al's parody version with tin cans would probably exceed that limit.
e. Viola could not use the compulsory license. The compulsory license does not authorize public performances, but only making and distributing recordings.

LIMITATIONS ON EXCLUSIVE RIGHTS IN COMPUTER PROGRAMS

Suppose Writer buys an authorized copy of a word processing program, which she gets on a CD. To use the program, she must put the CD into her computer. Her computer will copy all or part of the program into its temporary memory to run the program. Writer may also wish to copy the program onto her computer's hard drive or to make another copy as a backup. She might also need to make some changes to the program to run it on her particular system.

Section 117, sometimes called "computer fair use," authorizes her to make copies or adapt the program when the "new copy or adaptation is created as an essential step in the utilization of the computer program" or "such new copy or adaptation is for archival purposes only." 17 U.S.C. §117(a). Without the authorization of section 117, Writer arguably would be liable for infringing by making copies and by preparing a derivative work (adapting the program). But Writer must also stay within section 117's narrow scope. If a copy is made to use the program, it must be used in no other manner. If Writer's right to possess the copy ends, all archival copies or adaptations must be destroyed.

The two rights above apply only to the owner of an authorized copy of a computer program. Software copyright owners often seek to avoid application of section 117 by characterizing the transaction as delivery of possession of a copy of the program, with the copyright owner retaining ownership of the copy. Under this view, the recipient has whatever rights are provided for in the license but does not have any rights under section 117.

As with first sale, courts may look to economic reality to see whether a party is the owner of a copy. As the Second Circuit put it:

> We conclude that Titleserv owned copies of the disputed programs within the meaning of *section 117(a)*. We reach this conclusion in consideration of the following factors: Titleserv paid Krause substantial consideration to develop the programs for its sole benefit. Krause customized the software to serve Titleserv's operations. The copies were stored on a server owned by Titleserv. Krause never reserved the right to repossess the copies used by Titleserv and agreed that Titleserv had the right to continue to possess and use the programs forever, regardless whether its relationship with Krause terminated. Titleserv was similarly free to discard or destroy the copies any time it wished. In our view, the pertinent facts in the aggregate satisfy section 117(a)'s requirement of ownership of a copy.

Krause v. Titleserv, 402 F.3d 119, 124 (2d Cir. 2005).

Another provision facilitates maintenance and repair of computers. Under section 117(c), the owner or lessee of a computer may make or authorize the making of a copy of a program that the computer lawfully contains when such copy is made by activation of the computer to maintain or repair the computer. In plain words, the owner of a computer may authorize a technician to turn the computer on to service it, even if that causes the computer to make a copy of a copyrighted program that is lawfully contained in the computer. The copy must be used for nothing beyond maintenance and repair and must be destroyed after the maintenance and repair. The Federal Circuit has read the provision broadly by construing "maintenance" to cover a broad range of activities to support use of a program. *See Storage Tech. Corp. v. Custom Hardware Eng'g. & Consulting, Inc.*, 421 F.3d 1307 (Fed. Cir. 2005).

Examples

1. *OK?* Charlie owns a copy of PlumbCAD, computer-aided design software for hydraulic engineers. Which of the following would be authorized by section 117?
   a. The program has a few bugs, so Charlie fixes them by changing the code.
   b. Charlie adapts the program so that it will run on his iMac.
   c. Charlie rewrites and supplements the code considerably so that it can be used not just for hydraulic engineering but also for various other engineering tasks.
   d. Charlie makes a copy on tape to store in his basement in case his first copy is lost or destroyed.
   e. Charlie makes a copy to contribute to the software collection of the local engineering society.

Would it make a difference if the contract provided that Charlie paid for the program and had the right to retain and use his copy forever, but the vendor remained the owner of the program?

2. *109 plus 117.* Chops purchases a copy of a computer program from Bender. Bender bought the copy directly from its copyright owner, Abble. The program runs accounting services for a small business, and Chops intends to use it in his restaurant. Chops learns that the program needs to be adapted somewhat to run on his computer. Fortunately, the necessary documentation is supplied with the copy. Chops hires a grad student, who makes the necessary changes. Abble claims Bender infringed Abble's copyright by selling the copy to Chops because that infringed Abble's exclusive right to distribute copies to the public. Abble also contends that adapting the work infringes Abble's copyright because it constitutes the unauthorized preparation of a derivative work. In addition, Abble states that using the program violates the copyright because loading it on the computer and running it necessarily makes copies of large portions of the copyrighted code. Does Chops own a copy of a program he cannot use?

3. *Long-term temporary.* Custom Hardware provided support services for businesses that used copyrighted software. To monitor the operation of the software and to diagnose problems, Custom Hardware periodically activated the machines, thereby making copies of portions of the software. Custom Hardware would leave the copies in memory on the customer's computer for the duration of the support contract. The copyright owner contends that such usage goes beyond "maintenance and repair" and that the copies were not destroyed after maintenance and repair, as required by section 117. Is Custom Hardware protected by section 117(c)?

Explanations

1. a. Section 117 authorizes an adaptation that is "an essential step in the utilization." Fixing the bugs would qualify.
   b. Charlie would argue that adapting the program is necessary so it will run on the iMac; therefore, it is an "an essential step in the utilization of the computer program in conjunction with a machine." The vendor might take the position that the adaptation was not essential because Charlie could already run the program on his other machine. Section 117 has held to protect adaptation done to make a program run on new computers acquired by the program owner. *See Aymes v. Bonelli*, 47 F.3d 23, 26 (2d Cir. 1995) (holding that section 117 authorizes adapting program to run on successive generations of IBM

computers). The same reasoning would seem to apply to running it on machines with a different operating system, so Charlie would not be infringing.

c. This would seem to go beyond adaptations necessary to use the program, so section 117 would not protect Charlie. But he may still win, because preparation of the adaptations may not infringe the copyright in the computer program. Rather, the copyright owner would still have to show copying or preparation of a derivative work and overcome Charlie's fair use defense. This is an example of the fact that analyzing the applicability of specific limitations may not end the analysis.
d. Charlie would be protected by section 117, because the backup copy would be an "archival" copy.
e. Charlie might contend that the copy for the library is a protected "archival" copy. Section 117 does not define "archival," but courts are likely to look to the purposes of section 117 and hold that archival copies are backup copies or copies necessary for use (such as software libraries referenced by the program). This copy goes well beyond the purpose of section 117.

   If the contract provided that Charlie was not the owner, some courts would still treat him as the owner, but others might give effect to the parties' characterization, as discussed above.

2. Bender is the owner of a lawfully made copy, so first sale authorizes Bender to sell it. Chops is now the owner of a lawfully made copy of a computer program, which gives Chops the rights under section 117 to adapt it or make a copy, provided such steps are necessary to utilize the program on a computer. Here, such actions are necessary to utilize the program on Chops's computer, so Chops did not infringe.

3. In a case of first impression, the Federal Circuit construed section 117(c)'s exemption for maintenance and repair relatively broadly. *Storage Tech. Corp. v. Custom Hardware Eng'g & Consulting, Inc.*, 421 F.3d 1307 (Fed. Cir. 2005). The court held that relatively long-term copies were authorized under section 117 as copying done for the purpose of "maintenance" of the computers. In so doing, the court rejected a narrow reading of maintenance that would restrict it to replacement or tending of machine parts. Rather, "maintenance" could also include service for the software to keep it running. The court found statutory support in the reference to both "maintenance" and "repair," which suggests something more than basic parts repair was intended. This reading jibed with the purpose of the provision, which was to prevent software copyright owners from using their copyright to control ancillary markets for services. *See* Stephen McJohn, *Fair Use of Copyrighted Software*, 28 Rutgers L.J. 593 (1997).

ARCHITECTURAL WORKS

An "architectural work" is "the design of a building as embodied in any tangible medium of expression, including a building, architectural plans, or drawings. The work includes the overall form as well as the arrangement and composition of spaces and elements in the design, but does not include individual standard features." 17 U.S.C. §101.

When Congress amended the Copyright Act to specifically cover architectural works, it also added some quite specific limitations on their copyrights. One issue is that architectural works are part of the public landscape. If their copyrights were too broad, then it could be copyright infringement to make depictions of public places. One limitation responds to that. Once an architectural work has been constructed, its copyright does not "prevent the making, distributing, or public display of pictures, paintings, photographs, or other pictorial representations of the work, if the building in which the work is embodied is located in or ordinarily visible from a public place." 17 U.S.C. §120(a). If a building is visible from a public place, others may photograph or draw the building without infringing the copyright in its design, and they may distribute and display those pictures.

Note that an architectural work is the design of a building. The legislative history indicates that "buildings" include places that people enter (such as houses, temples, or schools), but not structures such as bridges and highways. Such structures would not be subject to the limitations in section 120.

Another issue is that architectural works are embodied in buildings. If the owner of the building alters or destroys the building, that could constitute preparation of an infringing derivative work. Such a right would effectively give the copyright in the architectural work a veto over future changes to the building, converting the intangible property of copyright to a species of real property, like a covenant or an easement. The second limitation addresses that concern: "Notwithstanding the provisions of section 106(2), the owners of a building embodying an architectural work may, without the consent of the author or copyright owner of the architectural work, make or authorize the making of alterations to such building, and destroy or authorize the destruction of such building." The owner of a home may build a family room on the back without infringing the copyright in the original architecture.

Examples

1. *The masked infringer?* A building in downtown Los Angeles is filmed and used as the Second Bank of Gotham in the film *Batman Forever*. The architect sues for copyright infringement. Are the producers liable? Would it matter if the building was not just an architectural work but had additional aesthetic features such that it was also a sculptural work?

2. *Hideaway*. Jeff designs a unique home, which he builds nestled in the woods on a large plot of land. He keeps the drawings, blueprints, and any photos private so that only a few people have seen his design. He is dismayed when *Architecture Weekly* runs photos of the building. Its photographer had chartered a small plane. Although trees surrounded the building, the pilot was able to fly at just the right angle to let the photographer get pictures of the building. Is *Architecture Weekly* protected by section 120?

3. *Building?* Frank designs and builds a sculpture of a convoy of soldiers, which is displayed in a public park. Is the sculpture a building—meaning that anyone can make and distribute images of the sculpture?

Explanations

1. There is no infringement. The design of the building is an architectural work, and the building is visible from a public place. Under section 120, there is no infringement by "the making, distributing, or public display of pictures, paintings, photographs, or other pictorial representations of the work." A movie qualifies as a pictorial representation, so there is no infringement. This is true even if the building qualifies as a sculptural work. Many architectural works would also be sculptural works. A rule that barred the public from making pictures of buildings with sculptural features would eviscerate section 120. *See Leicester v. Warner Bros.*, 232 F.3d 1212 (9th Cir. 2000). The court quoted highly relevant legislative history:

   > Architecture is a public art form and is enjoyed as such. Millions of people visit our cities every year and take back home photographs, posters, and other pictorial representations of prominent works of architecture as a memory of their trip. Additionally, numerous scholarly books on architecture are based on the ability to use photographs of architectural works.

   H.R. Rep. 101-735, at 22.

2. The privilege to make and distribute pictures applies if the building "is located in or ordinarily visible from a public place." The building is not in a public place. It is visible from a public place—certain points in the airspace above the building. A court might hold that is not "ordinarily visible" but rather visible only with extraordinary effort. (Although maybe that is changing in this age of satellite photographs available online.) If that is the case, then the limit in section 120 would not apply, and there would likely be infringement. Fair use would also not protect such commercial use of an unpublished work.

3. The legislative history indicates that "buildings" include places that people enter (such as houses, temples, or schools), but not structures such as bridges and highways. People do not enter the sculpture the

way they enter a house. A person who took a picture of the sculpture would likely be protected by fair use (discussed in the next chapter), but someone who made commercial use of an image of the sculpture might be infringing. Buildings are an exception to the general rule: publicly displayed works retain the full protection of copyright. *See Gaylord v. United States*, 595 F.3d 1364 (Fed. Cir. 2010).

LIBRARIES AND ARCHIVES

Section 108 authorizes libraries and archives to make and distribute copies of works for various purposes, subject to detailed conditions. The library may make three copies of a work from its collection for "preservation and security" or to deposit in another library. It may also make three copies to replace a lost or damaged copy if the work is not readily available elsewhere. The library may make a copy of a magazine article (or other small portion of a work) for a user's "private study, scholarship, or research." It may make a copy of the entire work for a user if the work is not obtainable elsewhere at a fair price.

The library must be open to the public or to researchers in a field. The copies must include a copyright notice (or a warning that the work may be copyrighted). There may be no commercial purpose to the reproduction. The library must also display warnings about copyright at its front desk or other appropriate place.

Section 108 does not define "library" or "archive." One could arguably extend those terms to businesses from video stores to online search engines to clipping services, but commercial enterprises could not gain section 108's protections simply by styling themselves as libraries or archives. Rather, section 108 only applies to copying and distributing done "without any purpose of direct or indirect commercial advantage." 17 U.S.C. §108(a)(1). Moreover, it only applies to "isolated and unrelated reproduction or distribution," not multiple or systematic copying. 17 U.S.C. §108(g).

OTHER LIMITATIONS ON THE EXCLUSIVE RIGHTS

The limitations above are not exhaustive. Others appear in various places in the Copyright Act. Some notable examples follow.

Under section 111 of the Copyright Act, if material is broadcast, cable companies may receive it and retransmit it to their customers by using a compulsory license. Internet streaming services were unsuccessful in convincing courts to extend to them the compulsory license for retransmission by cable systems.[1]

If someone plays the radio or television in a public place, that is technically a public performance of the works being broadcast. Section 110(5) provides that there is no infringement by "the public reception of the transmission on a single receiving apparatus of a kind commonly used in private homes, unless (i) a direct charge is made to see or hear the transmission; or (ii) the transmission received is further transmitted to the public." In addition, for establishments, section 110(5) has specific limits concerning the size of the premises and the nature of the equipment.

Section 1008, added as part of the Audio Home Recording Act of 1992, authorizes some noncommercial home recording of musical works by consumers. Notably, the provision applies only to certain categories of devices. In particular, it does not apply to recordings on general-purpose computers and so generally does not apply to downloading music from the Internet.

1. *Fox TV Stations, Inc. v. AereoKiller, LLC*, 851 F.3d 1002 (9th Cir. 2017). One wrinkle on the federal nature of intellectual property is that whether particular provisions, such as compulsory licenses, apply in the various United States territories may depend on whether specific legislation authorizing such an extension manages to make it through Congress. The representative from the Virgin Islands, although lacking a vote, may play an important role in providing the impetus for such legislation.

CHAPTER 14

Fair Use

Fair use lies at the heart of copyright law. Fair use is a flexible doctrine allowing use of copyrighted works without permission or payment. Determining whether a use qualifies as fair use requires a broad, multifactored decision-making process. The concept of fair use is extremely slippery, embodying both copyright doctrine and competing policy values. This flexibility often makes fair use a hard standard to apply in specific cases. Court decisions are sometimes hard to predict, making it often difficult to decide whether to rely on fair use.

Geologist made 60 copies of a recent copyrighted newspaper article and passed them out at her public lecture a month later to show the importance of the topic and diverging views of experts. Musician's new dance recording repeatedly used a three-second sample from a copyrighted 1960s hit song to evoke old memories and to contrast new musical styles and attitudes. Advocate's op-ed quoted four paragraphs from her opponent's recent copyrighted article to methodically demolish its argument. Google copies as much of the web as possible, and even scans libraries of books, to make a searchable database of the world's published knowledge. Do these various actions infringe copyright? It would depend whether a court considers them fair use. Each would probably be a close case, and the analysis would have to go more deeply into the facts. Whenever considering whether a copyright is infringed, one must always consider fair use. Fair use provides a broad but vaguely defined defense against copyright infringement. The statute specifies several factors to consider, but the question ultimately comes down to case law and policy considerations. Because fair use is so fact specific, it can be difficult for parties to decide whether a potential use is fair use. A teacher including material in a coursepack, a writer quoting lengthy passages from a letter, a documentary filmmaker who captures others' images or music in her footage, a student group that would like to show a film, the maker of a mash-up—such users often seek guidance about fair use. That raises the hazard that people will err on the side of caution, effectively adding to the scope of copyright—not to mention the dead-weight loss of uses that do not occur. *See* James Gibson, *Risk Aversion and Rights Accretion in Intellectual Property Law*, 116 Yale L.J. 882 (2007). Some have responded by drafting advice tailored to specific creators who frequently rely on use of other works. *See Documentary Filmmakers' Statement of Best Practices in Fair Use* and the *Code of Best Practices in Fair Use for Online Video*. Another possibility would be to have a Fair Use Board in the U.S. Copyright Office, with authority to declare a proposed use to qualify as fair use. *See* Michael W. Carroll. *Fixing Fair Use*, 85 N.C. L. Rev. 1087 (2007).

Under 17 U.S.C. §107, fair use of a copyrighted work is not infringement of the basket of exclusive rights granted under 17 U.S.C. §106 or the VARA rights in 17 U.S.C. §106A. The statute does not define "fair use." Rather, the court must first consider whether the use at issue falls into one of the specified favored uses: "criticism, comment, news reporting, teaching (including multiple copies for classroom use), scholarship, or research." 17 U.S.C. §107. Section 107 next requires the court to consider four factors:

1. the purpose and character of the use, including whether such use is of a commercial nature or is for nonprofit educational purposes
2. the nature of the copyrighted work
3. the amount and substantiality of the portion used in relation to the copyrighted work as a whole
4. the effect of the use on the potential market for or value of the copyrighted work

Weighing the factors, the court then decides whether fair use applies.

Fair use was first made part of the copyright statute as part of the Copyright Act of 1976. As part of the long process leading up to the enactment of the statute, in 1961 the Copyright Office provided several examples of cases held to be fair use:

> quotation of excerpts in a review or criticism for purposes of illustration or comment; quotation of short passages in a scholarly or technical work, for illustration or clarification of the author's observations; use in a parody of some of the content of the work parodied; summary of an address or article, with brief quotations, in a news report; reproduction by a library of a portion of a work to replace part of a damaged copy; reproduction by a teacher or student of a small part of a work to illustrate a lesson; reproduction of a work in legislative or judicial proceedings or reports; incidental and fortuitous

reproduction, in a newsreel or broadcast, of a work located in the scene of an event being reported.

Copyright Office Circular FL 102.

The Supreme Court has rested the constitutional place of copyright on fair use. In *Eldred v. Ashcroft*, one issue was whether Congress had violated the First Amendment's guarantee of freedom of speech by extending the terms of existing copyrights by 20 years. *Eldred v. Ashcroft*, 123 S. Ct. 769 (2003); *see also* Rebecca Tushnet, *Copy This Essay: How Fair Use Doctrine Harms Free Speech and How Copying Serves It*, 114 Yale L.J. 535 (2004). *Eldred* held that copyright protection is generally not subject to First Amendment scrutiny. The Court based this conclusion on several grounds. First, the Copyright Clause and First Amendment were adopted close together in time. This indicated that the Framers regarded copyright as consistent with the First Amendment. Second, the Court considered that copyright and the First Amendment were also consistent in effect. Copyright is a restriction on speech, but its purpose is the same as the First Amendment: to promote speech. By giving authors exclusive rights, copyright provides a strong incentive for the creation and dissemination of works. Third, copyright law has "built-in First Amendment accommodations." Copyright protects only creative expression. It is not copyright infringement to copy ideas from a copyrighted work. Copyright does not restrict communication of ideas. In addition, copyright also authorizes fair use of copyright works. Others may copy works for such purposes as education, criticism, news reporting, and research. Relying on these "traditional First Amendment safeguards" contained within copyright law, the Court held that First Amendment scrutiny is unnecessary where "Congress has not altered the traditional contours of copyright protection."

Fair use is a distinctive feature of U.S. copyright law. *See* Julie Cohen, Lydia Loren, Ruth Okediji, and Maureen O'Rourke, *Copyright in a Global Information Economy*, 492-496 (Aspen 2002). Countries often provide a number of specific, narrow exemptions to copyright protection, such as the face-to-face teaching exemption under the U.S. statute. Some countries allow a "fair dealing" exemption, similar to fair use but narrower in scope, but the sort of broad exemption for fair use in the United States is unusual and even leads some to raise questions about whether the United States is in compliance with its treaty obligations. *Id.*

SONY, HARPER & ROW, CAMPBELL & STEWART

Fair use is a notoriously troublesome doctrine because the rule provides little guidance about what weight to give the various factors. Accordingly, the voluminous case law is key in application of the fair use doctrine, especially in the four Supreme Court cases applying section 107.

In *Sony Corporation of America v. University City Studios*, 464 U.S. 417 (1984), the Court held fair use applicable to "time shifting": unauthorized home recording of television programs, done to watch the programs at a later time. The "nature of the use" factor had two aspects. The use was merely making copies of the work, a disfavored "reproductive" use, as opposed to a productive use (one where copies are made as part of a favored activity, such as education or creation of more creative works). But the use was a noncommercial and nonprofit activity (private recording for personal use), not a disfavored commercial use. The nature of the works varied because many programs were copied, but some were highly protected creative works. The amount copied was the entire work, which normally weighs against fair use. But that was undercut by the fact that the material copied had been broadcast for free viewing. By time shifting, consumers were merely watching the material at a different time. With respect to the final factor, the plaintiffs made no concrete showing of specific market harm or loss of value from the practice of time shifting. That was probably the key fact. Had the plaintiffs presented evidence that the practice of home taping was causing specific loss of viewership, reduction in advertising revenue, or other harm, the analysis might have been different.

In *Harper & Row, Publishers v. Nation Enterprises*, 471 U.S. 539 (1985), the *Nation* magazine managed to get a copy of President Gerald Ford's autobiography shortly before its publication. The *Nation* article included verbatim quotations amounting to some 300 words (from a manuscript of some 200,000 words), including portions of Ford's description of his thoughts at the time he pardoned former president Richard Nixon. As a result, *Time* magazine canceled its agreement to print prepublication excerpts from the book. The court held fair use inapplicable. The nature of the use was news reporting (a favored use), but it was also commercial (less likely to qualify). The *Nation* had also "knowingly exploited a purloined manuscript." The nature of the work was a factual work. Because facts are not protected by copyright, such works are more subject to fair use than works of fiction or fantasy. But the *Nation* not only copied facts but freely took expressive elements of the work. Moreover, the work was unpublished, which is a key factor against fair use. The amount used was small, only a few pages of a lengthy book. But the portion taken was the heart of the book, the section most interesting to potential readers. Moreover, the *Nation* could have freely copied the unprotected facts and ideas in the work. So it could have accomplished the favored use of news reporting without taking any protected expression. Finally, a specific market harm was shown—the loss of prepublication licensing revenue from *Time*. The factors taken together weighed against fair use. *Harper & Row* shows that even a favored use like news reporting on a historic event will not qualify as fair where other factors point heavily the other way (commercial use of an unpublished work, with demonstrated market harm, where the goal could have been largely accomplished by copying unprotected facts and ideas).

In *Campbell v. Acuff-Rose Music*, 510 U.S. 569 (1994), the Court addressed parody as fair use. The group 2 Live Crew made a rap parody version of Roy Orbison's song "Pretty Woman." By changing the lyrics and music somewhat, they inverted the viewpoint of the song. Their version was a cutting commentary on both the music and the worldview of Orbison's original. The lower court had rejected fair use, relying on the commercial nature of the use and the fact that the parody had used substantial amounts of the original. The Supreme Court reversed and remanded for a more nuanced analysis. A parody must borrow some from the original to make its point. The parody at issue was a criticism and commentary on the original "Pretty Woman," so was more likely to be fair use than a parody that simply took material to free-ride on the efforts of others. In addition, parody is a transformative use, meaning that defendants added independent creative material to the work. The nature of the work was a highly protected creative work, but such would normally be the case where parody is at issue. The amount taken was no more than necessary for the favored use of commentary, especially as the parody version departed from the original in both words and music. The Court held on remand that a key factual issue was whether there was a showing of market harm—that is, whether the rap parody version had decreased any potential licensing revenue for other versions that plaintiff would have authorized. The court noted that some market harms would not count: "When a lethal parody, like a scathing theater review, kills demand for the original, it does not produce a harm cognizable under the Copyright Act." The court also stated that there would be a presumption of market harm for "verbatim copying of the original in its entirety for commercial purposes." But in other circumstances, even commercial uses would not lead to an inference of market harm. *Campbell* shows that even extensive commercial use may qualify as fair, with several factors in the other direction ((1) a transformative use, (2) that also acts as criticism, (3) taking no more than necessary for the favored use, and (4) not making use of a specific market that the copyright owner would have exploited).

In *Stewart v. Abend*, 495 U.S. 207, 238 (1990), the Supreme Court held that it was not fair use for the producers of Alfred Hitchcock's film *Rear Window* to continue showing the film after their rights in the underlying story, "*It Had to Be Murder*," were terminated. *Stewart* was decided between *Sony* and *Harper & Row*. Although cited much less frequently than the three cases above, *Stewart* casts considerable light on fair use. *See* Stephen McJohn and Lorie Graham, *Thirty-Two Short Stories About Intellectual Property*, 3 Hastings Sci. & Tech. L.J. 1 (2011). As in the other cases, loss of potential licensing revenue was the determinative factor. In *Stewart*, the two parties to the case had been parties to a licensing transaction. The author agreed to sell the movie rights to Hitchcock for the entire effective copyright term. Hitchcock, however, had lost the movie rights back to the author's estate because of a quirky series of copyright cases. In effect, Hitchcock sought to use fair use to gain greater rights than had been gained in the transaction. There was an argument that continuing to allow Hitchcock to exploit the movie would be fair. The parties had agreed that Hitchcock would have the movie rights to the story permanently. Only because of the author's death and because of some complex decisions involving renewal of copyright did Hitchcock lose the bargained-for rights to the heirs. Allowing Hitchcock to continue showing *Rear Window* would not have prevented the heirs from making their own movie based on the story. Nevertheless, fair use was held inapplicable, on the theory that a party to a transaction is entitled to what the law grants from that transaction. If Hitchcock continued to show his film, then that would have a negative impact on the potential market for other films based on the same short story. The context of the market discussion, however, is quite different from the other cases. In the other three Supreme Court cases, the fair use issue arose between strangers, not parties who were disputing a previous transaction. Under *Stewart*, fair use will rarely allow a party to gain rights greater than the party gained by agreement.

The Court came back to fair use in a couple of key cases in the 2020s. *Google LLC v. Oracle America, Inc.*, 141 S. Ct. 1183 (2021), held that fair use authorized a certain amount of copying for the purpose of getting at unprotected functional matter. The Court held that Google's use of Oracle's Java SE API packages in its Android operating system constituted fair use. To translate that into English, it was fair use to copy snippets of the software code that runs Java, the software language, in order to write another software package that was compatible with Java. By copying those snippets, Google's Java could be used the same way as Oracle's Java, allowing easy transfer of skills for coders.

Some courts had read "transformative" to apply broadly. But the Supreme Court cut back on that in *Andy Warhol Foundation for the Visual Arts, Inc. v. Goldsmith*, 143 S. Ct. 1258 (2023)(holding that licensing an image of Prince derived straight from a copyrighted photograph was not fair use). Andy Warhol had made prints based on plaintiff's photograph of the musician Prince. The Warhol artworks were certainly treated differently than the photograph, but were not transformative, in the Court's view, because they were simply copies of the photograph.

ONE EXAMPLE: PHOTOCOPYING

As copying technologies improve, the scope of fair use may come into dispute. The topic of photocopying illustrates fair use well, as a widespread practice with considerable uncertainty as to the scope of protection. Classic examples of fair use involve photocopying. Section 107 specifically mentions the favored use of "multiple copies for classroom use." A social studies teacher reads an article in his morning paper that fits aptly with today's class. He makes 30 copies to hand out to his students. That would be fair use. The purpose is education. The use is impromptu and time was short, so there seems little likelihood that he could have licensed the use from the publisher. Therefore, there is no market harm, under the fourth factor. He did use the entire work. This would weigh against fair use somewhat but would be diminished if the entire work was relevant to the favored use of teaching. The nature of the work is probably a medium-protected work—a literary work with much unprotected material, such as facts, ideas, and nonoriginal material (such as quotes from others).

If we tweak the facts, the clear case of fair use becomes muddier. Suppose he saves the article and makes 30 copies next year for the class. Now there is sufficient time for him to have sought permission. Or suppose there is a month between reading the article and the day of the relevant class—and he has the school bookstore make copies and sell them to the students. Now there is a commercial aspect, as well as more time to seek permission.

Some courts will regard as persuasive authority the "Agreement on Guidelines for Classroom Copying in Not-for-Profit Educational Institutions with Respect to Books and Periodicals," a set of guidelines agreed on by many of the interest groups that participated in negotiations in connection with the 1976 Act. Making multiple copies for classroom use would be considered fair if it met various conditions. To summarize the key ones:

- brevity (copying is limited, such as a short poem or 1,000 words from a book)
- spontaneity (the teacher decides to use the work and has too little time to secure permission, and does not repeat the copying each term)
- cumulative effect (the practice does not become too widespread)
- no substitutions (copying does not reduce sales of works, or create anthologies, or substitute for works that are intended to be used up, like coloring books)
- cost (no charge to the student beyond actual copying costs)

The guidelines purport only to provide minimum standards, so copying that exceeds the guidelines may still be within fair use, but they provide relevant factors for courts to consider.

Recent decisions have denied fair use to systematic photocopying for commercial uses, even when associated with education or research. In *Princeton Univ. Press v. Michigan Document Services*, 99 F.3d 1813 (6th Cir. 1996) (en banc), the defendant was a commercial copy shop. It received course lists from instructors, including substantial segments of copyrighted works (such as a 90-page segment of a book). The copy shop bound the copies into coursepacks that it sold to students. The copy shop contended that the use qualified for fair use. It argued that it was making a favored educational use, that it was only copying a part of the works, and that there was no showing of a loss in sales of the books from which it copied. The copy shop acknowledged that it was not paying licensing fees but contended that if every possible loss of licensing were considered, then fair use would be defined out of existence.

The court viewed the factors quite differently. It held the relevant use was the defendant's commercial use as a copy shop, rather than the ultimate educational use by a student. Although the defendants used only portions of the works, they used substantial portions. Moreover, instructors would presumably choose the portions of greatest value. As to market harm, the court considered loss of licensing revenue to be highly relevant. This was especially true where other copy shops did in fact pay licensing fees to publishers. So this was not a case like *Sony* or *Harper*, where the copyright owner failed to show it would have exploited the market that the claimed fair use occupied.

Another leading photocopying case is *American Geophysical Union v. Texaco*, 60 F.3d 913 (2d Cir. 1994). Texaco subscribed to various scientific and technical journals. Texaco's library would purchase one copy of a journal and circulate it among its researchers. The library had an established practice of efficiently making copies of articles from the journals upon request from researchers. A researcher could have a copy made of an article that seemed relevant to her work and keep the copy on her office shelf. Texaco defended the practice as fair use. It was done for the favored purpose of research and was a "reasonable and customary practice." The works contained much unprotected material (such as facts and ideas), and at the time of the case, there was an established practice of selling individual articles.

The court held against fair use. It first held that although the use by researchers was not directly commercial, the ultimate purpose was Texaco's effort to develop commercial products. It rejected Texaco's argument that making copies of individual articles was a favored transformative use. Rather, the use was simply to make a copy for archival purposes, which weighed against fair use. The key factor again was effect on the potential market for the work. Although the publishers did not sell copies of individual articles, they did offer licensing of photocopying rights through the Copyright Clearance Center. The court explicitly held that the scope of fair use may change "when the means for paying for such a use is made easier." Read for all its worth, such language is very troubling, conjuring up a future where everything is available over the Internet for a fee, meaning that fair use shrinks up and disappears. But read in light of the specific facts of the case, the language is less troubling; for-profit corporations may be required to pay for copies of copyrighted works that they make to keep for reference.

The case does highlight the increasing ability of publishers to license works. First, they are working together collectively, just as music copyright holders have done for decades. The Copyright Clearance Center and other collective rights organizations seek to provide a route to seek licensing for photocopying and other uses. Second, technology may create means to provide licensing more efficiently, more specific to particular uses, and in a shorter time frame. How such developments affect fair use will likely be a continuing area of disagreement. If our social studies teacher sees an article in the paper today, and the bottom of the page lists a website for instant licensing permissions at a reasonable rate, some may question whether it is still fair use to run off 50 copies without permission.

SUMMING UP FAIR USE

Fair use is always a fact-based determination. A small amount of copying from a song into a musical: fair use.[1] Copying and editing a YouTube video to critique it: fair use.[2] Incorporating an old newspaper article in the video of a news report: not necessarily fair use.[3] But a number of general principles can be drawn from the cases. Note how the factors are interdependent.

Purpose and Character of the Use, Including Whether Such Use Is of a Commercial Nature or for Nonprofit Educational Purposes

Commercial uses are less likely to qualify, because there is likely to be market harm and because a commercial user is apt to bear the cost. Private, nonprofit uses are more likely to qualify but certainly do not have categorical immunity. Moreover, there is really a spectrum, because private uses may have a commercial quality if they substitute for purchases or if they are used for barter.

1. *Corbello v. DeVito*, 2017 U.S. Dist. LEXIS 91164, *57-58 (D. Nev. June 13, 2017).
2. Here, it is clear to the court that the Klein video does not serve as a market substitute for the Hoss video; anyone seeking to enjoy "Bold Guy v. Parkour Girl" on its own will have a very different experience watching the Klein video, which responds to and transforms the Hoss video from a skit into fodder for caustic, moment-by-moment commentary and mockery. Because the Klein video does not "offer[] a substitute for the original," it does not (and indeed, cannot) "usurp a market that properly belongs to the copyright-holder." *Infinity Broadcast Corp. v. Kirkwood* 150 F.3d 104, 110 (2d Cir. 1998). *Hosseinzadeh v. Klein*, No. 16-cv-3081 (KBF), 2017 U.S. Dist. LEXIS 134910, at *19-20 (S.D.N.Y. Aug. 23, 2017).
3. *Hirsch v. CBS Broad. Inc.*, 2017 U.S. Dist. LEXIS 123468 (S.D.N.Y. Aug. 4, 2017).

Uses specifically mentioned by the statute are favored: "criticism, comment, news reporting, teaching (including multiple copies for classroom use), scholarship, or research." But other uses may be favored. Productive uses, where works are used as part of another activity, are more likely to be fair use than reproductive uses, where the defendant simply uses the work. Transformative uses, where the work is used to make another creative work or the work is put to a different use, are highly favored.

Another favored type of use is one that attempts to exploit unprotected aspects of the copyrighted work. Reverse engineering may entail making copies of a computer program to study its nonprotected functional aspects or to create another program that will operate together with it. A work might be copied to disseminate the unprotected ideas or facts in the work, as opposed to its protected creative expression of those elements. Such a use is more likely to qualify for fair use where the copyright owner is attempting to censor others, as opposed to protect a market for the work.

Courts may also consider the good faith of a defendant's actions. Where the defendant made a good faith attempt to get permission to use a work, the court may weigh that in favor of fair use. If the defendant obtained a copy of the work through breach of contract, theft, or other bad faith actions, that will weigh against fair use. The copyright owner's motivations may also be relevant. A blogger was protected by fair use in posting an "unflattering" photo of a business person, where the subject had purchased the copyright to get the photo taken down.[4] Fair use defeated a city's assertion of copyright in its videos of city council meetings from recovering from a critic who posted portions, with subtitles and commentary.[5]

Nature of the Copyrighted Work

The more creative expression in a work, the more protection it has against fair use. Fair use applies more to thinly protected functional works (like computer programs or useful articles) and factual works (like databases) and nonoriginal works (like judicial reports or works that reproduce public domain works).

Unpublished works, under *Harper & Row*, are less subject to fair use. If a copy of an unpublished work has been obtained wrongfully, then this factor weighs even more strongly against fair use.

4. *Katz v. Google Inc.*, 802 F.3d 1178 (11th Cir. 2015); *see also* http://blog.ericgoldman.org/archives/2015/10/another-censorious-copyright-case-results-in-a-big-fee-shift-inglewood-v-teixeira.htm.

5. *City of Inglewood v. Teixeira*, 2015 U.S. Dist. LEXIS 143380 (C.D. Cal. Oct. 8, 2015).

Amount and Substantiality of the Portion Used in Relation to the Copyrighted Work as a Whole

Copying (or distributing or adapting or performing or displaying) the entire work is less likely to qualify for fair use than using only a portion. But fair use often protects use of the entire work, as in *Sony*. This is especially true if the work is thinly protected, where copying the entire work still copies only a little protected expression (as may occur with a computer program or database). The particular portion copied is important. There was no fair use in *Harper & Row* for copying less than 1 percent of a book when the copier chose the "heart" of the book. Whether the portion chosen is itself highly protected, creative expression is also relevant.

The key is whether the amount taken is appropriate to the favored use. There are several aspects to this. The first issue is whether the copier took an amount that fit the proposed use, for example, whether the reviewer quoted only sections relevant to her analysis of a book. The second issue is whether there was an alternative to taking the portion copied. *Harper & Row* again is key, with its argument that the magazine could largely have accomplished the favored purpose of news reporting by copying unprotected facts, ideas, and nonoriginal material. The third issue is whether the amount taken was likely to diminish a potential market for the copyright owner.

Effect of the Use on the Potential Market for or Value of the Copyrighted Work

The effect on the market for the work may be the factor that sways courts most. *See* Barton Beebe, *An Empirical Study of U.S. Copyright Fair Use Opinions, 1978-2005*, 156 Penn. St. L. Rev. 549 (2008). There are several ways to show market harm. Lost sales of the copyrighted work (or sales of copies of the work by the defendant) may be the most direct way, but other markets will count. The statute speaks of "potential market," so it is enough to show harm in a market that the copyright owner was likely to enter. In addition, under *Sony*, it may be sufficient to show that if the defendant's use became a widespread practice, the copyright owner would suffer market harm, but there must generally be a concrete showing. There is a presumption of market harm for "verbatim copying of the original in its entirety for commercial purposes." For other uses, mere speculative theories will not suffice. Rather, the copyright owner should make a concrete showing, such as by market surveys or other evidence.

Some types of market harm are not cognizable. Uses like criticism may decrease sales, but that does not weigh against fair use. Rather, it serves the underlying purpose of copyright to foster exchange of ideas. Likewise, uses like reverse engineering may permit copying of unprotected elements of the work. If use of unprotected elements leads to a product that buyers prefer, there is no cognizable market harm.

Finally, as commentators and courts have stressed, there is a tension between permitting fair use and permitting market mechanisms to develop. If photocopying were generally considered to be fair use, there would be no incentive to seek permission. If it is not considered fair use, then market mechanisms will develop to facilitate licensing, such as the Copyright Clearance Center. Music downloading is another area where some see conflict between free use and the development of permitted use. Courts are likely to struggle to find a balance.

That tension is illustrated by issues involving AI. Is it fair use to scrape tons of material off the Internet to use as sets of data to train AI programs? The argument in favor is that the practice is necessary to promote a useful new technology, does not cut into the licensing market for the works, and is transformative, in the sense that it allows creation of new works. The argument against is that the entire work is copied, the copying is done to access the expressive aspect of the works, and that other means can be found to get the necessary data—using material with permission or using material that is not under copyright.

Examples

1. *Sweet charity. Touchdown!* is a famous, beloved photo by Snapz. It captures three toddlers deliriously raising their arms in delight at some unshown performer. Snapz has earned considerable revenue from licensing various uses of the photo. He is surprised to find the photo being used on the front of Footie chocolate cookie boxes. When Snapz's agent contacts the seller of Footies cookies, she is informed that no permission was sought because the use is considered a fair use. Footie is a nonprofit company that sells cookies to fund various charitable activities. Millions of dollars are earned by selling Footies (with *Touchdown!* on the front), and all the money (other than expenses, which are rigorously minimized) goes to support a number of highly praiseworthy efforts, such as fighting infectious disease and aiding those harmed by earthquakes. Does the use of *Touchdown!* qualify as fair use?

2. *Kopy Kop Kop*. Photoshoppe, a commercial copy shop, makes coursepacks for students at a local university using reading lists provided by university instructors. Each coursepack contains several hundred pages of text from up to ten different sources. The sources range from textbooks to scholarly articles to newspaper articles. Most of the sources are under copyright, but Photoshoppe does not seek permission or offer to pay licensing fees. Photoshoppe refuses to seek licenses even when directly

contacted by the various copyright owners. Other copy shops in the area do seek permission and pay fees when making such coursepacks. Photoshoppe, however, takes the position that making and distributing the coursepacks is protected as fair use, as a noncommercial educational activity. Does fair use protect Photoshoppe?

3. *Reverse engineering*. SoMak sells a popular word processing program, Word Prefect. Word Prefect is sold to the public in its object code version, meaning it is sold in the form in which it is run on a computer and not the source code form that a software developer could easily read and modify. Strive, an engineer, purchases a copy of Word Prefect at a local office supply store. Strive then prints the object code version on several hundred sheets of paper. Strive spends several months studying the object code quite closely to see how the program functions. Strive then writes her own word processing program, Sendense. Strive is very careful only to copy unprotected, functional aspects of Word Prefect into Sendense. Her avowed purpose is to win over market leadership from Word Prefect.

   SoMak sues Strive, alleging infringement of the copyright in Word Prefect. Strive contends that she cannot have infringed because she copied only nonprotected elements. She then realizes that she did make a copy—she printed the program on paper—but she decides that fair use protects her. Does fair use apply?

4. *Trouble in parodies*. "Evermore," a ballad written and sung by Wangelis, is often heard on the radio. The song tells the tale of a modern Romeo and Juliet, set to soothing electronic sounds. Smiling Al, a popular comedian, uses the words and melody of the song for his recording "Mevermore." Al rewrites the words into an amusing tale of a trip to the Mount Mevermore, a mound in the Everglades. "Mevermore" uses the melody from "Evermore" but does not explicitly or implicitly comment on or criticize "Evermore." Rather, the use of the familiar tune from "Evermore" makes "Mevermore" more marketable. Because listeners know and like the tune, they are more likely to stay tuned and listen to the new version. When Wangelis claims infringement, Smiling Al claims that "Mevermore" is a parody and therefore protected under fair use. Does fair use protect this use?

5. *Clips*. Trailers Inc. makes movie trailers. When a movie is released to the public on video, Trailers gets a copy. It selects certain portions and edits them to get an entertaining trailer designed to get the consumers to rent the film. Trailers provides its trailers to video stores, for a fee, to show to their customers. Trailers also has customers among online video rental customers. Sued by the movie companies for copyright infringement, Trailers argues for fair use. First, the trailers do not substitute for the

movies. Second, they actually help movie sales by encouraging rentals. What's next, Trailers contends, suing the authors of book reviews? Does fair use protect Trailers?

6. *Thumbnails*. An Internet search engine helps users find images on the web. The search engine automatically browses the web, collecting as many images as it can. Using both humans and software, it compiles an index of keywords associated with the images. If a user types "Panda" into the search page, it will return all the pictures it has associated with the word "Panda." It does not show the original pictures but rather shows "thumbnail" versions. Thumbnails are small, low-resolution versions of the pictures. To view the original, the user can click on the link and be sent to the page where the original is found. A photographer who posts original photos on his site sues for infringement. Fair use?

7. *Panned*. Critic writes a review of *Slidder*, a new detective novel from bestselling author Austen. Critic makes ten verbatim quotations from the book of one to four sentences each. The review convincingly argues that Austen is simply recycling plotlines and characters from her previous books. The quotations are carefully selected to support Critic's argument. Critic's review is printed in newspapers across the land. *Slidder* becomes Austen's first book in years not to make the top of the bestseller charts. Austen blames Critic and sues for copyright infringement. She contends that fair use will not apply, where Critic's use of her very own words destroyed the market value of the work. Was demolition fair use?

8. *Extraction by copying*. Data Gatherer compiles property information for municipalities. The municipalities send out forms to their residents, with various questions about their real property (including such things as ownership, lenders, residents, use, renovations, and additions). When the forms come back, Data Gatherer's employees input them into a database, which is stored on computers in the municipal offices and may be accessed by the public and by municipal employees. Data Gatherer has made several creative choices about how to organize the information. The municipalities pay a fee to Data Gatherer.

   A rival compiler sends in workers who download the entire database and take the copy to their home office. There, they extract all the information into their own database. They do not ultimately copy Data Gatherer's creative arrangement of information, only the unprotected facts. But Data Gatherer claims infringement for the first copying, which was done to extract the information. Infringement or fair use?

9. *Purloined letter*. The CEO of Megacorp writes a lengthy, confidential letter to the board of directors describing in memorable fashion the events leading up to Megacorp's bankruptcy. The CEO's personal assistant leaks the letter to *Money Money* magazine, in clear breach of the terms of his

written employment contract. Before *Money Money* goes to press with an article excerpting much of the letter, the CEO seeks an injunction. When the magazine argues fair use, her attorneys respond that fair use cannot apply where the copy used was obtained illegally. Should a wrongfully obtained copy be subject to fair use?

10. *Whole lotta copying goin' on.* Defendant's work is a video documentary about Elvis Presley, which incorporated many copyrighted photographs, music excerpts, and clips from videos. Defendant spent much time and creativity in finding and selecting works to use in the documentary. Defendant artfully edited the documentary to make it an entertaining account of Presley's career, especially by relying heavily on the contemporary works. Defendant did not get permission from the many copyright owners. Established licensing practices would have permitted most of the uses, but at a considerable cost in fees.

11. *Fair use test?* Defendants publish the Seinfeld Aptitude Test (SAT). The book has multiple-choice, matching, and short-answer questions on the characters and incidents in the long-running television situation comedy *Seinfeld*. The book, in effect, takes the various entertaining aspects of the television program and puts them into book form. As its creator put it, to "capture Seinfeld's flavor in quiz book fashion." The book does not offer any independent analysis or criticism of the program, but it does test the reader/viewer's knowledge. *Seinfeld*'s producers have not made any attempts at creating their own quiz book. Would defendants qualify for fair use?

12. *Fair use zone.* Artist Richard Prince bought several copies of a book of photographs titled *Yes, Rasta*. Prince mounted 41 of the photographs on backer board and painted over various portions. Prince displayed his works, collectively called *Canal Zone*. The gallery reproduced the works in an exhibition catalog that it sold. Several of the paintings sold, for a total well into the millions of dollars. Another gallery, which had been planning to show the original photographs, canceled its exhibition. The second gallery feared the perception that it would be trying to piggyback on the use of the photos by Prince, a well-known appropriation artist. Is Prince protected by fair use?

13. *Hoist on their own petard.* Flunt, the publisher of *Grumble* magazine, is a strong opponent of presidential candidate Ellery. Flunt's minions create a two-page cartoon purporting to tell the story of Ellery's life but actually pushing various outrageous fictions. Ellery sues for libel but loses because of the latitude afforded by the First Amendment. Ellery then sends out thousands of fund-raising letters containing copies of the scurrilous cartoon to supporters. Supporters send plenty of money. Flunt, angry at providing fuel for Ellery's campaign, sues for copyright

infringement for making and distributing copies of the copyrighted cartoon. Flunt seeks to have all the funds raised paid over. Is Ellery protected by fair use?

14. *More multiple-choice tests*. The Chicago Board of Education creates a series of standardized multiple-choice tests. The tests are administered to students each year to assess their proficiency in various areas. The board carefully keeps the content of the tests private so it can reuse the tests. Ms. Brodie, a teacher, dislikes both the tests (thinking them poorly drafted and clumsily adapted to the courses students take) and standardized tests generally. One year, she takes all the tests administered to several grade levels of students at her school and distributes copies to the public. She claims fair use, arguing that making the tests public is the best way to criticize them and further the cause of education. Would she qualify for fair use?

15. *File sharing*. The company Napster creates and distributes file-sharing software. Consumers can download Napster for free. Consumers use Napster's software to download music from other Napster users. To get music from others, the Napster user makes music files available to others. The software could be used for many things, but by far its most common use is to trade copyrighted music. Holders of music and sound recording copyrights sue Napster for secondary copyright infringement. The music companies present concrete evidence that Napster has contributed to a loss of music sales. Napster contends that home music copying is protected as fair use, under *Sony*. Is it?

16. *Post and discuss*. Freeforall Forum runs a website devoted to the discussion of topical issues in politics, culture, and everything else. Freeforall finds articles of interest from newspapers, magazines, blogs, and other places. Freeforall posts the entire text, along with any pictures, on the Freeforall website. Freeforall gives correct attribution of source but does not seek permission from the copyright owners. Freeforall permits any visitor to the website to post comments. Freeforall's site gains in popularity each month, with more visitors and more posted comments. Articles are often available on Freeforall shortly after their original publication and are left there permanently for reference. Its website reflects extremely robust discussion about the issues at every level of argument, from philosophical analysis all the way up to pure invective.

    Freeforall does not seek any financial advantage. It does not run ads, sell information to businesses, or use the website or the information about its visitors in any other way. A number of copyright owners object, requesting that Freeforall simply post links to articles. Freeforall refuses on several grounds. Links often expire. Some of the material requires registration or even a paid subscription. Freeforall also posts text from paper works that are not available online. If the copyright owners sue, is Freeforall protected by fair use?

17. *Google Books*. Google undertakes a library digitization project. Google's plans are flexible, but suppose it takes the following approach: With the cooperation of several libraries, Google will scan their collections, book by book. Google will include the material in a huge database. Google users will be able to search the database using Google Books. A user will not be able to download the book's text but will get back only a few lines of text with each search result. The user may get links to places to buy the book (like Amazon.com) and advertisements keyed to the search and its results. To do this, Google will have to do a lot of copying (scanning, saving into the database, giving snippets to users, and more) of copyrighted works (as well as a lot of noncopyrighted works). Publishers object and suggest that Google negotiate licensing fees. Fair use?

    That question sparked a lot of online discussion. A Google search for "Google Books" and "fair use" yielded about 102 million results. Opinions were all across the spectrum. What do you think?

18. *That's gratitude for ya. Grateful Dead: The Illustrated Trip* tells the story, month by month, of the decades-long career of the band the Grateful Dead. It includes reproductions of many relevant artworks. Among them are thumbnail versions of seven concert posters, approximately two-by-three-inch versions of the large, highly creative posters. The publisher had sought permission from posters' copyright holder, the Bill Graham Archives, but was refused. There was no practice of paying licensing fees for such uses. Fair use?

19. *Flipendo Lexicon*. RDR Books seeks to publish the *Harry Potter Lexicon*, an encyclopedia listing terms, events, characters, and various other aspects of the *Harry Potter* books and movies. The encyclopedia sticks close to the text of the books, with its entries quoting many passages largely verbatim. The *Harry Potter* copyright holders seek an injunction. Among other reasons, *Harry Potter*'s author plans her own reference work. The *Lexicon*'s publishers argue fair use, on the theory that the work is a reference work, useful for research and scholarship; that the purpose of the work is transformative, like the protected parody in the "Pretty Woman" case; that the amount taken is appropriate; that the material taken was largely nonprotected factual material, relating what happened to whom in the books; and that the *Lexicon* would not hurt the huge market for *Harry Potter*.

20. *AWOL*. The U.S. Postal Service (USPS) commissioned a sculpture for the Korean War Veterans Memorial. In the agreement, the sculptor

adamantly retained the copyright. The USPS subsequently put a photo of the sculpture on a postage stamp, which sold millions of copies. The photographer had made the image of the snow-bedecked sculpture as a present for his father, a Korean War veteran. The USPS signed a license agreement getting permission only from the photographer. The sculptor was not consulted. Fair use?

21. *Sample.* Public Announcement's song "D.O.G. in Me" makes repeated use of a sample from George Clinton's "Atomic Dog." The sampled elements are "the use of the word 'dog' in a low voice as 'musical punctuation,' the rhythmic panting," and the refrain, "Bow wow wow, yippie yo, yippie yea." Many others paid to sample from "Atomic Dog," but Public Announcement did not. Fair use?

22. *Enlargement.* The Los Angeles County Sheriff's Department buys 3,663 licenses to use Wall Data's software but installs the software onto 6,007 computers, configuring its network so that no more than 3,663 copies will be in use at any one time. Fair use?

23. *Fair, Rasta.* Prince, a successful appropriation artist, tore prints of photos from a book titled *Yes, Rasta* and dramatically altered them with paint, printing, and pasted elements. After the altered prints are sold for gigantic sums, the photographer sues for infringement. Fair use?

24. *Fair clips?* Meltwater's Global Media Monitoring service enabled "users to monitor the news based on the presence of certain words or phrases in news articles appearing on the Internet and to receive excerpts of those news articles. Meltwater uses automated computer programs or algorithms to copy or 'scrape' an article from an online news source, index the article, and deliver verbatim excerpts of the article to its customers in response to search queries." Fair use?

25. *Coursepacks.* University professors make copies of excerpts of books and provide them to their students online. Fair use?

26. *Posting bills.* Would it be fair use for a nonprofit to copy and post online "private sector codes and standards [drafted] in order to advance public safety, ensure compatibility across products and services, facilitate training, and spur innovation," where such codes have been given legal effect by adoption by governmental agencies?[6]

27. *Sony?* VidAngel markets itself as a one-dollar movie streaming service. VidAngel purchased movies on DVDs, circumvented access controls, and copied the movie to permit streaming to customers. It characterized

6. *Am. Soc'y for Testing & Materials v. Public.Resource.Org, Inc.*, 2017 U.S. Dist. LEXIS 14623, *5 (D.D.C. Feb. 2, 2017).

its transactions with customers as selling the disc to the user for $20, streaming the movie, and then repurchasing it for $19, all the while maintaining physical possession of the disc, so the user was streaming their own copy. Fair use?

28. *Oracle again.* Recall from earlier in the book that it is unsettled whether the APIs for the Java programming language are protected by copyright. Google copies the Java APIs to write its own code to run Java, so that developers could use Java to write apps for the Android operating system distributed by Google. In plain English, APIs are snippets of software code that programmers use to tell software to do things. Was it fair use for Google to copy the Java APIs in order to write software that would run Java, a common practice in the software industry?

29. *Free for the picking?* Should good faith weigh in favor of fair use, if the user simply assumes that photographs (specifically, "Adams Morgan at Night") available online may be freely used?

Explanations

1. The use does not qualify as fair use. Indeed, although the ultimate purpose is to fund highly praiseworthy activities, every factor in the fair use analysis weighs against finding fair use here. It does not fall into one of the favored uses: "criticism, commentary, news reporting, teaching, scholarship, or research." The purpose is arguably charitable (indirectly), but the direct use is simply commercial. Moreover, the use simply reproduces the work without adding any creative expression, so that factor is at best neutral—and more likely weighs against fair use. The nature of the work is a highly protected creative work, which weighs against fair use. The amount copied is the entire work, again a strong factor against fair use. Finally, Snapz earns licensing revenue from various uses of the photo. The failure to pay him licensing while widely exploiting the work makes the fourth factor also weigh against fair use.

2. Under recent cases, a court would probably deny fair use. The nature of the work depends on the materials chosen for copying, but expressive texts are likely to be highly protected literary works. The purpose of the copy shop is commercial, and courts are not likely to consider the purpose of the students, who buy the coursepacks for educational purposes. The amount taken would often not be the whole work, but presumably the instructor would choose what she deemed to be important sections. Remember that *Harper & Row* denied fair use to a few hundred words copied from a book and deemed especially significant (although that was unpublished work, which is much less subject to fair use). The

last factor weighs strongly in favor of the copyright owners. Other copy shops do pay licensing fees, so the practice would cause the copyright holders market harm.

3. Strive has a strong argument that making a copy for purposes of reverse engineering is fair use. *See, e.g., Sony Computer Entertainment v. Connectix*, 203 F.3d 596 (9th Cir. 2000); *Atari Games v. Nintendo of Am.*, 975 F.2d 832 (Fed. Cir. 1992); *Sega Enters. v. Accolade*, 977 F.2d 1510 (9th Cir. 1992). The purpose of the use is commercial, but it is also research. Moreover, making a copy may sometimes be the only way to gain access to the unprotected functional aspects of works. The nature of the copyrighted work is a computer program, a functional work rather than a highly expressive work whose nature lies at the core of copyright. The amount copied was the entire work, but such intermediate copying was necessary to study the functional aspects, and none of the expressive aspects was copied into the final product. Finally, SoMak may lose sales, not because Strive is selling infringing copies but because Strive is selling noninfringing copies in legitimate competition. Such market harm does not weigh against fair use in the same way the loss of sales from the criticism in a book review or a parody does not weigh against fair use. The Supreme Court's decision in *Google* supports allowing copying for the purpose of getting at functional aspects of works.

4. Smiling Al is about to lose his smile. He is not protected by fair use. Parody can be protected by fair use, as in *Campbell*, but there is a key distinction in this case. The purpose of the parody in *Campbell* was, in part, commentary. The parody in *Campbell* was an effective critique of the very worldview of the copyrighted work. Here, the parody does not comment on or criticize the original work. Rather, the parody borrows the tune of the original to profit from its popularity, which verges on the very free-riding that copyright exists to reduce. The parody does add creative expression and somewhat transform the original work, but such elements would appear in almost any derivative work. *See also Dr. Seuss Enters. v. Penguin Books USA*, 109 F.3d 1394 (9th Cir. 1997) (*The Cat NOT in the Hat! A Parody by Dr. Juice*, the story of a famous criminal trial retold in the form of a parody of a famous children's book, was not protected by fair use because it merely used the original as raw material without commenting on it), and *Lombardo v. Dr. Seuss Enterprises, L.P.*, 279 F. Supp. 3d 497 (S.D.N.Y 2017) (parody of *How the Grinch Stole Christmas* did qualify for fair use, where it recontextualized the character of "Cindy–Lou Who—a symbol of childhood innocence and naiveté"). For a parody that was protected as fair use because it likewise commented on and criticized the copyrighted work, see *Mattel Inc. v. Walking Mt. Prods.*, 353 F.3d 792, 802 (9th Cir. 2003) (where Mattel marketed Barbie doll as a "symbol of American girlhood" with a glamorous lifestyle and engaged

in exciting activities, artist turned "this image on its head, so to speak, by displaying carefully positioned, nude, and sometimes frazzled looking Barbies in often ridiculous and apparently dangerous situations").

5. In *Video Pipeline, Inc. v. Buena Vista Home Ent.*, 342 F.3d 191 (3d Cir. 2003), the court rejected fair use. Although the distributor used only portions of the film, the other factors would weigh against fair use. To make the trailers entertaining, the distributor chose some of the best bits (like using the most interesting parts of the book in *Harper & Row*). The trailer would not substitute for the film (well, in most cases), but the distributor also foreclosed a potential market for the copyrighted works because film companies or other services would likely compete to provide trailers.

   In addition, Trailer's book review analogy is flawed. A trailer is not a review, using portions of the book as part of a critical discussion of the book. Rather, a trailer is a compilation of portions of the work.

6. Probably fair use. *See Kelly v. Arriba Soft Corp.*, 336 F.3d 811 (9th Cir. 2003). The use is commercial, especially if the search engine uses the service to sell advertising. The works are highly protected creative works. But the use is a productive use. The search engine made at least two copies (downloading a copy and making a thumbnail version). But the website permitted the downloading, and the thumbnail was no more than necessary for the favored productive use. There was also likely to be no harm to the potential market. The use did not serve as a substitute for the copyrighted works (because the thumbnails had greatly diminished resolution). Nor is there a market for licensing works to search engines.

7. Fair use. Critic did use protected expression without permission, but the factors would favor fair use. Critic made a favored use: criticism. The work was a highly protected creative work, but such works are certainly subject to criticism, so the factor would not weigh heavily. The amount used was not large and was also appropriate for the favored use. There was market harm but not a cognizable harm. The author lost sales not because Critic sold copies of the work but because Critic convinced people not to buy the work.

8. Fair use serves to implement the other limitations on the scope of copyright. Facts are not copyrightable, but a database of facts may be copyrightable because of the originality in selecting and arranging the data. Wholesale copying and distribution would be infringement because it would entail copying the protected elements of the database, but the copyright in the selection and arrangement should not make it impossible to copy unprotected elements. To extract facts, it might be necessary to make intermediate copies including protected elements. Provided that the copying of protected elements was done

only to gain access to unprotected elements and the scope of copying did not exceed that purpose, fair use would likely shield extractor from infringement claims. *See Assessment Techs. of WI, LLC v. WIREdata*, 350 F.3d 640 (7th Cir. 2003).

9. It will weigh against fair use if the defendant wrongfully acquired a copy. For example, in *Harper & Row*, the Court noted that the *Nation* had "knowingly exploited a purloined manuscript" in printing prepublication excerpts of President Ford's autobiography. Likewise, some courts have suggested that making copies for the purpose of reverse engineering a product can be fair use only if the copy was rightfully acquired. But even an illegally acquired copy may be subject to fair use, other factors permitting. *See NXIVM Corporation v. The Ross Institute*, 364 F.3d 471 (9th Cir. 2003), in which a seminar manual was obtained wrongfully and small portions were distributed on the Internet as parts of writings that critically analyzed the manual. The wrongful acquisition weighed against fair use, but the court held that the other factors were strong enough to overcome that. The defendant did not simply distribute copies of the manual. Rather, the defendant made a transformative use. He used no more than necessary for the favored use. The distribution of ideas is favored, and the suppression of such distribution using protection of their copyrighted expression is not.

   In our case, we would need to know more about *Money Money*'s article. Fair use is not precluded by the fact that the letter was obtained through breach of contract. But all factors must be weighed. The use is news reporting, a favored use. It could be a productive or even transformative use if the excerpts from the letter are integrated into a larger story, as opposed to simply reprinting excerpts. The amount taken would be key: whether it was appropriate for the favored use, and in particular whether the article could simply copy unprotected facts and ideas rather than copying original expression. Finally, it seems unlikely there would be cognizable market harm (unlike *Harper & Row*).

10. Courts will often find a disfavored commercial purpose even where the use has some aspects of reporting, historical writing, or other favored purposed. For example, in *Elvis Presley Enterprises, Inc. v. Passport Video*, 349 F.3d 622 (9th Cir. 2004), fair use did not protect documentary film's use of various excerpts from copyrighted works, where loss of licensing revenue was shown. The compilation of such works could be viewed as scholarship or even education, and is itself creative and somewhat transformative. The decisions about what to include, how to arrange it, and how to edit the whole are all creative choices. The documentary was presumably intended to further the discourse about a notable public figure. But the court held that the overriding commercial purpose of the endeavor put it into the disfavored category. The transformative

element was somewhat thin, for what the defendant used were literal clips from the materials, profiting from their creative, copyrighted aspects. Because the clips served the same entertainment value as the original, the factor would weigh against fair use. Although the clips were short in absolute terms, the plaintiff often used the "heart" of the works, because in making a documentary, one would naturally seek to use the best moments from the excerpted materials. The use of material without permission, for example, was likely to be deemed a loss of potential licensing revenue. Were such practice to become widespread, licensing of the materials would certainly suffer. *Elvis Presley* is representative of the reluctance of courts to allow large-scale use of copyrighted excerpts. It also represents the reluctance to extend fair use even to genuine works of scholarship and history, where the works also have a commercial element that benefits from use of the copyrighted works. Without question, fair use is not a cure for the obstacles that copyright creates for scholars and researchers. By contrast, use of eight seconds of the Chicago Bears' *Superbowl Shuffle* in a documentary film was held fair use, where the use was intended as factual and the court was cognizant of the risk of requiring documentary filmmakers to get permission, which would give censorship control to the subjects of documentaries. *Red Label Music Publ'g, Inc. v. Chila Prods.*, 388 F. Supp. 3d 975 (N.D. Ill. 2019).

11. The Second Circuit rejected the defense of fair use. *See Castle Rock Entm't v. Carol Publishing Group*, 150 F.3d 132 (2d Cir. 1998). The defendants argued that the book should qualify for fair use, for several reasons. They contended it was a transformative work (in that it took a television program and transformed it into a quiz book) and that it threw the program and its cultural place into a new light. In addition, the book was a favored educational work, both assessing and increasing the reader's knowledge of *Seinfeld*. Finally, *Seinfeld* had offered no book of its own, so there was no demonstrated loss of market.

    The Second Circuit rejected all those arguments. The book was not transformative, because it merely repackaged the entertaining aspects of the television program. It did not add any independent criticism or commentary and was unlike the parody in *Campbell*. Although it was a quiz book, its educational value was slight. Rather, it was a commercial work intended to benefit from the popularity of the program by copying its creative content. The nature of the work was a highly protected creative work, and the amount taken was substantial, forming the bulk of the quiz book. Finally, although the producers of *Seinfeld* had not created such a book, the SAT certainly had exploited a market the copyright owner "would in general develop or license others to develop," the relevant consideration under *Campbell*. The owner of the copyright in "Pretty Woman" might be unlikely to authorize a parody rap version of the song, but the owner of the *Seinfeld* copyrights might well authorize books that simply repackage the television program.

12. The Second Circuit held most of the works to be fair use. The use was deemed transformative: "Here, looking at the artworks and the photographs side-by-side, we conclude that Prince's images, except for those we discuss separately below, have a different character, give Cariou's photographs a new expression, and employ new aesthetics with creative and communicative results distinct from Cariou's." *Cariou v. Prince*, 714 F.3d 694, 707-708 (2d Cir. 2013).

13. Fair use. In particular, there was no market harm, where the supporters of the candidate would (arguably) not have been customers of the preacher's detractors. *See Hustler Magazine, Inc. v. Moral Majority*, 796 F.2d 1148 (9th Cir. 1986).

14. The court rejected fair use. The use was a favored use, criticism of the tests, but the tests were highly protected unpublished works, the value of which depended on their remaining unpublished. The amount taken was the entire tests. The favored purpose could have been accomplished without publishing the entire tests, either by publishing selected questions or by publishing an analysis that did not compromise their security. The defendant also acted in breach of her contract, which would weigh against fair use. *Cf. Chicago Board of Education v. Substance, Inc.*, 354 F.3d 624 (7th Cir. 2003).

15. The court held fair use inapplicable. *A&M Records, Inc. v. Napster, Inc.*, 239 F.3d 1004 (9th Cir. 2001). The first issue would be the nature of the use. Napster is a commercial entity, but the relevant use is the consumer's use. The Ninth Circuit characterized file sharing by consumers as a commercial use, hence disfavored in the fair use analysis. The court reasoned that by trading music, a consumer is providing music to some anonymous member of the public and receiving music free, which the consumer would otherwise pay for. In addition, the practice amounts to "repeated and exploitative copying of copyrighted works." By contrast, in *Sony*, consumers made copies for themselves simply to change the time of viewing.

    Whether the court was correct in terming the use by consumers as "commercial" might be questioned, but the use is certainly different from *Sony*. There, copyright owners authorized broadcasts to be viewed for free. Time shifting simply changed the time consumers viewed the program. File sharing, by contrast, allows consumers to avoid paying for music and to make copies for repeated listening.

    The nature of the works would be highly protected works. The works were copied in their entirety. Both factors would weigh against fair use.

The last factor is effect on the market. The court determined that market harm had been demonstrated, which would be a strong factor against fair use. In *Sony*, there was no such showing with respect to time shifting of television programming.

16. Freeforall Forum would not qualify for fair use. Cf. *Los Angeles Times v. Free Republic*, 54 U.S.P.Q. 2d 1453 (C. Dist. Cal. 2000). Freeforall would contend that fair use protects their activity as a not-for-profit, transformative use that fosters the favored purposes of criticism, comment, and news reporting. It does not charge for access, so it is not diverting revenues from the copyright owners.

    The first factor favors Freeforall. Even if it took donations, it did not charge visitors or advertisers and so would probably not be a commercial use. It does foster criticism, comment, and news reporting. But the other factors would weigh against fair use.

    As to the nature of the works copied, they were medium protected literary works containing much factual, nonoriginal, or otherwise nonprotected material. The amount of copying factor would weigh heavily against fair use. Freeforall copied the entire texts of articles. Its purposes of fostering comment could have been served by much less extensive copying. It could have copied all unprotected facts and ideas, but it saved itself the trouble by using wholesale copying. Likewise, it could have linked to the original sources for at least some pieces but instead copied the pieces to its own site.

    As to the final factor, there may not be a concrete showing of harm. But a court would likely conclude that of the many visitors to Freeforall's site, at least some were using that as a substitute for visits to the original site, costing advertising revenue and decreasing the popularity of the site (and its value). This factor would be even stronger if the copyright owners could bring forward specific market data, which is not unlikely given the bountiful data available.

17. There's a lot of room for argument on this one, because the general topic of fair use and the Internet is still very unsettled. Two sides of the argument might run this way:
    a. Of course it is fair use. The nature of the use is helping people to identify books that they are interested in. This is far from a merely reproductive use, but rather is a productive, if not transformative, use. It assists the free flow of ideas—a prime policy of copyright—without distributing more than a tiny amount of creative expression, because users only get a few lines of text with each search result. Two factors might weigh against fair use. Many of the works are highly protected creative works, and they are being copied in their entirety. But those are both undercut. The creative aspects, like the works as a whole, are copied only as part of facilitating research

and the dissemination of ideas. Those creative aspects are not distributed. Finally, there is no showing of an adverse effect on the market. The snippets in no way serve as a substitute for the books or even as a substitute for excerpts from the books—just like reverse engineering, by which you make an intermediate copy of the whole work to get at its unprotected aspects.

b. Of course it is not fair use. This is systematic copying of entire libraries, well beyond the scope of anything that ever qualified as fair use. No market harm? Google makes e-books by scanning the paper books. Google uses those e-books to compile indexes. Well, publishers already sell e-books and indexes to the contents of books. If Google wants electronic copies of the books or searchable indexes, it should buy them from the publishers or get permission to scan them. The use is commercial, just like the photocopying cases. The users may use Google Books for research or education, but Google is doing this as a commercial entity to sell advertising, accumulate useful marketing data, and establish itself as a key source of information—other people's copyrighted information. Finally, there is a clear showing of market harm. As Google's actions demonstrate, there is a demand for the use of copyrighted books in databases. We stand willing to negotiate a price.

Google adjusted its plans, announcing that it would suspend scanning for three months and honor requests by publishers to opt out of the project. *See Google Library Project Temporarily Halted to Allow Copyright Owner Response*, BNA Patent, Trademark & Copyright Journal, August 19, 2005. This leaves open the question of whether there would be infringement if Google scans a book where the publisher has not opted out. Certainly, willingness to omit books on request weighs in favor of good faith use and fair use, but that is only part of one of the factors.

The Second Circuit held that fair use protected copying by the Google Book project, which involved scanning libraries of books, putting the files in a database, permitting online text searches that returned snippets of the books. Although the database might conceivably cost some book sales, where such a snippet made buying the book unnecessary, that factor was outweighed by the valuable uses. "The search engine also makes possible new forms of research, known as 'text mining' and 'data mining.' Google's 'ngrams' research tool draws on the Google Library Project corpus to furnish statistical information to Internet users about the frequency of word and phrase usage over centuries. . . . It also allows researchers to comb over the tens of millions of books Google has scanned in order to examine 'word frequencies, syntactic patterns, and thematic markers' and to derive information on how nomenclature, linguistic usage, and literary style have changed over time." *Authors Guild v. Google, Inc.*, 804 F.3d 202, 209 (2d Cir. 2015).

However, the same court declined to extend those cases, in *Hachette Book Group, Inc. v. Internet Archive*, 63 F.4th 100 (2d Cir. 2023). There the Internet Archive's unauthorized scanning and lending of books was held to infringe the publishers' copyrights. The project, which took force during the pandemic, did not charge for copies and sought to limit lending to the same number of physical copies in its participating libraries. The use was held not transformative; it served the same purpose and did not add new expression, meaning, or message. The use was deemed commercial. There was no charge, but the Internet Archive solicited donations. Finally, lending was a substitute for the publishers' electronic and print books, and so caused market harm.

The digital age will continue to raise many issues of fair use. *See, e.g.*, Matthew Sag, *Copyright and Copy-Reliant Technology*, 103 Nw. U. L. Rev. (2009) (discussing technologies that rely on copying for nonexpressive uses, such as "search engines, plagiarism-detection software, reverse engineering and Google's nascent library cataloging effort").

18. Fair use. *See Bill Graham Archives v. Dorling Kindersley Ltd.*, 448 F.3d 605 (2d Cir. 2006). The nature of the use was both historical writing and transformative, because by setting the posters into the context of a timeline, it adapted them into another creative work. Defendants also showed good faith by attempting to get permission to use the works. As to the second factor, the copyrighted works were highly creative posters, which would weigh against fair use. But where the use is transformative, that weighs less heavily. Under the third factor, the amount used was the entire work, which again weighs against fair use, but the amount used was appropriate because the entire poster would be relevant to the timeline. Moreover, only thumbnail versions were used, as opposed to full-scale or high-quality reproductions, so the amount used was appropriate to the favored use. Finally, there was no showing of relevant market harm. The biography would not serve as a market substitute for the posters themselves, especially where the use was "thumbnail" reproductions of much lower resolution than the posters and having less visual quality. Nor was there shown to be regular market for such licensing.

19. The federal court in New York rejected fair use. *Warner Bros. Entertainment Inc. v. RDR Books*, No. 07 Civ. 9667 (S.D.N.Y. 2008). *Harry Potter*'s author cannot prevent others from writing reference books about the young magician's tales. Nor can she prevent copying of ideas and nonoriginal material (such as preexisting witchcraft lore that she used). Others may make fair use even of her original creative expression. But the *Lexicon* exceeded the bounds of fair use. The key factor was that the *Lexicon* used much more of her expression than necessary to provide a reference work. There was also a showing of potential market harm by her concrete plans to write an authorized *Harry Potter* reference.

20. Most photos of national monuments would qualify for fair use, but this use did not qualify, for several reasons. The use by the USPS was commercial (selling millions of stamps). The photographer's image was not held to be transformative, but rather simply a beautiful image of the sculpture in snow. Moreover, any transformative use was by the photographer, not by the USPS. In addition, the parties here were not strangers. The negotiated agreement did not grant the USPS the copyright, or a license to make derivative works. Fair use is not a way to transform the agreement itself. *See Gaylord v. United States*, 595 F.3d 1364 (Fed. Cir. 2010).

21. Infringement, according to some. The use was commercial. It was also transformative but did not criticize or comment on the original. Although the elements copied were small, they were among the most distinctive elements of the song. Market harm was shown by the many others who paid to license samples of the song. *See Bridgeport Music, Inc. v. UMG Recordings, Inc.*, 585 F.3d 267, 277-279 (6th Cir. 2009). By contrast, the Second Circuit held that rapper Drake was protected by fair use, for sampling "Jimmy Smith Rap," in Drake's hip hop song "Pound Cake." The court regarded it as a transformative use that used only a small portion and saw "no evidence that 'Pound Cake' usurps demand for 'Jimmy Smith Rap' or otherwise cause a negative market effect." *Estate of Smith v. Graham*, 799 F. App'x 36, 39 (2d Cir. 2020).

22. Infringement. "The Sheriff's Department could have bargained for the flexibility it desired, but it did not. Whenever a user puts copyrighted software to uses beyond the uses it bargained for, it affects the legitimate market for the product." *See* 447 F.3d 769 (9th Cir. 2006).

23. The Second Circuit held the adaptations were fair use, emphasizing that the use was "transformative" because it altered the original with "new expression, meaning, or message. . . . These twenty-five of Prince's artworks manifest an entirely different aesthetic from Cariou's photographs. Where Cariou's serene and deliberately composed portraits and landscape photographs depict the natural beauty of Rastafarians and their surrounding environs, Prince's crude and jarring works, on the other hand, are hectic and provocative." *Cariou v. Prince*, 714 F.3d 694 (2d Cir. N.Y. 2013). See also *Marano v. Metropolitan Museum of Art*, 844 F. App'x 436 (2d Cir. 2021) (holding that the Met's use of a photograph in an online catalog was fair use).

24. The court rejected fair use, looking primarily to the effect on the market for the copyrighted works: "By refusing to pay a licensing fee to AP, Meltwater not only deprives AP of a licensing fee in an established market for AP's work, but also cheapens the value of AP's work by competing with companies that pay a licensing fee to use AP content in the way that Meltwater does."

AP v. Meltwater U.S. Holdings, Inc., 931 F. Supp. 2d 537 (S.D.N.Y. 2013). Unlike typical search engines that return thumbnail versions of photographs or snippets of text, Meltwater provided the very information sought and so replaced the original works. Likewise, fair use did not protect a news clipping service, which charged clients for access to a searchable database of news clippings from others' copyrighted newscasts. *Fox News Network, LLC v. TVEyes, Inc.*, 883 F.3d 169 (2d Cir. 2018).

25. We need to know more, such as the length of the excerpts and whether there is a practical way for the university to get a license. All the fair use factors must be considered with the particulars of each use. *Cambridge Univ. Press v. Patton*, 769 F.3d 1232 (11th Cir. 2014).The court looked to whether practicable licensing agreements were available to universities. Where the works were not available to be licensed, such "electronic reserves" were more likely to be fair use. Where licenses were available, such as through the Copyright Clearance Center, fair use might still permit use of smaller portions. Under this case, by making copyrighted works available for licensing, a rights holder makes it less likely that unauthorized use would be fair use. One could see that as shrinking fair use because a publisher can inoculate its book against broad fair use by signing up with a licensing service. But one could also see it as benefiting users by encouraging publishers to make works available, which avoids the troublesome issue of figuring out how much use is fair—a little like buying copyright infringement insurance.

26. Well, the trial court held it was not fair use, because it would eat into the licensing control of those who expended efforts to create those useful works. Others would differ, on the theory that material drafted with the intent that it have legal effect should be free for republication. Indeed, on appeal (as noted earlier), the appellate court held that it could be fair use to post such standards online, and reversed and remanded for reexamination of the fair use issue; the court did not decide "the far thornier question of whether standards retain their copyright after they are incorporated by reference into law." *Am. Soc'y for Testing & Materials, et al. v. Public.Resource.Org, Inc.*, 896 F.3d 437, 441 (D.C. Cir. 2018).

27. The Ninth Circuit held that fair use did not apply. *Disney Enters. v. VidAngel, Inc.*, 869 F.3d 848, 862 (9th Cir. 2017). First, VidAngel did not stream an authorized copy of the movie, rather circumvented access controls and copying controls in order to make a digital copy from the DVD for streaming. Whether the customer owned the movie was not decisive. First sale authorizes one to distribute that copy, not to make more copies—otherwise one could buy one copy of a movie and make thousands of copies. Nor was the use transformative, because editing out content did not transform the work—and in any case users typically requested

little or no editing, but rather simply watched the movie. Nor did it qualify for time-shifting as under *Sony*, which involved a consumer copying a movie on a VCR for the consumer's later use. The Internet Archive case weighs against fair use, for a similar project with books, with less commercial purpose.

28. As discussed in the text above, the Supreme Court held that fair use protected Google. The use was commercial, but more importantly it was to make use of functional, nonprotected aspects. The use was transformative, in the sense that a new work was created. The amount of copying was that necessary to achieve the favored use. The market harm arose not from use of expressive elements, but rather nonprotected functional elements.

29. The Fourth Circuit thought not (reversing a decision that had quite alarmed photographers):

> But "regardless of the weight one might place on the alleged infringer's state of mind," we see no reason to tip the scales in Violent Hues' favor. Campbell, 510 U.S. at 585 n.18, 114 S.Ct. 1164. Whatever relevance good faith has to the fair use inquiry, Violent Hues has not offered any evidence that it acted in good faith. At best, Violent Hues appears to have acted negligently. Violent Hues' owner, Fernando Mico, stated that he believed the Photo was freely available. But contrary to Violent Hues' suggestion, this does not end the matter. For Mico did not explain why this belief was reasonable given that all contemporary photographs are presumptively under copyright, 17 U.S.C. § 302(a), and given his own acknowledgment that he downloaded the Photo from Flickr, which stated "© All rights reserved" in the Photo caption.

Brammer v. Violent Hues Prods., LLC, 922 F.3d 255, 266 (4th Cir. 2019).

CHAPTER 15

Moral Rights in Works of Visual Art

COMPARATIVE AND INTERNATIONAL CONTEXT

Franz sells the copyright in his novel to MegaPub. By publication, editors have metamorphosed Franz's tender tale of a struggling writer into a scary story of a hungry artist. Copyright law would not give Franz grounds to object. He sold the copyright, including the right to adapt the work. It would be different if Franz had sold a painting and its copyright (note that usually the artist just sells the painting and keeps the copyright). In the United States, copyright gives works of visual art special protection against modification, distortion, misattribution, and destruction, even where the artist has parted with the copyright.

Moral rights present a considerable difference between copyright law in the United States and many other jurisdictions. Many countries explicitly recognize several types of moral rights, including such things as rights of attribution (others must acknowledge the author and cannot wrongfully claim to be the author), rights of integrity (protecting against destruction or distortion of the work), and rights of disclosure (the right to decide whether and when a work will be published). *See* Robert Merges, Peter Menell, and Mark Lemley, *Intellectual Property in the New Technological Age*, 443 (Aspen 2003). Some give such rights as the right of withdrawal (to take a work such as a book off the market), the right to reply to criticism, and the right to resale royalties (aka "following rights," such as the right of a painter to receive a percentage if her work is sold, even long after she has sold the work). By contrast, copyright statutes in the United States have given little explicit recognition to moral rights, as such.

The different approach to moral rights is often cited as showing a fundamental difference in approach between U.S. copyright law and copyright law in other jurisdictions, especially Europe. Other jurisdictions may see copyright as a type of natural right. Because an author creates a work (a novel, a painting, some music), she should be able to control what happens to the work. The work is an expression of the author's personality. The author's reputation is tied to the work. Someone who injures the work, injures the author. In the United States, by contrast, copyright is thought to be less a matter of philosophy than of economics. Copyright law provides a basket of exclusive rights to provide an incentive for authors to create works.

The difference in approaches to moral rights was long considered a stumbling block to U.S. adherence to the Berne treaty, the leading international copyright law treaty. Berne requires its members to grant a measure of moral rights:

> Independently of the author's economic rights, and even after the transfer of the said rights, the author shall have the right to claim authorship of the work and to object to any distortion, mutilation or other modification of, or other derogatory action in relation to, the said work, which would be prejudicial to his honor or reputation.

Berne Convention for the Protection of Literary and Artistic Works, Art. 6bis. Berne, therefore, requires members to recognize an author's rights of attribution and integrity.

Effective 1989, the United States adhered to the Berne treaty. In doing so, Congress took what has been called a minimalist approach to moral rights. Congress could have broadly provided that all authors have rights of attribution and integrity with respect to their works. The general U.S. position, however, was that U.S. law already provided the protections required by Berne. Although the U.S. copyright statute did not explicitly grant rights of integrity and attribution, authors receive equivalent protections from various provisions of the copyright statute and other laws. If a work is distorted, for example, that could infringe copyright by creating a derivative work. Distortion of the work could violate the license under which the work was used, giving rise to a claim under contract law. Misattribution of authorship could violate trademark law as trademark infringement, false designation of origin, or simply false advertising. Misattribution or distortion that harmed the author's reputation could amount to defamation or unfair competition. In short, the United States did not amend its copyright statute to explicitly provide moral rights to copyright holders but instead relied on protections in existing law. Not long after joining Berne, however, Congress did provide such rights to "works of visual art," a narrow set of works, in the Visual

Artists Rights Act of 1990 (VARA), now set forth in section 106A of the Copyright Act.

The United States adhered to Berne without adding much in the nature of moral rights. What if a U.S. author felt that she was entitled to greater moral rights than U.S. law provides? Congress made clear that Berne is not self-implementing—meaning that individuals do not have rights that are enforceable under the Berne treaty itself. Rather, they have only the rights provided by U.S. domestic law. An author cannot sue in U.S. courts for violation of rights granted by Berne. What if one of the Berne countries believed that the United States did not provide sufficient protection for moral rights to meet the requirements of Berne? The Berne treaty does not provide an obligatory enforcement mechanism. Member countries can permit themselves to be subject to the jurisdiction of the International Court of Justice, but the United States has not done so for Berne. If one party to Berne believes another has fallen short, it can do little more than complain. The United States, for practical purposes, is the judge of whether it has met its obligations under the treaty. This is quite different from TRIPS, the treaty that brought intellectual property rights into the rubric of the World Trade Organization (WTO). As part of the WTO structure, TRIPS has a meaty enforcement procedure, providing for resolution of disputes and imposition of sanctions. The United States is also a member of TRIPS, which requires, among other things, that its members meet most of the requirements of the Berne treaty. A failure to meet a Berne requirement could result in the United States being subject to substantial penalties, but although TRIPS incorporates most of the Berne requirements, it specifically excludes Article 6bis with its rights of attribution and integrity.

RIGHTS UNDER THE VARA

Section 106A of the Copyright Act, entitled "Rights of Certain Authors to Attribution and Integrity," is the section of the copyright statute that gives the most explicit protection to moral rights. All copyright holders have rights under section 106, which provides for the exclusive rights of reproduction, adaptation, distribution to the public, public performance, and public display. Section 106A gives an additional set of rights to a narrow set of authors.

§106A. Rights of certain authors to attribution and integrity

(a) Rights of Attribution and Integrity.—Subject to section 107 and independent of the exclusive rights provided in section 106, the author of a work of visual art—

(1) shall have the right—

(A) to claim authorship of that work, and

(B) to prevent the use of his or her name as the author of any work of visual art which he or she did not create;

(2) shall have the right to prevent the use of his or her name as the author of the work of visual art in the event of a distortion, mutilation, or other modification of the work which would be prejudicial to his or her honor or reputation; and

(3) subject to the limitations set forth in section 113(d), shall have the right—

(A) to prevent any intentional distortion, mutilation, or other modification of that work which would be prejudicial to his or her honor or reputation, and any intentional distortion, mutilation, or modification of that work is a violation of that right, and

(B) to prevent any destruction of a work of recognized stature, and any intentional or grossly negligent destruction of that work is a violation of that right.

(b) Scope and Exercise of Rights.—Only the author of a work of visual art has the rights conferred by subsection (a) in that work, whether or not the author is the copyright owner. The authors of a joint work of visual art are co-owners of the rights conferred by subsection (a) in that work.

(c) Exceptions.—(1) The modification of a work of visual art which is the result of the passage of time or the inherent nature of the materials is not a distortion, mutilation, or other modification described in subsection (a)(3)(A).

(2) The modification of a work of visual art which is the result of conservation, or of the public presentation, including lighting and placement, of the work is not a destruction, distortion, mutilation, or other modification described in subsection (a)(3) unless the modification is caused by gross negligence.

(3) The rights described in paragraphs (1) and (2) of subsection (a) shall not apply to any reproduction, depiction, portrayal, or other use of a work in, upon, or in any connection with any item described in subparagraph (A) or (B) of the definition of "work of visual art" in section 101, and any such reproduction, depiction, portrayal, or other use of a work is not a destruction, distortion, mutilation, or other modification described in paragraph (3) of subsection (a).

(d) Duration of Rights.—(1) With respect to works of visual art created on or after the effective date set forth in section 610(a) of the Visual Artists Rights Act of 1990, the rights conferred by subsection (a) shall endure for a term consisting of the life of the author.

(2) With respect to works of visual art created before the effective date set forth in section 610(a) of the Visual Artists Rights Act of 1990, but title to which has not, as of such effective date, been transferred

from the author, the rights conferred by subsection (a) shall be coextensive with, and shall expire at the same time as, the rights conferred by section 106.

(3) In the case of a joint work prepared by two or more authors, the rights conferred by subsection (a) shall endure for a term consisting of the life of the last surviving author.

(4) All terms of the rights conferred by subsection (a) run to the end of the calendar year in which they would otherwise expire.

(e) Transfer and Waiver.—(1) The rights conferred by subsection (a) may not be transferred, but those rights may be waived if the author expressly agrees to such waiver in a written instrument signed by the author. Such instrument shall specifically identify the work, and uses of that work, to which the waiver applies, and the waiver shall apply only to the work and uses so identified. In the case of a joint work prepared by two or more authors, a waiver of rights under this paragraph made by one such author waives such rights for all such authors.

(2) Ownership of the rights conferred by subsection (a) with respect to a work of visual art is distinct from ownership of any copy of that work, or of a copyright or any exclusive right under a copyright in that work. Transfer of ownership of any copy of a work of visual art, or of a copyright or any exclusive right under a copyright, shall not constitute a waiver of the rights conferred by subsection (a). Except as may otherwise be agreed by the author in a written instrument signed by the author, a waiver of the rights conferred by subsection (a) with respect to a work of visual art shall not constitute a transfer of ownership of any copy of that work, or of ownership of a copyright or of any exclusive right under a copyright in that work.

Works Protected

The author of a "work of visual art" enjoys rights of attribution and integrity under 17 U.S.C. §106A. To be a work of visual art, the work must be a painting, drawing, print, sculpture, or photographic image (if the photograph was "produced for exhibition purposes only"). The provision does not provide a set of moral rights to authors generally. Such creative works as novels, poems, movies, and songs are not protected by section 106A, not to mention works like computer programs or useful articles. A work must also not be produced in great number—there can be no more than 200 copies, and the author must sign and number them all. 17 U.S.C. §101. Even visual works like drawings or photographs do not qualify if more than 200 copies are made, or even if individual copies are not specifically signed and numbered.

The statute explicitly excludes several categories of works with commercial or functional aspects. "Work of visual art" does not include

> [a]ny poster, map, globe, chart, technical drawing, diagram, model, applied art, motion picture or other audiovisual work, book, magazine, newspaper, periodical, data base, electronic information service, electronic publication, or similar publication.

17 U.S.C. §101. In addition, the rights do not apply to "any merchandising item or advertising, promotional, descriptive, covering, or packaging material or container." 17 U.S.C. §101.

The rights are also inapplicable if the work is a work for hire. Employees who create works of visual art do not have the protections of section 106A. If an employee paints a portrait as part of her work, she has neither VARA rights (because section 106A excludes works made for hire) nor the initial copyright (because the employer is deemed the author of the work). Of course, her contract may provide for a transfer of the copyright or oblige the employer to properly attribute her work or avoid distorting the work.

The VARA became effective on June 1, 1991. Its protections apply to works of visual art created after that date and works created before that date if the author had not transferred title to the work. It excludes protection for works created before June 1, 1991, if the author had sold or otherwise transferred title to the work.

In addition, the protections of section 106A apply only if the work itself is protected by copyright. The author would have no section 106A rights if the work had gone into the public domain because of a pre-1989 publication without a copyright notice or a failure to file a renewal of copyright or simply by expiration of the copyright. The VARA would also not apply if the work did not meet the substantive requirements for copyright: an original work of authorship fixed in a tangible medium of expression. But that is a low standard, so most works of visual art would qualify easily.

Some scope questions remain open. Is illegal graffiti protected against distortion, misattribution, and even destruction (for a work of recognized stature)? Courts are likely to limit protection for illegally created works, though one could see that protection against misattribution would not harm the building's owner, but preventing distortion or destruction might unduly burden one whose property was painted without permission. Another question is at what stage of a work protection vests. Courts have split on whether the VARA applies to an unfinished work.

So the VARA only applies to works of visual art. Authors of books, songs, photographs (if not limited to 200 prints) have no VARA rights.

Such authors may seek to protect themselves by contract. If the author licenses the copyright, they can use the license to forbid specified changes uses of the work.

Examples

1. *VARA protected?* Which of the following works would be protected by section 106A (aka the VARA)?
   a. The song "Pretty Woman."
   b. A Pulitzer Prize-winning photograph of a marathon winner taken by a news photographer for publication.
   c. An oil painting of the CEO of Megacorp painted by a Megacorp employee as part of her job.
   d. A lithographic print of a leaping lizard by Gratho. She made only 50 of the prints.
   e. A mural depicting the workers of the world made by the employees of a human rights organization for their headquarters. After the lease ran out, the property has been leased to a bank, which plans to paint over the mural.
   f. A 1966 painting by Picasso, which he sold in 1968.
   g. A 1966 painting by Picasso, which he never sold. It is out of copyright in the United States because of publication without a copyright notice in 1967.
   h. A creative painted banner depicting marathon runners made by an artist commissioned by Alligator Fuel Sport Drink. The banner was used as advertising at the Hendersonville Marathon.
   i. A 1990 painting by Ashley, which she sold in 1992 to a collector. Ashley also sold the copyright to the painting in 1993 to Alligator Fuel.
   j. *Falling Weather*, a still photograph by Geoff. He made only one print, for exhibition at his gallery.

2. *Unfinished*. Büchel, an artist, works on an installation in the Massachusetts Museum of Contemporary Art. In *Training Ground for Democracy*, visitors would play such roles as immigrants, activists, looters, and judges, working their way through installations ranging from a movie theater to an aircraft fuselage. The artist and museum, however, did not manage to finish the project together. When the museum proposed showing the unfinished work, the artist sued, claiming that would violate his rights under the VARA. Is an unfinished work protected?

3. *Burning question*. *La Contessa* is "a mobile replica of a 16th-century Spanish galleon for use at the Burning Man Festival." Extensively adorned, the bus still functioned as a bus, at least until the festival organizers banned the drivers for unsafe driving. Does VARA protect *La Contessa*?

Explanations

1. a. The VARA protects only "works of visual art," which must be a painting, drawing, print, sculpture, or photographic image. The song would not be protected.
   b. Photographs may be protected, but only if they are taken solely for exhibition purposes. News photos would not qualify, so the VARA does not protect this prize-winning photo.
   c. A work made for hire is not protected, even if it is a painting, drawing, print, sculpture, or photographic image.
   d. A limited-edition work may be protected, but only if the individual prints are consecutively numbered and signed by the author. That was not done here, so no VARA protection.
   e. A work made for hire is not protected, so not protected. *See Carter v. Helmsley-Spear*, 71 F.3d 77 (2d Cir. 1995).
   f. A work created before June 1, 1991, is protected only if the artist had not transferred title before that date. Picasso had sold it, so no protection.
   g. Works are not protected by the VARA if they are out of copyright, so no protection.
   h. The VARA does not protect "any merchandising item or advertising," so the banner would not be protected. *Cf. Pollara v. Seymour*, 344 F.3d 265 (2d Cir. 2003).
   i. The painting would be protected by the VARA. The fact that the author no longer owns the work or the copyright does not affect VARA rights (in post-1991 works).
   j. This photograph would be protected as a still photograph produced for exhibition purposes only.

2. The definition of "work of visual art" does not require a work to be finished. Not protecting unfinished works would leave a considerable gap. The court held that moral rights do apply to unfinished works, and so the artist had the right to protect his rights of integrity and attribution. *See Massachusetts Museum of Contemporary Art Foundation, Inc. v. Büchel*, 593 F.3d 38 (1st Cir. 2010).

3. Protected works include "painting, drawing, print, or sculpture," but not "applied art." The statute does not define "applied art." The Second Circuit reasoned that an object is applied art if it serves a useful function. A functional, adorned school bus was deemed applied art. *Cheffins v. Stewart*, 825 F.3d 588, 592 (9th Cir. 2016).

Scope of VARA Rights

The rights under section 106A track the general requirements of Berne 6bis to provide rights of attribution and integrity. Section 106A even draws much of its wording directly from Berne 6bis, but it also provides many limitations on those rights.

If Pamela paints a portrait, she has the rights to:

1. claim authorship of the work and prevent misattribution of her name as author to any work of visual art she did not create
2. prevent use of her name as the author in a manner that would be prejudicial to her honor or reputation, if the work has been distorted, mutilated, or otherwise modified
3. prevent intentional distortion, mutilation, or other modification of the work that would be prejudicial to her honor or reputation
4. if it is a work of recognized stature, to prevent destruction of the work

17 U.S.C. §106A(a).

In short, authors of works of visual art are generally entitled to receive attribution of authorship, prevent misattribution of authorship, and protect the work itself from intentional modification or destruction.

Each right is carefully circumscribed. The rights to prevent modification and to avoid attribution of authorship to modified works apply only where the author can show harm to her honor or reputation. The rights to prevent modification and destruction apply only to intentional or grossly negligent acts.

The right to prevent destruction has an additional requirement. The author of a "work of recognized stature" has the right to prevent any intentional or grossly negligent destruction of the work. How well known or critically acclaimed a work must be to be a "work of recognized stature" is not set out in the statute. Courts will likely look at such factors as (1) whether the work has been praised by experts such as other artists, curators, critics; (2) how well known the work has become; and (3) the artistic merit of the work (even though judges in copyright cases often shy away from aesthetic judgments).

The protections against distortion and destruction apply only to the work itself. Someone can make a distorted copy without infringing section 106A. They could also copy elements of the work into another work without infringing section 106A. Other acts that would harm the author's reputation would likewise not violate section 106A if they did not affect the physical work itself. Unfair criticism or slanted descriptions of the work, for example, would not fall within the scope of section 106A.

Works excluded from the category of works of visual art are also partially insulated from liability under the VARA. As stated above, VARA rights do not apply to many functional or commercial works, such as newspapers or advertisements. The "reproduction, depiction, portrayal, or other use" of a protected work of visual art in such a work is itself not subject to the rights of attribution, and such use of the work does not constitute "destruction, distortion, mutilation, or other modification" of the protected work. 17 U.S.C. §106A(c)(3).

One could argue that this is too narrow to meet Berne 6bis, which requires protection against "other derogatory action in relation to, the said work." Section 106A does not grant such protections as the right to reply to criticism (and such a rule in the United States might be difficult to square with the First Amendment).

The author has protections against only intentional modifications and intentional or grossly negligent destruction. The statute also expressly provides that modification that "is a result of the passage of time or the inherent nature of the materials" is not a violation. Likewise, modification that is the result of "conservation, or of the public presentation, including lighting and placement of the work" does not violate the statute unless caused by gross negligence.

Special provisions govern the situation where a work of visual art has been incorporated into a building. 17 U.S.C. §113(d). The author cannot prevent destruction or modification if the author consented to the installation before June 11, 1991, or consented in writing to installation with the risk of such removal. Otherwise, if the work can be removed without harming it, the building owner must first attempt to give 90 days' notice to the artist, who may remove the work at her own expense (and have ownership of the work). If the work cannot be removed without destruction or modification, then the artist retains the rights to prevent intentional modification or destruction—but those would still be subject to the requirements outlined above, such as prejudice to honor or reputation (to prevent intentional modification) or recognized stature (to prevent destruction).

The statute explicitly provides that VARA rights are subject to fair use. As discussed earlier, fair use of a copyrighted work does not infringe the copyright. Usually, fair use involves copying from the work for such favored purposes as education, research, criticism, or commentary. A parody version of a song or a novel may qualify for fair use when it criticizes or comments on the original. Applying fair use in the section 106A context would be interesting, because it would involve altering the work or misattributing authorship of the work. As yet, the case law on point is sparse.

VARA rights are not subject to the first sale doctrine. Under first sale, the owner of a lawfully made copy is entitled "to sell or otherwise dispose" of the copy without infringing the public distribution right in section 106(3). By its terms, however, that protection applies only to the section 106(3) rights. Section 109 does not authorize the owner of a lawfully made copy to dispose of the work in a way that would violate section 106A, such as destroying the work or distorting it. Likewise, the owner may display the copy without infringing the public display right in section 106(5). That right to display does not limit the rights in section 106A, but section 106A itself provides modification by "public presentation, including lighting and placement" of the work is not a violation.

The duration of VARA rights depends on the date of the work's creation. If the work was created before June 1, 1991, and the author had not transferred title before that date, then the VARA rights last as long as the copyright (potentially life plus 70 years). For works created after June 1, 1991, VARA rights endure for the life of the author. For joint works, the term is figured by using the life of the longest-lived author.

Examples

1. *How much protection?* Pamela painted a portrait of her niece, Vera. Pamela then sold the painting to Vera's mother, Maya. Which of the following would violate Pamela's VARA rights?
   a. Maya puts the painting on exhibition at a local gallery with a plaque stating that Maya painted the portrait.
   b. Maya covers the painting with a thin layer of transparent sealer, intended to prevent wear and tear to the painting. Pamela feels the sealer distorts the appearance of the painting.
   c. Maya lends the painting to the Museum of Bad Art, which exhibits it in a gallery of awful portraits of children. The museum puts an orange spotlight on the painting, making it look ghastly.
   d. Maya gets the painting back and uses her own paints to touch it up, changing the subject's expression and features and the overall mood of the painting. It makes the painting much worse. She then puts the painting on exhibit, attributing it this time to Pamela.
   e. Maya burns the painting on a chilly night.
   f. Gonzo takes a photo of the painting, uses software to widely distort it, and places the image online.

2. *Don't move.* A landscape artist created an integrated set of sculptures for a park. The owner of the park decided to remove the sculptures to make way for a new overall design of the park. The first artist argues that this would violate his right to the integrity of the work. Even if the sculptures were not physically modified or distorted in removing them, it would modify and distort the work as a whole, because it was an integrated, site-specific work of art. Removing it from its site, along with

the backdrop of the nearby oceanside, would be like painting over the background landscape in the *Mona Lisa*. Does the VARA prohibit moving the sculptures?

3. *Better to seek permission than forgiveness?* 5Pointz was a group of dilapidated warehouses. Artists created large graffiti paintings, with the permission of the buildings' owners. A leader selected works to preserve, and the 5Pointz appeared "in films, television, newspaper articles, blogs, and online videos, in addition to social media buzz." In time, the owners made plans to raze the buildings and develop the real estate. The artists asserted rights against destruction of their work. In response, the owners whitewashed the walls, destroying the 45 paintings. VARA liability?

Explanations

1. a. This would violate the right of attribution.
   b. The VARA provides that "modification of a work of visual art which is the result of conservation" does not infringe. The use of the sealant would be protected as a conservation measure.
   c. This may not violate the VARA. Placing it in the Museum of Bad Art might violate moral rights in some countries (as disparagement), but the VARA does not provide such rights. The VARA also provides that the "modification of a work of visual art which is the result of conservation, or of the public presentation, including lighting and placement, of the work is not a destruction, distortion, mutilation, or other modification. . . unless the modification is caused by gross negligence." The museum would argue that its lighting and placement of the work is protected, but it might qualify as gross negligence where an orange spotlight so changes the look of the work. The question would be whether the VARA extends the "modification" where there has been no change to the physical work itself. The statute does not define the terms, and there is little case law as yet. A possible defense would be fair use if the museum argued that it used the orange spotlight as commentary on the merits of the work.
   d. This would violate both the right of integrity (because Maya intentionally distorted and modified the work) and attribution (because the distorted work is attributed to Pamela in a manner prejudicial to her reputation).
   e. The VARA prohibits "destruction of a work of recognized stature." We do not have any facts suggesting that this is a work of recognized stature—critical acclaim, exhibition in museums (other than the museum of bad art), recognition by peers—so Pamela does not appear to have a right to prevent destruction.

f. The VARA rights against distortion and destruction under section 106A protect only the work itself, so Gonzo would not be liable under section 106A. He might, however, be liable for infringing the exclusive rights to make copies and to adapt the work (by making a derivative work), under section 106.

2. *Phillips v. Pembroke Real Estate, Inc.*, 459 F.3d 128, 137 (1st Cir. 2006), addressed this difficult conceptual issue about the scope of the right to prevent modification and distortion of the work. The court held that the case was addressed by the public presentation provision, which permits modification of "public presentation, including lighting and placement." The VARA does not give absolute protection to artistic integrity. Rather, with its various limitations and exceptions, the VARA represents a compromise between protecting the moral rights of artists and protecting the freedoms of others whose actions may affect the art. As the court put it, protecting outdoor art against any change in its lighting and placement could, in theory, put limits not just on the property owner but also on any neighbors whose use of their property could come within the scope of the artwork.

   Such a reading does not leave artists without legal protection. The VARA provides a gap-filling rule where the parties have not reached their own specific agreement. An artist may seek greater protection by agreement with the commissioning party. Such provisions could be made binding on future owners of the land through easements or covenants running with the land.

3. The works qualified as works of visual art. They also had attained "recognized stature," as evidenced by the curation and media attention. A building owner may destroy a work incorporated into a building, but only after giving 90 days' written notice—which was not done here. Rather, the owner deliberately destroyed the works before the dispute was settled. The court awarded the maximum statutory damages of $150,000 per work, for a total of $6,750,000. *See Castillo v. G & M Realty L.P.*, 950 F.3d 155 (2d Cir. 2020).

Who May Enforce VARA Rights

Berne provides that authors shall have rights of attribution and integrity "independently of the author's economic rights, and even after the transfer of the said rights." The VARA tracks this approach. Rights under the VARA are separate from ownership of the copyright and from ownership of the work itself. 17 U.S.C. §106A(e)(2). The author of a work, not the owner of the copyright or of the physical work itself, has VARA rights. If a painter sells her painting and sells the copyright as well, she still retains her VARA rights. Indeed, VARA rights may not be transferred, so any purported transfer of her rights would not be effective. Only the author has rights under the VARA, regardless of whether she still owns the copyright.

Although the rights are not transferable, they may be waived. The waiver must be in a writing signed by the author that specifically identifies "the work, and use of that work, to which the waiver applies." 17 U.S.C. §106A(e). The author may waive her VARA rights but must do so quite specifically in a signed writing.

The authors of a joint work of visual art are co-owners of the rights. A waiver of rights by one joint-waives such rights for all such authors. For joint works, therefore, one need obtain a waiver of rights from only one of the authors.

ALTERNATIVE SOURCES OF MORAL RIGHTS? HEREIN OF *DASTAR*

Section 106A provides protection for only a narrow category of works, but authors may also use other provisions of intellectual property laws to protect rights of integrity and attribution. Modification of a work, for example, could constitute preparation of a derivative work. Wrongly attributed works might also be infringing copies and could violate the new provision governing copyright management information, briefly discussed below. The right of termination (discussed below) prevents many authors from permanently giving up all rights in their work. More generally, trademark law and other areas of the law provide protections against some misattribution of works of authorship. Contract law can provide considerable protection. If a work is used in a way inconsistent with the permission granted by the author, there may be a breach of contract leading to damages and an injunction. *Cf. Gilliam v. American Broadcasting Companies*, 538 F.2d 14 (2d Cir. 1976).

If a work is published without consent of the author, there could be copyright infringement, and the Supreme Court has given considerable weight to the author's right of first publication. *Harper & Row, Publishers v. Nation Enterprises*, 471 U.S. 539 (1985). The right of withdrawal likewise can find some protection in the author's exclusive right to make copies and distribute copies. The rights of termination under section 203 of the U.S. copyright statute give something analogous to following rights. If a starving artist sells the copyright to his painting or novel, he has the inalienable right to reclaim it in 35 years. In addition, many states have moral rights laws. They are not preempted if they provide rights that are not equivalent to section 106A. 17 U.S.C. §301(f).

The U.S. Supreme Court, however, has held that the copyright statute limits trademark law as a source of rights of attribution. *See Dastar Corp.*

v. Twentieth Century Fox Film Corp., 123 S. Ct. 2041 (2003). In *Dastar*, plaintiff's copyrights in videos of historical works had expired. Defendants republished the videos after removing credits to the original producers. The *Dastar* court rejected the claim that such action misrepresented the "origin" of the videos in violation of the Trademark Act. Such a broad reading of origin would, in effect, give copyrighted works unlimited terms, because others could not publish the works even after they passed into the public domain. To preserve the distinction between copyright protection in the works and trademark law protection in indicia of source, the Court held that trademark law did not extend to mere use of public domain works.

Remember that contract law may provide some protection for moral rights. When licensing a work, the author may provide limits against changes or uses of the work. Playwrights, for example, often license plays with limits against changes in the play as performed under the license.

Example

1. *Iron hand.* Art Pictures sells thousands of copies of *Quack*, a book of photographs of ducks. Art Pictures holds the copyrights in all the pictures. Webby Crafts purchases several copies of the books. Webby cuts out various photos, glues them to decorative ceramic plates, applies a shiny gloss finish, and sells the mounted pictures in its boutique. Art Pictures knows it cannot sue under the VARA; this does not involve a limited edition of consecutively numbered photographic prints. But Art Pictures sues for infringement of its copyright, arguing that Webby has created unauthorized derivative works. Several chapters ago, we saw that courts differ on whether Webby is liable for infringing Art Pictures' exclusive right to prepare derivative works. How does this fit into the moral rights issue?

Explanation

1. As Judge Easterbrook put it, if this "counts as a derivative work, then the United States has established through the back door an extraordinarily broad version of authors' moral rights, under which artists may block any modification of their works of which they disapprove. No European version of droit moral goes this far." *Lee v. A.R.T. Co.*, 125 F.3d 580, 582 (7th Cir. 1997). The exclusive right to prepare derivative works can indeed protect authors against modification of their works, but if *any* modification of the work infringes the right to prepare derivative works, then the VARA would hardly be necessary. A better view is that preparation of an infringing derivative work requires preparation of a new work, with the requisite originality for it to qualify for copyright.

CHAPTER 16

Protections for Technological Measures and Copyright Management Information

Digital Rights Management (DRM) is a class of technologies that are used by hardware manufacturers, publishers, copyright holders, and individuals with the intent to control the use of digital content and devices after sale.

—*Digital Rights Management, Wikipedia, September 24, 2014, http://en.wikipedia.org/wiki/Digital_rights_management*

copy protection/n./: A class of methods for preventing incompetent pirates from stealing software and legitimate customers from using it. Considered silly.

—*Eric S. Raymond, The Jargon File, version 4.4.8, October 1, 2004, http://www.catb.org/jargon/html/C/copy-protection.html*

LEGAL PROTECTION FOR ANTICOPYING AND ANTIACCESS MEASURES

Copyright holders have long resorted to technical means to prevent or detect copying, from watermarked paper to digital watermarks. Early computer game programmers relied on obfuscation and slight format alterations, writing code such that copied games would not work correctly. To discourage circulation of unauthorized copies, some games required users to answer questions like "What is the first word on page 17 of the manual?" so one would need a copy of the manual to play the game. *See Copy Protection*, Wikipedia, October 22, 2014, http://en.wikipedia.org/wiki/Copy_protection. A user might need to register software, or have a special serial number, or plug in a dongle (a piece of encoded hardware). Videotapes, audio CDs, CD-ROMs, DVDs, and other media have likewise seen various attempts to control copying. The various devices and techniques prevented some copying. But just as they might frustrate some potential infringers, they also sometimes prevented use by authorized users. Historians, hobbyists, and archivists now sometimes struggle to circumvent copy protection devices on old software in order to study the old works.

More recently, digital rights management (DRM) technologies seek to both prevent unauthorized use and facilitate licensing systems. Ideally (from the point of the copyright holder), DRM would permit products to be efficiently licensed on different terms to different classes of users (one fee for individuals, one fee for companies), while preventing any use not authorized by the copyright owner. DRM could control how many times a work could be used and what levels of the work could be accessed and allow the copyright holder to remotely monitor or control use of the work. Users could benefit from these controls. By allowing copyright holders to tailor the products they offer, works could be made more widely available and consumers would have more choices.

Commentators raise many potential problems: DRM schemes—"crippleware" to critics—may prevent legitimate uses, such as fair use. DRM may lock up noncopyrightable elements of work by controlling access to them. DRM monitoring raises issues of privacy. Price discrimination between users may be unfair. The promises of DRM makers have not always withstood scrutiny by technologists. Various DRM systems have failed to work as promised, or have prevented users from getting promised content, or have even introduced potential bugs or security flaws into users' systems. DRM systems may also discourage innovation by discouraging adaptations and development of products that work together with existing products (although they may encourage innovation by hackers, both good and bad). *See* Jonathan Zittrain, *The Future of the Internet—and How to Stop It* (2008).

New types of protection for copyright owners were added to the Copyright Act in 1998 as part of the Digital Millennium Copyright Act (DMCA). Section 1201 now provides legal protection for two types of technological measures that copyright owners might use: anticopying technology and antiaccess technology. *See* 17 U.S.C. §1201. Such legal protection was said to be necessary (in addition to the practical protection provided by the technology itself) because electronic digital works are so easily copied and distributed. The legislation was also justified as necessary under the World Intellectual Property Organization Copyright Treaty, which requires members to

> provide adequate legal protection and effective legal remedies against the circumvention of effective technological measures that are used by authors in connection with the exercise of their rights under this Treaty or the Berne

> Convention and that restrict acts, in respect of their works, which are not authorized by the authors concerned or permitted by law.

WIPO Copyright Treaty, Art. 11, Obligations Concerning Technological Measures. Some commentators argued that the U.S. law already provided adequate legal protections through the broad definitions of the copyright holder's exclusive rights and through contributory infringement and vicarious liability. *See* Jessica Litman, *Digital Copyright* (2001).

The first class of protected technology is anticopying technology ("copying" is copyright lingo shorthand for the exclusive rights of the copyright holder to make copies, adapt the work, or publicly distribute, perform, or display the work). A copyright owner might use a technological measure to prevent copying of the work. Copy protection technology is frequently used on DVDs and video games, and less often on CDs and software generally. Streaming media may be used to allow a viewer to watch a movie without being able to make a copy of the movie. Older versions of copy protection included devices on software disks and videotapes to prevent copying (and accidental erasing). Someone in possession of a copy-protected item could use it, but could not make another copy (to the extent the anticopying device worked as intended—often the device is no more than a speed bump to a knowledgeable operator).

The other category of technological protection, antiaccess technology, is intended to prevent someone who has access to a copy of a work from being able to *effectively* access the work without permission. Pay-per-view movies are often transmitted in scrambled form. Some products in digital form are encrypted. One might have a copy of an encrypted e-book but be unable to read it without circumventing the antiaccess technology (that is, decrypting the copy). Such technology is intended to permit copyright holders to control the conditions under which the works can be used. Various rules (fees, amount of use, types of use, duration of the contract) could be implemented in code that limit access to the work.

Section 1201 has two types of prohibitions:

1. *anticircumvention rules*, which prohibit the circumvention of antiaccess technology
2. *antitrafficking rules*, which prohibit the making and selling of devices or services to circumvent either antiaccess technology or anticopying technology

See Digital Millennium Copyright Act of 1998, Copyright Office Summary.

Circumventing an antiaccess measure violates the statute, but circumventing an anticopying measure does not. The distinction was made on the theory that making unauthorized copies is often permitted by fair use, but (here some might well differ) fair use does not sanction unauthorized access. Moreover, where there is circumvention for purposes that are not protected by fair use, the copying could be copyright infringement anyway, making additional liability under section 1201 less necessary.

By contrast, the antitrafficking rules apply to both antiaccess and anticopying technology: Making or selling devices or services to circumvent either type of technology is prohibited. If I circumvent technology to make a copy of an e-book, I do not violate section 1201. If I circumvent technology to read the e-book, then I violate section 1201. If I sell goods or services to others for either purpose, I violate section 1201 (even, perhaps, if I sold my services to help them exercise their fair use rights).

The anticircumvention provisions may increase the copyright owner's legal control over copies no longer under her direct control. Under traditional copyright law, once an authorized copy was in the hands of others, the copyright owner's legal control over it was limited. The copyright owner had specified exclusive rights, which would be violated if someone made another copy, made a derivative work, or publicly performed the work. But under the first sale doctrine, the owner of the copy could publicly distribute or display the copy. Moreover, one could make many uses of the copy that did not fall with the exclusive rights. It is not copyright infringement to read a book, to privately perform a copyrighted work, or to copy unprotected material from a copyrighted work, but the anticircumvention provisions may allow copyright owners some legal control over the terms by which works are accessed.

A key issue will be how broadly courts construe the section 1201 protections. As discussed below, some courts may read the protections narrowly to apply only to the extent that someone seeks to defeat antiaccess or anticopying measures to infringe copyright. Other courts may construe the protections more broadly to find section 1201 violations even where the purpose of circumvention was to use uncopyrighted aspects of works or to make fair use of works. To put it very broadly, the argument might be framed as follows:

> Section 1201 should not be read to prohibit acts that are intended to exploit unprotected elements of works, or use those protected elements in a way that does not fall within the exclusive rights of copyright. Section 1201 should not apply where someone seeks to use functional aspects of works, or nonoriginal aspects of works, or seeks to make fair use of works, or simply uses the work in a way that falls outside the exclusive rights of copyright. Otherwise, that would extend the reach of copyright beyond its intended boundaries, perhaps even beyond the scope of Congress's powers, because Congress cannot give copyright protection to nonoriginal elements or to ideas. Suppose that an e-book contains the text of *Huckleberry Finn* (not copyrighted) as well as a page or so of new annotations. Maybe the annotated edition meets the minimal requirements for protection, because it has a few pages of new annotations added in.

> But if it is protected by antiaccess code, there should be no violation if someone simply wants to use the noncopyrighted text of *Huckleberry Finn*.

Versus:

> Of course section 1201 goes beyond the scope of protection in the existing Copyright Act. Otherwise, it would be superfluous. Rather, section 1201 is intended to allow copyright owners to determine the extent to which their copyrighted works are used. A copyright owner has no obligation to put her work out to the public at all. In the digital era, piracy is a huge risk to copyright owners. A work can easily be reproduced and distributed over the Internet. Section 1201 simply says that, if the copyright owner puts her work out to the public with technological controls on access or copying, then the statute will punish circumvention of antiaccess controls or trafficking in devices or services to circumvent antiaccess or anticopying technology. In other words, if someone gets a work subject to restrictions imposed by the copyright holder, she must respect those limitations.

Such general policies are likely to guide courts in interpreting the specific language of section 1201.

Anticircumvention Rule (Applies Only to Antiaccess Measures)

Section 1201 first prohibits circumvention of antiaccess technology: "No person shall circumvent a technological measure that effectively controls access to a work protected under this title." 17 U.S.C. §1201(a)(1)(A). In outline form, there is liability where:

a. the work is legally protected by the Copyright Act;
b. a technological measure effectively controls access to the work; and
c. a defendant circumvents the measure.

Whether a Work Is Legally Protected by the Copyright Act

Section 1201 applies only if the work is protected by the Copyright Act. Anticopying or antiaccess measures put on public domain works would not receive protection under section 1201. Section 1201 would not apply to works where the copyright had expired or the content was noncopyrightable (because it was nonoriginal, functional, or otherwise not qualifying for protection). But recall that some works, although largely unprotected, may have "thin" protection. A database of unprotectable facts may have sufficient originality in its selection and arrangement to qualify for protection.

A computer program is largely functional but nevertheless is likely to have protection at least against literal copying. Antiaccess or anticopying measures on such works may be protected under section 1201. This raises the hazard that a party could effectively get copyright protection on noncopyrighted material if section 1201 made it illegal to access the material.

Whether a Technological Measure Effectively Controls Access to the Work

To be protected by section 1201, a technological measure must effectively control access to a work. Protected antiaccess measures could include such technology as scrambling for cable movies, encryption of DVDs or CDs containing copyrighted content, and password protection for databases or online services.

A paradox arises when deciding which measures are protected. If an antiaccess measure is technologically successful, then legal protection would be unnecessary. If it completely prevented anyone from gaining access to the work, then the copyright owner could rely completely on the technological protection and need not worry about using legal measures. But the provision is designed to cover situations where antiaccess technology has not succeeded. The definition sets the bar for protection relatively low: A "technological measure 'effectively controls access to a work' if the measure, in the ordinary course of its operation, requires the application of information, or a process or a treatment, with the authority of the copyright owner, to gain access to the work." 17 U.S.C. §1201(a)(3)(B). The legislative history indicates that such protections would include encryption, scrambling, and authentication schemes (such as passwords).

The provision protects technology that controls "access" to a work. What constitutes access could be broadly or narrowly construed. The Federal Circuit took an approach that could significantly narrow the potential scope of the anticircumvention provisions. *Chamberlain Group v. Skylink Techs.*, 381 F.3d 1178, 1182 (Fed. Cir. 2004). It considered whether there was a section 1201 violation where a competitor sold a device that provided a "rolling code" necessary to activate a computer-controlled garage door opener. The plaintiff, a garage door maker, argued that the code was protected antiaccess technology because it was necessary to use the code in order to use the copyrighted program. Using the program, under this view, constituted making "access" to the copyrighted work.

The *Chamberlain* court rejected this view, holding that section 1201 applied only to limitations on access that are linked to copyright protection. It held that there was no "connection between Skylink's accused circumvention device and the protections that the copyright laws afford." The court reasoned that copyright does not protect the functional aspect of works but only their creative aspects. The device in question served only to activate the garage door opener, thereby triggering the function of the program, without copying any of its expressive aspects. Because the device did not serve to access the protected aspects of the work, it did not trigger the antiaccess provisions of section 1201. Hence, there was no liability for circumventing the code.

The Sixth Circuit has similarly rejected an attempt to use section 1201 to apply to protections against using a computer program, as opposed to making copies or other acts linked to copyright protection. *Lexmark Intl. v. Static Control Components*, 387 F.3d 522 (6th Cir. 2004). *Lexmark* considered whether a code sequence necessary to use a program on a printer qualified as a protected access control device. Someone in possession of a *Lexmark* printer could easily print a copy of the computer program, so the code sequence did not control access in the sense that it was an obstacle to getting a copy of the program. Rather, the code sequence was necessary to use the program, one of a number of programs that ran the printer. The court concluded that the code was not a protected access technology, because the code was not necessary to *access* the program; rather, it was necessary to *use* the program: "No security device, in other words, protects access to the Printer Engine Program Code and no security device accordingly must be circumvented to obtain access to that program code." The *Lexmark* decision rested on the difference between copyright law (which grants exclusive rights to make copies of works but does not give an exclusive right to use works) and patent law (which gives a stronger type of protection—an exclusive right to use the patented invention). If the copyright in a computer program could be used, via section 1201, to bar any unauthorized access to the program, then the copyright would effectively be an exclusive right to use the program.

If there is more than one way to access a work, then circumventing one barrier to access may not violate the anticircumvention provision. As *Lexmark* put it, "Just as one would not say that a lock on the back door of a house 'controls access' to a house whose front door does not contain a lock and just as one would not say that a lock on any door of a house 'controls access' to the house after its purchaser receives the key to the lock, it does not make sense to say that this provision of the DMCA applies to otherwise-readily-accessible copyrighted works." *Lexmark* held that the authentication sequence necessary to use a copyrighted program did not qualify as antiaccess technology because the code to the program was readily accessible by other means.

Lexmark and *Chamberlain* pose a significant barrier to companies attempting to use section 1201 to control aftermarkets, such as the markets for garage door openers and for printer cartridges. Under those cases, section 1201 may not be read to protect anticircumvention technology that is intended to govern use of products, as opposed to govern the exclusive rights under copyright. As *Lexmark* put it, "Nowhere in its deliberations over the DMCA did Congress express an interest in creating liability for the circumvention of technological measures designed to prevent consumers from using consumer goods while leaving the copyrightable content of a work unprotected."

By contrast, *Davidson & Assocs. v. Jung*, 422 F.3d 630, 641 (8th Cir. 2005), held that there was an anticircumvention violation where software developers used reverse engineering to create code that bypassed a "secret handshake" to play an online game. Unlike *Lexmark*, copies of the work were not readily accessible to the public. Unlike the program in a copy machine, the game program was not distributed to the public. Rather, users could access the game program only online. The *Davidson* court reasoned that the code not only affected noncopyrightable functional elements but also restricted access to creative expression and was therefore a protected antiaccess device.

Whether Defendant Circumvented the Measure

The prohibited acts are broadly defined. Circumvention is defined to mean "to descramble a scrambled work, to decrypt an encrypted work, *or otherwise* to avoid, bypass, remove, deactivate, or impair a technological measure, without the authority of the copyright owner." 17 U.S.C. §1201(a)(3)(A) (emphasis added). Various means of getting around a technological measure might fit under the statute. There could be liability for descrambling movies on cable TV, decrypting DVDs, or getting around password protection to gain access to a database of copyrighted music.

Not every act of hacking will constitute circumvention. Suppose that a copyrighted program controls a piece of machinery. Access to the program is controlled by encryption. The defendant makes a chip that can be used to replace the copyrighted program. The defendant plugs in the chip and is able to run the machinery. The defendant will not have violated section 1201, because the defendant did not circumvent the measure to gain access to the copyrighted work. The defendant simply replaced the copyrighted work without doing anything to the technological measure. *See Lexmark*.

There may be no violation where the defendant's acts did not facilitate infringement. *Storage Tech. Corp. v. Custom Hardware Eng'g & Consulting, Inc.*, 421 F.3d 1307, 1319 (Fed. Cir. 2005), held that there was no anticircumvention violation where the defendant accessed software to make use of the software permitted by the safe harbor for computer maintenance in section 117(c). Although the defendant circumvented a technological measure, the defendant's ultimate use was not infringement but rather authorized use of the software.

Unauthorized use of a work, by itself, is not circumvention of an antiaccess measure. The use of unauthorized passwords has split courts. Suppose a video game maker uses password protection to control access to the games. Each user must register, receive a password, and promise not to share the password with anyone else. One user tells the password to her friend, who then uses a copy of the game. In the view of some courts, the friend would not violate section 1201, because she did not circumvent the technological measure. Circumvention is "to descramble a scrambled work, to decrypt an encrypted work, or otherwise to avoid, bypass, remove, deactivate, or impair a technological measure." Rather, she used the measure according to its technical design (if not according to the legal rules). Other courts would hold that the friend circumvented the password protection technology, which exists to keep out those without authorized passwords.

One last requirement may sometimes hinge on contract law. There is liability for trafficking only for devices that circumvent technology "without the authority of the copyright owner." Suppose Business has purchased a copy of some expensive accounting software. Business, under the contract, is permitted to access the software. The software code contains access controls. Business hires an independent contractor to modify the software. If the contractor circumvents the access controls with the permission of Business, did it do so "without the authority" of the software vendor? In more general terms, can vendors of products use antiaccess measures to restrict the ability of others to deal with the vendors' customers? In addressing this question, courts may consider not just section 1201 but also contract law. Indeed, use of section 1201 to hinder competitors may constitute copyright misuse. *See* Dan L. Burk, *Anticircumvention Misuse*, 50 UCLA L. Rev. 1095 (2003). On the other hand, access given to customers should not open the door to unrestricted access to all comers.

Examples

1. *The poet didn't know it.* Delving through the archives, Researcher finds a long-lost 200-year-old poem, published only once in a local newspaper. Researcher wishes to strictly control circulation of the text. She encrypts a file containing the text of the poem and sends copies of the encrypted file to other researchers in the field. She separately sends them directions for decrypting the text. Interloper acquires a copy of the encrypted text by tricking one of the recipients. Interloper manages to decipher the encryption and gets a copy of the text. Has Interloper violated section 1201?

2. *Shell-fishing expedition.* Consulting Information has compiled a large database with information about the lobster industry. Consulting used considerable creativity in selecting and arranging the information. Consulting considers the database to be a valuable trade secret. It takes several measures to keep the information secure. Access is limited by encryption and password protection. Nevertheless, a competitor circumvents these technological measures and copies the entire database. Has the competitor

violated section 1201? What if the competitor had selectively copied only a small number of the entries in the database?

3. *Parton me!* Scruggs releases his new country music CD. This CD has special encoding. It will play in any consumer CD player, but the coding normally makes it impossible to make a copy of the CD. Fan borrows a copy of the CD and, after studying the encoding, manages to make another copy. Has Fan violated section 1201? Has Fan infringed copyright? Suppose that the code instead prevented someone from accessing the music on the CD. Would the answer be different?

4. *Maryland crab caper.* Sculptor keeps his latest creation, *Soft Shell Crab*, locked in a vault, protected with a combination lock. A burglar manages to enter the premises, jimmy the lock, and steal the sculpture. The burglar is certainly liable for trespass and conversion. Is the burglar also liable for violating section 1201?

5. *Fade to black.* Movie Co. sells copies of copyrighted movies on self-destructing DVDs. The DVDs are covered with a special type of volatile plastic. Once the DVD is removed from its case, it may be used for three days. After three days, the plastic degenerates and makes the DVD unviewable. The purpose of the technology is to simplify video rentals. Rather than renting videos for three days, stores simply sell videos that can be used for only three days. Chemist purchases such a DVD. She cleverly soaks it in a solution of preservative that nullifies the self-destructive property. She may now view the DVD as long as she pleases. Has Chemist violated section 1201?

6. *It's not just TV.* For a modest fee, Sharpie customizes cable service for homeowners (with permission from the cable company). By making a few choice adjustments to the homeowner's cable box, Sharpie allows the homeowner to access premium cable channels without paying the premium fee. Sharpie is sued for, among other things, violating section 1201. Sharpie argues that section 1201 is inapplicable. Section 1201 applies only if a technological measure effectively controls access to work. But, Sharpie argues, the cable scrambling does not effectively control access to the works. The scrambling is obviously ineffective, because Sharpie is so easily able to circumvent it. Would his argument succeed?

7. *Patients isn't a virtue.* Yonda the Yodeler operates a website that allows members to listen to her music online. For a small monthly fee, each member receives a password that allows unlimited access to Yonda's oeuvre. Patients, a thrifty and diligent fan, visits the website and tries several hundred times to guess a password. Finally, using a combination of Yonda's children's names, Patients guesses a valid password and is able to access the music. Has Patients violated section 1201?

8. *McBoxed into a corner.* McPix sells McBoxes, handheld electronic video game players, for a nominal price. McPix makes most of its money from selling game cartridges to use on the handheld players. An operating system computer program runs each handheld player. Only game cartridges sold by McPix will work with the computer program because of special coding in the program. A competitor cleverly builds game cartridges that, when inserted in a McBox, load another operating system computer program that runs the McBox and works well with any game cartridge. Has the competitor violated section 1201?

9. *Not my bad. Angry Burglars* is a popular, and copy-protected, video game. Jeremy hacks a copy and modifies the game to comic effect. Maddie uses the game to draw traffic to her website. Maddie has a license to use the game on her site, and the license does not prohibit using adapted versions, but is she liable for violating the anticircumvention provisions?

10. *Friend or foe?* Nitnik uses social engineering to walk past Dozey Corp.'s security desk. Walking amid the cubicles, Nitnik snags an employee's list of passwords. Nitnik uses one of the passwords to access a copyrighted database. Circumvention violation?

Explanations

1. Interloper has not violated section 1201, which prohibits circumvention of a technological measure that "controls access to a work protected under this title." The encryption did control access to the text of the poem, but the poem was not "a work protected under this title." A poem that had been published 200 years ago could not be under copyright. Section 1201 only applies to technological measures that protect works protected by the copyright statute.

2. The competitor has violated section 1201 by circumventing an antiaccess measure. The database is protected by copyright. Even though it consists mainly of noncopyrightable facts, it also includes copyrightable expression in the creative selection and arrangement of data. The competitor circumvented a measure controlling access to a copyrighted work, violating the anticircumvention rule.

   The result might be different if the competitor, after gaining access, had only copied a few facts (which are not protected by copyright), rather than the entire database. The copyright holder would argue that section 1201 prohibits circumvention without limiting it to circumvention that results in copyright infringement. But under *Lexmark* and *Chamberlain*, a court might hold that section 1201 does not prohibit circumvention intended only to exploit nonprotected elements of a work.

3. Circumvention of an anticopying measure does not violate section 1201, so Fan would not be liable under section 1201 for making an additional copy. The anticircumvention rule applies only to circumvention of antiaccess measures (not circumvention of anticopying measures), so the circumvention would not violate section 1201. By making the copy, Fan potentially infringes copyright—but may be protected by fair use or by the Audio Home Recording Act.

   Note that the answer would be different if Fan circumvented an antiaccess measure. That would potentially violate section 1201, which prohibits circumvention of antiaccess measures.

4. This example explores how broadly section 1201 can be read. The statute could be read to apply to this situation. The vault could be seen as a technological measure that effectively controls access to a copyrighted work. A measure controls access if the measure ordinarily "requires the application of information, or a process or a treatment, with the authority of the copyright owner, to gain access to the work." 17 U.S.C. §1201(a)(3)(B). To open a vault, it is usually necessary to use the correct combination to the lock. The burglar circumvented the lock by jimmying it open. Literally read, the statute could apply here. The counterargument would be that the statute was not intended to apply to this sort of situation and that the purpose of the statute should govern—not the broadest possible literal reading. Where the purpose was to steal a physical object, as opposed to doing something that would infringe copyright, courts might construe section 1201 to be inapplicable. This is all moot, of course, where the burglars are liable under various other criminal and civil theories.

5. The question here is whether the technological measure qualifies as an antiaccess measure, an anticopying measure (remember the anticircumvention rule applies only to antiaccess measures), or neither. Movie Co. might regard its special plastic as an antiaccess measure because it limits access to the work, but the definition applies to a measure that ordinarily "requires the application of information, or a process or a treatment" to gain access to the work. The degenerating plastic does not require information to give access; rather, it simply self-destructs three days after opening. One could again stretch the statutory language: To get access after three days, the chemist did have to apply a "treatment." But the better reading is probably that the measure falls into the second category, anticopying measures, because it "restricts or otherwise limits the exercise of a right of a copyright owner." Circumvention of anticopying measures does not violate section 1201. A court could also conclude that it falls into neither category.

6. Sharpie's argument would not succeed. The anticircumvention prohibition indeed applies only to a measure that "effectively controls access to a work." But that phrase is defined to mean a measure that ordinarily requires the application of information, a process or a treatment to get access. To "effectively control" does not mean that the measure is impossible or even difficult to get around. Awkwardly drafted, but it makes sense. There would not be a point to the statute if it protected only measures that were completely effective—because they would not need legal protection.

7. The question here is whether Patients has *circumvented* an antiaccess measure. Yonda would argue that Patients has circumvented the password protection technology. Circumvention is defined to mean "to descramble a scrambled work, to decrypt an encrypted work, or otherwise to avoid, bypass, remove, deactivate, or impair a technological measure, without the authority of the copyright owner." 17 U.S.C. §1201(a)(3)(A). Yonda would argue that Patients avoided or bypassed the requirement of an authorized password by guessing a password. Patients would argue that she did not "circumvent" it (in the sense of getting around it); rather, she used the technology. She submitted a password, it was accepted, and she was granted access—exactly the way the technology is supposed to work. One court has held in accord with Patients. *I.M.S. Inquiry Mgmt. Sys. v. Berkshire Info. Sys.*, 307 F. Supp. 2d 521, 532-533 (D.N.Y. 2004) ("Defendant did not surmount or puncture or evade any technological measure to do so; instead, it used a password intentionally issued by plaintiff to another entity"). Unauthorized use does not violate section 1201 if there is no circumvention.

8. The question again is whether the competitor has circumvented an antiaccess measure. It has removed the program containing the antiaccess measure and replaced it with another program. A court reading section 1201 narrowly would hold that rather than circumvent the measure, the competitor has simply removed it. In addition, the competitor did not try to access the computer program but simply deleted it. The better result would be that the competitor has not circumvented an antiaccess measure. Note that this assumes the code qualified as an antiaccess measure to begin with. A court might hold that if it simply controlled the *use* of the program, then it would not be protected under section 1201 because it did not control access in a way linked to the copyright holder's bundle of exclusive rights.

9. Where Maddie used the software only after the measures had been removed, she is not liable for circumvention. *MGE UPS Sys. v. GE Consumer & Indus. Inc.*, 612 F.3d 760 (5th Cir. 2010) (holding that there

is anticircumvention liability only where there is a showing that party engaged in circumvention, as opposed to used work after circumvention).

10. Some courts hold that using an unauthorized password is not circumvention of antiaccess technology. Rather, it is using the technology as intended, albeit without authority. Other courts regard the question more broadly, seeing use of the unauthorized password as circumvention of the password protection technology.

Antitrafficking Rules (Apply to Both Antiaccess and Anticopying Measures)

The antitrafficking rules apply to both antiaccess and anticopying technology. A defendant could be liable for selling software that circumvented anticopying codes in video game CDs or software that allowed the user to gain access to encrypted copyrighted games.

Anticopying Technology

What this book calls anticopying technology is really much broader. Section 1201 protects not just anticopying technology but also measures that protect any of the rights of the copyright owner. A technological measure "effectively protects a right of a copyright owner under this title" if the measure, "in the ordinary course of its operation, prevents, restricts, or otherwise limits the exercise of a right of a copyright owner under this title." 17 U.S.C. §1201(b)(2). It protects technology that prevents exercise of any of the copyright owner's rights: copying, making derivative works, public distribution, public performance, and public display.

Trafficking in Circumvention Devices/Services

Section 1201 prohibits trafficking in devices or services to circumvent either antiaccess or anticopying technology. The range of prohibited devices and services is broadly drawn, applying if the device or service:

1. is "primarily designed or produced for the purpose of circumventing," or
2. "has only limited commercially significant purpose or use other than to circumvent," or
3. is "marketed . . . for use in circumventing."

17 U.S.C. §1201(a)(2). The way defendant designed the device or service, what her customers use it for, and how defendant marketed it all provide independent bases for finding a violation of section 1201. Notably, a device or service with many legitimate uses could violate section 1201 if it was designed or marketed for circumvention. This approach prefigures the 2005 *Grokster* decision on secondary liability with its focus on the intent and marketing of the defendant.

The prohibited acts of trafficking include the "manufacture, import, offer to the public, provide, or otherwise traffic in any technology, product, service, device, component, or part thereof." The definition is broad. It would likely cover selling software intended to bypass access measures on video games, unauthorized cable boxes used to access cable TV without paying, or services by the hour to get around copy controls on digital content. Illegal trafficking in antiaccess technology was found where the defendant used his website to post computer code that could be used to decrypt DVDs, as well as link to other websites where the code was available. *See Universal City Studios v. Corley*, 273 F.3d 429 (2d Cir. 2002).

The definition is so broad that it can be plausibly read to reach such activity as publicizing information about the technology in DRM-protected products. Indeed, some companies have threatened DMCA actions against individuals who have publicly revealed security flaws in products. As a result, some have reported a chilling effect on technologists, with some reluctant to publish papers or report findings at conferences. Such a broad reading of the antitrafficking provision is unlikely to stand up to judicial scrutiny—but until the statute has been authoritatively read not to stifle such discussion, even the risk of litigation can be a considerable cost.

Courts Are Split on How Broadly to Read the Anticircumvention Rules

Some courts have held that there is a violation of the anticircumvention or antitrafficking rules only if the activity has a nexus to copyright infringement. *See, e.g., Chamberlain Group v. Skylink Techs.*, 381 F.3d 1178, 1182 (Fed. Cir. 2004). In this view, it would not be a violation to market software that unlocked a garage door opener or a video game if the party in possession of the work had authority to use it.

Ford Motor held that Autel did not violate the DMCA, by circumventing antiaccess measures in order to access diagnostic data in the vehicles. Autel copied data, but was not alleged to copy the aspects of a database that would be protected by copyright, which would be its selection, coordination, and arrangement of data.[1] *Ford Motor's* reading of the DMCA would narrow its scope, because the provisions would be violated only where a party was likely infringing copyright anyway. But the contrary reading would give copyright-like protection that would go well beyond copyright.

By contrast, some courts have directly rejected that interpretation. *See MDY Industries, LLC v. Blizzard Entertainment, Inc.*, 629 F.3d 928 (9th Cir. 2010). Copyright gives a set of exclusive rights (to make copies of the work, and to adapt, distribute, perform, or display the work). In addition, in this view, the DMCA created a new right to control access to the work, so circumvention to permit use beyond the scope of a license may violate the protections for access controls (because it permits unauthorized access), even if it does not cause infringement of copyright (because the users had a license, even though the circumvention allows them to use the software beyond the scope of the license). Under this approach, MDY was liable for selling Glider, software that allowed players of the online game *World of Warcraft* to use bots to play the game and progress more rapidly through levels. Glider circumvented certain technological controls that limited the uses of the *World of Warcraft* software. MDY did not infringe copyright, but it did violate the separate right to control access to the work.

Examples

1. *A rose by any other name*. Movie Company releases its latest blockbuster, *Botanic Gardens*, in the DVD format. Each DVD contains two types of digital rights management coding. One type of coding is intended to prevent the DVD from being copied. The other type of coding is a region code, which means it will play only on a DVD player built for the North American region. Idaho Software sells UNDVD, a program that allows users to circumvent both types of coding. Able uses UNDVD to make a copy of a *Botanic Gardens* DVD. Baker uses UNDVD to play the *Botanic Gardens* DVD on her home video game console. Which of the parties has violated section 1201?

2. *One plus one equals fun*. Mathematics Co. sells MathMad, a popular software package for mathematicians. The software has dozens of uses: solving equations, figuring out logic puzzles, drawing graphs, proving theorems,

1. *Ford Motor Co. v. Autel US, Inc.*, 2015 U.S. Dist. LEXIS 133201 (E.D. Mich. Sept. 30, 2015).

and so on. MathMad is marketed for use in all types of mathematics and related activity. Isaac, a video game enthusiast, uses MathMad to get around the copy protection coding on his favorite game, Ichabod. Isaac then posts a message to a newsgroup of similar fans, offering to sell his services to them to hack extra copies of Ichabod and other specific copyrighted games. Is Mathematics Co. liable for trafficking in anticircumvention services or products? Is Isaac?

3. *Grabbing the Minotaur by the horns.* Software Security launches its new product, Minotaur, a customizable digital rights management system that uses encryption, passwords, and various optical illusions. Minotaur is sold for use by music or video publishers to create pay-for-use systems for their respective products. Software Security announces that Minotaur's various security measures are "unbreakable" and offers a $100,000 bounty for anyone who can circumvent them. Within weeks, a computer science professor announces that he has figured out how to circumvent all Minotaur's security. He promises to release his analysis of Minotaur's flaws and algorithms to exploit them at an academic conference the following month. Software Security seeks an injunction, on the grounds that the professor would be trafficking in anticircumvention products or services. Would the professor violate section 1201 by making public the methods for defeating Minotaur's security measures?

4. *Is this a dagger which I see before me?* Modern copy machines are highly computerized. Commercial copiers are sold together with software that runs the machine, communicates with the user, and monitors dozens of parts. The software also interfaces with software that runs other components of the machine. For example, the toner cartridge also contains a microchip that monitors toner levels and temperatures and adjusts certain variables to keep the copies looking good. The copier software communicates with the toner software to keep the toner flowing for various sorts of jobs and to tell the user when the cartridge is due for replacing.

   Hexmark sells a line of business copy machines and replacement toner cartridges. The software on a Hexmark copy machine and the software on a Hexmark replacement toner cartridge interface using a "handshake" protocol. Unless the copy machine receives the correct handshake message from the cartridge software, it will not operate correctly. Macbeth competes with Hexmark in the market for replacement toner cartridges. To sell cartridges that will work on Hexmark machines, Macbeth programs its cartridges to send the correct handshake that the Hexmark copier will recognize. Hexmark sues Macbeth for violating section 1201, arguing that Macbeth is trafficking in a device to circumvent an antiaccess measure. Has Macbeth violated section 1201?

Explanations

1. This example is intended to clarify the categories of section 1201 liability. Section 1201 has one anticircumvention rule, which applies to circumvention of antiaccess measures. Section 1201 also has two antitrafficking rules, which apply to trafficking in devices/services to circumvent antiaccess measures or anticopying measures.

   The DVDs in the example have both antiaccess measures and anticopying measures. Idaho Software sells a program that allows users to circumvent both types of protection. Idaho would violate both of the antitrafficking provisions. Able used the software to circumvent the anticopying measure. This would not violate section 1201 because the anticircumvention rule applies only to antiaccess measures. (Of course, by making a copy, Able may be liable for copyright infringement.) By contrast, Baker uses the software to circumvent an antiaccess measure, and would be liable under section 1201.

2. Mathematics Co. is not liable for trafficking in anticircumvention services or products. For liability to obtain, the device or service must (1) be primarily designed or produced for circumvention, (2) have only limited commercial purpose other than circumvention, or (3) be marketed for circumvention. But MathMad does not fall into any of those categories. It is primarily designed for a whole host of mathematical uses, not just circumvention of the Ichabod copy protection. It has many commercial purposes other than circumvention. It also was not marketed for circumvention. The result would be different if Mathematics Co. behaved differently. If it sought to get into the circumvention business, by designing a product specifically for circumvention, or by marketing its existing products for circumvention purposes, then the Mathematics Co. would be liable.

   Isaac, by contrast, would be liable. He sells his services specifically for the purposes of circumventing anticopying measures.

3. This example, loosely based on a noted case, reflects the widespread concerns that the antitrafficking provisions have raised among computer scientists. The professor in question has become a leading commentator on legal and technical issues involving things like reverse engineering and DRM. (*See* http://www.freedom-to-tinker.com.) The argument that the professor violates section 1201 runs as follows. By publishing his analysis of Minotaur, the professor would enable others to circumvent Minotaur, which is an antiaccess measure. This would fall within the antitrafficking prohibition by providing a product or service that has no significant commercial purpose other than to circumvent Minotaur.

   That argument has several weaknesses. Publishing an academic analysis very likely would not be considered to be providing a product or service. Even if it were, the publication would not seem to fall into any of the three categories of trafficking. It is not designed for circumvention; rather, its purpose is to spread knowledge within the community of experts. It has purposes other than circumvention: increasing technical knowledge and warning others of possible flaws. One could argue that these purposes do not count because they are not commercial, but his activity in general is not commercial. Finally, he has not marketed the analysis for use in circumventing Minotaur.

The result might be different if he simply allowed others to download a program to circumvent Minotaur. The purpose would then be circumvention, not spreading knowledge about Minotaur.

4. This example is also loosely based on real events: the *Lexmark* case. Lawyers have crafted a number of arguments like this one to attempt to use the antitrafficking provisions as a device to limit the sales of interoperating products. A literal reading of the statute might indeed find a violation here, on the following theory: The program that runs the copy machine is a copyrighted work. The handshake protocol is an antiaccess or anticopying measure. The software on the replacement cartridge therefore is a product that circumvents the antiaccess measure, like password protection.

   A court could reject the argument on several theories. As commentators have strongly argued, this would stretch the statute well beyond its intended reach. A court could reason that the handshake protocol is not an antiaccess measure or anticopying measure but is simply a device for coordinating parts of a machine. To put that argument another way, the court could reason that the handshake protocol limits only purely functional, noncopyrightable aspects, and therefore does not trigger the statute. A court could also reason that the replacement cartridge software does not circumvent the handshake protocol but that it operates it exactly as it should. It permits the user to use her machine (as opposed to permitting an unauthorized user to listen to music she has not paid for).

Exemptions

Section 1201 contains a number of exemptions from liability. The list sounds like the sort of activities that are protected by fair use. One exemption applies to nonprofit libraries, archives, and educational institutions. Other exemptions apply to reverse engineering and encryption research. But the exemptions are so narrowly drafted that they are far from playing the broad role of fair use.

The exemption for nonprofit libraries, archives, and educational institutions, for example, allows circumvention of antiaccess measures under extremely limited circumstances. If a nonprofit institution is considering acquiring a copy of a work but cannot otherwise acquire a copy of the work to examine, it may circumvent antiaccess measures to get a copy it can examine. It can use the copy only to decide to see if it wants to permanently acquire a copy, and it must not retain that copy. The exemption applies only to the antiaccess prohibition; it would still violate the antitrafficking provisions for someone to provide software or services for the library to gain access to the copy. Rather, the library must presumably rely on the software hacking abilities of its staff to make use of the exemption, and, of course, if a library did such an activity (got access to a copy of a work for a brief period to decide whether to buy a permanent copy of the work), it is rather unlikely that anyone would have sued the library anyway. The exemption does little to protect the sort of activity that libraries are much more likely to encounter. If a library owns a copy of an encrypted work and wishes to get access for such purposes as education, archival preservation, or research, the exemption would be of no help.

The other exemptions are also limited. There is an exemption for reverse engineering, but one that would not cover the broad range of reverse engineering that would be protected by fair use. Reverse engineering means taking something apart (literally or figuratively) to see how it works. To reverse-engineer software, it is often necessary to make a copy of the software. To study software, one might print out a copy and peruse the code, make a copy to run the software and follow its behavior, or make a copy that may be analyzed by another piece of software. Such reverse engineering is done by people interested in learning about software for many reasons, from pure curiosity to interest in the technology to making similar products. Reverse engineering is directed to studying the functional aspects of works. Copyright does not protect functional aspects of works, so reverse engineering of many stripes qualifies as fair use with respect to copyright infringement.

But section 1201's reverse engineering exception is quite narrow: "a person who has lawfully obtained the right to use a copy of a computer program may circumvent a technological measure that effectively controls access to a particular portion of that program for the sole purpose of identifying and analyzing those elements of the program that are necessary to achieve interoperability of an independently created computer program with other programs." 17 U.S.C. §1201(f)(1). If someone has a copy of a computer program, she may circumvent antiaccess measures for the limited purpose of getting the program to work with other programs.

There is also an exemption for encryption research. A researcher may circumvent antiaccess encryption if that is necessary to study the encryption itself. In deciding whether the exemption applies, the court is told to consider whether the researcher disseminates her findings to other researchers (as opposed to potential infringers), whether she is a bona fide encryption researcher, and whether she asks permission of the copyright owner and shares her results with the copyright owner.

Another exemption serves to authorize self-help for privacy protection. It authorizes circumvention of antiaccess measures, provided such activity has the "sole effect of identifying and disabling" elements that collect or disseminate personally identifying information. Other exemptions authorize law enforcement activity, security testing, and access of minors to material on the Internet.

Section 1201 further authorizes the Librarian of Congress to effectively exempt a class of works from the antiaccess rule (not the antitrafficking rules), for periods of three years. As of 2024, the Librarian had exempted, among others, the following categories, which permit parties to circumvent controls on audiovisual works, for criticism or comment, for use in nonfiction multimedia e-books, for use in documentary films and other films where the use, for parody or biographical or historical work, or educational uses (such as Massive Online Open Courses)

- circumvent controls to make material available for captioning or to allow read-aloud function for disability services c
- enable wireless phones to execute software applications or connect to a wireless network, (also known as "jailbreaking")
- circumvent controls on computer programs, for purposes of good-faith security research
- circumvent controls to use obsolete video games
- circumvent controls on computer programs that operate 3D printers, to allow use of alternative material
- circumvent controls on computer programs, for purpose of investigating potential infringement of free and open-source computer programs
- circumvent technological measures for the purpose of diagnosing, maintaining, or repairing motorized vehicles
- circumvent access controls on computer programs embedded in commercial food preparation equipment (most notably, this enabled McDonald's franchisees to choose who could repair their ice cream machines)
- Circumvent controls on audiovisual and literary works, for the purpose of text and data mining for scholarly research and teaching

As with most of the other exemptions, these apply only to the anticircumvention rule. The antitrafficking rules may still impose liability for distributing software that accomplishes these tasks. The Librarian's exemptions may permit a person to jailbreak her iPhone or access a DVD to get a clip for a documentary or to get around an obsolete dongle on some old but useful software. The exemption would not authorize someone to post software to do those things online or to offer his or her services to people seeking to take advantage of the exemptions. The exemptions, on their face, give protection only to rather sophisticated users. Having said that, recall that courts are split on how broadly to interpret the antitrafficking provisions. Courts that read them narrowly (to prohibit trafficking only that has a nexus to copyright infringement) might likewise hold that trafficking is permitted where it permits someone to take advantage of an exemption.

Issues of Fair Use and Freedom of Speech

The section 106 exclusive rights of a copyright holder are subject to many limitations. The copyright does not protect unprotected elements, such as ideas, functional aspects, and nonoriginal elements. It is not copyright infringement to copy such unprotected elements from a copyrighted work. The rights of a copyright owner are further limited by the fair use doctrine. Another may copy (or make derivative works or publicly distribute, display, or perform) a copyrighted work, if the use is a fair use. The exclusive rights to publicly display and distribute the work are also limited by the first sale doctrine.

But section 1201 rights are not explicitly made subject to any of those limitations. In particular, the provision does not provide that antiaccess or anticopying technology may be circumvented for the purposes of fair use. Rather, section 1201 separates the section 1021 liability from copyright infringement: "Nothing in this section shall affect rights, remedies, limitations, or defenses to copyright infringement, including fair use, under this title." 17 U.S.C. §1201(c)(1). On its face, section 1201 could be read to prohibit circumvention or trafficking, even where the activity is intended to make fair use of copyrighted materials or to use unprotected elements of copyrighted works.

Section 1201 may permit copyright owners, in effect, to protect unprotected aspects of works. For example, under *Feist*, the facts in a database are not protected by copyright. If a company expended great resources in compiling a database, it would nevertheless not have copyright protection in the facts. Anyone who copied facts from the database would not infringe copyright, but some elements of the database may be protected. Provided that the compiler used a modicum of creativity, her selection and arrangement of the facts could qualify as protected expression. Other works also have "thin" protection. Works that are largely unoriginal or functional may have some creative elements that are protected by copyright.

If the work qualifies for copyright protection, then it would qualify also for the protections of section 1201. If the copyright owner encrypted the database to prevent unauthorized access or used digital rights management software to limit the number of copies made, then such technological measures could be protected by section 1201. If someone circumvented the antiaccess measure or provided services to circumvent either antiaccess measures or anticopying measures, then that could be held to violate section 1201. Under some readings of section 1201, this would be true even if the underlying activity would not have infringed copyright. If the purpose of the activity was to copy unprotected facts or ideas or to make an educational fair use, section 1201 would still be violated.

Although section 1201 does not contain an explicit fair use provision, courts may read fair use into the statute. The first federal appellate court to address section 1201 rejected that approach. *See Universal City Studios v. Corley*, 273 F.3d 429 (2d Cir. 2002). *Corley* declined either to read fair use into section 1201 or to analyze whether the lack of fair use would be an unconstitutional limitation on free speech. *Corley* relied on the proposition that "the Supreme Court has never held that fair use is constitutionally required, although some isolated statements in its opinions might arguably be enlisted for such a requirement."

In a case decided after *Corley*, however, the Supreme Court strongly indicated that fair use is indeed constitutionally required. *Eldred v. Ashcroft*, 123 S. Ct. 769 (2003), relied on fair use to uphold the constitutional status of copyright law. In upholding a copyright term extension, *Eldred* declined to apply strict scrutiny under the First Amendment to copyright legislation. Rather, *Eldred* held that First Amendment safeguards within copyright law, namely fair use and the idea/expression dichotomy, were sufficient to protect free speech interests. Accordingly, *Eldred* held that First Amendment scrutiny was unnecessary where Congress had not "altered the traditional contours of copyright."

Eldred could affect the application of section 1201 in two ways. First, courts could reason that at least some fair use must be read into section 1201, because fair use is such a central concept of copyright. Alternatively, the question would arise whether section 1201 is subject to strict scrutiny under the First Amendment. Strict scrutiny would apply where Congress had altered the "traditional contours of copyright." Commentators have widely described section 1201 as departing from traditional copyright protection. Section 1201 grants broader rights than traditional copyright without the traditional safeguards of copyright. The counterargument would be that section 1201 simply adapts a long-standing copyright tool (secondary liability) to a new class of copyrighted works.

The Federal Circuit considered *Eldred* in reading some fair use protections into section 1201:

> [A]s the Supreme Court recently explained, "Congress' exercise of its Copyright Clause authority must be rational." *Eldred v. Ashcroft*, 537 U.S. 186, 205 n.10, 154 L. Ed. 2d 683, 123 S. Ct. 769 (2003). In determining whether a particular aspect of the Copyright Act "is a rational exercise of the legislative authority conferred by the Copyright Clause . . . we defer substantially to Congress. It is Congress that has been assigned the task of defining the scope of the limited

> monopoly that should be granted to authors... in order to give the public appropriate access to their work product." *Id.* at 204-05. Chamberlain's proposed construction of section 1201(a) implies that in enacting the DMCA, Congress attempted to "give the public appropriate access" to copyrighted works by allowing copyright owners to deny all access to the public. Even under the substantial deference due Congress, such a redefinition borders on the irrational.

Chamberlain Group v. Skylink Techs, 381 F.3d 1178, 1200 (Fed. Cir. 2004).

The *Chamberlain* court also considered the potential effect on fair use, under the plaintiff's reading of the statute. "It would therefore allow any copyright owner, through a combination of contractual terms and technological measures, to repeal the fair use doctrine with respect to an individual copyrighted work—or even selected copies of that copyrighted work." In other words, there would be no effective ability to take advantage of the fair use doctrine, even with respect to a widely distributed work. Copyright holders would tilt the balance of protections under the statute.

In analyzing the application of section 1201, one should be aware that important questions remain to be addressed: whether courts will read fair use into the statute and whether courts will limit the reach of the statute to protect free speech rights. *See also* Dan L. Burk and Julie Cohen, *Fair Use Infrastructure for Copyright Management Systems*, 15 Harv. J.L. & Tech. 41 (2001).

In 2024, the DC Circuit rejected the argument that it violated the First Amendment to bar circumvention of controls on expressive works. The court reasoned that breaking technological controls was not a form of expressive conduct. *Green v. United States DOJ*, 2024 U.S. App. LEXIS 19261, at *30-31 (D.C. Cir. Aug. 2, 2024)("The First Amendment protects a right to read, but it does not grant unimpeded access to every reading material a reader might wish for. Similarly, the First Amendment does not guarantee potential fair users unfettered or privileged access to copyrighted works they seek to use in their own expression.").

Examples

1. *Today's trash, tomorrow's treasure.* The Pop Culture Museum preserves various passing fancies of American teenagers. Its video game vault has hundreds of video games. Museum is considering whether to acquire copies of several dozen games. It has copies of the games, but they all contain copy-protection and antiaccess technology. Museum's employees lack the technical expertise to get around the coding. Klever Consulting offers its services, for a fee, to get around the coding. Museum simply wants to view the games to see if it should pay to acquire permanent copies. If Museum hires Klever, would section 1201 be violated?

2. *Too smart for their own good.* Moozik sells CDs of music that have encryption coding, both to limit access to the music and to prevent unauthorized copying. The engineers at Sonic Labs decide to study Moozik's encryption coding. They buy several of Moozik's CDs and study them using several methods, such as visual inspection of the CDs and mechanized analysis of the contents of the CDs. The engineers manage to work around both the copy protection and the antiaccess protection. When Moozik accuses them of violating section 1201, the engineers respond that they were simply engaged in reverse engineering and are therefore protected by both fair use in copyright and the exemptions for reverse engineering and for encryption research in section 1201. Have they violated section 1201?

3. *Is it right to write?* Return to the example on page 362, about the professor publishing his analysis of a digital rights management system. Assume (contrary to the analysis above) that his publication potentially violated section 1201. Would he be protected by the encryption research exception, fair use, or the First Amendment?

Explanations

1. Klever might violate section 1201 if it was hired by the Museum and circumvented the antiaccess measures. This result may seem a little strange. If Museum itself circumvented the antiaccess measures, Museum would not violate section 1201. Museum would be able to use the exemption for nonprofit libraries, archives, and educational institutions, provided it stayed within the very narrow confines of the exemption. It circumvented the protection only to decide whether to acquire a copy, no other means to examine a copy was reasonably available, and the Museum retained the copy no longer than necessary for that purpose and used it for no other purpose. But the exemption (like most of the exemptions) applies only to the anticircumvention rule. It would not apply to violation of the antitrafficking rule. If Klever sold its services to circumvent the antiaccess measure, Klever would violate the antitrafficking rule and would not be protected by the exemption. A court that read fair use into section 1201, however, might hold that Klever is protected by fair use.

   This points to an important point about the exemptions. They are all narrowly drafted, and most of them give protection only with respect to the anticircumvention rule, not with respect to the antitrafficking rules. The exemptions, standing alone, are truly narrow and likely to afford little protection for many activities protected by fair use in the context of copyright infringement.

2. The engineers would not qualify for the reverse engineering exemption. It does not protect reverse engineering in general but applies only to a very narrow range of reverse engineering: circumventing an antiaccess measure "for the sole purpose" of analyzing it to create software that works with it. The engineers were not simply trying to build a compatible product; they were using reverse engineering to study the product generally.

   The engineers, however, may well qualify for the encryption research exemption. They would have to show that their purpose was to increase knowledge about encryption or to develop products and that they first sought permission before resorting to circumvention. In addition, the court is told to consider whether the engineers published their analysis for other researchers and disclosed the results to Moozik. So encryption research does get a little broader protection than other types of reverse engineering.

3. The encryption research exception applies only to the antiaccess rule, not to the antitrafficking rules, so it would not protect publication of the professor's analysis.

   Does fair use protect publication? Section 1201 does not appear to have any general fair use provision, so fair use would apparently not apply to any violation of section 1201. It is possible, however, that courts would read at least some fair use protection into the statute.

   Would the First Amendment apply? These are also uncharted waters, but the basis analysis runs as follows. First, even after *Eldred*, the First Amendment scrutiny will apply to protections that go beyond the traditional contours of copyright. The new antitrafficking provisions would seem to go beyond traditional copyright, unless a court sees them as simply an upgrade of secondary liability for the digital age. The question would then be, what level of First Amendment scrutiny would apply? This book leaves the specific analysis for future case law, but it is likely that the First Amendment would not permit the prohibition of publishing ideas about encryption products simply to protect the rights of copyright holders. Rather, more narrowly tailored protections would be required.

STANDING AND REMEDIES

Any person injured by a violation of section 1201 may bring a civil action under section 1203. A copyright holder who has used anticopying or antiaccess measures would have standing to sue an alleged violator of section 1201, but others may also have standing to sue because section 1203 does not require that the plaintiff be the copyright holder; she must only be "injured by a violation of section 1201." A cable company that uses scrambling to control access to movies may have standing to sue, even though the cable company does not own the copyright to the movies (it simply has permission to broadcast them).

The statute provides a range of remedies for violation of section 1201. The court may grant injunctions to prevent or restrain violations. 17 U.S.C. §1203(b). The court may also award actual damages and restitution of the violator's profits. 17 U.S.C. §1203(c). Rather than actual damages and profits, the plaintiff may elect statutory damages in the "sum of not less than $200 or more than $2,500 per act of circumvention, device, product, component, offer, or performance of service, as the court considers just." 17 U.S.C. §1203(c)(3). The court may also reduce or remit damages for innocent violations where the defendant reasonably did not know its acts constituted a violation. 17 U.S.C. §1203(c)(5). The statute also provides for criminal penalties where the violation is done "willfully and for purposes of commercial advantage or private financial gain." 17 U.S.C. §1204. The penalties are substantial: a fine of up to $500,000 and a prison term of up to five years for the first offense.

LEGAL PROTECTIONS FOR COPYRIGHT MANAGEMENT INFORMATION

Section 1202 protects the integrity of "copyright management information." Copyright management information is defined to include information identifying the work, such as the title, people such as the author, the copyright owner, performers, writers, and directors, and others, as well as terms and conditions for use of the work.

Section 1202 prohibits providing or distributing false copyright information or removing or altering copyright information with the intent to cause copyright infringement. This is a relatively high standard. Giving false information or altering existing information by itself will not violate section 1202. Only if there is intent to "induce, enable, facilitate, or conceal" copyright infringement is there a violation of section 1202.

One open issue is how broadly the protection for "copyright management information" extends. Protection could be limited to information in digital form. Under this approach, only information that served as part of an automated digital rights management system, such as encoded information about the work and its associated licensing information, would likely qualify, but one can read the statute broadly enough to cover information in any form. Under this view, it could violate the statute to remove printed material, such as a copyright notice or terms of use.

Example

1. *Sin of omission*. Clara pulls a photo offline and puts it on her personal website, to illustrate a joke to her family. That would be fair use. But if, in the process of posting the photo, she unknowingly stripped away the copyright notice, would she be liable for removing copyright management information?

Explanation

1. No. There is only a violation for removal or alteration with the intent to cause copyright infringement. Clara did not intentionally remove the information, nor did she intend to cause copyright infringement.

PART IV

Copyright Litigation

CHAPTER 17

Jurisdiction, Standing, and the Elements of an Infringement Action

JURISDICTION

"Arising Under" the Copyright Law

Copyright cases are federal cases. Federal trial courts have exclusive jurisdiction over any civil action "arising under" the copyright statute. 28 U.S.C. §1338. "Exclusive jurisdiction" means that federal trial courts can hear copyright cases and that state courts are excluded from hearing them.

A state law claim does not give a federal court jurisdiction to hear a case (although there may be another basis for jurisdiction, such as diversity of citizenship). Just because a copyright is involved in a case does not make it one "arising under" the copyright laws. Suppose Author sells book rights to Publisher, for a payment of 15 percent of Publisher's sales. Publisher sells millions of copies but never sends Author a check. Author's lawsuit against Publisher will simply be a state law contract action, for failing to pay the promised money. Change the facts, and it becomes a copyright infringement action: Publisher, without Author's permission, makes and distributes a movie out made from the book. Author sues. This time, Author would be suing for copyright infringement: infringing Author's reproduction, adaptation, distribution, and performance rights.

Sometimes there is an issue as to whether a case is a federal copyright case or simply a state law contract case. Suppose Author had signed a contract granting Publisher the right to make and distribute "books" for a fixed payment of $100,000. Publisher promises not to do anything beyond the scope of the license. Publisher sells plenty of paper books. Then Publisher makes and distributes the book in electronic form. Author sues, contending Publisher got the right only to publish the book in paper form. Is it a contract case about the scope of rights granted to Publisher? Or is it a copyright case about Publisher's infringement of Author's exclusive rights to, among other things, distribute the book in electronic form?

Under the most-followed test for resolving the issue, a case "arises under" the Copyright Act if:

1. the complaint is for a remedy expressly granted by the act (such as damages or an injunction as a remedy for copyright infringement), or
2. asserts a claim requiring construction of the act, or
3. presents a case where a distinctive policy of the act requires that federal principles control the disposition of the claim.

T. B. Harms Co. v. Eliscu, 339 F.2d 823, 828 (2d Cir. 1964).

In short, the court has jurisdiction if there is a claim for copyright infringement, or if the claim requires deciding how the Copyright Act would apply to the case, or if an important policy of the Copyright Act is at stake.

Registration of the Copyright as a Prerequisite for Filing an Infringement Suit

No registration is required to have a copyright. A work is copyrighted as soon as it is fixed in tangible form (or, for pre-1977 works, was published with a copyright notice or was properly registered), but (for U.S. works) registration is required before bringing a copyright infringement action. "No action for infringement of the copyright in any United States work shall be instituted until registration of the copyright claim has been made in accordance with this title." 17 U.S.C. §411(a). Foreign copyright holders are excused from the registration requirement.

There are three exceptions to the registration requirement (and a special rule for bootlegged recordings). First, it applies only to actions concerning "United States works," meaning works first published in the United States, unpublished works by U.S. residents, or works originating in a country that is not party with the United States to a copyright treaty. Second, it does not apply to an action for infringement under the section 106A moral rights in a work of visual art. Third, refusal by the Copyright Office to register the work does not prevent an infringement action. Rather, if the applicant has delivered the deposit, application, and fee in proper form and the Copyright Office has refused registration, then the infringement action may be brought. 17 U.S.C. §411(a).

The Supreme Court has applied the statute literally. There is no jurisdiction if an application has been filed but neither registration nor refusal has occurred yet. *Fourth Estate Pub. Benefit Corp. v. Wall-Street.com, LLC*, 139 S. Ct. 881 (2019). This can delay an infringement action. A copyright holder who has not registered must first file an application and wait for the registration to issue, which can take months. That delay, likely of some months, can be important in such time-sensitive markets as New York's fashion district or music community, where the holder of an unregistered copyright needs to shut down an infringer as quickly as possible. Likewise, if registration has been refused, there is no jurisdiction unless the applicant has delivered the deposit, application, and fee in proper form—so a defect in the application would bar a lawsuit. But some courts have held that "a plaintiff who files a copyright infringement lawsuit before registering with the Copyright Office may cure the section 411 defect by subsequently amending or supplementing its complaint once it has registered the copyright." *Positive Black Talk, Inc. v. Cash Money Records, Inc.*, 394 F.3d 357, 365 (5th Cir. 2004).

Reed Elsevier addressed a long-standing issue: whether registration of a copyright is a jurisdictional requirement to bring an infringement action or just a condition, which may be excused in some cases. *Reed Elsevier, Inc. v. Muchnick*, 559 U.S., 130 S. Ct. 1237, 176 L. Ed. 2d 18, 26-28 (2010). The distinction has great weight. If a requirement is jurisdictional, then failure to meet the requirement means that the action must be dismissed—even if the case is on appeal when the issue is first raised. It also means that parties (as in *Reed Elsevier*) who have not registered their works may not be parties to a lawsuit. This could considerably complicate resolution of issues that involve large number of copyrights, some registered and others not. In *Reed Elsevier*, the Supreme Court held that the provision was not jurisdictional. Therefore, a federal district court had jurisdiction over a class action brought by freelance authors claiming infringement by the Google Books project, even though not all the allegedly infringed works were registered. The Court, however, acknowledged that the statute generally requires registration before litigation, suggesting that the requirement will be relaxed only in unusual cases, which may enable courts to resolve otherwise nonjudiciable complex copyright issues.

Examples

1. *Federal or state court?* Suppose Wolfgang has registered the copyright in the musical work "Symphony with the Devil," listing himself as the author. Would there be federal jurisdiction over the following cases?
   a. Wolfgang sues a record company, alleging breach of contract because the record company has terminated its agreement to record and distribute the work.

b. Wolfgang sues another record company, alleging copyright infringement, seeking damages and an injunction because the record company has recorded and distributed the work without authorization.
c. Sally sues Wolfgang, alleging that she is a joint author of the work and therefore entitled to some of the royalties Wolfgang has collected. The suit will require interpreting the meaning of "joint author" and defining the duties of a joint author under the copyright statute.
d. Sally sues Wolfgang, alleging that he transferred ownership of the copyright to her. The issue in the case will be whether one of the parties breached their rather ambiguously drafted contract.

2. *No registration, no infringement?* Twain files a copyright infringement lawsuit against Austen, alleging that she infringed the copyright in Twain's book by making and selling unauthorized electronic copies. Austen files a motion to dismiss, on the grounds that Twain did not register his copyright until long after the alleged infringement occurred. Rather, Twain registered his copyright shortly before filing the infringement action. Should the suit be dismissed?

3. *Dangling pointer.* Airframe sues L-3, alleging infringement of a copyrighted software program. Before suing, Airframe dutifully registers its copyright and deposits a copy of the original 2003 version. In the litigation, Airframe alleges infringement by copying elements that were added to its 2009 version of the software. Infringement?

Explanations

1. a. No federal jurisdiction. Under *TB Harms*, the case arises under the Copyright Act if there is a claim for copyright infringement, if the claim requires construction of the act, or if a distinctive policy of the Act requires that federal principles control the disposition of the claim. None of those apply here, where there is simply allegation of breach of contract under state law.
   b. There is federal jurisdiction here, where the claim is for copyright infringement.
   c. There is probably federal jurisdiction, because deciding the claim entails construction of the act (interpreting the meaning of "joint author" and defining the duties of a joint author).
   d. There would be no federal jurisdiction. The case is about copyright ownership, like the last problem. But there are no copyright issues to decide, whereas the last problem required interpretation of "joint author" under the Copyright Act. Rather, the court will decide only state contract law issues.

2. Twain's suit should not be dismissed. Registration is not a condition for copyright protection. A work is copyrighted as soon as it is fixed in tangible form. Infringement of an unregistered copyright is still infringement (although if the copyright has been registered before the infringement, there are more remedies available, such as attorney's fees and statutory damages). Registration must be done before filing the lawsuit (for U.S. works).

3. A party must register the work before suing for infringement, and can only recover for infringement of the registered work. So L-3 is not liable. *See Airframe Systems Inc. f/k/a Airline Software Inc. v. L-3 Communications Corp.*, No. 10-2001 (1st Cir. 2011). This can raise practical issues with works like software, which are likely to exist in many versions. A party can register the various versions (as derivative works) and should be especially careful before initiating a lawsuit to see that a copy of the relevant version has been registered and deposited.

OWNERSHIP OF COPYRIGHT/STANDING

"Happy Birthday to You" is a staple of copyright lore. It illustrates how long copyright lasts, because the song was still subject to a registered copyright, despite being written in the 1920s (and using music from before then). Enforcement of the copyright illustrates the scope of the exclusive rights. It could be copyright infringement for restaurant staff to publicly perform "Happy Birthday to You" to a customer or for a scene in a movie to have a family sing the song at dinner over a cake. To avoid licensing fees, restaurants trained their staff to sing other songs, and screenwriters avoided birthday song scenes. The song also illustrates the possible murkiness of copyright ownership. In 2015, a court held that the Warner/Chappell, which had collected millions in royalties for more than eight decades for "Happy Birthday to You," could not prove that it had been transferred the copyright, a longstanding registration notwithstanding.[1]

Who can sue for copyright infringement? The copyright owner can: "The legal or beneficial owner of an exclusive right under a copyright is entitled . . . to institute an action for any infringement of that particular right committed while he or she is the owner of it." 17 U.S.C. §501(b). Some statutes give any person injured by a violation of the statute standing to sue. The Copyright Act takes a narrower approach.

1. *Marya v. Warner/Chappell Music, Inc.*, 131 F. Supp. 3d 975 (C.D. Cal. 2015).

The plaintiff must own some of the rights under the copyright at the time of the alleged infringement. The plaintiff must be the "legal owner," someone that owns the copyright or that owns one of the exclusive rights. If Author has sold Publisher the exclusive right to publish her book, then both Author (as owner of the remaining rights) and Publisher (as owner of the exclusive book publication rights) would have standing to sue for infringement. The plaintiff may also be a "beneficial owner," one who has sold her legal rights but retained an interest in the copyright. If Author sold her copyright to Publisher in exchange for 10 percent of any revenue that Publisher got from the work, Author would be a beneficial owner. If Author sold her copyright for $100,000 cash, then Author would no longer be a legal or beneficial owner and would not have standing to sue if the copyright were infringed. Someone who is less than the legal owner of the copyright has no standing to sue. DRK Photo, who represented numerous photographers, sued publishers, alleging unauthorized use of the photographer's work. But DRK Photo did not have standing to sue, because it did not own the copyrights, but rather had merely received nonexclusive rights to license their work and to sue for infringement.[2] So copyright has stricter standing requirements than many other areas of the law. If someone owes Bank a debt, Bank can sell the debt to Collector, who can enforce it. With copyright, one cannot simply assign the right to sue for infringement.

Standing is limited to the copyright owner(s) at the time of infringement. A nonowner of the copyright has no standing to sue, even if she created the work, owned the copyright before the infringement, or has a nonexclusive license from the copyright owner. In addition, the assignment of a claim for copyright infringement does not give the assignee standing to enforce the claim. Suppose Pirate infringes Author's copyright. Author assigns to Bank the valuable claim for infringement. Bank owns the claim but does not own any of the exclusive rights under the copyright and therefore does not have standing to enforce the claim. Only if Author agrees to bring the action can Bank get paid. If Author does not agree, Bank is left with an unenforceable right. Someone taking an assignment of a copyright infringement claim should be sure to get a prior agreement from the copyright holder to enforce the claim.

Standing is therefore intertwined with ownership of copyright. Suppose a nefarious professor infringes by copying from another academic's work. The owner can sue for copyright infringement: Is that the other professor, or her university? That will depend on whether she and her university agreed who would own copyright—and if they did not, whether it was a work made for hire—an issue that people have different opinions on.

2. *John Wiley & Sons, Inc. v. DRK Photo*, 882 F.3d 394 (2d Cir. 2018).

Special issues arise in class actions, in which a number of plaintiffs seek to sue on behalf of a class of parties. There's considerable uncertainty about the application of copyright to the planetary copying machine known as the Internet. One way to resolve uncertainty is to settle a lawsuit. The question in the Google Books case was whether settlement of a class action could bind parties who had not joined the affected class. *See Authors Guild v. Google Inc.*, No. 1:05-cv-08136-DC (S.D.N.Y. 2011). Google embarked on an ambitious effort to scan millions of books, working together with several university libraries. The Author's Guild filed a class action against Google, claiming that the wholesale copying of books without permission and displaying of snippets to those searching Google Books was copyright infringement. Google responded that fair use applied. Before any decision on the merits, the parties reached a settlement. The agreement provided that Google could continue scanning books, sell subscriptions to the database of books, and earn advertising revenue in connection with searches of the database. A Books Rights Registry would be established to track use of works and provide royalties to copyright holders. Libraries, universities, and other institutions could subscribe for access to the digital library. Google agreed to pay some $125 million toward establishing the framework. In return, authors would no longer be able to sue Google for infringement, unless they opted out of the agreement by 2012.

The court declined to approve the settlement, for several reasons. The agreement effectively settled the issue of orphan works, books whose copyright holder was not readily identified. This issue, the court reasoned, was one within the powers of Congress to address. The settlement, which would be binding on anyone who did not opt out, settled disputes far beyond the actual parties to the litigation. In addition, the named parties were not representative of the class of authors and other copyright holders affected.

Examples

1. *No standing*. Homer travels across the United States, posting an account of his journey on a blog. Cicero, a small book publisher, enjoys the account and asks Homer for permission to publish the story in book form. Homer tells Cicero to go right ahead. After Cicero has printed several thousand copies, he learns that another publisher has also begun marketing the story in book form without Homer's permission. Cicero can show that this has cost Cicero thousands of dollars in orders. Does Cicero have standing to sue the other publisher for copyright infringement?

2. *Shut out*. Writer is an employee of Movie Studio. She writes a screenplay, *Dara, Tara, and Dana*. Because the screenplay is a work made for hire, the author, and therefore copyright owner, is Movie Studio. The screenplay circulates around the movie industry but does not become a film. Writer

learns that another studio made *Danny, Tammy, and Randy*. Writer gets a copy and sees that it was copied wholesale from her work. The movie has gone nowhere—it was neither released to theaters or on DVD—but the other writer got paid handsomely. Writer asks Movie Studio to sue for infringement. Movie Studio does not want to sue but assigns Writer any rights that Movie Studio has to sue for infringement. Writer figures she can sue for infringement: She created the work, and she owns the cause of action. Does she have standing to sue? What if Movie Studio also assigned her the copyright?

3. *Notwithstanding*. Websites, bloggers, and commenters often post stories cut and pasted from media websites. That may be infringement, or it may be fair use. Righthaven purchased rights to sue for many alleged infringements and filed hundreds of actions, but Righthaven did not purchase any of the exclusive rights. Copyright holders might be willing to sell their rights to sue for infringements (past and future) for either a specified payment or a percentage of the proceeds. That would allow the copyright holder to have income without playing the role of enforcer, which could be costly not just financially but also to its reputation. But the copyright holder may be reluctant to transfer the entire copyright, or even the exclusive rights most likely to be infringed. That would take away its control over the exploitation of the work and also bar certain forms of exploitation of the work. Did Righthaven have standing to sue for the alleged infringement?

Explanations

1. Cicero does not have standing to sue. Only the owner of one or more of the exclusive rights has standing to sue for infringement of the copyright. Cicero got a nonexclusive license from Homer, so Cicero is not the owner of an exclusive right and therefore lacks standing. Some statutes give standing to sue to any person injured by a violation of the statute. Copyright infringement has a narrower standing requirement.

2. Writer does not have standing to sue. *See Silvers v. Sony Pictures Entm't*, 402 F.3d 881 (9th Cir. 2005) (en banc)(holding writer of screenplay, who received assignment of an accrued claim for copyright infringement but had no legal or beneficial interest in the copyright itself could not institute an action for infringement). The plaintiff must be the legal or beneficial owner of any of the exclusive rights at the time of infringement. Writer did not and does not own any of the exclusive rights. She created the work, but the copyright owner is Movie Studio. She owns the cause of action—but she must own one of the exclusive rights to bring the action.

   Even if Movie Studio assigned her the copyright, the result should be the same. The owner of an exclusive right may sue for "any infringement of that particular right committed while he or she is the owner of it." The alleged infringement occurred while Movie Studio owned the copyright at the time of infringement, so only it would have standing to sue for that infringement. If the copyright was assigned to Writer and there was post-assignment infringement, then Writer would have standing to sue for that infringement.

3. A number of defendants settled, but once defendants started to resist, several courts held that Righthaven had not received transfer of sufficient rights to sue. *Righthaven L.L.C. v. Hoehn*, 716 F.3d 1166 (9th Cir. 2013). An assignment of rights to sue for copyright infringement without conveyance of actual exclusive rights does not give standing to sue for infringement. The narrow rule for standing in copyright cases makes it difficult to structure an entity that is solely in the business of enforcing copyright infringement. Some courts awarded attorney's fees against Righthaven. At last report, one of Righthaven's major partners had terminated their agreement, stating on reflection, "It was a dumb idea."

   Another question is who can be defendants? *AF Holdings, LLC v. Doe*, 752 F.3d 990 (D.C. Cir. 2014), rejected the practice of suing numerous John Does for copyright infringement as part of the practice of what the court itself termed "porno-trolling." The plaintiffs had purchased the copyright to a pornographic film, *Popular Demand*, and sued 1,058 anonymous defendants, identified only by IP address. The suit alleged that they had all downloaded the film using the BitTorrent service. But defendants may be joined under Federal Rule of Civil Procedure 20(a)(2) for an action "with respect to or arising out of the same transaction, occurrence, or series of transactions or occurrences." Downloading the same file months apart as part of different BitTorrent swarms was not the same transaction or series of transactions any more than "two individuals who play at the same blackjack table at different times."

ELEMENTS OF THE PLAINTIFF'S CASE

"To establish infringement, two elements must be proven: (1) ownership of a valid copyright, and (2) copying of constituent elements of the work that are original." *Feist Publns., Inc. v. Rural Tel. Serv. Co.*, 499 U.S. 340, 361 (1991).

Ownership of a Valid Copyright

A plaintiff must show ownership of the exclusive right allegedly infringed. This has several parts to it. First, the work must have a valid copyright. We have seen a number of ways that a work may be not copyrighted. It may lack originality; it may not have been fixed in a tangible medium of expression; it may be a government work; it may be denied copyright because all parts of it infringe on an earlier work; it may be noncopyrightable because it does not have creative elements beyond its functional aspects. The work might also be out of copyright. Its term could have expired (especially pre-1924 works), no renewal may have been filed (for pre-1963 works), or it may have been published without the necessary copyright notice (for pre-1989 works).

Second, the plaintiff must own the right allegedly infringed. This requires determining who the copyright first belonged to, which would be the author or authors. But the author or authors are not necessarily the actual creators of the work. For a work made for hire, the copyright belongs initially to the hiring party. Then, ownership of the copyright may have been transferred by assignment of the copyright, an exclusive license, operation of law (such as death or bankruptcy), or otherwise. In addition, any transfer of an interest in the copyright may have been terminated, meaning the rights would revert to the author or successors.

In many cases, the plaintiff need not bring forward much evidence to show the foregoing. Rather, timely registration gives rise to a presumption that the copyright is valid and belongs to the registrant: "In any judicial proceedings the certificate of a registration made before or within five years after first publication of the work shall constitute *prima facie* evidence of the validity of the copyright and of the facts stated in the certificate." 17 U.S.C. §410(c). It is a relatively weak presumption: "The evidentiary weight to be accorded the certificate of a registration made thereafter shall be within the discretion of the court." 17 U.S.C. §410(c). Courts readily consider evidence that the copyright is not valid or that the registrant does not own it. So in a case where any facts are contested, the registrant must bring forward evidence supporting her side and should not just rely on the presumptions arising out of registration.

Copying of Constituent Elements of the Work That Are Original

The plaintiff must prove that defendant infringed the copyright by copying copyrighted elements of the work. This can involve two questions: whether defendant copied (termed "actual copying") and whether the defendant copied protected elements (termed "misappropriation").

Actual Copying Versus Independent Creation

The plaintiff must show that the defendant infringed one of the plaintiff's exclusive rights under 17 U.S.C. §106. (Violations of moral rights under 17

U.S.C. §106A are also copyright infringement, discussed in an earlier chapter.) The copyright owner must show that the plaintiff reproduced the work in a copy or phonorecord, adapted the work, or publicly distributed, displayed, or performed the work. Note that copyright infringement need not be for commercial purposes, result in financial gain, be deceptive, involve improper acts, or even be knowing or intentional. The defendant is liable even if he did not know he was using copyrighted material. But the defendant's acts must infringe one of the exclusive rights.

In doing so, the defendant must have *actually copied* from the copyrighted work. This means that the defendant made a literal copy of the work, created a work by working from the copyrighted work, or worked with the copyrighted work in mind. The defendant need not have consciously copied. Former Beatle George Harrison was held to have infringed in recording "My Sweet Lord" because he subconsciously copied from "She's So Fine."

But without actual copying, there is no infringement. Independent creation is not copyright infringement. If George Harrison had not copied from "She's So Fine," there would be no liability—even if the two songs had been identical.

Sometimes, there is a factual dispute about actual copying. The defendant may be a musician, writer, or moviemaker. The plaintiff claims that the defendant copied her work. The defendant will contend that she created the work independently without copying from the plaintiff.

To determine whether actual copying took place, the fact finder looks to several factors. One is the degree of similarity between the works. The more similar the works, the more likely it is that the defendant copied. If two songs are somewhat alike, that may mean it is somewhat likely that the defendant copied. By contrast, if two 400-page novels are strikingly similar, down to line-for-line narration of fictional events, then it is highly likely that one was copied from the other. Another factor is the degree of access that the defendant had to the plaintiff's work. The more access, the more likely it is that the defendant copied rather than created her work independently. If the plaintiff's book was sitting in the defendant's office while the defendant wrote the screenplay, that increases the possibility that the defendant copied. The fact finder also considers evidence of independent creation by the defendant or others. If the defendant can show notes or drafts created during production of the work or has witnesses testify about the defendant's making contemporaneous descriptions of her travails in working out the details of the work, that raises the likelihood that the defendant did not copy from the plaintiff. In some cases, the defendant can establish that her work was completed before the plaintiff created her work—which proves that the defendant did not copy from the plaintiff's work. The defendant can also show independent creation if the defendant copied not from the plaintiff's work but from the work of a third party. Suppose the author of *Southern Dell* claims copyright infringement by the author of *Mint Tulips*, showing many similar elements in the two books. But the defendant shows she simply copied all of those elements from *Huckleberry Finn*, which is no longer under copyright. The defendant did not copy from *Southern Dell* and therefore would not be liable for copyright infringement. No copying, no infringement. In many cases, the fact finder will consider all three categories—degree of similarity, degree of access, and evidence of independent creation—in deciding whether the defendant copied from the plaintiff's work.

Examples

1. *"You're the One for Me."* Plaintiff alleges that Defendant record company copies his song "You're the One (for Me)" to make a song titled "You're the One." Both songs, like many others, use "you're the one for me" in the lyrics. The melodies are vaguely similar—"their relationship is something more akin to that of second cousins, twice removed"—but those similarities are shared by many songs already in the public domain. They both use harmonic progression, a common composing technique. They both repeat the same note three times (as do many other songs). There is little evidence that Defendant had access to Plaintiff's song, beyond the fact that Plaintiff delivered one copy of it to a sometime coworker. By the same token, Defendant has little evidence of independent creation, such as tapes from the recording session. Is there sufficient evidence to get to a jury?

2. *"How Deep Is Your Love?"* Ronald Selle composed the song "Let It End" and performed it with his band a few times in the Chicago area. Selle sent a tape and sheet music to a number of music companies but received no response other than getting his material returned. Selle applied for and received a copyright registration. A couple years later, Selle heard another song, "How Deep Is Your Love?", by the group the Bee Gees. That song was a huge seller and featured in a Hollywood hit, *Saturday Night Fever*. Selle sued for copyright infringement.

   The two songs were similar in many ways. Many notes were "identical in pitch and symmetrical position." Many of the "rhythmic impulses" were also the same. But there is no evidence that the Bee Gees ever had access to Selle's song, with its very limited distribution. There is also considerable evidence of independent creation, from witnesses and from tapes capturing some of the evolution of the Bee Gees' composition of their song. Is there sufficient evidence to support a finding of actual copying?

3. *Gotcha, Grouch?* Reality Realty publishes a monthly newsletter with information about all real estate transactions in Sesame City. Grouch publishes a weekly magazine with similar info, which Reality strongly suspects

is copied from its newsletter. Grouch does not copy the selection and arrangement of information or any of Reality's clever text. To test its theory, Reality includes a fictitious transaction, a sale of 727 Boeing Avenue for $123,456, from Marilyn Monroe to Charles DeGaul, which duly shows up in Grouch's next newsletter. Will that prove infringement?

4. *Online*. Design Basics publishes its architectural designs on a public website. If another architect draws somewhat, but not strikingly, similar plans, could a jury infer that there was copying from Design Basics?

Explanations

1. The evidence would not be sufficient to support a finding of actual copying. *See Johnson v. Gordon*, 409 F.3d 12, 24 (1st Cir. 2005). The court will consider similarity between the works, Defendant's access to Plaintiff's works, and evidence of independent creation. Here, the slight similarities are no more than would occur by coincidence: use of a hackneyed phrase, vaguely similar melodies, common compositional techniques, and use of a note three times. There is also no substantial evidence of access to the work. Plaintiff would not meet the burden of showing actual copying.

2. The court held there was insufficient evidence to show actual copying. *See Selle v. Gibb*, 741 F.2d 896, 900 (7th Cir. 1984). There was a high showing of similarity but no showing of access and considerable evidence of independent creation. For a plaintiff to succeed by showing similarity alone, the similarity would have to be so great that it could be explained only by copying. If two lengthy symphonies were absolutely identical, one must have been copied from the other. But things other than copying from Selle's song could cause the similarity between two songs.

3. It will not prove infringement. It proves actual copying because the similarity can be explained only by copying, but actual copying alone is not infringement; there must also be copying of copyrighted expression. The facts of a real estate transaction are not copyrightable—and this was represented as fact, so would not be protected under the doctrine of copyright estoppel.

4. No. The "existence of the plaintiff's copyrighted materials on the Internet, even on a public and "user-friendly" site, cannot by itself justify an inference that the defendant accessed those materials. It follows that a plaintiff who cannot show striking similarity and whose evidence of access reduces to the mere existence of a website cannot survive summary judgment on a copyright infringement claim." *Design Basics, LLC v. Lexington Homes, Inc.*, 858 F.3d 1093, 1108 (7th Cir. 2017).

Misappropriation Versus Permissible Copying

Suppose the fact finder decides that the defendant copied from the plaintiff's copyrighted work—or the defendant admits copying. That does not end the case. Copying from a copyrighted work is not necessarily infringement. Copying noncopyrighted material is not copyright infringement.

As discussed above, many aspects of copyrighted works are not protected by copyright: ideas, facts, functional aspects, nonoriginal elements, government works, infringing material, and other elements are not copyrightable. Someone may copy such elements from a copyrighted work without infringing (although, as earlier chapters discuss, distinguishing protected expressive elements from the unprotected elements can be difficult). An author who copies ideas from another author's novel is not liable for copyright infringement. A software developer may copy the unprotected method of operation of a software package. A filmmaker may copy the unprotected facts set forth in a history book. In addition to proving copying, the plaintiff must show that the defendant copied protected expression.

Examples

1. PhantomAlert alleged that Google infringed copyright, by copying "Points of Interest," including traffic conditions, speed restrictions, and police-monitors, from PhantomAlert's database of navigation information. Infringement?
2. Towle sells unauthorized replicas of the Batmobile, from the comics and movies. Copying—but copying of protected material?

Explanations

1. The first copyright statute of the United States covered only books, maps, and charts. The extent of copyright protection for maps has been litigated, albeit sporadically, ever since. The issue of maps is a classic teaching example for copyright classes. Facts are not subject to copyright, because they do not originate with the author, even if she discovers them. Facts may be selected or arranged in a creative fashion, which would trigger copyright protection. So a map, although it portrays facts, may have sufficient creativity to be copyrighted.

   But here Google copied not the entire map, but only information that was "inherently factual, involving 'traffic conditions, speed restrictions, and police-monitors,' that is, objective facts that can be discovered and reported." *PhantomALERT, Inc. v. Google Inc.*, 2015 U.S. Dist. LEXIS 167754 (N.D. Cal. Dec. 14, 2015). There was actual copying, but not infringement, because only noncopyrightable material was copied.

In pre-*Feist* days, when facts could be protected by copyright, one mapmaker set a copyright trap by portraying a fictitious town, Agloe, on its maps. A competitor with Agloe on their map must have copied. As an unintended side result, someone opened an Agloe General Store in that location and a small community sprang up.[3] The fictional town begat a real one.

2. Copying a character would not be infringement if the character was not original (a stock character magician in a suit and hat) or an idea. But a character may be sufficiently creatively expressed to be protected. The court applied this test:

> First, the character must generally have "physical as well as conceptual qualities." Second, the character must be "sufficiently delineated" to be recognizable as the same character whenever it appears. Considering the character as it has appeared in different productions, it must display consistent, identifiable character traits and attributes, although the character need not have a consistent appearance. Third, the character must be "especially distinctive" and "contain some unique elements of expression."

DC Comics v. Towle, 802 F.3d 1012, 1021 (9th Cir. 2015). The Batmobile was sufficiently characterized, even though inanimate, to pass the test for protection.

Substantial Similarity

Copying need not be literal to give rise to liability (except for infringement of a sound recording copyright). Only substantial similarity is required for infringement. As previous chapters discuss, protected elements of a work go well beyond the exact form of the copyrighted work. A writer who paraphrases another novel, or a photographer who closely models her photo on another may be liable.

Substantial similarity is a factual issue but is guided by several legal principles. In deciding whether two works are substantially similar, the fact finder should consider only similarities involving protected elements. If defendant has copied ideas, facts, functional matter, or other nonprotected elements, those elements should be disregarded. Only original creative expression that was copied is relevant to the infringement determination.

A court may consider the question: Substantially similar from whose point of view? To some people, every heavy metal song may seem substantially similar to every other heavy metal song. In typical cases, the

3. *See* John Green, Paper Towns (2008).

question would be whether the works are substantially similar to an ordinary observer. But where a work is targeted to a particular audience, then the fact finder may consider whether that audience would find the works substantially similar. Courts have used this approach where the relevant market is more sophisticated (such as musicians working in a particular genre) or even less sophisticated, such as children. *See Lyons Partnership v. Morris Costumes*, 243 F.3d 789 (4th Cir. 2001) (holding that whether a defendant's dinosaur Halloween costume was substantially similar to a copyrighted work featuring Barney (the famous purple dinosaur) should be determined from the viewpoint of the young children to whom such works are targeted). Some courts will allow expert testimony to assist the fact finder.

Whether two works are substantially similar is sometimes a difficult analysis to put into words, especially with nonverbal elements such as melodies in music and shapes in artworks. Some courts frame the question in terms of whether defendant has copied the "total concept and feel" of the copyrighted work. This standard, however, is somewhat troubling. Ideas are not copyrighted. Section 102(b) specifically denies protection to any "*concept*, principle, or discovery, regardless of the form in which it is described, explained, illustrated, or embodied" (emphasis added). Copying of a concept is not infringement. In addition, "total concept and feel" might misleadingly suggest that the two works overall must be similar, but copying of small sections may still be infringement. The "total concept and feel" test, then, might be better framed. The real issue is whether the defendant copied identifiable protected elements—because that is what constitutes copyright infringement.

Example

1. *Captive audience.* Rearden has the copyright on software, MOVA Contour Reality Capture Program, a "program for capturing the motion of the human face to create images used in motion pictures. . . . The MOVA Contour system captures 'an actor's performance frame-by-frame, and then creates original Contour Program output files based on the performance, frame-by-frame.'" Another party uses the software without permission, working with actors and directors to create files for use in animation. For Disney's *The Beauty and the Beast*, the "film's romantic hero, the Beast, was a CG (computer graphics) character played by actor Dan Stevens, with every human subtlety of his facial performance carried through to the animal-like CG face of the Beast by a unique Oscar-winning visual effects ('VFX') technology)." The unauthorized use infringed. But did Disney infringe by using the outputted files?

Explanation

1. The court held that the outputted files did not infringe the copyright in the software that made them, just as a story written in Word will not infringe the copyright in Word. Only if the program does the lion's share of creating the work will the output infringe. Here, the actors and directors contributed substantially to the creation of the files. *Rearden LLC v. Walt Disney Co.*, 2018 U.S. Dist. LEXIS 28903, at *13 (N.D. Cal. Feb. 21, 2018).

De Minimis Copying

"De minimis non curat lex." The law does not care about trivial things. Some courts hold that where defendant made only trivial use of the copyrighted work, there is no infringement. Where a copyrighted illustration appeared briefly, out of focus, in the background of a commercial, there was no infringement. *See Gordon v. Nextel Commc'ns*, 345 F.3d 922, 925 (6th Cir. 2003).

The de minimis rule has been applied by some courts—and rejected by others—to the widespread practice of "sampling" from other recordings. The Sixth Circuit held that the de minimis rule would not apply to sound recordings; rather, any literal copying from a copyrighted sound recording would potentially infringe unless it qualified for fair use. The repeated use of the brief segment ("'dog' in a low voice as 'musical punctuation,' the rhythmic panting, and the Bow Wow refrain") was infringing and not fair use. *See Bridgeport Music, Inc. v. UMG Recordings, Inc.*, 585 F.3d 267 (6th Cir. 2009). By contrast, the Ninth Circuit held no infringement, where the producers of Madonna's song "Vogue" copied "a 0.23-second segment of horns from an earlier song, known as Love Break, and used a modified version of that snippet when recording Vogue." *VMG, LLC v. Ciccone*, 824 F.3d 871 (9th Cir. 2016). Along those lines, sampling of a simple three-note sequence was held too trivial to support a finding of substantial similarity to the musical work. *See Newton v. Diamond*, 349 F.3d 591 (9th Cir. 2003). Led Zeppelin did not infringe by copying a few notes from "Taurus" into "Stairway to Heaven." *Skidmore v. Led Zeppelin*, 952 F.3d 1051, 1071 (9th Cir. 2020) ("We have never extended copyright protection to just a few notes. Instead we have held that 'a four-note sequence common in the music field' is not the copyrightable expression in a song. *Granite Music Corp. v. United Artists Corp.*, 532 F.2d 718, 721 (9th Cir. 1976). In the context of a sound recording copyright, we have also concluded that taking six seconds of the plaintiff's four-and-a-half-minute sound recording—spanning three notes—is de minimis, inactionable copying. See Newton, 388 F.3d at 1195–96.").

DEFENSES

Fair Use

The defense of fair use plays a huge role in copyright. Fair use is a potential issue in most contested cases. The contours of fair use play an important role in setting the boundaries of copyright law itself. Fair use (discussed in more detail in its own chapter) is not infringement. Whether a use qualifies as fair depends on four factors: the purpose and character of the use, the nature of the copyrighted work, the amount of the copyrighted work used, and the effect on the potential market for or value of the copyrighted work.

Misuse

Courts have identified several settings where misuse of copyright might bar enforcement. A copyright holder might leverage copyright protection into related markets, such as by requiring purchasers of a copyrighted program also to purchase service contracts, or to agree not to buy competitor's products, or to agree not to compete with the copyright holder. A copyright holder might attempt to use copyright to gain property-like control over noncopyrightable elements, like ideas, facts, or functional elements. A plaintiff might bring a baseless infringement action to coerce a defendant with few resources to defend the suit. As yet, there is relatively little case law setting out the content of the misuse doctrine in specific fact settings.

Courts have applied misuse where it clearly limited competition without precompetitive justifications. Misuse applied where a software license for telephone switching software limited use to customers using the licensor's cards and effectively prohibited competitors from using licensed software to test and develop competing software. *See Alcatel USA, Inc. v. DGI Techs., Inc.*, 166 F.3d 772 (5th Cir. 1999). Misuse applied where a publisher of medical books sold them under the condition that buyers not use competing books. *See Practice Mgmt. Info. Corp. v. Am. Med. Ass'n*, 133 F.3d 1140 (9th Cir. 1998). But courts have generally given copyright holders leeway in contracting for limitations on the use of the work.

Example

1. *Peasgood's Nonsuch.* Psystar builds and sells computers that run Apple's software for Macs. Psystar bought a copy of the operating system Mac OS X Snow Leopard. Psystar then added a bootloader and kernel extension so the software would run on non-Apple computers. Psystar then loaded the adapted Snow Leopard on the computers built by Psystar and sold

them as Open Computers (originally OpenMacs, until Apple objected on trademark grounds). With each computer, Psystar included an unopened copy of Snow Leopard, purchased from Apple. Apple sues for copyright infringement because Psystar has made copies of Snow Leopard, adapted it, and distributed copies to the public. Even though Psystar has purchased a copy of Snow Leopard for each computer it sells, its actions violate the Snow Leopard license, which limits the use of Snow Leopard to Apple computers. Psystar raises the defense of copyright misuse, arguing that Apple cannot hinder competitors by limiting the use of copies it has sold. Misuse?

Explanation

1. The court held that Apple had not misused its copyright. The court first held that Apple had not sold copies of Snow Leopard, but merely had licensed them, so its license terms were valid restrictions. The court next concluded that, unlike the cases where misuse had been applied, Apple did not attempt to "stifle" competition: "Apple's SLA does not restrict competitors' ability to develop their own software, nor does it preclude customers from using non-Apple components with Apple computers. Instead, Apple's SLA merely restricts the use of Apple's own software to its own hardware. . . . Psystar produces its own computer hardware and it is free to develop its own computer software." The court's analysis seemed to consider other factors: Apple might have valid reasons to seek to control the quality of computers using Apple's software, and Apple does not have market power in the market for personal computers. Along with the first sale cases involving software licenses, *Apple* gives considerable leeway to copyright holders in placing restrictions on the use of their works, provided that buyers agree to those restrictions. *See Apple Inc. v. Psystar Corp.*, No. 10-15113 (9th Cir. 2011).

Statute of Limitations

A civil action under the Copyright Act must be "commenced within three years after the claim accrued." 17 U.S.C. §507. Where a defendant has fraudulently concealed infringement, the limitations period may be tolled (meaning plaintiff can sue up to three years from when she learned of the infringement). Some courts also apply the doctrine of "continuing wrong," allowing recovery for infringing acts more than three years before the suit was filed, where the acts were part a continuing course of action. Owners have latitude in deciding when to sue, as long as it is within three years. Courts have applied a discovery rule, meaning plaintiff must sue within three years of discovering the infringement, not necessarily within three years of when the infringement occurs.[4]

The Supreme Court has held that equitable doctrine of laches cannot bar a copyright claim brought within the statutory period of limitations. *Petrella v. MGM*, 134 S. Ct. 1962 (2014). Laches applies where the plaintiff delayed unreasonably in bringing the action and the alleged infringer was prejudiced by that delay. *Petrella* rejected its application in copyright cases, for which Congress has set a specific time limit.

Example

1. *Rambling tale.* Around 1974, Kid Ory heard Country Joe McDonald's "Fixin' to Die a Rag." He quickly decided that the song infringed his copyright in "Muskrat Ramble" but did not take legal action. As the years passed, Country Joe invested in performing, distributing, and marketing the song and reaped some returns. In 2001, the copyright in "Muskrat Ramble" passed to Ory's daughter, Babette Ory. Finally, in 2004, Babette Ory sued for infringement. To avoid the three-year statute of limitations, she alleged infringement on the basis of a recent rerecording of the song. Most of the people involved in the original recordings had died, and all of the evidence was long gone. Would laches apply?

Explanation

1. Laches would not bar the suit, even if there was unreasonable delay by the plaintiff that caused prejudice to the defendant. The Supreme Court in *Petrella* made laches inapplicable in copyright cases.

Sovereign Immunity

Sovereign government, like the federal government, states, and Native American tribes, have immunity for some causes of action. Was North Carolina liable where it posted online, without permission, videos made of a sunken ship of the pirate Blackbeard? The Supreme Court has held

4. *See Warner Chappell Music, Inc. v. Nealy*, 601 U.S. 366, 368, 144 S. Ct. 1135, 1137 (2024) (assuming but not deciding that discovery rule applies, and holding that if discovery rule allowed plaintiff to recover for infringement more than three years before suit, then plaintiff could also recover resulting damages more than three years before suit).

that Congress cannot generally make states (and state bodies such as state universities) liable for copyright infringement, although it may impose liability on states where such infringement amounts to a due process violation:

> But going forward, Congress will know those rules. And under them, if it detects violations of due process, then it may enact a proportionate response. That kind of tailored statute can effectively stop States from behaving as copyright pirates. Even while respecting constitutional limits, it can bring digital Blackbeards to justice.

Allen v. Cooper, 140 S. Ct. 994, 1007, 206 L. Ed. 2d 291 (2020).

Declaratory Judgment Actions

Where someone has been threatened with a copyright infringement claim, he or she can resolve the uncertainty by bringing action himself or herself, seeking a declaratory judgment of no infringement. The requirements to bring an action are a little different. The plaintiff need not own the copyright (he or she is the one accused of infringing the copyright), and the copyright need not be registered (the accused infringer cannot register the copyright). Rather, jurisdiction requires that there be an actual controversy between the parties. An example of the use of a declaratory judgment involved the works of James Joyce. The Joyce estate liberally threatened copyright infringement actions against anyone who so much as quoted a few words from Joyce's writings, even though such use is the very embodiment of fair use. The threats made it difficult for those writing about Joyce to find willing publishers. A literary scholar brought a declaratory judgment action, winning not just a decision upholding the application of fair use, but also an award of attorney's fees, meaning that the Joyce estate ended up having funded the litigation against itself. *See* Karen Sloan, *James Joyce Estate Agrees to Pay Plaintiff's Fees in Fair Use Dispute*, Nat'l L.J., September 30, 2009.

Example

1. *Clarify*. Kane is developing a movie based on Sherlock Holmes stories that were published before 1923 and are therefore out of copyright. The author's estate contends that would be copyright infringement because post-1922 stories are still under copyright. But the estate does not sue, leaving the question hanging. Can Kane use judicial process to clarify the rights rather than invest in making the movie and then defending an infringement lawsuit?

Explanation

1. Kane would have standing to file a declaratory judgment action. There is an actual controversy, because the estate has asserted that the movie would infringe and threatened to sue for infringement. *See Klinger v. Conan Doyle Estate, Ltd.*, 755 F.3d 496 (7th Cir. Ill. 2014).

CHAPTER 18

Secondary Liability and Immunity for Website Operators

Infringers often get assistance and guidance from others. Someone who sells unauthorized CDs of copyrighted music needs equipment and blank CDs, music to copy, a place from which to sell the CDs, and customers. The copyright music owner could sue the seller of the unauthorized CDs, but she might also like to be able to sue the pirate's suppliers, landlord, customers, and employees. That would give her more people, with deeper pockets, from whom to recover damages. It might also make people less likely to deal with copyright infringers. But imposing such liability too broadly could have considerable costs. If landlords had to vet and monitor their tenants, that would raise the costs of renting for all (in both dollars and decreased privacy). Likewise, if sellers of blank CDs, computers, and music equipment were liable for infringement by their customers, they would somehow have to pass on their costs (whether through higher prices to all customers, vetting and monitoring customers, lower returns to investors, lower prices to their own suppliers, or through their own sacrifice of profits). The same issues arise in considering whether online services should be liable for the activity of their users. In general, risks of copyright liability can deter technological innovation, cultural interchange, and investment. Too little copyright liability can create incentives for infringement and decrease incentives for creation and authorized distribution of works. Setting the boundaries of secondary infringement implicates many competing values and the balancing of many costs and benefits.

Copyright law recognizes two types of secondary liability: contributory infringement and vicarious liability. "One infringes contributorily by intentionally inducing or encouraging direct infringement and infringes vicariously by profiting from direct infringement while declining to exercise a right to stop or limit it." *MGM Studios Inc. v. Grokster, Ltd.*, 125 S. Ct. 2764, 2776 (2005) (citations omitted). The copyright statute does not specifically provide for secondary liability. Rather, courts have recognized the doctrines and given some definition to their boundaries.

There is no secondary liability without a direct infringer. Neither vicarious liability nor contributory infringement applies unless someone has directly infringed: They made a copy of the copyrighted work, adapted it into a derivative work, publicly distributed the work, or performed or displayed the work. Suppose an engineer makes copies of a video game to reverse-engineer it. If the engineer qualifies for fair use, she is not liable for copyright infringement. Her employer would not be secondarily liable because there is no direct infringer.

Suppose Boss has Employee make and sell 1,000 unauthorized copies of a popular computer program and give the proceeds to Boss. Boss did not directly infringe, because she did not make or distribute copies, but Boss is liable under both contributory infringement and vicarious liability theories. She controlled Employee and profited directly from the infringement, and she induced Employee to act. Only vicarious liability would apply if Employee had done the acts on her own initiative as part of her job with Boss and sold the infringing copies for Boss's profit. Only contributory infringement would apply if Boss had talked a friend into making and selling the copies. In short, contributory infringement requires a higher showing of knowledge, while vicarious liability requires a higher showing of control.

Secondary liability can lower the cost of copyright enforcement. Suppose that there is a widespread practice of individuals using the Internet to sell, swap, or give away unauthorized copies of copyrighted works (could be music, film, games, or e-books). Enforcing the copyright against direct infringers may require finding them, identifying them, filing and litigating many actions, and trying to enforce remedies against a range of individuals, some of whom may be judgment-proof or simply hard to pin down. Getting judgments against a few file shares may discourage many others. However, it may be less costly and more effective if a copyright owner could sue the online service providers or distributors of the file-swapping software. Such corporate defendants may be easier to locate, be less numerous, and have deeper pockets. In short, it is easier to shut down the operator of a file-sharing network than pursue thousands of file sharers.

But of course there are countervailing costs. Potential secondary liability can increase the costs of legitimate technological innovation. File-sharing networks, for example, can have plenty of productive purposes other than copyright infringement, but their developers' potential secondary liability is presently rather uncertain, and uncertainty imposes costs.

Likewise, copyrighted works are subject to fair use and other limitations, which may be cut back through fear of secondary liability. Courts have sought to balance competing interests in shaping the bounds of secondary liability.

Employers and others that supervise or hire should think of the risk of secondary liability. Universities now often have copyright policies to reduce the risk of infringement by faculty, staff, and students.

VICARIOUS INFRINGEMENT

Suppose that Gamey Retail operates a large gaming arcade. Located on the premises is a booth, which Gamey leases to Pyrite Productions. Pyrite sells video games and gives 25 percent of its revenue to Gamey as rent. Under the lease, Gamey has the right to control Pyrite's operations. But Gamey pays little attention to what Pyrite does, other than cashing the weekly checks from Pyrite. Unknown to Gamey, Pyrite makes so much money because it sells unauthorized copies of copyrighted games. When the copyright owners turn up and object, Pyrite absconds with its remaining proceeds, leaving Gamey as the only available defendant. Gamey might contend that it should not be liable for copyright infringement. It has not directly infringed, because it did not make copies, adapt the works, distribute copies to the public, perform the works publicly, or display the works publicly. It did not even know about the infringing activity.

But Gamey would be liable for vicarious infringement, "which allows imposition of liability when the defendant profits directly from the infringement and has a right and ability to supervise the direct infringer, even if the defendant initially lacks knowledge of the infringement." *Grokster, Ltd.*, 125 S. Ct. at 2776, citing *Shapiro, Bernstein & Co. v. H.L. Green Co.*, 316 F.2d 304 (2d Cir. 1963) (department store vicariously liable for direct infringement by contractor operating record department). The theory behind vicarious liability is that a defendant should not profit from infringement by someone she controls. The rationale is similar to respondeat superior in tort law. Vicarious liability requires direct financial benefit. Just providing Internet access for a fee is not a direct financial benefit.[1]

1. *Entertainment v. Cox Communs., Inc.*, 93 F.4th 222 (4th Cir. 2024):

> "An internet service provider would necessarily lose money if it canceled subscriptions, but that demonstrates only that the service provider profits directly from the sale of internet access. Vicarious liability, on the other hand, demands proof that the defendant profits directly from the *acts of infringement* for which it is being held accountable."

A key aspect is that vicarious liability does not require knowledge of the direct infringement. An employer, a landlord, or a party hiring an independent contractor may all be liable for copyright infringement, even where they lack knowledge of the direct infringement.

Vicarious liability has two important limitations. First, it applies only if the defendant gets a direct financial benefit. The classic example is the defendant landlord. Suppose landlord rents an apartment at market rates. The tenant brings in some high-tech machinery and makes thousands of pirated music CDs. The landlord would not be liable for vicarious infringement because it did not profit directly from the infringement. It simply received the same rent any other tenant would pay. Likewise, suppose an employee used her employer's equipment to make and sell infringing copies of a video game, and the employee pocketed all the money. The employer would not be vicariously liable, because the employer did not profit from the infringement.

The direct financial benefit need not be a specific percentage of the direct infringer's revenue. In the dance hall cases, owners of dance halls were vicariously liable for the direct infringement by dance bands performing copyrighted works without permission. A dance hall owner could directly benefit, because the unauthorized use of popular tunes increased the admission paid and the refreshments sold.

The second key limitation is that the defendant must have the "right and ability to supervise the direct infringer." Suppose that Gamey had sold part of its property outright to Pyrite, who then used it as an illicit production facility. If Gamey had no control over Pyrite, then Gamey would not be liable, even if Pyrite were using part of its ill-gotten gains to pay the purchase price on the property. There are several ways that the right and ability to supervise can be shown. There may be a formal contract granting those rights. There could be an employment contract or commission that implicitly gives the hiring party control over the hired party. There may be a less formal relationship, such as where a promoter organizes and controls a concert. There may be the necessary control where one party supplies goods or services (such as software or online services) necessary to the direct infringer's activities on an ongoing basis.

Both direct financial benefit and ability to control are necessary. A party is not vicariously liable if it gets a direct financial benefit but lacks ability to control. A shareholder, for example, may benefit from a corporation's infringement. But if the shareholder lacks the ability to control, it would not be liable. *See Softel, Inc. v. Dragon Med. & Sci. Communs.*, 118 F.3d 955, 971 (2d Cir. 1997) (rejecting vicarious liability based solely on defendant being the president and a shareholder of direct infringer). Likewise, one that controls but does not get a direct financial benefit is not vicariously liable.

Examples

1. *Community music*. The Town of Plumby allows nonprofit groups to use its town hall without charge. The Plumby Players, a group of local musicians, sign the standard agreement, promising to repair any damage, finish all activities by 10 P.M., and comply with all relevant laws and any directions from Town. Any violation allows Town to terminate Players' use of the town hall. Players play a series of concerts over the course of the summer, charging no admission to the sparse but enthusiastic audience. The music is mostly under copyright, but Players do not seek or need permission, because such nonprofit performances are authorized by section 110(4) of the Copyright Act. A copyright owner sues Town, claiming that the protections of section 110 say nothing about secondary liability. Is Town liable?

2. *Community theater*. Town permits similar use of the town hall by the Plumby Hambs, a group of local actors. The actors perform a series of copyrighted plays over the summer. Unlike the musicians, the actors are probably infringing, because section 110(4) authorizes only nonprofit performances of *nondramatic* musical and literary works. We will also assume fair use does not protect them. If the actors are direct infringers, is Town secondarily liable?

3. *Commercial music*. The Town of Plumby strikes a deal with a promoter. The promoter rents the town hall, its occupancy subject to Town's rules and instructions. The promoter further agrees to obey all laws, including getting any necessary permission from copyright holders. The promoter agrees to pay 25 percent of its revenue to Town. The promoter holds a summerlong talent contest called Plumby Idol. Locals compete by performing well-known songs. Unbeknownst to Town, no copyright permissions are sought. The promoter is gone with its share of the proceeds by the time the copyright holders complain. Town responds that it did not participate in or even know about the infringement and even specifically prohibited it. Is Town liable?

4. *Off Broadway*. The Sherbert Theater Company rents out its theater to an impresario. The parties sign a typical lease known as a "four walls agreement." Sherbert receives its typical weekly lease payment and relinquishes all control of the theater to the impresario—who then stages *The Lion King* without asking Disney. Is Sherbert liable?

5. *Hand to hand, peer to peer*. Cherry Auction promotes and organizes a swap meet. Vendors pay a daily fee to Cherry Auction and occupy small booths in premises controlled and patrolled by Cherry Auction. Cherry Auction has the contractual right to terminate vendors. Customers pay an

admission fee to Cherry Auction, stroll around, and patronize vendors. Customers often pay Cherry Auction for parking and refreshments. An important draw to customers is the fact that many of the vendors sell attractively priced unauthorized recordings of copyrighted music.

6. *Napster (prelude to Grokster)*. Napster facilitates music sharing by distributing software and providing online services. Once a user downloads Napster's free MusicShare software and registers with Napster, she can make her music files available to others, search the directory on Napster's website for music, and download the music from other users by sending a request to Napster, which establishes a link between the two users. Napster does not charge users for its software or services. It plans to make revenue from its user base through things like advertising and targeted e-mail. Users are subject to Napster's terms of use, including Napster's right to terminate accounts and services at any time. As Napster knows, most of the music swapped using Napster is under copyright. Is Napster vicariously liable?

Explanations

1. Town is not liable. There is no secondary liability without a direct infringer. The musicians are not infringing, because section 110 protects their conduct. Town does not need to come within section 110. Town itself is not a direct infringer, because it did not make copies, adapt the works, or publicly distribute, display, or perform works. It cannot be secondarily liable without a direct infringer.

2. This time there is a direct infringer. Town is vicariously liable only if it "profits directly from the infringement and has a right and ability to supervise the direct infringer." The plaintiff must show both elements: direct financial benefit, and right and ability to control. Town has the second (right and ability to control) but not the first, because it does not get a financial benefit. It is therefore not vicariously liable.

3. This time Town is vicariously liable because there is both direct financial benefit (its share of the proceeds) and control (promoter's occupancy subject to Town's rules and instructions). The fact that Town had no knowledge of infringement does not save it. For vicarious liability, there is no need to show knowledge of the direct infringement. There is liability "even if the defendant initially lacks knowledge of the infringement." *MGM Studios Inc. v. Grokster, Ltd.*, 125 S. Ct. at 2776.

4. Sherbert is not liable. There is no vicarious liability without the right and ability to control. Unlike the Town of Plumby, which retained the right to direct its tenants, Sherbert relinquished all control to the tenant. *See Robert Stigwood Group, Ltd. v. Hurwitz*, 462 F.2d 910 (2d Cir. 1972). Even

if it had control, there may not be the requisite direct financial benefit, where Sherbert received its customary rent, as opposed to a stake in the infringing activity. Note that the result could be different if Sherbert had knowledge of the infringement. Then it might be liable for contributory infringement (discussed below).

5. Cherry Auction was liable for vicarious infringement. *See Fonovisa, Inc. v. Cherry Auction, Inc.*, 76 F.3d 259 (9th Cir. 1996). There was the necessary right and ability to control. It promoted and organized the swap meet and controlled the vendors through the right to set rules, patrol the grounds, and terminate vendors' occupancy. There was also the necessary direct financial benefit. There was no set percentage of sales. But the availability of unauthorized copies at great prices was a draw to customers. Because there were more customers, Cherry Auction received more revenue from vendor rental fees, customer admissions, parking fees, food sales, and other sources. Cherry Auction was not like a landlord who happened to have a tenant that engaged in infringing activity. Rather, Cherry Auction was like a dance hall owner, where infringement acted to "enhance the attractiveness of the venue to potential customers."

6. The Ninth Circuit regarded Napster as an online equivalent to Cherry Auction: "Napster's failure to police the system's 'premises,' combined with a showing that Napster financially benefits from the continuing availability of infringing files on its system, leads to the imposition of vicarious liability." *A&M Records v. Napster, Inc.*, 239 F.3d 1004, 1024 (9th Cir. 2001). The necessary direct financial interest obtained in that the availability of infringing material was a draw for users, and increased numbers of users were critical to Napster's future revenue. Napster did not charge users, but when more users came to download copyrighted works, more advertising and other sources of revenue could be tapped. Napster was like the swap meet promoter or dance hall operator. The court held the requisite right and ability to control was also present. Napster "has the ability to locate infringing material listed on its search indices, and the right to terminate users' access to the system. The file name indices, therefore, are within the 'premises' that Napster has the ability to police."

CONTRIBUTORY INFRINGEMENT

"One infringes contributorily by intentionally inducing or encouraging direct infringement." *MGM Studios Inc. v. Grokster, Ltd.*, 125 S. Ct. 2764, 2776 (2005). Contributory infringement can take several forms, applying to "one who, with knowledge of the infringing activity, induces, or materially contributes to the infringing conduct of another." *Gershwin Publishing v. Columbia Artists Management*, 443 F.2d 1159 (2d Cir. 1971).

Unlike vicarious infringement, knowledge of the infringing activity is required for contributory infringement. If the defendant merely has general control over the direct infringer or helps in the creation or distribution of a work without knowledge of infringement, the defendant will not be liable for contributory infringement. Note that there is not a bright line between vicarious and direct infringement. A defendant may be liable on both theories (as in *Napster*).

The contributory infringement cases can be divided into cases where the defendant acted together with the direct infringer and those where the defendant provided a device used by the direct infringer. *See* Goldstein, *Copyright* §6.1. In the first type of case, a defendant may act together with the direct infringer by such conduct as selecting infringing materials for inclusion in a film, suggesting changes during the composition of a song, or granting a license (without authority) to use copyrighted material. *Id.* Likewise, a defendant that supervises infringing activity may be liable for contributory infringement, such as the manager of a radio station who supervises the music director and the station's day-to-day activities. *Id.* In many of these cases, the defendant will have such involvement in the infringing activity that it is liable as a direct infringer as well.

The second category is contributory infringement by providing a device or service that is used for infringement. Technological innovations in copying, performing, and distribution technology offer both social benefits and threats of copyright infringement. Courts have struggled with each new generation of technology, from player pianos to cassette tapes to photocopy machines to videocassette recorders to the Internet, that global machine for making and distributing copies. These cases raise important policy considerations. The Supreme Court has sought

> a sound balance between the respective values of supporting creative pursuits through copyright protection and promoting innovation in new communication technologies by limiting the incidence of liability for copyright infringement. The more artistic protection is favored, the more technological innovation may be discouraged; the administration of copyright law is an exercise in managing the trade-off.

MGM Studios Inc. v. Grokster, Ltd., 125 S. Ct. 2764, 2775 (2005). The Court's decisions in *Sony* and *Grokster* will affect copyright holders, technologists, and consumers.

In *Sony Corp. of America v. Universal City Studios*, 464 U.S. 417 (1984), the Court adopted a standard from patent law: Simply selling a "staple article or commodity of commerce suitable for substantial noninfringing purposes" is not contributory infringement. Sony was not liable for selling videocassette recorders, which had substantial noninfringing purposes: recording of television programs where the copyright holders did not object and recording of programs to watch at a different time, which was held to be fair use. Xerox is not liable, because there are many noninfringing uses of photocopy machines. Sellers of blank CDs are not liable, because blank CDs can be used to store plenty of things other than pirated works. But the breadth of the safe harbor was vague. Under *Sony*, a defendant that merely distributes a device is not liable if it has "substantial" or "commercially significant" noninfringing uses. Unclear is whether the device need merely be capable of such noninfringing use or whether actual noninfringing use is required. And if noninfringing use must be shown, how much: Ten percent of users? Fifty percent?

The Court next addressed contributory liability some twenty years later in *MGM v. Grokster*. Grokster, like Napster, distributed software used by consumers to swap music files. Grokster worked differently. With Napster, users searched for music on directories on Napster's servers and downloaded from other users only by sending requests to Napster, who then would link the two users. In short, everything went through Napster. Grokster, by contrast, simply distributed software, which users could then use to share music without going through Grokster. Grokster argued that it was protected by the *Sony* safe harbor rule. It could not be contributorily liable for distributing software, because the software had substantial noninfringing uses (sharing of music where the copyright holder did not object or of noncopyrighted music or of other works).

The *Grokster* court held that *Sony* was inapplicable. In its view, *Sony* held that a defendant could not be liable *merely* for distributing a device that had substantial noninfringing uses. But Grokster did not merely distribute its software; it also promoted its use for infringing purposes. The *Grokster* court focused on the element of intent in contributory infringement: "*Sony's* rule limits imputing culpable intent as a matter of law from the characteristics or uses of a distributed product. But nothing in Sony requires courts to ignore evidence of intent if there is such evidence, and the case was never meant to foreclose rules of fault-based liability derived from the common law." 125 S. Ct. at 2779. The Court formulated a standard for addressing cases that went beyond distribution of a device: "We hold that one who distributes a device with the object of promoting its use to infringe copyright, as shown by clear expression or other affirmative steps taken to foster infringement, is liable for the resulting acts of infringement by third parties." 125 S. Ct. at 2770. The court emphasized that

> mere knowledge of infringing potential or of actual infringing uses would not be enough here to subject a distributor to liability. Nor would ordinary acts incident to product distribution, such as offering customers technical support or product updates, support liability in themselves. The inducement rule, instead, premises liability on purposeful, culpable expression and conduct, and

> thus does nothing to compromise legitimate commerce or discourage innovation having a lawful promise.

125 S. Ct. at 2780.

The court saw a number of factors that would support a conclusion that Grokster had not just knowledge of infringement but also acted with the object of promoting infringement with its software. First, Grokster offered itself to consumers as a successor to the shut-down "notorious file-sharing service, Napster." It offered software designed to be similar to Napster, sought to divert requests to Napster to its own site, and derived its name from Napster. Second, it did not attempt "to develop filtering tools or other mechanisms to diminish the infringing activity using their software." Third, its advertising sales were dependent on high-volume use, which was in turn dependent on the availability of downloads of copyrighted music.

Grokster should not be read too broadly. A party may finance an infringing transaction without being liable for contributory infringement. Credit card companies were not liable for processing credit card payments to infringing websites despite having knowledge of the existence of ongoing infringement. *See Perfect 10, Inc. v. Visa Int'l Serv. Ass'n*, 494 F.3d 788, 796 (9th Cir. Cal. 2007). Providing credit card payment services was not a material contribution, because it did not have a direct connection to the infringing activity. Providing financing made it easier for the businesses to continue in operation but did not directly cause the infringing activity. There is a distinction between parties like credit card companies, which provide services that generally facilitate commercial transactions, and entities like search engines or user-created content sites, which actually make copies of copyrighted material and direct consumers to websites. If one of the latter continues to host infringing material after notice, it is more likely to be held liable. But there must be knowledge of specific infringing material. Just general knowledge that infringing material is on the site will not give rise to liability, unless there are simple measures available to identify and remove infringing material. Giganews was not liable for infringement by its users, where the only means to identify and remove the material were "onerous and unreasonably complicated." *Perfect 10, Inc. v. Giganews, Inc.*, 847 F.3d 657, 671 (9th Cir. 2017).

Examples

1. *Special orders.* Audio Phil buys sound recordings on CD from Rouge Records. Audio Phil e-mails a list of CDs that he would like for his collection. Rouge then locates a recording of the music, makes an unauthorized copy, and mails it to Audio Phil. Phil knows that he is getting unauthorized copies—that's why the price is so low. Indeed, Phil often sends along information to help Rouge locate a recording to copy, whether the

local music library or a collector. Sued for infringement, Phil responds that he has not infringed any of the copyright holders' exclusive rights: He did not make or distribute phonorecords. Is Audio Phil liable?

2. *Tailor made.* Abdallah sells "time-loaded" cassette tapes to his customers, who are in the business of making and selling unauthorized copies of copyrighted music. Blank cassettes usually come in specific lengths, such as 45, 60, 75, or 90 minutes. If the CD you are copying is 68 minutes, then a 60-minute tape is too short and a 75-minute tape leaves blank space—more costly for the maker and an annoyance to the consumer. Abdallah fulfills orders from customers for tapes of specific length. He knows that his customers are making phonorecords without permission. Is Abdallah liable for infringement?

3. *Seek and ye shall find.* Users can find almost anything online using Google. Some use Google to find sites that allow them to download copyrighted music. Google does not promote such use. In general, Google gets more revenue if it has more users, whether they are googling people, searching for music, or anything else. After *Grokster*, is Google liable for contributory infringement?

4. *Substitute.* F2F appears not long after the Supreme Court opinion in *Grokster*. F2F is a new provider of file-sharing software, very similar to Grokster. Like Grokster, F2F allows decentralized file sharing, about 90 percent of which is copyrighted music. Indeed, F2F's similarities win it many of Grokster's former users. Like Grokster, F2F gets revenue from advertising, which depends on the volume of use. Unlike Grokster, there is no record of F2F making statements encouraging its use for copyright infringement. Is F2F liable for contributory infringement?

5. *Freebird.* A small group of volunteers develop and distribute Freenet file-sharing software. Unlike Grokster, which anyone could join, a Freenet group is open only to trusted members. Freenet uses encryption to resist monitoring by outsiders, just as old-time secret societies had secret handshakes. The developer of Freenet has primarily political purposes, such as "helping dissidents in countries where computer traffic is monitored by the government." John Markoff, *File Sharers Anonymous: Building a Net That's Private*, New York Times, August 1, 2005. But he also scorns copyright, preferring free sharing of all information, and recognizes that a leading use of Freenet may be for "darknet" distribution of infringing copies of work. *Id.* If some groups use Freenet to swap music, games, and software, are the developers of Freenet liable for contributory infringement?

6. *One bad applet.* Wonka Software hires Charlie to work on development of its Chocmatica software package. Charlie signs an employment contract, agreeing to abide by Wonka's regulations and agreeing that Wonka can

fire him with or without cause at any time. Over the next few months, Charlie contributes significant portions of code to the Chocmatica product. Chocmatica goes live and sells like hotcakes. It then turns out that Charlie had not written any of the code but had simply cut and pasted long portions of code from software of his prior employer. Wonka argues that it is not vicariously liable because it did not get a direct financial benefit, the link between Charlie's coding and the sales of Chocmatica being too indirect. Wonka also argues that it is not contributorily liable because it lacked knowledge of Charlie's activity. Is Wonka liable?

Explanations

1. Audio Phil is not liable for direct infringement, but he is liable for contributory infringement. Contributory infringement applies to "one who, with knowledge of the infringing activity, induces, or materially contributes to the infringing conduct of another." *Gershwin Publishing v. Columbia Artists Management*, 443 F.2d 1159 (2d Cir. 1971). Audio Phil knowingly induced Rouge to make the infringing recordings, and also contributed by helping locate recordings to use.

2. Abdallah would be liable. Cf. *A&M Records v. Abdallah*, 948 F. Supp. 1449 (C.D. Cal. 1996) (pre-*Grokster*). The tapes arguably have substantial noninfringing purposes, but that would not matter in a case like this, in which Abdallah had ongoing knowledge of the infringement and marketed his goods to people for the purpose of infringement. Under *Grokster*, he would be liable for contributory infringement and not be able to use the protection of *Sony*.

3. Google would not be liable for contributory infringement. Unlike Grokster, it did not market its services for infringement or depend on infringement as the basis of its business. There is no showing that Google had the necessary "object of promoting its use to infringe copyright, as shown by clear expression or other affirmative steps taken to foster infringement," which is the standard set by *Grokster*. If a search engine was specially designed and marketed to facilitate online infringement, there could be a different result.

4. Here, there was no expression by F2F promoting infringing activity, unlike in *Grokster*. The question would be whether supplying a substitute for Grokster's service, software that was used primarily for infringement, as with Grokster, would be sufficient to meet the standard set by the *Grokster* court. In other words, whether actions alone would be sufficient to constitute promotion, or whether words are also required.

5. This example also calls for interpreting the *Grokster* standard. The purpose of Freenet is not to promote copyright infringement, but rather

more generally to allow free sharing of information without the knowledge of outsiders. If the developers take no active steps to promote the use of Freenet for copyright infringement, then there would seem to be no liability under *Grokster*. By contrast, an advertising-supported website that urged a user to download movies using BitTorrent and provided technical support was liable for inducement of copyright infringement. *Columbia Pictures Indus. v. Gary Fung*, 710 F.3d 1020 (9th Cir. 2013).

6. This example is a red herring as a reminder. There is no need here to go into the analysis of contributory or vicarious liability. Chocmatica is liable as a direct infringer for making and distributing infringing copies.

PROVIDERS OF INTERNET ACCESS AND ONLINE SERVICES: IMMUNITY FOR INFRINGEMENT BY CUSTOMERS (HEREIN OF TAKEDOWNS AND PUTBACKS)

A frequent sight on YouTube: "This video is no longer available because of a copyright claim" by a music company, news source, or other copyright claimant. Users of websites often infringe: posting copyrighted material to YouTube, sharing copyrighted music, cutting and pasting stories, and so forth (as always, fair use might apply in some cases). Congress has provided immunity for infringement to online service providers on the condition that they act to take down material they know is infringing and respond to takedown notices sent by copyright holders. "Service providers" is defined broadly in the statute to cover anyone who provides online services or network access, so it would cover parties that provide Internet access, like Comcast, and websites that provide content or other services, like YouTube and Amazon. 17 U.S.C. §512(k)(1). That is why, when looking for a video on YouTube, we often find a screen simply stating that the work has been taken down by request of the copyright holder. If a service provider were held responsible for all copyright infringement by its customers, the liability could be large. Copies of music, video, text, images are all made in the course of transmitting, hosting, and providing other services for customers. Section 512 offers service providers protection at a certain cost. They receive limits on liability for certain types of copying if they take certain actions designed to reduce the amount of infringement (such as responding to takedown notices) and facilitate suits against customers who infringe. In other words, service providers like YouTube have a program for taking down possibly infringing videos to avoid liability for copyright infringement—not just for the removed videos but also for other infringing videos. Section 512 limits the liability of service providers for several categories of copying that are frequently made in the operation and use of computer networks:

- copies made in transmission, routing, or providing connections
- caching
- copies made by users
- copies made using information location tools (such as searching and linking)

To gain the protection of the last two safe harbors (copies made by users and information location tools), a service provider must adopt and implement certain policies. In general, the service provider must take down material when it has actual knowledge of infringement. In addition, it must have a procedure to receive notification of alleged infringement by users and take specified actions to remove infringing materials and terminate accounts of repeat infringers. *See Ellison v. Robertson*, 357 F.3d 1072 (9th Cir. 2004) (America Online not entitled to rely on safe harbors where it "allowed notices of potential copyright infringement to fall into a vacuum and to go unheeded" by failing to update e-mail address for notification of alleged infringement); *EMI Christian Music Group v. MP3tunes, LLC*, 840 F.3d 69 (2d Cir. 2016) (no immunity for online service provider who was not scrupulous in canceling accounts of repeat infringers). The service provider must accommodate technical measures used to protect works. In appropriate circumstances, it must terminate the account of repeat infringers. §512(i). That accounts for another frequent message on YouTube: "This video is no longer available because the YouTube account associated with this video has been terminated due to multiple third-party notifications of copyright infringement." Some providers must respond to certain subpoenas intended to identify infringing customers.

To take advantage of the safe harbors, a service provider must act if it is "aware of facts or circumstances from which infringing activity is apparent." 17 U.S.C. §512(c)(1)(A)(ii). This duty is not triggered if the notifications of alleged infringement do not meet the requirements of the statute, because such notices cannot be deemed to impart such awareness. The statute only requires a service provider to act when it knows or should know about copyright infringement. *See Capitol Records, LLC v. Vimeo, LLC*, 826 F.3d 78 (2d Cir. 2023)(not willful blindness, where site responded to takedown orders systematically, even if some infringing material remained on the site). In addition, the service provider is not required to monitor its customers' activity or to actively police for potential copyright infringement. *See Perfect 10, Inc. v. CCBill, LLC*, 488 F.3d 1102, 1112 (9th Cir. 2007). To be protected for secondary copyright infringement liability, a service provider must have a reasonably implemented notice and takedown policy.

The standard is quite malleable, with that classic word for legal standards, "reasonable." Courts have held such a policy to require the provider to have a working notification system, to have a procedure for dealing with DMCA-compliant notifications, and not to actively prevent copyright owners from collecting information needed to issue such notifications. Note that courts may be forgiving of small ISPs that have programs which are not as efficient and formal as their corporate cousins. *See Ventura Content, Ltd. v. Motherless, Inc.*, 885 F.3d 597 (9th Cir. 2018).

There are some safeguards in the takedown procedure. The takedown notice must:

- contain a signature from some entity authorized to act on behalf of the copyright owner
- identify the work
- identify infringing material
- provide contact information
- provide a good faith statement that the material is not authorized by the copyright owner or by the law

Parties may be liable for lack of good faith in issuing takedown notices. A party could be liable if it issued a notice where it did not hold the copyright, where it had authorized the use, or where the use was clearly fair use. *See Lenz v. Universal Music Corp.*, 801 F.3d 1126 (9th Cir. 2015). Universal Music sent such a takedown notice to YouTube, where Lenz had posted a video of her toddler dancing, with Prince's "Let's Go Crazy" playing in the background. *Lenz* held that a sender of a takedown notice may be liable for bad faith, if they send it without considering whether fair use authorized the posting. Many of the millions of takedown notices are generated by software, meaning that copyright owners may need to adjust their software to avoid possible liability.

Sending a notice for works not under copyright (such as very old books or government records) or works that are known to have been removed could rise to liability.

On receiving the takedown notice, the service provider will generally take down the material to maintain its immunity. It may choose to keep the material up if it deems the takedown notice to be insufficient or the material not to infringe (such as where fair use applies). If it takes the material down, it will notify the user. The user may respond with a putback notice, stating in good faith that the material is not infringing. If the sender of the takedown does not file an infringement suit within 10 to 14 days, the service provider must put the material back up or have possible liability to the user if the takedown was unwarranted and not permitted by the terms of service.

Dealing with takedown notices can take considerable resources. YouTube receives more than 10,000 takedown notices per month (mostly for music). YouTube (and its owner, Google) has an automated system to process the notices—many of which are automatically generated by software searching on behalf of copyright owners.

The takedown process applies only to allegations of copyright infringement. Failure to respond to allegations of trademark (such as postings offering counterfeit clothes) or patent infringement is not covered by these rules. A party that makes a claim of trademark infringement would not affect the service provider's liability for copyright infringement (if the service provider did not respond) and would not be liable (under the copyright statute) if the allegation was ill founded.

Examples

1. *Blind eye?* A number of television and movie companies sued YouTube for secondary copyright infringement. YouTube responded to takedown notices. YouTube also took down specific material it knew was infringing, even without receiving a takedown notice. But YouTube did not police the site to find and take down infringing material. Is YouTube immune?

2. *Take that.* Iago is jealous of his competitor Othello's successful parody video business. Othello makes short animated parodies of famous movies and posts them on YouTube, along with craftily placed advertisements. Iago sends takedown notices, falsely claiming power to act for the movies' copyright holders. Iago also knows the videos are protected by fair use (as parodies that directly comment on the relevant movies). Does Othello have any recourse?

3. *Volunteer trouble.* Users send photographs to the LiveJournal website. Volunteer moderators, controlled by LiveJournal, review posts and delete posts, depending on whether they deem them to comply with the site's standards. Most of the photographs posted infringe. Is LiveJournal shielded from liability?

4. *14 strikes?* In order to have immunity for copyright infringement by its users, an ISP must implement a reasonable notice and takedown procedure and must terminate repeat infringers' accounts. Cox Cable wants to have immunity, but is reluctant to terminate fee-paying accounts, so it terminates users only after 14 instances of infringement, and even then might simply issue one more final warning. Will Cox Cable maintain immunity?

Explanations

1. YouTube does have immunity. *See Viacom International Inc. v. YouTube Inc.*, 676 F.3d 19 (2d Cir. 2012). The court rejected the argument that awareness that infringement was common on the site gave YouTube actual knowledge of infringement. Rather, the court held it sufficient that an online service provider responds to "knowledge of specific and identifiable infringements of particular individual items," not just general knowledge of infringement. *Viacom* has considerable impact because it does not require service providers to actively seek out and take down infringing material. It simply requires them to respond when they gain knowledge of the infringement. Other courts have followed this interpretation. *See Capitol Records Inc. v. MP3tunes LLC*, No. 1:07-cv-09931-WHP-FM (S.D.N.Y. 2011).

2. Iago is doubly liable. He falsely represented to act on behalf of the copyright owner. He also falsely stated that use of the material was not permitted by the copyright owners or *by law*—but fair use permits the use. The statute explicitly provides liability for false representations about whether the material is infringing. It would likely be read to apply liability for the other misrepresentation.

3. The court held that LiveJournal could be liable. *Mavrix Photographs, LLC v. LiveJournal, Inc.*, 853 F.3d 1020 (9th Cir. 2017). It remanded for the trial court to determine whether the photos were posted by users or by moderators. Immunity only applies for posts by users. If by users, immunity would not apply if LiveJournal was aware of the infringing posts, which in turn could depend on whether the moderators were agents of LiveJournal. So online service provider immunity can involve tricky balances.

4. No. To have immunity, an ISP must have a program to receive and act on takedown notices and to terminate repeat infringers, in substance, not merely in form. "Cox failed to qualify for the DMCA safe harbor because it failed to implement its policy in any consistent or meaningful way—leaving it essentially with no policy." *BMG Rights Mgmt. (US) LLC v. Cox Commc'ns, Inc.*, 881 F.3d 293, 305 (4th Cir. 2018).

CHAPTER 19

Remedies

A copyright owner has a set of exclusive rights. How valuable those are depends on what remedies are available for infringement. As some put it, remedies are what you get when you win a lawsuit. Remedies measure the exclusive rights in copyright. A court may award a range of remedies for copyright infringement: actual damages and profits, an injunction governing the infringer's future behavior, and impoundment and destruction of unauthorized copies, even the equipment used to make them. 17 U.S.C. §504. If the copyright owner registered her copyright in timely fashion, she has two more options: She may choose to seek statutory damages, rather than actual damages, and she may seek attorney's fees.

Remedies are linked with formalities. Statutory damages and attorney's fees are available only if the copyright was registered at the time of infringement (or was registered no later than three months after first publication, and infringement occurred after publication). 17 U.S.C. §412. Registered copyrights are somewhat stronger in enforcement than unregistered copyrights. In addition, if a work was published without a copyright notice before March 1, 1989, someone who innocently infringed, believing the work was not copyrighted, is not liable for damages. 17 U.S.C. §405(b).

Different remedies are important in different categories of cases. Take three possible infringers: Alpher made 50 copies of a year-old physics journal article (unregistered copyright) and handed them out at an academic conference; Bethe downloaded 1,000 songs (copyrights registered); Gamow, about to release a Hollywood movie titled *Big Bang*, learned of a claim that the screenplay was lifted bodily from a short story (copyright registered). In each case, one issue would be whether there is copyright infringement. Alpher may be protected by fair use. Bethe may show the downloading was authorized. Gamow may prove the screenplay was written independently of the short story. But each defendant (and plaintiff) would also consider if there is infringement, what remedies are likely to apply?

Alpher may not be too worried. Alpher may be liable for actual damages, but the lost sales of 50 copies of a journal article may not be too scary. Alpher did not make any profits, so there would be none to hand over. The court might order an injunction against further distribution and even order destruction of the infringing copies—but Alpher may not care about distributing any more copies or the fate of the copies already distributed.

Bethe may be more concerned. Actual damages for 1,000 songs, supposing the court awarded $1 per song, could be $1,000 dollars, which is bad enough. Because the copyright was registered, however, the plaintiffs may elect instead to receive statutory damages in the amount of $750 to $30,000 per work, or in the range of $750,000 to $30 million, if the songs are separate works. *See BMG Music v. Gonzalez*, 430 F.3d 888 (7th Cir. 2005) (upholding award of statutory damages of $22,500, based on $750 per song for thirty songs against an individual who downloaded copyrighted songs from the Internet). For willful infringement, the court can even raise the range to $150,000 per work. To make it worse, a court may award attorney's fees for infringement of a registered copyright, and Bethe would therefore have to pay the plaintiff's lawyers, adding insult and more injury. In cases where a service provider is liable for infringement by its customers, that could involve thousands of works infringed, meaning statutory damages of millions.

Gamow might be less concerned about statutory damages. Even for willful infringement (and we have no facts yet that suggest willfulness), the maximum is $150,000 where there was only one work infringed. That may be well within the budget of a Hollywood movie. But rather than statutory damages, the plaintiff may elect actual damage and profits attributable to the infringement. This could include the fee that a screenwriter for such a film would get. If the court finds that movie's success sprang principally from elements copied from the story, profits to be handed over could be millions of dollars. Attorney's fees might also be awarded. Moreover, unlike Alpher and Bethe, Gamow would fear an injunction, which would shut down his use of the movie. Likewise, impoundment and destruction of infringing copies would be hard to bear (although rarely awarded in this sort of case).

In short, remedies play a key role in assessing the real-world impact of copyright.

DAMAGES AND PROFITS

Actual Damages

The successful plaintiff is entitled to an award of damages and disgorgement of profits: "The copyright owner is entitled to recover the actual damages suffered by him or her as a result of the infringement, and any profits of the infringer that are attributable to the infringement and are not taken into account in computing the actual damages." 17 U.S.C. §504. The monetary award serves two purposes: "Damages are awarded to compensate the copyright owner for losses from the infringement, and profits are awarded to prevent the infringer from unfairly benefiting from a wrongful act." House Report No. 94-1476. Defendants are liable "jointly and severally," meaning that each defendant may be liable for the entire amount of damages award. If six defendants are liable, for example, their respective liability is not limited to one-sixth of the award.

Damages to the plaintiff could come in many forms. There could be lost revenue from fewer sales of the copyrighted work or fewer sales of derivative works or related products. There could be loss of licensing opportunities or damage to the plaintiff's overall business. Damages could include payment of the licensing fee that the copyright owner would have charged the defendant for the use in question. Such a "hypothetical transaction test" is often used in patent cases and can apply in copyright as well. In computing damages, courts may look to the actual price for the work or assess a fair market value for licensing such a work. In any case, the statute makes clear that causation must be shown, allowing recovery for damages suffered "as a result of the infringement." The burden is on the plaintiff to show damages, not just to request speculative monetary awards.

A jury awarded Oracle some $1.3 billion as damages for copyright infringement. The courts, however, overturned the damages award. The court reasoned that Oracle had not presented sufficient evidence on which to calculate the lost licensing revenue. Oracle was entitled to whatever licensing fee the parties would have agreed to in a hypothetical transaction but "offered no evidence of the type on which plaintiffs ordinarily rely to prove that they would have entered into such a license, such as past licensing history or a plaintiff's previous licensing practices." Oracle did not show "actual use of the copyrighted works, and an objectively verifiable number of customers lost as a result." Nor did Oracle show another basis for calculation, such as licensing practices by other companies in the industry. *Oracle*, however, provides guidance for future litigants by showing the sort of evidence that will support a damages verdict. *See Oracle Corp. v. SAP AG*, 2014

U.S. App. LEXIS 16840 (9th Cir. Aug. 29, 2014) (affirming trial court's decision to overturn verdict). A court applied the hypothetical transaction test and looked at previous license agreements in holding the U.S. Postal Service liable for $684,844.94 for using an image of the Korean War Memorial without the authorization of its sculptor. *Gaylord v. United States*, 112 Fed. Cl. 539 (Fed. Cl. 2013).

In addition to damages, the plaintiff is entitled to recover "any profits of the infringer that are attributable to the infringement." The statute does not allow double counting here, limiting recovery to profits "not taken into account in computing the actual damages." If the defendant sold 1,000 copies of a book, the plaintiff cannot argue for damages (1,000 lost sales) in addition to recouping the defendant's profits from those 1,000 sales. But the defendant must have profited in a separate market, as by making a film from a book or using photographs in an advertisement.

Figuring relevant profits may be straightforward: For unauthorized sales of a book, profits might simply be the infringer's book sales minus its costs. But for other cases, apportionment may be required. Where a short story is used to make a movie, some of the movie's profits may be attributable to use of the story, but some may be a result of other elements, such as box office appeal of the stars, special effects, marketing campaigns.

Actions outside the United States do not infringe the U.S. copyright in a work, but some courts will allow damages for overseas activity where the damages flow from infringement within the United States. *See L.A. News Serv. v. Reuters TV Intl.*, 149 F.3d 987 (9th Cir. 1998).

A special provision governs businesses that infringe copyright by receiving transmissions of works, such as a business that had a radio or TV on and was too big to qualify for protection under section 110(5). A defendant who makes an unreasonable claim of protection under section 110(5) may be liable for additional damages, set by doubling the licensing fee the defendant should have paid over the previous three years.

Statutory Damages

Statutory damages are key to copyright litigation and licensing practice. If a bar has been playing dozens of copyrighted songs without a license, actual damages may be difficult to prove. But statutory damages could easily run into hundreds of thousands of dollars. That gives considerable leverage to the representatives of the copyright holders in negotiating a license or in litigation. Statutory damages are available only if the copyright had been registered at the time of infringement, so that provides a strong incentive to register copyrights (and recall registration is relatively simple and inexpensive).

Actual damages and profits in many settings may be small or difficult to prove. If the copyright was registered at the time of infringement (or within three months of publication, for infringement of a published work), the plaintiff may choose instead to receive statutory damages:

> [T]he copyright owner may elect, at any time before final judgment is rendered, to recover, instead of actual damages and profits, an award of statutory damages for all infringements involved in the action, with respect to any one work, for which any one infringer is liable individually, or for which any two or more infringers are liable jointly and severally, in a sum of not less than $750 or more than $30,000 as the court considers just.

17 U.S.C. §504(c).

A copyright holder may be entitled a damages award, even where she does not prove damages. Damages may be difficult to prove in many cases of infringement. The possibility of statutory damages may roughly compensate copyright holders and deter some potential infringers, who might otherwise be effectively immune from suit. Statutory damages have also been justified as a means to counter a possible underenforcement problem, because copyright owners often have little means to detect whether their works are being used with permission, where such use may be widespread, private, and beyond the knowledge of the copyright holder. *See* Roger D. Blair and Thomas F. Cotter, *Intellectual Property: Economic and Legal Dimensions of Rights and Remedies*, 77-78 (2005).

For each work infringed, the court is to award between $750 and $30,000. *Id.* In deciding on the amount to award, the fact finder has broad discretion to consider such factors as whether defendant knew she was infringing, financial benefits such as profits or reduced expenses, the number of infringing acts, the amount of copyrighted material used, harm to the copyright holder, and deterrent to other potential infringers. *Cf. Feltner v. Columbia Pictures TV*, 523 U.S. 340 (1998) (holding that defendant has right to jury trial on factual issue of amount of statutory damages). The statute further provides that for willful infringement, the range may be increased to $150,000 per work. Willful infringement requires "(1) that the defendant was actually aware of the infringing activity, or (2) that the defendant's actions were the result of 'reckless disregard' for, or 'willful blindness' to, the copyright holder's rights." *Island Software & Computer Serv. v. Microsoft Corp.*, 413 F.3d 257, 263 (2d Cir. 2005).

The court may also reduce the range to $200 for innocent infringers where the "infringer was not aware and had no reason to believe that his or her acts constituted an infringement of copyright." *Id.* This innocent infringer defense is not available, however, if the copyright notices appeared on copies of the work accessible to the defendant. 17 U.S.C. §402(d). *See Maverick Recording Co. v. Harper*, 598 F.3d 193 (5th Cir. 2010). The statutory damages may be zero dollars for certain specified infringers (such as employees of libraries) who reasonably believed they were protected by fair use. 17 U.S.C. §504(c).

A key practical point is that there may be an award of statutory damages per work infringed. Some defendants infringe only one work, such as an author who copies from another author's book. But some defendants copy lots of works, like a music pirate who might sell hundreds of different titles. The statutory award may be much greater in such cases.

It is not always clear how many works have been infringed. The statute addresses some cases: "For the purposes of this subsection, all the parts of a compilation or derivative work constitute one work." One can read this provision two ways. One way is to read it as a limitation: a defendant who copies *Best Short Stories of 2006* is liable for one award of statutory damages (for copying the compilation), not an award for each story in the book. *See XOOM v. Imageline*, 323 F.3d 279, 285 (4th Cir.). Some, however, read it to authorize one award for infringing the compilation copyright but also an award for each work in the compilation. *See* Goldstein, *Copyright*, §12.2.2.1(a). That reading seeks to give effect to the underlying purpose of statutory remedies but seems hard to square with the words of the statute.

Another unsettled question arises when the compilation itself is not copied, but rather only parts that also appear outside the compilation are copied. If three songs appear on the same compilation CD, it is not settled whether copying them independently (as by downloading them from different sites) would infringe one or three works. Other sorts of works raise similar issues. One court held that each episode of a weekly television program was a separate work. *See Columbia Pictures Indus. v. Krypton Broad. of Birmingham, Inc.*, 259 F.3d 1186, 1193 (9th Cir. 2001). *Krypton* applied a commonly used test: whether the purported work "has an independent economic value and is, in itself, viable."

The statute specifies a range of $750 to $30,000 per work (up to $150,000 for willful infringement, down to $200 or even zero for some innocent infringers). It does not specify how the court should decide on a number within that range. Courts look at many factors: harm to the plaintiff and to the value of the copyright, the defendant's good faith or lack thereof, the nature of the works, and effects on third parties.

Statutory damages (and attorney's fees) are available only if the copyright was registered at the time of infringement or shortly after publication. That may be the most compelling reason to register a copyright, because it makes it much stronger to enforce. Registration after infringement will not give a right to statutory damages. What if someone infringes before registration, and continues to infringe after registration. Some courts hold that there may be no statutory damages if any infringement preceded registration, even if the infringement is different in nature. That approach supports the incentive for early infringement. *S. Credentialing Support Servs., L.L.C. v. Hammond Surgical Hosp., L.L.C.*, 946 F.3d 780, 787 (5th Cir. 2020).

Courts are struggling to determine the limits on statutory damages. In two noted cases involving music downloading, juries awarded hefty statutory damages: $1.92 million for 24 songs and $675,000 for 30 songs, respectively. *Capitol Records Inc. v. Thomas-Rasset*, 680 F. Supp. 2d 1045 (D. Minn. 2010); *Sony BMG Music Entertainment v. Tenenbaum*, 721 F. Supp. 2d 85 (D. Mass. 2010). Both courts reduced the awards to some $2,250 per song. On the appeal in *Sony*, the First Circuit held that the trial court erred in holding the award to be unconstitutional, as offending due process. Rather than addressing the thorny constitutional issues (due process, Seventh Amendment), the trial court should have first applied the common-law rule of remittitur, which allows a court to reduce an excessive award (and give the plaintiff a choice of accepting the reduced award or having a new trial). *See Sony BMG Music Entertainment v. Tenenbaum*, No. 10-1883 (1st Cir. 2011). Statutory damages can add up. Where Cox Communications permitted widespread music infringement by its subscribers, the resulting lawsuit implicated some 10,017 copyrights; the jury awarded statutory damages of $99,830.29 per work, for a total over one billion dollars (although the judgment was adjusted downward for some overlap in the works, such as limiting damages to one award per work, even if it had multiple copyright owners). *See Sony Music Entm't v. Cox Commc'ns, Inc.*, No. 1:18-CV-950-LO-JFA, 2020 WL 3121306, at *26 (E.D. Va. June 2, 2020).

Punitive Damages

Courts are split on whether punitive damages may be awarded in federal copyright cases. They are subject to constitutional limitations. The Sixth Circuit held that an award of $3.5 million in addition to compensatory damages of $3,66,939 was impermissibly excessive. *See Bridgeport Music, Inc. v. Justin Combs Publ'g*, 507 F.3d 470 (6th Cir. Tenn. 2007). Courts will look to whether "the harm caused was physical as opposed to economic; the tortious conduct evinced an indifference to or a reckless disregard of the health or safety of others; the target of the conduct had financial vulnerability; the conduct involved repeated actions or was an isolated incident; and the harm was the result of intentional malice, trickery, or deceit, or mere accident." *Id.*, citing Supreme Court authority.

Note that such infringement judgments may not be dischargeable in bankruptcy, unlike unsecured debts generally. Statutory damages awarded in bankruptcy for copyright infringement, along with damages for trademark infringement, were held nondischargeable where the defendant knowingly participated in the sale of devices to view television programs without authorization.[1] In addition, judgments can have a long reach, sufficient to get assets located in other jurisdictions.[2]

Bankruptcy?

Suppose Music Company gets a big damages award against Downloader. Downloader has few assets. Can Downloader file bankruptcy and get the damages award discharged, along with any other debts that Downloader has? Not all debts are dischargeable in bankruptcy. The Bankruptcy Code does not specifically address liability for intellectual property infringement. Rather, courts apply the general standard, that a debtor may not be discharged for debt that arising out of "willful and malicious injury." How that applies in intellectual property cases has not been fleshed out by the courts.

Examples

1. *No harm, no foul.* Isaiah, an art student, posts an abstract design on his website. One day, he sees it on the cover of Taylor's best-selling novel, *Monopoly Topology*. At trial, witnesses for both sides agree that the cover design did not affect sales of the novel. Indeed, most buyers saw the cover only after buying or ordering the book. A typical artist's commission for such a cover would have been $1,000. Isaiah's attorney argues that damages should be a mere ten cents a copy. At 10 million copies sold, that would amount to $1 million. Anything less, she argues, would fail to discourage publishers from stealing. What damages should the court award?

---

1. As described above, Debtor's conduct—the sale of TVpads by the deliberate promotion of their use to infringe Plaintiffs' rights—was wrongful and without just cause. He knew, or should have known, that Plaintiffs were losing revenues because of this activity. Moreover, Debtor's actions to remove channel listings from the website, his use of a pseudonym, and his solicitation of advice from SEO as to how to reduce the appearance of his own involvement, demonstrate that Debtor was conscious at all times of the risks inherent to this business. Because the Debtor directed and facilitated others' infringement of Plaintiffs' copyrights and trademarks, the Court finds that his conduct was malicious, as well as willful, as required by § 523(a)(6). *China Cent. TV v. Bhalla* (In re Bhalla), 573 B.R. 265, 279 (Bankr. M.D. Fla. 2017).

2. *See Koehler v. Bank of Bermuda Ltd.*, 12 N.Y.3d 533, 541, 911 N.E.2d 825, 831 (2009):

> In short, the principle that a New York court may issue a judgment ordering the turnover of out-of-state assets is not limited to judgment debtors, but applies equally to garnishees. Consequently, we conclude that a court sitting in New York that has personal jurisdiction over a garnishee bank can order the bank to produce stock certificates [of a Bermuda corporation, namely those of the Reef Resort] located outside New York, pursuant to CPLR 5225(b).

2. *No better late than never*. Maria makes copies of all the photos made by Isabella, some 200 in all. Isabella considers suing for copyright infringement. She realizes that she will have little to show by way of her actual damages or Maria's profits, but statutory damages would run $750 to $30,000 per work. The copyrights have not been registered, so she decides to quickly register them to qualify for statutory damages. Would that work?

3. *Restitution*. Evil Studio steals a screenplay, *Shark Gallery*, written by Ian, and makes a big-budget movie. The customary fee for such a screenplay would be $5 million. Evil Studio bungles the making and marketing of the movie and loses millions. When Ian sues, Evil Studio gladly agrees to an injunction, happy to take the stinker off the market. But, it evilly argues, no damages may be awarded, because the movie was a loser. Correct? Does it matter in this case whether the copyright was registered at the time of infringement?

4. *How many works?* Over a long career, Avigit's many photographs appear in various publications and exhibitions. Avigit retains the copyrights and registers them all. He finally publishes his favorite 1,000 images in a single book. Standish, without permission, copies dozens of them from the book for use in a clothing catalog. The range of statutory damages is $750 to $30,000 per work infringed (up to $150,000 for willful infringement, down to $200 for an infringer that reasonably believed she was not infringing, and down to zero for some such as library employees). How many works were infringed here: dozens of copyrights in photographs or one copyright in a book of photographs?

5. *Stretch*. Polar Bear shoots whitewater kayaking video and licenses it to Timex for promotion of watches. Timex likes the footage so much that the company keeps using it beyond the expiration of the license to promote Expedition Watches. Polar Bear seeks damages, arguing that it might otherwise have sold $200,000 worth of a video, *PaddleQuest*. It was unable to produce the video and market it, because Timex did not forward funds for additional use of the footage. In addition, Polar Bear argues that Timex made indirect profits from using the footage because it enhanced the value of the Expedition Watch brand, even where it was not used in advertising. A jury awards Polar Bear all of those damages. Should the court sustain the award?

6. *Sticky debt*. Wheeler runs a profitable business, selling illegal counterfeit cable boxes to thrifty homeowners to enjoy cable television and premium movies for free. Eventually, Wheeler is on the wrong end of a large jury verdict for copyright infringement. Can Wheeler get the debt discharged in bankruptcy?

Explanations

1. The work was evidently unregistered at the time of infringement, so statutory damages and attorney's fees are not available. Isaiah is entitled to actual damages and recovery of profits attributable to the infringement. Proven actual damages appear to be no more than \$1,000, the commission that would have been paid. No recoverable profits are shown, because none of the book's profits are attributable to the infringement. His argument for ten cents a copy is really a request for punitive damages — but the statute makes no allowance for punitive damages, only for compensation (actual damages) and restitution (recovery of profits). The result would be different if he could show more actual damages (damages to him or the value of the work, or a higher lost licensing fee).

2. Registration now will not lead to statutory damages for Maria's past infringement. Statutory damages and attorney's fees are only available if the copyright was registered at the time of infringement (or was registered no later than three months after first publication, and infringement occurred after publication). 17 U.S.C. §412. The works were unregistered at the time of infringement. The three-month period for recently published works applies only to infringement of published works. This example shows that if the copyright owner wishes to have statutory damages and attorney's fees available, she must register in a timely fashion.

3. A court would likely award Ian \$5 million in damages. The successful plaintiff is entitled to actual damages and to defendant's profits attributable to the infringement. Had the movie made profits, the court would have had to determine which portion was attributable to use of the screenplay (as opposed to other factors, such as the contribution of the director, actors, and marketers). Defendant had no profits here, so there would be none to disgorge. But Ian is also entitled to recover damages. A good way to show damages is the fair market value of the infringing use. The customary screenplay fee would be \$5 million, so the court would likely award that.

   The damages award would not be affected if the copyright was unregistered. Infringement gives a right to actual damages and profits, whether the copyright was timely registered or not. (Note that Ian will be required to register as a precondition to bringing suit, but that may be done after infringement.) If the copyright was timely registered, the plaintiff may elect to receive statutory damages instead of actual damages and profits. Statutory damages would not be available if Ian had not registered — but the maximum award of statutory damages is \$150,000, even for willful infringement (which there was here). Ian would prefer actual damages of $5 million.

4. This example raises an unsettled question of interpreting the statute. Standish would argue that he infringed only one work: the book, which was a compilation containing the various photographs. The statute provides, "For the purposes of this subsection, all the parts of a compilation or derivative work constitute one work." Standish would argue that the various photographs were parts of the compilation, so he only is liable for one award of statutory damages.

   Avigit would argue that he is not claiming infringement in the compilation copyright. He does not contend that Standish copied the selection, arrangement, or coordination of the photographs. Rather, he is suing for infringement in each of the dozens of individual photographs. Some courts would apply the test, whether the purported work has an independent economic value and is, in itself, viable. The various photographs would qualify as separate works because they appeared separately in publications and exhibitions. Under this approach, Standish would be liable for a separate award of statutory damages for each photograph.

5. The award was overturned for lack of a causal connection. The theory that had the money arrived, Polar Bear would have funded a successful campaign to sell the video, was "pie in the sky." More concrete evidence is required. The infringer is also liable for a portion of profits attributable to the infringement, but the indirect profit theory was likewise too thin. Rather, a basis for apportioning such profits must be shown. *See Polar Bear Productions v. Timex Corporation*, 384 F.3d 700 (9th Cir. 2004).

6. Such intentional infringement would likely be held nondischargeable, as "willful and malicious injury." *China Cent. TV v. Bhalla (In re Bhalla)*, 573 B.R. 265, 281 (Bankr. M.D. Fla. 2017).

INJUNCTIONS

The court may "grant temporary and final injunctions on such terms as it may deem reasonable to prevent or restrain infringement of a copyright." 17 U.S.C. §502. Although copyright injunctions used to be almost automatic, courts now apply the same general standards for injunctions as other cases. A common approach is to consider three factors: (1) the threat of irreparable harm to the moving party, (2) the balance of harm between this harm and the harm suffered by the nonmoving party if the injunction is granted, and (3) the public interest. *Taylor Corp. v. Four Seasons Greetings, LLC*, 403 F.3d 958, 967 (8th Cir. 2005). For a preliminary injunction, a court will likely also consider the probability of success on the merits.

In practice, courts readily grant injunctions in copyright cases. The copyright owner has the exclusive right to use the work, and courts will often enjoin infringers from continuing unauthorized uses. But a court may decline to grant an injunction, for example, where the infringing use is a small portion of the defendant's work, so the harm from forbidding the defendant to use the work considerably outweighs any harm to the plaintiff. Sometimes a court will refrain from enjoining the defendant, provided that a reasonable licensing fee is paid for continued use. *See, e.g.*, *Salinger v. Colting*, 607 F.3d 68 (2d Cir. 2010) (permitting possible continuing publication of infringing sequel to *Catcher in the Rye*, subject to payment of damages). Issues of free speech may come into play when an injunction would have the effect of unduly burdening the defendant's ability to express herself or to disseminate ideas. In a related vein, an injunction should not prevent the use of uncopyrighted elements of a work, such as nonoriginal elements, ideas, and functional aspects.

Beyond the question of whether to grant an injunction, the court must decide the scope of the injunction. The injunction should not be too broad or narrow but instead should be tailored to fit the infringement and protect the interests of the parties. For example, rather than enjoining all further use of a film, the court may enjoin further use of the portions containing infringing elements.

The availability of injunctive relief is a powerful tool for the copyright owner. Suppose a movie is held to infringe the copyright in a song or in a short story. If the soundtrack infringes the copyright in a song, the moviemakers may be able to edit the soundtrack and then continue distribution. If the entire screenplay copies from a short story, then an injunction against further infringement means ceasing further distribution. That gives a powerful incentive to reach a settlement with the story copyright owner.

Example

1. *Enjoin?* The animated film *Phlogiston* contains a 30-second scene that made considerable unauthorized use of *Fireworks*, a painting by Sarah Jane. Sarah Jane seeks actual damages, profits, and an injunction against any further distribution or performance of the film or any derivative works based on the film. The film has been shown at a few previews but has not yet been commercially released. The studio argues that an injunction should not be awarded where only 30 seconds of a one-hour film infringes. Rather, damages would be appropriate. Should *Phlogiston* be shut down?

Explanation

1. A court would likely consider (1) the threat of irreparable harm to the moving party, (2) the balance of harm between this harm and the harm suffered by the nonmoving party if the injunction is granted, and (3) the public interest. The third factor, public interest, may matter less here than with such works as textbooks or medical journals. The issue would be the balance of harm to the parties. Sarah Jane may be harmed by widespread release of the infringing use of her work. Damages would somewhat reduce the harm to her. A complete injunction could be very harmful to the studio if it meant that the film could not be used at all. It would appear, however, that the court could choose something in the middle—an injunction that the film could not be distributed or performed until the 30-second infringing sequence was removed or replaced with a noninfringing version. The court would need more facts here (going to potential damage to Sarah Jane's artistic reputation and to the studio's situation). The example serves simply to show that injunctive relief is a matter of equity rather than mechanics and can be tailored.

ATTORNEY'S FEES AND COSTS

In its discretion, the court may award costs to the prevailing party. "Costs" are limited to specified expenses like copying or translation fees, and do not include larger expenses like fees for attorneys and expert witnesses. 17 U.S.C. §505; *Rimini St., Inc. v. Oracle USA, Inc.*, 139 S. Ct. 873, 878-879, 203 L. Ed. 2d 180 (2019). In exceptional cases, successful plaintiffs and successful defendants may seek attorney's fees, and the same standard should govern both. *See Fogerty v. Fantasy, Inc.*, 510 U.S. 517 (1994). *Fogerty* did not set a standard for the award of fees but approvingly cited consideration of such factors as "frivolousness, motivation, objective unreasonableness (both in the factual and in the legal components of the case) and the need in particular circumstances to advance considerations of compensation and deterrence." As with statutory damages, fees are awarded against infringers only if the copyright was registered at the time of infringement or within three months of publication.

Unreasonableness in infringement or in litigation may support an award of fees to the other party. Fees may be awarded where defendant makes an unreasonable defense, such as claiming fair use for a purely commercial use with no redeeming fair use factors or denying facts defendant knew to be true. Fees may be awarded when the plaintiff lacked a reasonable basis for an infringement claim, such as claiming infringement where only an idea was copied, claiming infringement with no basis to show copying, or claiming infringement in an obviously noncopyrighted work (like a work published in 1910 or a work created by a federal employee). Fees were awarded against an overly persistent plaintiff even when the defendant copied protected expression and when defenses of fair use or de minimis infringement were clearly applicable. *See Computer Corp. v. Ergonome Inc.*, 387 F.3d 403 (5th Cir. 2004) (claiming infringement by use of minimal portions of a work with no impact on market for copyrighted work).

The Supreme Court has emphasized that, even if a party takes a reasonable position, it may be subject to attorney's fees awards for other reasons. A "court may order fee-shifting because of a party's litigation misconduct . . . or to deter repeated instances of copyright infringement or overaggressive assertions of copyright claims, again even if the losing position was reasonable in a particular case." *Kirtsaeng v. John Wiley & Sons, Inc.*, 136 S. Ct. 1979, 1988-1989 (2016).

IMPOUNDMENT AND DISPOSITION OF INFRINGING ARTICLES

Infringing copies and equipment used to make them may be ordered impounded and destroyed. The court at any time "may order the impounding, on such terms as it may deem reasonable, of all copies or phonorecords claimed to have been made or used in violation of the copyright owner's exclusive rights, and of all plates, molds, matrices, masters, tapes, film negatives, or other articles by means of which such copies of phonorecords may be reproduced." 17 U.S.C. §503(a). At final judgment, the court may order destruction or other disposition of such articles, including having them delivered to the plaintiff. 17 U.S.C. §503(b). Impounding will not be ordered in every case. An infringing tattoo, as some have noted, will probably be left in place. Even infringing books may be left alone if other remedies are available.

CRIMINAL LIABILITY

"Warning: The unauthorized reproduction or distribution of this copyrighted work is illegal. Criminal copyright infringement, including infringement without monetary gain, is investigated by the FBI and is punishable by up to five years in federal prison and a fine of $250,000." You have undoubtedly seen this warning on your rented DVD of *The Muppets Take Manhattan*.

Criminal sanctions may indeed apply. There is criminal liability for "any person who infringes a copyright willfully either (1) for purposes of commercial advantage or private financial gain, or (2) by the reproduction or distribution, including by electronic means, during any 180-day period, of 1 or more copies or phonorecords of 1 or more copyrighted works, which have a total retail value of more than $1,000." 17 U.S.C. §506. The standard for liability is high. The Ninth Circuit held that criminal copyright liability requires that the defendant knew of the illegal nature of the activity. *United States v. Liu*, 731 F.3d 982 (9th Cir. 2013).

There are also criminal sanctions aimed at preventing piracy of copyrighted works. It is a felony to make an unauthorized recording of a movie in a movie theater. *See* 18 U.S.C. §2319B. It is a crime to distribute unauthorized copies of a work prior to commercial distribution if the work is a computer program, musical work, motion picture, or other audiovisual work, or sound recording. 17 U.S.C. §506(a)(1)(C). Videotaping in the local megaplex or passing around copies of a movie not yet out on DVD may lead to jail time.

CHAPTER 20

Three State Law Theories and Federal Preemption

This chapter discusses some state law theories related to copyright and the extent to which the federal copyright statute preempts state law.

CONTRACT LAW AND IDEA SUBMISSIONS

How to get legal protection for an idea? The best bet is to get others to promise not to use or disclose the idea, before telling them your idea. Mere ideas are not protected by copyright, patent, or trademark law. The owner of a copyright has the exclusive right to make copies of the work, distribute the work publicly, adapt it, display copies publicly, or perform the work publicly. But copyright protects only creative expression, not ideas (no matter how original and creative). Likewise, a patentee has the right to exclude others from using, making, offering to sell, selling, or importing the invention. But mere ideas are not patentable; the invention must be reduced to practice as a product or process. A trademark owner may exclude others from using her symbol in a manner that is likely to confuse consumers, but trademark law likewise does not protect ideas. A valuable idea might have sufficient potential commercial value to be a trade secret, but trade secret does not grant the owner exclusive rights in the idea. He has trade secret protection against misappropriation of the idea, but only if he keeps the idea secret, using reasonable security measures. Once the idea becomes public, anyone may use it.

Contract law can be used to gain some partial protection for ideas, provided the parties so agree (implicitly or explicitly). An inventor might share her ideas with potential investors subject to a nondisclosure agreement, a contract by which the recipients of the information agree not to use it. More broadly, employees, investors, and others in a firm often sign contracts controlling their use of ideas: nondisclosure agreements, noncompete agreements, assignments of rights concerning works and inventions. That way, ideas may be circulated within the firm, with contract law giving some protection against the ideas being disclosed. *See* Oren Bar-Gill and Gideon Parchomovsky, *Intellectual Property and the Boundaries of the Firm* (2004) (suggesting that intellectual property law affects the optimal size of the firm because pre-patent innovation must be carried out within the boundaries of a single firm).

Here we focus on the idea submission cases. The lack of protection for ideas can pose a problem for someone who has an idea she believes is valuable. Someone might have an idea for a movie, book, or children's toy. To exploit the idea, she might need to convince a movie studio, publisher, or manufacturer to produce the proposed item. If she discloses an unprotected idea, the recipient could simply make the movie, book, or toy and sell it without paying her for it. If the idea is unprotected, the recipient does not need the creator's permission and is not obliged to pay her royalties.

Contract law can be used not to give exclusive rights against the world (like a copyright, patent, or trademark) but to impose an obligation on the recipient of the idea. The submitter could offer to disclose the idea to the studio, publisher, or manufacturer, subject to an agreement to share the proceeds of the movie, book, or toy.

In a typical idea submission case, the submitter alleges that he submitted a valuable idea that the recipient used without paying compensation required by an explicit or implicit obligation. Courts have many sources of law to apply to such fact patterns, including contract, unjust enrichment, fiduciary relations, property, and fraud. Here we discuss just some of the contract law rules that courts have employed in idea submission cases.

Courts apply several contract doctrines but with common threads. Courts may require that the idea be novel and concrete, that the parties have an express or implied agreement, and that the recipient has actually used the idea submitted. The standards for novelty and concreteness vary considerably. An idea may not be novel if the recipient already knew it, could easily have developed it herself, or could have gotten it elsewhere. A higher standard of novelty might require that the idea also be strikingly creative. Concreteness will not be met if the idea is too vague or preliminary to be of any specific use. A higher standard may require that the idea be developed into a commercialized form.

As discussed below, courts look to the requirements listed above in applying contract law doctrine to idea submission cases.

Two practical points: First, someone who has an idea for a movie or for a product might want the studio or a venture capitalist to sign a nondisclosure agreement before hearing the idea. But the studio and venture capitalist are likely to say, "If you want to see if we are interested in your idea, pitch the idea. But we do not sign nondisclosures, as a matter of policy. That's much more litigation risk than we want." Second, getting legal protection for an idea is often not necessary. Businesses often succeed not because they were the first with an idea, but rather they followed through on the idea and did all the other things (marketing, refining, networking, . . .) that make a business succeed (and maybe had some luck).

WAS A CONTRACT FORMED?

Express Contract: Offer and Acceptance, Definiteness

The requirements of offer and acceptance provide several hurdles for a submitter to overcome to show a binding contract. Ideas are often submitted in a manner that does not amount to an offer to enter into a contract. The submitter may just send in the idea, send in the idea with a request for payment, or leave the question of compensation to the judgment of the recipient. If the idea is not concrete, an intended offer may be too vague to be the basis of a contract.

Even if the idea is submitted as part of a clear offer to enter into a contract, the recipient may clearly reject the offer. She may make an acceptance, but one that varies the terms; without an acceptance that matches the offer, courts may hold no contract formed. The submitter may also claim that the recipient accepted the offer by conduct, by using the idea. But when the idea was not novel or concrete, the court may hold that there was no acceptance by conduct. Suppose the nonoriginal idea was to make a film from a best-selling detective novel. If the recipient studio did indeed make the film, a court could hold that it nonetheless did not accept the contract by taking such an obvious course of action. The idea may also be too vague to have been accepted by conduct. Likewise, if the recipient's project is different from the idea submitted, there is no acceptance by conduct. There are few cases where someone has proven damages from stealing an idea.

Consideration

If the idea submitted is not valuable (because it was not novel and concrete), the consideration necessary for a binding contract may not be shown. Consideration is a notoriously elusive doctrine in contract law. But when one party to the transaction gives nothing of value to the other, courts can use the requirement of consideration to hold that there was no binding contract, even if an express agreement was made.

Implied Contract

In many idea submission cases, there is no express offer and acceptance of a legally binding contract. In some circumstances, courts hold that an implied agreement exists, as evidenced from the conduct of the parties and the surrounding circumstances. Courts look to such factors as industry custom, whether the recipient encouraged submission of the idea, previous dealings between the parties, any confidential relationship between the parties, the status and commercial sophistication of the parties, and the nature of the idea and the relevant business. A commonly used test is whether a reasonable person in the recipient's position would have considered that the idea was submitted subject to an implicit condition that use of the idea would require compensation.

DID THE DEFENDANT USE THE SUBMITTED IDEA?

If the defendant does not use the submitted idea, there may be no obligation to pay, even if a binding contract was made. Suppose Writer and Studio agree that Writer will submit an idea for a movie to Studio, contingent on a fee and acknowledgment in the credits of the film. Writer's idea is a comedy based on the nineteenth-century comic novel *Diary of a Nobody*. But Studio already has such a project under way, with someone working on the screenplay and others choosing a cast. Because Studio did not get the idea from Writer, a court may hold it did not use Writer's idea and there is no liability to pay. The result might be the same if Studio subsequently made a movie based on a nineteenth-century comic novel—but a different one than suggested.

If the idea submitted is not novel and concrete, it may also be difficult to show that the defendant used the idea. If the idea is not novel, the defendant may likely have gotten the same idea from another source. If the idea is vague or preliminary, it is difficult to show that the defendant actually used that particular idea.

DID THE SUBMITTER PERFORM THE PROMISED CONTRACTUAL OBLIGATION?

If the idea is not novel and concrete, the submitter may have failed to live up to her obligation under the contract. Suppose Consultant offers to sell a valuable new manufacturing process to Business, contingent on Business paying Consultant a percentage of revenue. After the agreement is made, Consultant submits a process that is already well known in the industry (and so not novel) or is very vague. Consultant's failure to produce an idea that matched its representations breaches the contract, relieving Business of the obligation to pay.

AVOIDING CONTRACTUAL OBLIGATIONS

As noted above, some firms maintain policies to ensure that they are not deemed to have explicitly or implicitly agreed to contracts with idea submitters. Venture capitalists frequently make clear that they will not sign nondisclosure agreements when they hear "pitches" of business ideas. Otherwise, a venture capitalist might turn down an investment in one company and then find itself unable to invest in others that have similar ideas. A movie studio, music company, or book publisher may have a policy of sending back unsolicited manuscripts or tapes without reading or hearing them to avoid any possible obligation to the authors. It might also save some time—but pass on some opportunities. The fact that ideas are unprotected, in some cases, makes it more difficult for the creator of the idea to share it with others. The alternative—ownership of abstract ideas—would result in much greater restrictions on the flow of ideas.

Examples

1. *No-brainer.* Tenzing successfully builds and sells ice axes for mountaineering under the brand name K1. Tenzing's sales have been increasing at 10 percent per year for the past six years. Edmund, an engineer and marketing consultant, reads an article in a finance magazine lauding Tenzing's operation. Edmund approaches Tenzing and offers to give him a suggestion that will increase Tenzing's sales by 10 percent, on the condition that Tenzing pays a hefty finder's fee. Tenzing agrees to the transaction. Edmund then says, "Just keep doing what you are doing. Success breeds success." Tenzing continues to operate his business without substantial changes, just as he had planned before speaking with Edmund. Tenzing's sales increase by 10 percent in the next year. Is Tenzing contractually bound to pay Edmund's hefty fee?

2. *Molehill?* Margaret, the CEO of Mortar Products, is concerned about whether her company is keeping up with the times. Mortar has made and sold essentially the same line of building supplies for more than a decade. Mortar advertises regularly in trade magazines, featuring its slogan ("Good old dependable Mortar"), some endorsements by well-known builders, and rather prosaic listings of its products and their prices. Margaret and her management team are considering expanding into new product

areas and introducing a snazzy new advertising campaign. Margaret hires Lourdes Consulting Group to conduct a thorough marketing survey. The parties draw up a detailed contract, specifying the tasks Lourdes will perform (customer surveys, focus groups with leading buyers, benchmark comparisons with various companies, drafting of possible marketing campaigns). Lourdes and her associates spend several thousand hours compiling data and analyzing it. They draft a report detailing their findings and presenting a plan of action. In sum, the plan is for Margaret to avoid any substantial changes in the way the business is run. The present product lines are increasingly profitable. If Mortar were to expand into new product lines, it would be difficult to win market share, and the necessary investment in manufacturing and distribution facilities would be prohibitive. Even the marketing campaign should remain unchanged. The research shows great affection and trust among prospective buyers for the campaign. Margaret reads the report with great interest. She decides to follow the advice. She informs Lourdes, however, that she will not pay the fee because the report did not tell them to do anything they were not already doing. Is Margaret contractually obliged to pay the fee?

3. *Dear reader*. Phisto, a computer scientist, figures out an elegant way to write a short program that gets rid of advertising for Internet users. Phisto submits an article to a computer science journal, detailing his method. He also posts the paper on his website. In the first footnote to the paper, Phisto includes the following language: "Anyone who uses my method hereby agrees to pay me the modest fee of $365 per year, $1 a day, for avoiding all those annoying ads." Such a condition is highly unusual in the area. Rather, the information in published academic articles is generally considered to be free for whatever uses readers find. Phisto's paper becomes widely circulated among software developers, many of whom use it to write programs putting the method to work. The programs are in turn widely distributed and are often included with web browsers. Soon, millions of people are using programs that incorporate Phisto's method. Are they all obliged to pay Phisto $1 a day?

Explanations

1. Tenzing is not contractually bound to pay Edmund's hefty fee. A court would very likely hold that the idea was not sufficiently novel and concrete to support the creation of a binding obligation. Edmund's suggestion was completely obvious and based on no particular useful information. It may also be too vague to meet the concreteness requirement. Edmund's knowledge of Tenzing's operations was limited to reading a magazine article, so when Edmund advised him to continue his course of action, that advice had little specific content to it.

A court might use the lack of novelty and concreteness to apply any of several doctrines. It might hold that Edmund did not provide the necessary consideration for a binding contract, that Edmund's offer was too vague to form a binding contract, or that Tenzing did not use Edmund's obvious idea (but rather that Tenzing would have done the same thing without the suggestion).

2. Margaret is contractually obliged to pay the fee. This case involves both an idea submission and a contract for other services. Lourdes's performance of the various research services alone entitles her to at least compensation. In addition, the ideas submitted did not lack novelty and concreteness. Rather, they were well-supported arguments for choosing between various alternatives, for a specific business under specific circumstances. The plan of action could be described as obvious, but the suggestion was based on considerable research and analysis. Unlike the last case, the parties had a clearly drafted contract that specified their respective duties in detail. The suggestion had value because it was based on the research and analysis. Margaret clearly did use the idea (as well as the fruits of the research and analysis). Lourdes gave consideration—not just the suggestion but also the considerable resources used in compiling and analyzing data. So here, the court would hold that the various contract law requirements were met and that Margaret was obliged to pay for the specific, agreed-on services that she received.

3. Phisto is not entitled to payment from any of the people using his idea—neither the developers who wrote his method into their programs nor the users who used those programs. This case illustrates the fact that even if an idea is novel and concrete, submission of the idea to others who use it does not always entitle the submitter to compensation. There must be other circumstances to give rise to an express or implied obligation to pay for the idea. Phisto submitted his idea in a form that would make it part of public knowledge without any obligation to pay on the part of others. He did include the language "Anyone who uses my method hereby agrees to pay me the modest fee of $365 per year, $1 a day for avoiding all those annoying ads." Others did subsequently use the method, but a court would be unlikely to hold that this amounted to either an express or implied contract.

   The circumstances of submission were not such as to create an implied obligation. The method was published in an academic journal, in which writers and readers normally understood information to be free for use. The recipients had no confidential relationship with Phisto and had not encouraged him to submit commercially useful information. Indeed, most users did not have any direct contact with Phisto. No one made an express verbal acceptance of the contract. A court also would not find acceptance by conduct. Once the method had been published, it was widely known information among the public. Use of public information does not constitute acceptance of a contract (the doctrines of consideration or offer and acceptance could be used here). Otherwise, Phisto would effectively have the right to exclude others from using his publicly known process.

MISAPPROPRIATION

The tort of misappropriation (not to be confused with misappropriation of a trade secret) comes from *International News Service v. Associated Press*, 248 U.S. 215 (1918). AP and INS were two competing news services. AP, a cooperative of newspapers, expended considerable resources in gathering news and distributing news reports to its member newspapers throughout the United States. INS systematically obtained copies of the reports as quickly as possible and wired the information to its client newspapers. INS acted so quickly that its clients often received the reports as quickly as the local AP member newspaper.

The Court held that INS was liable for the tort of misappropriation, under federal common law, without defining the scope of the tort. A number of states later adopted the tort under state common law. Some cases interpreted the tort broadly to grant a right against the taking of valuable information where such taking seemed to violate business ethics. Other cases construed it very narrowly. The drafters of the third Restatement of Unfair Competition even advocated the rejection of the misappropriation tort because it was ill defined and covered material better left to other law such as copyright and patent.

The leading case now is *National Basketball Association v. Motorola*, 105 F.3d 841 (2d Cir. 1997). Motorola transmitted to its pager customers the latest information about NBA basketball games while the games were still in progress.

The *NBA* court held that to avoid preemption by the federal copyright act (preemption is discussed later in this chapter), the misappropriation tort survived under New York law in only a narrow version, applying where:

1. A plaintiff generates or gathers information at a cost
2. The information is time sensitive
3. A defendant's use of the information constitutes free-riding on the plaintiff's efforts
4. The defendant is in direct competition with a product or service offered by the plaintiffs
5. The ability of other parties to free-ride on the efforts of the plaintiff or others would so reduce the incentive to produce the product or service that its existence or quality would be substantially threatened

Motorola's conduct did not fall within such a narrowly defined tort. In particular, the fifth element was clearly not met. Motorola providing information over pagers did not threaten the existence of the NBA, even if the NBA's ability to create a competing service was hampered.

Examples

1. *Database.* Info LLC compiles white-page telephone books. Info spends considerable resources in gathering the names, addresses, and telephone numbers of everyone in a town, arranging the information alphabetically by name, and printing and distributing the phone books. Info gives the books away and makes money from selling advertisements in the books. Data LLC, a competitor, buys copies of the phone books from recipients. Data uses machines to disassemble the books and scan the information at much less cost than Info needed to compile the information. Data publishes and sells its own phone books. Is Data liable for misappropriation under the *NBA* test?

2. *The edge.* Punter News is a news service for stock market traders. Punter has dozens of sources and long-standing relationships with many important people in the finance world. Punter is often the first news service to get wind of developments that will affect stock prices. Punter charges a very high fee to subscribers. In return, Punter sends news out to subscribers as quickly as possible, 24 hours a day, and makes special efforts to reach subscribers wherever they are. The subscribers agree to use the information for their own trading purposes but not to share the information with others. One of Punter's subscribers is Levon Investing. Punter learns that Marta, an administrator at Levon, has used her access to Punter's reports to trade for her own account over the past several years. Marta has made many thousands of dollars in profits from this activity. Marta is aware that her use violates the terms on which the information is provided to Levon. Her conduct also violates her contract with Levon because it is contrary to Levon's employee regulations. Is Marta liable to Punter for the tort of misappropriation under the *NBA* test?

Explanations

1. Data is not liable for misappropriation under the *NBA* test. Most of the elements are met: Info gathered the information at a cost, Data's use probably constitutes free-riding because Data put little effort into getting the information, and Data and Info are in direct competition. But there is no showing that Data meets the last element, that the ability of people to make such use of the information would drastically reduce the incentive to gather the information. And the second element is clearly not met. The information is not time sensitive; to the contrary,

the information in a phone book is intended to remain useful for a long period of time. So not all of the necessary elements are met here. The case illustrates the fact that *NBA* leaves only a very narrow tort of misappropriation.

2. Marta is not liable to Punter for misappropriation. One element is that the defendant be in direct competition with a product or service offered by the plaintiff. But Marta does not offer a product or service that competes with Punter. She is simply buying and selling stock, rather than selling products or services. Marta is breaching her contract with Levon and knows her use violates the terms on which the information is provided. But the misappropriation tort does not depend solely on the wrongfulness of the defendant's conduct. Rather, as formulated by *NBA*, it requires meeting several very specific limitations. Note that some earlier cases may have applied misappropriation here, reasoning that Marta used valuable commercial information in an unethical manner. But the trend, exemplified by *NBA*, is away from such a broad formulation.

RIGHT OF PUBLICITY

Name, Image, and License rights are now a staple of commerce, for example by changing the economics of college sports. States are increasingly recognizing a right of publicity, an exclusive right to the commercial exploitation of one's identity. *See generally* J. Thomas McCarthy, *The Rights of Publicity and Privacy* (2d ed. 1987 and Supp.). Several policies support such a right. A right of publicity can create an incentive for people to do things that make them well known and create a demand for uses of their identity. The right can also be seen as preventing free-riding on the goodwill of others and as enforcing a moral right to control the exploitation of one's identity. The right can serve a role similar to trademarks to prevent consumer deception about an individual's association with goods and services. Historically, the right of publicity is often considered to be an extension of the right of privacy.

Other policy considerations weigh in the other direction, toward limiting the scope of the right to publicity. Like copyright, the right of publicity is a restraint on expression. Identities are material for speech, from entertainment to art to news reporting to gossip. The subject matter most interesting to people is people. To the extent that individuals control expression concerning them, avenues of expression are foreclosed, so a delicate balance is at stake.

The scope of the right of publicity varies considerably from state to state (and in many respects remains undefined). Some of the key issues in defining the extent of the right to publicity follow.

Whether the State Recognizes the Right of Publicity

Most states have adopted a right of publicity cause of action through case law or statute, but a number of states have not. Generally, these states have not definitively rejected the cause of action. More often, the highest court in the state has not decided the issue.

Who Has a Right of Publicity?

The right of publicity could be applied only when the individual has become well known. If an individual has not been the subject of publicity, one who uses her image for commercial purposes may not be undercutting uses that would have been made. The right could also be limited to its incentive rationale. If the right is an incentive to acts that gain acclaim, it could be limited to individuals who have earned fame through their achievements or professional efforts, as opposed to more accidental celebrities. But the general approach has been to extend the right to all individuals, even if there exists little public interest in a particular individual.

How Broadly the Protected Identity Is Defined

The right could be restricted to the use of one's name and likeness. The trend, however, is to recognize more broadly many ways in which individuals may be recognized. The right can apply to names, identifying phrases such as nicknames or catchphrases, voice, style of speaking, visual likenesses broadly defined (such as a silhouette or even a robot dressed, coifed, and posed in a way to bring a particular celebrity to mind).

States agree that whether the protected modes are broadly or narrowly defined, the characteristic at issue must be one that could identify the subject. If an anonymous individual has the name Carla Peirce, her right of publicity is not infringed if a character coincidentally named Carla Peirce is featured in advertisements because the public would not link the fictional Peirce with the real one. By contrast, it is less settled whether the likeness need be one that would be used by the public to actually identify the person. Suppose the face of an unknown person is used in a commercial, and the public has no idea who she is. Whether that invokes the right of publicity is a question unsettled in most jurisdictions.

How Broadly the Exclusive Right to Commercial Exploitation Is Defined

The right can be applied to uses of the subject's identity in advertising goods or services, but it could also be extended to a whole spectrum of commercial uses.

Duration of the Right

The term of protection may be set in many ways: the time in which the subject is well known to the public, a given term of years, the lifetime of the subject, the lifetime of the subject plus a given term of years, or even a perpetual right that would pass from generation to generation.

Assignability

Depending on how the right is categorized, this may govern whether the right is an assignable piece of property or an inalienable right.

Scope of Limitations to the Right

By definition, the right of publicity is a limitation on freedom of expression. Accordingly, some states have expressly recognized such exceptions as news reporting, commentaries, or parodies. When the right is understood very broadly, the First Amendment can also come into play as a restriction. The California Supreme Court has formulated a balancing test, holding that the First Amendment trumps the right of publicity when "the work in question adds significant creative elements so as to be transformed into something more than a mere celebrity likeness or imitation." *Compare Comedy Iii Prods. v. Gary Saderup*, 25 Cal. 4th 387 (Cal. 2001)(right of publicity infringed by sale of T-shirts bearing mere likeness of Three Stooges without transformative element) and *Winter v. DC Comics*, 30 Cal. 4th 881, 885 (Cal. 2003)(First Amendment prevents right of publicity action by blues musician brothers where characters in comic book were based on brothers but were transformed into "villainous half-worm, half-human offspring").

The right can also be subject to limitations similar to those in copyright, such as first sale. If an item bearing a person's likeness were sold, then the owner would likely have the right to display or further distribute the item without infringing the right of publicity.

Examples

The states of Broadonia and Narrovania have each recently enacted statutes creating a right of publicity. The Broadonia statute reads:

> Every person, living or dead, shall have the exclusive right to any commercial exploitation of her name, likeness, voice, signature, or any other symbol, representation or combination thereof that could identify her. Such right shall have the attributes of personal property and shall endure for the life of the individual plus 50 years. Anyone who infringes this right shall be liable for damages and attorney's fees. Mere references to such person for literary, cultural, news reporting, critical, or entertainment purposes shall not fall within such right, where such reference does not have a commercial purpose.

The Narrovania statute reads:

> Every well-known person shall have the exclusive right to use her name or face, where the sole purpose of such use is to advertise goods or services. Such right shall not be assignable or survive the owner of the right.

1. *Bandwagon*. Eagle Iron wins several professional golf tournaments in a row and becomes nationally famous. Green Beer runs television advertisements that consist of close-ups of Eagle's face as she plays while a voice in the background extols the relaxing powers of Green Beer ale. Eagle has not given permission for the use of her image. Is Green Beer liable under the law of Broadonia? Of Narrovania? Would the result be different if rather than a famous golfer, Green Beer had just used close-ups of the face of an obscure golf fan?

2. *Shape*. Eagle continues to have great success. Every time she wins a tournament, she raises her putter over her head in a distinctive celebratory gesture. Instant Products begins to sell a T-shirt that bears a simple photo of Eagle making her well-known gesture. The photo quality is too poor to make the face recognizable, but most viewers of the photo instantly recognize Eagle as the only person who makes such a gesture standing on a golf green. Is Instant Products liable under the law of Broadonia? Of Narrovania? Would the result be different if the photo were simply a stock photo of Eagle's face?

3. *Truer than life*. Widget is a character in Otter's new novel, *Look-In*. To get the book published, Otter sold the copyright to Bond for several thousand dollars. Widget, a college student struggling to find her identity, strikes a chord with students nationwide. Soon Agent authorizes an animated film to be made based on Otter's book. After the film is released, Agent sells a license to Carrie's Phone Cards to use the face of Widget, copied from the film, in phone card advertising. Otter, aghast at the commercialization of Widget, files an action to enjoin the advertising. Otter acknowledges that

he has sold the copyright to the book but claims that, as the creator of Widget, he owns Widget's rights to publicity. Would Otter succeed under the Broadonia statute? The Narrovania statute?

Explanations

1. Green Beer is liable under both the Broadonia and the Narrovania statute. Eagle Iron's face is used prominently in television advertisements while beer is praised in the background. Under the Broadonia statute, that constitutes "commercial exploitation" of her likeness. Under the Narrovania statute, that constitutes the requisite use of her face, where the sole purpose is to advertise goods or services.

   If an obscure subject had been chosen, the result would be different under the Narrovania statute, which only applies to well-known persons. But the result would be the same under the Broadonia statute. The use of the individual's face constitutes commercial exploitation of her likeness when the entire commercial is made of close-ups of the individual's face. The Broadonia statute does not require that the public be able to actually identify the person whose likeness is used.

2. Instant Products may be liable under the Broadonia statute but is not under the Narrovania statute. The Narrovania statute does not apply because it applies only to uses of the subject's name or face. Here, the T-shirt does not use Eagle's name or face.

   The Broadonia statute requires "commercial exploitation" of a representation that would identify Eagle. The T-shirt does include the necessary identifying representation because the figure in the photo is readily identifiable as Eagle. The issue is whether using the representation on T-shirts qualifies as commercial exploitation of the identifying representation. Putting her figure on T-shirts and selling them may constitute the necessary commercial exploitation, but a court might reason that the statute is not intended to reach every commercial activity that invokes an individual. The statute does contain an exception for "mere references" for various purposes provided there is no commercial purpose. The making and selling of T-shirts seems to have a commercial purpose and also does not fit clearly into one of the protected purposes. But "commercial exploitation" might be read to include only uses of the subject's identity in advertising or similar uses.

   In addition, the use of the image on T-shirts is an expressive use and not "commercial speech," which receives limited First Amendment protection. So, although the case law is as yet unsettled, it may be unconstitutional to grant exclusive rights that would so restrict expression concerning individuals.

If the T-shirt used a stock photo of Eagle's face, the analysis would be similar under the Broadonia statute, although the argument for "commercial exploitation" might be a little stronger. Under the Narrovania statute, the issue would be closer. The photo of the face (unlike the photo of the gesturing figure) falls within the protected uses of name or face. But the Narrovania statute is limited to cases in which the sole purpose is to advertise goods or services. Here, the image appears on the goods themselves. The image serves as the product itself—although it might also be used to advertise the product wherever the T-shirts are exhibited for sale—so the sole purpose is not advertising, and the use would not fall inside the Narrovania statute.

3. Otter would not succeed under either statute. The question is whether a fictional person has a right of publicity. The Broadonia statute grants rights to "[e]very person, living or dead." The Narrovania statute grants rights to "[e]very well-known person" and provides also that the right does not survive the subject. Both statutes appear to apply only to actual human beings, as opposed to fictional persons (such as characters in works of fiction) or to strictly legal persons (such as corporations). So there is no right to publicity with respect to Widget.

FEDERAL PREEMPTION BY THE COPYRIGHT ACT

The federal government and the states both have the power to regulate in the area of intellectual property. Under the Constitution, federal law is the supreme law of the land. To the extent that federal law preempts regulation in an area, state law is invalid. Courts apply three types of preemption:

1. *Explicit preemption*: A federal statute may expressly preempt state law in the relevant field, completely or partly.
2. *Field preemption*: If federal law occupies the entire field, there is no room for application of state law.
3. *Conflict preemption*: State law is preempted if (a) it would be impossible to comply with both state and federal law, or (b) state law stands in the way of accomplishment of the objectives of the federal law.

The preemptive reach of the copyright statute is considerable. In preempting state law, the drafters of the present Copyright Act sought national uniformity in copyright, as opposed to a patchwork of state statutes: "One of the fundamental purposes behind the copyright clause of the Constitution, as shown in Madison's comments in The Federalist, was to promote national uniformity and to avoid the practical difficulties of determining and enforcing an author's rights under the differing laws and in the separate courts of the various States." House Report No. 94-1476. In addition, copyright law represents many balances struck between incentives to authors and the rights of users of works. Such a balance would be upset if states could have their own copyright laws, with different rules on such matters as fair use and first sale.

Copying information potentially violates many types of state law, such as contract law (by using the information in violation of contractual limits or without paying agreed compensation), trade secret law (by obtaining the information through misappropriation of a trade secret), rights of publicity (by making commercial use of something that identifies an individual), unfair competition (by selling copied products), or the tort of misappropriation (by copying valuable information). The federal Copyright Act preempts some state regulation of rights against copying, and likewise may preempt territorial law, such as Puerto Rico and the U.S. Virgin Islands, and tribal law of Native American groups.

Explicit Preemption

The Copyright Act expressly preempts state law granting equivalent rights. 17 U.S.C. §301(a). Under section 301, the Copyright Act exclusively governs

> all legal or equitable rights that are equivalent to any of the exclusive rights within the general scope of copyright as specified by section 106 in works of authorship that are fixed in a tangible medium of expression and come within the subject matter of copyright as specified by sections 102 and 103.

Section 301 does not preempt state rights that are not equivalent to federal copyright rights (such as state law governing ownership of a painting, as opposed to ownership of the copyright in the painting), state rights in unfixed works (such as a common-law copyright in a dance that has not been fixed in a tangible form), or state rights that do not fall within the scope of copyright (such as rights to inherit the painting).

Come Within the Scope of Copyright as Specified by Sections 102 and 103

There is no preemption of matter that is outside the subject matter of copyright. To take a notable example, sound recordings were not subject to federal copyright protection until 1972. Section 301 specifically provides that state protection of pre-1972 sound recordings is not preempted. The New York Court of Appeals has held that New York law recognizes a perpetual ownership right in pre-1972 sound recordings. *See Capitol Records, Inc. v. Naxos of America*, 4 N.Y.3d 540 (2005).

Courts generally have read "the scope of copyright" to include matter protected by copyright, but also subject matter that the Copyright Act leaves unprotected. As the legislative history put it, "As long as a work fits within one of the general subject matter categories of sections 102 and 103, the bill prevents the States from protecting it even if it fails to achieve Federal statutory copyright because it is too minimal or lacking in originality to qualify, or because it has fallen into the public domain." House Report No. 94-1476. The fact that the Copyright Act leaves subject matter unprotected does not mean that it is free for the states to grant rights in the subject matter. Rather, the effect is that the matter is left in the public domain, for copyright purposes. A state law that granted copyright-like protection in nonoriginal material would be preempted. *See ATC Distrib. Group, Inc. v. Whatever It Takes Transmissions & Parts, Inc.*, 402 F.3d 700, 713 (6th Cir. 2005) (Copyright Act preempts state law cause of action for copying parts numbers, even if numbers were noncopyrightable). Otherwise, state law would upset the balance set by federal copyright law.

Equivalent to Any of the Exclusive Rights Within the General Scope of Copyright

Section 301 bars state rights that are "equivalent" to any of the section 106 exclusive rights (the right to make copies, adapt the work, distribute the work to the public, perform the work publicly, and display the work publicly). To decide whether a right is equivalent, most courts use the "extra element" test. The court determines whether the state right would be infringed by an act that would potentially infringe a federal copyright or whether infringement of the state right required showing additional substantial elements. Suppose a state law prohibits making unauthorized copies of paintings. Anyone who makes an unauthorized copy violates both state and federal law. The rights are equivalent, and so the state statute is preempted. Suppose the state statute, by contrast, prohibits fraudulently selling unauthorized copies of paintings. The additional element of fraudulent intent is not required by copyright. The state right is not equivalent here and is not preempted.

Whether rights are equivalent is not always clear, because preemption applies broadly to any rights "within the general scope of copyright." Courts usually require that there be a substantial difference in the state right to avoid preemption. Suppose a state law prohibits unauthorized copying of paintings done for commercial gain. The element of commercial gain is not required for copyright infringement, but because that additional element makes little difference to the substance of the right, the state right is still substantially equivalent and therefore preempted. Likewise, the Copyright Act preempts a state law unjust enrichment claim based on using a screenplay and a novel to make movie without compensation. Although "enrichment" is not an element of a copyright infringement action, the suit was essentially enforcing "the right of adaptation—i.e., the right to prepare or authorize preparation of a derivative work based on a novel or screenplay." *Briarpatch Ltd., L.P. v. Phoenix Pictures, Inc.*, 373 F.3d 296, 306 (2d Cir. 2004).

In considering equivalence, courts also consider which parties are subject to the right. For example, a contract may provide limitations on the use of information that are similar to the section 106 rights. The recipient of information may agree that she will not make copies or distribute or adapt the information. A leading decision held that such a contractual right is not equivalent to a right under copyright because it applies only to the contracting parties and is not an exclusive right against the rest of the world. *See ProCD v. Zeidenburg*, 86 F.3d 1447 (7th Cir. 1996). Commentators have argued that if the information is widely licensed subject to such restrictions (such as mass-market software), the restriction may be functionally equivalent to an exclusive right.

In Works of Authorship Fixed in a Tangible Medium of Expression

Before the 1976 Act, federal copyright applied primarily to published works, although some unpublished works could be copyrighted through registration. State copyright law generally applied to unpublished works. Congress changed that balance in 1976, expanding federal copyright protection to works as soon as they were fixed in a tangible form. The preemption provision likewise preempts state copyright law, except as to "unfixed" works—those not fixed in tangible form. As the legislative history notes, this leaves some (not many) works to state copyright law protection: "Examples would include choreography that has never been filmed or notated, an extemporaneous speech, 'original works of authorship' communicated solely through conversations or live broadcasts [that were not recorded], and a dramatic sketch or musical composition improvised or developed from memory and without being recorded or written down." House Report No. 94-1476.

Conflict Preemption

In addition to express preemption under section 301, state law is subject to conflict preemption. The first type of conflict preemption (impossible to comply with both federal and state law) is rare with such subject matter, but the second type of conflict preemption (state law obstructs accomplishment of objectives of federal law) has been raised in several areas.

Courts have regularly applied federal copyright rules to supplant contract law that conflicts with specific provisions of the Copyright Act. The requirements of a signed writing for a transfer of copyright ownership under section 204 will control, even where the parties would have had an enforceable oral agreement under state law. Likewise, a party may exercise its rights under the Copyright Act to terminate a license or transfer of copyright, even if applicable state law would have made the agreement permanent.

Case law is struggling with preemption in other areas. Suppose a photographer makes a photograph of some surfers. The photo is used in an advertising campaign with permission of the photographer, who owns the copyright. Do the surfers have a cause of action under the right of publicity, or are rights in use of the photo governed exclusively by federal copyright law? *Downing v. Abercrombie & Fitch*, 265 F.3d 994 (9th Cir. 2001), held that the surfers' rights of publicity were not preempted. As the right to publicity expands, such possible conflicts are likely to increase. Courts could well hold that the federal copyright statute would preempt such a broad reading of the state right of publicity. Otherwise, there could be conflict between how federal copyright law and state right of publicity law permit uses and allocate rights. *See* Jennifer E. Rothman, *Copyright Preemption and the Right of Publicity*, 36 U.C. Davis L. Rev. 199 (2002).

Another type of conflict arises with respect to using copyrights as collateral for loans. Whether the creditor should protect her rights by filing in the copyright office or in the state U.C.C. office remains unsettled. *See World Auxiliary Power v. Silicon Valley Bank*, 303 F.3d 1120 (9th Cir. 2002) (holding that federal law preempted perfection of security interests in registered copyrights but not in unregistered copyrights).

Contracts often contain restricted use clauses that are permitted by copyright law. Software licenses might contain clauses prohibiting reverse engineering, which otherwise would be fair use. Database licenses may prohibit copying or distribution of facts, which are not protected by law. Nondisclosure agreements likewise prohibit restrictions on noncopyrightable material, such as functional matter, facts, or ideas. Most cases have upheld contractual restrictions against preemption arguments. *See, e.g.*, *ProCD*, *supra*. But some courts have limited enforceability of state law rights that appear to conflict with copyright policy. *See Vault Corp. v. Quaid Software Ltd.*, 847 F.2d 255 (5th Cir. 1988) (applying preemption to enforcement of software license terms when license effectively denied rights provided by section 117 of the Copyright Act). Conflict preemption remains a relatively unsettled area.

Examples

1. *Author's rights.* A new Broadonia statute provides that any poet has the exclusive right to sell copies of her poems or to read them in public once she has written the poem down or otherwise preserved it. Shakes, a poet, seeks to enforce his rights under the statute against a literary magazine that printed one of his poems without permission. The magazine contends that the federal statute preempts the Broadonia statute. Shakes responds that the Broadonia statute is not preempted because it

is entirely consistent with the federal statute. Both grant rights to the authors of poems. Is the Broadonia statute preempted? Would it make a difference if the Broadonia statute applied only to poems that had not been written down or otherwise preserved in a stable form by the poet (that is, to poems saved only in the poet's mind)?

2. *Unauthorized biography*. Broadonia passes a statute granting each person the exclusive right to make or sell any book based on the person's life. Anyone making or selling a book about someone without permission is liable for a percentage of the receipts from the work. The statute expressly provides that it does not apply to copying of expression that is protected by copyright, but rather only to use of facts involving the person. Does federal law preempt the statute?

3. *Broken promise*. Zosoft sells widely used software for processing digital images. To use the software, the user must click on "yes" to the click-wrap agreement. One clause of the agreement provides that the user agrees not to copy any aspect of Zosoft's software into other software. Myrtle buys a copy of the software and greatly admires how well it works. Myrtle then develops her own digital image software for the commercial market, copying several functional aspects of Zosoft's software. Zosoft sues for breach of contract. Myrtle contends that federal law preempts enforcement of the contract. Is Zosoft's cause of action preempted?

4. *Characters are people too*. Broadonia expands the scope of its right to publicity statute by granting a right of publicity to fictional characters in books, films, or other works. The Broadonia statute provides that there shall be a right of publicity for any fictional character encompassing the exclusive right to make or distribute any work that contains the character. Such right belongs to the author of the work in which the fictional character first appears. Years ago, Downpike sold the copyright to her first novel, which features the hard-boiled detective Annie Asphalt. The buyer of the copyright has just published a sequel to the novel and released a movie based on the novel, both featuring Annie Asphalt. Does federal law preempt Downpike's cause of action under the Broadonia statute?

5. *Preemption of misappropriation?* Theflyonthewall.com collected investment recommendations made by major financial institutions and published the information before the financial institutions themselves made them public. Sued for state law misappropriation, Theflyontheall.com argued that the federal copyright statute preempted any state law liability. Does it?

6. *Zombie lawsuit?* Montz spoke with some TV producers to sell his "idea for a television show that would follow a team of paranormal investigators conducting field investigations." They did not hire him, but later on, they produced *Ghost Hunters*, which Montz deemed to be an incarnation

of his idea. Under California law, when a writer discloses a script idea to a producer, there may be an implied contract that the writer will be compensated if the idea is used. The producers argued that federal law preempted a suit based simply on copying ideas. Federal copyright law permits copying of ideas, so state law cannot forbid it. Can Montz proceed?

7. *Following rights*. The California Resale Royalties Act required that when works of fine art are resold, 5 percent must go to the artist. Any conflict with federal copyright law?

8. Former professional football players file suit, alleging that commercial use of footage from their playing days infringes their right of publicity. Preemption?

Explanations

1. The Broadonia statute is preempted under section 301 of the Copyright Act. It is unnecessary to consider conflict preemption or field preemption. The Copyright Act expressly preempts certain state rights such as this Broadonia statute. Under section 301, the Copyright Act preempts any state right that is
   a. equivalent to any of the section 106 exclusive rights,
   b. a work of authorship fixed in a tangible medium of expression, and
   c. comes within the scope of copyright as specified by sections 102 and 103.

   The rights under the Broadonia statute meet all three requirements. The rights are equivalent to the section 106 rights to distribute the work to the public and perform the work publicly. The rights are in a fixed work of authorship, having been written down or otherwise preserved. Poetry comes well within the scope of copyright.

   The Broadonia statute would not be preempted if it applied only to poetry that the author had not preserved in tangible form. As listed above, section 301 preemption applies only to works that are fixed in a tangible medium of expression. Field preemption and conflict preemption would also be inapplicable to unfixed works. Rather, states remain generally free to regulate copyright in unfixed works (a narrow category of works).

2. The Broadonia statute is probably preempted. It is not clear that section 301 preemption applies. The Broadonia statute does grant a right equivalent to section 106 rights (a right to make copies or distribute works to the public) that comes within the scope of copyright, but the right arguably is not based on a work of authorship that is fixed in tangible form; it is based only on intangible facts relating to the life of a person. One

might conclude, however, that the statute gives the subject a copyright once the ideas have been fixed in the form of a book written by someone else. In any case, the statute surely is invalid under conflict preemption because it grants exclusive rights to make and distribute works using certain facts, exactly the sort of material that the Copyright Act seeks to keep in the public domain. It does not have any extra elements such as deception and so is equivalent to granting a copyright in facts.

3. This case gives an example of an area that is presently unsettled, the extent to which contract law may be used to obtain rights that copyright law does not grant. Contracts frequently protect information that is not protectable by copyright (such as facts, ideas, or functional matter) or reduce user rights granted by copyright (such as fair use or first sale rights). Courts generally have upheld such restrictions. *See, e.g., Bowers v. Baystate Techs*, 302 F.3d 1334, 1343 (Fed. Cir. 2002)(holding no preemption of "shrinkwrap" contract that prohibited any reverse engineering of the software covered by the agreement); *Davidson & Assocs. v. Jung*, 422 F.3d 630 (8th Cir. 2005) (same). But the issue is far from settled.

   When only a few parties are subject to the contract, such private agreements seem to have little conflict with copyright law—and indeed often further copyright law by enabling efficient licensing of copyrighted works. As both legal and technological licensing techniques continue to refine control over information, however, there may be more cases in which (as in patent law) courts hold that contractual restrictions are unenforceable in light of federal copyright law policy (or other federal law, such as antitrust). So there is no clear answer to this case. Courts generally have upheld contractual restrictions that exceed the exclusive rights of copyright, but where the lines may be drawn awaits further development of the case law. A court could hold that enforcement of the agreement not to copy would conflict with the federal policies in the Copyright Act by effectively giving exclusive rights in noncopyrightable elements and is therefore preempted.

4. The federal copyright statute would preempt Downpike's state law cause of action. The Broadonia statute gives the author of a fictional work the exclusive right to make or distribute any work that contains the character. Such an exclusive right is equivalent to some of the exclusive rights of federal copyright law (the rights to make copies, adapt the work, and distribute copies). It would be preempted under section 301 of the Copyright Act.

5. The court held that federal copyright law would preempt liability for simply copying information in this case, following the *NBA v. Motorola* case discussed earlier with respect to the tort of misappropriation. *Barclays Capital Inc. v. Theflyonthewall.com Inc.*, 99 U.S.P.Q.2D (BNA) 1247 (2d Cir.

2011). Federal copyright law allows copying of facts, nonoriginal expression, and other noncopyrightable elements. *Theflyonthewall.com* addresses the "ghostly presence" of *International News Service v. Associated Press*, 248 U.S. 215 (1918), under which misappropriation of "hot news" might supply a cause of action. The Second Circuit held that "hot news" might still survive where it was sufficiently different from the federal copyright law, but the tort would be very narrow. It would only apply where free-riding allowed the defendant to produce a product in direct competition for lower cost. But the plaintiffs here were financial institutions, making the recommendations as part of a broader business providing financial services. They were not in *direct* competition with the seller of investment tips; nor would their entire business be at risk if the recommendations would be prematurely made public. Under *Theflyonthewall.com*, it will be difficult to impose liability simply for copying information (as opposed to using improper means to obtain information, which will still be subject liability under such theories as trade secret misappropriation or breach of contractual promises not to disclose information).

6. Copyright did not preempt the state law claim because it had as "an added element: an agreement to pay for use of the disclosed ideas." *Montz v. Pilgrim Films & Television Inc.*, 98 U.S.P.Q.2D (BNA) 1569 (9th Cir. 2011) (en banc).

7. In the courts' view, the California law conflicted with federal copyright's first sale doctrine, which authorizes the owner of a copy (including the original) of a work to resell it, free of obligations to the copyright holder. As the trial court put it, "Because the CRRA disrupts Congress's efforts to balance the interests of copyright holders and downstream consumers, it must be preempted." *Estate of Graham v. Sotheby's, Inc.*, 178 F. Supp. 3d 974, 988 (C.D. Cal. 2016). The appellate court agreed that the California law conflicted with the federal first sale doctrine:

> In short, the CRRA does not merely grant an additional right beyond what federal copyright law already provides but fundamentally reshapes the contours of federal copyright law's existing distribution right. This runs counter to § 301(a), which precludes "all legal or equitable rights that are equivalent to any of the exclusive rights within the general scope of copyright," even if they are not precisely within the contemplation of the Copyright Act.

Close v. Sotheby's, Inc., 894 F.3d 1061, 1071 (9th Cir. 2018). Some might differ. *See* Lorie M. Graham & Stephen M. McJohn, *Intellectual Property's First Sale Doctrine and the Policy Against Restraints on Alienation*, 7 Tex. A&M L. Rev. 497 (2020) (arguing that the Supreme Court has grounded the copyright's first sale doctrine on the policy against restraints on alienation, and that the modest resale royalty right under California law did not operate as an unreasonable restraint on alienation).

8. The court held that the federal copyright statute preempted state law right of publicity claims brought by former professional football players against NFL Films. *Dryer v. National Football League*, 814 F.3d 938 (8th Cir. 2016). The court reasoned that their claims would be the state law equivalent of copyright claims. The court distinguished the case where an announcer's voice had been used in advertising, because that was a commercial use of the identity, as opposed to the sort of expressive use that copyright protects. *Dryer* viewed the player's claims as analogous to claims brought by actors in a movie: "If [a] performer [in a copyrighted recording] later objects to the reproduction or performance of that recording in an expressive, non-advertising use, then the claim is one of copyright infringement, not of infringement of the right of publicity."[1]

   Others might differ. Football players, unlike actors or musicians, are not performing a copyrighted work. Football games are not scripted, nor was this based on some claimed copyright in the choreography of the plays. Rather, the relevant copyright was in the game footage. The court placed weight on the fact that NFL Films had permission to make the films. But the players were not claiming to hold copyright in the films as authors; rather, they were alleging that use of the films infringed their state law rights of publicity. A sounder way to resolve the case may have been an issue the court did reach, whether the First Amendment would bar such a broad interpretation of the state law right of publicity.

---

1. *Dryer v. NFL*, 814 F.3d at 943 (quoting, in parenthetical, J. Thomas McCarthy, *The Rights of Publicity and Privacy* §11.55 (2d ed. 2013)).

APPENDIX

Review Topic: Copyright and Art Works

We can review some key topics in copyright law by looking at its application in the area of fine art—how copyright law might raise issues for galleries and museums.

SUBJECT MATTER

What does it take for a work of art to be protected by copyright? It must be an original work of authorship fixed in a tangible medium. The vast majority of works would meet that modest standard. If Pablo paints a painting of three dancers, whether Pablo is a master or a novice, his work would be original: made by Pablo with at least a minimal spark of creativity. "Original" in the art world might mean a highly creative work, but in copyright law it takes just a little creativity. Indeed, even if Pablo copied another painting, Pablo might make a few creative choices that would meet the originality requirement. If Pablo made an exact copy, then the necessary creativity might be lacking. Ironically, that would require greater technical skill than simply making a slapdash copy, whose departures from accuracy might supply the necessary originality. If Pablo copied a copyrighted work, of course, Pablo's work could be denied copyright as an infringing work.

Works of art fall comfortably within the categories of works of authorship. With a minimal spark of creativity, we can think of an artwork in a museum that would fall into any of the categories listed in 17 U.S.C. §102:

(1) literary works;

René Magritte's painting of a pipe, including the words, "Ceci n'est pas une pipe" (This is not a pipe). A literary work is any work "expressed in words, numbers, or other verbal or numerical symbols," 17 U.S.C. §101.

(2) musical works, including any accompanying words; such as the title song in *Death Is Elsewhere* (2019), "a seven-channel video installation by the acclaimed Icelandic artist Ragnar Kjartansson." It was installed at the Metropolitan Museum of Art in New York:

> Filmed around the time of the summer solstice shortly after midnight in southern Iceland, Death Is Elsewhere features male and female pairs of twins (Kjartansson's frequent collaborators: the musicians Gyða and Kristín Anna Valtýsdóttir, and Aaron and Bryce Dessner of the National), performing the title song against a landscape of sublime natural beauty, as they move continuously across seven screens, encircling the viewer.

(3) dramatic works, including any accompanying music;

Dramatic works are typically plays, operas, other works where performers get into character. There exists a genre of Performance Art. In Chris Burden's work "*Shoot*," 1971, he walked into the F Space gallery in Santa Ana, California, and had a friend shoot him in the arm with a rifle, a little more gory than initially planned.

(4) pantomimes and choreographic works, choreographic notes;

(5) pictorial, graphic, and sculptural works;

Magritte's "Ceci n'est pas une pipe" would also fall into this category, which emphasizes that the categories are quite overlapping.

(6) motion pictures and other audiovisual works;

Many works of video art appear in museums and galleries. The overlapping of categories is again illustrated here: "*Shoot*" was filmed. *Death Is Elsewhere* was a video.

(7) sound recordings;

The Museum of Modern Art in New York has an archive of sound recordings. A genre of Sound Artists work specifically with sound, often recording it to preserve it—or not recording it, to preserve spontaneity. In 2013, MoMA put on "Soundings: A Contemporary Score," its first major exhibition dedicated to sound art.

(8) architectural

Architectural drawings are themselves often exhibited in museums or sold in galleries.

We should also remember that the foregoing categories, although they cover almost everything, are not necessarily exclusive. An art work composed of smells might not fall into any of the foregoing, but could still qualify as a copyrightable work of authorship.

The third requirement, fixation, is met with most artworks simply by creating them. In making a painting, a sculpture, a print, a mobile, a photograph, the artist necessarily fixes the work in a tangible medium, thereby securing copyright, even if copyright is the furthest thing from their mind. Some artworks, however, are less tangible. "*Shoot*" consisted of the artist being shot in the arm. That had tangible effects on him, but did not fix the overall work. However, the work was filmed, and fixation in any form suffices. Writing a detailed description—such as in words or pictograms—would have sufficed. But without fixation, there would be no copyright. Another artist could have shot themselves in the arm without a copyright to infringe—although the wound would be worse than an infringement judgment. Conceptual art often involves abstract ideas, which may not be put in a tangible form and so might not be copyrighted. They could, however, be recorded in video, words, drawings, or otherwise.

The limitations on copyright, especially the nonprotection of ideas, are important in art. Copyright allows the free flow of ideas, because ideas are not copyrighted. Picasso's career illustrates that, as he freely copied ideas from others in Cubist, Symbolist, and Surrealist movements. He also copied many ideas from African indigenous art, which illustrates that indigenous culture receives lamentably little protection under intellectual property law. Functional aspects of work are also not protected by copyright. This limit plays little role in many areas of art. But artworks like mobiles and sculpture often have functional aspects that are worth copying. The nonprotection of functional aspects may be important for museums such as the Owls Head Transportation Museum, which displays functional works such as automobiles, airplanes, and even the Pocock rowing shell. Such works are important but so functional that copyright would give little if any protection against copying. Rather, the inventors would have to seek patent protection (as many did, using both utility and design patents). Some artworks do have functional aspects. Conceptual artist Sol LeWitt created works that were sets of instructions for creating works, such as Wall Drawing #118: "On a wall surface, any continuous stretch of wall, using a hard pencil, place fifty points at random. The points should be evenly distributed over the area of the wall. All of the points should be connected by straight lines." Those instructions are relatively abstract, and could yield many different works. Someone who implemented that work would likely not infringe, because they were copying only functional aspects and the abstract idea. If the instructions were much more detailed, then there might be copying of expression by implementing them.

Some artworks are not under copyright because they are government works, i.e., works made by federal employees. Many of the great Depression-era photos were taken by photographers hired by the federal government and so are not under copyright. Anyone can make copies and sell them without infringing copyright.

OWNERSHIP AND LICENSING

Art provides a classic example of the copyright ownership rules. Suppose Frankenthaler painted a painting and sold it to Gagosian Gallery. Who owns the painting? Gagosian Gallery, bought and paid for. Who owns the copyright to the painting? Frankenthaler. The author owns the copyright initially, and she has done nothing to transfer ownership of the copyright. Sale of a copy (here, the painting) does not automatically include transfer of the copyright, although the parties can agree otherwise. In the art business, that is rare. From the major galleries in New York to smaller galleries in upstate New York to Bermuda and on to London and Paris, galleries typically do not bargain for ownership of the copyright. So if the gallery wishes to make copies, such as for marketing, it would need permission from the artist (express or implied) or to rely on fair use. Few artists would sue a gallery for promoting their work, but artists can be touchy. Museums likewise do not generally hold the copyright in the works they display, so promotion of copyrighted works could require a license or at least crossed fingers.

Some artworks are works made for hire, with the copyright automatically belonging to the hiring party. But the Supreme Court's decision in *Reid* shows that the work-for-hire rule is narrow, applying only to employee works. Someone who commissions a sculpture or painting does not own the copyright if the artist is an independent contractor. A hiring party that wants to own not just the physical work but also the copyright should negotiate for that in the contract.

Joint works are relatively uncommon in the world of art. Even artists who rely heavily on others in the production process generally would be treated as sole authors. A studio worker may do some of the actual work in producing a sculpture or painting, but will not qualify as a joint author without a showing that the parties intended her to be treated as a joint author. Collective works play a role in art, not so much in the gallery or museum, but in settings like books containing collections images of multiple works.

Until 1989, copyright in the United States depended on the author using a copyright notice when publishing or displaying the work. Artists often did not concern themselves with such formalities, and so many artworks went into the public domain. As noted, artists often did not care.

Jackson Pollock could still sell his paintings whether he held the copyright or not, and did not need copyright to maintain his market. Others might be able to copy without infringing, but still could not produce a genuine Jackson Pollock. In 1977, Congress changed the law so that copyright vested automatically when a work was put in tangible form. But the author could still lose copyright by publishing without a notice. Finally, in 1989, Congress changed the law so that copyright notice is no longer required to secure copyright. The United States took the rule followed by most countries (and required by the Berne Convention, the leading copyright treaty) that copyright does not depend on compliance with formalities.

Another formality for copyright protection survived a little longer. Authors could lose their copyright for failure to renew the copyright after the first 28 years. In 1992, Congress made renewal automatic, so it is only a hazard for works published before 1964.

Like other works, the copyright in an art work may be registered. Registration is not required to secure copyright. Registration does make the copyright stronger, because the remedies of statutory damages and attorneys' fees are available only for registered works. Deposit of two copies is required with registration. A sculptor need not make two full-size copies to send to the Copyright Office. Rather, the regulations allow a flexible approach to submit copies in reasonable form, such as images.

Copyright has long but limited duration. For pre-1977 works, copyright lasts 95 years. So works from the 1920s may still be under copyright, provided the copyright owner complied with the requirement of copyright notice on publication and the renewal requirement 28 years later. So determining the copyright status of a work may not be simple. Works published more than 95 years ago are not under copyright. Museums or galleries that have collections of pre-twentieth-century art, then, have little concern with copyright. They make photos, reproductions, and miniatures of the pieces in the collection without seeking a license from anyone.

Although most attention falls on sale of physical artworks, copyright licensing plays a role in the art world. An artist may agree in a licensing agreement for others to make use of the work, whether an exclusive license or a nonexclusive license (such as permission to use an image of the work in a book, maybe even on the cover). Even works that do not qualify for copyright may be licensed. A conceptual artist might enter into a licensing agreement granting others permission to perform the work. Indeed, for abstract conceptual works, where there is no physical work to buy and sell, museums have been known to acquire the work for their collection by getting an exclusive license to the work. Such a license would not be a copyright license (if the work was a noncopyrightable abstract idea) but rather a contract.

Many artists license their works under Creative Commons licenses. These allow others to make and distribute copies of the works, provided that further restrictions are not put on the new copies. Creative Commons licenses may be tailored: a photographer who puts her photos online under a CC license may determine whether others may adapt the work and whether others may make commercial use of the work. Museums and galleries that put works online may likewise do so under a CC license. They may need permission to do so. As noted above, authority to do so belongs to the copyright holder, which is likely the artist.

Copyright's termination rules allow authors to terminate licenses after 35 years (for post-1976 works). That is important in areas like music, where songwriters are now getting back the rights to songs they sold in the 1980s and 1990s. But because copyright is less important in fine art than other areas, termination is likewise less important. An artist who sold her works cheap in 1989 cannot terminate the sale 35 years later. That was a sale of the object, governed by property law, not a transfer of copyright, subject to the termination under copyright law.

Many foreign artists lost their U.S. copyright due to failure to comply with the U.S. formalities of copyright notice and renewal. Foreign authors, including artists, were given restoration rights in 1994, as part of trade negotiations. Picasso had lost his U.S. copyright in the great painting *Guernica*, but his estate gained the right to restore the copyright. U.S. authors, however, did not get restoration rights.

The gallery or museum does not generally own the copyright in the works it displays. If someone infringes the copyright, the gallery or museum would have no copyright infringement claim. Does it have the right, as many do, to prohibit visitors from taking pictures of the works? Not from copyright law, but as owner of the premises, the gallery or museum can set the rules under which it gives permission for others to enter. On the flip side, a gallery or museum does not own the copyright and so may lack authority to give permission to visitors to take pictures. Nevertheless, galleries very often permit or even encourage visitors to take pictures of the pictures. Technically, they may be inducing infringement—but may well figure that the artist would approve of encouraging interest in the work. A careful gallery may address the issue in a contract with the artist when acquiring the work.

EXCLUSIVE RIGHTS AND INFRINGEMENT

The copyright holder gets a basket of rights under 17 U.S.C. §106:

(1) to reproduce the copyrighted work in copies or phonorecords;
(2) to prepare derivative works based upon the copyrighted work;

(3) to distribute copies or phonorecords of the copyrighted work to the public by sale or other transfer of ownership, or by rental, lease, or lending;
(4) in the case of literary, musical, dramatic, and choreographic works, pantomimes, and motion pictures and other audiovisual works, to perform the copyrighted work publicly;
(5) in the case of literary, musical, dramatic, and choreographic works, pantomimes, and pictorial, graphic, or sculptural works, including the individual images of a motion picture or other audiovisual work, to display the copyrighted work publicly; and
(6) in the case of sound recordings, to perform the copyrighted work publicly by means of a digital audio transmission.

An artist who copied another's work in a painting and sold it to a gallery could thus infringe the reproduction right (also known as the right to make copies), the derivative work right (or adaptation right), the distribution right, and the display right. The gallery could then itself infringe the display right and the distribution right, by showing and selling the painting. The gallery would be liable even if it did not know of the copying. Infringement has no state-of-mind requirement (intent, knowledge, recklessness), beyond the minimal requirement of some volitional act that infringes one of the rights.

For most artists, copyright infringement is not an issue. They may be influenced by others, but copying ideas or common themes is not infringement. Sometimes artists do copy more closely. In particular, some artists copy directly from other works, sometimes termed appropriation art. The question then would arise, whether fair use authorizes the copying. Courts have been relatively favorable, as long as they can find some transformative element to the copying, as opposed to simply using the other work as raw material.

Fair use is central to the creation of art. A gallery in Camden, Maine, exhibited a painting that was itself a painting of an Andy Warhol painting, depicted as curling up at the corner. The painting copies from Warhol's copyrighted work, but would qualify as a transformative fair use. Warhol's painting itself relied on fair use, being a copy of a famous photograph of a celebrity. So an art work may represent multiple generations of fair use, because transformative copying is key to art. Likewise

Galleries and museums, like libraries and used booksellers, benefit from the first sale doctrine. First sale allows the owner of an authorized copy to display or distribute the work without infringing. First sale allows museums to display works without infringing. For example, the National Museum of African American History and Culture has many artifacts on display that may be copyrighted. The museum need not get permission to display them, as long as it owns them or has authority from the owner. Note that first sale is limited to the display and distribution rights. First sale would not authorize the museum to perform a work. So it might need permission to play a video or song—or it might be covered by fair use, for a nonprofit, educational, and historical use. Galleries may likewise rely on first sale. Often the gallery has permission from the artist to display the work, because the gallery works with the artist. But galleries also acquire works. The gallery does not need the permission of the artist to display or to sell the work. California enacted a resale royalty right, which required galleries to pay a percentage to artists upon resale of the work. The courts, however, held that California preempted the federal copyright act, on the theory that it conflicted with federal first sale rights.

The art world must consider a special form of protection that only applies to a "work of visual art," defined as a painting, drawing, sculpture, or a print or photo in limited edition of 200 copies or fewer. Section 106A gives rights of attribution and integrity to authors of works of visual art. So a painter will have a cause of action under 106A against someone who misattributes authorship of a painting, or distorts it. For a work "of recognized stature," there is also a right to prevent destruction of the work. So fine art gets a narrow set of moral rights not granted to other works like songs and novels. Not all artworks fall under the definition of "work of visual art." Conceptual or performance art—like "Shoot"—may not receive protection under 106A. A work of sound art would not be a work of visual art, without some visual component. But those works still have the basket of rights under copyright if they meet the originality, work of authorship, and fixation requirements.

Index

Index